ECONOMIC EVIDENCE IN EU COMPETITION LAW

European Studies in Law and Economics Series

1. *Group Litigation in European Competition Law. A Law and Economics Perspective*, Sonja E. Keske
2. *Behavioural Economics in Consumer Policy*, Hanneke Luth
3. *Ex-Post Liability Rules in Modern Patent Law*, Rosa Castro Bernieri
4. *Competition and Innovation in the EU Regulation of Pharmaceuticals: The Case of Parallel Trade*, Claudia Desogus
5. *The Law and Economics of Organ Procurement*, Fırat Bilgel
6. *Law and Economics in the RIA World. Improving the use of economic analysis in public policy and legislation*, Andrea Renda
7. *Regulatory Competition in European Corporate and Capital Market Law*, Lars Hornuf
8. *Economic Criteria for Criminalization: Optimizing Enforcement in Case of Environmental Violations*, Katarina Svatikova
9. *Definition of the Relevant Market. (Lack of) Harmony between Industrial Economics and Competition Law*, Hila Nevo
10. *Patents as Protection of Traditional Medical Knowledge? A Law and Economics Analysis*, Petra Ebermann
11. *Rethinking the New York Convention. A Law and Economics Approach*, Shen Wei
12. *Towards a Better Assessment of Pain and Suffering Damages for Personal Injuries*, Vaia Karapanou
13. *Comparative Analysis of Merger Control Policy. Lessons for China*, Jingyuan Ma
14. *Does Law Matter for Economic Growth? A Re-examination of the 'Legal Origin' Hypothesis*, Guangdong Xu
15. *Committed to Reform. Pragmatic Antitrust Enforcement in Electricity Markets*, Małgorzata Sadowska
16. *Civil Liability of Securities Underwriters. Enforcing the Gatekeeping Function*, Olia Skripova
17. *Banking Regulation in Times of Crisis. An Economic Analysis from Turkey and Russia*, Deniz Akün Ergun

ECONOMIC EVIDENCE IN EU COMPETITION LAW

Mitja Kovač
Ann-Sophie Vandenberghe
(eds.)

intersentia
Cambridge – Antwerp – Portland

Intersentia Ltd
Sheraton House | Castle Park
Cambridge | CB3 0AX | United Kingdom
Tel.: +44 1223 370 170 | Fax: +44 1223 370 169
Email: mail@intersentia.co.uk
www.intersentia.com | www.intersentia.co.uk

Distribution for the UK and Ireland:
NBN International
Airport Business Centre, 10 Thornbury Road
Plymouth, PL6 7 PP
United Kingdom
Tel.: +44 1752 202 301 | Fax: +44 1752 202 331
Email: orders@nbninternational.com

Distribution for Europe and all other countries:
Intersentia Publishing nv
Groenstraat 31
2640 Mortsel
Belgium
Tel.: +32 3 680 15 50 | Fax: +32 3 658 71 21
Email: mail@intersentia.be

Distribution for the USA and Canada:
International Specialized Book Services
920 NE 58th Ave. Suite 300
Portland, OR 97213
USA
Tel.: +1 800 944 6190 (toll free) | Fax: +1 503 280 8832
Email: info@isbs.com

ISBN 978-1-78068-286-0
D/2016/7849/18
NUR 828

British Library Cataloguing in Publication Data. A catalogue record for this book is available from the British Library.

'What role does economics play in cases of competition law? What role could it play? And what role should it play? But do scholarly experts and judges agree on these viewpoints? In this book an impressive variety of topics is covered and surprising insights are gained. Thus it really covers recent and partly controversial developments in the EU regarding the handling of competition law cases on a national as well as an EU level – something experts in the field must not miss.'

Wolfgang Weigel, Chair, The Joseph von Sonnenfels Center for the Study of Public Law and Economics and Department of Economics, University of Vienna

'Economics is the study of scarcity. Law is the study of rights. Un-fortunately, law and economics scholarship that is practical and focused on problems from the courtroom is scarce. This volume makes it right. It combines the legal experience of experts and judges in several European countries and the rigor of economics. The result is an indispensable tool for anyone interested in EU competition law.'

Shai Dothan, Associate Professor of International and Public Law, iCourts – the Centre of Excellence for International Courts, Faculty of Law, University of Copenhagen

PREFACE

Competition law has formed an important area of European law since the establishment of the European Union. However, the enforcement of EU competition law relies to a great extent on national courts and tribunals which are faced with ever increasing challenging responsibility given the dynamic nature of this area of law. Also the interplay of EC competition law and national law, especially national procedural law and employment of economic evidences, poses them with various challenges. In this light, the aim of this book is to identify practices for coping with these challenges to enable more efficient enforcement and application of EU competition law and also to stimulate transnational processes of mutual judicial-scholarly dialogue.

This book represents a direct outcome of a unique judicial-scholarly-expert research group in competition law and economics bringing together several European judges (from Belgium, Croatia, Czech Republic, Germany, Hungary, Lithuania, The Netherlands, Portugal, Rumania, Slovakia, Slovenia and United Kingdom), experts and selected outstanding scholars which identified the most triggering inefficiencies, problems of the economic evidence in EU competition law enforcement practice in different Member States. This book represents the outcome of this expert research group, providing a broad assessment of identified problems, inconsistencies, inefficiency, legal practice, cases, application of economic evidence and responding mitigating tools and interpretation techniques.

Contributions cover the most intriguing and challenging issues faced by practitioners and judges enforcing and litigating competition cases throughout the EU Member states (addressing current case law, enforcing practices, standards of proof and current developments in relation to economic evidence). The problem identification comes from judges, national experts and national enforcement authorities (bottom up approach) and reflects real obstacles in current EU competition law practices. Identified obstacles and issues are then addressed in chapters by several outstanding scholars and influential Supreme Court Judges.

This book could not have been made without the enthusiastic collaboration of our authors. They were all wiling to contribute on a relatively short notice for which we are immensely grateful. We would like also to express our sincere gratitude to Anna Gerbrandy, Krijn de Veer and Ton van den Brink from Utrecht University, Faculty of Law, Europa Institute, to Oda Essens from the Competition

Authority of The Netherlands, to Jacques Steenbergen the Director of Competition Authority of Belgium, to Tomas Rymeikis from Lithuania and to Mitja Kocmut from KBL law firm (Ljubljana, Slovenia) for their substantive insights and suggestions.

Our special gratitude goes also to Professor Roger van den Bergh from Erasmus University of Rotterdam for his extraordinary, fascinating, inspiring and path-breaking series of "Ljubljana lectures" which we have been privileged to follow and admire.

We are especially indebted to and would like to express our sincere gratitude for their precious substantive comments, insights, reflections, feedbacks, suggestions, discussions and inspiration to the following judges: Nina Betetto, Judge and Vice-President of the Supreme Court of Slovenia (Slovenia); Diana Magdalena Bulancea, Judge at the Court of Appeals of Rumania, Bucharest (Rumania); Ana Boularot, Judge at the Court of Appeal of Lisbon (Portugal); Karin Butscher, Judge at the Landgericht Frankfurt am Main (Germany); Jakub Camrda, Judge at the Supreme Administrative Court of Czech Republic (Czech Republic); Beatrix Crnogorac, Judge at the Commercial Court in Zagreb (Croatia); Rolf Danckwerts, Judge at the Richter am Landgericht Lehrbeauftragter an der Humboldt-Universität zu Berlin (Germany); Miodrag Djordevic, Judge at the Supreme Court of Slovenia (Slovenia); Marc Fierstra, Judge at the Supreme Court of The Netherlands (Netherlands); Jasna Golubić Vargec, Judge at the Commercial Court in Zagreb (Croatia); Djordje Grbovic, Judge at the District Court of Ljubljana (Slovenia); Herman van Harten, Deputy Judge, District Court of The Hague (The Netherlands); Tina Jakupak, Judge at the Commercial Court in Zagreb (Croatia); Maja Josipović, Judge at the Commercial Court in Zagreb (Croatia); Hendrik Kerkmeester, Judge at the Commercial Chamber at the Court of Appeals Amsterdam and Associate professor at the University of Antwerp Faculty of Law (The Netherlands); Andras Kovacs, Judge at the Administrative-Labour Department of the Supreme Court of Hungary (Hungary); Viktorija Lovrič, Judge at the Supreme Court of Croatia (Croatia); Gorana Aralica Martinović, Judge at the High Commercial Court of Croatia (Croatia); Arjen Meij, Judge and Chamber President at the General Court of the European Union from 1998 until 2010, current Judge at the Court of Appeal of The Hague, The Netherlands and Professors of International and European Law at the University of Luxemburg and Utrecht University, Faculty of Law (The Netherlands); Polona Mlakar Adam, Judge at the District Court of Ljubljana (Slovenia); Beatrix Ocsai, Judge at the OIT Hungary (Hungary); Jan Passer, Judge at the Supreme Administrative Court of Czech Republic and Charles University, Praha (Czech Republic); Veerle Roets, Judge at the Rechtbank van Koophandel Gent (Belgium); Ramute Ruskyte, Judge at the Supreme Court of Lithuania (Lithuania); Marcus Smith, Q.C., Judge and Chairman of the U.K. Competition Appeal Tribunal Court of Appeals (CAT), London (United

Kingdom); Lidija Smolar, Judge at the District Court of Ljubljana (Slovenia); Lucia Sousa, Judge at the Court of Appeal of Lisbon (Portugal); Ron Stam, Judge at the Supreme Court of The Netherlands (The Netherlands); Arunas Sutkevicius, Judge at Lietuvos vyriausiasis administracinis teismas (Lithuania); Iva Karin Šipek, Judge at the Commercial Court in Zagreb (Croatia); Pavel Trna, Judge at the Supreme Administrative Court of Czech Republic (Czech Republic) and Jaap de Wildt, Judge at the Court of Appeals Rotterdam (The Netherlands).

We are also grateful to Anja Bergant, Jaka Cepec, Sandra Durasevič, Lea Perovšek, Martina Petan, Urška Potočnik, Aljoša Valentinčič, Katarina Zajc, Tadeja Žabkar and Vesna Žabkar for their daily, round-a-clock care and immense organisational support. Special thank goes to Leeanna Whirl for her excellent English editing service. We are also fully indebted to Nika Kristina Butina for her tremendous help with fine-tunning of footnotes and bibliographies. This is also the place to thank the publisher Intersentia on behalf of all contributing authors in particular to Tom Scheirs as the responsible publisher officer.

We could not have completed this book without the cooperation and support of the Supreme Court of the Republic of Slovenia (Ljubljana, Slovenia) which hosted our research meetings and plenary discussions.

Finally, thanks are due to the European Commission Directorate General for Competition that has generously supported our Faculty of Economics University of Ljubljana (Slovenia) and Utrecht University Faculty of Law, Europa Institute (The Netherlands) in pursuing a pan-European research project of identifying problems and overcoming obstacles in enforcing EU competition law. One of the related objectives of the research project was also the education of national judges in the context of the public and private enforcement of the European competition rules, including articles 101 and 102 of the Treaty with the emphasis on the economic analysis incumbent in these articles and the enforcement of state aid rules. The goal was to ensure the coherence and consistency in the enforcement of these rules by discussing the practical issues arising in the enforcement of EC competition law in the national courts of the selected Member States and encouraging a debate on these issues aimed at establishing solutions in the form of best practices of the Member States involved. Project also promotes a judicial-scholarly dialogue and creates coherence and consistency in the enforcement of European competition law.

However, this research-training project had also an unintended but highly beneficial, fruitful and rewarding side-effect. Namely, the issue of the proper and effective employment and assessment (understanding) of economic evidences in daily decision-making in competition cases across European Union appeared as one of the most triggering problems that European judiciary is facing while enforcing common EU competition rules and deciding daily competition cases.

This book hence represents a real positive, beneficial externality and reflects the collective wisdom and ideas of European judges, experts and scholars developed in this project over the past four years. We all hope that you will enjoy it.

Ljubljana – Rotterdam, September 2015
Mitja Kovač and Ann-Sophie Vandenberghe

This book could not have been made without extensive financial and organisational support from the European Commission Directorate General for Competition.

European
Commission

What we do need is more dialogue. Like English river Thames that flows in both directions, out to the sea and in to the England with an incoming tide we need dialogue between judges and scholars, judges of national courts and judges of two European supranational courts. We need to pursue many forms of dialogue and judges across Europe shall adopt an international perspective on their work and to be alive to legal and academic issues in other jurisdictions.

Lady Justice Mary Arden, at 106th annual SLS conference,
University of York, 2015

CONTENTS

LIST OF CONTRIBUTORS

Roger van den Bergh, Professor of Law and Economics at the Erasmus University of Rotterdam, Faculty of Law, Rotterdam Institute of Law and Economics (The Netherlands).

Rosamaria Bitetti, Associate professor at LUISS Guido Carli University, Instituto Bruno Leoni (Italy).

Jaka Cepec, Assistance professor at the University of Ljubljana, Faculty of Economics, Department of economic theory and policy (Slovenia).

Miodrag Dordevic, Judge at the Supreme Court of Slovenia (Slovenia).

Michael Faure, Professor of International and Comparative Environmental Law at Maastricht University Faculty of Law and Professor of Comparative Private Law and Economics at the Erasmus University of Rotterdam, Faculty of Law, Rotterdam Institute of Law and Economics (The Netherlands).

Jasminka Pecotic Kaufman, Associate professor at the University of Zagreb Faculty of Economics (Croatia).

Hendrik Kerkmeester, Judge at the Commercial Chamber at the Court of Appeals Amsterdam (The Netherlands) and Associate professor at the University of Antwerp Faculty of Law (Belgium).

Jonathan Klick, Professor of law at the University of Pennsylvania, Faculty of law, Professor of empirical legal studies at Erasmus University of Rotterdam, Faculty of Law and a Maurice R. Greenberg Visiting Professor of Law at Yale University, Yale Law School (USA).

Ayşe Gül Kökkılınç, Professor at the Dokuz Eylül University Izmir, Faculty of Law (Turkey).

Mitja Kovač, Associate professor at the University of Ljubljana Faculty of Economics, Department for economic theory and policy (Slovenia).

Claire Leger, Post-doctoral researcher at the Université Paris Ouest Nanterre la Défense (France).

Vlatka Butorac Malnar, Assistance professor at the University of Rijeka, Faculty of Law (Croatia).

Francisco Marcos, Professor of law at the IE Business School, Instituto de Empresa, Madrid (Spain).

Arjen Meij, Judge and Chamber President at the General Court of the European Union from 1998 until 2010, current Judge at the Court of Appeal of The Hague, The Netherlands and Professors of International and European Law at the University of Luxemburg and Utrecht University, Faculty of Law (The Netherlands).

Danilo Sama, Professor of competition law at LUISS Guido Carli University of Rome (Italy).

Anastasia Shastitko, Assistance professor at the Lomonosov Moscow State University (Russia).

Marcus Smith, Q.C., Judge and Chairman of the U.K. Competition Appeal Tribunal Court of Appeals (CAT), London (United Kingdom).

Rok Spruk, Researcher at the Utrecht University, Faculty of Humanities, Department of economic and social history (The Netherlands).

Ann-Sophie Vandenberghe, Associate professor at the Erasmus University of Rotterdam, Faculty of Law, Rotterdam Institute of Law and Economics (The Netherlands).

Ana Vlahek, Associate professor at the University of Ljubljana Faculty of Law (Slovenia).

Katarina Zajc, Professor of law and economics, University of Ljubljana Faculty of Law (Slovenia).

Sabina Zgaga, Assistance professor at the University of Maribor, Faculty of criminal justice and security (Slovenia).

REVIEWERS

Prof. Dr. Michael G. Faure (Erasmus University Rotterdam),

Prof. Dr. Luigi A. Franzoni (University of Bologna) and

Prof. Dr. Stefan Voigt (University of Hamburg).

GENERAL INTRODUCTION

Miltja Kovač and Ann-Sophie Vandenberghe

This book is motivated by two developments in EU competition law: first, the wider role for national courts to apply and enforce EU competition law, and second, the increasing use of economic theory and economic evidence in competition cases. Since regulation 1/2003[1], national courts play a key role in the enforcement of European competition policy in a variety of scenarios. Some courts act as review courts, hearing appeals which are brought against decisions of the national competition authorities and some courts have jurisdiction over law suits between two private parties, such as actions relating to contracts or actions for damages. The provisions of EU competition law are to a significant extent vague or open-textured, and thus leave scope for different interpretations as to the precise legal content to be applied in specific cases. In a decentralized system where rules are applied by competition authorities and courts from different countries, there is a risk that the rules are not applied uniformly. However, the European Commission is committed to assisting national courts in order to ensure a coherent application of the provisions throughout Europe. The increasing use of economic theory and economic evidence in competition cases is a reflection of the economic approach to competition law. Since the late nineties the Commission has indicated to favor the economic approach to competition law over a pure legal-formalistic approach.[2] The economic approach essentially boils down to a functional interpretation of competition law which means that rules are construed so as to achieve the objective of welfare maximization. This objective would only be randomly achieved, at the expense of numerous errors, if economic thinking and market dynamics would be ignored.[3] Competition law must therefore be guided by economic analysis,

---

1 Council Regulation (EC) No 1/2003 of 16 December 2002 on the implementation of the rules on competition laid down in Articles 81 and 82 of the Treaty [2003] OJ L1/1. Articles 81 and 82 of the then EC Treaty have since (without any modification) become Articles 101 and 102 TFEU.

2 Commission Notice on Guidelines on vertical restraints [2000] OJ C291/1, Commission Notice on Guidelines on the application of Article 81 of the Treaty to horizontal cooperation agreements [2001] OJ C3/2, Commission Notice on Guidelines on the application of Article 81(3) of the EC Treaty [2004] OJ C101/97.

3 Speech by Mario Monti," A reformed competition policy: achievements and challenges for the future", Centre for European Reform, Brussels, 28 October 2004, http://ec.europa.eu/competition/publications/cpn/2004_3_1.pdf.

otherwise the law acts blindly upon forces it does not understand and produces results it does not intend.[4] Economic analysis can inform competition law about how a decision model should look like (i.e. which questions to ask and in what order, when evaluating whether a competition infringement exists) in order to minimize the social costs of decision errors. A type I error (false positive) exists when competition authorities or courts conclude that a particular act is illegal where in reality the act is good from a social welfare perspective. A type II error (false negative) exists when competition authorities or courts conclude that a particular act is legal whereas in reality the act is bad from a social welfare perspective. Hence, an improvement of the economic analysis enhances the quality of competition law by making it less error-prone. Under modern EU competition law, cases are increasingly decided through an examination of the effects of the challenged activity on social welfare as judged by modern economic theory and sophisticated statistical analyses. Economics offers a set of insights, suggestions, practical tests, econometric and statistical techniques that make the application of the law more effective and efficient. Such techniques and insights enable the generation of robust economic evidence that may be employed in order to support and strengthen the arguments presented in competition cases.

The thesis of this book is that the decentralization of EU competition law increases the importance of the economic approach. Ideally, the economic approach enhances transparency and legal certainty, and has harmonizing effects, by providing a coherent analytical framework for decision-making and by relying on objective economic standards and tools, when measuring the impact of an agreement or practice on social welfare or efficiency. However, there are reasons to doubt that current EU-wide competition law practice fully corresponds with that ideal. Heavy reliance on economic evidence in competition cases may seem indicated, or contraindicated, by the many economic mistakes that courts have made in those cases.[5] Moreover, the courts have often misunderstood the core concepts and theories, and also mishandled economic evidence.[6] The use of economic theory and economic evidence in competition cases, their appropriate interpretation, meaning, impact, usefulness and validity are among the most challenging issues that judges and legal practitioners are facing in their daily decision-making. Questions, for example, of how courts and other decision-making bodies should employ economic evidence and what weight (and credibility) should be attached to such evidence where different experts offer different suggestions have still to be addressed thoroughly. Much still needs to be done to improve the effective employment of economic evidence and of economic experts in competition cases. The aim of the

---

4 Bork, The Antitrust Paradox: A policy at war with itself (basic books,1978), p. 97.

5 Posner, 2001, at 294. See also Posner, 2011.

6 Stigler, J. George, "The Dominant Firm and the Inverted Umbrella," in "The Organization of Industry" 39, 1968.

book is twofold: first to find out which obstacles and objections (of a principled, practical, informational, institutional, legal or other nature) may stand in the way of a full-fledged application of the economic approach in competition cases and second, to provide tools for judges and legal practitioners to employ economic evidence in a more effective, predictable way so as to overcome the identified, EU-wide obstacles in enforcing EU competition law.

The quality of competition law is best served by an integration of competition law and competition economics. This implies – to use the words of Lord Denning from the introductory quote – that both lawyers and economists have to learn to become amphibious if they wish to keep their heads above water. For judges who have to evaluate economic assessments this implies preparing for a new role: that of gatekeepers regarding expert economic expert to avoid junk science from entering the court room. There is also room for improvement on the side of the economists. Economic analysis is useful to legal scholars when it offers clear and intuitive practical guidance. This requires that the economic approach is consequently converted into a full decision-making model for solving legal cases. The Commission in its guidelines provides a fundamental analytical framework. The framework could be improved by making it more complete and consistent, and by a full and consequent integration of economic insights.

This book consists of 19 chapters which all address the importance, implications, practices, problems and the role of economic evidence in EU competition law. It includes contributions on the use of the economic approach in the application and enforcement of EU competition law in different countries, including mainly EU member states (Slovenia, the Netherlands, Spain, the U.K., Croatia), but also candidate member states (Turkey) and third countries (Russia). The choice to select contributions from different countries follows from the decentralization of the enforcement of EU competition law. The contributions are written by scholars who are experts in the field of competition law and economics as well as by judges who can provide first-hand information on the use of economic evidence in practice. Some contributions discuss the use of the economic approach at a more fundamental level, others discuss the economic approach as applied to a specific case in a particular country. The book is not limited to a particular subfield of competition law, but covers the area of competition law at large, including state aid. This reflects the fact that also the European Commission has gradually expanded the application of the economic approach to all areas of competition law. Finally, the book covers issues on the substance of competition law as well enforcement issues. An optimal enforcement structure is as important as an optimal content of competition law. Enforcement levels should be high enough to create sufficient incentives to stick to the rules and there is some evidence that competition rules are under-enforced.

The book is divided into five parts. Part I deals with economic methods in competition law; Part II deals with different types of economic evidence in competition law; Part III discusses insider trading, cartels and criminalization of such behaviour; Part IV reflects on preliminary rulings and state aid controls; whereas Part V offers discussions on economic evidence, enforcement problems and national courts. Here follows a short description of the individual chapters.

In Chapter 1 of Part I, Roger Van den Bergh focuses on the more fundamental question whether more economics implies better competition law. Professor Van den Bergh actually opens an avenue for further scholarly research by stressing the critical question of whether more economics in European competition law is too much or not enough. Van den Bergh argues that this answer depends on the goal(s) that competition rules are trying to achieve. These goals may be either economic or non-economic, but even in the first case there is not such a thing as 'the right' economic approach. The answer to the question how much and which kind of economics must be used in competition law entirely flows from the particular policy goal that has been chosen. A lot of economics is missing if the goal of EU competition law is fostering total welfare. However, the assessment changes if not total welfare but the protection of consumers' interests is advanced as the goal of EU competition law. Besides total welfare and consumer welfare, there exists a third economic approach: competition rules may be seen as instruments to preserve the competitive process as such and guarantee economic freedom of market participants. Van den Bergh also analyses some of the objections raised by competition lawyers, competition authorities and judges to a full-fledged economic approach to competition law. While some of these objections can be discarded as inappropriate, two of them have to be taken seriously. First, the level of abstraction of economic models make them mathematically sophisticated but, at the same time, inapt to capture the essence of real-life markets. Second, the application of competition rules in practice imposes limitations on the use of economics that are often overlooked in the economists' profession. Economic approaches which are technically refined may point in the direction of potentially different outcomes. Such analyses, as Van den Bergh argues, may be unsuited for application by competition authorities and judges since they collide with 'rule of law' requirements of clarity, predictability and legal certainty. In spite of its potential benefits, an extended application of economic approaches may also increase the administrative costs of the legal system. After all, as van den Bergh suggests, competition law is more than applied micro-economics and also the use of economics in antitrust law must pass a cost-benefit test.

Jonathan Klick in Chapter 2 addresses the issue on the value of training in quantitative methods for judges. Modern competition law disputes frequently involve decisions that hinge on quantitative or theoretically sophisticated economic evidence. The U.S Supreme Court's Daubert ruling left federal judges in the clear role of gatekeepers regarding expert evidence. While such a gatekeeper function is necessary to prevent junk science from entering the court room, few judges have backgrounds sufficient to prepare them for this function. Courses on statistics, economics, and finance are almost entirely absent in legal education programs even though judicial analysis of these matters affects untold resources throughout the world on a daily basis. Klick also argues that reliance on a judge's own ambition to be a better consumer of scientific and quantitative evidence is overly optimistic; nor will institutional safeguards remedy the knowledge deficit of judges worldwide. The available evidence according to Klick actually suggests that judges desire the training that would be necessary to fill in these gaps. Klick also offers ample evidence that such training can lead to improved judicial decision making. Namely, the evidence regarding judicial desire is related to the publication of the Federal Judicial Center's Manual on Scientific Evidence in the wake of the Supreme Court's Daubert ruling which left federal judges in the clear role of gatekeepers regarding expert evidence. Qualitative evidence suggests that judges are indeed interested in easily available, well-done resources to improve their ability to make judgments regarding the kind of sophisticated quantitative evidence that arises in modern cases. Further, there are indications that the influence of the FJC's work spread beyond the nominal audience of the federal judiciary, potentially improving the work of state judges as well. Klick concludes with a call for providing judges with attractive and low-cost educational opportunities and resources that has the potential to mitigate the gaps they otherwise have in their backgrounds. Expanding such opportunities both in the US and in EU will according to Klick likely generate a very high social return.

In Chapter 3, Rok Spruk extensively discusses reliable research methods in applied econometrics for competition law. Spruk in his chapter seeks to fill the gap between qualitative aspects of the competition law and the quantitative analytical background of judicial decision making in the area of competition law. His chapter focusses on how the tools of applied econometrics can be utilized to help investigators, judges and policymakers disentangle the very essential questions on whether and to what extent the proposed change in the competition law can influence the outcomes of interest and how such experiments can be validated. Moreover, Spruk's chapter provides an introductory treatment in applied econometric methods for antitrust investigators by focusing on the most common tools such as (i) linear regression analysis, (ii) panel data econometrics and (iii) difference-in-difference analysis. In the modern econometric paradigm, these tools allow judges and investigators establish the determinants and predictors of cartel-based collusion, abuse of state aid and also facilitate a broader understanding on how policy changes can be exploited to determine its effectiveness or failure.

Part III of this book deals with general topics of economic evidences in competition law. In the first chapter, Chapter 4, Judge and Professor Kerkmeester argues that the way judges handle economic evidence very much depends on the institutional context. Justice Kerkmeester also points out that in administrative law, even without an economic background, judges are able to handle economic evidence if they apply their normal procedural rules. Moreover, because of the interrelation of economic and legal issues, they probably can do so better than a court-appointed expert would. However, he also suggests that it still might be useful to teach judges on economics in order to take away possible prejudices and to make judges feel more at ease when economic evidence is involved. Besides basics of the methodology of economics and its applications in administrative law, attention should be, according to Judge Kerkmeester, paid to practical examples, preferably based on the "best practices" of other national judges.

Next chapter deals with the applicability of behavioural law and economics evidence in courtrooms. Mitja Kovac summarizes in Chapter 5 the insights that behavioural law and economics have brought to discussion and concludes that such behavioural evidence might indeed shed additional light on the market outcomes and that indeed might be employed by modern EU courts as an additional tool to assess the anti-competitive practices of certain market players. However, he concludes that considering behavioural insights does not yet require a fundamental shift of current competition policy.

In Chapter 6, his Justice Marcus Smith, Q.C. in his outstanding chapter discusses puzzling and highly significant issues of judges, their *ex ante* decisions, evidence and related proof. Justice Smith discusses the evidential difference between *ex ante* and *ex post* regulation and presents a breath-taking analysis of the recent decision in the 08x Case and the related approach of Ofcom and his findings.

Chapter 7 on law and economics evidence in competition law, written by Katarina Zajc, surveys the literature on economic analysis of competition law, offers an empirical analysis of related case law and discusses the use of economic tools and evidence in competition cases litigated in the Republic of Slovenia. Surprisingly, Zajc founds that although the Notice sets the SSNIP test as the primary test of the relevant market and only then (as a secondary method) considers qualitative indicators, the Slovenian authorities think otherwise. She argues that regardless of the hierarchy of tests, introduced by the Supreme Court and the CPO, the SSNIP test should already be the primary tool because it is rigorous and the only one that leads to clear results. According to Zajc employing qualitative indicators leaves the reader of the decisions with a bitter taste of doubt over the correctness of the decision.

Part III. of this book deals with insider trading, cartels and criminalization. In the first chapter, Chapter 8, Michael Faure and Claire Leger provide an insightful and an outstanding analysis of the criminalization of insider trading at the EU level. Faure and Leger argue that there is currently little evidence that the enforcement of insider trading laws at Member State level would be ineffective, as far as 27 out of the 28 EU Member States have criminal law to back-up insider trading legislation. Hence, the added value of European legislation in this respect might be limited. According to Faure and Leger the mere imposition of criminal sanctions at EU level will not guarantee that problems with the effective enforcement of insider trading law, that would currently exist in the Member States, would be solved. Moreover, the Commission refers to a current 'ineffective enforcement' of insider trading law, but there is not much empirical proof that is provided to back this up. They conclude that economic theory casts doubt on whether there is effectively a need of imposing criminal sanctions at European level; the contents of the proposal is moreover to a large extent incompatible with fundamental principles of criminal law.

Sabina Zgaga offers in Chapter 9 a very different, purely legal, but highly sophisticated analysis on the criminalization of EU competition law. Zgaga in her chapter surveys the arguments for regulating and enforcing criminal responsibility in addition to the responsibility for misdemeanours in cases of unlawful restriction of competition in Slovenia and to critically assess current Slovenian legislation. She also proposes that the unlawful restriction of competition and, thereby violations of primary rules are classified as misdemeanours, for which the undertakings and their responsible persons should be held responsible. Violation of competition law should be according to Zgaga classified also as a criminal act, defined by national criminal legislations or potentially even European law. Two separate, but also intertwined forms of legal responsibility could therefore arise in the case of the restriction of competition.

In Chapter 10, Danilo Sama discusses cartel detection and collusion screening and provides an empirical analysis of the London metal exchange. Danilo Sama argues that in order to detect and fight cartel conducts, the best scenario for competition agencies would be of course the possibility to analyze detailed information on firms' costs and prices, being the price-cost margin a robust indicator of market power. However, information on firms' costs is rarely available. In this context, as pointed out by his analysis of the London Metal Exchange, quick tests such as Benford's Law can only be helpful to inspect markets where price patterns show signs of collusion. Given the budget constraints to which antitrust watchdogs are commonly subject to, a such price screen could be set up, just exploiting the data available, as warning system to identify cases that require the opening of an investigation. Nevertheless, Sama also stresses out that Benford's Law, as any other statistical test, cannot be adopted as investigative tool in any circumstance, since not all real data are expected to obey the law at issue. The risk otherwise is to fall into false-positive assessments. In any case, as Sama argues, what seems certain is the fact that such a useful instrument, if not employed by competition authorities, will be surely used by firms to further disguise and mystify cartel activities.

Francisco Marcos addresses extensively damages claims in the Spanish sugar cartel in Chapter 11. Sama looks at the € 5 million award for damages caused by the cartel as one of the most relevant developments in private enforcement of competition law in Spain to date. The final decisions on the case by the Spanish Supreme Court include several relevant rulings that will mark civil redress for victims of competition violations in Spain in the future. Marcos' investigation shows that the Supreme Court holdings are in line with the new Directive 2014/104/EU of 26 November 2014 on certain rules governing actions for damages under national law for infringements of the competition law provisions of the Member States and of the EU. Firstly, it has clarified the legal force that prior public enforcement decisions by competition authorities as a ground for follow-on private litigation claims. Secondly, it has also spelt out the assessment of expert forensic opinions in court. Finally, it delineated how the conventional civil rules on compensation apply to these claims, leaving room for the passing-on defence to operate if proof enough is provided by the defendants.

Part IV of this book deals with preliminary rulings and state aid control. In Chapter 12 his Justice and professor Arjen Mei provides a marvellous and insightful discussion of state aid cases in national courts and on the role of European Commission. Justice Mei offers a picture of EU State aid control as an intriguing system of multilevel administration and judicial activity. Interestingly, it is the very meeting point of the distinct and complementary roles of the Commission and national courts in the application of the notion of State aid that triggers the delimitation of those roles in the DHL v FFH Case. Furthermore, Justice Mei also argues that the national courts seem to be picking up their particular role within the framework of each Member State's autonomous, but adapting national procedural system. This development is enhanced by the Commission's policy to the effect of providing for extensive regulatory frameworks and reducing the number of cases dealt with by the Commission. The shift in the activity of the Commission towards a role of amicus curiae in State aid proceedings in national courts, however, will as Justice Mei argues, require close scrutiny.

In Chapter 13 Jaka Cepec discusses the issues of restructuring the concept of state aid. His chapter offers an overview of the Rescue and Restructuring State Aid Guidelines with an emphasis on the criteria that must be met for R&R State Aid to be in compliance with the TFEU rules on competition law. Cepec argues that the main, practical implication of the New Guidelines consists of making it more difficult for companies to be eligible for rescue and restructuring aid and to comply with the compatibility criteria for Commission approval.

In the final chapter of Part IV, Chapter 14, Ayşe Gül Kökkılınç reviews the literature on Turkish EU accession process and provides an elaborated analysis of judicial review and state aid in the current Turkish competition law.

The final part of this book, Part V., consist of five chapters that offer varied perspectives on the particular issues of economic evidences and related enforcement problems encountered by specific national courts, competition authorities and lawmakers. Rosamaria Bitetti in Chapter 15. argues that a competition policy informed by weak economic models might stop the movement of innovation, and that one should accept that, at least until the night has fallen and we can better understand the new economy, we should have a cautionary approach to competition law. In Chapter 16. Jasminka Pecotic Kaufman and Vlatka Butorac Malnar indentify the turning point in Croatian competition law – that has been the entry into force of the Interim Agreement which made possible the coming into force of article 70 SAA, which in turn, provided for the application of EU competition law in Croatia. After initial challenges, the practice of applying EU rules became stable after the Constitutional Court's decision to approve the practice of the Competition Agency in relying on EU law by qualifying EU rules as 'an auxiliary means of interpretation.'

Anastasia Shastitko, in Chapter 17, analyzes the employment of economic evidence and related enforcement problems in the Russian competition law. Her investigation confirms that an economic analysis increases the durability of cases. However, this evidence is according to Shastitko not enough to conclude that the usage of economic analysis leads to higher social costs. The benefits and costs of its application should be weighted in order to analyze the effect on social welfare. She also shows that economic analysis is an important argument in litigation and that it increases the probability of antitrust authority to make out a case. Thus if a decision about application of economic analysis is based on its weight in litigation, its application should be extended. But the antitrust authority of Russia seems to underestimate the role an economic analysis could play in litigation. The investigation of the demand for economic analysis in Russia revealed that it is used mostly in cases under article 10 (abuse of dominant position). Hence the Russian antitrust authority is more likely to be obliged to use an economic analysis than be aware of its real power.

In Chapter 18 Ana Vlahek analyses focal elements of current regulation of private enforcement of antitrust in Slovenia. She focuses on the relevant European legal framework, in particular on the new Directive 2014/104 and its travaux preparatoires, as well as on relevant national legislation. Article 62 of the Prevention of Restriction of Competition Act of 2008 (PRCA-1) setting down some specific rules as regards antitrust damages lawsuits, and other, more general pieces of Slovenian legislation relevant in proceedings of private enforcement of antitrust are also presented and are assessed through the prism of the new directive. Further, her chapter elaborates on the status quo of private enforcement of European and national antitrust in Slovenia and tries to find reasons for its inefficiency. Relevant follow-on and stand-alone private lawsuits that are or were pending before Slovenian courts that are analysed in the final chapter, also mirror the challenges of Slovenian judiciary in private antitrust enforcement proceedings.

In the last chapter, Chapter 19, Justice Miodrag Dordevic calls for the establishment of a system that would ensure that the competition in the common market is not distorted, Articles 101 and 102 of the Treaty must be according to Justice Dordevic applied effectively and uniformly in the European Community. In order to ensure the effective enforcement of the Community competition rules and the proper functioning of the cooperation mechanisms, it is, in Justice Dordevic's view, necessary to develop the best practices in international competition law enforcement proceedings.

BIBLIOGRAPHY

Bishop, Simon and Mike Walker, "The Economics of EC Competition Law: Concepts, Application and Measurement," 3rd ed., Sweet & Maxwell, 2010.

Bork, R., The antitrust paradox. A policy at war with itself, Basic Books, New York 1978

Carlton, W. Denis, Gertner, H. Robert, and Andrew M. Rosenfield, "Communication among Competitors: Game Theory and Antitrust," 5 George Mason Law review 423, 1997.

Carlton, W. Dennis, "A Reexamination of Delivered Pricing System," 23 Journal of Law and Economics 51, 1983.

Corts, S. Kenneth, "On the Competitive Effects of Price-Matching Policies," 15 International Journal of Industrial Organization 283, 1997.

Griffin, M. James and William S. Neilson, "The 1985–87 Oil Price Collapse and afterwards: What does Game Theory add?," 32 Econ. Inquiry 543, 1994.

Pindyck, S. Robert, "Gains to Producers from the Cartelization of Exhaustible Resources," 60 Rev. Econ. & Stat. 238, 1978.

Posner A. Richard, "Antitrust Law," 2nd ed., Chiacago University Press, 2001.

Posner A. Richard, "Economic Analysis of Law," 8th ed., Wolters Kluwer, 2011.

Shepard, Andrea, "Price Discrimination and retail Configuration," 99 Journal of political Economy 30, 1991.

Tirole Jean, "The Theory of Industrial Organization," Harvard University Press, 1988.

Stigler, J. George, "The Dominant Firm and the Inverted Umbrella," in "The Organization of Industry" 39, 1968.

Sugden, R., "A Theory of focal Points," 105 Econ. J. 535, 1995.

PART I

ECONOMIC METHODS IN COMPETITION LAW

CHAPTER 1

THE MORE ECONOMIC APPROACH IN EUROPEAN COMPETITION LAW: IS MORE TOO MUCH OR NOT ENOUGH?

Roger VAN DEN BERGH

1. INTRODUCTION

In the recent past, economic theories have had an increasing impact on the application of competition rules at both sides of the Atlantic Ocean. The impact of economics has been most clearly visible in the United States of America (US), where competition law is commonly called antitrust law.[1] Whereas the impact of economic theories on antitrust law became visible in the US already from the 1970ies onwards, the impact of modern industrial organisation theory[2] on competition law in the European Union (EU) is a more recent phenomenon. It took until the launch of the so-called More Economic Approach (MEA) by the European Commission in the late 1990ies before economics started to make its way in the enforcement of the competition rules. Today, economic insights have become indispensable for every day antitrust practice. Competition law practitioners often are so heavily busy investigating the intricacies of the economics of competition that they lose out of sight the more fundamental questions about the use of economic theories in antitrust enforcement. This article takes on the latter issues and asks the important question whether more economics also implies better competition law.

Before assessing the MEA, a crucial preliminary question is whether competition law pursues only economic goals. Economic commentators often take the economic goals of antitrust law for granted and, in their analyses, they use sophisticated economic models to prescribe an optimal competition policy.

---

1 In this chapter the terms competition law and antitrust law are used interchangeably.

2 Industrial organization theory is the branch of micro-economics, which studies behaviour of firms in markets. It includes price theory, contestable markets theory, game theory, and transaction cost theory. For an introduction to economic approaches of competition law, see R. Van den Bergh and P. Camesasca, op.cit., p. 54–104.

In this way competition law is transformed into applied micro-economics.[3] Such an approach is far from evident when the history of the competition laws is taken into consideration. In the US, antitrust law has experienced more and less economically oriented cycles. In the early days of US antitrust, protection of individual competitors and structural interventions in markets were widely accepted. This approach led to welfare losses by protecting inefficient small retailers or prohibiting mergers that could have achieved important economies of scale. The picture changed dramatically when these interventionist views were criticised by the Chicago School, which stressed the protection of the competitive process, rather than the protection of competitors, as an instrument of increasing total welfare. Today, the goals of allocative efficiency (total welfare) and consumer welfare have become dominant in the US. Consequently, industrial organisation theory has become indispensable for a proper understanding and application of the US antitrust rules.

The picture is different at the other side of the Atlantic. The history of EU competition law shows a multitude of goals for competition law. The enforcement of the competition rules started with a clear focus on the goal of market integration, which is a broad political objective. At the same time emphasis was put on safeguarding the competitive process and the protection of economic freedom. The latter goals were based largely on the views of the Ordoliberal School, which is a legal-economic approach to competition law that does not have its equivalent in the history of US antitrust law. Later, EU competition law gradually evolved towards efficiency goals and, recently, policy makers stress above all the goal of increasing consumer welfare. At the same time, a wide variety of political goals (market integration, levelling the playing field for industry in Europe) remains prominently present in the policy statements of the European Commission. On top of this, the European Commission continues to emphasise the interdependence of competition policy with other EU policies (environmental policy, social policy…). Obviously, if the goal to be achieved is not defined in micro-economic terms, the stylised economic models developed in price theory and game theory will not be able to provide appropriate guidance to EU competition law.

The structure of this chapter is as follows. After this introduction, section two focuses on the different goals of competition law. A discussion of the multiple objectives of EU competition law is needed since the choice of an appropriate economic theory for solving an antitrust problem is crucially dependent on the goal that competition rules are trying to achieve. Section three argues that there is not (yet) enough economics included in the MEA, under the (strong) assumption that EU competition law aims at increasing total welfare and should, therefore, be in harmony with insights from industrial organisation

3 For example, the title of Motta's excellent textbook on industrial organization theory suggests that competition policy is not different from competition economics. See M. Motta, op.cit.

theory. Two examples will be given to illustrate the broad range of disharmonies. The first example relates to the persisting differences in the legal treatment of vertical restraints, which are inconsistent with economic insights from transaction cost theory. The second example is the blatant inconsistency between the damage compensation that can be claimed by victims of antitrust violations and the real economic size of the harm, as it should be calculated from a total welfare perspective. Section four stresses that there are different economic approaches to competition law. A lot of (alternative) economics may be missing if not the total welfare paradigm but a different economic approach is chosen to guide competition policy. Section five contrasts an economic approach to competition problems with the demands of the legal system. It investigates why competition law practitioners and judges may be reluctant to adopt a purely economic approach. Concerns exist with respect to the underlying assumptions of economic approaches and hidden value judgements. Even if the 'right' economic methodology is chosen, benefits of increased economic consistency may be outweighed by losses caused by increased legal uncertainty and higher administrative costs of the legal system. Section six concludes.

2. THE GOALS OF COMPETITION LAW: AN UNRESOLVED PUZZLE

In his seminal work, *The Antitrust Paradox*, Judge Robert Bork wrote: "Antitrust policy cannot be made rational until we are able to give a firm answer to one question: what is the point of the law–what are its goals? Everything else follows from the answer we give."[4] This quote stresses that the relative importance of economic theory in applying competition law is dependent on the goals that competition law is attempting to serve. If competition law only pursues economic goals, an economic approach is more apparent than if the objectives to be achieved by competition law are non-economic by nature. Here the problem starts. Competition law may serve a multitude of goals, comprising both economic and non-economic objectives. But even if the goals of competition law were purely economic, confusion about the objectives of the antitrust rules would not automatically disappear.

If the analysis is restricted to economic goals, there are no less than three different perspectives. The first view, which is commonly associated with the Chicago School, sees total welfare as the only goal of antitrust law. Defined in static terms, the total welfare goal refers to the maximisation of productive and allocative efficiency. As will be further explained below, the analysis may be broadened to include dynamic efficiency, but this will lead to difficult trade-offs.

4 R. Bork, op.cit., p. 50.

The second view is currently very popular among competition authorities. It stresses that, next to efficiency goals, competition law should above all foster consumer welfare. The main difference between the first and the second view is that the latter puts emphasis on the negative distributional effects of market power. It is not in the first place the allocation effect of monopoly (lower production, deadweight-loss) but above all the price effect (higher consumer prices) that justifies antitrust intervention.[5] A third view, which has its roots in the ordoliberal tradition of EU competition law, advances the protection of individual economic freedom as the central goal of competition law. In this section, the total welfare view is contrasted with the consumer welfare view. The discussion of the ordoliberal approach is postponed to section 4 of this paper.

2.1. TOTAL WELFARE VERSUS CONSUMER WELFARE

The most difficult contemporary trade-off results from the potential conflict between the efficiency goals stressed by economists, and the consumer welfare goal so much cherished by competition authorities. For a proper understanding of the potential conflicts between, on the one hand, the goals of economic efficiency and the consumer welfare goal, on the other, one needs to be familiar with three different efficiency concepts and their potential incompatibility: two static concepts (productive efficiency, allocative efficiency) and one dynamic concept.

First, productive efficiency refers to a situation in which sellers maximise output by using the socially optimal number and quality of inputs in the production process. In a perfectly competitive market firms produce at minimum efficient scale; this advantage gets lost under monopoly since the output reducing monopolist does not achieve potential productive efficiency gains. In sum, productive efficiency implies maximisation of output given the availability of inputs through cost minimisation. Allocative efficiency is a different notion. It is also denoted as the 'total welfare standard', since it describes a situation where both producer surplus and consumer surplus are maximised. Producer surplus is the difference between the cost of production and the selling price that manufacturers receive. Consumer surplus is the difference between what buyers would be willing to spend for acquiring a good and what they actually pay. Total welfare is achieved in a perfectly competitive

5 Under monopoly some consumers pay too high prices (price effect); this can be seen as an undesirable transfer of wealth from the consumers to the monopolist. Other consumers, who would have purchased the product at a competitive price, cease buying the product. This leads to a deadweight loss, since the potential profits of additional sales are not captured by the monopolist. Compared to a perfectly competitive market, monopoly changes a part of the consumer surplus into producer surplus, whereas another part of the consumer surplus is lost completely.

market, where firms produce what buyers want and are willing to pay for. In such market, the outcome is called Pareto-optimal since no seller or buyer can be made better off without someone being made worse off. By contrast, monopoly causes welfare losses and distributional effects that may be undesirable. On top of the loss of productive efficiency mentioned above, a part of the consumer surplus is transferred to the monopolist. This is the price effect of monopoly: consumers have to pay *supra*-competitive prices for acquiring goods. Next to the price effect, there is the allocation effect of monopoly. The monopolist ceases production when marginal cost exceeds marginal revenue. In this way, buyers who are willing to buy goods at a price higher than the (profit-maximising) monopoly price do not receive additional quantities of the monopolised good. As a consequence, neither the producer (who does not make additional profits) nor the consumer (who does not get supplies) gains; the ensuing loss is called 'deadweight loss'.

The notions of productive and allocative efficiency are static concepts; they are all based on an economic equilibrium analysis. The analysis of dynamic efficiency does not focus on the price or allocation effects of monopoly but on the optimal degree of innovation in markets. From the latter perspective a monopoly is not necessarily a bad thing. The prospect of monopoly rewards that awaits the most innovative companies is in itself a great spur to competition. Prohibiting monopoly prices may suppress dynamic competition and hinder innovation in rapidly evolving technological markets. As long as monopoly positions are temporary and excessive profits are eroded by newcomers offering more innovative products, a process of 'creative destruction'[6] will guarantee dynamic efficiency in the long run. Outside the mainstream literature, which is criticised often for its static view of competition, the literature taking a dynamic perspective on competition puts emphasis on dynamic efficiency and monopoly power is redefined as immunity from competitive threats.[7]

The concepts of efficiency explained above are fundamentally different and their simultaneous implementation in antitrust practice necessitates trade-offs. An example can illustrate this. A merger may enable the post-merger firm to reduce the average costs of production. However, at the same time the merger may enhance market power and enable the post-merger firm to charge *supra*-competitive prices. On the one hand, the merger may thus produce benefits in the form of productive efficiencies. On the other hand, the merger may cause harm through price increases leading to allocative inefficiencies. The ensuing welfare trade-off, which was first analysed by Nobel Prize laureate Oliver Williamson, may be solved if total welfare is the goal of competition law. As long as the size of the cost savings (the productive efficiency rectangle) is larger than the loss caused by the allocation effect of increased market power (the

6 This concept goes back to J. Schumpeter, op.cit.

7 See for example C. Kirchner, op.cit.

deadweight loss triangle), the merger increases total welfare.[8] In this case, the normative criterion of Kaldor-Hicks efficiency[9] may be applied since the gains of the post-merger firm are so large that it could potentially compensate the consumers who have to pay higher prices.

The welfare trade-off becomes more complicated when not total welfare but consumer welfare is advanced as the goal of competition law. It should immediately be added that consumer welfare is not a concept that is employed as such in industrial organisation theory. In price theory, the notion of consumer surplus is defined as the difference between the competitive price and the price that consumers would be willing to pay. This consumer surplus is maximised in a perfectly competitive market. By contrast, under monopoly a part of this surplus is transferred to the producer and another part gets lost. If competition law aims at maximising consumer surplus, anti-competitive practices may be outlawed because of the undesirable distributional consequences of monopoly. Turning back to the above merger example, it is clear that consumer welfare may conflict with the total welfare goal. Those who object to the distributional consequences of monopoly power will not advocate allowing a merger because the post-merger firm could potentially compensate the losses of consumers. If competition law is used as an instrument of redistribution, one will object to the price increases and the merger will be allowed only if consumers also get their share of the cost savings and will be effectively better off afterwards, or if prices remain at least constant after the merger.

How are the potentially conflicting goals of efficiency and consumer welfare balanced against each other in everyday competition practice? Unfortunately, EU policy makers do not always make us much wiser about the economic goals to be achieved by competition law and how the different goals should be ranked in case of conflicts. Statements of the European Commissioners for Competition often mention the goals of consumer welfare and efficient allocation of resources alongside each other, without paying attention to the possible interpretation problems and unavoidable trade-offs. A typical example of such statements is the following quote from former Commissioner Kroes: "Our aim is simple, to protect competition as a means of enhancing consumer welfare and ensuring an efficient allocation of resources. An effects based approach grounded in solid economics, ensures that citizens enjoy the benefits of a competitive dynamic market economy"[10] Unfortunately, simplicity is not a characteristic of competition policy when the rules aim at two different, potentially conflicting, goals. Moreover, the reference to a competitive market economy brings also

---

8 O. Williamson, op.cit.

9 Kaldor-Hicks efficiency implies that policy changes generate gains that are sufficiently large, so that those who gain could potentially compensate those who lose. Notice that this criterion requires only potential compensation. Effective compensation would satisfy the Pareto criterion, implying that nobody gets worse-off.

10 N. Kroes, op. cit.

dynamic efficiency into the picture. Allocative efficiency, consumer welfare and dynamic efficiency do not always go together. Without explicitly recognising the potential conflicts and ranking the opposing goals competition law risks remaining inconsistent and unpredictable.

2.2. FURTHER COMPLICATIONS: A BROADER CONSUMER WELFARE CONCEPT AND NON-ECONOMIC GOALS

Looking for a definition of consumer welfare, maximisation of consumer surplus is not the only possible goal of competition law. Consumer welfare may be interpreted in a broader sense. The concept may encompass not only increases of consumer surplus but also 'freedom of choice', so that consumers may choose among a large variety of goods those products which best fit their preferences. Economic analysis typically focuses upon price whereas other elements of consumer choice, such as quality and variety, are not directly addressed. The mainstream economic view accepts price as a proxy for quality but alternative approaches give a different content to the notion of consumer welfare. In a broader definition, not only prices but also quality, variety and innovation (dynamic efficiency) may be considered.[11] In addition, by stressing freedom of choice for consumers, a link may be established with ordoliberal thoughts. The freedom for business people to choose how to compete and their freedom to select trading partners[12] may find its corollary in the freedom of consumers to find the best quality among a variety of suppliers.

The complications caused by diverging conceptions of efficiency and consumer welfare are not yet the end of the competition law puzzle. The picture gets further complicated when statements of policy makers or decisions of competition authorities reveal non-economic goals. In the EU, these statements include the political goal of market integration but also goals of industrial policy[13], environmental policy[14], and employment objectives.[15] EU competition law thus pursues a multitude of economic, political, social and moral goals. But

11 R. Lande, op. cit.

12 As indicated by Erich Hoppmann, the two components of freedom of competition are 'Freiheit im Parallalprozess' and 'Freiheit im Austauschprozess'. See: E. Hoppmann, op. cit.

13 Competition policy is a key element to foster the competitiveness of European industries and to attain the goals of the Lisbon strategy; see: Working together for growth and jobs: A new start for the Lisbon strategy COM (2005) 24,2.

14 European Commission, 25th Annual Report on Competition Policy, Brussels, 1995, para 85; Decision of 21.12.1994 [1994] OJ L 378/37 Philips/Osram; Decision of 24.01.1999 [2000] OJ L 187/47, paras 55 et seq.

15 Decision of 23.12.1992 [1992] OJ L 20/14, para 23 Ford/Volkswagen; Decision of 29.04.1994 [1994] OJ L 131/15, para 27 *Stichting Baksteen*. The last case is the only decision in which the European Commission accepted price restraints to counter the effects of an economic crisis. This decision seemed to be isolated from the main of EU competition goal but could get new support in the context of the current economic crisis. The experience of the earlier crisis in

even if competition law aims only at economic objectives, competition authorities and judges will not be able to escape from difficult trade-offs in the absence of a unifying single economic goal. Given this multi-valued tradition, a one-dimensional economic approach to competition law is not obvious. As a first step to bring more clarity and increase predictability, one could consider confining competition law goals to economic objectives and pursuing other goals through different legal instruments (public regulation, contract law, consumer law). A more demanding alternative is rethinking the goals of competition law and eventually rank them by using a constitutional economics perspective.[16] Within the limits of this paper these difficult questions cannot be further elaborated but the competition goal puzzle should always be kept in mind when the inconsistencies of current EU competition law are revealed.

3. EU COMPETITION LAW ASSESSED FROM A TOTAL WELFARE PERSPECTIVE

If the maximisation of total welfare (eventually corrected from a distributional perspective[17]) is seen as the goal of EU competition law, the MEA is still far away from how an economically optimal competition law would look like. An economics based application of competition rules may be defended since it is less prone to errors (false positives and false negatives[18]) than a purely legalistic approach. Economic analysis may function as a kind of guarantee for high-quality competition law and, from a total welfare perspective, it is advisable to extend its application to the areas of competition law where it has not yet fully

the nineteen-thirties warns against such policy. Crisis cartels, which were allowed during the New Deal, turned out to be counter-productive.

16 W. Kerber, op.cit.

17 The goal of competition law may be defined as the maximization of productive and allocative efficiency. If productive efficiency increases, competition rules may require that a part of the ensuing cost efficiencies is passed on to consumers in the form of lower prices. In this way, not only producer surplus but also consumer surplus increase. Consumer welfare, understood as an increase in consumer surplus, may thus function as a correction to a total welfare approach that maximizes the sum of producer and consumer surplus without taking account of distributional effects. EU competition law fits the latter description, since it requires that an equitable part of the efficiency benefits is passed-on to consumers (see the wording of Art. 101 (30 TFEU).

18 A false positive refers to the prohibition of a type of conduct that is welfare increasing and should, therefore, have been allowed. Examples include a prohibition of predatory pricing that puts an end to beneficial price competition and a prohibition of a merger generating efficiencies, which outweigh its anti-competitive consequences. False negatives are the opposite of false negatives; they entail the approval of anti-competitive practices that cannot be justified by efficiency savings. Examples include the legalization of vertical minimum price fixing even in the absence of an efficiency justification (such as protection against free-riding) and the approval of a merger causing substantial price increases without off-setting productive efficiencies (marginal cost savings).

penetrated. In this way the cost of errors may be minimised. Within the limited scope of this paper, a full discussion of the remaining disharmonies between industrial organisation theory and competition law is not possible. Two examples must suffice to illustrate the remaining disharmonies. First, similar (potentially anti-competitive) practices are treated differently, even though there is no economic justification for the ensuing inconsistencies. In the field of vertical restraints, the persisting prohibition of vertical minimum price fixing is the clearest example of these inconsistencies. Second, damages awards remain far below the welfare costs of monopoly. The recent proposal of the European Commission on cartel damages claims[19] does not address this problem.

3.1. THE INCONSISTENT TREATMENT OF VERTICAL RESTRAINTS

For a long time, both in the US and the EU, competition rules relating to vertical restraints were dominated by technical legal distinctions rather than economic analysis.[20] From the 1960ies onwards, economists have pleaded in favour of an effects-based approach focusing on both the potential anti-competitive effects and efficiency benefits of vertical restraints. This implies not only that formalistic rules based on the legal form of the business relationships must be avoided. It also leads to a rejection of simple rules such as *per se* (il)legality of (certain types of) vertical restraints. Any legal rule must take into account that vertical restraints have an ambiguous impact on economic welfare, depending on the context in which they are used.[21]

EU competition law in the field of vertical restraints has always been characterised by a high degree of regulatory intervention. The outcome of the last two revisions (1999, 2010) has been re-regulation rather than deregulation. Nevertheless, in the literature Regulation 2790/1999 was welcomed as a considerable improvement on the 'old style' system. Since the 'new style' block exemption no longer contains a white list, the 'strait-jacketing' effect is avoided, so it was argued.[22] In spite of the uncertainties flowing from the definition of relevant markets, the use of a market share cap has been judged as in line with the MEA, in order to escape from the discredited and formalistic regulations of

19 Proposal for a Directive of the European Parliament and of the Council on certain rules governing actions for damages under national law for infringements of the competition law provisions of the Member States and of the European Union, COM (2013) 404, 11.6.2013.

20 V. Verouden, op.cit., p. 525–575.

21 The old Regulations contained both black lists of illegal clauses and white lists containing clauses that did not infringe competition law. To avoid the use of grey clauses, legal counsels gave their clients the advice to include only white clauses in the distribution contracts. This had a strait-jacketing effect.

22 R. Whish, op. cit., p. 898.

the past.[23] Regulation 330/2010 is largely shaped after its predecessor: it contains a safe harbour clause based on the market shares of both supplier and buyer and a 'black list' of clauses that are presumed illegal. Contrary to the opinion that the new approach to vertical restraints is better in line with insights from economic analysis, a more critical view is presented here. There is no perfect harmony between competition economics and competition law. EU competition law adopts a strict market share test. As it will be explained below, market shares are at best a proxy of market power and the market share/market power paradigm is no perfectly reliable way of detecting welfare-reducing antitrust infringements. The same applies, even with more force, to the 'black list': even though this list provides (some) legal certainty to firms, it does so at the expense of aggravating economic inconsistencies.

It must be acknowledged that the design of an optimal legal regime for vertical restraints is not an easy task, because of the ambiguous effects of these restrictions. In spite of these difficulties, the following two policy lessons may be advocated upon the basis of a full-fledged economic analysis. First, the economic consequences of vertical restraints, and not their legal form, should be decisive in judging their conformity with the competition rules. Both price restraints and non-price restraints may have positive as well as negative impacts on economic efficiency, depending on the context and their purposes. On the one hand, vertical restraints reduce transaction costs of contracting parties by minimising uncertainty and coping with opportunistic behaviour. On the other hand, anti-competitive effects may be caused if vertical restraints strengthen horizontal collusion or enhance market power through foreclosure. Second, different types of vertical restraints can be substitutes for each other, so that there is no economic reason for distinct rules. A prohibition of a particular type of vertical restraints will create a substitution effect towards other vertical restrictions of competition. If such a substitution is inspired only by legal reasons, EU competition law may impose inefficient distribution patterns and cause economic waste.[24]

Every single word of the economic analysis of vertical restraints applies to both non-price restraints and price restraints. For this reason, a distinct legal treatment of vertical minimum price fixing is not justified from a total welfare perspective. On the one hand, several efficiency explanations may be given for the use of vertical minimum price fixing. Next to the popular free-rider

23 R. Whish, op.cit., p. 907.

24 The most extreme substitution effect occurs when manufacturers opt for full vertical integration (hire salespersons as employees) to escape from the prohibitions of contractually imposed restraints. Both vertical restraints and vertical integration aim at curing the same inefficiencies but the latter may do so only at higher costs. Moreover, also the anti-competitive effects may be more worrisome since it may be more difficult to undo vertical integration than to change the terms of distribution contracts.

rationale[25], vertical restraints may be explained as a contract enforcement mechanism[26], a method of risk-spreading[27] or a device to guarantee efficient provision of distribution services[28] If vertical minimum price fixing is illegal, manufacturers have several alternatives at their disposal, such as territorial restraints, selective distribution and refusals to deal. This creates scope for a substitution effect, which may imply that manufacturers are forced by the legal system to choose a less efficient alternative to organize the distribution of their products.

The economic wisdom on vertical restraints has been fully absorbed in US antitrust law but not in EU competition law. Since the 1977 Supreme Court's decision in *State Oil* v. *Khan* the rule of reason is applied with respect to maximum resale price maintenance.[29] Full consistency with insights from economic analysis has been achieved 10 years later with the *Leegin* decision.[30] In the latter case, the US Supreme Court also abolished the *per se* prohibition of minimum resale price maintenance. The 'rule of reason', which allows for taking into account the economic effects of practices challenged under the US antitrust laws, now governs all vertical restraints.[31] In this way, a different treatment of certain categories of vertical restraints, for which there is no economic reason, is avoided. With the judgment of the US Supreme Court in *Leegin* the different approaches in US case law on vertical restraints have been reconciled with each other and reduced to a unitary regime. Clearly, the US approach is superior to the EU approach for reasons of internal consistency; it also conforms to the total welfare paradigm as a guiding normative principle of antitrust law.

Conversely, the EU approach towards price restraints is not in harmony with the lessons from economic analysis. Vertical minimum price fixing is the first

25 L. Telser, *op.cit.*; An extension of the free-riding theory is the quality certification theory; see H. Marvel and S. McCafferty, *op.cit.*

26 B. Klein and K. Murphy, *op.cit.*

27 P. Rey and J. Tirole, *op.cit.*

28 B. Klein, *op.cit.*

29 *State Oil Co v Barkat U. Khan and Khan and Associates Inc*, 118 S.Ct. 275 (1997). Since June 2001 EU competition rules also distinguish between the legal assessment of minimum resale prices and that of maximum resale prices (See Regulation 330/2010 [2010] OJ L 102/1 and Guidelines on Vertical Restraints, [2010] OJ C 130/1) Maximum resale price maintenance may be efficiency enhancing since it is a device to fight against problems of double marginalization arising under conditions of successive monopolies. Since the elimination of double monopoly mark-ups benefits consumers as well as firms, the antitrust prohibition should not be applied to price ceilings used to fight double marginalization problems. The double monopoly mark-up is particularly relevant in exclusive distribution agreements. Distributors who have been granted an exclusive territory will enjoy market power which may enable them to increase prices above competitive levels. In contrast with the treatment of vertical maximum price fixing, the EU approach towards vertical minimum price fixing does not follow current economic wisdom.

30 *Leegin Creative Leather Products, Inc. v PSKS, Inc.*, 127 S.Ct. 2705 (2007).

31 With respect to non-price restraints, the rule of reason has been applied since the late 1970s. See: *Continental TV Inc v GTE Sylvania Inc*, 433 U.S. 36 (1977).

clause mentioned on the black list of Regulation 330/2010. Admittedly, the Guidelines create an opening for assessing efficiency benefits of minimum resale prices. More particularly, resale price maintenance is seen as a helpful instrument to induce better distributors' efforts when a manufacturer introduces a new product. The European Commission adds that the goal of protecting pre-sales services may be important when experience or complex products are sold. However, the parties must "convincingly demonstrate that the RPM agreement can be expected to not only provide the means but also the incentive to overcome possible free-riding between retailers on these services and that the pre-sales services overall benefit consumers as part of the demonstration that all the conditions of Article 101 (3) are fulfilled."[32] In spite of this very cautious opening towards potential legality, the heavy burden of proof makes it unlikely that firms will be able to successfully plead an efficiency defence. The result is a *quasi per se* prohibition, which is at odds with insights from welfare economics.

3.2. CARTEL DAMAGES: UNDER-DETERRENCE AND LACK OF COMPENSATION

Horizontal price-fixing is the most serious infringement of the antitrust laws. Even though economists disagree about the welfare implications of vertical restrictions of competition, potential abuses of dominant firms and the economic impact of mergers, they all[33] subscribe to the view that cartels cause substantial welfare losses. These losses are equal to those of monopoly: i) prices are set above competitive levels, thus causing a redistribution of consumer surplus to the producers (price effect), and ii) consumers buy less goods even though additional purchases would be utility maximising for them (allocation effect). The estimated costs of monopoly amount to a non-negligible part of the gross domestic product.[34] Hence, if total welfare is the goal of the competition rules, one would expect a policy aiming at effective deterrence of horizontal price cartels to prevent the welfare losses of price fixing. To achieve this goal, public enforcement is superior to private enforcement. The superiority of public enforcement is due to several reasons: information advantages of competition authorities in discovering cartels (including leniency programs), fine-tuning of sanctions, and the need to overcome the rational apathy problem.[35] Effective deterrents of price conspiracies include an optimal mix of high (criminal) fines, imprisonment and disqualification of company directors. From a total welfare perspective deterring price-fixing is always better than compensating the losses of consumers, since

32 Guidelines on Vertical Restraints [2010] OJ C 130/1, at 225.
33 The only exception is the Austrian literature, see section 4.2 of this paper.
34 K. Cowling and D. Mueller, *op.cit.*
35 For a more elaborate discussion, see: R. Van den Bergh, *op.cit.*

the latter cannot easily be identified and compensation will remain imperfect. At best, private enforcement through damages claims could play a secondary role by strengthening the deterrence effect of fines.

The enforcement model of EU competition law does not correspond with the above economic insights. On the one hand, public enforcement is considered more important than private enforcement. As a consequence, the newly proposed Directive on actions for damages under national law for the infringement of the competition rules includes a number of provisions that should protect the effectiveness of leniency programmes. Potential whistle-blowers may have fewer incentives to step forward if they run the risk of having to pay substantial damages, even though they enjoy immunity or reduction of fines. To counteract this outcome, the proposed Directive limits the extent of the duty to compensate. Leniency recipients must compensate only the losses suffered by their direct and indirect purchasers, except in case of insolvency of the other cartel member. On the other hand, the European Commission does not mention deterrence (effective detection and sanctioning) but compensation as the main goal of the proposed Directive, Consequently, US-style remedies including opt-out class actions, treble damages and contingency fees are not considered since they would pursue primarily an objective of deterrence. The consequence of this political balancing act may be that neither deterrence nor compensation will be achieved.

Effective deterrence implies that cartel members are forced to internalise the full social costs of their behaviour. Apart from the transfer of consumer surplus, which is a distributional issue, legal rules should aim at internalising the deadweight loss of monopoly and the costs of rent-seeking to achieve a monopoly position. Fines will often under-deter since the detection rate is low (approximately 15 per cent).[36] Follow-on actions for damages may add to the deterrence effect, provided that they are sufficiently large to capture the allocative efficiency loss. From a total welfare perspective, the most blatant economic inconsistency is that damages relate to the redistribution of consumer surplus and not to the welfare losses of monopoly. On top of this, effective deterrence requires that the collective action problem is solved and that the amount of compensation is multiplied to take account of the low probability of detection. Neither of both measures is proposed by the European Commission. Opt-out class actions and punitive damages are regarded as not reconcilable with European legal traditions. Unfortunately, opt-in collective actions are likely to attract only a low number of participants and are thus no effective means of internalising the costs of monopolies. Similarly, single damages do not correct

---

36 The probability of a successful prosecution of a price cartel is at most between 13 and 17%. See: P. Bryant and E. Eckhard, *op.cit.*

for the low detection rate of horizontal cartels and are thus equally inefficient since they are unable to internalise the social loss caused by price conspiracies. In addition, opt-in collective actions are not effective instruments to compensate consumers in cases of wide-spread losses; only opt-out mechanisms could achieve this goal. In sum, the policy choices made by the European Commission contradict insights from welfare economics. Only arguments based on the legal tradition of EU Member States may explain the current and future enforcement picture.

4. THE MISSING ECONOMICS IN THE MORE ECONOMIC APPROACH

The MEA adopted by the European Commission is a choice in favour of a particular economic approach. It tries to align EU competition law with US antitrust law, which is dominated by the total welfare paradigm. To fully appraise the MEA, it is important to acknowledge the existence of other economic approaches to competition law. Following the central tenets of the Ordoliberal School, one may define the goal of competition law as the protection of the competitive process and the economic freedom of market participants. Protection of freedom of competition thus constitutes a third economic approach, next to the views that competition law should aim at total welfare or consumer welfare. Ordoliberal views may lead to normative guidelines that are different from the principles deduced from total welfare (or consumer welfare) analysis. The MEA has been criticised also for neglecting dynamic approaches to competition. In particular, the consumer welfare approach may be judged too static since it stresses short term effects on consumer prices, while neglecting beneficial dynamic effects (innovation) in the long run. Below, ordoliberalism and dynamic theories of competition are further commented upon. Clearly, if one prefers one of the latter approaches to the total or consumer welfare standard, the MEA is in need of different economics.

4.1. ORDOLIBERALISM

It is likely that many mainstream industrial organisation theorists will disagree when the Ordoliberal Freiburg School is mentioned as an alternative economic approach to competition. They may argue that ordoliberalism did not contribute to economic theory and that the broad set of ordoliberal policy recommendations lacks a strong theoretical underpinning. This may be true but, in spite of that, it cannot be denied that ordoliberalism had a profound impact on thinking about competition issues in the EU. Ordoliberal writers developed a unique and valuable approach to identifying the most suitable form of competition policy and developed guidelines to formulate the most appropriate legal rules. Many of the ordoliberal insights remain valid up until today.

Any history of EU competition law that fails to take into account the influence of the Freiburg School would be seriously incomplete. It is an often heard misunderstanding that in the after-war period the allied occupation authorities imported US antitrust law in Europe and that the European competition rules were shaped after the prohibitions of the US Sherman Act, – at that time the world-wide guiding example of antitrust law. Economic history tells us a different story. The original articles 85 and 86 of the Treaty establishing the European Economic Community (EEC) were not a by-product of US post-war debates on competition law but aimed at a goal that is extraneous to US antitrust law: the achievement of market integration by eliminating private trade barriers between the six original Member States. The Freiburg scholars exerted, – either directly or indirectly –, an important influence on the process of European unification; it was through their impact that competition rules were enshrined in the original EEC Treaty. A key concept of the Freiburg School was that competition should protect individuals from private economic power and that this freedom, next to political freedom, must be part of the economic order envisioned by society's economic constitution (*Ordnungspolitik*). Consequently, the EEC Treaty itself fixed the rules for the functioning of an economic system and awarded a key role to competition.[37] The ordoliberals of the Freiburg School accepted the main idea of classical liberalism, viewing economic freedom as the corollary of political freedom. Different from the classical liberal view, they did not put thrust on an unregulated market to generate the benefits of competition. Instead, they stressed the need of a legal framework regulating the market behaviour of cartels and dominant firms, which must be enforced by an independent competition authority.

Neither a standard economic theory, nor a US policy prescription thus lies at the basis of the EU competition rules. Europe did not follow the Harvard School (or at a later stage the Chicago School) but its own peculiar economic School of thought, the Freiburg School. Clearly, EU competition law has never been in complete harmony with ordoliberal views, but major competition cases decided by the European Court of Justice have been influenced by ordoliberal thoughts.[38] Economic commentators will likely (and some of them even happily) see the end of ordoliberalism with the introduction of the MEA in the late nineties. However, even though the European Commission adopted much of US-style economics, many relics of Ordoliberalism remain present in today's EU competition law. The

37 N. Giocoli, *op. cit.*

38 The 'special responsibility' of dominant firms was mentioned in a number of leading cases, including ECJ, Case 322/81, *Michelin v. Commission* [1983] ECR 3461, at para. 57.

differences are most clearly visible in the field of abuse of dominant position (Article 102 TFEU). Imposing increased liabilities on powerful market players is a peculiar characteristic of EU competition law that is absent in rules of US antitrust law, which embrace the total welfare perspective. When protecting economic opportunities of smaller rivals is a major concern, strict prohibitions of refusals to deal and tying practices logically follow. The more tolerant approach of US antitrust law towards those practices can be better understood when market power is seen as a reward for superior efficiency and not solely as a source of antitrust liability. Obviously, broad prohibitions of refusals to deal and tying inspired by ordoliberalism may cause inefficiencies that a competition law aiming at total welfare wants to avoid.

4.2. DYNAMIC APPROACHES

Traditional concepts of industrial organisation theory relate to actual competition; efficiency criteria (productive and allocative efficiency) assess market outcomes in static terms. According to dynamic views, competition can also exist in a latent or potential form. An example may illustrate the conflict between allocative efficiency and dynamic efficiency. Firms which sell superior products may enjoy market power enabling them to charge *supra*-competitive prices, thus causing allocative inefficiencies. However, the additional profits may be used to finance costly R&D projects, which may lead to important innovations and higher quality products that better satisfy consumers' wishes. A competition policy aiming at dynamic efficiency may accept temporary monopoly profits in spite of the price effect and allocation effect of the enhanced market power enjoyed by the most innovative firm.

Although Schumpeter already endorsed the notion of potential competition, above all the economists of the Austrian School have elaborated this concept.[39] This School's approach implies that the exploitation of monopolistic positions is rendered impossible by the existence of potential competition (new firms, or pre-existing large firms in competing countries), at least in the long run. More recently, the attention which Schumpeter and the Austrians devoted to potential competition has taken formal shape in the theory of contestable markets. A combination of ordoliberal insights and a dynamic approach to competition can be found in the work of Hoppmann. Each of these approaches is briefly discussed in turn.

In Schumpeter's work[40] competition is regarded as a dynamic process of 'creative destruction'. Pioneer firms introduce new products and new production methods, thereby opening up new markets. The dynamism of these firms

39 See for example: D. Reekie, *op.cit.* and D. Armentano, *op.cit.*

40 J. Schumpeter, *op.cit.*

initially gives them a temporary monopoly position in the market, but at the same time stimulates others to imitate them. These successive innovations and imitations promote economic progress. Seen from the perspective of competition as a dynamic process, deviations from the perfect competition model, such as product differentiation and lack of market transparency, are pre-requisites for the 'workability' of that process. Whereas in price theory monopoly is unambiguously considered to be something bad, this is no longer the case in a dynamic view. Indeed, monopolies are seen as a decisive factor in promoting competition. Apart from cost reductions, dynamic considerations may indicate a preference for more concentrated market structures, – even though in static terms this is allocatively inefficient. A more fragmented market structure may be allocatively efficient, but at the same time inhospitable to innovation. The question of how to take technological progress into account is one of the most heavily discussed topics in industrial organisation. Ever since the time Schumpeter presented the issue of a possible link between market structure and the rate of innovation, as well as firm size and innovation, implying that it would be advisable to allow for higher market shares in innovation markets, this has been a prolonged field of controversy. Arrow showed that, theoretically, a monopolist has less incentive to invest in innovation than a new entrant or a firm in a competitive industry.[41] Empirical evidence, however, still fails to demonstrate any definitive relationship between firm size, market concentration, and the pace of innovation.[42] The individual circumstances of the industry under scrutiny weigh heavily on the relation between firm size and innovation.[43]

Von Hayek defended the position that numerous interventions by competition law, such as determining the optimum size for firms, or the degree of workable competition, and the requirement that costs must be justified, are vacuous and erroneous. Costs, prices, and market results cannot be determined by market simulations but are revealed by competitive forces. It is the task of the competitive process itself to find out the best products and production methods. The price system provides market participants with important signals that enable them to adapt to events and circumstances of which they are unaware. This basic insight, which initiated a Copernican revolution in economics, has far-reaching consequences for competition policy. To remain in business, firms must constantly obtain information about market conditions and how they change. Individual firms hold important economic information in an extremely non-aggregated way. No single economist, administrator, or judge can answer the relevant questions of competition policy better than the competitive process itself. Von Hayek rejects both a prohibition against cartels and the control of

41 K.J. Arrow, *op.cit.*

42 F. Scherer, op. cit., p. 1416. Recent empirical work arguing a positive correlation between product market competition and productivity growth includes S. Nickell, *op. cit.*

43 Roberts and S. Salop, *op. cit.*

abuses by firms in a dominant position because of their negative effects on the dynamic competitive process.[44] According to the Austrian view, interference by competition law must be avoided because of its potentially negative effects on the competitive incentive system.

The conceptual approach of freedom of competition elaborated by Hoppmann has identified a different notion of restrictions of competition. According to Hoppmann, freedom of competition embraces two components: on the one hand, the freedom to emulate the performance of competitors and to introduce innovations (*Wettbewerb im Parallelprozess*) and, on the other hand, the freedom to choose one's trading partners (*Wettbewerb im Austauschprozess*). Only forms of conduct which significantly restrict freedom of competition by fostering unreasonable market power should be prohibited by competition law. Legal prohibitions should be formulated as *per se* rules in order to minimise legal uncertainty for firms. Hoppmann's advocacy of *per se* rules was criticised, because it is difficult to give a description of practices which are, by their very nature, restrictive of competition.[45] Other proponents of the concept of freedom of competition have argued that the requirements of justice and legal certainty do not require *per se* rules, but can also be satisfied by the formulation of abstract rules that do apply in a general way and are sufficiently stable.[46]

5. OBSTACLES TO AN ECONOMIC APPROACH

There are different reasons why competition lawyers, officials of competition authorities and judges may be hesitant to adopt a full-fledged economic approach to competition law. First, they may subject to the cognitive bias that an economic approach boils down to an adoption of Chicago views, which are seen as ultraliberal and politically biased in favour of the interests of large industry groups. Second, they may have great difficulties in accepting the results of economic analysis that are counter-intuitive and contradict common expectations and ideas. Third, competition lawyers and judges may feel that the assumptions of (mathematically complex) economic models are far away from real-life cases. Fourth, even though they may agree that law and economics cannot be separated in the antitrust field, lawyers may stress that economic arguments must find their place within the existing legal framework and have to be rejected if they do not satisfy the demands of the 'rule of law'. Each of these counterarguments merits further discussion. The first two objections (Chicago antipathy and contra-intuitiveness) must be discarded as inappropriate. By contrast, the other two objections (unrealistic models, demands of the legal

44 F.A. von Hayek, *op.cit.*
45 For an overview, see; R. Clapham, *op.cit.*
46 6 D. Schmidtchen, *op.cit.*

system) need to be taken seriously. Each point of criticism will be discussed in turn.

5.1. THE CHICAGO SCHOOL'S BAD REPUTATION IN EUROPE

In European discussions about competition policy the term Chicago has a negative connotation and shooting at Chicago remains a popular sport. By contrast, in the US Chicago economics has established itself as a main component of industrial organisation theory. The Harvard paradigm and the Chicago paradigm are not incompatible as organising principles and may, therefore, be used as complementary rather than as mutually exclusive. The Harvard School argued that a concentrated market structure has a negative impact on the conduct of firms in the market and on ultimate market performance, given that high concentration goes hand in hand with high profit margins for firms. In the US, this structure-conduct-performance paradigm led to a very interventionist antitrust law in the 1960ies and 1970ies. The Chicago School reacted to this interventionism by postulating the rival paradigm of economic efficiency. Firms grow big because they are more efficient than their rivals and persistent market concentration is the result of the need to achieve minimum efficient scale and not of collusion. The relevant test to assess market performance is not its relation with market structure but rather whether high profits in a concentrated industry are earned by large (more efficient) firms alone or also by small (less efficient) firms, which hide under the price umbrella of the monopolist. Modern industrial organisation accepts both views and, in this way, it preserves the valuable insights of both Schools without their immoderations or excesses. It is now widely accepted that high profits may be the consequence of either collusion in concentrated markets or higher efficiency. It all depends on the characteristics of various industries. Game theory has contributed a lot in discovering the conditions that need to be satisfied to enable stable (tacit) collusion in oligopolistic markets. Transaction cost theory has further clarified why concentration (in particular, vertical integration) may be efficient. Rather than throwing the Chicago views overboard, these new insights have integrated them in a broader and more refined theoretical framework.[47] Unfortunately, in the EU references to the Chicago School still imply pejorative connotations that conjure up images of firms unjustly enriched from exploiting consumers. In this way, the child is often thrown away with the bathwater and useful insights may get lost.

---

47 The limited scope of this contribution does not allow an in-depth discussion of the post-Chicago approach to competition law. For an interesting collection of articles, see A. Cucinotta, *op.cit.*

5.2. THE COUNTER-INTUITIVE RESULTS OF ECONOMIC ANALYSIS

Insights from economic theories on competition are often counter-intuitive; they contradict what seems obvious and thus provoke easy criticisms. It is not easy to understand why vertical minimum price-fixing may be beneficial to consumers. After all, consumers pay higher prices than would prevail in a competitive market. If prices increase, this seems sufficient evidence of the negative consequences for consumers who must pay *supra*-competitive prices. Is it at all thinkable that consumers profit from higher prices? The answer to this question is a surprising 'yes'.

If price increases are the result of exploiting market power, they raise competition concerns. However, price increases are not necessarily anti-competitive. The crucial, though counter-intuitive, explanation is that minimum resale price maintenance may guarantee the provision of pre-sales and post-sales services and, more generally, that it may enable an efficient distribution of consumer goods. These explanations of resale price maintenance are pro-competitive rather than anti-competitive. In the absence of minimum resale price maintenance specialised retailers are vulnerable to free-riding by discount stores and, for this reason, may abstain from providing costly sales services.[48] A manufacturer may wish to increase sales of his products by asking retailers to optimally display the products, provide information and free demonstrations. These services obviously add to the retail price. If consumers can take advantage of the pre-sales services provided by a specialised retailer and then buy at a discount store from another retailer who offers no such services, there would be little incentives for retailers to provide the desired services. This would lead to an overall decrease in demand, which entails not only lower profits for the manufacturer but also a reduction of services supplied to consumers.

The typical answer to the above argument is that resale price maintenance is also imposed for products (such as shampoo and men's underwear) for which average consumers do not demand additional services. However, the quality certification theory may explain resale price maintenance also for products that are not complex. A retail store selling fashion articles (such as clothing, shoes or perfume) may develop a reputation of exclusivity, so that consumers who regularly shop there receive a quality certification from the specialised retailers. Discount stores may free-ride on these investments if they carry the same products. In such a case, minimum retail prices protect fashionable stores and guarantee the sale of luxury products that are valued by consumers.[49]

Another example for showing that the counter-intuitive conclusions of industrial organisation theory hinder its acceptance in legal circles is the case

48 L. Telser, *op.cit.*

49 H. Marvel, S. McCafferty, *op.cit.*

against product tying. There are two popular objections to tying. First, there is the perceived fact of coercion. Critics argue that tying induces consumers to purchase tied products that they do not necessarily desire. If products are offered as a package, consumers willing to buy a separate product may not get supplies. Second, the 'leverage argument' holds that firms may extend their dominant power in the tying market, where they already earn monopoly profits, into a competitive tied market. Using their leverage power, dominant firms would thus earn a second monopoly profit. A firm which is a dominant supplier of machines (for example, printers) may tie the sale of the machine to the purchase of complementary products (for example, ink) or services (for example, maintenance contracts). Both arguments are largely erroneous. Tying arrangements are wide-spread in the economy and can be found also in competitive markets. Consumers are not 'coerced' to buy shoes with laces, smart-phones with preloaded software or cars with in-built radios. They usually prefer the bundled product, instead of incurring high search costs. Also the leverage argument has been shown to be wrong. A monopolist firm cannot earn a second monopoly profit on a secondary product, since the resulting package price will induce the consumers to switch to alternative suppliers. Since the consumer cannot separate the price of the tying product and the tied product (s) he will consider the package price as too high; consequently the monopolist firm will lose sales in the tying market since it can no longer sell at the profit maximising price.[50] Even though these arguments may be convincing, it is likely to remain difficult for competition lawyers, enforcement authorities and courts to accept the above conclusions since they go against common beliefs and seem to favour producers' interests over those of consumers. However, the simple fact that a theory provides conclusions that contradict everyday wisdom should not detract from its value for explaining and predicting real-world outcomes. If we always could trust our intuitions, scientific research would become redundant.

5.3. UNREALISTIC MODELS

An often heard objection to the use of economics is that economic models, which are often mathematically sophisticated, are too far away from real-life markets in

50 An example may further clarify this. Assume a firm in a dominant position who is selling a tying product at a price of 100 euro, which enables the firm to earn a (first) monopoly profit. In a competitive market the tied product is sold at a price of 20 euro. Charging a *supra*-competitive price of 30 euro would increase the package price from 120 to 130 euro. If the consumer pays 130 euro, the dominant firm will earn two monopoly profits instead of one. However, the firm cannot leverage its monopoly power of the tying market into the tied market. Any price exceeding 100 euro for the tying product will not be profit-maximizing and may incite buyers to switch suppliers. Since the consumer may think that the monopoly price of the tying product has increased, (s)he may decide to stop buying the tying product from the firm that makes use of tying arrangements.

order to be used in competition decisions. On this point there seems to exist a widening gap between lawyers and economists. This unfortunate state of things is partly due to misunderstandings on the lawyers' side and some misplaced arrogance on the economists' side. On the one hand, lawyers must realise that economic models are not aiming at giving a description of reality. Economic models predict outcomes on the basis of assumptions, which try to capture the driving decision variables of economic actors. Hence, the strength of a model is not its descriptive but its predictive value. Moreover, predictive statements should not be confused with normative statements. On the other hand, economists should not simply discard the lawyers' concern by stating that lawyers must improve their mathematical skills to better understand economics. Economic models should not leave lawyers cold and perplexed, in particular because of inaccessible mathematics. On the contrary, they should lead to results that lawyers may recognise as real-world outcomes. If a model does not provide predictions that are consistent with observed market behaviour, there is nothing wrong with the lawyer who does not understand the mathematics but the problem lies with the economist who has used a model based on purely theoretical assumptions.

In a recent paper, Bishop has expressed serious concerns about the increased use of sophisticated economics. He observes two detrimental developments in the application of economics in competition policy: an increased reliance on theoretical possibilities and the use of superficially more complex models and techniques. Both give less and less regard to observed behaviour and detract attention away from the central issue of understanding how competition really works. Bishop formulates three criteria that economic analysis must satisfy to become a good basis for policy decisions. The economic model being used must reflect the key features of the industry under investigation. The model must provide hypotheses that can be tested empirically using market evidence. Ultimately, the model must be able to explain observed competitive behaviour.[51] Bishop's arguments may be surprising, since he is a well-known competition economist from whom one would expect a plea in favour of an increased use of economics in competition law. However, his paper does not argue against the use of economic reasoning, but stresses that real-world competition may not be ignored if a widening gap between economists and lawyers is to be avoided.

5.4. THE DEMANDS OF THE LEGAL SYSTEM

5.4.1. Administrative Costs and the Need for 'Simple' Rules

Even if competition lawyers, officials of competition authorities and judges are receptive of the insights offered by industrial organisation theory, the specific

[51] S. Bishop, *op. cit.*

demands of the legal system (in particular, procedural law) may inhibit the use of economic arguments. The European Commission argued that "economic theory cannot be the only factor in the design of policy. (...) Strict economic theory must take place in the context of existing legal texts and jurisprudence".[52] In real-life antitrust cases, economic arguments may not be sufficiently convincing to satisfy the legal burden of proof. Economic models mostly rely on very specific assumptions and reach conclusions that lose their validity when one of the assumptions is replaced by an alternative assumption. Today, game theory provides an almost unmanageable amount of economic models showing different equilibria. The fact that game theory does not provide unequivocal answers probably explains why so far it has had no impact on judges. By contrast, the Chicago School with its bright-line, simple answers to complex legal questions exerted a very strong influence upon the US Supreme court. The practical manageability of economic theories thus seems to determine their success in antitrust cases, even though with a narrow 5–4 majority in *Leegin*.

If economic analysis shows that a particular practice may have both pro-competitive and anti-competitive consequences, why not adopt a legal standard that looks at all relevant factors to determine the reasonableness of a restraint? Why not allow an efficiency defence in all areas of competition law to improve the welfare outcomes of policy-making? The answer is that the legal system needs simple rules; a full consideration of all potential efficiency benefits and possible anticompetitive consequences leads to extremely complicated assessments and unpredictable outcomes. A rule-of-reason does not give an immediate answer to the question what must be proven to establish antitrust liability. A full consideration of efficiencies poses serious problems of proof, particularly if it must be shown that consumers receive a fair share of those benefits. This may explain why US antitrust law moves towards a 'structured rule-of-reason', which may include market share criteria or rebuttable presumptions; it also may clarify the use of black lists in EU competition law.

5.4.2. *A Telling Example: Definition of the Relevant Market*

The outcome of competition cases heavily depends on the calculation of market shares and the ensuing establishment or rejection of market power. As a consequence, the quality of competition law is directly determined by the reliability of the market definition used. Competition lawyers who take a look at leading textbooks in industrial organisation may be surprised to see that there is no chapter devoted to market definition. This should not come as a shock, though. The concept of the relevant market is a legal construct that has no direct relation to the economic concept of market power. Economists define market power as the ability of a firm to elevate its prices above the competitive level for a

52 Green Paper on vertical restraints in EC competition policy, COM/96/0721 Final, at para. 86.

sustained period of time without losing so many customers that the price increase becomes unprofitable.[53] A direct way of assessing market power is the calculation of the Lerner index, which measures to what extent prices deviate from marginal costs.[54] Compared to the latter assessment, market shares are no more than an indirect way of assessing competitive constraints and, depending on the quality of market definition, a more or less reliable proxy of market power. Since in practice it is often impossible to establish market power directly (since information about marginal cost cannot be obtained), competition law has opted for an indirect approach. Unfortunately, in many cases the definition of the relevant market has caused severe criticisms, since it turned out to be influenced by subjective considerations and sometimes seemed inspired by the desire to achieve a predetermined result.

In a thought provoking article, Kaplow severely criticises the current market definition process in antitrust law. Given its many pitfalls, Kaplow concludes that market definition should simply be abandoned. His arguments consist of four prongs. First, market shares are relevant to infer market power in homogeneous goods markets only. Once markets are redefined to include imperfect substitutes, one needs a new mechanism for translating market shares into market power. The only correct way to do so requires invalidating the formerly established market definition. Second, making market power inferences from market shares presupposes some sort of benchmark for interpreting market shares. Discussions of market shares often operate on the implicit assumption that each share level is associated with some benchmark amount of market power. However, a given market share does not imply a unique level of market power. A market share approach would need a standard reference market, which could be either an average market or an abstract, hypothetical market. Up until now, there have been no attempts in antitrust law to construct such a reference market. Third, the market definition exercise may yield conflicting market definitions. The decision-maker may then select the definition which is least prone to error and provides a market power inference that is as close as possible to the actual level. In this way, the decision process presumes that the best estimate of market power is already available, which is ironic since the whole point of market definition is adequately assessing market power. Alternatively, the decision-maker may choose the market definition that provides the best legal answers, in which case the process is circular and superfluous. Fourth, antitrust practice shows a strong focus on cross-price elasticity, rather than on the market elasticity of demand which is directly relevant to proper market power inferences.[55] As will be explained below, Kaplow's criticisms also apply to EU competition law,

---

53 D. Carlton and J. Perloff, *op.cit*, p. 642.

54 In a perfectly competitive market price is equal to marginal cost and the Lerner index is zero. Under monopoly the Lerner index equals 1. The values in between indicate the degree of market power.

55 L. Kaplow, *op.cit.*

In its 1997 Notice,[56] the European Commission has tied the traditional method of market definition to the economic concept of the SSNIP. The relevant market may be defined in a thought-experiment asking which products and geographic regions a hypothetical monopolist would need to control in order to impose a Small but Significant and Non-Transitory Increase in Price (for example, a price increase of 5–10 per cent lasting for two years). The SSNIP-text has a clear economic appeal. However, this conceptual framework has not removed the tension between the economic theory of market power and everyday antitrust practice. The EU Commission's 1997 Notice on market definition is a very peculiar document; one does not escape the impression of new theories and techniques being injected into an orthodox legal straight-jacket. At the outset, the Commission repeats the traditional legal definition of the relevant market, related to functional interchangeability of products.[57] The explicit adoption of the hypothetical monopolist test seems to imply that the Commission intends to put more weight on economic analysis in the market delineation exercise. However, Kaplow's criticisms remain intact: the SSNIP applies to heterogeneous goods markets; there is no indication of a standard reference market and too much emphasis on cross-elasticity. The core criticism remains that market power is not defined directly; the SSNIP continues the tradition of an indirect approach to market power by identifying the products and geographic regions that may exert competitive pressure on the company under investigation.

Theoretical as well as empirical developments in the US have initiated an evolution that could lead to putting less emphasis on the role traditional methods of market definition play in determining the market players' positions and, ultimately, market power. In the field of merger control, the US Guidelines state that: "Where sufficient data are available, the Agencies may construct economic models designed to quantify the unilateral price effects from the merger. These merger simulation methods need not rely on market definition.[58] As stated above, the market share/market power paradigm may bring forth convincing conclusions in markets distinguished by homogeneous goods but this no longer holds when goods are differentiated or branded[59] and market shares do not confer trustworthy information on the market's competitive situation.[60] Initially cultivated as a means of assessing merged companies' incentives to raise differentiated goods' prices post-merger, the unilateral effects approach

56 Commission Notice on the definition of the relevant market for the purposes of Community competition law [1997] OJ C 372/5.

57 Idem, paras 7–8.

58 US Horizontal Merger Guidelines, US Department of Justice and the Federal Trade Commission, p. 7.

59 Products can be differentiated in a number of ways, including characteristics relating to the product itself (such as by brands, physical characteristics, or utility for the end user), or relating to how and to whom the product is sold (such as by channel of distribution, customers, or being sold as a cluster). See, for an overview, J. Keyte, *op.cit.*, p. 701.

60 Compare R. Schmalensee, *op.cit.* and E. Chamberlin, *op.cit.*, p. 86–87.

comprehensively diminishes the need for delineating relevant markets. As noted by Stigler and Sherwin, the hypothetical monopolist test coupled with a judgment concerning the level and changes in concentration is not in any way easier than asking directly whether the merger under investigation will result in an increased price.[61]

Merger simulation models use data on existing firm behaviour to predict how that behaviour will change in response to a merger. In practice, the use of merger simulation is a highly technical and data-intensive process. To make the mathematics manageable, it may require the use of strong, sometimes questionable, assumptions about the way in which consumers make choices and in which competitors interact. Looking at the practice of merger control, one will notice that the use of simulation models comes at a high cost. It is the availability of data, rather than the seriousness of competitive distortions that seems to determine the use of these techniques. Competition authorities use simulation models often in the context of mergers in branded consumer goods industries due to the availability of scanner data.[62] It is unlikely that these are the industry sectors where competitive distortions are the most serious. Given the large volumes that they buy, supermarkets may use their buying power to resist price increases by suppliers. From a competition policy perspective, it may thus be preferable to investigate industry sectors where such 'countervailing power' does not exist.

A further problem is that for reasons of manageability, competition authorities may prefer the use of the simplest available technique. An example is the UPP (Upward Pricing Pressure) indicator, which eliminates the need to make an assumption about the shape of demand. The application of this test requires the calculation of diversion ratios and gross margins. Neither the measurement of diversion ratios between individual firms, nor the definition and measurement of the appropriate margin are straightforward exercises. Moreover, the UPP model ignores the dynamic aspects of competition. For these reasons, Bishop warns against the "false and dangerous sense of precision" that the UPP (and other pricing tests) may give. Although the market share/market power paradigm is subject to many criticisms, the traditional approach accommodates a more wide-ranging view of available evidence. Also, it does not require the calculation of parameters (such as diversion ratios) that are difficult to measure. Coming back to Kaplow's criticisms, one may conclude that his remarks are theoretically valid but that also the practical implementation of econometric techniques exhibits a number of drawbacks, due to difficulties of measurement and manageability requirements. Hence, it is too soon to abandon traditional ways of market definition.

---

61 G. Stigler and R. Sherwin, *op.cit.*

62 D. Gore et al., *op.cit*, p. 214–215.

6. CONCLUSIONS

It is now possible to answer the question asked in the title of this article. This answer depends on the goal(s) that competition rules are trying to achieve. These goals may be either economic or non-economic, but even in the first case there is not such a thing as 'the right' economic approach. The answer to the question how much and which kind of economics must be used in competition law entirely flows from the particular policy goal that has been chosen. A lot of economics is missing if the goal of EU competition law is fostering total welfare. Salient examples of the refusal to adopt insights of modern industrial organisation theory include the prohibition of vertical minimum price-fixing and the absence of damages claims for compensating the deadweight loss of monopoly. However, the assessment changes if not total welfare but the protection of consumers' interests is advanced as the goal of EU competition law. Consumer welfare as such is not a concept borrowed from economic theory. The related concept of consumer surplus defines consumers' benefits as the difference between the competitive price and what consumers are willing to pay. In the antitrust context consumer welfare may be given a broader meaning, which includes not only low prices but also freedom of choice. If the latter notion is used, mainstream industrial organisation theory does not always offer clear-cut policy recommendations. The tensions between the total welfare and the consumer welfare standards point at the limits of an economic approach that does not incorporate distributional concerns. Besides total welfare and consumer welfare, there exists a third economic approach: competition rules may be seen as instruments to preserve the competitive process as such and guarantee economic freedom of market participants. Because of historical and political reasons, EU competition law contains a mix of different economic approaches and, therefore, runs a serious risk of inconsistencies.

The European Commission's More Economic Approach (MEA) is not hospitable to alternative economic approaches, such as the Austrian School and a 'revitalised' ordoliberalism. Current EU competition economics puts emphasis on short-term price effects and does not sufficiently incorporate dynamic approaches. Mainstream economics rejects ordoliberalism because it is neither formalised nor empirical. Nevertheless, there is a clear ordoliberal legacy in EU competition law (particularly Article 102 TFEU). From a policy perspective, it is not sufficiently demonstrated why a total welfare approach is superior and ordoliberal thoughts should be abandoned entirely. Dynamic approaches warn against an interventionist policy in innovative markets, because of a pervasive knowledge problem within competition authorities. On top of this, modern industrial organisation theory does not provide convincing answers if competition law is aiming at political goals or non-economic objectives. The clearest example is the goal of market integration, which is a central part of the

European political agenda and may be pursued even if noticeable inefficiencies in the organisation of production and distribution ensue. In sum, there is an urgent need for clarifying the goals of competition law and the hierarchy between those goals. Dependent on those goals there be may not be enough economics in EU competition law, but there may also be already too much or inappropriate economics in the MEA.

This article has indicated many reasons why competition lawyers, competition authorities and judges may be hesitant to accept the major conclusions of modern competition economics. First, the pejorative connotation associated with Chicago School arguments has stalled the entry of competition economics into EU competition law by several decades. Second, the relevant economic analyses contain counter-intuitive conclusions that are difficult to accept by lawyers who are used not to think in economic terms. The third reason relates to the level of abstraction of economic models that make them mathematically sophisticated but, at the same time, inapt to capture the essence of real-life markets. Fourth, the application of competition rules in practice imposes limitations on the use of economics that are often overlooked in the economists' profession. Economic approaches which are technically refined may point in the direction of potentially different outcomes. Such analyses may be unsuited for application by competition authorities and judges since they collide with 'rule of law' requirements of clarity, predictability and legal certainty. In spite of its potential benefits, an extended application of economic approaches may also increase the administrative costs of the legal system. After all, competition law is more than applied micro-economics and also the use of economics in antitrust law must pass a cost-benefit test.

BIBLIOGRAPHY

Armentano, D., Antitrust and monopoly; Anatomy of a policy failure, 2nd edition, The Independent Institute, Oakland 1990.

Arrow, K., Economic welfare and the allocation of resources for invention, in: NBER, ed., The rate and direction of inventive activity: economic and social factors, 1962, p. 609–626.

Bishop, S., Snake-oil with mathematics is still snake-oil: why recent trends in the application of so-called "sophisticated" economics is hindering good competition policy enforcement, in: European Competition Journal, 9 (2013) 1, p. 67–77.

Bork, R., The antitrust paradox. A policy at war with itself, Basic Books, New York 1978

Bryant, P. and Eckhard, E., Price fixing: the probability of getting caught, in: The Review of Economics and Statistics,73 (1991), 3, p. 531–536.

Carlton, D. and Perloff J., Modern Industrial Organization, 3d edition, Addison-Wesley, Reading, Mass., 2000.

Edward H. Chamberlin: Product heterogeneity and public policy, in: American Economic Review, 40 (1950) 2, p. 85–92.

Clapham, R., Das wettbewerbspolitische Konzept der Wettbewerbsfreiheit, in: H. Cox, U. Jens and K. Markert (eds), Handbuch des Wettbewerbs, Vahlen, München, 1981, p. 129–148.

Cowling, K. and Mueller, D., The social costs of monopoly power, in: Economic Journal, 88 (1978) 352, p. 727–748.

Cucinotta, A., Pardolesi, R. and Van den Bergh, R., Post-Chicago developments in antitrust law, Edward Elgar, Cheltenham, 2002.

Giocoli, N., Competition versus property rights: American antitrust law, the Freiburg School, and the early years of European competition policy, in: Journal of Competition Law and Economics, 5 (2009) 4, p. 747–786.

Gore, D., Lewis, S., Lofaro, A. and Dethmers, F., The economic assessment of mergers under European competition law, Cambridge University Press, Cambridge, 2013.

Friedrich A. von Hayek: Grundsätze einer liberalen Gesellschaftsordnung, in: ORDO Jahrbuch für die Ordnung von Wirtschaft und Gesellschaft, 18 (1967), p. 11–33.

Hoppmann, E., Das Konzept der optimalen Wettbewerbsintensität. Rivalität und Freiheit des Wettbewerbs: Zum Problem eines wettbewerbspolitisch adäquaten Ansatzes der Wettbewerbstheorie, in: Jahrbücher für Nationalökonomie und Statistik, 179 (1966), p. 286–323.

Hoppmann, E., Marktmacht und Wettbewerb, Mohr Siebeck, Tübingen, 1977.

Kaplow, L., Why (ever) define markets?, in: Harvard Law Review, 124 (2010), p. 438–517.

Kerber, W., Should competition law promote efficiency? Some reflections of an economist on the normative foundations of competition law, in: Josef Drexl et. al (eds), Economic theory and competition law, Edward Elgar, Cheltenham, 2009, p. 93–120.

Keyte, J., Market definition and differentiated products: the need for a workable standard, in: Antitrust Law Journal, 63 (1995), p. 697–729.

Kirchner, C., Goals of antitrust revisited, in: D. Schmidtchen et al. (eds), The more economic approach to European competition law, 2007, p. 7–26.

Klein, B. and Murphy, K., Vertical restraints as contract enforcement mechanisms, in: Journal of Law and Economics, 31 (1988) 2, p. 265–297.

Klein, B., Assessing resale price maintenance after Leegin, in: Einer Elhauge (ed.), Research handbook on the economics of antitrust laws, Edward Elgar, Cheltenham, 2012, p. 174–200.

Kroes, N., European competition policy – Delivering better markets and better choices, Speech at European consumer and competition day, London, 15 September 2005, available at http://ec.europa.eu/competition/speeches/index_2005.html.

Lande, R., Consumer choice as the ultimate goal of antitrust, in: University of Pittsburgh Law Review, 62 (2001), 3, p. 503–525.

Marvel, H. and McCafferty, S., Resale price maintenance and quality certification, in: RAND Journal of Economics, 15 (1984), 3, p. 346–359.

Motta, M., Competition Policy. Theory and Practice, Cambridge University Press, Cambridge, 2004.

Nickell, S., Competition and corporate performance, in: Journal of Political Economy, 104 (1996), 4, p. 724–746.

Rey, P. and Tirole, J., The logic of vertical restraints, in: American Economic Review, 76 (1986) 5, p. 921–939

Reekie, D., Industry, Prices and Market, Wiley, New York, 1979.
Roberts, G. and Salop, S., Dynamic analysis of efficiency benefits, in: World Competition, 19 (1996) 5, p. 13–17.
Schmidtchen, D., Fehlurteile über das Konzept der Wettbewerbsfreiheit, in: ORDO Jahrbuch für die Ordnung von Wirtschaft und Gesellschaft, 39 (1988), p. 111–135.
Scherer, F. M., Schumpeter and plausible capitalism, in: Journal of Economic Literature. 30 (1992), p. 1416–1433.
Schumpeter, J., Capitalism, Socialism and Democracy. 3rd Edition, 1950 republished by HarperCollins, New York, 2008.
Schmalensee, R., Another look at market power, in: Harvard Law Review, 95 (1982), p. 1789–1816.
Stigler, G. and Sherwin, R., The extent of the market, in: Journal of Law and Economics 28(1985) 3, p. 555–585.
Telser, T., Why should manufacturers want fair trade, in: Journal of Law and Economics, 3 (1960), p. 86–105.
Van den Bergh, R. and Camesasca, P., European Competition Law and Economics: A Comparative Perspective, 2nd Edition, Thomson/Sweet&Maxwell, London, 2006.
Van den Bergh, R., Private Enforcement of European competition law and the persisting collective action problem, in: Maastricht Journal of European and Comparative Law, 20 (2013) 1, p. 2–34.
Verouden, V., Vertical agreements and Article 81(1) EC; The evolving role of economic analysis, in: Antitrust Law Journal, 71 (2003) 2, p. 525–575
Whish, R., Regulation 2790/99: the Commission's new style block exemption for vertical agreements, in: Common Market Law Review, 37 (2000) 4, p. 887–924
Williamson, O., Economies as an antitrust defense: the welfare trade-offs, in: American Economic Review 58 (1968) 1, p. 18–36.

CHAPTER 2
THE VALUE OF TRAINING IN QUANTITATIVE METHODS FOR JUDGES

Jonathan Klick

1. INTRODUCTION

Judges face a significant skills gap that threatens to undermine their ability to properly adjudicate civil matters. Although modern disputes frequently involve decisions that hinge on quantitative or theoretically sophisticated economic evidence, few judges have backgrounds sufficient to prepare them for these decisions. Courses on statistics, economics, and finance are almost entirely absent in legal education programs even though judicial analysis of these matters affects untold resources throughout the world on a daily basis.

With few exceptions, the individuals who sort into law do not have scientific or quantitative backgrounds. In the US, the majority of law school applicants have undergraduate degrees in the humanities and the non-quantitative social sciences.[1] In most of the rest of the world, where law is a first degree, the situation is likely even worse. Judges are not unaware of this problem. Tasked by the Supreme Court with serving as the gatekeeper with respect to scientific evidence, the 9th Circuit opinion in the follow up to *Daubert* laments: "As we read the Supreme Court's teaching in *Daubert*, therefore, though we are largely untrained in science and certainly no match for any of the witnesses whose testimony we are reviewing, it is our responsibility to determine whether those experts' proposed testimony amounts to 'scientific knowledge,' constitutes 'good science,' and was 'derived by the scientific method.'"[2]

In a presentation at the 2008 symposium "The Supreme Court and Useful Knowledge", Linda Greenhouse, the Pulitzer Prize winning reporter who

---

1 See Nieswiadomy, Michael, LSAT Scores of Economics Majors: The 2008–2009 Class Update (June 25, 2009). Available at SSRN: http://ssrn.com/abstract=1430654 or http://dx.doi.org/10.2139/ssrn.1430654.

2 Daubert v. Merrell Dow Pharms., Inc., 43 F.3d 1311, 1316 (9th Cir. 1995).

covered the Supreme Court for the *New York Times* from 1978 to 2007, concluded "A good judge is not necessarily one who knows everything, but one who is willing to learn."[3] Presumably judges do want to get these issues "right", and while most are likely willing to learn[4], at least in theory, reality often gets in the way.

Given the demands placed upon judges in most jurisdictions, it is unlikely they will have resources or the inclination to remedy this shortcoming despite recognising the problem, especially in an environment where the remuneration of judges appears to fall short of compensating them for doing even the bare minimum. As the U.S. Chief Justice, John Roberts, notes repeatedly, poor judicial pay is already depleting the ranks of the federal judiciary.[5] Under such circumstances, it is unreasonable to think judges will be motivated to incur the expense of improving their facility with scientific evidence on their own. Also, given that the gap between judicial pay and private practice pay is largest in the area of corporate law, it is likely that those with some background knowledge of finance and microeconomics will be especially under-represented within the judiciary.

As recognised by the Court in *Daubert*, however, it is not reasonable to simply hope that the adversarial posture of the US courts will lead to a scenario where sound science (or statistics, or economics, etc.) trumps bad science. Junk science can always be dressed up in elegant-sounding claims, wherein the more charismatic expert with the more aesthetically pleasing flow charts beats the bumbling but methodologically sound expert.

Inquisitorial systems generate their own problems with respect to scientific or quantitative evidence as well. While such systems may be less susceptible to manipulation due to hired-gun experts in the courtroom, the problem does not go away as the parties in front of the judge will have used such experts in framing the dispute and preparing their arguments. Further, even if the judge in such a system can rely on a hopefully disinterested court-appointed expert for guidance, lacking any background skills in these areas, the judge will be poorly positioned

3 Greenhouse, Linda (2010), "How Do Judges Know What They Know?" *Proceedings of the American Philosophical Society*, 154(3): 287–293.

4 However, many judges may view this as a practical impossibility or even beyond the scope of their duties. David L. Faigman quotes a remarkable line by Justice Brennan from *Craig v. Boren* (429 U.S. 190 (1976)) while rejecting statistical evidence: "There is no reason to belabor this line of analysis. It is unrealistic to expect either members of the judiciary or state officials to be well versed in the rigors of experimental or statistical technique. But this merely illustrates that proving broad sociological propositions by statistics is a dubious business..." Faigman expresses shock at this statement, suggesting that it would be unthinkable that a Supreme Court justice would be as willing to disclaim any ability to read history, or presumably a similar unwillingness to wrestle with arguments grounded in tools from the liberal arts. See David L. Faigman, Judges As "Amateur Scientists", 86 Boston University Law Review 1207, 1210–1211 (2006).

5 For the first public instance of this, see John Roberts, 2005 Year-End Report on The Federal Judiciary 3 (2006).

to choose an adequately trained expert. Beyond that, often the core of a dispute involves judging how relevant a scientific finding or literature is in answering a particular legal question. Non-legal experts are often ill equipped for such inquiries that require some familiarity with both the science and the law.

Thus, reliance on a judge's own ambition to be a better consumer of scientific and quantitative evidence is overly optimistic; nor will institutional safeguards remedy the knowledge deficit of judges worldwide. While this challenge may seem insurmountable, the potential to educate judges has been demonstrated in the U.S. setting.

The available evidence suggests that judges desire the training that would be necessary to fill in these gaps. There is also evidence that such training can lead to improved judicial decision making. The evidence regarding judicial desire is related to the publication of the Federal Judicial Center's Manual on Scientific Evidence in the wake of the Supreme Court's *Daubert* ruling which left federal judges in the clear role of gatekeepers regarding expert evidence. Qualitative evidence suggests that judges are indeed interested in easily available, well-done resources to improve their ability to make judgments regarding the kind of sophisticated quantitative evidence that arises in modern cases. Further, there are indications that the influence of the FJC's work spread beyond the nominal audience of the federal judiciary, potentially improving the work of state judges as well.

As the following discussions demonstrate, providing judges with attractive and low-cost educational opportunities and resources has the potential to mitigate the gaps they otherwise have in their backgrounds. Expanding such opportunities both in the US and abroad will likely generate a very high social return.

2. REFERENCE MANUAL ON SCIENTIFIC EVIDENCE

Beginning in the early 1990s, there was a general recognition that there was a need to educate federal judges in matters related to scientific evidence. One manifestation of this was the creation of the Federal Judicial Center's Science and Technology Resources Center (STRC). In addition to developing educational programs, the STRC was tasked with developing a handbook on science and technology for judges.[6]

The perceived need for this kind of guidance was heightened when the Supreme Court abandoned the traditional Frye rule in *Daubert v. Merrell Dow*

6 For background on these developments, see Carnegie Commission on Science, Technology, and Government (1993), Science and Technology in Judicial Decision Making: Creating Opportunities and Meeting Challenges.

Pharmaceuticals, Inc.[7] Whereas the *Frye* rule had limited the inquiry regarding the admissibility of scientific evidence to asking whether the evidence was generally accepted in the relevant academic community, *Daubert* demanded that judges themselves serve a gatekeeper function, evaluating the soundness of the underlying methodology used by the expert to arrive at her conclusions. This inquiry involved a determination of whether the underlying methods were reliable and whether they were appropriately applied in the given legal context (i.e., is the application relevant to the legal point being advanced by the evidence).

While the Court did provide some potential indicators of methodological soundness (i.e., whether the expert's theory could be tested/falsified; whether the theory had been subjected to a peer review process; whether the error rate of an expert's empirical method was known; acceptance in the relevant scientific community), the discretion of the judge in making these determinations was left quite broad. This discretion point was later made clear in *General Electric Co. v. Joiner* which held that the appellate standard on an admissibility determination under *Daubert* is abuse of discretion.[8] The final case in the *Daubert* trilogy, *Kumho Tire Co. v. Carmichael*, made clear that this standard applied even to fields like economics and finance, in addition to the hard sciences.[9]

The Federal Judicial Center published the first Reference Manual on Scientific Evidence in 1994, with subsequent editions published in 2000 and 2011. The manual, written with the aim of being accessible to individuals with no scientific or quantitative training, includes chapters on statistics, multiple regression, survey research, microeconomics, epidemiology, and toxicology, among other technical fields.

The judiciary embraced this manual. In preparation for the third edition, the Federal Judicial Center engaged in survey research which found that judges at both the state and federal levels consult the manual when they are faced with scientific or technical evidence. This reinforces the FJC's view that the manual has been highly successful based on the fact that it has sold more than 100,000 copies. Even this latter evidence is likely understated, given that the manual is available for free in an electronic format.[10] In its assessment of the impact of the manual, the Federal Judicial Center concludes: "The Manual continues to be an extremely important resource for judges handling cases in which scientific evidence plays a role. While no manual for general distribution can anticipate and address the particular questions a judge or jury may need to decide, the Manual appears to provide a general introduction that can help judges dealing with scientific issues pertaining to the subject of a dispute. The Manual has

7 509 U.S. 579 (1993).
8 522 U.S. 136 (1997).
9 526 U.S. 137 (1999).
10 For more information on this claim, see Committee on the Evaluation of the Reference Manual on Scientific Evidence; National Research Council, Evaluation of the Reference Manual on Scientific Evidence: Letter Report (2009).

gained a reputation for providing judges with a frame of reference to approach such disputes with confidence and with a sufficient level of comfort to listen, learn, and ultimately make a decision on a matter involving scientific content."[11]

This conclusion accords with some empirical evidence on the matter suggesting that judges have become much more comfortable in questioning expert evidence during the period where this manual has been available. A 2001 RAND study found that post 1994, federal judges were more likely to challenge expert evidence and to ultimately exclude said evidence.[12]

While RAND speculated that this was a function of the more demanding *Daubert* rule, this conclusion is found to be lacking in work comparing federal and state courts in this period. A 2005 *Virginia Law Review* article by Edward Cheng and Albert Yoon, found no meaningful difference between state jurisdictions retaining the old Frye rule and state courts adopting the Daubert rule as well as federal courts. Their study focused on analysing changes in removal rates to federal court after Daubert is adopted. The intuition behind this research design is that if judges are more demanding under Daubert regarding scientific evidence, defendants will have a stronger incentive to remove the case to federal court when a plaintiff files in a state court operating under Frye than if the plaintiff files in a state court that has already adopted Daubert. They find no evidence of a differential effect, stating, "[Daubert] has a vanishingly small effect on removal rate. DAUBERT contributes only five-thousandths of a percentage point to a state's removal rate, and the result is statistically insignificant. This result suggests that, in making removal decisions, defendants place little weight on whether a state follows Frye or Daubert."[13]

For Daubert to not make a difference between state and federal court practice, as found in Cheng and Yoon, but to have been associated with increasing scrutiny at the federal level, as found in the RAND study, it is likely the case that state courts were becoming increasingly demanding as well. While we cannot be certain judges were more demanding due to their reliance on the Reference Manual on Scientific Evidence, the survey results collected from judges by the Federal Judicial Center surely indicate that the judges themselves claim the manual has had an effect.

However, as the RAND study makes clear, this increasing scrutiny may not necessarily imply that judges are handling scientific evidence better. Perhaps during this period, judges were excluding evidence that is scientifically valid. While a systematic study of this possibility is likely impossible, since it would require making independent determinations regarding an unmanageable number of evidence determinations by scholars with expertise in both law and

---

11 Id, 16.

12 See Lloyd Dixon and Brian Gill (2001), Changes in the Standards for Admitting Expert Evidence in Federal Civil Cases Since the Daubert Decision, RAND Monograph Report.

13 Edward K. Cheng and Albert H. Yoon, Does Frye or Daubert Matter? A Study of Scientific Admissibility Standards, 91 Virginia Law Review 471, 498 (2005).

science, there is some indirect evidence that the state of science in the courtroom was actually improving in this time period.

In data collected by Eric Helland and Jonathan Klick for their 2012 article "Does Anyone Get Stopped at the Gate? An Empirical Assessment of the Daubert Trilogy in the States",[14] they too confirm the Cheng and Yoon result that Daubert itself does not make much of a difference on objective indicators of an expert's quality (publication record, years of experience, affiliation with a top 10 university) but they do find that these indicators are improving everywhere, Daubert adopters and non-adopters alike, over time, suggesting that the increasing demands identified by RAND are likely the result of an improvement in the rigor of the evidence that gets admitted.

Again, this improvement in the demands made by judges in the post-Daubert era shows up in both state and federal courts. While there are likely many factors driving this, judges themselves appear to credit the Reference Manual on Scientific Evidence. However, the FJC's survey results suggest that the judges believe they could substantially benefit from actual training in the topics covered in the manual. Specifically, the FJC commented, "Judges expressed interest in educational programs that would allow them to work through material encountered at Daubert hearings. A Science for Judges Program on Evidence-Based Medicine attempted to accommodate this desire by placing participants in small break-out groups to analyse studies from speaker presentations. Judges liked this format. The advantages of this model might be harnessed using interactive computer exercises dealing with, for example, statistical issues.[15] While the FJC has organised some limited training sessions, this demand goes largely unmet via public channels. There are, however, more extensive privately-financed programs that apparently generate substantial improvements to judicial human capital.

3. THE EFFECT OF TRAINING IN ANTITRUST LAW

Competition law is an area where sophisticated quantitative and theoretical evidence largely determine the outcome of a given case. Given judicial backgrounds, competition law is also an area where the skills gap is likely to be quite large.

There is a systematic treatment of the effects of this kind of training on the sophistication of judges in the area of antitrust law. In a 2011 article in the

14 Eric Helland and Jonathan Klick, Does Anyone Get Stopped at the Gate? An Empirical Assessment of the Daubert Trilogy in the States, 20 Supreme Court Economic Review forthcoming (2012).

15 Committee on the Evaluation of the Reference Manual on Scientific Evidence; National Research Council, Evaluation of the Reference Manual on Scientific Evidence: Letter Report (2009), 12.

Journal of Law and Economics, Michael Baye and Joshua Wright analyse data on the effect of attending judicial training seminars organised by the Law and Economics Center of George Mason University and performance in antitrust cases.[16] Their study analysed 714 antitrust cases over the period 1996–2006, suggesting a fairly broad sample unlikely to be inordinately affected by a few idiosyncratic judges or cases.

Antitrust is an area where judges are especially likely to be under-prepared. Modern antitrust law has departed substantially from its historic approach of applying per se rules to challenged activities. Under modern law, most cases are decided via a rule of reason approach that examines the effect of the challenged activity on consumer welfare as judged by modern economic theory and sophisticated statistical analyses. Presumably because of this, an ABA survey found that less than one fourth of antitrust economists responded that judges usually understand the economic issues in an antitrust case.[17]

For a measure of performance, Baye and Wright examine the appeals rate on the assumption that a higher quality decision at the trial stage is less likely to be appealed. They also code the decisions according to their economic complexity, focusing on whether the case involved complicated econometric evidence, game theory, or other elements requiring greater economic sophistication.

In short, after controlling for trends over time, they find that cases decided by judges who have gone through training programs were about 10 percent less likely to be appealed, and this result is statistically significant. The basic result holds even when the authors control for the specific type of antitrust case (e.g., merger, monopolisation, etc.), the plaintiff type (private, DOJ, FTC, or state Attorney General), and the federal circuit where the case was decided. Interestingly, this effect was most pronounced in the more simple cases, suggesting that the value of the training is primarily in remedying fairly basic skills deficits. To reinforce confidence in the positive effects of judicial training, Baye and Wright replicate their results after including controls for the antitrust experience of the judge, the political party of the judge, and a measure of whether the judge has an advanced degree. These controls mitigate concerns that the results are driven by certain judges, who might happen to be naturally better positioned to write a high quality antitrust opinion, being more likely to attend programs at the Law and Economics Center. By including a measure of experience, Baye and Wright are also able to conclude that "on the job training" does not appear to be as effective as basic judicial training.

---

16 Michael R. Baye and Joshua D. Wright (2011), "Is Antitrust Too Complicated for Generalist Judges? The Impact of Economic Complexity and Judicial Training on Appeals", *Journal of Law and Economics*, 54(1): 1–24.

17 See Baker, Jonathan B., and M. Howard Morse. 2006. Final Report of the American Bar Association Antitrust Division Economic Evidence Task Force. Chicago: American Bar Association. www.abanet.org/antitrust/at-reports/01-c-ii.pdf.

While the effect of privately financed judicial training has not been studied systematically in other areas, these antitrust results suggest that an expansion of such opportunities could significantly improve judicial performance. A better equipped judiciary is likely to improve social welfare substantially.

4. CONCLUSION

Every day judges are asked to make extremely important decisions, potentially worth millions of dollars, which hinge on complicated determinations involving scientific and quantitative evidence. Judges are generally ill-equipped to make these determinations. Basic economics, statistics, and science are subjects that are absent in legal education throughout the world. Judges generally do not have the time, resources, or inclination to get themselves up to speed on these issues, much to the detriment of legal outcomes.

Fortunately, there are some reasons to be optimistic. The popularity of the FJC's Reference Manual on Scientific Evidence shows that judges will avail themselves of cheaply available high quality resources. The performance of judges who receive privately funded training gives even more reason to be optimistic, as demonstrated clearly in the antitrust area.

Given the importance of a well-trained judiciary, in the context of underfunded judicial systems, there should be an attempt to expand these educational opportunities and to encourage judges to make use of them.

BIBLIOGRAPHY

Baye R. M. and Wright J. D., Is Antitrust Too Complicated for Generalist Judges? The Impact of Economic Complexity and Judicial Training on Appeals, in: Journal of Law and Economics, 54 (2011) 1, p. 1–24

Cheng E. K. and Yoon A. H., Does Frye or Daubert Matter? A Study of Scientific Admissibility Standards, in Virginia Law Review, 91 (2005) p. 471, 498

Greenhouse, L., How Do Judges Know What They Know? Proceedings of the American Philosophical Society, 154 (2010) 3, p. 287–293

Helland E. and Klick, J., Does Anyone Get Stopped at the Gate? An Empirical Assessment of the Daubert Trilogy in the States, in Supreme Court Economic Review, 20 (2012)

Kassirer, J., Committee on the Evaluation of the Reference Manual on Scientific Evidence; National Research Council, Evaluation of the Reference Manual on Scientific Evidence: Letter Report, 12 (2009)

CHAPTER 3
RELIABLE RESEARCH METHODS IN APPLIED ECONOMETRICS FOR COMPETITION LAW

Rok Spruk

1. INTRODUCTION

One of the most pressing questions in modern social science is whether a legal and policy change can influence the legal and economic environment which governments in the European Union and United States strive to create to provide a level-playing field. Historically, EU competition law has aimed at controlling collusion and other anti-competitive practices that harm the benefit of consumers, preventing the abuse of dominant market position, controlling mergers and acquisitions and use all disposable means to prevent adverse effects of state aid. Article 102 of the Treaty on the Functioning of European Union stipulates that "any abuse by one or more undertakings of dominant position within the common market or in substantial part of it shall be prohibited as incompatible with the common market insofar as it may affect trade between Member states." The nature of the competition law essentially concerns normative aspects of decision-making with respect to what competition law shall strive for. However, the quantitative background of the competition law often remains unclear since judges, investigators and policymakers typically possess little information and know-how on the quantitative empirical analysis of policy and legal changes and how these changes affect the institutional environment. The aim of this chapter is to fill the gap between qualitative aspects of the competition law and the quantitative analytical background of judicial decision making in the area of competition law. The chapter focusses on how the tools of applied econometrics can be utilised to help investigators, judges and policymakers disentangle the very essential questions on whether and to what extent the proposed change in the competition law can influence the outcomes of interest and how such experiments can be validated. The chapter provides an introductory treatment in applied econometric methods for antitrust investigators by focusing on the most common tools such as (i) linear regression analysis, (ii) panel data econometrics and (iii) difference-in-difference analysis. In the modern econometric paradigm, these tools allow judges and investigators establish the determinants and predictors of cartel-based collusion, abuse of state aid and also facilitate a broader understanding on how policy changes can be exploited to determine its effectiveness or failure.

2. A BRIEF CRASH COURSE IN LINEAR REGRESSION

Linear regression analysis comprises the most fundamental and the most widely accepted tool in applied econometrics and it is concerned with whether a change in one variables can cause a change in another variable. Regression techniques are essential in answering some of the most puzzling questions and dilemmas posed by competition authorities and judicial experts since these techniques enable both the estimation and validation of the model rather than descriptive analysis which fails to control for the causal relationship between the investigated variables.

Population regression model, where the researcher is interested in whether an array of controllable factors explain the desired outcome of interest, can be constructed:

$$y = \alpha_0 + \alpha_1 x_1 + \alpha_2 x_2 + \ldots + \alpha_k x_k + u \qquad (1)$$

where y denotes the outcome of interest which the investigator aims to explain and the variables $x_1 x_2 x_k$ are explanatory variables, independent variables of control variables used by the researcher to explain the variation and dynamics in the outcome of interest.[1] In principle, the researcher can construct a model with k independent variables since overspecifying the underlying regression model can inevitably lead to specification bias, rendering the regression analysis inconsistent. The outcome of interest is also called the dependent variable since the key assumption surrounding the regression model advocates a direct relationship between a vector of independent variables $X = \{x_1, x_2, \ldots x_k\}$ and the outcome of interest whether the latter is conditioned by the set of explanatory variables. The effect of each independent variable on the dependent variable is captured by the underlying coefficient. In population regression model in (1), the coefficient α_1 describes the effect of x_1 independent variable on the dependent variable, y. Similarly, the coefficient α_2 captures the effect of x_2 independent

1 The terms control variables, explanatory variables and independent variables will be used interchangeably throughout the discussion in the text.

variable on the outcome of interest. Regression coefficients represent both parameter estimates of the effect of independent variables on the dependent variable and the magnitude of the effect since some explanatory variables can exhibit greater influence on the outcome of interest. The term α_0 represents the autonomous regression component which designates the level of the dependent variable when the effect of control variables is excluded. The variable u represents the unobserved variation in the dependent variable which is not captured by the explanatory variables in the specified population regression model and is also called the stochastic component. It contains a broad array of factors affecting the variance of the dependent variables, not captured by the set of explanatory variables. The key task of applied econometrics is to estimate the underlying parameters in the population regression model and establish the causal relationship between the independent variable and the outcome of interest with the sufficient number of control variables. By default, the behaviour of the population regression model can only be estimated using a sample of observations which allows econometrician to estimate the vector of unknown parameters $\alpha = \{\alpha_1, \alpha_2, \ldots \alpha_k\}$ which can reveal the information on how the independent variables influence the outcome in question since. Economists typically assume that the population regression model in (1) is true for a disposable sample of observations. The sample of observations is used to construct the sample regression model and estimate the unknown parameters, describing the relationship between the independent variables and the outcome of interest, also called the target variable.

The goal of the applied econometrician is to provide reasonably unbiased and consistent estimates of unknown regression coefficients. This goal facilitates the quality of regression estimates to be used both as evidence and the source of inference by judges, competition authorities and investigators. Such a task cannot be accomplished without the set of fundamental assumptions on the regression model construction and estimation which facilitate both the unbiasedness and consistency of the estimated unknown coefficient. The key assumption underlying the regression model concerns the relationship between stochastic disturbances (u) and the vector of control variables$X = \{x_1, x_2, \ldots x_k\}$. The first step towards consistently and unbiasedly estimated unknown regression coefficients is to achieve the exogeneity of control variables. When control variables are correlated with the stochastic component, the variance in the outcome of interest is driven by the unobserved random error which precludes the exogeneity condition. When the exogeneity assumption fails, the sample regression model suffers from ill-designed specification and cannot be used for explanatory and causal inference on the effects of explanatory variables on the dependent variable. The exogeneity condition implies that the expected value of the stochastic disturbances conditional on the vector of explanatory variables is zero:

$$E(u|x_1,x_2,...x_k) = 0 \tag{2}$$

which allows us to establish the validity of the population regression model and its sample counterpart. The exogeneity condition is often referred to as conditional mean independence since the mean value of the error term should be independent of the variation in the vector of explanatory variables used to explain the variance in the outcome of interest. Suppose the investigator is interested in whether the independent variable x_1 affects the target variable y in a simple bivariate relationship:

$$y = \alpha_0 + \alpha_1 x_1 + u \tag{3}$$

where the coefficient $\alpha_0$denotes the mean value of the target variable when the effect of independent variable x_1 is excluded, the regression coefficient α_1 denotes the partial effect of x_1 on y and the term u captures the stochastic component or the unobserved variance of the outcome of interest. Regression coefficients as displayed in (1) and (2) are estimated using the ordinary least squares (OLS) method which is the most commonly exercised and the most widely used method in investigating causal relationship between the independent variables and the outcome of interest. Let $\hat{\alpha}_0$ and $\hat{\alpha}_1$ denote the sample estimates of population regression coefficients in the sample regression model:

$$\hat{y}_i = \hat{\alpha}_0 + \hat{\alpha}_1 x_{1i} + u_i \tag{4}$$

where $\hat{y}_i$ is the estimated level of the outcome of interest for i-th observation, x_{1i} is the observed independent variable and u_i is the unobserved or stochastic component of the outcome of interest. Sample regression coefficients represent OLS estimates of unknown population parameters. The partial effect of the explanatory variable $\hat{\alpha}_1$ and the autonomous component $\hat{\alpha}_0$ are used to predict the level of the dependent variable purely as an outcome of the variation in the level of independent variable. The central tenet of the regression analysis is the difference between the observed versus predicted value of the dependent variable. Consistency and unbiasedness of the estimated coefficients depends on the difference between observed versus predicted level of the dependent variable. The OLS method of estimating the regression coefficients in the model specification is based on the minimisation of the difference between the observed and predicted value of the outcome of interest. In this respect, the stochastic component denotes the residual of the regression model which characterises the unobserved variance in the dependent variable once the effect of explanatory variables is controlled for. The residual denotes the difference between prior observed value of the dependent variable (y_i) and its posterior predicted value ($\hat{y}_i$) implied by the effect of x_{1i} on y_i:

$$\hat{u}_i = y_i - \hat{y}_i = y_i - \hat{\alpha}_0 - \hat{\alpha}_1 x_{1i} \tag{5}$$

The OLS sample estimates of unknown population parameters are obtained by minimising the residual sum of squares across the set of disposable observations:

$$\sum_{i=1}^{n} \hat{u}_i^2 = \sum_{i=1}^{n} (y_i - \hat{\alpha}_0 - \hat{\alpha}_1 x_{1i})^2 \tag{6}$$

The minimisation of the sum of squared residuals involves the derivation of the estimator of unknown parameters. OLS estimator of the underlying population regression model is obtained by differentiating (6) with respect to the coefficients $\hat{\alpha}_0$ and $\hat{\alpha}_1$ and setting first-order derivatives to zero which yields:

$$\hat{u} = \frac{1}{n}\sum_{i=1}^{n} \hat{u}_i = \frac{1}{n}\sum_{i=1}^{n} (y_i - \hat{\alpha}_0 - \hat{\alpha}_1 x_{1i}) = 0 \tag{7}$$

$$\frac{1}{n}\sum_{i=1}^{n} x_{1i}\hat{u}_i = \frac{1}{n}\sum_{i=1}^{n} x_i(y_i - \hat{\alpha}_0 - \hat{\alpha}_1 x_{1i}) = 0 \tag{8}$$

First-order conditions through ordinary least squares in (7) and (8) establish the system of two normal linear equations with two unknown parameters, $\hat{\alpha}_0$and $\hat{\alpha}_1$. Considering first-order conditions and emphasising both unknowns gives the OLS sample estimator of unknown population regression parameter:

$$\hat{\alpha}_1 = \frac{\sum_{i=1}^{n} (x_{1i} - \bar{x}_1)(y_{1i} - \bar{y})}{\sum_{i=1}^{n} (x_{1i} - \bar{x})} \tag{9}$$

$$\hat{\alpha}_0 = \bar{y} - \hat{\alpha}_1 \bar{x} \tag{10}$$

where $\bar{x}_1$ and $\bar{y}$represent the mean values of the independent and dependent variable. The OLS estimator in (9) essentially captures the partial effect of the explanatory variable on the outcome of interest and denotes the respective effect in the regression model whereas the second unknown in (10) captures the autonomous regression term which designates the predicted value of outcome of interest when the effect of the independent variable is not controlled for. The main interest in the realm of regression analysis lies in the magnitude of $\hat{\alpha}_1$ as a sample counterpart of the unknown population regression coefficient. Sampling distribution can be constructed for $\hat{\alpha}_1$ which yields the distribution of all possible outcomes for regression coefficient for large samples of equal size. The construction of sampling distribution for the sample regression coefficient is a necessary but insufficient condition for consistent and unbiased estimator properties. Since sampling distribution exhibits a variance when the size of the sample increases indefinitely, first-order conditions for OLS estimator derivation in (7) and (8) imply the smaller the variance of the estimator, the more accurate the estimate of unknown population parameter. The set of OLS estimators of unknown regression parameters $\{\hat{\alpha}_0, \hat{\alpha}_1, \ldots \hat{\alpha}_k\}$ where $k = 1, 2, \ldots K$, is unbiased if the expected value of each coefficient is equivalent to the prior unknown population regression parameter when sample size increases asymptotically:

$$E(\alpha_k) = \alpha_k \tag{11}$$

2.1. BUILDING BLOCKS OF LINEAR REGRESSION MODEL

The OLS estimator yields unbiased estimates of unknown parameters in population regression model in (1) when four essential assumptions underlying the regression model are met. First, the regression model should exhibit the linearity in parameters which allows both the straightforward minimisation of the sum of squared residuals and partial effect estimation. Second, the regression model should be estimated on the basis of a randomly drawn sample from a population whose behaviour can be described the regression equation. In non-random sampling, the regression estimates capture only a subset of the underlying population and are therefore biased by default. Third, the expected value of the stochastic disturbance in the regression model should be zero conditional on the variance of independent variables to ensure conditional mean independence or the exogeneity condition. When the unobserved component is non-zero, $E(u|x_1, x_2, \ldots x_k) \neq 0$, the exogeneity assumption fails since the stochastic component does not enter the model independently of control variables and the OLS estimates are no longer unbiased. And fourth, the regression model should exhibit no perfectly collinear relationship between independent variable to ensure sampling variation in each variable for the OLS method to yield unbiased estimates of the unknown population coefficients.[2]

One of the most essential questions arising from the OLS sample estimate of the population regression concerns the share of variance in the outcome of interest accounted for by the variation in the independent variable. This question penetrates nonetheless important and sometimes central dilemmas in antitrust policy. How much variance in the likelihood of market power abuse is explained by the firm-specific extent of price fixing? What is the share of variance in the likelihood of cartel collision accounted for by the size of R&D expenditure? Such questions can be answered by computing goodness of fit criteria for the

2 Greene 2008. See also Wooldridge 2009; and Verbeek 2012.

underlying regression model where the investigator aims at explaining the outcome of interest using the vector of plausible control variables conditioning the predicted value of the dependent variable.

2.2. GOODNESS OF FIT CRITERIA IN REGRESSION ANALYSIS

The most commonly used goodness of fit measure is the coefficient of determination or put simply R^2. Using R^2, the researcher can establish the share of variance in the outcome of interest between units in the sample explained by the independent variables. The computation of R^2 is routinely performed by modern econometric software packages such as STATA, EViews, Limdep and others but it is nevertheless important to understand the mechanics and interpretative issues behind it. The R^2 coefficient is computed as the difference between the maximum extent of variance explained by the independent variables and the ratio between residual sum of squares and total sum of squares:

$$R^2 = 1 - \frac{\sum_{i=1}^{n} \hat{u}_i^2}{\sum_{i=1}^{n} (y_i - \bar{y})^2} \tag{12}$$

where $\sum_{i=1}^{n} \hat{u}_i^2$ denotes the sum of squared residuals from the regression model and $\sum_{i=1}^{n} (y_i - \bar{y})^2$denotes the total sum of squares between observed (y) and predicted value ($\bar{y}$) of the dependent variable. The coefficient can range from 0 to 1 since the underlying independent variables can explain either no variance in the outcome of interest or its entire variance. Lower values of R^2 coefficient indicate a poorer fit of the model whereas higher values correspond to a better fit of the model. For instance, $R^2=0.45$ indicate that the independent variables account for the 45% of the variance in the outcome of interest and indicate a reasonably moderate fit of the model since the vector of explanatory variable accounts for about a half of the entire variation in the dependent variable. An important caveat regarding the R^2 should be kept in mind since investigators oftentimes attempt to manipulate the goodness of fit criteria by artificially inflating the coefficient to present a better fit of the model. The R^2 increases automatically when additional control variables are included in the regression model. Such ill-suited and manipulative empirical strategy leads to over-specifying the underlying model and falsifying the true population model. The problem of manipulative variable addition can be overcome be Theil R^2 which is adjusted for the difference between the number of observations and the number of estimated parameter which is known as degrees of freedom.[3] Adjusted R^2 never increases with the inclusion of irrelevant variables and helps investigators detect the flaws of ill-suited empirical strategy since the magnitude of adjusted R^2 can decrease if extra control variables without any relevance are added to the regression model. Theil R^2 is a modified coefficient of the original R^2:

$$R^2 = 1 - \frac{\sum_{i=1}^{n} \hat{u}_i^2 / (n - k - 1)}{\sum_{i=1}^{n} (y_i - \bar{y})^2 / (n - 1)} \tag{13}$$

where n denotes the number of observations and k represents the number of estimated parameters. The difference between sample size and number of estimated parameters is known as the number of degrees of freedom. The investigator should necessarily consider both measures when judging the evidence and conducting the empirical inference from the econometric analysis since only such cautious approach allows the detection of ill-suited and possibly manipulative empirical strategy which renders the estimates implausible.[4]

2.3. OMITTED VARIABLE BIAS

One of the most pertinent issues in the estimation of the population regression model with OLS estimator is the situation in which the investigator omits the independent variable from the vector of control variable that supposedly belongs to the true model. The problem of excluding a relevant variable or underspecifying a model is known as omitted variable bias. The failure to address omitted variable bias leads to inconsistently estimated partial effects since a key independent variable belonging to the population regression model is omitted from the vector of conditioning variables.[5] In such circumstances, the omitted control variables exhibited either overestimated or underestimated effects implied by regression coefficients. Consider a true multiple regression model with two explanatory variables:

$$\hat{y}_i = \hat{\alpha}_0 + \hat{\alpha}_1 x_{1i} + \hat{\alpha}_2 x_{2i} + u_i \tag{14}$$

where $\hat{y}_i$ is the outcome of interest, x_{1i} and x_{2i} are the independent variables influencing the behaviour of $\hat{y}_i$ and u_i is the residual, capturing the stochastic component of the variance in $\hat{y}_i$. The coefficients$\hat{\alpha}_0$, $\hat{\alpha}_1$ and $\hat{\alpha}_2$ denote the unknown population parameters estimated by the OLS method. Suppose the

3 Theil 1971.
4 Maddala and Lahiri 2009.
5 Angrist and Pischke 2009.

relevant variable x_{2i} is excluded from the regression model which subsequently boils down to the simple bivariate regression model:

$$\tilde{y}_i = \tilde{\alpha}_0 + \tilde{\alpha}_1 x_{1i} + u_i \tag{15}$$

where the coefficients $\tilde{\alpha}_0$ and $\tilde{\alpha}_1$ denote biased effects on the outcome of interest $\tilde{y}_i$ whose behaviour is inadequately described by the conditioning variable as a result of omitting the variable x_{2i}. Since x_{2i} comprises the true population regression model, the omission from (15) subsumes the relevant variable into the unobserved residual:

$$u = \alpha_2 x_{2i} + v \tag{16}$$

where the residual is composed of x_{2i} and the structural stochastic component, denoted by v. Omitting a variable from the population regression model when it supposedly belongs to it, triggers both the unbiasedness and inconsistency of the estimated regression coefficients. The relevance of the omitted variable in the regression model can be inspected from the regression of omitted variable (x_2) on the included variable (x_1):

$$x_2 = \delta_0 + \delta_1 x_1 + \varepsilon \tag{17}$$

where ε denotes the residual term. The size of omitted variable bias depends chiefly on the correlation between x_2 and x_1. Since the sample population model yields unbiased estimates under linear parameters, random sampling, conditional mean independence and no perfect collinearity between independent variables, the underlying parameters from the sample regression function $\{\hat{\alpha}_0, \hat{\alpha}_1, \ldots \hat{\alpha}_k\}$ would be unbiased for the coefficients in true population model $\{\alpha_0, \alpha_1, \ldots \alpha_k\}$. Since the extent of omitted variable bias depends on the correlation between x_1 and x_2, the bias of sample regression coefficient from (15) can be decomposed:

$$E(\tilde{\alpha}_1) = E(\hat{\alpha}_1 + \hat{\alpha}_2 \delta_1) = E(\hat{\alpha}_1) + E(\hat{\alpha}_2)\delta_1 = \alpha_1 + \alpha_2 \delta_1 \tag{18}$$

when x_1 and x_2 are uncorrelated so that $corr(x_1, x_2) = 0$, reduced-form regression of the omitted variable on the included variable in (17) implies $\delta_1 = 0$ which suggests that the size of omitted variable bias corresponds to the estimated effect of the included variable on the outcome of interest since $E(\tilde{\alpha}_1) = \hat{\alpha}_1 = \alpha_1$. In most cases of omitted variable bias, the opposite is true since the omitted variable typically exhibits a strong and persistent relationship with the included independent variable since $\delta_1 \neq 0$ underline the persistent of bias resulting from the underspecification of regression model. Bias from under-specified model depend on the strength of the relationship between the omitted and the included variable. When the omitted variable essentially comprises the true population model and exhibits a strong direct and indirect effect on the outcome of interest, the size of the bias corresponds to the difference between the biased population regression coefficient and its true counterpart:

$$Bias\{\tilde{\alpha}_1\} = E(\tilde{\alpha}_1) - \alpha_1 = \alpha_2 \delta_1 \tag{19}$$

where the size of the bias increases proportionately with the estimated effect of the included independent variable on the omitted variable as advocated by (17). The relative size of the bias is conditioned by the difference between the expected effect with the omitted variable and the true effect in the population model. Several types of biases can be inferred from (18) and (19). When the size of the bias is denoted by $E\hat{\alpha}_j - \alpha_j$ and sample regression estimates advocate $E\hat{\alpha}_j - \alpha_j > 0$ omitting a relevant variable generally overestimates the true population model since the estimated coefficient is biased upward. On the other hand, when $E\hat{\alpha}_j - \alpha_j < 0$ omitting a relevant variable from the set of control variables leads to underestimated population parameters since the underlying population regression coefficient is biased downward. When the effect of omitted variable on the outcome of interest is positive, excluding a relevant variable can lead to upward biased effect of $\tilde{\alpha}_1$ in supposedly true but underspecified model in (15) if the correlation between the included and omitted variable is positive or downward biased effect if the correlated between the two is negative. Conversely, when the relationship between the omitted variable and the dependent variable is inverse, the underlying sample regression coefficient $\tilde{\alpha}_1$ in (15) is biased downward provided that the correlation between the included and omitted variable is greater than zero and biased upward when the correlation between the two is negative. Table 1 summarises omitted variable bias when a relevant variable x_2 is excluded from the sample regression model when it belongs to the true model.

Table 1. Summary of Omitted Variables Bias in Sample Regression Coefficients when Relevant Independent Variables Are Excluded from the True Model

	$\text{corr}(x_1, x_2) > 0$	$\text{corr}(x_1, x_2) < 0$
$\alpha_2 > 0$	Upward bias	Downward bias
$\alpha_2 < 0$	Downward bias	Upward bias

2.4. HOMOSCEDASTICITY AND RESIDUAL VARIANCE DISTRIBUTION

The main goal of the empirical research is pre-determined by the quality of the research strategy in various attempts to disentangle policy dilemmas using the tools of applied econometrics. When OLS method is applied to establish regression coefficients in a sample model which is supposedly true for the population at large, estimates of population parameters will be consistent as long as the specified model exhibits linearity in parameters, random sampling method, conditional mean independence and no perfect collinearity between independent variables. Under such conditions, OLS method will yield unbiased estimates of the unknown population parameters.

The key assumption underlying the OLS regression model involves the exogeneity of the residual or stochastic component which captures the systematic variance in the outcome of interest not accounted by observable explanatory variables. For a truly unbiased estimator of unknown parameters, the exogeneity of the stochastic component is a necessary but insufficient assumption since the conditional mean independence does not address the possible distribution of the residual term across the sample. Residual distribution across groups in the sample can be either (i) homoscedastic when the residual distribution is constant, or (ii) heteroscedastic when the residual distribution differs between groups. Homoscedasticity of the residual term is therefore both the necessary and sufficient condition for a truly unbiased estimator of unknown parameter since this assumption is used to impose the restriction on the distribution of the residual term. Define the variance of the residual term:

$$\operatorname{var}\left(u \mid x_1, x_2, \ldots x_k\right) = \sigma^2 \tag{19}$$

which implies that the residual term u is constantly distribution conditional on the variation in the vector of explanatory variables $\{x_1, x_2, \ldots x_k\}$and where $\hat{\sigma}^2 = \sum_{i=1}^{n} \hat{u}_i^2/n - (k+1)$ denotes the sum of squared residuals divided by the number of degrees of freedom and is an unknown parameter estimates by OLS method in a randomly drawn sample. When the homoscedasticity assumption in (19) is not satisfied by the research or experimental design the variance of the OLS estimator for regression coefficient is biased and inconsistent. Consider a multiple OLS regression model in (14). When the distribution of residual term is not constant across groups, the variance of the underlying $\hat{\alpha}_1$ regression coefficient

$$\operatorname{var}(\hat{\alpha}_1) = \frac{\sigma^2}{\left(1 - R_j^2\right) \sum_{i=1}^{n} (x_i - \bar{x})} \tag{20}$$

is biased and inconsistent estimator of a true unknown population parameter which renders the OLS estimation strategy unfeasible and where R_j^2 is the coefficient of determination from auxiliary regression of x_1 on all other independent variables and where σ is assumed to be unknown to the researcher.

Under homoscedastic distribution of the residual term, it follows immediately that the sigma parameter from a randomly drawn sample is an unbiased estimator of the unknown population parameter since $E(\hat{\sigma}^2) = \sigma^2$. The consequences of violating the homoscedasticity assumption also preclude the reliance on classical statistical tests of hypotheses to perform inference on the estimated parameters.[6] Necessary adjustments of the estimation strategy to account for possible heteroscedastic distribution of error variance and statistical tests will be discussed below.

OLS estimator of unknown population parameters yield as an unbiased estimate of the true value when the model is characterised by linearity in parameters, randomly drawn sampling, conditional mean independence and no perfect collinearity. Unfortunately, unbiasedness does not necessarily imply consistent. The consistency of OLS estimator is crucially conditioned by assumption on the exogeneity of stochastic disturbance since one the main postulates of the regression model implies the zero mean value of the unobservable factors conditional on the vector of observables $E(u|x_1,x_2,\ldots x_k) = 0$. Since the assumption of strong exogeneity is too powerful to be imposed on the experimental research and the underlying design, weak exogeneity assumption still allows consistent OLS estimate of the true population parameter. Under weakly exogenous stochastic disturbance, when$E(u) = 0$, the unobservable stochastic component should be uncorrelated with the observable independent variables which implies$\text{cov}(x_1,u) = 0$. When zero covariance between the unobserved factors and observable independent variable holds, it can be shown that when sample size increases asymptotically, the OLS estimator $\hat{\alpha}_1$ will consistently estimate the population coefficient α_1. The probability limit of OLS estimator:

$$\underset{N\to\infty}{\text{plim}}\ \hat{\alpha}_1 = \alpha_1 + \frac{\text{cov}(x_1,u)}{\text{var}(x_1)} \tag{21}$$

suggests that when $\text{cov}(x_1,u) = 0$, an indefinite increase in the size of the sample will yield plim $\hat{\alpha}_1 = \alpha_1$ for a sufficiently large sample and, as a resulted, the OLS sample estimator will be both valid and asymptotically normally distributed.

2.5. INFERENCE AND HYPOTHESIS TESTING FROM REGRESSION ANALYSIS

Once the OLS regression analysis satisfied the five criteria for an unbiased estimator of a true parameter unknown to the econometrician, the estimated

6 Davidson and MacKinnon 1993.

regression coefficients can be used for formulating the hypotheses underlying the behaviour of groups in the sample. Statistical inference lies at the centre of investigator's interest in conducting regression analysis to articulate hypotheses about the behaviour and estimated effects. Quantitative inference based on statistical tests and appropriate distribution are also the only valid approach towards constructing and testing the hypotheses involving either single or multiple parameters describing how the independent variables influence the outcome of interest once other factors, either observed and unobserved, are controlled for.

Suppose the judge is presented the evidence by competition lawyers who presents supposedly compelling arguments and quantitative evidence in favour of the plaintiff that the behaviour of the defendant has violated the competition code in a given country. On the other side, the defendant refuses to accept the claim by the plaintiff and suggests that the inference on the type of alleged behaviour is false and ill-suited. How can a judge infer the causal relationship between the defendant's behaviour with respect to the outcome of interest depends on the validity of statistical inference from the estimated parameters?

The validity of the inference is conditioned chiefly by the behaviour of the residual term which captures the unobserved factors affecting the dependent variable. For a valid statistical inference from the estimated parameters, the residual term or the stochastic component of the outcome of interest as advocated by (14) must follow a normal Gaussian-style distribution. A normal distribution of the residual term implies that in repeated sampling the mean value of the residual will be zero and its distribution across groups will be constant, as indicated by the homoscedasticity assumption. Such an assumption is inevitably strong and powerful since the zero mean value of the residual basically advocates that in large and asymptotically valid samples, the outcome of interest will remained unaffected by the stochastic (residual) component which contains the array of unobserved factors in the underlying regression model. Normally distributed residual term in repeated sampling and as the sample size increases asymptotically with zero mean value and homoscedastic distribution implies$u \sim \mathbb{N}(0, \sigma^2)$ where $\mathbb{N}$ denotes the assumed Gaussian-style normal distribution. When the four critical assumptions and the homoscedasticity assumption are satisfied, the estimated OLS regression coefficient from (14) will be asymptotically valid as the size of the sample would increase indefinitely and will yield a true population parameter since $\hat{\alpha}_j \sim \mathbb{N}\left(\hat{\alpha}_j, \mathrm{var}(\alpha_j)\right)$.

Similarly, a test statistic for the magnitude and significance of estimated regression coefficients can be derived based on the normality assumption for the residual term:

$$\frac{\hat{\alpha}_j - \alpha_j}{\sqrt{\text{var}(\hat{\alpha}_j)}} \sim \mathbb{N}(0, \sigma^2) \qquad j = 0, 1, \ldots k \tag{22}$$

where $\hat{\alpha}_j$ is the estimated regression coefficient and α_j is the hypothetical population parameter which the investigators wants to test and $\text{var}(\hat{\alpha}_j)$ is the variance of the estimated regression coefficient from (20). A typically first-hand approach by the experimental researcher or investigator is to test whether the estimated coefficient is statistically different from zero. When the estimated coefficient is statistically significant and different from zero, the coefficients can be used with validity to conduct inference on the behaviour of groups in the sample. Conversely, when the estimated coefficient does not differ significantly from zero, the independent variable pertaining to the regression coefficient does not influence the outcome of interest since the estimated value of the coefficient does not differ statistically from its hypothesised value. When the difference between estimated regression coefficient and its hypothetical value is zero, imposing a claim on the valid non-zero effect on the independent variable on the outcome of interest is simply invalid.

Equation (22) can be used for testing the formulated hypotheses in the underlying regression model. But since the sum of squared residuals from the regression is unknown by default, the true variance of the regression coefficient $\hat{\alpha}_1$ is also unknown and the sampling variance of OLS estimator can be safely used to apply the hypothesis testing to the appropriate distribution assuming the normality of the stochastic component distribution between groups. Equation (22) follows a Student t-distribution:

$$\frac{\hat{\alpha}_j - \alpha_j}{\sqrt{\text{var}(\hat{\alpha}_j)}} \sim t_{n-k-1} \tag{23}$$

where t denotes the t-distribution with $n - k - 1$ degrees of freedom where n is the effective sample size and k is the number of estimated parameters in the regression model. The resulting test statistic is often called **t-statistic** or simply **t-test**. Testing whether the estimated coefficient differs from the hypothesised value, as shown by (22) and (23), allows either the judge, lawyer or the researcher to articulate the hypotheses underlying group behaviour in the randomly drawn sample. Articulating hypotheses is carried out in two steps. First, null hypothesis is established where the investigator supposes that the estimated regression coefficient and the resulting effect of x_j variable on the outcome of interest y is zero. Second, an alternative hypothesis is constructed which contradicts the claim of the null hypothesis which yields the assertion that the estimated effect of x_j on y is non-zero and valid accordingly. A null hypothesis on the behaviour of the single parameter can be written as $\text{H}_0 : \alpha_1 = 0$ whilst the appropriate alternative hypothesis is $\text{H}_1 : \alpha_1 \neq 0$ which suggests that the investigator principally tests whether the effect of x_1 on y as captured by $\hat{\alpha}_1$ in (14) is essentially zero in a true population model which yields the t-statistic:

$$T = \frac{\hat{\alpha}_1 - 0}{\sqrt{\text{var}(\hat{\alpha}_1)}} \quad (24)$$

which is known **as standard error of regression coefficient** and follows T-distribution with $n - k - 1$ degrees of freedom when $H_0: \alpha_1 = 0$ is true. Once the null (H_0) and alternative (H_1) hypothesis are formulated and appropriately framed in the research question, the investigator specifies significance levels. Significance level denotes the maximum accepted conditional probability of rejecting the null hypothesis when its claim is true in a population at large which is known as type-I error. Significance level denotes the maximum accepted probability of committing an error, i.e. rejecting the null hypothesis when it is, in fact, true in a population model. A clever and well-designed research strategy aims at keeping the maximum accepted conditional type-I error probability as low as possible to provide a valid inference. Significance level also indicates the threshold at which null hypothesis is rejected. Let significance level be denoted by γ. A common rule of thumb in statistics and applied econometrics is to set significance level at 5% which implies that$\gamma = 0.05$. Significance level is basically the probability of obtaining a test statistic on the hypothetical value of the regression coefficient at least as extreme as the estimated value when null hypothesis is true. Therefore, 5% significance level ($\gamma = 0.05$) suggests that researcher allows 5% probability of rejecting the null hypothesis when the latter is true which suggests. In addition, at 1% significance level ($\gamma = 0.01$), the investigators allows only 1% probability of rejecting the null hypothesis when it is actually true. Based on test statistics in (23) and (24), the probability of rejecting the null hypothesis can be estimated for an infinite number of regression coefficients in either simple bivariate or multiple regression model. The probability of rejecting the null for each coefficient is also widely known as **p-value.** Obtaining a probability of at least as extreme as the observed one is equivalent to the test of statistical significance of estimated coefficients in repeated sampling. In particular, p-value (P) for a concrete estimated coefficient denotes the percentage of correctly obtained estimates as the ones estimated in the original regression once sample size would increase indefinitely. Therefore p-value below 5% suggests that the estimated coefficient would be equivalent in 95% of the repeatedly drawn random samples and the p-value below 1% indicates that the estimated coefficient would be equivalent to the obtained estimate in 99% of the repeated randomly drawn population. A simple decision rule suggests that, if the p-value for regression coefficient is below the specified critical threshold, $P < \gamma$, the null hypothesis $H_0: \alpha_1 = 0$ is rejected. If the p-value for regression coefficient is above the specified critical threshold, the null hypothesis fails and is therefore not rejected, giving validity to the alternative hypothesis$H_1: \alpha_1 \neq 0$.

Hypothesis testing on a single parameter can easily be extended to the hypothesis test on multiple parameters since this a common interest of the investigator presenting the evidence. Testing credible and verifiable hypotheses on multiple regression coefficients at the same time invokes testing for joint significance of regression coefficients and largely indicates both the plausibility and feasibility of the regression model specification with respect to explaining the behaviour in the outcome of interest by the set of observable independent variables. In a multiple regression model:

$$\hat{y}_i = \hat{\alpha}_0 + \hat{\alpha}_1 x_{1i} + \hat{\alpha}_2 x_{2i} + u_i \tag{25}$$

Testing for joint significance of estimated regression coefficients also invokes the plausibility of independent variables with respect to explaining the behaviour in the outcome of interest. In this respect, testing for joint significance involves a formal statistical test on whether both variables jointly rather than individually account for the variation in the dependent variable. Null hypothesis for joint significance of both observable independent variables can be articulated in a similar fashion,$H_0 : \hat{\alpha}_1 = 0, \hat{\alpha}_2 = 0$ whereas the alternative hypothesis suggests the null hypothesis is not true or,H_1: not true. The null hypothesis contains two simple linear restrictions on the multiple regression model. Using the OLS estimator, the restricted regression model is estimated under null hypothesis whilst the unrestricted model is estimated under the alternative hypothesis. The difference between the two models can be tested by invoking the distribution and behaviour of residual term under null hypothesis and its alternative counterpart. Under the null hypothesis in restricted model, the residual term is equivalent to the single regression through the origin with $\hat{\alpha}_0$ as the only term incorporated in the model while under alternative hypothesis, the residual term is obtained with independent variables x_{1i} and x_{2i}. A test statistic can be applied by computing the sum of squared residuals in restricted versus unrestricted model known as F-statistic or simply F-test:

$$F= \frac{\left(\sum_{i=1}^{n}\hat{u}_i^2\right)_{\text{Restricted}} - \left(\sum_{i=1}^{n}\hat{u}_i^2\right)_{\text{Unrestricted}} /q}{\left(\sum_{i=1}^{n}\hat{u}_i^2\right)_{\text{Unrestricted}} /(n-(k+1))} \tag{26}$$

where q is the number of linear restrictions according to null hypothesis, n is effective sample size, k is the number of estimated parameters, $\left(\sum_{i=1}^{n}\hat{u}_i^2\right)_{\text{Restricted}}$ is the sum of squared residuals in a restricted model specified in accordance with null hypothesis and $\left(\sum_{i=1}^{n}\hat{u}_i^2\right)_{\text{Unrestricted}}$ is the sum of squared residuals in unrestricted model constructed as suggested by the alternative hypothesis. When the computed p-value for the F-test exceeds the critical threshold $P > |\gamma|$determined by the researcher or requested by the judge, the null hypothesis is not rejected which claims the validity to the alternative hypothesis since the evidence suggests that the residual variance does not differ between the model with observable variables and the model without observables. When the computed p-value is below the critical value, $P < |\gamma|$, null hypothesis can be rejected since the residual variance differ significantly between the model according to the null and the model under alternative hypothesis which suggests that both observable independent variables exhibit jointly significant effect on the outcome of interest.

2.7. INTERPRETING REGRESSION COEFFICIENTS AND FUNCTIONAL FORMS

The mechanics of regression analysis constitutes the essential part of deriving the coefficients describing the response of the dependent variable to a presumably exogenous change in the observable explanatory variables. One the key assumptions imposed on the sampling variance of OLS coefficient concerns the linearity of parameters whereas oftentimes researchers construct independent variables in different units of measurement. For instance, if an investigator is interested in the effect of firm size on the likelihood of contract breach, she might denote firm size as the right-hand-side variable in logarithmic unit to avoid infinitesimally small magnitude of regression coefficients. A similar setting applies to the dependent variable which is often expressed as a logarithm as a result of large variation in the outcome of interest. Transforming the underlying regression model and selecting the most appropriate specification is known as the **functional form.** Consider a simple multiple regression model:

$$\hat{y}_i = \hat{\alpha}_0 + \hat{\alpha}_1 x_{1i} + \hat{\alpha}_2 \log x_{2i} + u_i \tag{27}$$

where x_{2i} variable is measured in logarithmic unit as a result of a priori large observed variance. Transformed specification of multiple regression model in (27) is known as linear-logarithmic or simply *lin-log model* because a dependent variable is measured on the original scale whereas an independent variable is transformed on the logarithmic scale. In order to translate the interpretation of the regression coefficient back onto the original scale, the coefficient has to be divided by 100 to derive the true effect of transformed independent variable on the outcome of interest since a unit change in the log-transformed variable is associated with doubling the outcome of interest. In a multiple regression model:

$$\log \hat{y}_i = \hat{\alpha}_0 + \hat{\alpha}_1 x_{1i} + \hat{\alpha}_2 \log x_{2i} + u_i \tag{28}$$

where both the dependent and independent variable are measured in logarithmic units, the transformation of the effect of x_{2i} on $\hat{y}$ is not necessary since both variables are denoted in the same unit. In such circumstances, the estimated effect $\hat{\alpha}_2$ corresponds to the percent effect and indicates what happens to the dependent variable if x_{2i} either increases or decreases by one unit. When a dependent variable is log-transformed and an independent variable is measured on the original scale:

$$\log \hat{y}_i = \hat{\alpha}_0 + \hat{\alpha}_1 x_{1i} + \hat{\alpha}_2 x_{2i} + u_i \quad (29)$$

the coefficients on the effect of independent variables on the outcome of interest $\hat{\alpha}_1$ and $\hat{\alpha}_2$ represents the effect on the log-transformed level of dependent variable. In these conditions, the effect of a unit change in variables x_{1i} and x_{2i} on $\hat{y}_i$ is obtained by multiplying each coefficient by 100. Table 2 summarises the overview of interpreting regression coefficients when either dependent or independent variables are denoted in a different measurement unit.

Table 2. A Summary of Regression Coefficient Interpretation

Form of dependent variable	Form of independent variable	Dependent variable	Independent variable	Interpretation of coefficient
Level	Level	Y	X	$\Delta y = \alpha_j \Delta x$
Level	Log	Y	log(x)	$\Delta y = (\alpha_j / 100)\% \Delta x$
Log	Level	log(y)	X	$\Delta y = (100 \cdot \alpha_j)\% \Delta x$
Log	Log	log(y)	log(y)	$\% \Delta y = \alpha_j \% \Delta x$

2.8. A NOTE ON NON-LINEARITY

Consider linear multiple regression model specification of a simple unconstrained function where the investigators aims at establishing the observable determinants of participation in cartel agreement:

$$q_{1i} = \beta_0 + \beta_1 P_{1i} + \beta_2 P_{2i} + \beta_3 S_i + u_i \quad (30)$$

where q_{1i} denotes the latent likelihood of engaging in cartel agreement for firm i, P_{1i} is the price of good 1 for i-th firm, P_{2i} is the price of good 2 for i-th firm, S_i is the size of the firm and u_i is the unobservable stochastic component of engaging in cartelised market agreement. Suppose the investigator is interested in the effect of prices of good 1 and 2 and the firm size on the likelihood of engagement. Based on the prior evidence, the investigator assumes that the effect of firm size on the likelihood differs depending on the size of the firm since larger firms would be more significantly more likely to initiate and establish cartel agreement in a given industry than smaller firms whereas very large firms might avoid the engagement in cartelised agreement as antitrust investigators might easily detect the participation in such agreements or presumably because very large firms have already paid significant fines in previous cases and tend to avoid such agreements once the judgment has been ruled against them. Such effects and patterns can be invoked by constructing non-linear regression model whilst still applying the OLS estimator. Suppose the investigator assumes a quadratic relationship between firm size and the likelihood of cartel agreement and posits the modified non-linear regression model:

$$q_{1i} = \hat{\beta}_0 + \hat{\beta}_1 P_{1i} + \hat{\beta}_2 P_{2i} + \hat{\beta}_3 S_i + \hat{\beta}_4 S_i^2 + u_i \tag{31}$$

where the specification is augmented by the quadratic term of firm size for i-th firm S_i^2 in the disposable sample. The effect of firm size on the likelihood of participating in the cartel depends on the sign of linear and quadratic coefficient on the size of the firm. When the estimated model specification in (30) yields $\hat{\beta}_3 > 0$ and $\hat{\beta}_4 < 0$ below the critical significance threshold, the pattern suggests a hump-shaped relationship between firm size and the likelihood of participating in the cartel which indicates that medium-sized firms are most likely to engage in a cartel compared to small and large firms. On the other hand, when the evidence indicates $\hat{\beta}_3 < 0$ and $\hat{\beta}_4 > 0$below critical significance level, the estimated model specification advocates U-shaped relationship suggesting that either small or very large-sized firms are most likely to participate in the cartel whereas the minimum likelihood is observed for medium-sized firms. F-test can be applied straightforward to examine the joint significance of the estimated regression coefficients $\hat{\beta}_3$ and $\hat{\beta}_4$ under the null hypothesis $H_0 : \hat{\beta}_3 < 0, \hat{\beta}_4 > 0$ versus the alternative hypothesis $H_1 : H_0$ not true and tested as shown in (25).

The most inherent feature of non-linear regression model is the allowance for the estimation of marginal effects of non-linear variables such as firm size. The estimation of marginal effects in market demand function as shown in (31) allows the investigator to establish the critical threshold of the non-linear variable beyond which the likelihood of engaging in cartelised agreement is most likely to diminish or expand. Therefore, non-linearity in independent variables enables the prediction of minimum and maximum level of the outcome of interest as a result of the cross-group variation in the independent variable such as firm size (31). The marginal effect of firm size on the likelihood of participation can be estimated from underlying regression model:

$$E(q)_i = \hat{\beta}_0 + \hat{\beta}_1 P_{1i} + \hat{\beta}_2 P_{2i} + \hat{\beta}_3 S_i + \hat{\beta}_4 S_i^2 + u_i \tag{32}$$

where the operator E denotes the expected likelihood of participating in the cartel. The marginal effect of firm size is invoked by taking the first-order derivative of the expected likelihood with respect to firm size which yields:

$$\frac{\partial E(q)_i}{\partial S_i} = \hat{\beta}_3 + 2\hat{\beta}_4 S_i \tag{33}$$

The key implication of the estimated marginal effect is that its magnitude and direction change for each observation in the sample. The optimum level of firm size where the likelihood of participation is either at the maximum or minimum level is derived by inverting (32) and solving for S which implies$S_i^* = \hat{\beta}_3/2\hat{\beta}_4$. The predicted marginal effect is evaluated at mean or selected values of independent variables that the investigator wishes to examine. One of the most perpetrating directional assumptions is whether the marginal effect is zero which would contradict the non-linearity in the estimated effect of firm size on the likelihood of participation in the cartel. Zero marginal effect hypothesis is tested by constructing a null hypothesis for (32) which yields $H_0: \hat{\beta}_3 + 2\hat{\beta}_4 \overline{S}_i = 0$ versus the alternative hypothesis$H_1: \hat{\beta}_3 + 2\hat{\beta}_4 \overline{S}_i \neq 0$. Consequently, the null hypothesis for zero marginal effect is examined with an extended Student t-test for non-linear hypothesis on zero marginal effect:

$$t = \frac{\left(\hat{\beta}_3 + 2\hat{\beta}_4 \log\overline{S}\right) - \left(\beta_3 + 2\beta_4 \log\overline{S}\right)}{\sqrt{\mathrm{var}\left(\beta_3 + 2\beta_4 \log\overline{S}\right)}} \tag{34}$$

where the null hypothesis features the inference on non-linear combination of the estimated effects of firm size on the likelihood of cartel participation. Antitrust investigators are often interested in whether particular firms under investigation are more likely than its within-industry or cross-industry peers to be involved in the cartel-based agreements. The researcher can investigate firm-specific effects on this type of likelihood by constructing **dummy variables**. A dummy variable is also known as indicator variable since it denotes binary and categorical outcomes which can influence the outcome of interest to significant degree. Binary dummy variables take two values either one or zero whereas categorical dummy variables can take several values for categorical outcomes. For instance, a binary dummy variable takes the value$D_{1i} = 1$ if the observation in the sample is the firm 1 and $D_{1i} = 0$ otherwise. When the investigator assumes firm 1 is significantly more likely to engage in cartelised agreements, a dummy variable for this firm can be constructed and added to the cross-sectional regression model:

$$q_i = \hat{\beta}_0 + \hat{\beta}_1 P_{1i} + \hat{\beta}_2 P_{2i} + \hat{\beta}_3 S_i + \hat{\beta}_4 S_i^2 + \hat{\beta}_5 D_{1i} + u_i \tag{35}$$

where the coefficient $\hat{\beta}_5$ indicates whether firm 1 is more likely than other firms to participate in the cartel. If the estimates indicate $\hat{\beta}_5 > 0$ and significant coefficient, firm 1 is indeed more likely to engage in cartel agreements whereas statistically significant estimated coefficient $\hat{\beta}_5 < 0$ indicates otherwise. Typically, researcher construct multiple dummy variables based on the underlying conceptual and theoretical framework as well as literature review. For instance, the investigator could add further dummy variables for antitrust violations, ownership type, union status and other relevant characteristics. Since antitrust investigators are typically interested in the likelihood of cartel participation for all respective firms in the sample, a naïve approach would suggest the construction of dummy variables for each firm. Despite its appeal, such approach is not plausible since it exacerbates perfect collinearity among independent variables and thus violates one of the four underlying assumptions for OLS sample estimator to yield unbiased estimates of unknown population parameters which renders the OLS as best linear predictor both biased and inconsistent. Perfect collinearity can be overcome by selecting a single firm as a reference category and construct dummy variables for other firms which still allows unbiased and consistent estimate of the unknown parameters.

A commonly invoked question by the alleged authorities is whether the effect of independent variable differs between firms. For instance, the effect of price structure on the likelihood participation in the cartel might differ across firms since the price structure in a given market in some firms is significantly more likely to encourage cartelised agreements that the price structure in other firms. Such effects can be inspected by constructing interaction terms between dummy variables and independent variables. Consider a multiple regression model for the latent likelihood of cartel participation:

$$q_i = \hat{\beta}_0 + \hat{\beta}_1 P_{1i} + \hat{\beta}_2 P_{2i} + \hat{\beta}_3 S_i + \hat{\beta}_4 S_i^2 + \hat{\beta}_5 D_{1i} + \hat{\beta}_6 P_{1i} \cdot D_{1i} + u_i \tag{36}$$

where the variable $P_{1i} \cdot D_{1i}$ is the interaction term between price structure for good 1 and the dummy variable for firm 1 and the regression coefficient $\hat{\beta}_6$ reveals whether price structure for good 1 in firm 1 is significantly more likely predict the likelihood of participating in the cartel. Similar interaction terms can be constructed in other relevant context. In a multiple regression model with interaction terms, the model specification should consist of both dummy variable (D_{1i}) and the price structure (P_{1i}) as independent variables for the interaction term ($P_{1i} \cdot D_{1i}$) to yield consistent and meaningful estimate. Interaction terms also facilitate the inspection on whether the effect of interacted independent variable is different between treatment group indicated by the dummy variable, such as a single firm, and the control group which comprises firms not indicated by the dummy variable. Assuming a regression model:

$$E(q_i) = \hat{\beta}_0 + \hat{\beta}_1 P_{1i} + \hat{\beta}_2 P_{2i} + \hat{\beta}_3 S_i + \hat{\beta}_4 S_i^2 + \hat{\beta}_5 D_{1i} + \hat{\beta}_6 P_{1i} \cdot D_{1i} + u_i \tag{37}$$

the marginal effect of price increase on the outcome of interest can differ between treatment group and control group as a result of the interaction term. Since treatment group comprises either a single firm or a group of firms in the sample whereas control group encompasses other firms or group of firms, the interaction term enables the investigator to examine whether or not the effect of a change in the price structure on the likelihood of cartel participation is the same for all firms alike. The marginal effect of a change in price structure from (37) is established by taking first-order derivative of the conditional expectation function:

$$\frac{\partial E(q_i)}{\partial P_{1i}} = \hat{\beta}_1 + \hat{\beta}_6 \cdot D_{1i} \tag{38}$$

where the directional sign of $\hat{\beta}_6$ advocates the persistent of firm-specific rather than general effect of a change in price structure on the likelihood of cartel-based agreements. Binary outcomes can augmented by constructing categorical dummy variables for more than simply two categories to investigate the effect of firm size on the likelihood of participation in the cartel either independent or in interaction with other observable explanatory variables. Suppose category dummy variables are constructed for three distinct firm size groups with the probability distribution scheme:

$$D_{ji} = \begin{cases} D_{1i} = 1 \text{ if } 0 \leq S < 5 \text{ and } 0 \text{ otherwise} \\ D_{2i} = 1 \text{ if } 5 \leq S < 10 \text{ and } 0 \text{ otherwise} \\ D_{3i} = 1 \text{ if } 10 \leq S < 15 \text{ and } 0 \text{ otherwise} \end{cases} \tag{39}$$

where firms with size $S > 15$ serve as reference category for the three categorical groups to avoid perfect multicollinearity and still allow for unbiased and consistent estimate of respective regression coefficients. Probability distribution scheme in (38) allows us to construct and augment the multiple regression model:

$$q_i = \hat{\beta}_0 + \hat{\beta}_1 S_i + \hat{\beta}_2 S_i^2 + \hat{\beta}_3 D_{1i} + \hat{\beta}_4 D_{2i} + \hat{\beta}_5 D_{3i} + u_i \tag{40}$$

where the coefficients $\hat{\beta}_3$, $\hat{\beta}_4$ and $\hat{\beta}_5$ denote the effect of respective firm size group on the likelihood of participation in the cartel relative to the largest firms as reference category. The inclusion of firm size groups in the underlying multiple regression model can be flexible if the investigator aims at direct estimate of the categorical dummy variable which otherwise serves as reference category. In such circumstance, the investigator must choose another group as reference. Each estimated regression coefficient on the categorical dummy variable in (39) denotes the difference in the outcome of interest relative to the reference category and ceteris paribus on overall firm size.

2.9. ADJUSTING THE REGRESSION MODEL FOR HETEROSCEDASTICITY

When the variance of unobserved stochastic component is violated as in (20), the OLS sampling variance estimator for regression coefficients in the linear multiple regression model:

$$y = \alpha_0 + \alpha_1 x_1 + \alpha_2 x_2 + \ldots + \alpha_k x_k + u \tag{41}$$

yields biased and inconsistent effect since the variance of the residual term is not constant across groups. Under linearity in parameters, random drawn sample, exogenous residual term and no perfect collinearity among independent variable, the sample regression coefficient $\hat{\alpha}_k$ is an unbiased estimator of its unknown population parameter α_k which yields$E(\hat{\alpha}_k) = \alpha_k$. When the homoscedasticity assumption on the distribution of residual variance across observations$\text{var}(u| x_1, x_2, \ldots x_k) = \sigma^2$is violated so that $\text{var}(u| x_1, x_2, \ldots x_k) \neq \sigma^2$, it follows immediately $E(\hat{\sigma}^2) \neq \sigma_2$ which implies that the variance of the sample regression coefficient $\text{var}(\hat{\alpha}_k) = \hat{\sigma}^2/(1 - R_j^2)\sum_{i=1}^{n}(x_i - \bar{x})$ is biased and inconsistent even when the size of the sample increases indefinitely and the test statistic on the significance of the regression coefficient $\frac{\hat{\alpha}_j - \alpha_j}{\sqrt{\text{var}(\hat{\alpha}_j)}}$ does not follow the t-distribution and further hinges on the violation of normality assumption which renders classical statistical hypothesis testing invalid and unreliable. The heteroscedasticity of the residual variance can be appropriately adjusted to arrive at unbiased and consistently estimated regression coefficient. The correction of the model when it suffers from heteroscedasticity has been proposed by Breusch and Pagan[7] (1979) in two seminal contributions. The adjustment of the model is a necessary step towards consistently estimated unknown parameters as well as plausible and valid statistical inference on the estimated parameters. The presence of heteroscedasticity in the multiple regression model can be inspected by applying Breusch-Pagan test. Consider first a simple unconstrained multiple regression model:

$$y = \alpha_0 + \alpha_1 x_1 + \alpha_2 x_2 + \ldots + \alpha_k x_k + u \tag{42}$$

where the researcher should obtain the residuals by predicting the level of the dependent variable based on the estimated regression coefficients. Obtained residuals should be used to perform the second-stage regression of the squared residual on the set of independent variables from (41):

7 Breusch and Pagan 1979.

$$\hat{u}_i^2 = \alpha_0 + \alpha_1 x_1 + \alpha_2 x_2 + \ldots + \alpha_k x_k + v_i \tag{43}$$

where v_i denotes the second-stage residual term. Under the null hypothesis, the investigator assumes that independent variables exhibit no effect on the residual term in which case such evidence would largely indicate homoscedasticity. When one or more independent variables exacerbate statistically significant effect on the unobserved stochastic component, the estimated regression of squared residual term on the set of explanatory variables indicates the violation of homoscedasticity assumption since the residual is obviously not independent from the explanatory variables. The investigator should apply the F-test to test the null hypothesis vs. alternative hypothesis:

$$H_0 : \hat{\alpha}_1 = \hat{\alpha}_2 = \ldots = \hat{\alpha}_k = 0 \text{ (no heteroscedasticity)} \tag{44}$$

$$H_1 : H_0 \text{ not true(heteroscedasticity)} \tag{45}$$

If the null hypothesis is rejected in favour of its alternative in (45), the constructed multiple regression model can still allow for possible heteroscedasticity by computing the valid variance matrix estimator for the necessary adjustment:

$$\text{var}(\hat{\alpha}_k) = \frac{\sum_{i=1}^{n} \hat{r}_{ij} \hat{u}_i^2}{\sum_{i=1}^{n} \hat{u}_i^2} \tag{46}$$

where $\hat{r}_{ij}$ is the i-th residual from regressing x_k on all other independent variables. Covariance matrix estimator in (46) is known as Huber-White or Eickner-Huber-White variance matrix estimator which adjusts the standard errors of regression coefficients to allow for possible heteroskedastic distribution of residual variance.[8] The adjustment for heteroscedasticity is a necessary step in the empirical design of the investigation which enables the investigator to arrive at credible, consistent and unbiased inference on the statistical significance of the underlying regression coefficient and should be performed routinely disregarding a prior assumptions on whether homoscedastic assumption is met or not.

3. ESSENTIALS OF PANEL DATA ECONOMETRICS

The mechanics of econometric analysis so far has been based on cross-sectional analysis where the researchers performs a regression analysis based on a given sample at a certain point in time. Despite its usefulness and widespread application, cross-sectional analysis ignores the temporal dimension of the

---

8 Eickner 1967. See also Huber 1967, and White 1980.

outcome of interest since it disallows the observation of the dependent variable both across groups and over time. Such empirical strategy is possible by constructing a **panel** which exhibits observations on both dependent and independent variables at multiple years. The neglect for joint temporal and cross-sectional dimension leads to the lack of control for unobserved effects both across space and time. Estimation strategy without the control for unobserved effects inevitably leads to (i) omitted variable bias, and (ii) inconsistently estimated effect of independent variables on the dependent variable. Unobserved effects across space are commonly known as **fixed-effects, unobserved heterogeneity** or simply **heterogeneity bias** since unobserved effects necessarily imply a degree of heterogeneity between groups with respect to the outcome of interest. Similarly, unobserved effects across time are known as time-fixed effects which allow the investigator to control for unobserved shocks to the outcome of interest and therefore tackle intertemporal omitted variable bias.

Consider a simple panel-data regression model:

$$\hat{y}_{it} = \hat{\alpha}_0 + \hat{\alpha}_1 P_{1it} + \hat{\alpha}_2 P_{2it} + a_i + u_{it} \quad (47)$$

where the outcome of interest $\hat{y}$ is observed for i-th firm in the sample and across t time periods, P_{1it} and P_{2it} are the prices of good 1 and 2 observed for i-th firm across t periods, and u_{it} is the residual term. The variable a captures unobserved (fixed) effects across firms. It allows the control for unobserved spatial shocks in the outcome of interest which are otherwise not contained in the effect of independent variables. Fixed-effects across space facilitate the comparison of partial effect of each firm's unobserved effects on the outcome of interest. Unobserved spatial effects for $i = 1, 2, \ldots k$ number of firms in the panel-data regression model can be written as:

$$a_i = \hat{\beta}_1 D_{1i} + \hat{\beta}_2 D_{2i} + \ldots + \hat{\beta}_k D_{ki} = \sum_{i=1}^{k} \hat{\beta}_i D_i \quad (48)$$

where D_{1i} is a dummy variable for firm 1, D_{2i} is a dummy variable for firm 2, and D_{ki} is a dummy variable for k-th firm in the panel. Firm-specific dummy variable capture unobserved effects across space in the panel which can affect the outcome of interest to a significant degree. The key assumption underlying the panel data regression model implies the exogeneity of the residual term with respect to the independent variable$E(u_{it} | x_{1it}, x_{2it}, \ldots x_{kit}) = 0$. When the residual term is exogenous, panel data estimators allow consistent and reasonably unbiased estimates of unknown population parameters both across space and time. The most typical question posed by the investigator concerns what would have happened to the panel data regression model if unobserved effects were zero, suggesting that firm-fixed effects do not affect the outcome of interest. In such circumstances, zero fixed-effects assumption$E(a_i | x_{1it}, x_{2it}, \ldots x_{kit}) = 0$

suggests that these effects are purely random and advocate the construction of panel data regression model with **random effects**:

$$\hat{y}_{it} = \hat{\alpha}_0 + \hat{\alpha}_1 P_{1it} + \hat{\alpha}_2 P_{2it} + v_{it} \quad (49)$$

where the residual term is composed of the classical stochastic disturbance u_{it} and fixed-effects component a_i, which implies $v_{it} = a_i + u_{it}$. Hausman has developed a specification test which allows the investigator to test whether fixed-effects and random-effects model estimates differ systematically.[9] Suppose $\hat{\beta}^{FE} = \{\hat{\beta}_1, \hat{\beta}_2, \ldots \hat{\beta}_k\}$ is a vector of panel regression coefficients estimated with fixed-effects estimator where $E(a_i | x_{1i}, x_{2i}, \ldots x_{ki}) \neq 0$ and let $\hat{\beta}^{RE} = \{\hat{\beta}_1, \hat{\beta}_2, \ldots \hat{\beta}_k\}$ be a vector of regression coefficients obtained by using random-effects estimator with the assumption on zero fixed-effects$E(a_i | x_{1i}, x_{2i}, \ldots x_{ki}) = 0$. Hausman test is conducted by comparing the spatial and intertemporal distribution of fixed-effects vs. random-effects regression coefficients with the test statistic:

$$H = \frac{\left(\hat{\beta}^{FE} - \hat{\beta}^{RE}\right)^2}{\text{var}\left(\hat{\beta}^{RE} - \hat{\beta}^{FE}\right)} \sim \chi_k^2 \quad (50)$$

which follows the chi-squared distribution χ^2 with the number of degrees of freedom equal to the rank of the matrix $\text{var}\left(\hat{\beta}^{RE} - \hat{\beta}^{FE}\right)$ denoted by k. Under the null hypothesis, the investigators assumes random effects $\text{H}_0: E(a_i | x_{1i}, x_{2i}, \ldots x_{ki}) = 0$ whereas the alternative hypothesis prefers fixed-effects estimator since $\text{H}_1: E(a_i | x_{1i}, x_{2i}, \ldots x_{ki}) \neq 0$. Under the null hypothesis, random effects estimator is preferred since its main advantage is higher efficiency whereas the alternative hypothesis prefers fixed effects estimator which achieves greater consistency. When $\text{H}_0: E(a_i | x_{1it}, x_{2it}, \ldots x_{kit}) = 0$true, random effects estimator is both consistent and efficient whilst under H_1 random effects estimator is inconsistent. Fixed-effects estimator is consistent but inefficiency when H_0 is true whereas when H_1 is true, fixed-effects estimator is still consistent. A common rule for the rejection of the null hypothesis is 5% significance level or $\alpha = 0.05$.

When fixed-effects estimator is preferred, the investigator should proceed with the specification of the panel data regression with both unobserved firm-fixed and time-fixed effects. The former controls for unobserved heterogeneity across space whilst the latter tackles the unobserved heterogeneity over time and controls for possible intertemporal shocks to the outcome of interest. Assume a panel-data regression model with firm-fixed effects and time-fixed effects:

[9] Hausman 1978.

$$\hat{y}_{it} = \hat{\alpha}_0 + \hat{\alpha}_1 P_{1it} + \hat{\alpha}_2 P_{2it} + a_i + \tau_t + u_{it} \tag{51}$$

where the term τ_t captures unobserved time-fixed effects. The intertemporal component of time-fixed effects essentially consists of time dummy variables for each time period t in the panel which implies $\tau_t = \delta_1 + \delta_2 t_{1t} + \delta_2 t_{2t} + \ldots + \delta_k t_{kt} = \sum_{t=1}^{k} \delta_t t_t$ and where it is a priori assumed based on Hausman or alternative specification tests[10] that fixed-effects is the preferred estimator, $E(\tau_t | x_{1it}, x_{2it}, \ldots x_{kit}) \neq 0$ and $E(a_i | x_{1i}, x_{2i}, \ldots x_{ki}) \neq 0$. An alternative to the model with unobserved effects is a panel-data regression model with lagged dependent variable as originally proposed by Arellano and Bond:

$$\hat{y}_{it} = \hat{\alpha}_0 + \hat{\theta}_1 y_{it-1} + \hat{\alpha}_1 P_{1it} + \hat{\alpha}_2 P_{2it} + a_i + u_{it} \tag{52}$$

where y_{it-1} is one-period lagged value of the dependent variable and the regression coefficient $\hat{\theta}_1$ captures the persistence of state dependence.[11] Arellano-Bond estimator in (52) based on the assumption that fixed effects are correlated with the dependent variable and can be overcome by constructing a dynamic linear panel-data regression model with lagged dependent variable where unobserved effects are already controlled for without specifying and decomposing fixed effects separately. Since demeaning is used to estimate the regression coefficients, Arellano-Bond estimator effectively eliminates the unobserved effect a_i. Dynamic panel data estimator is based on simple unrestricted generalised methods of moments (GMM) estimator for the regression parameters. Both methods, either fixed-effects modelling assumptions or Arellano-Bond estimator yield consistent estimates of unknown parameters. Compared to fixed-effects estimator, Arellano-Bond estimator is especially designed for multiple panels with few periods and the investigator has to impose the assumption of no serial correlation in residual term u_{it} to yield consistent estimates of the regression parameters.

4. EMPIRICAL ANALYSIS OF POLICY CHANGES: DIFFERENCE-IN-DIFFERENCE ESTIMATION

One of the most commonly asked questions in the competition law is whether policy changes are effective and whether such change influence the outcome of interest. Multiple questions arise from judging the effectiveness of policy changes. Has European Commission's trail against Microsoft permanently mitigated price-fixing behaviour of software producers? Has the training of competition

10 Mundlak 1978.

11 Arellano and Bond 1991.

judges in the empirical methods delivered more efficient decision-making and has it improved its quality and substance? Does information disclosure by plaintiff and the defendant before the trail significantly shortens the length of judicial procedure? These are only few questions which pervade the minds of competition judges and lawyers. Although these questions are qualitative in its origin, the investigator cannot answer these questions without using a quantitative empirical analysis in which she exploits policy changes and examine whether these changes influence the outcome of interest or the target variable.

Quantitative empirical analysis of exploiting policy changes is commonly known in applied econometrics as **difference-in-difference estimation strategy**. In this setup, the investigator is interested in whether an exogenous policy change affects the outcome of interest. Such affect necessarily depends on which groups such as firms or individuals, are affected by policy change and which of them remain unaffected. The group affected by a given policy change is referred to as **treatment group** whereas the unaffected group is known as **control group** since it remains uninfluenced by the exogenous policy change (Imbens & Wooldridge, 2009). Suppose the investigator is interested in whether the outcome of interest differs between treatment and control group of firms in the aftermath of policy change and posits the following model:

$$y_{ijt} = \hat{\alpha}_0 + \hat{\beta}_1 D_{ikt} + a_i + \tau_t + u_{ijt} \tag{53}$$

where y_{ijt} is the dependent variable for i-th firm in country j at time t and D_{ikt} is a simple dummy variable for the treatment group, denoted by k, a_i are firm-fixed effects, τ_t are time-fixed effects and u_{ijt} is the stochastic disturbance. For the sake of simplicity, assume that the panel consists of two periods, t=1 and t=2 and that the investigator is interested in the average difference in the outcome of interest between firms in country 1 (s=1) and country 2 (s=2). Difference in difference estimator can be derived by computing individual mean values for the outcome of interest for firms in s=1 and s=2 and observe the difference in the behaviour of the dependent variable over time:

$$\begin{aligned}(y_{11} - y_{22}) - (y_{21} - y_{22}) &= \left[(a_1 + \tau_1 + \beta D_{11} + \overline{u}_{11}) - (a_1 + \tau_2 + \beta D_{12} + \overline{u}_{12})\right] - \\ &\left[(a_2 + \tau_1 + \beta D_{21} + \overline{u}_{21}) - (a_2 + \tau_2 + \beta D_{22} + \overline{u}_{22})\right] = \\ &\hat{\beta}_1(D_{11} - D_{12}) + \hat{\beta}_1(D_{22} - D_{21}) + \overline{u}_{11} - \overline{u}_{12} + \overline{u}_{22} - \overline{u}_{21}\end{aligned} \tag{54}$$

where y_{11}, y_{22}, y_{21} and y_{22} denote the outcome of interest for firms in country s=1 and s=2 between time t=2 and t=1, the dummy variables D_{11}, D_{12}, D_{21}, and D_{22} denote treatment status between firms over time. The key interest lies in the coefficient $\hat{\beta}_1$ which indicates the difference in the outcome of interest between the treated and non-treated group. Under strict exogeneity assumption on the treatment status:

$$E[(\bar{y}_{11} - \bar{y}_{12}) - (\bar{y}_{21} - \bar{y}_{22})] = \hat{\beta}_1(D_{11} - D_{12}) + \hat{\beta}_1(D_{22} - D_{21}) \tag{55}$$

assume that the firms in country s=2 receive treatment in period t=2, $D_{22} = 1$ whilst firms in country s=1 receive no treatment and therefore comprise control group, so that $D_{11} = D_{12} = D_{21} = 0$. The coefficient $\hat{\beta}_1$ is **difference-in-difference estimator** and denotes **average treatment effect** of an exogenous policy change on the treated relative to control group. Difference-in-difference estimator is simply the average difference in the outcome of interest between treatment group and control group after the policy change has been implemented:

$$\hat{\beta}_1 = (\bar{y}_{11} - \bar{y}_{12}) - (\bar{y}_{21} - \bar{y}_{22}) \tag{56}$$

All assumptions underlying the consistency and unbiasedness of the OLS estimator apply to the difference-in-difference estimator (DiD). The central tenet of DiD estimator is the parallel trend assumption which requires that the difference between pre-treatment and post-treatment period is the same for all groups participating in the DiD experiment alike. Under parallel trend assumption, the treatment effect of policy change is equivalent to the difference between observed value of the outcome of interest and assumed value with parallel trends if there had been no treatment at all. Parallel trend assumption is both necessary and sufficient condition for DiD estimator to yield consistently estimated effects of policy change. Parallel trend assumption is violated when factors other than treatment change in the treatment group but not in the other group at the same time. To assure the accuracy of DiD estimates, the composition of firms or other group should remain unchanged over time. Moreover, the researcher should not excluded systematically important control variables affecting the outcome of interest at the same time to partial out the effect of unobserved factors at the same time.

Figure 1 summarises parallel trend assumption. The blue line corresponds to the behaviour of the dependent variable for the treatment group s=1 between t=1 and t=2 periods whereas the downward sloping black line corresponds to the direction of the assumed counterfactual which provides a check on whether the treatment goes against the establish facts about the outcome of interest. The behaviour of outcome of interest between periods t=2 and t=1 as the difference between treatment group and control group constitutes the first counterfactual upon the assumption of what would have happened to the trend in the control group had it received no treatment at all. Validity of DiD non-experimental setting depends chiefly on the assumption that trends for the treatment and control group would have been the same in the absence of treatment. Table 3 provides a summary of difference-in-difference effects of exogenous policy change by comparing the average difference between firms in country s=2 versus country s=1 before policy change (t=1) and after policy change (t=2).

Figure 1. Parallel Trend Assumption in Difference-in-Difference Estimation Strategy

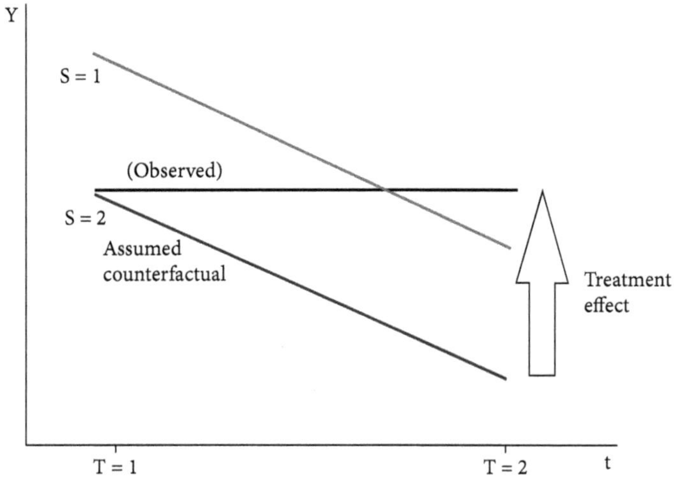

Table 3. Summary of Difference-in-Difference Effects

Y_{st}	Treatment Group S = 2	Control Group S = 1	Difference
Post-Treatment t = 2	y_{22}	y_{12}	$y_{12} - y_{22}$
Pre-Treatment t = 1	y_{21}	y_{11}	$y_{11} - y_{21}$
Change	$y_{21} - y_{22}$	$y_{11} - y_{12}$	$(y_{11} - y_{21}) - (y_{12} - y_{22})$

Consider a simple difference-in-difference estimate of exogenous policy change which affects the treatment group wherein the investigators aims at disentangling the causal effects of policy change on the treated:

$$y_{ist} = \hat{\beta}_0 + \hat{\alpha}_1 T_t + \hat{\alpha}_2 S_{is} + \hat{\delta}_1 (T_t \cdot S_{is}) + u_{ist} \quad (57)$$

where y_{ist} is the outcome of interest for i-th firm in s-th country at time t, T_t is a treatment status for the policy change affecting the treated firms, S_{is} is a dummy variable for the policy change, and $T_t \cdot S_{is}$ is an interaction term between policy change at time t and the treatment group S. The coefficient $\hat{\beta}_0$ indicates the expected outcome of interest before the policy change common to all firms in the panel:

$$\hat{\beta}_0 = E(y|T = 0, S = 0) \quad (58)$$

The coefficient $\hat{\alpha}_1$ encompasses the difference in expected outcome of interest between pre-treatment and post-treatment period common for all firms alike. This coefficient indicates the degree to which a given policy change alters the dependent variable:

$$\hat{\alpha}_1 = E(y|T = 1, S = 0) - E(y|T = 0, S = 0) \tag{59}$$

The coefficient $\hat{\alpha}_2$ denotes the difference in the expected outcome of interest between treatment group s=1 and control group s=0 before the policy change has taken place which allows the investigator to observe the relative difference in the dependent variable disregarding the effect of policy change:

$$\hat{\alpha}_2 = E(y|T = 0, S = 1) - E(y|T = 0, S = 0) \tag{60}$$

The coefficient $\hat{\delta}_1$ is the DiD coefficient and the key parameter of interest in the analysis of policy change. The coefficient indicates the difference in the expected outcome of interest between treatment group and control group in the post-treatment period when the effect of policy change has already taken place. The coefficient also indicates the degree to which policy change has influenced the outcome of interest once the assumed counterfactual is taken into account:

$$\hat{\delta}_1 = [E(y|T = 1, S = 1) - E(y|T = 0, S = 1)] - [E(y|T = 1, S = 0) - E(y|T = 0, S = 0)] \tag{61}$$

DiD coefficient is also known as average treatment effect since it represents the level of effectiveness of policy change which is judged solely by the average outcome of interest between the treated and non-treated group with respect to policy change. Alternatively, DiD coefficient can be computed by taking the difference in the outcome of interest between treatment and control group ($y_{11} - y_{21}$) and the difference in the outcome before treatment and after treatment took place ($y_{12} - y_{22}$):

$$\hat{\delta}_1 = (y_{11} - y_{21}) - (y_{12} - y_{22}) \tag{62}$$

DiD estimation strategy conveys important implications for the econometric analysis of policy changes. Table 4 presents a practical guide to the conduct of DiD analysis of policy change. In DiD panel data model specification in (56), the coefficient $\hat{\beta}_0$ amounts to the expected outcome in control group in the pre-treatment period, the coefficient $\hat{\beta}_0 + \hat{\alpha}_1$ amounts to the expected outcome in the control group after treatment whilst the coefficient $\hat{\alpha}_1$ indicates the outcome difference in the control group post-treatment vs. pre-treatment period. Before treatment takes place, the expected outcome for treatment group amounts to $\hat{\beta}_0 + \hat{\alpha}_2$, and the post treatment levels amounts to $\hat{\beta}_0 + \hat{\alpha}_1 + \hat{\alpha}_2 + \hat{\delta}_1$. The coefficient $\hat{\alpha}_1 + \hat{\delta}_1$ indicates the expected outcome in treatment group after policy change vs. before policy change. Before policy change, $\hat{\alpha}_2$ represents the difference in expected outcome before treatment and control group whilst $\hat{\alpha}_2 + \hat{\delta}_1$ indicates the difference in the post-treatment period. Average treatment effect $\hat{\delta}_1$ is the key parameter of interest as it designates the difference in the outcome between treatment and control period after the policy change compared to the period before policy change.

Table 4. Difference-in-Difference Estimator

	Pre-Treatment	Post-Treatment	Pre vs. Post
Control Group	$\hat{\beta}_0$	$\hat{\beta}_0 + \hat{\alpha}_1$	$\hat{\alpha}_1$
Treatment Group	$\hat{\beta}_0 + \hat{\alpha}_2$	$\hat{\beta}_0 + \hat{\alpha}_1 + \hat{\alpha}_2 + \hat{\delta}_1$	$\hat{\alpha}_1 + \hat{\delta}_1$
Treatment vs. Control Group	$\hat{\alpha}_2$	$\hat{\alpha}_2 + \hat{\delta}_1$	$\hat{\delta}_1$

SUMMARY

A sensible research design of non-experimental DiD analysis where the investigator exploits policy change to determine whether the change has systematically influenced the outcome of interest encompasses the control for confounding variables. In this example, confounding variables represent the factors affecting the outcome of interest independently of the treatment status and policy change so that these factors are common between treatment and control group. The selection of confounding control variables is based either on the theoretical reasoning and/or literature review which depends on both the type and scope of DiD analysis. Augmenting DiD model specification with confounding variables leads to:

$$y_{ist} = \beta_0 + \alpha_1 T_t + \dot{\alpha}_2 S_{is} + \delta_1 (T_t \cdot S_{is}) + a_i + \tau_t + X'_{ist}\eta + u_{ist} \qquad (63)$$

where $X = \{x_{1ist}, x_{2ist}, \ldots x_{kist}\}$ represents the vector of k confounding variables which influence the outcome of interest independently of the policy change S and treatment status and should be controlled to exclude the possibility of omitted variables bias and still arrive at consistent and unbiased estimate of average treatment effect which allows investigators to determine whether a particular policy change has been effective or not.

5. CONCLUSION

In this chapter, several essential tools in applied econometrics have been discussed. The focal point of the discussion has combined core building blocks of the analysis and how the methods of applied econometrics can help experts in competition law, judges and investigators answer some of the most intricate and puzzling dilemmas in the field. Linear OLS regression analysis, panel data regression analysis with unobserved effects and difference-in-difference methods still comprise the core methods used in applied econometric analysis. Although OLS regression analysis can in most cases yield unbiased and consistent results if all underlying assumptions are met, its main shortcomings, such as the inability to exploit the intertemporal dimension across observations can be overcome by applying simple panel data econometric methods where the investigator can tackle the unobserved heterogeneity among groups in the sample both across space and time. Oftentimes, antitrust investigators, competition lawyers and judges are interested in whether legislative changes of competition policy have been effective. Although investigators are tempted to compare the outcomes in question before and after policy change, such naïve approach neglects the common trend in the outcome of interest over time. Quantitative evaluation of policy changes can be overcome by applying difference-in-difference analysis which has been discussed in this chapter and which comprises a simple, yet intuitive and powerful tools of econometric analysis, helping judges and investigators uncover whether policy changes have achieved desired outcomes.

BIBLIOGRAPHY

Angrist, J.D. and Pischke, J.S., Mostly Harmless Econometrics: An Empiricist's Companion, Princeton University Press, New Jersey, 2009.

Arellano, M. and Bond, S., Some Tests of Specification for Panel Data: Monte Carlo Evidence and an Application to Employment Equations (1991), Review of Economic Studies 58, 277-297.

Breusch, T. and Pagan, A., "A Simple Test for Heteroskedasticity and Random Coefficient Variation" (1979), Econometrica 47, 1287-1294.

Davidson R. and MacKinnon, J.G., Estimation and Inference in Econometrics, Oxford University Press, New York, 1993.

Eickner, F., Limit Theorems for Regressions with Unequal and Dependent Errors (1967), Proceedings of the Fifth Berkeley Symposium on Mathematical Statistics and Probability 1, 59-82. University of California Press, Berkeley.

Greene, W.H., Econometric Analysis. 6th Edition. Pearson International, Upper Saddle River, 2009.

Hausman, J.A., "Specification Tests in Econometrics" (1978), Econometrica 46, 1251-1271.

Huber, P.J., The Behavior of Maximum Likelihood Estimates Under Nonstandard Conditions (1967), Proceedings of the Fifth Berkeley Symposium on Mathematical Statistics and Probability 1, 221-233. University of California Press, Berkeley.

Imbens, G.W. and Wooldridge, J.M., Recent Developments in the Econometrics of Program Evaluation (2009), Journal of Economic Literature 47, 5-86.

Maddala G.S. and Lahiri K., Introduction to Econometrics. Wiley, London, 2009.

Mundlak Y., On the Pooling of Time Series and Cross Sectional Data (1978), Econometrica 56, 69-89.

Theil H., Principles of Econometrics. Wiley, London, 1971.

Verbeek M., A Guide to Modern Econometrics. Wiley, London, 2012.

White H., A Heteroskedasticity – Consistent Covariance Matrix Estimator and a Direct Test for Heteroskedasticity (1980), Econometrica 48, 817-838.

Wooldridge J.M., Introductory Econometrics: A Modern Approach, 4th Ed., South-Western Cengage Learning, Boston, 2009.

PART II

ECONOMIC EVIDENCES IN COMPETITION LAW

CHAPTER 4

ECONOMIC EVIDENCE IN COMPETITION LAW: THE EXPERIENCE FROM A NATIONAL ADMINISTRATIVE COURT

Hendrik KERKMEESTER

1. INTRODUCTION

In this contribution it will be argued that the way judges handle economic evidence very much depends on the institutional context. In the first paragraph, a number of relevant factors concerning this context will be discussed. In the second paragraph, the focus is on a number of common misperceptions among economic experts advising at a national court. In the third paragraph, a number of observations will be made about how judges handle economic evidence. In the fourth paragraph, it will be explained why, in spite of possible miscommunications between judges and economic experts, economic evidence often plays an unavoidable role in court proceedings. This will be followed by paragraph 5 in which a number of examples will be given and paragraph 6 in which a conclusion will be drawn.

It should be clear in advance, that this contribution is written from a particular institutional context – an administrative higher court, where all judges have had a legal education, but may have some economic background as well – and that the conclusions drawn may not hold in other contexts. Nevertheless, the conclusion will be a positive one: improvement is always possible, but administrative may be quite able to work with economic evidence.

2. THE INSTITUTIONAL CONTEXT

How do judges handle economic evidence? It should be obvious that the answer to this question depends on the institutional context the judge is working in. This contribution draws on ten years of experience in the Dutch Court of

Appeal for Trade and Industry (College van Beroep voor het bedrijfsleven). It is the highest administrative court in the Netherlands dealing with economic administrative law, such as energy law, competition law, and telecommunications law. The last ten years the use of economic evidence took a flight, not only in competition law, but in particular in energy law due to the introduction of the so-called method decisions regulating natural monopolies in the distribution of electricity and gas, and in telecommunications law due to the introduction of market analyses covering parts of the telecommunications market.

1.1. ADMINISTRATIVE COURT

The Court of Appeal for Trade and Industry is an administrative law court. This implies that it has to make judgments on decisions made by administrative bodies. Therefore, one of the parties always is the administrative body involved, for example a regulatory authority. This body confronts one or more parties that filed an appeal against its decision. There might as well be one or more third parties, which have a direct interest in the decision taken by the administrative body.

One of the implications is that the parties are not regarded as equal. This observation does not so much refer to the issue that the administrative body may be in a stronger position than its counterparty. Of course, this is often the case, for example when a citizen – like a farmer – confronts the Ministry of Agriculture. In many cases involving economic evidence, however, parties may be more equal if it comes to issues like having the means of hiring top lawyers and economic experts. Often, it is even the case that the appealing party – that may be a large energy or telecommunications company – is able to put much more money into the legal proceedings than the administrative body can afford to do.

The most important remark in this context is, however, that a starting point is that the decision of the government body is assumed to be lawful, unless it is proven to be likely that it is not lawful. The administrative body generally has a margin of appreciation and the judge has to decide whether it stayed within the borders of this margin, and for example not whether the decision of the body was the best possible decision.

Traditionally, a Dutch administrative court was not supposed to come up with a final decision to be put into the place of a decision by an administrative body that it had annulled. In case of annulment of an unlawful decision, it was send back to the administrative body to repair it or to replace it by a new decision, taking the judicial decision into account. Although there have been recent changes in Dutch administrative law on this topic and a court is now supposed to come up with a final decision of its own that replaces the annulled decision if it is able to do so, in complicated economic matters the possibilities for a court to come up with a final judgment are still limited. To start with, a requirement for a court that intends to come up with a final decision is that it should be clear that no other decision can possibly be taken. The consequence is that the court cannot refer the case to an economic expert that should determine the final outcome of the case. This is a considerable difference with for example civil law proceedings where, after the court has determined a number of principles on which damages should be based, it may hire an economic expert to calculate the amount of damages to be awarded.

The Court of Appeal for Trade and Industry is not only a court of appeal, it is – besides the Central Council of Appeal (social security and civil servant law) and the Council of State (all remaining topics in administrative law) also one of the three highest administrative courts in The Netherlands. A consequence is that its judgments have an effect on the interpretation of administrative law that goes beyond the specific economic issues on which it is competent.

1.2. NATIONAL COURT

The Court of Appeal for Trade and Industry is a national court, as are the competent courts in the 27 other member states of the European Union. Most of the debates on the use of economic evidence focus on proceedings before the European courts in Luxembourg. What is stated in those debates is, however, of limited relevance in the national context.

A first issue is the ability of the court to appoint an independent expert. To start with, national procedural law must allow this. Moreover, at the level of a national court financial means tend to be limited. It may be that one or more of the parties involved were able to afford the hiring of an economic expert, but this is not to say that this also holds for the court itself. This is particularly relevant if the use of economics is concerned, since the issue often requires empirical data that may be quite costly to obtain.

A second issue is the amount of economic knowledge available at the court. In particular if it is not a specialised court, a national court often lacks judges and clerks with an economic background. A possible solution that is applied in some countries is to allow for lay judges sitting on a case.

As a matter of consequence, the way in which economic evidence will be handled will vary from country to country. The judges involved in the case may range from (lay) judges who are professional economists to administrative lawyers, who are generally reluctant to interfere with decisions of administrative bodies and are so in particular whenever matters arise that they do not understand.

1.3. THE SPECIFIC COMPETENCE OF THE COURT OF APPEAL FOR TRADE AND INDUSTRY

In the ten years that are covered by this contribution, the Court of Appeal for Trade and Industry never appointed an economic expert itself. As set out in paragraph 1.1, this is partly due to peculiarities in administrative law where a different type of questions has to be answered than is the case in civil law proceedings. This is not to say, however, that administrative law as such does not leave room for court-hired experts. The Central Council of Appeal generally appoints a medical expert in cases where to experts hired by the parties come up with different opinions about the medical position of the appealing party. The Council of State regularly requests the advice of the impartial Stichting Advisering Bestuursrechtspraak voor Milieu en Ruimtelijke Ordening (StAB) that advises on issues of environmental law.

The difference can partly be explained by financial reasons. A medical report as required in social security cases usually will usually cost an amount in the order of several hundreds of euros. An economic report is likely to have a price tag that is considerably higher. Most important, however, is that it is extremely hard for a judge to determine who is right if two medical experts contradict each other. Likewise, a judge will not be able to measure or estimate which level of noise or pollution a new road will cause. In the case of two conflicting economic experts, however, a judge may well be able to compare their arguments on the merits. Economic models and empirical research always come with a verbal explanation that is understandable. The point is that economics is essentially logic, and a judge if he surmounts possible reluctance concerning numbers possibly is able to judge which economist came up with the most coherent argument.

2. COMMON MISPERCEPTIONS OF ECONOMIC EXPERTS

Many judges may be unfamiliar with economic evidence, but many economic experts may be unfamiliar with law in general and court proceedings in particular. In this paragraph, I will refer to a number of common misperceptions in this context.

2.1. THE COURT WILL SOLVE OUR SCIENTIFIC DISPUTE

The most obvious cases in which different schools of thought oppose each other in the courtroom tend to be criminal cases where statistical evidence is involved. Classical statisticians may confront Bayesians and it is unlikely that they will find a common ground. They may look for the court, not only to decide the guilt or the innocence, but thereby who is on the right side in the scientific debate as well.

Emotions will not run as high between opposing economic experts at a court, but still it might be the case that the experts hired by the parties come from a different scientific background. It must be clear that a judge is not interested in which view on economics in general is the better one. The only thing that counts is whether they shed light on an issue that the judge has to solve and which he cannot decide upon by only using the familiar legal means. Whether the Capital Asset Pricing Model is the best way of calculating the rate of return that a regulated monopoly is allowed to make on its investments, is not of interest for an administrative judge. If it is a widely accepted method, the application of it falls within the margin of appreciation of the administrative body, and the focus will only be on whether the method has been applied correctly and consistently.

An interesting question in this context is whether or not a judge will be impressed by the academic standing of the economic experts before his court. Is it helpful to hire a Nobel Prize winner as an expert? Once upon a time an economic expert complained that a court had not allowed him the equal amount of time as his opponent and blamed that on the fact that the opponent was a university professor, while he had a lower rank.

It would be too blunt to dismiss these claims out of hand. Lawyers are used to arguments based on authority and when judges do not grasp the issue before them, they may be inclined to rely on reputation as a tiebreaker. However, in particular in administrative proceedings it is doubtful that arguments based on authority will have this tiebreaking effect. More important is the starting point that the decision of the administrative body is assumed to be lawful. The mere fact that the expert of the appealing party is a famous economist cannot make this decision unlawful. An example is a case in which a professor of economics argued that on the basis of his knowledge a variable should be determined at the level of 3 per cent, rather than 5 per cent as the administrative body had done. There was no doubt that this economist was more famous in academia than his colleagues working at the administrative body, but the court did not regard this as relevant. The starting point was that the 5 per cent was to be regarded as unlawful, unless it was likely that it was based on empirical evidence that was widely disputed or on a way of reasoning that was internally inconsistent or on any other argument of which the logic could be examined by the judge.

2.2. THE COURT WILL LOOK FOR THE RIGHT ANSWER

To a layman it goes without saying that a judge is looking for the truth, in particular if it comes to issues of evidence. Economists are laymen and they are likely to share this belief.

However, administrative procedure is not about finding the truth. In the first place, in many regulatory cases a prediction of the future is involved. It may, for example, concern developments on the telecommunications market in the coming three years. Who is telling the truth can simply not be determined in such a case. Even if the judgment in the case for some reason is delayed until the period on which the prediction sees is over and the administrative body turned out to be wrong, this does not necessarily imply that the decision was unlawful. The court will decide ex tunc, which is to say that it will determine whether the administrative body was allowed to make its decision on the basis of the facts as they were at the time the decision was taken.

In the second place, it is not to the court to determine which decision would have been the best one. The court will not look for the right answer, but will regard a reasonable answer as sufficient. As long as the administrative body stayed within its margin of appreciation there is no ground for the judgment that is decision was unlawful.

In the third place, the court generally is under the obligation to decide on the basis of the grounds of appeal of the parties. It may be clear to the court that a party would win its case if it would come up with a certain argument, but the party may nevertheless lose if for one reason or another it does not raise this particular point. There are circumstances under which a court decides at its discretion to complement the legal arguments of a party, mainly if a party has no legal experience and is not represented by a lawyer. This is, however, very unlikely to occur if economic evidence is concerned. In those cases parties are represented by experienced lawyers, who are supposed to be able to further the interests of their clients. If they fail to come up with a certain ground they may even have a good reason not to do so, for example because a deal has been made between the administrative body and the represented party, implying that a legal ground will not be put before the court in exchange for leniency in another dispute.

Finally, and probably most importantly, there are obligations to furnish (and dispute) facts. Important is who is to furnish the facts in the first place and undisputed facts are regarded as true, even if they are not. Therefore, the starting point of analysis may weigh heavily on the outcome, sometimes even to the point that where you start is where you get. An example is the importance of whether a market for telecommunications is included in the Commission Recommendation on relevant product and service markets within the electronic communications sector susceptible to ex ante regulation in accordance with Directive 2002/21/EC or not, or not anymore. In the 2003 Recommendation the market for broadcasting transmission services, to deliver broadcast content to end users, was mentioned as market 18. The Dutch telecommunications authority nevertheless did not subject this market to a market analysis. The interested parties appealed this decision and won their case before the Court of Appeal for

Trade and Industry on the basis that the authority had not sufficiently argued why it deviated from the Recommendation. The authority took a new decision, still not analysing the market at hand. The same parties as before appealed this new decision, on the basis of essentially the same arguments as in the previous case. Now they lost, not because the market had changed considerably or the authority came with better arguments, but simply because time had passed and in the 2007 Recommendation market 18 was no longer included. The obligation to furnish facts had shifted from the authority to the parties and that turned out to determine the outcome of the case.

2.3. THE ISSUE AT HAND IS AN ECONOMIC ISSUE

There may be cases in which a clear economic issue can be separated from the legal issues in a case. For example, in a tort case all legal issues concerning unlawfulness, accountability and causation may have been settled and only the calculation of damages remains. It is conceivable in such a case that an economic expert will be appointed by the court to make those calculations.

In most administrative procedures, however, separating economic from legal issues will be impossible. The most important reason is the one mentioned above: the court will decide on the extent of the margin of appreciation of the administrative body and the economic issue can only be judged about in this context.

An illuminating example of the diverging concepts in law and economics refers to a case in which the regulatory authority had to set rates for mobile terminating access. Essentially, the choice was between plus BULRIC that would allow the regulated parties to recover all their costs, including fixed and common costs and the more restrictive pure BULRIC. The authority painstakingly argued that pure BULRIC would maximise welfare. This probably was indeed the case, but welfare maximisation simply was not the legal requirement, however important it may be in economics. What was a legal requirement, was that the decision would be proportionate. It should not go further than necessary to solve the problem at hand. The authority itself had stated that plus BULRIC was sufficient to solve the anti-competitive behaviour to which it was a remedy, so the court could easily determine that the more intrusive pure BULRIC was not proportionate.

2.4. WE KNOW WHAT IS IMPORTANT TO DECIDE A CASE

The economic expert is hired to give his opinion on certain aspects of the case. Usually this is only a small part of the total and it may not be relevant because the appeal already fails for another – say procedural – reason. Definitely, it is unlikely that the economic expert has a complete overview of the case. To start with the expert probably does not know the grounds of appeal given by the lawyers that define the borders of the judgment of the court. On the basis of those grounds, the replies to those ground by the other party, the replies to those replies and the oral pleadings, the court has a picture of what already has been cleared up and of what are the remaining issues. The questions it will pose to the experts are aimed at clarifying those remaining points, and the content of those questions is the only possible clue for the expert of determining what is of interest to the court.

An illuminating example of a case in which an economic expert thought otherwise, is a hearing in which the court asked an expert a question and this expert replied that he did not find this question interesting and started to talk about a different issue. Obviously, it was the court that knew what was of interest for deciding the case and the expert missed the opportunity to shed a light on this issue that was favourable for his client.

3. ISSUES YOU FIND IN THE COURTS, NOT IN THE (ECONOMIC) BOOKS

Judges and economists have different ways of looking at a case and the judges are the ones that decide which procedure will be applied. In this paragraph a number of issues will be mentioned that may come up in the judicial mind and tend to be overlooked by economic experts.

3.1. JUDICIAL COLD FEET AND THE FLIGHT TO PROCEDURAL ISSUES

Almost all administrative judges have an excellent understanding of procedural law, less of them have a comparable level of insight as to the merits of the case. Many administrative judges will spend at least two hours inventing procedural reasons if that would save them one hour of looking at the merits. Their willingness to spend time finding ways to circumvent economics is probably even higher.

The court may refuse standing to parties, for example arguing that the issue at hand has not explicitly mentioned in the charter of the collective organisation by the court or that a competitor does not have a direct interest in the case. They may work through the decision of the administrative body to find procedural issues that have not even been raised by the parties, not so much to find an issue that they have to raise on its own motion (if a procedural issue of that importance is at hand it will almost certainly be brought forward by the interested party) but to find terrain where they feel at ease. Judges have an incentive to kick the can down the road: a reason to send a complicated decision back for repairment on a minor procedural issue because that would delay deciding on the merits with possibly a number of years.

A procedural issue that is particularly important in the context of economic expert evidence is the following. The court may insist that the lawyer for the party involved cannot suffice with referring to an economic report, but must explicitly integrate the relevant conclusions of this report in the legal grounds that were put forward. For example, if a regulated party does not agree with the percentage of the WACC that is used to calculate its tariffs, the lawyer takes a risk if he refers to an economic report where arguments are given why the WACC has not been determined correctly. The court may simply refuse to take a look at the report, as happened in one of the cases before the Court of Appeal for Trade and Industry.

3.2. JUDGES CAN DIGEST LASAGNE BUT NOT SPAGHETTI

The procedural issue raised at the end of paragraph 3.1 may look harsh, but it should be understandable. Administrative judges deciding on a complicated case are not eagles taking a helicopter view, they are moles gradually working their way through the darkness. They decide step-by-step on the basis of the legal grounds issued by the parties. Usually, this is the only way to keep a complicated case manageable.

Market analyses in telecommunications law provides an illuminating example. The market share of a telecommunications operator may be relevant for the market definition as well as for having significant market power on a defined market, and for the ability to practice anticompetitive behaviour at that market. In a market analysis every aspect touches a number of other aspects, like strands of spaghetti on a plate. A judge cannot digest this. The case can only be decided layer by layer, like lasagne if one eats it from the top down. The court will start with all legal grounds raised against the market definition, thereafter start with deciding on the grounds concerning market dominance and so on. This implies that if market share is important for several layers of the market analysis, this has to explained in every layer separately. Good economic arguments may fail if they are not brought in at the right place.

A related issue is that judges prefer to tick boxes over taking a more holistic view. This may for example explain why judging on the basis of whether a market share was above or below 50 per cent was so popular. The alternative of judging whether considering a thorough and overall analysis of the economic characteristics of the relevant market a party may be able to behave to an appreciable extent independently of competitors, customers and ultimately consumers (see point 78 of the Commission guidelines) is much more complicated. In the first market analysis cases brought before Court of Appeal for Trade and Industry parties came with extensive reports arguing that the market share of the Dutch incumbent KPN was just above 50 per cent, without explaining why a market share of 50,5 per cent would make KPN so much more powerful than a market share of 49,5 per cent. Apparently it was thought no such an explanation was needed, because the court would simply tick the box. When it became clear that – in spite of the extra efforts that would take – the court would rule on the basis of an analysis as referred to in point 78 of the Commission guidelines, the content of the economic reports changed.

3.3. THE REQUIREMENTS OF THE TEXTBOOKS, MAY BE TOO COSTLY IN PRACTICE

The economic textbooks are clear about the demands on economic evidence. It should be equally clear that courts will not set the same demands. It is not realistic to hold administrative bodies to the degree of economic sophistication that the textbooks require. Some relevant economic data may be impossible to obtain, or it may be too costly to do so. A court may take into account that the administrative body has limited means, and that this also limits the standard it is held against.

An example follows from the jurisprudence of the Court of Appeal for Trade and Industry on the SSNIP-test. The court started with accepting that under certain circumstances a SSNIP-test in the form of a thought experiment would suffice. In a next case it judged that the outcome of the test might be so evident that quantification of the variables in the test is not required. The third mitigation was that in cases where quantification of the test was possible, the regulatory authority was not held to provide exact numbers but in certain circumstances could suffice with an interval indicating the margin of uncertainty.

4. HOW, NEVERTHELESS, ECONOMIC EVIDENCE IS ABLE TO CREEP IN

The possible reluctance of judges in matters concerning economics and the limited understanding of legal procedure stand in the way of the use of economic evidence, so much should be clear after the first three paragraphs.

Nevertheless, the experience at the Court of Appeal for Trade and Industry is quite positive. There are several factors that contribute to the influence that economic evidence often has in cases brought before the court. The first factor to be mentioned is that in a number of cases economic evidence is hard to avoid, even if judges would be tempted to do so. The second factor is that the way economic experts operate in practice often is very helpful in putting forward information that is useful to decide about a case.

4.1. THE UNAVOIDABILITY OF ECONOMICS

The first point to be mentioned here is that the object of the judgment of the court is the decision that is taken by the administrative body, e.g. a competition or telecommunications authority that has decided on a merger or has analysed a telecommunication market. Among the employees of such an authority are not lawyers, but many economists as well. In cases as mentioned, those economists are likely to take the lead as to the merits of the case. They will make use of the textbook economics they learned at university to analyse the situation at hand and to decide on issues like how the market should be defined, whether an undertaking is dominant on that market, which type of anticompetitive behaviour could occur and how to remedy that behaviour. The consequence is that economic theory is the backbone of the decision, albeit that the lawyers have been looking over the decision in order to make it judgment proof. If the court is not allowed to limit itself to procedural issues but is required to judge on the merits of the case, it therefore cannot avoid judging about economics.

The second point is that many economic insights implicitly or explicitly have been accepted in European law. An example on the implicit side is formed by insights on the drawbacks of monopoly, compared to full competition. The theory that monopolies may lead to allocative inefficiency is underlying the price regulation of natural monopolies when a competition authority is trying the mimic the competitive price. The theory that monopolies may lead to productive inefficiency is underlying the determination of the x-factor, the discount to the regulated price that is set on the basis of the idea that it will force a regulated natural monopoly to become more efficient.

Judges who did not even get a basic training in economics may overlook the implicit economic points mentioned above, but cannot overlook the explicit reference to economic concept in decisions of the European Court of Justice or in all kind of Recommendations and Guidelines. An important example are the Commission guidelines on market analysis and the assessment of significant market power. A judge may personally be sceptic about the SSNIP-test as an appropriate means of defining a market, but may nevertheless accept the test since it is explicitly mentioned in those guidelines.

The third point has already mentioned before in a different context. If an issue more or less can be separated from the other issues in a case, for example the assessment of damages suffered by private parties due to price-fixing, and economic theory offers an appropriate method of assessing those damages, economics is hard to avoid.

4.2. WHY ECONOMIC EXPERTS TEND TO BE HELPFUL

The fact that economic experts are no lawyers may make them feel and look like strangers in court proceedings, but definitively has some advantages.

The first point to be mentioned is that in most cases the experts work for a highly reputed bureau like Analysys Mason, Dialogic, Ecorys, Frontier, Lexonomics, Nera, or Oxera. Typically for those bureaus is that they have an incentive to keep their high reputation, to work according to scientifically accepted standards and that in the next case they may be hired by the party they are now opposing. Those factors contribute to a considerable degree of objectivity, that often may even bring them to argue points that are not in the interest of the party they report for. A party is very likely to find a lawyer that is willing to defend any point that is in his interest and probably also a lone university professor of economics who will do the same, but this is not easily the case with bureaus like mentioned.

The second point is that the kind of economics used in court is not the most controversial one. Economists probably never will agree on issues like whether Keynes or Hayek had the correct view on macroeconomics, but if it comes to microeconomics (as often is the case in court proceedings) there may be more common ground. If it comes to a complicated legal issue, there are almost always at least two interpretation that can be convincingly pleaded by able lawyers, but debates between economists have at least some chance of leading into the direction of agreement. For example, concrete calculations are very likely to be correct, but if not, the other party's expert will point that out and the first party's expert will admit the mistake.

The third point is that, unlike lawyers, economic experts are very likely to give frank answers to questions posed by the court. If a lawyer senses that a straight answer will not be in the interest of his client, he will use his capabilities to beat about the bush. Partly because he has not be trained to circumvent uneasy questions, and partly because he does not as well as the lawyer oversee the consequences of an honest answer for the judgment on the case, the economic expert will react in a way that is likely to shed an objective light on the case. A useful trick for the court is to ask a question that because of its technical nature cannot be answered by the party's lawyer but will be referred to the expert and then observe the nonverbal communication of the lawyer during the answer to the question. Even the most stoic lawyers have difficulties hiding their emotions if the expert comes with an answer that is not in accordance with the position this lawyer has been defending.

The points mentioned above usually lead to court proceedings with the following tendency. After a party issues a report, the other party is allowed to react, and the first party to reply to this reaction. Parties can thereafter clarify their position at an oral hearing. The debate tends to concentrate on the issues that from an economic point of view are contentious, showing the real problems. The rule of thumb that is useful for the court is not exactly "the latest party to say something in an issue wins", but if a plausible critical remark is not refuted in a reply the judge should be alert. An example is a case in which the expert hired by a telecommunications operator came up with economic models aiming to show that mobile operators have the incentive to charge each other low terminating tariffs. The regulatory authority reacted with a well-argued reply that those models were based on assumptions that did not hold in the particular case. The telecommunications operator could have replied that the assumptions were realistic after all or explain why if did not matter whether they were realistic or not. However, it did not do so and the court drew the conclusion that the points made by the operator did not hold against the defence of the authority.

5. WHAT JUDGES ARE ABLE TO DO

In ten years and many cases with economic expert evidence the Court of Appeal for Trade and Industry never had to appoint an independent economic expert to solve the case. So the conclusion is justified that usually judges are able to decide on the issues brought forward by the experts hired by the parties. In this paragraph a number of representative cases will mentioned by way of illustration.

5.1. USING COMMON PROCEDURAL RULES TO FURNISH FACTS

One of the complications concerning the use of economic evidence is that much economic information, for example about the market share and costs of a telecommunications operator, may be confidential information. This information may be classified as accessible to the court, but hidden from the competitors of this operator. The consequence is that this information cannot be the subject of a discussion between the experts of the parties and the court is left on its own when judging about this information.

In a certain judgment the Court of Appeal for Trade and Industry remarked that the use of confidential information was acceptable because this information could be checked by the court. In following cases parties argued that the calculations on tariffs made by the regulatory authority could not be correct, but that they could not say exactly why because of the confidentiality of the information. Referring to the judgment just mentioned, parties argued that it now was up to the court to find out what exactly went wrong. Of course this was requiring an effort that the court could not and should not perform. The court judged that of course it would assess the confidential information if required to do so, but that this did not relieve parties from the burden to furnish the facts that they were able to bring forward in spite of the confidentiality and to clarify as far as possible what could be the possible causes of tariffs not being at the desired level. The consequence was that either appeals could be dismissed because parties remained too vague about their grounds of appeal, or the parties provided the information needed by the court in order to know where to look and what to find in the confidential information, making the case manageable.

5.2. USING PREVIOUS CASES AS PRECEDENTS

In method decisions in energy law and in market analyses in telecommunications law, after the end of a regulatory period of usually three years a new analysis is made, supported and opposed by new economic reports. If the court in every case would start from scratch when judging about these reports, this would amount to a task that is too time consuming. The solution is to state that in principle the court will decide like it did in the previous round of regulation, unless a party makes clear why the law and/or the facts have changed in the meantime and why this change is requiring a different decision. This focus on differences leads to a considerable decrease in workload for the court.

5.3. FINDING INCONSISTENCIES

The economic reasoning in the decision of a regulatory authority often contains inconsistencies. A probable cause is that the decision is long and complicated and that several teams within the authority have been working on it. Moreover, there is always the time pressure to publish the decision before the start of the new regulatory period, leaving little time to do the final editing of the decision.

An example is a case where the regulatory agency applied a SSNIP-test. The decision contained a more or less theoretical part, which probably was written by a team in which the economists had the overhand. In this part the requirements were stated the SSNIP-test should fulfil. These requirements included an answer to the question whether the price of unbundled access to the copper network of the regulated telecom operator could be profitably raised by 5 to 10 per cent, or too many clients would switch to unbundled access to glass (Fibre-to-the-Office) to make this raise in price profitable. When it came to applying the SSNIP-test, however, the authority did not answer this question. It just posed that it thought it to be likely that a considerable part of the group that was able to switch from copper from glass would switch indeed in the case of a price raise. The regulated party objected that the authority should have calculated at which degree of switching the price raise would not be profitable (critical loss) and consequently relate this degree to the degree of switching that had occurred in practice (actual loss). This requirement was in accordance with the demand that the authority itself had stated in the earlier part of its decision. The court concluded that the decision should be quashed on this point.

It is interesting to note that if the regulatory authority had argued in the first part of the decision that applying a textbook SSNIP-test was not possible in this case but that it would apply a reasonable alternative, the court possibly would have judged that the choice for this alternative method fell within the margin of appreciation of the authority and the decision might have been upheld.

A comparable example is a case in which the decision by the regulatory authority contained several, conflicting, definitions of predatory pricing. The authority first gave a definition of predatory pricing as using retail pricing under average variable costs for a considerable time in order to move competitors out of the market or to deter entrance and added that this strategy was aimed at a recoupment of the losses suffered thereby by raising the prices later on. Later in the decision, however, the authority doubted about the relevance of recoupment and argued that predatory pricing is a strategy that directly leads to profit optimisation. Consequently, the authority presented an economic report explaining how the use of zero pricing for calls terminated at the regulated party's own network could be profit maximising. The court concluded that this could not proof possible incentives for predatory pricing, because the authority had given a definition in its decision that was not consistent with the definition of predatory pricing that apparently was used by the economic expert.

5.4. CONTRADICTING THE PRINCIPAL

Of course, many statements and conclusions in economic reports are in accordance with the interests of the party that ordered the report. Mainly for the reasons stated in paragraph 4.2, however, it also often happens that an economist contradicts the interest of his principal. He may regard intellectual honesty or his reputation as more important than winning the case, or simply overlook the consequences of his statement. A court should be alert in such cases, because one can safely conclude that a statement that violates the interest of the principal is more likely to be true than a statement that is in accordance with this interest.

An example relates to a debate between parties whether the market for a number of old-fashioned PSTN-telephone lines, belongs to the same market as do modern ISDN-lines that allow a comparable number of phone calls at the same time. The regulatory authority had concluded that this was not the case, to which a number of parties objected.

The authority had based its decision on the reasoning that multiple PSTN is a legacy-service that dated from the time ISDN had not yet been introduced. Whenever extension of capacity was needed, a company would add one or more PSTN-lines. If the company would start anew and have the choice between

PSTN and ISDN, however, it would choose the latter since ISDN is considerably cheaper. The parties opposing this view presented the report of an expert. The expert did not dispute that ISDN is a cheaper way of using several telephone lines at the same time than PSTN. Rather, he argued by means of an example that the costs and hassle of switching from PSTN to ISDN is not outweighed by the lower costs of ISDN. The court concluded that the expert opinion supported the decision of the authority and dismissed the legal grounds of the parties who had hired the expert.

6. CONCLUSION – WHAT IS NEEDED TO REMOVE OBSTACLES

The conclusion of this contribution is that in administrating law, even without an economic background, judges are able to handle economic evidence if they apply their normal procedural rules. Moreover, because of the interrelation of economic and legal issues, they probably can do so better than a court-appointed expert would.

Still, it might be useful to teach judges on economics in order to take away possible prejudices and to make judges feel more at ease when economic evidence is involved. Besides basics of the methodology of economics and its applications in administrative law, attention should be paid to practical examples, preferably based on the "best practices" of other national judges.

At the same time, it would be useful if economic experts would be taught on issues like the elements of administrative procedure and on how to present economic evidence in order to be effective.

CHAPTER 5
COMPETITION LAW AND BEHAVIOURAL EVIDENCE IN A COURTROOM?

Mitja Kovač

1. INTRODUCTION

How do legal decisions and legal norms actually affect people and their daily behaviour? What people and general population do in response to certain judicial decisions and legal norms? What is actually behavioural law and economics, what is the "traditional" rational choice assumption and what are their main implications, assumptions, suggestions and how to employ them into the daily decision-making? What are the main behavioural economic evidences and insights for competition law? Can behavioural economics and the distilled behavioural evidences serves as a gap filler in explaining real world evidence that neoclassical economic theory cannot explain? Are they ready for the main EU competition law stage? Could judges employ such behavioural economic evidences in their daily decision-making? This chapter attempts to address precisely those issues and seeks to provide answers, suggestions and implications for competition law practitioners and daily judicial decision making in employing behavioural economic evidences and related insights.

In the last two decades, social scientists and law and economics scholars have learned a great deal about how people actually make their decisions. The newly developed field of economics, which was inspired by a triggering difference between the predicted and actual behaviour of rational, self-interested, risk averse person, the behavioural economics, borrowing from psychology and sociology to explain decisions inconsistent with traditional economics, has revolutionised the way economists (and to lesser extent also lawyers) view the world.[1] It is often argued that over the last decade a behavioural economics has,

1 Diamond, Peter and Hannu Vartiainen, *Behavioral Economics and its applications*, Princeton University Press, 2007.

while gradually becoming a mainstream,[2] fundamentally changed the way economists and to a lesser extent, with the development of behavioural law and economics, also lawyers conceptualise the world.[3] Moreover, policy-makers, regulators, judges and competition authorities are increasingly looking to the lessons from behavioural economics to help them determine whether markets are working in the interest of consumers. Competition authorities have for example considered the implications of behavioural economics as a gap filler, as a tool to assess critically the traditional assumptions of specific antitrust policies,[4] to revisit fundamental competition questions[5] and to assess how behavioural economics will affect the degree of convergence/divergence of competition law in EU Member States.[6]

This chapter is a synthesis of the literature on the central attributes of behavioural law and economics evidences and its applications to the field of EU competition law. Section 2 provides a synthesis on the concepts of rationality and on the nature of economic reasoning. Section 3 provides a brief summary on the notion of behavioural law and economics. Section 4 offers general implication and evidences of non-rational behaviour, Section 5 provides examples of the employment of behavioural law and economics' evidences in antitrust cases, Section 6 argues that behavioural economics should, despite its merits and incremental benefits, be used with caution, and, finally, Section 7 concludes.

2. ON THE NATURE OF ECONOMIC REASONING

In order to fully appraise the scope and possible impact of behavioural evidences in court room and having in mind that this book is written primarily for lawyers and judges a short introduction in to the nature of economic reasoning and "traditional" rational choice economics has to be offered. Namely, many judges, lawyers and surprisingly even some students of business and management still think that economics is the study of economic depressions, deflation, inflation, underemployment, globalisation, exploitation, austerity, quantitative easing, banking, elasticity and other mysterious phenomena remote from the day-to-day concerns of the legal and economic system.[7] However, the domain of economics, as the queen of social sciences, is

---

2 Lovallo, Dan, Sibony Oliver, *The Case of Behavioral Strategy*, McKinsey Q. 30, 2010.

3 For an excellent survey see Akerlof, Geoffrey, "Behavioral Macroeconomics and macroeconomic behaviour", 92 *American Economics Review 1*, 2002, pp. 411–33.

4 For example merger review, abuse of dominant position and cartel prosecutions.

5 What is a competition, what should be the goals of an optimal competition law and what should be the consequent relevant legal standards.

6 Stucke, Maurice, *Hearing on Competition and Behavioral Economics*, Directorate for financial and enterprise affairs Competition Committee, DAF/COMP/WD(2012)12, 2012.

7 See for example Posner, A. Richard, *Economic Analysis of Law*, 7th ed., Aspen Publishers, 2011.

much broader and economics itself may be actually regarded as a science of human behaviour. The traditional, orthodox economics is science of rational choice in a world in which resources are limited in relation to human needs and rests on the assumption that a man is a rational, wealth-maximising, self-interested and risk averse person.[8] Traditional economics hence assumes that a man rationally maximises his ends in life (self-interest). This concept of "rational wealth-maximisation" should not be confused with conscious calculation and economics is not a theory about consciousness.[9] Human behaviour is in this respect rational when it conforms to the model of rational choice (whatever the state of mind of that chooser is). This concept is objective rather than subjective and rationality means to traditional economist little more than a disposition to choose, consciously or unconsciously, an apt means to whatever ends the chooser happens to have.[10] Rationality is hence merely the ability and inclination to use instrumental reasoning to get on in life. Some economists employ also term "bounded-rationality" to describe the rationality of rational persons who face positive costs of acquiring, absorbing, processing and of using the information (transaction costs) available to them to make their decisions.[11] The term "bounded rationality" was actually introduced by Herbert Simon in 1955 and refers to the cognitive limitations facing decision-makers in terms of acquiring and processing information.[12] In other words, it may be argued that almost all human decisions are actually "boundedly-rational" since they are made in the world of imperfect information and positive transaction costs.

Moreover, the concept of self-interest should also not be confused with selfishness, since misery and the happiness of other people might be part of one's satisfactions.[13] Evidently, economics also assumes that man is a rational utility maximiser in all areas of life, not just in his economic affairs (i.e. not only when they are engaged in buying and selling). This concept of man as a rational, wealth maximising, self-interested individual person also implies that people respond to incentives in generally predictable way. For example, if a person's surroundings change in such a way that she could increase her satisfaction by

8 Gary Becker argues that all human behaviour can be viewed as involving participants who maximize their utility, have stable preferences and accumulate an optimal ex ante amount of information and other inputs in a variety of markets. Consequently the task of law and economics is then to determine the implications of such rational maximizing behaviour in and out of markets, and its legal implications for markets and other institutions; Becker, S. Garry, *The Economic Approach to Human Behaviour*, University of Chicago Press, 1976.

9 Posner, *supra* note 3, at 3.

10 Ibid.

11 See e.g. Herbert, A. Simon, "Theories of Bounded Rationality", in McGuire, C.B., and Ray Racher (eds.), *Decision and Organisation*, North-Holland, 1972, pp. 161–176.

12 Simon, A. Herbert, "A Behavioral Model of Rational Choice", 69 *Q.J.Econ.* 99, 1955.

13 Economists, however, in order to avoid potential confusion speak about "utility" rather than of self-interest; Ibid.

altering her behaviour, she will do so.[14] This rational-choice concept that encompasses the traditional economic analysis has been in recent years challenged on several grounds besides the very superficial one that it does not describe how people think about or describe their decisions.[15] Of course, this conventional "rational" approach does not assume at all that persons have always perfect information and consequently also persons which do not have perfect information *ex ante* are still making, in the light of their imperfect information, *ex ante* rational decisions. If the *ex ante* costs of acquiring and processing more information exceed the expected benefits of having more information and in making better decision, then decisions made under such circumstances are actually still rational ones, though they might *ex post* appear as completely irrational ones. Moreover, if one would in such circumstances strife for perfect *ex ante* information then this kind of behaviour would be actually an irrational one or at least inefficient one. Finally, one should also note, that economics as a science is concerned with explaining and predicting aggregates rather than behaviour of each individual person.[16]

3. WHAT IS BEHAVIOURAL LAW AND ECONOMICS?

The observed behavioural inconsistencies and apparent shortcomings of the conventional economic approach have induced some scholars to investigate the underlying motivation behind the behaviour of people in order to improve existing theories and make more accurate predictions. Simon's pioneering work and introduction of "bounded-rationality"[17] has been followed by several

---

14 For a detailed discussion on fundamental concepts of law and economics, values, utility and efficiency apprehensible to lawyers see e.g. Cooter, Robert and Thomas Ulen, *Law and Economics*, 6th ed. Princeton Hall, 2011; Posner, A Richard, *Economic Analysis of Law*, 7th ed., Aspen Publishers, 2007.

15 Of course, one should note that the assumptions of traditional economic theory are one-dimensional and pallid when viewed as descriptions of human behaviour. Yet, as Posner (2007) states, the abstraction and generalization is the essence of scientific inquiry and economics, as the queen of social sciences aspires to be scientific. For example, it is evident that the economic theory of certain legal institution (i.e. prohibition of the abuse of dominant position), rule or branch of law will never be able to explain completely every deviation, complexity and confusion of that analysed phenomena that it seeks to illuminate. Yet, this lack of realism in the sense of descriptive completeness, perfection is a precondition of theory and every theory that sought to reproduce the complexity pf the empirical world in all of its assumptions would not be a theory, but, as Posner insightfully observes, a description; Posner, *supra* note 3, at p. 17 et seq.

16 For the discussion, counter arguments and other serious objections (e.g. systematic departures, hyperbolic discounting, endowments effects) see Posner at p. 18 et seq.

17 Simon, *supra* note 8.

significant contributions[18] and in the end of 1970 the field of behavioural economics was established. In 1979 Kahneman and Tversky published their ground-breaking article on prospect theory in which they introduced fundamental concepts in relation to reference points, loss-aversion, utility measurement and subjective probability judgements.[19] This seminal work has been followed by Thaler's contribution on a positive theory of consumer choice where the concept of mental accounting has been introduced.[20] These pioneering work has been afterwards expanded and elaborated further by numerous scholars.[21] Today the behavioural economics is far from a uniform methodological approach differing substantially on the nature of assumptions, the value of empirical evidence and conclusions regarding rationality, efficiency and optimisation. In recent years this trend has been expanded even further with, for example, the introduction of experimental economics[22] and neuro-economics.[23]

Moreover, this resurgence of psychology in economics has also inspired some legal scholars to employ additional scholarship in both cognitive psychology and behavioural economics, which suggest that human behaviour often deviates from rational choice in systematic and predictable ways, to explain legal phenomena and to argue for legal reforms.[24] This novel approach (methodology)

---

18 See for example Markowitz, Harry, "The Utility of Wealth", 60 *Journal of Political Economy* 2, 1952; Markowitz, Harry, "Portfolio Selection", 7 *Journal of Finance* 1, 1952, pp. 77–91; Allais, Maurice, "Fondements d'une Théorie Positive des Choix Comportant un Risque et Critique des Postulats et Axiomes de L'Ecole Américaine", 21 *Econometrica* 4, 1953, pp. 503–546; Schelling, C. Thomas, *Strategy of Conflict*, Harvard University Pres 1960; Ellsberg, Daniel, "Risk, Ambiguity and the Savage Axiom", 75 *Quarterly Journal of Economics* 4, 1961, pp. 643–669.

19 Kahneman, Daniel and Amos Tversky, "Prospect Theory: An Analysis of Decisions under Risk", 47 *Econometrica* 263, 1979.

20 Thaler, Richard, "Toward a positive theory of consumer choice", 1 *Journal of Economic Behavior and Organization* 1, 1980, pp. 39–60.

21 For an excellent synthesis on the behavioural scholarship see for example Sunstein, R. Cass, *Behavioral Law and Economics*, Cambridge University Press, 2000.

22 Experimental economics has been pioneered by Vernon Smith who argues that economics should ne enriched by experimental methods that would offer additional insights into human psychological processes and would also enable us to control for the relevant variables which would consequently provide more specific and reliable conclusions; see e.g. Charles R. Plott and Vernon L. Smith, *Handbook of Experimental Economics Results*, Elsevier, 2008.

23 Neuroeconomics refers to the use of empirical evidence relating to brain activity in order to come to conclusions relating to economic behaviour (this research method is for example employing positron emission tomography, functional magnetic resonance imaging, regional cerebral blood flow *etc.*) and its finding might be relevant for decision-making heuristics, learning processes and the role of emotions. See for example Camerer, Colin, Loewenstein, George and Drazen Prelec, "Neuroeconomics: How Neuroscience Can Inform Economics", *Journal of Economic Literature* Vol. XLIII, 2005, pp. 9–54; Ross, Don, "Neuroeconomics and economic methodology", in John B. Davis, D.W. Hands and Uskali Mäki (eds.), *The Handbook of Economic Methodology*, Edward Elgar, 1998.

24 This behavioural approach to law has infiltrated the legal literature in such diverse areas as tax law, administrative law, environmental law, criminal law, civil procedure, corporate

is now known as the behavioural law and economics.[25] It has changed fundamentally the way that economists (and to some extent also lawyers) conceptualise the world and represents an umbrella of approaches that seek to extend standard economics framework to account for relevant features of human behaviour that are absent in the standard economics framework.[26] In the last decade, behavioural economics, borrowing from psychology and sociology to explain decisions inconsistent with traditional economics, has hence revolutionised the way economists view the world (especially in the field of applied economics-finance and consumer behaviour). Behavioural law and economics argues that persons display bounded rationality and that (a) suffer from certain biases, such as over-optimism and self-serving conceptions of fairness, (b) follow heuristics, such as availability, that lead to mistakes; c) display incomplete self-control that induce persons to make decisions that are in the conflict with their long-term interest,[27] and (c) they behave in accordance with prospect theory rather than expected utility theory.[28] Moreover, people might have bounded willpower and they might be tempted and myopic.[29] Furthermore, people might be concerned by the well-being of the others and this concern and their self-conception can lead them in the direction of cooperation at the expense of their material self-interest.[30]

The task of behavioural law and economics is, as argued by Jolls, Sunstein and Thaler, to explore the implications of actual (not hypothesised) human behaviour for the law and the lawmaker.[31] According to Teck, Noah and Camerer behavioural economics actually increases the explanatory power of economics by providing it with more realistic psychological assumptions.[32] Behavioural economics approach extends rational choice and equilibrium

securities law, tort law and contract law; Langevoort, C. Douglas, "Behavioral Theories of Judgment and Decision Making in Legal Scholarship: A Literature Review 51 *Vand. L. Rev. 1499*, 1998, Vol. 51, Issue 6 (November 1998), pp. 1499–1540.

25 Generally see Sunstein, R. Cass, "Behavioral Law and Economics", Cambridge University Press, 2000.

26 Diamond, Peter, and Hannu Vartiainen, *Behavioral Economics and its Applications*, Princenton University Press, 2007.

27 E.g. addictive behaviour, undersaving and procrastination.

28 Jolls, Christine, Sunstein, R. Cass, and Richard H. Thaler, "A Behavioral Approach to Law and Economics", in Sunstein, R. Cass (ed.), *Behavioral Law and Economics*, Cambridge University Press, 2000, pp.13–58. See also Jolls, Christine, "Behavioral law and economics", in Diamond, Peter, and Hannu Vartiainen (eds.), *Behavioral Economics and its Applications*, Princeton University Press, 2007, pp. 115 *et seq.*

29 *Ibid.*

30 *Ibid.*

31 Jolls, Christine, Sunstein, R. Cass, and Richard H. Thaler, "A Behavioral Approach to Law and Economics", in Sunstein, R. Cass (ed.), *Behavioral Law and Economics*, Cambridge University Press, 2000, pp.13–58.

32 Teck H. Ho, Noah Lim, and Colin F. Camerer, "How 'Psychological' Should Economic and Marketing Models Be?", 43 *Journal of Marketing Research* 3, 2006, pp. 341–344.

models and does not advocate at all abandoning these models entirely.[33] Jolls, Sunstein and Thaler also suggest that behavioural insights shall be employed in order to better explain both the effects and the content of the law.[34] Such insights should be employed to help the lawmaker to achieve specified ends, such as deterring socially undesirable behaviour. Yet, one might also argue that all of the discussed behavioural insights and observed inconsistencies could be also neatly explained from the conventional law and economics perspective. Observed patterns, behavioural biases might actually be a result of the completely rational *ex ante* decision making[35] which has been made in a world of positive transaction costs and asymmetric information. In other words, the employed methodological framework, assumptions and definitions might determine also the lawyers' normative and positive analysis, conclusions and suggestions.

4. GENERAL IMPLICATIONS AND EVIDENCES OF NON-RATIONAL BEHAVIOUR

As discussed previously conventional law and economics assumes that people exhibit rational behaviour: that people are risk-averse, self-interested utility maximisers with stable preferences and the capacity to optimally accumulate and assess information. However, a large body of social science literature demonstrates that these assumptions are not always accurate and that deviations from rational behaviour are often semantic.[36] Based on this evidence Jolls, Sunstein and Thaler[37] claim that people exhibit bounded rationality[38], bounded self-interest, and bounded willpower. Behaviourists offer ample evidence that cognitive limitations force actors to employ relatively simple decision-making strategies which may cause actors to fail to maximise their

33 Teck H. Ho, Noah Lim, and Colin F. Camerer, "How 'Psychological' Should Economic and Marketing Models Be?", 43 *Journal of Marketing Research* 3, 2006, pp. 341–344.

34 Jolls, Sunstein and Thaler, *supra* note 14, at p. 13 *et seq.*

35 Rationality does not presuppose zero costs of acquiring and processing information or zero transaction costs.

36 Ann-Sophie Vandenberghe, "Behavioral approaches to contract law", in Gerrit De Geest (ed.), *Contract Law and Economics*, Vol. 6, Encyclopedia of Law and Economics, 2nd ed., Edward Elgar, 2011.

37 Jolls, Christine, Sunstein, R. Cass, and Richard H. Thaler, "A Behavioral Approach to Law and Economics", in Sunstein, Cass R. (ed.), *Behavioral Law and Economics*, Cambridge University Press, 2000.

38 The concept of bounded rationality was introduced by professor Herbert Simon (1955) and refers to the fact that there are critical psychological limits on human cognition; Simon, A. Herbert, "A Behavioral Model of Rational Choice", 69 *Quarterly Journal of Economics* 1, 1955, pp. 99–118. Se generally Wilkinson, Nick, *An Introduction to Behavioral Economics*, Palgrave Macmillan, 2008.

utility. What follows is a brief synthesis of these general implications, heuristic and biases that are of the particular relevance to the law.

Firstly, persons are averse to extremes which gives rise to compromise effects. For example, as Sunstein argues, almost everyone of us has had the experience of switching to the second most expensive dish on the food-menu and of doing so partly because of the presence of the most expensive dish.[39] In other words, persons might have great difficulties judging probabilities, making predictions and cope with uncertainties. This aversion to extremes might also have an impact on legal advocacy and judgement as well as for predictions about the effects of the law. Juries and judges may for example choose a compromise solution which depends on what alternatives are actually made available. Availability heuristics[40] introduced by Kahneman and Tversky is another source of our errors in relation to risk perception, since persons tend to judge the probability of a future event based on the ease with which instances can be brought to mind.[41] Hence, people might weight disproportionally salient, memorable or vivid evidence, despite the fact that they might have better, scientific sources of information.[42] Slovic and Lichtenstein identified anchoring and adjustment as another source of human errors, arguing that there is a tendency to make probability judgements on the basis of an initial value-anchor, to resist altering such a probability estimate, even when pertinent new information comes to light.[43] People also suffer from the overconfidence, self-serving bias and over-optimism.[44] Moreover, people also tend to over-estimate the occurrence of low probability risks and under-estimate the occurrence of high-probability risks. For example we all experienced a prevailing fear of flying (and having a crash) while aeroplane is taking off from the airport although the probability of an accident is a minor one, whereas we never think about having a car accident while driving our cars although the probability of such an event is a

39 Hence the framing of choices matters; Sunstein *supra* note 26.

40 For an excellent survey see Ann-Sophie Vandenberghe, "Behavioral approaches to contract law", in De Geest, Gerrit, *Encyclopedia of Law and Economics*, Edward Elgar, 2011.

41 Kahneman and Tversky, 1974.

42 From the availability heuristics Fischhoff derived the notion of hindsight bias, explaining that we usually imagine events that have actually occurred (our grand mom's stories) than counterfactual events that did not (theoretical illustration in books on economic depression etc.) and that people than have a tendency to overestimate the probability that they previously attached to events that happened later; Fischhoff, B., "Hindsight Foresight: The effect of outcome knowledge on judgment under uncertainty", *Journal of Experimental Psychology: Human Perception & Performance* 1, 1975, pp.288–299. See also Fischhoff, B., and Beyth, R., "'I knew it would happen': Remembered probabilities of once-future things", 13 *Organizational Behaviour and Human Performance* 1, 1975, pp. 1–16.

43 Slovic, P., Lictensteln, S., "Comparison of Bayesian and regression approaches to the study of information processing in judgment", 6 *Organ. Behav. Hum. Perfom.* 4, 1971, pp. 649–744.

44 Humans on average belief that good things are more likely than average to happen to them and bad things are less likely than average to happen to them. This then leads to self-serving bias where persons interpret information in ways that serve their interest or preconceived notions. See also Vandenberghe, *supra* note 41.

significant one. Simply, we think that such risks are less likely for materialise to ourselves than for others. This notions is in behavioural economics described as the "optimistic bias".[45] Humans actually tend to be optimistic but this over-optimism can lead us to make fatal mistakes. Namely, if people tend to believe that they are relatively free from risks, they may lack accurate information even if they know statistical facts and hence this optimistic bias might be an argument for the paternalism in law-making.

Secondly, literature offers ample evidence of hindsight biases where people often think in hindsight, that things that happened were inevitable, or nearly so.[46] People also tend to like the *status-quo*, and they demand a great deal to justify departures from it.[47] Such *status-quo* bias actually explains the sheer resistance towards legal, economic and structure reforms in current EU member states. People actually evaluate situations largely in accordance with their relation to a certain reference point and the departed gains or losses from that reference point are prevailing in their decision to change the *status-quo* position.

Thirdly, the identified endowment effect introduced by Thaler stands for the principle that people tend to value goods more when they own them than when they do not.[48] A consequence of such an endowment effect is, according to Thaler, the "offer-asking gap", which is the empirically observed phenomenon that people will often demand a higher price to sell a good that they already possess than they would pay for the same good if they did not possess it at present.[49] Kahneman and Tversky explain all of this observed patterns and inconsistencies as a result of "loss aversion" where losses from a reference point are valued more highly than equivalent gains.[50] Hence, making one option the status quo or endowing a person with a good seems to establish a reference point from which people depart from only very reluctantly, or if they are paid a large sum.[51] Thaler explains this endowment effect as a simple underweighting of opportunity costs.[52]

The previously discussed endowment effect, status-quo bias and default preference might, as argued by Vandenberghe, undermine the central premise of conventional law and economics where fully informed individuals allowed to exercise free choice will maximise their own utility, and thus social welfare,

---

45 Kahneman and Tversky, *supra* note 42.
46 Sunstein, *supra* note 26.
47 Ibid.
48 Thaler, *supra* note 18.
49 *Ibid.*
50 Kahneman and Tversky, *supra* note 42.
51 *Ibid.*
52 Hence, if out of pockets losses are viewed by persons as losses and opportunity costs are viewed as foregone gains, the former will be more heavily weighted and people's decision making will reflect that weighting. Thus as Thaler advances, a person would be willing to pay more in opportunity costs to keep a good that he already possesses than he would be willing to spend in received income (out-of-pocket money) to acquire the good; Thaler, *supra* note 20.

when transaction costs are low.[53] Under such assumptions, legal systems might not maximise social welfare by simply following the standard assumptions of economics and allow markets to operate whenever possible.[54] However, one should note that the assumption of zero or at least very low transaction costs is never satisfied and that the transaction costs are actually always positive, very often even prohibitive.[55] Moreover, the general assumption of zero transaction costs in economic models might actually represent one of the main shortcomings of some of the modern economics scholarship. The "new institutional economics" for example is actually attempting to address exactly those shortcomings and investigates the world of positive transaction costs and the impact of legal and economic institutions upon the paths of economic growth. Namely, transaction costs, as defined by Coase, are actually the costs of functioning of the system of economic exchanges (allocation of resources)[56] and in the daily world of positive transaction costs the law (i.e. the costs of the legal system) play a crucial role in the pursuit of efficiency, maximisation of social welfare and have a significant impact on the wealth of nations.[57]

To sum up, the behavioural law and economics argues that people, while making their daily decisions, display a) bounded rationality; b) they suffer from certain biases, such as over-optimism and self-serving conceptions of fairness; c) they follow heuristics, such as availability, which leads to mistakes; and d) they behave in accordance with prospect theory rather than expected utility theory.[58] Moreover, according to Jolls, Sunstein and Thaler people also have bounded willpower, are boundedly self-interested, they can be tempted and can be even myopic.[59] They insightfully also argue that people are on average concerned about the wellbeing of others, even strangers in some circumstances and this self-conception might lead them in the direction of cooperation at the expense of their material, narrowly defined, rational self-interest.[60]

---

53 Vandenberghe, *supra* note 41.

54 *Ibid.*

55 This is also one of main misunderstandings of original Coase's work, since Coase was actually never interested in the world of zero transaction costs but always in the world of positive transaction costs. Despite this, economists generally devote their attention to the world of zero transaction costs (so called Coase theorem). See Coase, Ronald, *Essays on economics and economists*, University of Chicago Press, 1994; and Coase, Ronald, "The new institutional economics", 88 *The American Economic Review* 2, 1998, pp. 72–74.

56 Coase, Ronald, "The problem of social cost", 1 *Journal of Law and Economics* 3, 1961, pp. 1–44.

57 For a quantification and the impact of the costs of the legal systems upon the economic growth and the consequent wealth of nations see Kovač, Mitja and Rok Spruk, "Institutional development, transaction costs and economic growth: evidence from a cross-country investigation", *Journal of Institutional Economics*, FirstView Article, 2015.

58 Jolls, Christine, Sunstein, R. Cass, and Richard H. Thaler, "A Behavioral Approach to Law and Economics", in Sunstein, Cass R. (ed.), *Behavioral Law and Economics*, Cambridge University Press, 2000.

59 *Ibid.*

60 *Ibid.*

5. COMPETITION LAW AND BEHAVIOURAL LAW AND ECONOMICS: IMPLICATIONS, CASES AND INSIGHTS

Previously discussed behavioural law and economics' insights have induced lawmakers and competition authorities in pursue of competitive markets to focus both on supply and also on demand side of the markets. Obviously, on the supply side a lawmaker should focus on competition between suppliers and induce them to innovate, provide low prices, high quality and choice. However, on the demand side, well-informed, confident, rational, wealth maximising, self-interested and effective consumer play a crucial role in private enforcement of this market competition. Yet, as it follows from our previous discussion this assumptions might not be satisfied and hence the operation of the competitive market might be severely impaired. Namely, if consumers indeed suffer from discussed heuristics, biases, bounded rationality, self-interest and willpower, or behave in accordance with prospect theory than they might not be able to make rational decisions and suppliers, while reacting to this behavioural biases of their consumers, might have minor incentives to supply these consumers with what they truly desire and might instead exploit these biases in order to extract rents (rent-seeking behaviour). Such rent-seeking behaviour represents a stark source of inefficiencies which severely reduce social wealth and hence calls for an immediate regulatory response.

Consequently, lawmakers are increasingly aware of that consumer biases and are accordingly designing behavioural tools for making markets working better.[61] For example, the UK Office of Fair Trading (further on as OFT),[62] which might be at this moment from the behavioural perspective regarded as one of the progressive frontrunners, has identified four categories of bias that are most relevant to competition policy.[63]

Firstly, OFT identifies[64] *framing biases*, including the relative utility,[65] *default bias* where consumers adopt default options and *placement bias* where consumers may choose the option placed at the top of the list.[66] Secondly, there

---

61 See generally Fatas, Enrique and Bruce Lyons, "Consumer Behaviour and Market Competition", in Mehta, Judith (ed.), *Behavioural Economics in Competition and Consumer Policy*, ESCR Centre for Competition Policy, 2013; and Niels, Gunnar, Jenkins, Helen and James Kavanagh, *Economics for Competition Lawyers*, Oxford University Press, 2011.

62 Matthew Bennett, John Fingleton, Amelia Fletcher, Liz Hurley and David Ruck, *What does Behavioural Economics Mean for Competition Policy?*, United Kingdom Office of Fair Trading, 2010.

63 For an extensive discussion on behavioural policy interventions in consumer policy see Luth, A. Hanneke, *Behavioural Economics in Consumer Policy: The Economic Analysis of Standard Terms in Consumer Contracts Revisited*, Intersentia, 2010.

64 Reported also in Gunnar, Jenkins and Kavanagh, *supra* note 56 at pp. 469.

65 Consumer's utility is affected by reference points.

66 Bennett, Fingleton, Fletcher, Hurley and Ruck, 2010, *supra* note 57.

are processing-power biases, including *choice overload* where consumers make choices on sub-sets of information, *representational biases* where consumers employ visible value as an indicator of hidden value and rules of thumb where consumers are imitating behaviour and choices made by other consumers. Thirdly, Bennett, Fingleton, Fletcher, Hurley and Ruck also point at the time-inconsistency biases, which consists out of: a) *projection bias*, where consumers expect to feel the same tomorrow as they do today; b) over-optimism, where consumers overestimate how much they will use a product or underestimate how much it will cost; and d) hyperbolic discount bias where consumers value today disproportionately more than tomorrow.[67] Fourthly, OFT identifies also the *loss-aversion bias* where consumers value something more after having owned it than before owning it.[68]

Moreover, according to Niels, Jenkins and Kavanagh consumers while making their decisions are actually passing throughout three main stages: a) firstly they need to access information about various offers available in the market; b) secondly they have to access and process these offers in a well-reasoned way;[69] and c) finally they have to act upon this information and analysis by purchasing the good or service that offers the best value.[70] Of course suppliers, sellers and companies might seek to take advantage of such identified biases at each of these three stages. As reported by Gunnar, Jenkins and Kavanagh, sellers may also make it more difficult for consumers to compare offers by obfuscating prices,[71] partitioning them in separate prices for products and for deliveries, increasing their complexity or even employing price promotions and frames all in order to substantially distort, divert consumers' price perceptions, purchase intentions, their demand and their decision making.[72] For example Morowitz has offers several real-life examples of instances where partitioned pricing have influenced consumers' purchasing decisions[73] Furthermore, OFT's experimental research shows that indeed such

67 *Ibid.*

68 *Ibid.*

69 OFT for example argues that this stage is the most prone for abuses since consumers may be here sensitive to framing effects, may be poor at assessing future, have limits to their processing ability, look at limited sub- sets of information and employ heuristics to make their decisions; Bennett, Fingleton, Fletcher, Hurley and Ruck, 2010, *supra* note 57.

70 Gunnar, Jenkins and Kavanagh, *supra* note 56 at pp. 469.

71 For example in the U.S. Federal Trade Commission's ('FTC') case on bulletproof vests, the association of bulletproof vest manufacturers adopted a rule that prevented comparative advertising. Under this rule, no member could represent that another member's vests had failed certification testing, even if the advertising claim were true. The FTC determined that the rule had the impact of restraining quality competition, obviously a key competitive parameter in bulletproof vests; Federal Trade Commission, Personal Protective Armor Ass'n, Fed. Reg., 59, 19,019, 1994.

72 Gunnar, Jenkins and Kavanagh, *supra* note 56 at pp. 469.

73 Morwitz, V., Greenleaf, E., Shaelev, E., and E.J. Johnson, *The Price does not Include Additional Taxes, Fees and Surcharges: A review of Research on Partitioned Pricing*, 2009; and the seminal study by Morwitz, V.G., Greenleaf E.A. and Johnson, E.J., "Divide and

partitioning practices[74] have adverse effects on consumer choice and that most of them do have a significant impact upon consumer welfare. Hence, they may amount to abusive practices and consequently reduce competition within a particular market and also distort the operation of the common EU market.[75] Gabaix and Laibson for example suggest that if there is a sufficient proportion of "myopic" customers, competition does not induce firms to unshroud information about add-on prices.[76] Furthermore, behavioural scholars argue that the presence of consumer biases might affect also competitive interactions between markets where companies might lever the market power from a market in which it is dominant into one in which it faces competition.[77]

Behavioural economics therefore show the importance of making use of 'smarter information' – thinking carefully about its framing, the context in which information is read, and the ability of consumers to understand it. A report for the OFT highlighted the positive story around 'traffic light' information in food labelling.[78] Here, for example a simple (and consequently less detailed) information on nutritional value of food led to better outcomes than a full list of food ingredients and nutritional value.[79] Consequently, such biases are than a direct source of inefficiencies, might directly hinder competition in the affected market and might also have a negative impact upon competitive interactions between the markets (e.g. tying, bundling). In this respect OFT also suggests that in the presence of consumer inertia, endowment effects and default biases, even small switching costs might have a significant effect on consumer behaviour, whereas foreclosure through tying and bundling might be even more feasible that it would be in the absence of such behavioural effects.[80]

Behavioural law and economics literature generally employs the notorious EU Microsoft case[81] as an illustration of such cognitive bias, which focused on Microsoft's bundling of Windows Media Player with its Windows operating system. This bundling practice and related behavioural evidences are also an example of behavioural evidences that played a significant role in court's decision making. Namely, Microsoft held a dominant position in the operating system

Prosper: Consumers' Reactions to Partitioned Prices", 35 *Journal of Marketing Research* 1, 1998, pp. 453–63.

74 OFT investigated drip pricing, sales, complex pricing, bait pricing and time limit offers (London Economics, 2010).

75 OFT's report suggests that the consumer's errors are generated by the behavioural biases (largely the endowment effect) and cognitive errors; London Economics 2010.

76 Gabaix, X., and D. Laibson, "Shrouded Attributes, Consumer Myopia and Information Suppression in Competitive Markets", 121 *Quarterly Journal of Economics* 2, 2006, pp. 505–40.

77 Niels, Jenkins and Kavanagh, *supra* note 56 at pp.470.

78 Bennett, Fingleton, Fletcher, Hurley and Ruck, 2010, *supra* note 57.

79 Office of Fair Trading, (April 2008), Assessing the effectiveness of potential remedies in consumer markets, Economic Discussion Paper, OFT994, 4.39–4.42.

80 Bennett, Fingleton, Fletcher, Hurley and Ruck, 2010, *supra* note 57.

81 COMP/C-3/37.792 Microsoft.

market and competitors were struggling to gain a bigger market share in the emerging media player market. Microsoft bundled his Media Player as a default application through which all media would play an individual purchased when an individual consumer purchased a personal computer.[82] From the traditional rational choice perspective this bundling should not be regarded as anything problematic since rational consumers would quickly log on internet and download an alternative media player that would be cheaper or even free of charge. However, as identified by OFT "when viewed through behavioural lenses, it becomes clear that consumers are significantly less likely to switch from the preloaded Microsoft programs that might otherwise be expected.[83] In this context, a strategy to foreclose could move from being unlikely to being much more plausible."[84] This pre-installation of Media Player on Windows has then been in the light of this behavioural evidences by EU Commission indeed regarded as an abuse of a dominant position.[85] Commission held that "... Microsoft actually created the potential for leveraging since, on the demand side users who find Windows Media Player pre-installed on their PC's are...in general less likely to use alternative media players as they already have an application which delivers media streaming and playback functionality, whereas on the supply side an aspect to consider is that, while downloading is in itself a technically inexpensive way of distributing media players, vendors must expend resources to overcome end-users inertia and persuade them to ignore the pre-installation of Windows Media Player."[86]

In other words, such bundling would discourage investment in all technologies in which Microsoft could conceivably take an interest in the future and would deter users to use third-party media players and other original equipment manufacturers to pre-install such media players on client's personal computers.[87] Such tying would consequently weaken competition among media

82 Reported in Niels, Jenkins and Kavanagh, *supra* note 56 at pp. 471.

83 Microsoft was probably acquainted with a behavioural insight that firms and consumers may have different preferences over the default option of to opt-out or to opt-in (if many consumers opt for the default option than this provides firms or their products that are the default options a significant competitive advantage). Microsoft then preferred having its inferior media player as the default choice, thereby requiring consumers to opt out (and many consumers then indeed stick with the default media player. Moreover, Microsoft generated additional annoying factors (of course not per se justifying a finding of foreclosure) where for example: a) consumers could not delete Microsoft's Media Player (MMP) and hence the computer memory taken by MMP was unavailable for other purposes; and b) Microsoft's software was devised to override the consumer's default setting (if a specific consumer used an alternative player) and reappear when consumer used Microsoft's web browser, Internet Explorer, to access media files streamed over the internet; Case T-201/04, Microsoft Corp. v. Comm'n, 2007 E.C.R.II-3601.

84 OFT, 2010.

85 EU Commission decision of 24th March 2004 relating to a proceeding under Art. 102 of the Treaty on Functioning of EU (TFEU).

86 *Ibid* at 845 and 870.

87 Case T-201/04, Microsoft Corp. v. Comm'n, 2007 E.C.R.II-3601.

players in such a way that the maintenance of an effective competitive structure would not be ensured in the near future.[88] This behavioural insights and evidences on the behavioural biases that consumers face have afterwards been an implicit ground for finding that Microsoft abused his dominant position in EU.[89]

Discussed Microsoft case shows how the behavioural evidences are of relevance in standard Article 101 and 102 TFEU competition cases. Yet, United Kingdom's Office of Fair Trading (OFT) made an unique step further and tried to improve market functioning also through a demand-side remedies and not merely via supply-side remedies as traditionally done by competition authorities in other EU Member States. Namely, OFT argues that a standard antitrust policy is not well designed to address the demand-side effect of consumer biases and that other complementary tools to classic antitrust should be also introduced.[90] For example, OFT suggests employment of consumer policy, market studies, investigations and even the potential for authorities to advocate legislation in a particular market. These market studies and investigations are designed to examine consumer behavioural biases that might distort competition. They focused at most possible features of consumer biases such as the extended warranties on electrical goods, personal current accounts, store cards, home credit and payment protection insurance.[91] The OFT also emphasises that this does not necessarily mean more intervention but rather smarter and more efficient intervention.[92] Such behavioural remedies may encourage consumers to make choice rather than letting them to remain inert or simply opt for the default.[93] Moreover, in instances of the efficient outcomes for consumers, the policy maker should set, in order to reduce transaction costs, as the default exactly this efficient outcome, without restricting consumers' ability to choose the alternative.[94]

However, Competition Commission of United Kingdom while investigating personal current accounts in Northern Ireland identified that consumers actually generally do not actively search for alternative personal current

---

88 *Ibid.*

89 Such behavioural evidences have afterwards been also employed in a subsequent case on the bundling of the Microsoft Internet Explorer web browser with Windows. See Commission's decision of 16 December 2009 relating to a proceeding under Art. 102 of the Treaty on the Functioning of the European Union and Art. 54 of the EEA Agreement; Case COMP/39.530 Microsoft (tying), notified under document C (2009) 10033, 2010, OJ C36/7.

90 OFT, 2010.

91 OFT, 2010.

92 OFT follows the so called "liberal paternalistic" approach, where an intervention works to some extent with consumers' flawed preferences and decision-making abilities, rather than necessarily trying to correct them; Niels, Jenkins and Kavanagh, *supra* note 56 at pp. 473.

93 Employed remedy in the previously discussed Microsoft Internet Explorer case can be used as an illustration of such a behavioural remedy; *Ibid* at pp. 473.

94 The employment of automatic enrolment in pensions schemes which address the behavioural problem of inertia in pension savings and which simultaneously preserve the choice for savers to opt out of such a scheme might be seen as an example of such a, "behaviourally driven" policy.

accounts.[95] Investigation also showed that customers are generally not particularly interested in personal current accounts and that 80% of those surveyed who had not switched bank gave as a reason the fact that they had been with their current provider for a long time.[96] If such outcomes are driven by flaws in the consumer's information sets and decision-making abilities then this might be regarded as a point of alert, but if such outcomes are mere quirks in consumer's preferences (and consumers actually do not care about a product) then authorities should generally not intervene.

Moreover, it should be also stated that the developing behavioural economics' theory should be complemented, supported and verified with significant empirical evidences. For example, when a competition authority would like to intervene in a certain market it should have significant empirical evidence both on the nature and extent of biases present and of the effects on consumers of any remedies put forward.[97] Hence, while designing demand-side remedies one should obtain significant empirical evidence (via reliable consumer surveys and experiments) of their likely effects on consumers. In the absence of such reliable evidence authorities' market interventions should be addressed cautiously and it should not be enough to merely assert that such biases exist and that a specific remedy will correct them.

Furthermore, behavioural evidences could be also employed to predict competitive consequences in reviewing proposed mergers and determining the deterrent effect of increasing sanctions for price-fixing cartels. Namely, in assessing proposed mergers competition authorities generally assume that actual marketplace behaviour comports with rational, profit-maximising behaviour.[98] The key question that agencies address in merger cases is the so called SSNIP test. To find the relevant market, the US Department of Justice has introduced a test that is currently being used by anti-trust authorities worldwide.[99] In this test the merging companies' customers are asked what would happen if the prices of the merging companies' products increased by a small but significant non-

95 Competition Commission (United Kingdom), *Market Investigation into Personal Current account Banking Services in Northern Ireland – Provisional Findings*, 2006.

96 *Ibid.*

97 Competition authority should via consumer surveys and experiments provide exact evidence of how consumers would respond to a certain remedy, whether it would benefit them and how this would weigh against the loss of convenience to consumers. See e.g. *Barclays Bank plc v. Competition Commission* (2009) CAT 27, Judgment of 16 October 2009.

98 This includes at least five other assumptions: a) the relevant anticompetitive effects would manifest themselves as higher prices; b) anticompetitive effects are likely only in highly concentrated markets; c) even in highly concentrated markets, anticompetitive effects are unlikely given certain economic conditions (e.g. big buyers or sellers that would discipline any non-cost-based price increase post-merger); d) anticompetitive effects are unlikely, absent high entry barriers; and e) many companies merger to generate significant efficiencies; Stucke, *supra* note 7 at 7.

99 See Motta, Massimo, *Competition Policy: Theory and Practice*, Cambridge University Press, 2009, at p. 102 *et seq.*

transitory amount (SSNIP) in order of five to ten percent.[100] If the answer to such question is yes then. This SSNIP question is actually asked in order to define the relevant market, which than helps the competition authority in addressing the ultimate question of whether the merger facilitates the exercise of market power. If the SSNIP test inquiry suggests a broad product or geographic market, then the merging parties' market shares and the industry concentration levels are likely to be lower and the authority will generally allow the merger.[101]

6. BEHAVIOURAL COMPETITION LAW AND ECONOMICS IN A COURTROOM: NOT READY FOR THE MAIN STAGE?

Previous discussion undoubtedly illustrates a promising avenue of the behavioural competition law and economics as one of the latest entry in the continuing series of economic approaches to competition. As emphasised, the behavioural antitrust, which introduces irrationality into the analysis of firms and markets has started to develop several years ago and have argued that individuals attempt to overcome the impossibility of collecting and processing all available information through the extensive use of heuristics (rule of thumb) and associated cognitive biases (anchoring, availability and representativeness).[102]

However, while the behavioural literature has discovered a large number of heuristics and cognitive biases it may not be, as Roger van den Bergh in his path breaking work convincingly shows, immediately clear which of these forms or irrationality are relevant for competition policy,[103] Namely, much of the behavioural economic literature according to van den Bergh documents instances of consumer irrationality,[104] yet competition law while aiming at improving the functioning of markets focuses not on the consumer irrationality but on the firm's behaviour.[105] Competition law and economics must hence provide economic evidence that irrationality affects decisions made at the collective level of firms. In this respect van den Bergh, undisputed authority and a founding father of law and economics in Europe, identifies two particular

100 See for example US Horizontal Meger Guidelines, U.S. Department of Justice & federal Trade Commission, 2010. The US Department of Justice refers to a 5% increase in prices, whereas the EC and the UK guidelines refer to a 5–10% increase.

101 Motta, *supra* note 100.

102 See e.g. Herbert A. Simon, "A Behavioral Model of Rational Choice", 69 *Q.J.Econ.* 99, 1955; Kahneman and Tversky, *supra* note 42.

103 Van den Bergh, Roger, "Behavioral Antitrust: Not Ready for the Main Stage", 9 *Journal of Competition law and economics* 1, 2013, pp. 203–229.

104 From a normative perspective shows how consumer decisions could be debiased by rules of consumer law.

105 Van den Bergh, *supra* note 104.

problems resulting from disposing of the rationality assumption in the domain of competition policy: a) in competition law it is not the behaviour of individual consumers[106] but that of firms which is regulated and there are reasons to doubt that problems of irrationality diagnosed in experiments with individuals manifest themselves in the same way within firms; and b) even if firms act irrationally it may remain unclear how cognitive biases impact the competitive process.[107] Hence, the results of behavioural antitrust may be ambiguous and might not allow conclusions about the effects of firm's conduct on market outcomes. Firms have actually better ways of overcoming cognitive biases (in order to survive on the competitive markets they must over-come them) than individual consumers and the scope of irrationality at the firm's level remains an unresolved puzzle. Moreover, empirical evidence that individuals act irrationally cannot simply be extrapolated to firms.[108] Furthermore, s serious shortcoming relates to the ambiguity of the predictions of behavioural economics. Van den Bergh shows that it will not always be possible to recognise potential cognitive biases *ex ante* and to predict what effects they will have upon different decision-makers.[109] In addition, protecting firms from the consequences of their irrationality (as is the case in consumer law where one attempts to protect consumers from irrationality through debiasing and libertarian paternalism) is, as van den Bergh states, hardly reconcilable with the goals of competition rules that aim at guaranteeing the efficiency of markets and consequently also at the maximisation of social wealth.[110]

However, an integration of behavioural insights into the normative debate might be considered by assuming the existent welfare goals proposed by mainstream economics on competition (allocative and dynamic efficiency) are accepted. As showed in the previously discussed Microsoft case behavioural law and economics may by providing additional behavioural evidence contribute to the normative assessment of debated EU competition law's issues and in the daily decision-making. One could for example list vertical minimum price fixing, predatory pricing and tying as the most promising fields where behavioural evidence might significantly contribute to the effective problem solving and in shaping efficient policy responses.[111] However, one should also note that the insights from behavioural economics that are relevant for antitrust

106 Those issues are addressed by the field of consumer protection. See e.g. Thaler, H. Richard, Cass R. Sunstein, *Nudge. Improving Decisions about Health, Wealth and Happiness*, Yale University Press, 2008.

107 Van den Bergh, *supra* note 104.

108 Experiments in laboratories focusing on persons not representative of the business community that are conducted in an artificial setting may lack relevance in the competition context; van den Bergh, *supra* note 104.

109 In addition, the direction in which biases may affect the decisions will not be clear if the decision-makers are vulnerable to different biases that work in opposite directions; *Ibid.*

110 *Ibid.*

111 For an extended analysis see van den Bergh, *supra* note 104.

practice are not entirely new or can be otherwise also explained by modern developments in mainstream competition economics. Moreover, van den Bergh convincingly shows that behavioural economics should be used with great caution, since an unlimited irrationality assumption could easily lead to excessive interventionism, just as the unlimited rationality assumption caused a too lenient antitrust policy in the past.[112] Van den Bergh also suggests that the crucial question for competition policy and for the courts addressing competition issues is which factors cause anti-competitive consequences and not whether market players are rational or irrational.[113]

7. CONCLUSION

Last decades have witnessed a steady growth of a new economic discipline – behavioural economics. In the last decade, behavioural economics, borrowing from psychology and sociology to explain decisions inconsistent with traditional economics, has hence revolutionised the way economists view the world (especially in the field of applied economics-finance and consumer behaviour). Behavioural law and economics argues that persons display bounded rationality and that (a) suffer from certain biases, such as over-optimism and self-serving conceptions of fairness, (b) follow heuristics, such as availability, that lead to mistakes; c) display incomplete self-control that induce persons to make decisions that are in the conflict with their long-term interest, and (c) they behave in accordance with prospect theory rather than expected utility theory. Moreover, people might have bounded willpower and they might be tempted and myopic. Furthermore, people might be concerned by the well-being of the others and this concern and their self-conception can lead them in the direction of cooperation at the expense of their material self-interest. Behavioural economists thus study boundedly rational choice behaviour and biases in the assessment of risks, costs and benefits.

By incorporating those irrational insights into the traditional economic analysis of markets behavioural competition law and economics enriches discussion and contributes to the learning process of all stakeholders. These new behavioural insights have induced lawmakers and competition authorities on the both side of the Atlantic Ocean in pursue of competitive markets to focus both on

112 *Ibid.*

113 Before running to any normative conclusions, behavioural antitrust scholars will need to develop theoretical models that take account of different market characteristics, the distribution of irrationality across markets and the extent to which firms may overcome irrational behaviour. If not all firms are subject to the same cognitive biases, the affected firms must be identified and one should also then identify in which circumstances decision making is shaped by a specific cognitive bias. In this respect coping with ambiguous outcomes remains a daunting task; *ibid.*

supply and also on demand side of the markets. Obviously, on the supply side a lawmaker should focus on competition between suppliers and induce them to innovate, provide low prices, high quality and choice. However, on the demand side, well-informed, confident, rational, wealth maximising, self-interested and effective consumer play a crucial role in private enforcement of this market competition. Yet, as it follows from our previous discussion this assumptions might not be satisfied and hence the operation of the competitive market might be severely impaired. Namely, if consumers indeed suffer from discussed heuristics, biases, bounded rationality, self-interest and willpower, or behave in accordance with prospect theory than they might not be able to make rational decisions and suppliers, while reacting to this behavioural biases of their consumers, might have minor incentives to supply these consumers with what they truly desire and might instead exploit these biases in order to extract rents (rent-seeking behaviour). Such rent-seeking behaviour than represents a stark source of inefficiencies which severely reduce social wealth and hence calls for an immediate response.

Previously discussed cases show that behavioural economics might indeed shed additional light on the market outcomes and on the anti-competitive practices of certain market players. However, on the theoretical level behavioural economics has not yet produced a sufficiently large set of theorems to support a general unifying theory of antitrust. Such unified theory should be than documented empirically, by replicating laboratory experiments in the real market settings. One should note, that both are still far out of sight.

Moreover, it must be also clear that considering behavioural insights does not require a fundamental shift of current competition policy. Behavioural competition law and economics should be hence seen as a mere, highly welcomed, additional toolbox for judges and practitioners, which should be in order to avoid excessive interventionism employed with extreme caution in daily decision-making. As Roger van den Bergh brilliantly stated: "Behavioural economics is not (yet) ready for the main stage."[114]

BIBLIOGRAPHY

Allais, Maurice, "Fondements d'une Théorie Positive des Choix Comportant un Risque et Critique des Postulats et Axiomes de L'Ecole Américaine", 21 *Econometrica* 4, 1953, pp. 503–546.

Akerlof, Geoffrey, "Behavioral Macroeconomics and macroeconomic behaviour", 92 *American Economics Review* 1, 2002, pp. 411–33.

Becker, S. Garry, *The Economic Approach to Human Behaviour*, University of Chicago Press, 1976.

114 *Ibid.*

Bennett, Matthew John Fingleton, Amelia Fletcher, Liz Hurley and David Ruck, *What does Behavioural Economics Mean for Competition Policy?*, United Kingdom Office of Fair Trading, 2010.

van den Bergh, Roger, "Behavioral Antitrust: Not Ready for the Main Stage", 9 *Journal of Competition law and economics* 1, 2013, pp. 203–229.

Camerer, Colin, Loewenstein, George and Drazen Prelec, "Neuroeconomics: How Neuroscience Can Inform Economics", *Journal of Economic Literature* Vol. XLIII, 2005, pp. 9–64.

Coase, Ronald, *Essays on economics and economists*, University of Chicago Press, 1994.

Coase, Ronald, "The new institutional economics", 88 *The American Economic Review* 2, 1998, pp. 72–74.

Coase, Ronald, "The problem of social cost", 1 *Journal of Law and Economics* 3, 1961, pp. 1–44.

Cooter, Robert and Thomas Ulen, *Law and Economics*, 6th ed. Princeton Hall, 2011.

Diamond, Peter and Hannu Vartiainen, *Behavioral Economics and its applications*, Princeton University Press, 2007.

Ellsberg, Daniel, "Risk, Ambiguity and the Savage Axiom", 75 *Quarterly Journal of Economics* 4, 1961, pp. 643–669.

Fatas, Enrique and Bruce Lyons, "Consumer Behaviour and Market Competition", in Mehta, Judith (ed.), *Behavioural Economics in Competition and Consumer Policy*, ESCR Centre for Competition Policy, 2013.

Federal Trade Commission, Personal Protective Armor Ass'n, Fed. Reg., 59, 19,019, 1994.

Fischhoff, B., "Hindsight Foresight: The effect of outcome knowledge on judgment under uncertainty", *Journal of Experimental Psychology: Human Perception & Performance*, 1, 1975, pp.288–299.

Fischhoff, B., and Beyth, R., "'I knew it would happen': Remembered probabilities of once-future things", 13 *Organizational Behaviour and Human Performance* 1, 1975, pp. 1–16.

Gabaix, X., and D. Laibson, "Shrouded Attributes, Consumer Myopia and Information Suppression in Competitive Markets", 121 *Quarterly Journal of Economics* 2, 2006, pp. 505–40.

Herbert, A. Simon, "Theories of Bounded Rationality", in McGuire, C.B., and Ray Racher (eds.), *Decision and Organisation*, North-Holland, 1972, pp. 161–176.

Herbert, A. Simon, "A Behavioral Model of Rational Choice", 69 *Q.J.Econ*. 99, 1955.

Jolls, Christine, Sunstein, R. Cass, and Richard H. Thaler, "A Behavioral Approach to Law and Economics", in Sunstein, R. Cass (ed.), *Behavioral Law and Economics*, Cambridge University Press, 2000, pp.13–58.

Jolls, Christine, "Behavioral law and economics", in Diamond, Peter, and Hannu Vartiainen (eds.), *Behavioral Economics and its Applications*, Princeton University Press, 2007, pp. 115 et seq.

Jolls, Christine, Sunstein, R. Cass, and Richard H. Thaler, "A Behavioral Approach to Law and Economics", in Sunstein, R. Cass (ed.), *Behavioral Law and Economics*, Cambridge University Press, 2000, pp.13–58.

Kahneman, Daniel and Amos Tversky, "Prospect Theory: An Analysis of Decisions under Risk", 47 *Econometrica* 263, 1979.

Kovač, Mitja and Rok Spruk, "Institutional development, transaction costs and economic growth: evidence from a cross-country investigation", *Journal of Institutional Economics*, FirstView Article, 2015.

Langevoort, C. Douglas, "Behavioral Theories of Judgment and Decision Making in Legal Scholarship: A Literature Review", 51 *Vand. L. Rev.* 1499, 1998, Vol. 51, Issue 6 (November 1998), pp. 1499–1540.

Lovallo, Dan, Sibony Oliver, "The Case of Behavioral Strategy", *McKinsey Q.* 30, 2010.

Luth, A. Hanneke, *Behavioural Economics in Consumer Policy: The Economic Analysis of Standard Terms in Consumer Contracts Revisited*, Intersentia, 2010.

Markowitz, Harry, "The Utility of Wealth", 60 *Journal of Political Economy* 2, 1952.

Markowitz, Harry, "Portfolio Selection", 7 *Journal of Finance* 1, 1952, pp. 77–91.

Morwitz, V., Greenleaf, E., Shaelev, E., and E.J. Johnson, *The Price does not Include Additional Taxes, Fees and Surcharges: A review of Research on Partitioned Pricing*, 2009.

Morwitz, V.G., Greenleaf E.A. and Johnson, E.J., "Divide and Prosper: Consumers' Reactions to Partitioned Prices", 35 *Journal of Marketing Research* 1, 1998, pp. 453–63.

Motta, Massimo, *Competition Policy: Theory and Practice*, Cambridge University Press, 2009, at p. 102 et seq.

Niels, Gunnar, Jenkins, Helen and James Kavanagh, *Economics for Competition Lawyers*, Oxford University Press, 2011.

Office of Fair Trading, "Assessing the effectiveness of potential remedies in consumer markets", Economic Discussion Paper, OFT994, 4.39–4.42, 2008.

Posner, A. Richard, *Economic Analysis of Law*, 7th ed., Aspen Publishers, 2011.

Posner, A Richard, *Economic Analysis of Law*, 7th ed., Aspen Publishers, 2007.

Plott, R. Charles and Vernon L. Smith, *Handbook of Experimental Economics Results*, Elsevier, 2008.

Ross, Don, "Neuroeconomics and economic methodology", in John, B. Davis, D. W. Hands and Uskali Mäki (eds.), *The Handbook of Economic Methodology*, Edward Elgar, 1998.

Schelling, C. Thomas, *Strategy of Conflict*, Harvard University Pres 1960.

Simon, A. Herbert, "A Behavioral Model of Rational Choice", 69 *Quarterly Journal of Economics* 1, 1955, pp. 99–118.

Slovic, P., Lictensteln, S., "Comparison of Bayesian and regression approaches to the study of information processing in judgment", 6 *Organ. Behav. Hum. Perform.* 4, 1971; pp. 649–744.

Stucke, Maurice, "Hearing on Competition and Behavioral Economics", Directorate for financial and enterprise affairs Competition Committee, DAF/COMP/WD(2012)12, 2012.

Sunstein, R. Cass, *Behavioral Law and Economics*, Cambridge University Press, 2000.

Teck H. Ho, Noah Lim, and Colin F. Camerer, "How 'Psychological' Should Economic and Marketing Models Be?", 43 *Journal of Marketing Research* 3, 2006, pp. 341–344.

Thaler, Richard, "Toward a positive theory of consumer choice", 1 *Journal of Economic Behavior and Organization* l, 1980, pp. 39–60.

Thaler, H. Richard, Cass R. Sunstein, *Nudge. Improving Decisions about Health, Wealth and Happiness*, Yale University Press, 2008.
Vandenberghe, Ann-Sophie, "Behavioral approaches to contract law", in Gerrit De Geest (ed.), *Contract Law and Economics*, Vol. 6, Encyclopedia of Law and Economics, 2nd ed., Edward Elgar, 2011.
Wilkinson, Nick, *An Introduction to Behavioral Economics*, Palgrave Macmillan, 2008.

CHAPTER 6

JUDGES, *EX ANTE* DECISIONS, EVIDENCE AND PROOF

Marcus SMITH, Q.C.

1. THE EVIDENTIAL DIFFERENCE BETWEEN *EX ANTE* AND *EX POST* REGULATION

Regulation in the competition world can be "*ex ante*" (i.e. before the event) or "*ex post*" (i.e. after the event). An example of the latter, *ex post*, form of regulation is where a regulator finds that there has, in the past, been an infringement of competition law by an undertaking. The continuation of the infringement is prohibited, and the past occurrence of the infringement sanctioned.

An example of the former, *ex ante*, form of regulation exists where a regulator seeks in advance to prevent anti-competitive conduct from arising at all. An example of such a form of regulation (indeed, one of the most extreme forms of *ex ante* regulation) is the price control, which fetters the freedom of an undertaking to set its own prices for the goods and services it sells. Unsurprisingly, under European law, the ability of a regulator to impose price controls is heavily circumscribed.[1]

Naturally, the decision of a regulator (whether *ex ante* or *ex post*) is subject to judicial control. This essay considers one particular difficulty which a court may face, particularly when reviewing the *ex ante* decision of a regulator. That difficulty relates to evidence. Fundamental to the rule of law upheld throughout the EU is the principle that regulatory decisions affecting undertakings cannot be made without a proper basis. In the case of *ex post* decisions, the exercise of determining whether there has or has not been an infringement of competition law is essentially a backward-looking one: looking at past events or circumstances, does the evidence disclose an infringement?

Although such exercises are without doubt difficult, involving complex questions of evidence-gathering and the assessment of that evidence, at least

1 One area where the power exists is in the telecommunications sector, where the "national regulatory authorities" of the various EU Member States have this power.

there is a factual framework (what actually happened in the past) that can assist the regulator in making its decision, and the court, when reviewing the regulator's decision.[2]

That factual framework may not exist where a regulator is contemplating *ex ante* regulation. Although it may very well be the case that there exists – at the time of the decision – a situation which may be regarded as anti-competitive, the fact is that even in such a case, the evidence of the effect of the *ex ante* remedy being proposed by the regulation may be lacking. This issue arose and was considered in *British Telecommunications plc v Telefonica O2 UK* ([2011] CAT 24 (Competition Appeal Tribunal); [2012] EWCA Civ 1002 (Court of Appeal); [2014] UKSC 42 (Supreme Court). For reasons that will become apparent, I shall refer to this case as the "*08x*" case.

2. THE *08X* CASE

The facts of *the 08x* case, in brief, are these. Telephone communications providers – whether operating a network of fixed lines or providing mobile services – offer their customers what is known as "end-to-end" connectivity: a caller subscribing to one network can call someone subscribing to another, different, network without more. Obviously, this entails the call being routed though the networks of different communications providers, and each of those communications providers will incur costs in providing this service.

Generally speaking, in the United Kingdom, it is the caller who pays for a call. Thus, it is the communications provider originating the call who receives payment. That originating communications provider will remunerate the other communications provider (the terminating provider) and any intermediate providers involved in routing the call to the person being called. Such charges are called "termination" charges. They are agreed pursuant to a overarching agreement between all communications providers in the United Kingdom known as the "standard interconnect agreement".

One exception to the "caller pays" principle are so-called "08" numbers. Although – at least at the time of the *08x* decisions – there was no legal mechanism for enforcing this, numbers beginning "080" were supposed to be free to the caller; numbers beginning "0845" were supposed to be charged at the rate for local calls (no matter how remote the call); and numbers beginning "0870" were supposed to be charged at the national rate. This is how Ofcom,[3]

2 It should not be thought that I am contending that there is a wholly water-tight distinction between *ex ante* and *ex post*. Counter-factual assessments in *ex post* cases may very well involve the types of uncertainty that are here being considered in the *ex ante* context; and there may well be cases where there is sufficient evidence to be able to assess the implications of *ex ante* regulation quite precisely.

3 The Office of Communications.

the UK's national regulatory authority for communications, described the numbers, although (as I have noted) Ofcom did not at the time of the *08x* case have the legal power to ensure that calls made on these numbers were charged in accordance with their description.

The purpose of "08" numbers is to enable the holder of the number, the person being called, to encourage calls on this number by ensuring that calls are either cheaper than they ordinarily would be (as in the case of "0845" and "0870" numbers) or else completely free to the caller (as in case of "080" numbers). The holder of the number pays the terminating communications provider a hosting fee in order to offer this service and – in the precise reverse of other types of calls – the originating communications provider receives a part of this hosting fee as an "origination" payment.

As between fixed line communications providers, the system worked as I have described. As between fixed line terminators (specifically, and in particular, British Telecommunications plc ("BT")) and mobile originators, it did not. This was because mobile communications providers did not charge their customers in accordance with the description of the "08" numbers their callers were calling. BT responded initially by reducing the origination payments it made to mobile communications providers (and, ultimately, these were reduced to zero), and then introduced what it described as "ladder pricing" for the termination of "08" calls.

The term ladder pricing was used because the termination charge was stepped, with charges increasing like steps on a ladder. Which particular "step" a mobile communications provider found itself on, depended upon how much that communications provider charged its customers. The higher the charge to the customer, the higher BT's termination charge.

Perhaps unsurprisingly, the mobile communications providers objected to this new form of pricing. In particular, it was asserted that BT's prices were not, and could not (by definition) be reflective of its costs.

However, because of the terms of the standard interconnect agreement, BT was entitled to impose its new tariffs on other communications providers, subject to an appeal to Ofcom, pursuant to its "dispute resolution procedure". Accordingly, a number of mobile communication providers appealed BT's new tariffs to Ofcom pursuant to its dispute resolution procedure.

3. THE COMMON REGULATORY FRAMEWORK AND DISPUTE RESOLUTION

Regulation of the communications sector in the UK is, for the most part, laid down in the Communications Act 2003, which implements within the UK a pan-European regulatory scheme known as the "Common Regulatory

Framework". In the words of Lord Sumption,[4] "[t]he objective of the scheme is to ensure end-to-end connectivity on a common basis throughout the EU, without distortions arising from anti-competitive behaviour or restrictions arising from national law or practices. It is contained in a number of Directives, all issued on 7 March 2002". Two of these Directives are the "Framework Directive" (Directive 2002/21/EC) and the "Access Directive" (Directive 2002/19/EC). The Access Directive contains a provision (in Article 20) regarding the resolution of disputes between communications providers by the national regulatory authority. In the case of the UK, this dispute resolution procedure is implemented in sections 190*ff* of the Communications Act 2003.

Although dispute resolution may – and very often does – embrace simply the adjudicative function of determining the rights and obligations of the parties to the dispute, it is quite clear that dispute resolution under the Common Regulatory Framework and under the Communications Act 2003 can be far wider than this: the dispute resolution procedure allows the national regulatory authority not merely to determine disputes in the traditional sense of adjudication, but to resolve disputes that may not be about legal rights at all by creating new rights, and imposing them on the parties to the dispute. In short, dispute resolution has a regulatory function, although of course that function needs to be exercised circumspectly.[5]

4. THE APPROACH OF OFCOM AND OFCOM'S FINDINGS

The question before Ofcom was, quite simply, whether BT's new prices should be permitted or not. Ofcom decided that it would permit the changes to be made only if they were "fair and reasonable". Whether the new prices were "fair and reasonable" was to be judged by three governing principles:

(1) *Principle 1.* Mobile network operators should be able to recover their efficient costs of originating calls to the relevant numbers.
(2) *Principle 2.* The new charges should *(i)* provide benefits to consumers, and *(ii)* not entail a material distortion of competition.
(3) *Principle 3.* Implementation of the new charges should be reasonably practicable.

---

4 Giving the judgment of the Supreme Court in [2014] UKSC 42 at [4].
5 As to which, see [2014] UKSC 42 at [15]. See also the decision of the CAT at [2011] CAT 24 at [179]*ff*.

As Lord Sumption noted, all of the principles can be related to objectives set out in the Framework Directive,[6] and no-one challenged this as an appropriate analytical framework. Indeed, all of the courts hearing the appeal from Ofcom's decision, found this framework to be appropriate.

The harder question was whether BT's tariffs satisfied these three principles. Here, the debate focussed on Principle 2*(i)*. Ofcom found Principle 1 to be satisfied; it found Principle 3 not to be satisfied, but was overruled on this point by the Competition Appeal Tribunal, and this point was not appealed further; Ofcom considered that although it had some concerns in relation to Principle 2*(ii)*, the risk of a material distortion of competition arising from the changes was "relatively low".[7]

Principle 2*(i)* – also known as the "welfare" test – in this case turned on a number of different effects:

(4) First, was the effect on consumer prices for calls to 08 numbers. Essentially, the question was whether BT's ladder pricing would cause the prices charged by mobile communications providers for calls to 08 numbers to fall, increase, or stay the same. This was referred to as the "direct effect".
(5) Second, was the extent to which any revenue gains by BT (if any – to a large extent this would depend on the nature of the direct effect) would feed back to the consumer in the form of lower charges or a higher standard of service on the part of hosts of 08 numbers. This was referred to as the "indirect effect".
(6) Thirdly, and finally, was what was known as the "mobile tariff package effect". This effect is based on a phenomenon accepted by economists to exist where undertakings offer multiple different goods or services. Essentially, the effect predicts that mobile communications providers deprived of one revenue stream (the extent of such deprivation would depend upon the direct effect) would seem to seek to compensate themselves by seeking to raise prices elsewhere.[8]

Ofcom concluded that the size of each of these effects was fundamentally known. It could not be said whether there was, or was not, a consumer benefit. That – after hearing a great deal of factual and economic evidence – was also the conclusion of the Competition Appeal Tribunal,[9] and this conclusion was accepted before both the Court of Appeal and the Supreme Court.

---

6 [2014] UKSC 42 at [20].

7 See [2014] UKSC 42 at [20] to [22]. The conclusion in relation to Principle 3 was no doubt influenced by the fact that BT did not have a dominant position or significant market power in relation to the hosting of calls on 08 numbers.

8 For this reason, the effect is often referred to as the "waterbed" effect: in a waterbed, if you push down in one place, the bed rises in another place.

9 See [2011] CAT 24 at [379] and [2014] UKSC 42 at [23].

5. DEALING WITH "KNOWN UNKNOWNS"

The welfare effect of BT's ladder prices were "known unknowns". And this was not through any lack of effort: the matter was investigated in depth both by Ofcom and during an "on the merits" review of Ofcom's decision by the Competition Appeal Tribunal. Despite such investigation, the effect remained unknown.

The question was how to treat such an "unknown". The Competition Appeal Tribunal put the point as follows (at [396]):

> "The crucial question is what is a regulator to do in the context of such uncertainty? Essentially, the regulator has two choices:
>
> (1) To prevent change unless it can be demonstrated that the change is beneficial – in which case it may well be said that the dead hand of regulation is constraining behaviour which may actually be beneficial to consumers. We stress that our conclusion regarding Principle 2(i) was that the welfare assessment was inconclusive, not that consumers would be harmed.
> (2) Alternatively, to allow change despite the uncertainty, even though there is a risk that the change may result in a disbenefit to consumers, recognising that an undue fetter on commercial freedom is itself a disbenefit to consumers."

Ofcom took the first course, concluding that Principle 2 was not satisfied because BT could not positively demonstrate that its proposed tariff changes would be beneficial to consumers. Accordingly, Ofcom decided that BT's new tariffs should not be allowed.

This decision was appealed to the Competition Appeal Tribunal, which – whilst substantially accepting Ofcom's factual conclusions regarding the welfare test – disagreed with Ofcom's conclusion that Principle 2 was not satisfied. Essentially, the CAT found that the proposed change in tariffs should be allowed, despite the "known unknown":

> "[447] If, therefore, the test to be applied is whether the [new tariffs] can be shown to provide benefits to consumers, then that test is not met. However, we do not consider this to be the correct test in the circumstances of the present case, because it places undue importance on Ofcom's policy preference [ie, consumer welfare], at the expense of the two other relevant factors that we have identified as forming a part of Principle 2 (namely Principle 2(ii) [the risk of a distortion to competition arising from restricting communication providers' commercial freedom to price] and BT's private law rights.
> [448] We consider that whilst Ofcom's welfare analysis could override these other factors, it should only do so where it can clearly and distinctly be demonstrated that the introduction of the [new tariffs] would act as a material disbenefit to consumers. In short, given the presence of the two other factors which we have identified, it is not enough for the welfare analysis to be simply inconclusive. The welfare analysis must demonstrate, and demonstrate clearly, that the interests of consumers will be disadvantaged."

The Competition Appeal Tribunal was influenced by three factors in particular, in addition to the inconclusiveness of the welfare analysis. Lord Sumption summarised these as follows:[10]

> "The CAT allowed BT's appeals. The tribunal agreed with the approach embodied in Ofcom's three principles, but they had a different starting point. In their view, BT was entitled to change its charges for three reasons. I list them in the order in which they will be addressed below. The first was that BT had a contractual right to vary its charges, subject to Ofcom's determination if the dispute resolution procedure was operated. The second was that the introduction of innovative charging structures was itself a mode of competing, and that interference with it would restrict competition. The third was that "price control is an intrusive form of control which elsewhere in the 2003 Act can only be introduced by SMP condition" (para 442). It was therefore inappropriate for Ofcom to use its dispute resolution powers as a way of controlling the charges of a [communications provider] like BT which did not have significant market power in a relevant market."

The Supreme Court essentially endorsed the CAT's approach. Lord Sumption emphasised the importance of any existing agreement:[11]

> "When Ofcom is resolving a dispute about a proposed variation of charges under an existing agreement, it is performing a mixture of adjudicatory and regulatory functions. The terms of the interconnection agreement are the necessary starting point for this process. If there is no contractual right to vary the charges, it is difficult to see how Ofcom can approve a variation unless it is necessary to achieve end-to-end connectivity (for example to enable operators to recover their efficient costs) or to achieve the Article 8 objectives. If there is a contractual right to a variation, but the proposed variation is not consistent with the Article 8 objectives, Ofcom may reject the variation. It may also modify any terms which created an entitlement inconsistent with the Article 8 objectives. If there is a contractual right to a variation which is consistent with the Article 8 objectives, Ofcom's function when the right is challenged is to give effect to it."

The starting point, therefore, is the contract, which in this case (as I have noted) permitted BT to make these changes. Lord Sumption then considered the welfare test in Principle 2*(i)* in this light:[12]

> "In my opinion, it is not consistent with either the contract or the scheme of the Directives for Ofcom to reject charges simply because they might have adverse consequences for consumers, in the absence of any reason to think that they would. It is not consistent with the contract because it prevents BT from exercising its

[10] [2014] UKSC 42 at [25].
[11] [2014] UKSC 42 at [34].
[12] [2014] UKSC 42 at [43].

> discretion to alter its charges in circumstances where there is no reason to suppose, and Ofcom has not found, that the limits of that discretion have been exceeded. It is inconsistent with the scheme of the Directives because it involves applying an extreme form of the precautionary principle to a dynamic and competitive market, in a manner which is at odds with the Directives' market-oriented and essentially permissive approach. Logically, given the inherent difficulty of forecasting the extent of any direct or indirect effects, and the practical impossibility of forecasting the mobile tariff package effect, it would rule out any increases in termination charges other than those justified by reference to underlying costs. On this point, therefore, I think that the CAT were right and that the Court of Appeal were wrong to overturn them.

The Supreme Court also agreed that the likely anti-competitive effects of restraining price changes were a relevant consideration, although this received relatively little analysis in the Supreme Court because the Supreme Court considered this conclusion to be "a factual judgment which it [the CAT] was perfectly entitled to make.

It was, moreover, an economic judgment by an expert tribunal which had received a substantial amount of additional evidence, including economic evidence. Since appeal lay to the Court of Appeal only on points of law, the CAT's findings on the distortion of competition liable to result from the rejection of the new charging structure were not open to rejection on appeal".[13]

The Supreme Court did not consider it necessary to consider the third point, that of the absence of a dominant position.

Thus, BT's tariffs were permitted to stand.

13 [2014] UKSC 42 at [46].

CHAPTER 7

LAW AND ECONOMICS' EVIDENCE IN COMPETITION LAW: JURISPRUDENCE IN SLOVENIA

Katarina Zajc

1. INTRODUCTION

This chapter discusses the use of economic tools in competition matters in Slovenia, dealt with by the Competition Protection Office (CPO), the Administrative Court and the Supreme Court in the relevant product market. I overviewed all the decisions that I have found published in different databases on the internet, and analysed a selection of 82 decisions, of which 66 were made by the CPO, 3 of the Administrative Court and 3 were the decisions of the Supreme Court.[1] Unfortunately I did not have access to the case files and I could assess the use of economic tools and their significance only on the basis of the reviewed decisions which might not have mentioned all the methods used to analyse the relevant product market. According to the analysed decisions, some explicitly mention certain economic analyses or methods used. However, some of them only mention that they examined the market and it is not clear what kind of methods were used. It is interesting that only two of the cases examined explicitly mention the SSNIP test, which in the EU (at least since 1997), as well as, in the U.S. (since 1982), is one of the most well-established economic tools in the field of competition law analysis and should be the primary test for determining the size of the relevant market in Slovenia also.

---

1 The decisions have been reviewed and selected on the basis of whether it is a procedural decision or a decision on the merits with the procedural ones being eliminated, as well as those not dealing with defining the relevant market. Of course, it is conceivable that there are many more decisions on the merits besides the ones reviewed, since some may not be published in the Ius-info database or on the CPO website, which at some point, stopped adding complete decisions to its website and now only attaches the operative part of the decisions. Of the decisions referred to in the EU cases, I reviewed the EU cases also, but did not cite them separately.

2. ECONOMIC ANALYSIS OF LAW IN THE ANTITRUST

The ideal world in which Pareto equilibrium[2] is achieved is a world of pure competition, in which allocation[3] and distribution balance[4] is achieved. Goods are distributed in such a way that the distribution of goods or means of production, which would improve the position of one market participant (consumer or supplier), without aggravating the position of another, is not possible. Consumers are in the best possible world, suppliers can freely enter or exit the market, goods are homogeneous, and all participants have perfect information. The number of suppliers and consumers on the market is such, that none of them alone can influence the price. The consequence of such a market situation is the lowest possible market prices (which in the balance are also equal to average costs), goods are produced efficiently and motivate innovation. In such circumstances, the interference of the regulator would not improve the welfare of consumers and producers, because it is already maximised.

The conditions of limited competition bring about a situation where prices are higher than marginal costs, the quantity of goods offered in the market is smaller than in pure competition, dead loss also occurs, where part of the consumer profit is lost for society as a whole.[5] In conditions of limited competition the consumers and society as a whole are thus worse off than under conditions of pure competition and the regulator or the state has the ability to intervene in the market and increase the well-being of society as a whole.

In the real world, pure competition is only an idea. Goods are not homogeneous, market entry or exit is expensive, and market participants do not have perfect information. Despite imperfections most markets are ruled by competition, at least in the long term, which is much closer to pure competition than, for example a monopoly. Nevertheless, competition law has a major influence on the market situation, on the behaviour of competitors, and the prosperity of society as a whole, because in some situations competition is rather limited.[6]

---

2 Pareto equilibrium is an ethical criterion, according to which the goods of all individuals are added up and on the basis of this sum the well-being of society as a whole is measured (Bajt, Štiblar, 2002).

3 The prices of goods and means of production are equal to marginal cost.

4 A certain quantity of goods is produced with the least possible cost or the maximum number of goods is produced with certain costs.

5 Dead losses in conditions of pure competition is part of consumer profit that is received by consumers.

6 See also Elhauge and Gerardin, 2007.

3. ECONOMIC TOOLS AND COMPETITION LAW

3.1. GENERAL

The use of economic tools in competition law has long had a prominent role in the jurisprudence of the United States, but is only slowly coming to the forefront in the EU, even though great progress has supposedly been made in the last decade.[7, 8] Not only is there a difference between use or non-use of economic analysis, the objectives of competition policies are different. While the objective of competition law in the U.S. is just to achieve efficiency and in doing so protecting consumers, in the EU there are two objectives of competition law, namely the unity of the market and efficiency, which in certain situations can exclude each other.[9]

In the United States Supreme Court, Judge Brandeis first mentioned economic analysis in competition cases as early as 1931.[10] Since then, the use of economic analysis has become increasingly standard.[11] It is also interesting that the use of economic analysis of law has adjusted to the findings of theory in the field of industrial organisation and is in standard use since at least 1968, when they released the Guidelines on horizontal mergers, and certainly since 1982, when the U.S. Department of Justice (DOJ) issued revised guidelines on horizontal mergers, which were significantly different from the guidelines in 1968 and contained Instructions for the use of the SSNIP test as the primary tool for determining the size of the relevant market.[12, 13]

The EU has in some ways introduced the "economic" thinking in 1997, with the adoption of the Commission notice on the determination of the relevant market for the purposes of EU competition law (hereinafter The Notice).[14, 15]

---

7 It is also interesting that the rules of competition in the United States are changed when it comes to changes in economic theory in the field of competition law (Kovačič, 1992).

8 See also Van den Bergh, 2007.

9 See Cayseele and Van den Bergh, 2000.

10 See case Standard Oil Co. of New Jersey. United States, 221 U. S. 1 (1911).

11 See criticized decisions, but also those that extensively used economic analysis of law: (i) United States v. Aluminium Co. of Am., 148 F.2d 416 (2d Circ. 1945), United States v. United Shoe Marc. Corp., 110 F Suppl. 295 (D. Mass. 1953), Brown Shoe Co. v. United States, 370 U. S. 294 (1962).

12 So we know Harvard school, which dominated until the seventies and was then taken over by the Chicago School (see case United States v. General Dynamics Corp., 415 U.S. 486 (1974), and Continental TV, Inc., v GTE Sylvania, Inc., 433 U.S. 36 (1972)), and later the New institutional school (Kovačič, 1992).

13 The Guidelines from 1992 are now used: www.ftc.gov/bc/docs/horizmer.shtm, which were jointly issued by the Federal Trade Commission (FTC) and the Department of Justice.

14 UL C 372, 9. 12. 1997.

15 Point 17 of The Notice defines the SSNIP test: "The question to be answered is whether customers of the involved companies, taking into account a small (5 to 10 percent) but permanent relative price increase of the examined products and areas would already switch to available substitutes or to suppliers located elsewhere. If there were enough substitutes to

With The Notice, the Commission has exceeded the qualitative analysis of the relevant market and introduced the quantitative method, the SSNIP test (Small but Significant Non-transitory Increase in Price). It should be noted that The Notice still "prescribed" that qualitative methods should also be used, such as characteristics of goods, intended use of goods, consumer preferences, differences in prices, and similar attributes, although it is understood that the SSNIP test should be used primarily against other quantitative and qualitative analysis (Bishop and Walker, 2010).

Although the Commission has "prescribed" a rigorous test to determine the relevant market, the EU practice is still criticised, because it is said to be lacking in the use of the SSNIP test and other quantitative methods, which are available for determining the relevant market.[16]

3.2. ECONOMIC METHODS OF DETERMINING THE RELEVANT MARKET[17]

In the following I will concentrate only on the methods of defining the relevant market in accordance with The Notice.[18] Based on the review of Slovenian decisions I have found that this is the most widely used concept in the reviewed decisions.[19]

3.3. THE DEFINITION OF THE RELEVANT MARKET AND THE SSNIP TEST

The Notice defines relevant markets (point 7 of The Notice): "*A relevant product market comprises of all those products and / or services, which the consumer considers interchangeable or replaceable, based on the products' characteristics, their prices and their intended use.*" A relevant Geographic market (point 8 of The Notice) is: "*The relevant geographic market comprises of the area in which companies are involved in the supply and demand of products or services, in which*

---

render the price increase unprofitable because of the resulting loss of sales, the additional substitutes and areas are included in the relevant market. This would be done until such a set of products and geographical areas would be established, that a small, but permanent increases in relative prices would be profitable. Equivalent analysis is applicable in cases concerning the concentration of purchasing power, where the supplier represents the starting point, and the price test is used to determine the existence of alternative distribution channels or retail outlets for the products of the supplier… ."

16 See for example Van den Bergh, 2007.

17 In the following I will concentrate mainly on the relevant product market and not so much on the geographical.

18 The methods are summarized by Bishop and Walker, 2010.

19 Adapted from Bishop and Walker, 2010.

the conditions of competition are sufficiently homogeneous and which can be distinguished from neighbouring areas because the conditions of competition in these areas are significantly different. "

The standard test for defining the relevant market is the SSNIP test, which was first proposed in the U.S. horizontal merger guidelines (U.S. Horizontal Merger Guidelines) in 1982 and modernised in 1992. In 1997 it was also adopted by the EU as part of The Notice.[20] The relevant market could be defined as a market of goods, on which a hypothetical supplier could raise the price, so that his profit would increase, so this is the market it "pays" to monopolise, as the supplier, when he raises the price, does not lose all his consumers. The relevant market in accordance with The Notice is thus a market in which a hypothetical monopolist (who represents all the suppliers in a given market) could permanently raise prices by 5 to 10 percent and in doing so increase his profits while the prices of other commodities would remain unchanged. The SSNIP test therefore defines the size of the market where the supplier or suppliers offer their goods.

Whether the rise in prices will also cause an increase in profit for the monopolist, and by how much, depends on what happens with the volume of sales of goods (which of course falls, but the question is for how much) when the price rises. If the decline in volume in percentage points is smaller than the percentage increase of the price, the price increase has a positive effect on profits. If the opposite is the case, the profit falls.[21] The decrease in quantity when the price rises is affected by demand interchangeability, supply interchangeability, and potential competition.[22] If there is demand interchangeability and if a hypothetical monopolist raises the price consumers shift to other goods, which are relatively cheaper, and so there is no rise in profit. If on the other hand there is no such interchangeability, the rise in price does not deter all consumers from the good, that had its' price raised, it may happen that the profit of the hypothetical monopolist will not fall. It is important to note that, it is not necessary that all consumers are diverted to another good, but it is enough to shift marginal consumers.[23] Even if there is no demand interchangeability, a particular market does not "pay" to monopolise, if there are such suppliers who can be quickly diverted to the production of the same goods as our hypothetical

---

20 Adapted from Bishop and Walker, 2010.

21 To see how much the sold quantity can drop when the price is raised and consequently profit also falls, critical loss can be calculated. See page 116, Bishop and Walker, 2010.

22 Since potential competition is generally not taken into account when determining the relevant market, I will neglect it from hereinafter.

23 In Case 27/76 United Brands Co. and United Brands Continental BV v Commission (1978) ECR 207, the Commission argued that the banana market is a specific market, since young children and older people (i.e. those who do not have teeth) do not have an adequate substitute for bananas. The right question we must ask ourselves is how big is the share of consumers considered certain goods as substitutes and how they respond to changes in relative prices.

monopolist. This happens if the potential supplier already has all the resources required to redirect production.[24]

If it is determined that the profit of a hypothetical monopolist, when he raises the price, does not rise, this means that there are certain substitutes on the market that make it impossible for the monopolist to raise prices, because consumers will shift to them. A market in which the relevant market is determined by the SSNIP test should be increased and use the SSNIP test again to determine that such an increased market is the relevant market.

The SSNIP test, although it is only a quantitative measure of the relevant market, also has disadvantages. Among them the most famous is the cellophane error and also the toothless error.[25] In the cellophane case, the U.S. Supreme Court was aware of the fact that Du Pont had high elasticity of demand, which usually means that it cannot raise prices, since it would mean the loss of most customers.[26] It is possible Du Pont already raised prices to their maximum level (because of its market power) and that additional raising of price would mean such a large loss of customers that profits would be reduced (its profit is thus already maximised considering its market position). In order to avoid the cellophane error, the SSNIP needs to be applied to prices that the supplier would set in conditions of pure competition and not in actual conditions, where it is already charging the highest possible prices, since it is maximising the profits. The Commission is aware of this, which is why it has already adjusted the instructions regarding calculating the price elasticity and determining interchangeability to the cellophane error (point 19 of The Notice).[27]

3.4. AN EMPIRICAL ANALYSIS

In recent years the Commission has increasingly used the empirical analyses, which of course also allows it to use the SSNIP test. The Commission considers it the primary test of relevant market; it is advisable to also use other quantitative and empirical tests, of course.[28]

The price tests includes the price correlation, while the empirical tests includes the Granger causality, co-integration and the single root test. Also used is the analysis of price elasticity (critical loss), which helps us in calculating the SSNIP test, and other methods, which will only be listed, as well as methods that

---

24 See Case 6/72 Europemballage Corp. and Continental Can Co. Inc. v. Commission (1972) ECR 215.

25 United States of E.I. du Pont de Nemours & Co. (1956) 351 U. S. 377.

26 A small rise in price percentage-wise brings with it a very large reduction in demand for quantity, which means that in this way, the supplier's income is usually reduced.

27 Other misconceptions are detailed in Bishop and Walker, 2010 (page 131 et seq.).

28 One of the reasons is also the opening of offices of the chief economist at the Commission (Chief Economist's Team).

will not be mentioned, however, the literature, where they are addressed will be mentioned.

3.4.1. Direct SSNIP Test – Critical Loss and Critical Elasticity

The first step for the SSNIP test is to determine the price elasticity of demand of the hypothetical monopolist, and then it is necessary to determine how much the costs of the supplier are reduced, because it decreases the supply of goods to the market, since it raised the price. It may happen that despite the fact that revenues of the monopolist fall when it raises the price, the costs are reduced, since it supplies less, which of course in turn means that it is still profitable for the monopolist to increase the price. To summarise, for any difference between price and costs the following applies: the lower the self-price elasticity, the higher the probability that two goods constitute two distinct markets; and for a given self-price elasticity, the greater the proportion of variable costs in the price, the greater the chance that raising the price will be profitable.

Once we have this information, we may ask, how many sales would the hypothetical monopolist loose (how much less could it sell) before the price increase would become unprofitable. When we get an answer, we know whether the conditions for calculating the SSNIP test are met. In order to determine whether the test SSNIP requirements are satisfied, it is further necessary to calculate critical elasticity using the following formula: $1 + t / m + t$, where m is the difference between the price and the costs and t is percent increase of the price. If the self-price elasticity is lower than the outcome of the fraction, then the monopolist could permanently increase the price by more than 5 to 10 percent and still make a profit.[29]

3.4.2. Price Correlation

Among price tests, price correlation is the simplest, but it has certain weaknesses.[30] With price correlation the parallel movement of prices of various goods is analysed through time.[31] Where prices are positively correlated, we see they are moving similarly. The higher or more positive the correlation ratio, the more the prices are interrelated and the more likely it is, that both goods form a relevant market, although this test does not answer the question, whether both goods form a relevant market. It may be that, despite the high

29 If the elasticity along the demand curve is not constant, but, for example, linear, which means that the demand varies along the curve, the formula is modified to read as follows: $1 / m + 2 t$.

30 Suppose a random link (spurious correlation), benchmarking, floating exchange rates, various time delays and the number of repetitions.

31 A good econometric estimate of the elasticity of demand or supply is of course of higher quality, but also much more expensive.

positive correlation ratio, only one of the analysed goods form a relevant market.[32]

3.4.3. *Granger Causality*

It tells us which of the variables analysed is dependent and which is the independent variable. In the case of competition this means that if two goods form a relevant market, then one might expect one good influences the other and vice versa. It should be emphasised that even if we find Granger causality between the goods, this does not mean that these goods form a relevant market, the result only tells us that the goods are interchangeable (i.e. a substitute for each other) to a degree.

3.4.4. *Co-integration Analysis*

Co-integration measures any strong correlation between individual variables, which should also reflect on their interchangeability. Data series are used for estimates of interchangeability between the prices. The prices of two goods are co-integrated if the combination of two types of prices are stable and indicates a long-term trend of integration and stability.[33]

3.4.5. *Single Root Test*

If we assume that two goods form a relevant market, we can expect that there is a long-term price equilibrium between them, which means that if, for example shock affects the price of one good, but not the other, the prices will, after a certain period of time, come back to the long-term equilibrium. Single root test shows the long-term balance between the prices of goods. Even this test has advantages and disadvantages and should be considered together with other analyses that define the relevant market.

In calculating the relevant market it is also important to use studies of tenders in the public procurement processes or other tenders, as well as shock analyses[34] and stock exchange case studies.[35]

---

32 The Commission, for example, used the price correlation in the following cases: IV / M 190 Nestle / Perrier (1993) 4 C.M.L.R., M17; (1992) OJ L356 / 1, IV/M430 Proctor & Gamble / VP Schikedanz (1994) OJ L354/33, COMP/M.2187 CVC / Lenzing (2000), COMP/M4439 Ryanair / Aer Lingus (June 27, 2007), COMP / M. 4980 ABF / GBI Business (2008).

33 See also Repas, 2010.

34 Shock analysis review and explore how the industry or sectors react to economic and other shocks and what these can tell us about the similarities between different industries or sectors. See IV/M430 Proctor & Gamble / VP Schickendanz (1994) OJ L354/32.

35 There are studies of price concentrations, case studies, simulations of mergers, Cournot models, and models of negotiation and auctions, analysis of transport costs, all of which are transparently listed and explained in Bishop and Walker, 2010.

4. REVIEW OF PRACTICES IN SLOVENIA

The Notice states the SSNIP test is the primary test for determining the relevant market given, but The Notice also says that, when quantitative methods are not available, qualitative methods are still to be used and this include considering the characteristics of goods, intended use of goods, consumer preferences, differences in price, and others. Below I will review decisions by individual state bodies and identify the analysis of the relevant market and any other economic analyses that have been made.

4.1. THE COMPETITION PROTECTION OFFICE

From the 21 CPO decisions it is evident that when defining the relevant product market the CPO often relies on similar cases in the EU (which often also does not apply the SSNIP test for determining the relevant product market) and qualitative elements of defining the relevant product market as defined by The Notice, but not on the analytical and empirical methods, as addressed by The Notice, the theory and the practice. The above is clear from decisions no. 306–21/2005–92, 306–1/2008–84, 306–1/2008–84, 30723–1/01–9, 3073–4/01, 306–168/2007–57, 3072–4 / 00–24, 30724–5/03–7. In two of the cases that are examined (30724–5/03–7 and 30724–7/2003–8, 3072–11/2003–44), the CPO did not deal with the definition of the relevant market, because it relied on an agreement, which is in line with the decision of the Supreme Court no. X Ips 70/2010. It is also interesting that in one of the examined cases, the CPO decided that it was not bound by the opinion of the state bodies and regulations regarding the relevant product market (3072–14/02/62),[36] however in two cases it based itself on Slovenian legislation (30724–1/01–9, 306–125/2005–80). The above mentioned would not be objectionable if the CPO, when it did or did not rely on regulations or opinions, would support its' analysis with quantitative evidence or the SSNIP test, but this did not happen. In the following two cases (3072–4/03–206 and 3072–4/03–184) the CPO did not directly apply the SSNIP test, but one of the analyses did measure the point elasticity of demand for certain services and found that the self-price elasticity is somewhere between 0.7 to 0.9. As we have seen from the above explanation (see point 3), the measurement of self-price elasticity is only a small fraction of the mosaic that defines the relevant market on the basis of the SSNIP test. In another case (3072–4/03–206 and 3072–4/03–184) the CPO asked itself whether consumers at home would switch to foreign suppliers, if the supplier would increase home prices by 5 to 10 percent, but found the transition to be inefficient in terms of cost and therefore unrealistic. It is not clear whether they also got the data to calculate the test. In

36 In this case, one party submitted two analytical studies.

two cases (3073-2/99-52 and 3073-9/2002-50) the CPO based the interpretation of the relevant product markets on surveys and questionnaires that it sent out, but it is not clear whether they were also processed analytically. The richest in economic and legal analysis are cases 306-21/2005-92 and 306-178/2007-189, but the SSNIP test is not mentioned in either of them. Decision 306-14/2006-100 is also interesting as this is where the CPO explicitly stated that it did not opt for the SSNIP test, as the examined elements (location, amount of price rise, price, timely availability of the rise, charfcxr'edswc cct market. It would be interesting to know whether the clients submitted the SSNIP test in the proceeding, and if not, why not, because all five of them alleged that the CPO did not properly determine the relevant market.

4.2. THE ADMINISTRATIVE COURT

I reviewed four decisions made by the Administrative Court.[37] In one of the decisions the Administrative Court only confirmed the definition of the relevant market as determined by the CPO, without adding its own reasons, even though the parties of the procedure challenged the definition of the relevant product market (U 1155/2004). In the other two decisions, the interpretation of the separation or unity of the market would be much easier and rigorous, if the court had the SSNIP test available. Since it seems it did not have it or as it explicitly stated in one of the decisions, that there is no need for it, it had a very hard time explaining the size of the relevant market, which was not very convincing.[38]

4.3. THE SUPREME COURT

There are not many decisions by the Supreme Court that address the relevant product market in the database of Ius-Info. I would mention three. Two of them are interesting, because (as I understand them) the Supreme Court ruled that The Notice does not oblige the CPO to use the SSNIP test, but allows the use of

37 There are very few Administrative decisions in the field of competition law in the Ius-Info database. When I eliminated those who had dealt with procedural issues and those who have not dealt with the definition of the relevant market, I only got four decisions that were relevant to the analysis.

38 "The Court finds, that the defendant in the contested decision provided adequate reasons, why it could establish the relevant market by assessing characteristics, price and intension of service and that further tests (such as the SSNIP) ware not necessary for this purpose, and also responded to the comments of banks in relation to the determination of the relevant market." Case U 581/2007.

other alternative methods (U 1286/2003 and X Ips 749/2007).[39, 40, 41] In the third case the Supreme Court emphasised that when it comes to agreements between parties, from which a clear objective of restricting competition is evident, the bodies making the decisions in the proceedings does not need to determine the relevant market, but may use the definition of the relevant market included in the agreement itself (X Ips 70/2010).

5. CONCLUSIONS

In this article I addressed the use of qualitative and quantitative tests of the relevant product market in Slovenia from a theoretical and a practical standpoint. Unfortunately, I did not get to inspect the files of individual cases, so I could only draw my own conclusions on the usage of various methods for defining the relevant market, unless they were expressly specified in the decision. The review is therefore inescapably incomplete, and can perhaps even be unfair and overly critical of certain Slovenian institutions. Nevertheless, it appears that although the Notice sets the SSNIP test as the primary test of the relevant market and only then (as a secondary method) considers qualitative indicators, the Slovenian bodies think otherwise, which is similar to the bodies in the EU. In my opinion, regardless of the hierarchy of tests, introduced by the Supreme Court and the CPO, the SSNIP test should already be the primary tool because it is rigorous and the only one that leads to clear results. Using qualitative indicators leaves the reader of the decisions with a bitter taste of doubt over the correctness of the decision.

BIBLIOGRAPHY

Bajt, A. and F. Štiblar, *Economics, Economic Policy and Analysis*, GV Publishing, Ljubljana 2002.

Bishop, S. and M. Walker, *The Economics of EC Competition Law: Concepts, Application and Measurement*, 3rd ed., Sweet & Maxwell, 2010.

39 "In this regards it states on what basis its conclusions are founded, both in terms of determining the relevant markets as well as concerning the assessment of concentrations and its effects. From the justification of the decision it follows that in determining the relevant markets, both product and geographic, it took into account the criteria set out in the Instruction. The methodology demanded by the second plaintiff, is not prescribed as mandatory in the Instruction. It is also not prohibited, neither in the determination of the relevant market nor in the assessment of the effects, the use of survey results as input data or the use of certain data or the manner of their collection." Judgment U 1286/2003, Ius-Info.

40 Let me just say that the file contained the SSNIP test, at least according to unofficial data, so that it was available to all authorities who decided in the matter.

41 "The same in both acts described demand and supply interchangeability, potential competition and barriers for entry on market is accepted as established (but not exclusive) criteria for the definition of the relevant market (at the time of deciding by the Office)." Matter X Ips 749/2007.

Cayseelle, Van P. and R. Van der Bergh, "Antitrust Law", in *Encyclopedia of Law and Economics*, Boudewijn Bouckaert editor and Gerrit De Geest, Edward Elgar Publishing, University of Ghent in 2000.

Elhauge, E. and D. Gerardin, *Global Competition Law and Economics*, Hart Publishing, Oxford and Portland, Oregon in 2007.

Glick, M., A., DJ, and DG Cameron, Mangum, "Importing the Merger Guidelines Market Test and Section 2 Cases: Potential Benefits and Limitations", 42 Antitrust Bulletin 121, 1997.

Kovacic, W., E., "The Influence of Economics on Antitrust Law", *Economic Inquiry*, April 1992.

Lyons, B., editor, "Cases in European Competition Policy", *The Economic Analysis*, Cambridge University Press, New York 2009.

Muris, J.T., 12 *George Mason Law Review*, 1, 2003.

Commission Notice on the definition of relevant market for the purposes of Community competition law (97 / C 372/03).

Repas, M., "The economic approach of determining the relevant market in EU competition law", *LeXonomica – Journal of Law and Economics*, Vol. II, no. 1, June 2010.

Horizontal merger guidelines, www.ftc.gov / bc / docs / horizmer.shtm 1992.

Van Den Bergh, R., The "More Economic Approach" and European Competition Law: Is "More" best buy "Enough?", http://esnie.org/presentations/111.html 2007.

PART III

INSIDER TRADING, CARTELS AND CRIMINALISATION

CHAPTER 8
AN ANALYSIS OF THE CRIMINALISATION OF INSIDER TRADING AT EU LEVEL

Michael G. Faure and Claire Leger

1. INTRODUCTION

Traditionally it was considered that the EU has no competence in the area of criminal law. However, the European Commission increasingly noticed that in some cases Member States formally implemented European Directives, but did not seriously enforce the national legislation implementing the EU Directives. For that reason the European Commission increasingly sought to force Member States to sanction violations of national legislation implementing EU law with criminal sanctions. This desire of the Commission was backed up by the European Court of Justice in the decision of 13 September 2005 where it decided that when the application of effective, proportionate and dissuasive criminal penalties by the competent national authorities is an essential measure for combating serious environmental offences, criminal law may be prescribed on the condition that it is necessary in order to ensure that the rules which it lays down on environmental protection are fully effective.[1]

Meanwhile, the European Commission has used these powers in the environmental area with the so-called Environmental Crimes Directive of 19 November 2008[2] and through Directive 2009/123 on Ship Source Pollution of 21 October 2009.[3] These powers of the EU to force Member States to use criminal law have now also been laid down in the Lisbon Treaty.[4]

---

1 See European Court of Justice, Decision of 13 September 2005 in case C-176/03.

2 Directive 2008/99/EC on the protection of the environment through criminal law (OJ L328/28) of 6.12.2008. It had to be implemented by 26 December 2010 by the Member States.

3 Directive 2009/123 on ship-source pollution (OJ L280/52) of 27.10.2008. It had to be transposed by 16 November 2010.

4 More particularly in Article 83. This will be further developed below in II A 4.

Although initially limited to the domain of environmental criminal law, the Commission apparently intends to broaden EU criminal law also to the area of economic law and more particularly to insider trading. The Directive on criminal sanctions for market abuse 2014/57/EU entered into force the 3 July 2014.[5] The idea is to introduce minimum rules on criminal offences which have to be transposed into national criminal law and applied by the criminal justice systems of the Member States. The reason for the Commission to come with this initiative is that today Member States' enforcement practices significantly diverge. The Commission argues that this may provide incentives for persons to carry out market abuse in Member States which do not provide for criminal sanctions for these offences or provide weak enforcement.

This Directive is in line with the policy of the Commission to increasingly introduce common EU minimum criminal law standards, arguing that only the criminal law can demonstrate social disapproval of a qualitatively different nature compared to administrative sanctions or compensation mechanisms under civil law.[6]

The goal of this chapter is to critically analyse this Directive concerning criminalisation of insider trading at EU level from a legal and from an economic perspective. We will argue that even if in particular circumstances the criminal law may be indicated, the question also arises whether it should be introduced at EU level. The economic theory of federalism, which analyses the division of labour between the Member States and the EU level, is used to analyse whether criminalisation should be implemented at EU level.[7] We further examine whether this Directive is consistent with fundamental principles of European criminal law. An alternative would obviously be to respect the subsidiarity principle and to allow Member States to decide on the necessity of criminalisation in particular circumstances.

This chapter hence contributes to the economic theory of federalism by indicating whether such a criminalisation should be imposed at a European or rather at a Member State level. This study therefore will have practical and policy implications as well since it allows to critically analyse insider trading, using economic analysis, on the Directive on criminal sanctions for market abuse.

The remainder this chapter will be structured as follows: the policybackground for harmonisation of criminal and insider trading laws in the EU, the contents of the Directive on criminal sanctions for market abuse are sketched (2). The study further addresses the question whether criminalisation of insider trading should be realised at EU or rather at member state level

5 Directive on criminal sanctions for market abuse 2014/57/EU (OJ L173/179) of 12.6.2014.

6 This motivation was *inter alia* explicitly used in the preamble to Directive 2008/99/EC on the protection of the environment through criminal law (OJ L328/28) of 6.12.2008.

7 For an overview of the economics of federalism see *inter alia* Van den Bergh, R., 2000. Towards an Institutional Legal Framework for Regulatory Competition in Europe, *Kyklos* 53, 435–466.

according to the economics of federalisation (3). Then the Directive is compared to fundamental principles of criminal law in order to identify a few problems of a qualitative nature (4). Section 5 concludes.

2. LEGAL AND POLICY BACKGROUND: CONTEXT OF THE DIRECTIVE ON CRIMINAL SANCTIONS FOR MARKET ABUSE

2.1. HARMONISATION OF CRIMINAL LAW IN THE EU

2.1.1. Criminal Law, a Traditional State Sovereignty Matter

Criminal law is one of the fundamental expressions of State sovereignty: the right to punish. It intrinsically expresses fundamental values of the society by determining the censurable behaviours. The criminal procedure is the process through which criminally sanctionnable conduct can be made an offence. Beyond that, the holding of a criminal trial and the realisation of criminal sentences might require and imply that certain fundamental freedoms be infringed.

Therefore, criminal law results in the confrontation of the State's right to punish and the guarantee of citizens' civil liberties. For these reasons, the rules relating to criminal law fall within the competence of the legislature. Parliamentary democratic oversight is strongly involved in its elaboration. This corresponds to the legality principle in criminal law which inter alia holds that the legislature should determine the conditions for criminal liability.

Indeed, criminal law actually embodies fundamental values of the society such as culture, religion, history, etc. Within the EU, it differs from one country to another. Consequently, as presented in the report of the European Securities and Markets Authority (ESMA) the same behaviour might not be equally punished in different Member States, procedures might not correspond to the same demands, and the nature of sanctions might diverge significantly.[8]

Before the entry into force of the Lisbon Treaty, introducing the Treaty on the Functioning of the European Union (TFEU) an explicit legal basis for ordering Member States to introduce criminal sanctions was lacking. There was therefore long time a hesitation of the European institutions to become active in this domain of the criminal law.

This changed with the decision of the Court of Justice of 13 September 2005 in case C-176/03 where the Court had argued that although 'as a general rule,

8 See ESMA, 26.04.2012. *Report: Actual Use of Sanctioning Powers under MAD, ESMA/2012/270*(European Securities and Market Authority, Paris).

neither criminal law nor the rules of criminal procedure fall within the community competence', 'the last-mentioned finding does not prevent the community legislature, when the application of effective, proportionate and dissuasive criminal penalties by the competent national authorities is an essential measure for combating serious environmental offences, from taking measures which relate to the criminal law of the Member States which it considers necessary in order to ensure that the rules which it lays down on environmental protection are fully effective'.[9] In a second decision of the Court of Justice of 23 October 2007 in case 176/03 the Court, however, specified: 'By contrast, and contrary to the submission of the Commission, the determination of the type and level of the criminal penalties to be applied does not fall within the community's sphere of competence'.[10] With that decision, it was made clear that within the conditions set by the decision of 13 September 2005 the Commission may prescribe the use of criminal penalties (if the necessity conditions are fulfilled and the topic falls within its sphere of competence). However, the EU level is clearly not competent, so it was held by the Court, to 'determine the type and level of the criminal penalties to be applied'.[11]

The European Commission has used the powers that were given to her as a result of this case law with the promulgation of the Environmental Crime Directive of 19 November 2008[12] and the directive on Ship-Source Pollution of 21 October 2009.[13] Both directives had already to be implemented by the end of 2010. Since then, the landscape has changed considerably as a result of the extension of the powers in the domain of criminal law under the Lisbon treaty.

2.1.2. *The Lisbon Treaty*

In 2009, the Lisbon Treaty[14] introduced specific competences for European Union in the domain of criminal law, providing for a new legal framework for criminal legislation and giving a strong role to the European Parliament, the European Council and the European Court of Justice. The new legal framework under the Lisbon Treaty aims at providing means to develop a consistent and coherent EU criminal law legislation. It allows the Member States to work

---

9 Par. 48 of the decision of the Court of Justice of 13 September 2005 in case C-176/03.

10 Par. 70 of the decision of the Court of Justice of 23 October 2007 in case 176/03.

11 For further details see Faure, M., 2008. The Continuing Story of Environmental Criminal Law in Europe after 23 October 2007, *European Energy and Environmental Law* 17, 68–75.

12 Directive 2008/99/EC on the protection of the environment through criminal law (OJ L328/28) of 6.12.2008.

13 Directive 2009/123/EC amending Directive 2005/35/EC on ship-source pollution and on the introduction of penalties for infringements (OJ L280/52) of 27.10.2009.

14 The Lisbon Treaty amended the Maastricht Treaty (Treaty on European Union) and the Treaty of Rome (Treaty establishing the European Community) which form the constitutional basis of the European Union. The Treaty of Rome was renamed the Treaty on the Functioning of the European Union (TFEU) (OJ C326/47) of 26.10.2012.

together with the Institutions[15] by providing national parliaments a stronger role in the field of criminal law than in the context of other EU policies.[16] They can give their views on proposals, and monitor the respect of the principle of subsidiarity.[17] Moreover, the Lisbon Treaty made the Charter of Fundamental Rights legally binding.[18]

Finally, when a Member State considers that a proposal dealing with criminal or criminal procedure touches upon fundamental aspects of its national criminal justice system it has the option to refer the proposal to the European Council.[19]

Article 83 of the Treaty on the Functioning of the European Union (TFEU) defines the substantive competences of the European Union in criminal matters by providing two specific legal basis for substantive criminal law.[20]

First of all, according to Article 83(1) of the Treaty on the Functioning of the European Union (TFEU),[21] the EU can adopt directives providing for minimum rules regarding the definition of criminal offences for the so-called listed "Euro crimes": terrorism, trafficking in human beings and sexual exploitation of women and children, illicit drug trafficking, illicit arms trafficking, money laundering, corruption, counterfeiting of means of payment, computer crime and organised crime. The Euro crimes are crimes that are considered as meriting an EU approach because of their serious nature and cross-border dimension.

---

15 COM(2011) 573 final of 20.9.2011, p.4.

16 See Protocol on the role of national parliaments in the European Union (OJ C83/203) of 30.3.2010.

17 OJ C 326/47 of 26.10.2012 art. 5 and Protocol on the application of the principles of subsidiarity and proportionality OJ C83/206 of 30 of March 2010, article 7(2): "Where reasoned opinions on a draft legislative act's non-compliance with the principle of subsidiarity represent at least one third of all the votes allocated to the national Parliaments in accordance with the second subparagraph of paragraph 1, the draft must be reviewed."

18 Communication from the Commission "Strategy for the effective implementation of the Charter of Fundamental Rights by the European Union" COM(2010) 573 final of 19.10.2010.

19 TFEU (OJ C326/47) of 26.10.2012 art. 83(3), Communication from the Commission to the European Parliament, the Council, the European Economic and Social Committee and the Committee of the Regions "Towards an EU Criminal Policy: Ensuring the effective implementation of EU policies through criminal law" COM(2011) 573 final of 20.09.2011, p.4.

20 Miettinen, S., 2012. *Criminal Law and Policy in the European Union*(Routledge). p.42.

21 TFEU (OJ C326/47) of 26.10.2012 art. 83(1): "The European Parliament and the Council may, by means of directives adopted in accordance with the ordinary legislative procedure, establish minimum rules concerning the definition of criminal offences and sanctions in the areas of particularly serious crime with a cross-border dimension resulting from the nature or impact of such offences or from a special need to combat them on a common basis. These areas of crime are the following: terrorism, trafficking in human beings and sexual exploitation of women and children, illicit drug trafficking, illicit arms trafficking, money laundering, corruption, counterfeiting of means of payment, computer crime and organised crime. On the basis of developments in crime, the Council may adopt a decision identifying other areas of crime that meet the criteria specified in this paragraph. It shall act unanimously after obtaining the consent of the European Parliament".

The Directive 2014/62/EU on the protection of the euro and other currencies against counterfeiting by criminal law[22] was adopted on the basis of this article.

Article 83(2) TFEU[23] allows the European Parliament and the Council, on a proposal from the Commission, to establish 'minimum rules with regard to the definition of criminal offences and sanctions if the approximation of criminal laws and regulations of the Member States proves essential to ensure the effective implementation of a Union policy in an area which has been subject to a harmonisation measure'.

In addition, article 325(4) of the Treaty provides for the specific possibility to take measures to fight against misuse of EU public money and to prevent fraud affecting the financial interests of the Union.

The Directive on criminal sanctions for market abuse, that constitutes the starting point for this contribution, is based on this new article 83(2) TFEU. In addition on 20 September 2011, the Commission issued a Communication 'Towards an EU Criminal Policy: Ensuring the effective implementation of EU policies through criminal law', intending to provide, inter alia, some specific guidance regarding article 83(2) of the TFEU.[24] It is mentioned that this article provides the possibility for EU institutions to determine which EU policies require the use of criminal law as an additional enforcement tool.

Article 83(2) explicitly requires a test of whether criminal law measures are 'essential' to achieve the goal of an effective policy implementation. According to the mentioned Communication on EU criminal policy, in order to establish that the effective implementation of a specific EU policy requires the use of criminal law, the Commission has to carry out an assessment of the national enforcement regimes in place, "based on clear factual evidence",[25] and of the added value of

22 Directive 2014/62/EU on the protection of the euro and other currencies against counterfeiting by criminal law (OJ L151/1) of 21.5.2014 replacing Council Framework Decision 2000/383/JHA.

23 TFEU (OJ C326/47) of 26.10.2012 art. 83(2): "If the approximation of criminal laws and regulations of the Member States proves essential to ensure the effective implementation of a Union policy in an area which has been subject to harmonization measures, directives may establish minimum rules with regard to the definition of criminal offences and sanctions in the area concerned. Such directives shall be adopted by the same ordinary or special legislative procedure as was followed for the adoption of the harmonization measures in question, without prejudice to Article 76".

24 COM(2011) 573 final of 20.9.2011, p. 6.

25 See COM(2011) 573 final of 20.9.2011, p. 8: "To establish the necessity for minimum rules on criminal law, the EU institutions need to be able to rely on clear factual evidence about the nature or effects of the crime in question and about a diverging legal situation in all Member States which could jeopardise the effective enforcement of an EU policy subject to harmonisation. This is why the EU needs to have at its disposal statistical data from the national authorities that allow it to assess the factual situation. As part of its follow up action, the Commission will develop plans to collect further statistical data and evidence to deal with the areas covered by Article 325(4) and Article 83(2)".

common EU minimum criminal law standards[26], taking in account the principles of necessity, proportionality[27] and subsidiarity. In this Communication, market abuse is the first policy area cited amongst the ones for which EU criminal law is desirable. Once the need for criminal law established, the next step concerns the concrete criminal measure to adopt at EU level.

Under article 83 of the Treaty, EU legislation is limited to 'minimum' rules on criminal law. Consequently, a full harmonisation is impossible. Moreover, the article 83(2) TFEU mentions that the objective to reach is an 'approximation of criminal laws and regulations of the Member States', meaning a reduction of the differences between the national systems.[28] Nevertheless, according to the principle of legal certainty and proportionality, it is important to clearly define what conduct may be considered criminal, as well as the result to be achieved through the implementation of EU legislation.

The concept of 'minimum' rules would gain to be clarified[29] to avoid any ambiguity. Regarding sanctions, EU criminal law can require Member States to take effective, proportionate and dissuasive criminal sanctions for a specific conduct. The Commission's interpretation of 'minimum rules' is clear: several documents specify that 'EU law sometimes specifically determines which types and/or levels of criminal sanctions are to be made applicable'.[30] In each case, the

---

26 See COM(2011) 573 of 20.9.2011, p. 3.

27 The Institutions have to establish a test of whether criminal law measures are "essential" to achieve the goal of an effective policy implementation It implies that the legislators need to analyse whether measures other than criminal law measures could not sufficiently ensure the Policy implementation and whether criminal law could address the problem more effectively; COM(2011) 573 of 20.9.2011, p. 7. Moreover, the condition of necessity applies on the level of deciding which criminal law; measures to include in a particular legislative instrument. The Article 49 of the Charter of Fundamental Rights "the severity of the penalty must not be disproportionate to the criminal offense" applies here; COM(2011) 573 of 20.9.2011, p. 8. See further Groenhuijsen, M., Ouwerkerk, J., 2013. *Ultima ration en criteria voor strafbaarstelling in Europees perspectief* (Kluwer, Deventer). p. 258.

28 COM(2011) 573 of 20.09.2011, p. 9.

29 See Miettinen, S., 2012. *Criminal Law and Policy in the European Union* (Routledge). p. 44: "The choice of instruments and their inherent limits will also remain a point of contention. Express provisions on approximation refer to directives as the legal instrument by which the Union may create minimum rules. Given substantial limitations to the directive as an instrument, and to the potential lack of direct effect to instruments containing minimum rules, the question arises whether any provisions on the new Area of Freedom, Security and Justice (AFSJ) may allow directly applicable rules on criminal law to be created in the form of Regulation, or whether either these or other competences ostensibly outside the AFSJ can be exercised to circumvent AFSJ references to directives. If the narrative on the development of EU criminal competences can be seen as a contest between the centralizing effects of EU law and the desire of the Member States to retain criminal law as a relatively decentralized policy area, then Lisbon has changed the rules but has not ended the game. What, for example, are 'minimum rules'?".

30 The possibility to make a proposal in the field of criminal law including type and level of criminal sanctions included in EU directive appears in the COM(2011) 573 final of 20.9.2011, p. 8: "Regarding sanctions, "minimum rules" can be requirements of certain sanction types (e.g. fines, imprisonment, disqualification), levels or the EU-wide definition of what are to be

EU instrument may only determine which sanctions have to be made 'at least' available to the judges in each Member State.[31]

2.2. HARMONISATION OF EU INSIDER TRADING LAW

The EU aims at creating a single common market[32], through harmonisation, towards an ideal of federation. Nevertheless, political and cultural differences persist. Moreover, member states are usually sceptical about giving total control to a central body. Consequently, the EU usually uses flexible legal instruments only binding in relation to the "result that is to be achieved"[33]: directives.[34] National regulators can thereby keep the control over implementation. The existing EU legislation in the domain of financial law is largely restricted to administrative sanctions and measures. Member States enjoy hence still considerable autonomy in the choice and application of sanctions at national level.

The harmonisation of the European Union securities regulation started in the 80's with a legislative framework for common market exchanges,[35] introducing

considered aggravating or mitigating circumstances"; It also appears in the Communication of the Commission on reinforcing sanctioning regimes in the financial services sector, COM(2010) 716 final of 8.12.2010, p. 14: "Any proposals in the field of criminal law should aim at ensuring appropriate coherence and consistency across different sectors, in particular when considering the type and level of criminal sanctions included in EU directives"; The European Commission page dedicated to the criminal law policy is also specifying that "The EU can adopt directives providing for minimum rules regarding the definitions of criminal offences, i.e. rules setting out which behaviour is considered to constitute a criminal act and which type and level of sanctions are applicable for such acts", *available at* http://ec.europa.eu/justice/criminal/criminal-law-policy/, accessed 21.7.2014.

31 COM(2011) 573 final of 20.9.2011, pp. 8–9.

32 Treaty of Amsterdam (OJ C340) of 10.11.1997 art. 2.

33 TFEU (OJ C326/47) of 26.10.2012 art. 249.

34 See COM(2010) 716 final of 8.12.2010: Previous to the reforms of the MAD, the European directives and regulations in place in the area of financial law dealt with four principal issues: (1) coordination of the power to impose sanctions between several Member States; (2) obligation for Member States to provide for the application of appropriate administrative sanctions and measures and ensure that they are effective, proportionate, and dissuasive; (3) sanctions for specific infringements; (4) provision for the authorities to publish the measures and sanctions under certain circumstances.

35 The Admission Directive, Council Directive 79/279/EEC (OJ 1979 L66/21) of 05.3.1979; the Listing Particular Directive, Council Directive 80/390/EEC (OJ 1980 L100/1) of 17.3.1980; the Interim Reports Directive, Council Directive 82/121/EEC (OJ 1982 L66/21) of 2.1982; the Major Share-holdings Directive, Council Directive 88/627/EEC (OJ 1988 L348) of 12.12.1988; consolidated in 2001 by the Consolidated Admission and Reporting Directive, Council Directive 2011/34/EC (OJ 2001 L184/1) of 28.5.2001; The 1985 White Paper, COM(85) 310 of 14.6.1985; the Single European Act (OJ 1987 L 169) of 29.6.1987; the Single Market Programme; the Undertaking for Collective Investments in Transferable Securities Directive, Council Directive 85/611/EEC (OJ 1985 L375/3) of 12.1985; the Public Offers Directive,

a model of mutual recognition and minimum harmonisation aimed at consolidating the internal market and opening the European market for investments. Amongst these measures, the 1989 Insider Dealing Directive[36] was the first to prohibit insider trading at EU level.

In 1999, the Commission adopted the Financial Action Service Plan (FASP).[37] The idea of this Plan was to promulgate 42 legislative measures, among which was the Market Abuse Directive (MAD).[38] This MAD was ultimately promulgated in 2003. Some years after the adoption of the FASP the so-called Lamfalussy process[39] gave place to the creation of a new first level general legislative framework for European financial markets,[40] complemented by a series of more detailed second level legislative measures,[41] providing technical details relative to the Market Abuse Directive.[42] The European Securities Committee (ESC)[43] and the Committee of European Securities Regulators (CESR)[44] were created.

Adopted in early 2003, the Market Abuse Directive (MAD) 2003/6/EC introduced a comprehensive framework to tackle insider dealing and market manipulation practices. In order to ensure the enforcement of Directive 2003/6/EC, Member States were required to implement appropriate administrative measures and sanctions. This requirement did not imply any consequences on Member States' criminal dispositions.

Council Directive 89/298/EEC (OJ 1989 L124) of 17.4.1989; Investment Service Directive, Council Directive 93/22/EEC (OJ 1993 L141) of 10.5.1993.

36 Council Directive 89/592/EEC (OJ 1989 L334) of 13.11.1989.

37 Financial services: Implementing the Framework For Financial Markets: Action Plan, COM(99) 232 of 11.05.1999.

38 Commission Directive 2003/6/EC of the European Parliament and of the Council on insider dealing and market manipulation of the 28.01.2003.

39 The Committee of Wise Men, Final Report of the Committee of Wise Men On The Regulation of European Securities Markets (2001).

40 First level legislation involve the EU Commission, Council and Parliament.

41 Second level legislation involve the EU Commission, the European Securities Committee and the Committee of European Securities Regulators.

42 Directive 2003/124/EC implementing Directive 2003/6/EC of the European Parliament and of the Council as regards the definition and public disclosure of inside information and the definition of market manipulation; Directive 2003/125/EC implementing Directive 2003/6/EC of the European Parliament and of the Council as regards the fair presentation of investment recommendations and the disclosure of conflicts of interest; Directive 2004/72/EC implementing Directive 2003/6/EC of the European Parliament and of the Council as regards accepted market practices; Regulation (EC) No. 2273/2003 on Market Abuse.

43 Commission Decision establishing the European Securities Committee, COM(2001) 1493 of 06.06.2001. The ESC is constituted of officials of Member States government and Commission officials.

44 Commission Decision establishing the Committee of European Securities Regulators, COM (2001) 1501 of 06.06.2001. The CESR is constituted of representatives of Member States' national regulators and Commission representatives.

Nevertheless, according to the Commission, the current system did not achieve the effective protection of the financial markets[45] as desired. In December 2010, the European Commission issued a communication on "Reinforcing sanctioning regimes in the financial services sector".[46]

The European Securities and Markets Authority (ESMA)[47] replaced the Committee of European Securities Regulation on the 1st of January 2011. ESMA's work on securities legislation aims at contributing to the development of a single rulebook in Europe by improving co-ordination and co-operation amongst securities regulators, as well as acting as an advisory group to assist the European Union Commission. ESMA is in charge of issuing guidance on the common operation of the Market Abuse Directive.

2.3. DIRECTIVE ON CRIMINAL SANCTIONS FOR MARKET ABUSE

The first aspect of this reform of the legislative framework for market abuse regulation at EU level consists of a Regulation,[48] which basically replaces the MAD and incorporates major elements of the Directives implementing it. This Regulation implies modifications to the prohibition, to the supervisory[49] and enforcement powers[50] as well as to the administrative measures and sanctions[51], directly applicable by the Member States. The Commission justified this choice with the fact that a Regulation is the most appropriate legal instrument to define the market abuse framework within the Union because it actually reduces the regulatory complexity related to the diversity of legislation across the Union.

---

45 Proposal for Directive on criminal sanctions for insider dealing and market manipulation COM(2011) 654 of 20.10.2011, p.3. Recitals in the preamble to the Directive on criminal sanctions for market abuse 2014/57/EU (OJ L173/179) of 12.6.2014.

46 Communication of the Commission on reinforcing sanctioning regimes in the financial services sector, COM(2010) 716.

47 Www.esma.europa.eu/.

48 Regulation (EU) No 596/2014 (OJ L173/1) of 12.6.2014.

49 Siems, M., Nelemans, M., 2012. The Reform of the EU Market Abuse Law: Revolution or Evolution, *The Maastricht Journal of European and Comparative Law* 19, 195–205, p. 10.

50 See Regulation (EU) No 596/2014 (OJ L173/1) of 12.6.2014 art. 23 "Powers of competent authorities", art. 25 "Obligation to cooperate", art. 26 "Cooperation with third country": Cross-border cooperation will be reinforced.

51 Regulation (EU) No 596/2014 (OJ L173/1) of 12.6.2014 art. 23 Chapter 5 "Administrative measures and sanctions", art.30: "(h) maximum administrative pecuniary sanctions of at least three times the amount of the profits gained or losses avoided because of the infringement, where those can be determined (...) (i) in respect of a natural person, maximum administrative pecuniary sanctions of at least € 5,000,000 (...) (j) in respect of legal persons, maximum administrative pecuniary sanctions of at least € 15,000,000 or 15% of the total annual turnover of the legal person according to the last available accounts approved by the management body".

Indeed, it would offer greater legal certainty for those subject to the legislation across the Union, introducing a harmonised set of core rules, thereby contributing to the functioning of the Single Market.[52]

Secondly, the Directive on criminal sanctions for market abuse was adopted on the basis of the article 83(2) TFEU.[53] The motivation is that today Member States use divergent criminal measures to enforce the prohibition of insider trading. The Commission argues that this may provide incentives for persons to carry out insider trading in Member States which provide weak measures for this offence.[54]

This Directive is in line with the policy of the Commission to increasingly introduce common EU minimum criminal law standards, arguing that only the criminal law can demonstrate social disapproval of a qualitatively different nature compared to administrative sanctions or compensation mechanisms under civil law.[55]

Because the Commission can only address criminal matters by the way of directives, it produced a Directive which only addresses approximation in insider trading criminal matters and general minimum rules.

The Directive requires Member States:

- to take the necessary measures to ensure that insider dealing constitutes a criminal offence (not the case in one country: Bulgaria)[56] …
- …when committed intentionally (Art.3) (not the case in 10 Member States: Cyprus, Germany, Denmark, Spain, Finland, Latvia, Malta, Netherlands, Sweden, United Kingdom)[57],
- to take the necessary measures to ensure that the criminal offences are subject to 'effective, proportionate and dissuasive' criminal sanctions (Art. 5),
- to ensure that insider trading is punishable by a maximum term of imprisonment of at least four years (Art.7) (Not the case 7 Member States:

52 Preamble to the Regulation (EU) No 596/2014 (OJ L173/1) of 12.6.2014 art. 23 "Powers of competent authorities".

53 Directive on criminal sanctions for market abuse 2014/57/EU (OJ L173/179) of 12.6.2014.

54 Recital 7 in the preamble to the Directive on criminal sanctions for market abuse 2014/57/EU (OJ L 173/179) of 12.6.2104.

55 Recital 6 in the preamble to the Directive on criminal sanctions for market abuse 2014/57/EU (OJ L173/179) of 12.6.2104. This was *inter alia* also mentioned in the preamble to Directive 2008/99/EC on the protection of the environment through criminal law (OJ L328/28) of 6.12.2008.

56 ESMA, 26.04.2012. *Report: Actual Use of Sanctioning Powers under MAD, ESMA/2012/270*(European Securities and Market Authority, Paris), p. 73.

57 Ibid. p.112 "Is proof of intent required in order to have a guilty verdict in a market abuse case? No: Cyprus, Germany, Denmark, Spain, Finland, Latvia, Malta, Netherlands, Sweden, United Kingdom".

Belgium, France, Lithuania, Luxembourg, The Netherlands, Estonia and Hungary)[58],

- to ensure that legal persons can be held liable for criminal insider trading (Art. 8) (not the case in 8 Member States: Bulgaria, Czech republic, Germany, Greece, Luxembourg, Poland, Portugal, Sweden).[59]

Moreover, the article 12 of the Directive holds that by 4 July 2018 the Commission should provide a report to the European Parliament and the Council on the application of the Directive and, if necessary, on the need to amend it, in particular with regard to the appropriateness of introducing common minimum rules on types and levels of criminal sanctions.[60]

3. CRIMINALISATION OF INSIDER TRADING AT A EU LEVEL?

The question addressed in this section is whether this criminal law should be mandated at EU level. Yet an analytical complication is that the question whether criminalisation should be promulgated at EU level cannot be seen separately from the question whether insider trading and market manipulation laws themselves should be harmonised at EU level.[61] The latter question is no longer an issue which will be addressed for the simple reason that insider trading has been regulated at EU level. However, the mere fact that the norm (in this case prohibition of insider trading) has been promulgated at EU level does not necessarily imply that the enforcement measure (criminal law) should be prescribed at EU level as well. Recently, van Zeben has rightly indicated that as far as the allocation of competences within a federal system like the EU is concerned, one should distinguish between competences for standard setting (making the norm) implementation and enforcement, whereby in both cases a choice between allocation to the central level or the Member State level based on

58 Ibid. p. 105: The maximum length of imprisonment for insider dealing violations is less than four years in Belgium, France, Lithuania, Luxembourg, The Netherlands, Estonia and Hungary.

59 Ibid. p. 73: "Market Abuse can not give rise to criminal sanctions: Bulgaria, Czech republic, Germany, Greece, Luxembourg, Poland, Portugal, Sweden".

60 See COM(2011) 573 final: Minimum rules with regards to the definition of sanctions, according to the Communication of the European Commission, "rule out the possibility of full harmonization" (p. 7) but at the same time "Regarding sanctions, "minimum rules" can be requirements of certain sanction types (e.g. fines, imprisonment, disqualification), levels or the EU-wide definition of what are to be considered aggravating or mitigating circumstances".

61 A similar problem arises when discussing the desirability of harmonization of procedural law. This issue is also strongly related to the harmonization of the substantive private rules as well. See on that issue. Visscher, L., 2012. *A Law and Economics View on Harmonization of Procedural Law*(Springer), pp. 65–91.

economic criteria would be possible.[62] The question therefore can be asked whether the mere fact that the norm itself (prohibition of insider trading) has been promulgated at EU level should necessarily imply that the method of enforcement (i.e. use of the criminal law) should be harmonised as well.[63]

These questions are addressed by first briefly looking at the economic criteria for centralisation (3.1), then looking at the issue from a European legal perspective by simply asking whether this Directive is actually necessary to solve a particular problem (3.2). Section 3.3 will address the contents of the Directive, more particularly by comparing it with fundamental principles of criminal law.

It should, however, be mentioned that it may be difficult to apply the economic criteria of federalism to the case of criminalisation for the simple reason that those criteria have been developed mainly to examine whether there would be arguments in favour of centralisation of normative legal standards (prohibition of insider trading), not so much for the question whether enforcement measures would have to be harmonised as well. In that respect, only the general need for harmonisation of the method of enforcement (criminalisation) is questioned.

3.1. ECONOMICS OF FEDERALISM

The economics of harmonisation provides a relevant framework for questioning whether harmonisation is desirable, depending on the characteristics of a certain domain. The assessment is made on the basis of three criteria: inter-jurisdictional externalities, jurisdictional competition and transaction costs. Internal markets and benefits of differentiation perspectives offer interesting complementary arguments.

3.1.1. *Transboundary Externalities*

Internationalisation of the world's securities market has challenged traditional notions of regulation and enforcement.[64] In order to ensure operational and

62 See Van Zeben, J., 2014. *Competence Allocation and Regulatory Functioning. A Study of the European Emission Trading Scheme* (Cambridge University Press).

63 Recently, Klip rightly held that at a European level the subsidiarity principle should therefore also be considered as a criterion for criminalization See Klip, A., 2012. European Criminal Policy, *European Journal of Crime, Criminal Law and Criminal Justice* 20, 6–7.

64 See Geiger, U., 1998. Harmonization of Securities Disclosure Rules in the Global Market – A Proposal *Fordham Law Review* 66, 1785–1836. pp.1786–1787. Choi, S. J., 2001. Assessing Regulatory Responses to Securities Market Globalization, *Theoretical Inquiries in Law* 2, 613–647. See IOSCO, 1998. *IOSCO Report: Causes, Effects and Regulatory Implications of Financial and Economic Turbulence in Emerging Markets* (Emerging Markets Committee of The International Organization of Securities Commissions). p.63: "What these developments suggest is that the environment of securities regulation no longer appears to be limited in

informational efficiency of their market, domestic regulators have to deal with cross-border cases. As a direct effect of the globalisation, financial and technological innovations, cross-border activities, cross-asset effects and broader financial and economic policy issues are changing.[65] However, this does not necessarily imply that Member States should be able to externalise harm to other Member States, for example if one Member State decided to criminalise insider trading when another would not. Externalisation would only be a reason for centralisation if Member States could, by not criminalising insider trading externalise the harm resulting from insider trading to other Member States. There is no evidence whatsoever that this is a serious risk.

3.1.2. *Race-to-the-Bottom*

A second argument is that there may be a race-to-the-bottom in the enforcement of insider trading laws. This scenario implies that some Member States would not be interested in seriously enforcing insider trading law, for instance by enforcing it through very weak mechanisms in order to attract particular managers of corporations that would be eager to engage in insider trading. There is, however, no evidence that such a race-for-the-bottom should take place in this geographical zone. Indeed, despite the numerous divergences, insider trading is actually criminalised in all of the Member States except for Bulgaria. Some, and more particularly Roberta Romano, have on the contrary advocated the likelihood of a race-to-the-top scenario.[66]

3.1.3. *Transaction Costs*

Divergences from one country to another regarding sanctions and enforcement of insider trading laws may create transaction costs for issuers and financial institutions when obtaining information, and when undertaking actions to comply with host countries regulation, in addition to complying with home

---

scope (...) A major implication for regulators in these jurisdictions therefore, is that they will have to consider whether the regulatory framework within which they operate has sufficient capacity and appropriate structure to accommodate a wider and more complex set of objectives". *Available at:* www.sc.com.my/clients/sccommy/Links/ioscosept98.pdf.

65 IOSCO, 1998. *IOSCO Report: Causes, Effects and Regulatory Implications of Financial and Economic Turbulence in Emerging Markets* (Emerging Markets Committee of The International Organization of Securities Commissions). p.63: "This has certain implications for securities regulators – and particularly for emerging market regulators. It is likely that they would be increasingly expected to deal with issues outside of their traditional scope of responsibilities, in particular, those involving cross-border activity, cross-asset effects and broader financial and economic policy issues".

66 Romano, R., 1985. Law as a Product: Some Pieces of the Incorporation Puzzle, *Journal of Law, Economics and Organization* 1, 225–283. Van den Bergh, R., Visscher, L., 2008. *Optimal Enforcement of Safety Law*(Rotterdam).

country regulations.[67] The costs associated to the divergence of regimes may reduce the advantages of investing internationally and may thereby prevent investors and companies from participating in the international securities market. From this point of view, harmonisation could be beneficial.[68] However, in the particular field of criminal insider trading matters, there is so far little empirical evidence supporting that substantial transaction cost savings could constitute a strong argument in favour of a harmonisation of enforcement method.

3.1.4. *Benefits of Differentiation*

Finally, economic analysis of harmonisation and law and economics of federalism have often pointed out the substantial benefits of differentiated legal rules. First of all, differentiated legal rules allow the satisfaction of heterogeneous preferences. In this respect, one advantage of decentralisation is to enable Member States to provide for rules which best serve the rules preferred by the local population.[69] As already mentioned, this dimension is particularly important in criminal matters. Another benefit of differentiated rules is that, through the application of different legal rules, substantial learning effects can be obtained.[70] A disadvantage of harmonisation at European level is that these learning effects would disappear.[71]

3.2. IS THE DIRECTIVE NECESSARY?

3.2.1. *Curing the Implementation Deficit?*

Of course, the perspective from the European Commission may be a totally different one than the economics of federalism. Starting point for the European Commission is not the economic theory that would address e.g. whether there

---

67 This is one of the arguments made by the Danish scholar Lando in favour of harmonised private law. Lando, O., 1993. *Die Regeln des Europäischen Vertragsrecht* (Nomos, Baden Baden). pp. 473–474.

68 Van den Bergh, R., Visscher, L., 2008. *Optimal Enforcement of Safety Law* (Rotterdam). Zhao, L., 2008. *Securities Regulation in the International Environment* (University of Glasgow, Glasgow). p. 101.

69 Van den Bergh, R., Visscher, L., 2008. *Optimal Enforcement of Safety Law* (Rotterdam). p.21. Romano, R., 1985. Law as a Product: Some Pieces of the Incorporation Puzzle, *Journal of Law, Economics and Organization* 1, 225–283. p. 281: "a centralized system could impose a welfare loss on firms, to the extent that it would be difficult to duplicate the important transaction-specific assets that serve to safeguard the interests of the parties".

70 See *inter alia* Van den Bergh, R., 2000. Towards an Institutional Legal Framework for Regulatory Competition in Europe, *Kyklos* 53, 435–466.

71 See Visscher, L., 2012. *A Law and Economics View on Harmonization of Procedural Law* (Springer), pp. 84–85.

are interjurisdictional externalities or a race-to-the-bottom, but whether criminal law is needed to encourage the compliance with EU directives, in this case concerning insider trading. This idea to criminalise insider trading should hence be seen within the context of the general worry at EU level that there is a considerable implementation deficit with respect to EU law, although this is stronger in some areas than in others. Therefore, a major focus of European law during the past thirty years has been on the issue how implementation of European law can be improved by requiring a correct implementation from Member States. In this respect, we can e.g. point at evolutions in case law:

- Although Member States remain free in the choice of instruments for the implementation of a directive, case law holds that these sanctions in case of a violation of implementing legislation should at least be effective, proportional and dissuasive.[72] Hence, one can now find in many directives the obligation for Member States to provide sanctions which are 'effective, proportionate and dissuasive'.[73]
- Case law also held that the lack of effective prosecution against violators of implementing legislation can be considered as a violation of European law.[74] Hence, Europe has increasingly received effective remedies to cope with the implementation deficit. However, most recently, starting with the environmental crimes directives we mentioned in the introduction, the EU now also wishes to cure the implementation deficit by forcing Member States to choose a particular type of sanction, in this particular case the criminal law.[75] The assumption is hence that the implementation deficit is largely due to an enforcement deficit at Member State level. The question can, however, be asked whether a harmonisation of the criminal law, as currently proposed, is indeed necessary to guarantee a correct implementation of European law and in this particular case the Insider Trading Directive.

An ESMA report presents enforcement of insider trading laws data about 15 Member States for which the information was available for the years 2008, 2009 and 2010.[76] As far as insider dealing is concerned, all the Member States provide

---

72 See ECJ 21 September 1989, case C-68/88 (Greek Corn).

73 This is also the formula used in article 7 of the Directive on criminal sanctions for market abuse 2014/57/EU (OJ L173/179) of 12.6.2104.

74 ECJ 9 December 1997, case C-265/95 (Spanish Strawberries).

75 A few years ago, Corstens and Pradel, two leading legal scholars in criminal law in Europe, still wrote: 'Such a method requiring Member States to use criminal penalties is compatible with neither the character of a directive, nor the opinion that the communities do not have authority to require Member States to impose criminal penalties'. This statement was obviously written in a time before the Lisbon Treaty. See Corstens, G., Pradel, J., 2002. *European Criminal Law* (Kluwer Law International, The Hague).

76 ESMA, 26.04.2012. *Report: Actual Use of Sanctioning Powers under MAD, ESMA/2012/270* (European Securities and Market Authority, Paris).

criminal sanctions except for Bulgaria.[77] Moreover, one can observe that the 15 countries for which data is available display a total number of 155 criminal sanctions[78] imposed over the entire period; higher than the total of 101 administrative sanctions. This information as such does not provide any indication on the effectiveness of the enforcement system as it is currently employed in the Member States. In order to know whether there is an enforcement deficit one would also need information on the number of violations, which is actually lacking. The data provided by ESMA hence do not as such support a finding that the enforcement of insider trading prohibition in the Member States would currently show large deficiencies.

3.2.2. *Effectiveness Doubtful*

All Member States, with the exception of Bulgaria, do have criminal sanctions, but that there may be considerable differences in modalities of sanctions. The question arises whether that is necessarily a problem. Sanctions do not only differ between Member States as far as insider trading is concerned, but for many other crimes as well. This very often has to do with the legislative tradition concerning criminal law in the various Member States. However, these differences do not indicate that the system of enforcement in one Member State would necessarily be more effective than in another. In this respect, it should be stressed that the sanctions provided for in legislation often just provide for the maximum penalties, but are not related to what is effectively imposed by judges. There would, from an economic perspective, only be a problem if the sanctions provided in legislation would be of such a nature that it is, taking the economic criteria into account, impossible to impose effective sanctions for insider trading in practice.

Finally, it should also be stressed that the current Directive will, at least in the first phase, imply little change. The Directive will merely force Member

77 Bulgaria does not provide criminal sanctions for market manipulation either. See Document of the Council of Europe, 'Bulgaria Progress report and written analysis by the Secretariat of Core Recommendations', p.6: "According to the Bulgarian authorities, at present, a new Concept for Criminal Policy of the Republic of Bulgaria was adopted in July 2010. The above mentioned Concept envisages the elaboration and adoption of a new Penal Code. One of the main purposes of the new Penal Code is to address the necessity to criminalize modern types of criminal activity, including those provided for under the international agreements undertaken by the Republic of Bulgaria. The timescale for the drafting and adoption of the new Penal Code is estimated to be 2014.", It is understood that market manipulation and insider trading are taken into consideration in the concept of the new Penal Code; *available at* www.coe.int/t/dghl/monitoring/moneyval/Evaluations/Progress%20reports%202y/MONEYVAL(2011)5_ProgRep2_BLG.pdf.

78 ESMA, 26.04.2012. *Report: Actual Use of Sanctioning Powers under MAD, ESMA/2012/270* (European Securities and Market Authority, Paris). pp. 41, 91, 111: Number of monetary and non-monetary sanctions imposed on natural and legal persons.

States towards criminalisation which, with the exception of Bulgaria, all Member States already do. Regarding the modalities of this criminalisation, for all other Member States, as far as the sanctions are concerned, two things may change. First the Directive requires to provide for criminal liability of legal persons (which is not the case in 8 Member States currently in Europe).[79] Second, the Directive requires the establishment of "intent" to prove a guilty criminal insider trading (which is not the case in 10 Member States).[80] Third, the Directive requires a punishment of a maximum term of imprisonment of at least four years (not the case in 7 Member States).[81] The remaining differences will hence remain into existence and would only change if the European Commission would use its powers according to article 12, introducing common minimum rules on the types and levels of criminal sanctions. However, even if that were the case, one always has to take into account that it still will be impossible to constrain the prosecution policy of public prosecutors nor the discretionary powers of the judiciary as far as the application of penalties is concerned. Even if one were hence, according to article 12, to harmonise the rules on types and levels of criminal sanctions, this may to a large extent remain a symbolic window dressing operation that should not necessarily change anything in the practice of the Member States.

It can therefore be concluded that this attempt to harmonise the method of enforcement of insider trading laws through criminalisation at a EU level will be largely symbolic with limited effects as far as the sanctions that will be imposed in practice on insider trading are concerned.

3.2.3. *No Convincing Justification*

The motivation provided by the European Commission to justify criminalisation at EU level can also be criticised. A first argument in favour of criminal sanctions at EU level is that 'the sanctions currently in place to fight market abuse offences are lacking impact and are insufficiently dissuasive which results in ineffective enforcement of the Directive'.[82] In line with this argument, the Directive supports that 'the adoption of administrative sanctions by Member States has proven to be insufficient to ensure compliance with the rules on preventing and fighting market abuse' and that 'the availability of criminal sanctions for at least

---

79 Ibid. p. 73: Bulgaria, Czech Republic, Germany, Greece, Luxembourg, Poland, Portugal and Sweden.

80 Ibid. p. 112: "Is proof of intent required in order to have a guilty verdict in a market abuse case? No: Cyprus, Germany, Denmark, Spain, Finland, Latvia, Malta, Netherlands, Sweden, United Kingdom".

81 Ibid. p. 105: The maximum length of imprisonment for insider dealing violations is less than four years in Belgium, France, Lithuania, Luxembourg, The Netherlands, Estonia and Hungary.

82 COM(2011) 654 final, p. 2.

serious market abuse across the Union, cannot be sufficiently achieved by the Member States'.[83]

First, there is no empirical basis for this strong statement.[84] Second, since we mentioned that the Directive merely forces criminalisation in one Member State, introduces criminal liability for legal entities in 8 Member States, introduces a higher threshold for mens rea (intend) for 10 Member States, and increase the maximum term of imprisonment for 7 Member States it remains a puzzle how the Commission thinks that merely providing theses changes will change the 'ineffective enforcement of the Directive'. Third, the Directive argues that the current 'different approaches by Member States undermine the uniformity of conditions of operation in the internal market' and even argues that perpetrators would be able 'to carry market abuse in jurisdictions which do not provide for criminal sanctions for those offences'.[85] Basically, the Directive here relies on a race-to-the-bottom argument. As we mentioned, the only Member State for which this holds true is Bulgaria. However, the mere absence of criminalisation should not by definition mean that Bulgaria does not effectively enforce the prohibition of insider trading. In the hypothesis of the Directive, Bulgaria should then become a 'insider traders haven' for which there is no empirical proof whatsoever. Fourth, the Directive stresses the importance of criminal law 'to demonstrate a stronger form of social disapproval compared to administrative penalties (...) and send a message to the public and to potential offenders that competent authorities take such behaviour very seriously'.[86] This shows that the Commission believes strongly in the 'stigma' effect of the criminal law on which economic literature had serious doubts. Moreover, since 27 out of 28 Member States already had criminal law in place before the entry into force of the Directive on criminal sanctions for market abuse, questions can be asked on the added value of European action in this respect. Finally, the importance of criminal law is also stressed to 'improve deterrence as they demonstrate to potential offenders that the authorities take serious enforcement action'. Again, this strongly stresses the symbolic value, not only of criminalisation, but also of criminalisation at EU level. All in all, the main arguments of the Directive are of abstract and symbolic nature since they mainly rely on consultations and

83 Recital 6 in the preamble to the Directive on criminal sanctions for market abuse 2014/57/EU (OJ L173/179) of 12.6.2104.

84 The Directive refers for instance to the evaluation of the national regimes for administrative sanctions under Directive 2003/6/EC. The call for evidence on the review of the Market Abuse Directive launched by the Commission on 20 April 2009 actually mainly focused on the scope of the Market Abuse Directive and did not particularly contribute to the assessment of the necessity to introduce criminal sanctions at EU level.

85 Recital 7 in the preamble to the Directive on criminal sanctions for market abuse 2014/57/EU (OJ L 173/179) of 12.6.2104.

86 Recital 6 in the preamble to the Directive on criminal sanctions for market abuse 2014/57/EU (OJ L173/179) of 12.6.2104.

conferences.[87] Furthermore the impact assessments provided together with the Directive provides a weak support.[88] In that respect, questions can be asked on the real effectiveness of this entire enterprise. This aspect is particularly sensitive since it raises some concerns regarding the compliance with the legal basis of the Directive. Indeed, article 83(2) TFEU calls for a clear reliance on empirical data regarding the essential need of introducing criminal sanctions.[89] The approximate interpretation of the Article 83(2) TFEU is criticisable since the first Directive adopted on this basis opens the field.

3.2.4. Inconsistency with European Policy

Finally, it should also be mentioned that it is remarkable that the European Commission is in this area (of insider dealing and market manipulation) stressing the need to introduce criminal sanctions, whereas in another domain, more particularly competition policy, apparently another strategy is followed. Competition policy in Europe has for years been based on an administrative sanctioning by the European Commission without criminal penalties. Many have stressed the importance to introduce criminal penalties to be applied to severe violations of competition law, like hard core cartels,[90] but these voices have not been heard.[91]

Moreover, in the area of competition policy increasing attention is now given to possibilities of private enforcement and methods to provide incentives to potential plaintiffs to bring suits in the area of competition law (like introducing treble damages, class actions etc.) are now also discussed in the area of competition policy.

It is striking that in this related domain of insider dealing the European discussion on enforcement mechanisms seems to focus on criminalisation and not e.g. on ways of improving private enforcement in order to increase

---

87 Miglietti, M., 2013. The New EU Criminal Law Competence in Action: The Proposal for a Directive on Criminal Sanctions for Insider Dealing and Market Manipulation, *IES Working Paper 5/2013*, 1–37. pp. 27, 29: "it is possible to affirm that the consultations and the conferences did not provide a 'clear factual evidence' of 'the added value of common EU minimum criminal law standards'".

88 Commission Staff Working Paper Impact Assessment SEC(2011) 1217 final of 20.10.2011, p.57: "In accordance with article 83 (2) of the Treaty (TFEU), the introduction of a requirement for criminal sanctions to address market abuse *is likely to lead* to increased successful prosecution of market abuse offences and to contribute to ensuring the effective functioning of the internal market". This statement underlines the fact that the "necessity requirement" of the article 83(2) is not fulfilled. See ibid. p. 27.

89 COM(2011) 573 final of 20.9.2011, p. 6.

90 Wils, W., 2005. Is Criminalization of EU Competition Law the Answear?, *World Competition* 28, 117–159.

91 For an overview of the enforcement of EU competition policy see Van den Bergh, R., Faure, M., 2011. *Critical Issues in the Enforcement of the Anti-Monopoly Law in China: a Law and Economics Perspective*(Edward Elgar, Cheltenham). pp. 54–75.

deterrence. This not only shows that there is apparently little consistency in the general enforcement strategy at EU level, but also that the Commission should probably learn from the experience with competition policy to look at ways, other than criminalisation, to improve enforcement. In that way, criminal law could truly remain an *ultimum remedium*. Moreover, the introduction of criminalisation at EU level may not only be ineffective and unnecessary; it also conflicts with fundamental principles of criminal law.

4. CONFLICTS WITH PRINCIPLES OF CRIMINAL LAW

The question can equally be asked to what extent the contents of the proposal for a directive aiming at the criminalisation of insider trading is compatible with substantive principles of criminal law. There are increasingly general principles of criminal law that are defined in legal doctrine. An interesting attempt in that respect is for example provided by the Manifesto on European Criminal Policy[92] published in 2009 by the European Criminal Policy Initiative aimed at clarifying the major principles of criminal law rooted in European law: the principle of a legitimate purpose, the *ultima ratio* principle, the principle of guilt, the principle of legality, the principle of subsidiarity, and the principle of coherence. We will now examine to what extent the current proposal of the European Commission corresponds with those fundamental principles.

4.1. THE PRINCIPLE OF PROPORTIONALITY

From an overall point of view, the principles of legitimate purpose, the *ultima ratio* principle and the principle of guilt may be perceived as directly emanating from the principle of proportionality.

First, of all the principle of proportionality is a fundamental principle of European law stated in the third paragraph of Article 5 TFEU 'Any action by the Community shall not go beyond what is necessary to achieve the objectives of this Treaty.' From this principle directly results the requirement of a legitimate purpose principle: the resort to criminalisation at EU level could be regarded as proportionate and legitimate only if a fundamental legal interest, worthy of protection against socially harmful conduct of significant degree,[93] can be

92 *Available at* www.zis-online.com/dat/artikel/2009_12_383.pdf, accessed 21.7.2014.

93 Kaiafa-Gbandi, M., 2011. The Importance of Core Principles of Substantive Criminal Law for a European Criminal Policy Respecting Fundamental Rights and the Rule of Law, *European Criminal Law Review* 1, 6–33. p. 15: "The requirement of a fundamental interest that is harmed in a socially significant way would be of particular usefulness in determining when the EU shall be justified in employing criminal law means to effectively implement its policies

justified. In that respect the need to reach the objectives of the EU cannot constitute a good motivation for harmonisation. Of course, it should be observed that fundamental legal interests may eventually differ and diverge at national and European levels.

Second, the *ultima ratio* principle is absolutely major in this context. The EU is now competent to bind its Member States as to the minimum standards of criminal law to larger extent than ever thanks to the new article 83(2). These new competences should call for great caution. With respect to the application of the *ultima ratio* principle any criminal law proposal at EU level should come with a requisite burden to ensure that it is used as a last resort to protect fundamental interests.[94] Setting minimum standards in criminal matters should be a last resort, meaning that the EU tried every other solution before. The question arises whether administrative sanctions could not be at least equally effective to ensure the effective implementation of the Union's policy in the insider trading field. Wouldn't administrative law be sufficient to ensure an equivalent protection? Previous legislative initiatives should be carefully assessed. The adoption of criminal dispositions at EU level should be based on the experience that other sanctions are insufficient.[95] Criminal law should be used as an additional means. Finally, some commentators argue that harmonisation may be perceived as encouraging a movement towards an increased repression[96], making criminal law a principle remedy.

In that respect, it should be noted that the fact that the Regulation provides for administrative sanctions for non-criminal actions is consistent with the idea that there is a softer alternative to criminal law at EU level. However, both the Regulation and the Directive were adopted at the same time. This may demonstrate that all the means were not explored and tried *before* resorting to criminal law. Improvement of the 2003 MAD does not automatically imply the need to resort to criminal law.

Third, according to the principle of guilt (*nulla poena sine culpa*), a criminal sanction can only be imposed when a criminal act has affirmatively been proven

---

under article 83(2) TFEU". Elholm, T., 2011. The Manifesto on European Criminal Policy in 2011, *European Criminal Law Review* 1, 86–103. p. 87: "The legislative powers of the EU in relation to criminal law issues should only be exercised in order to protect fundamental interests if: (1) These interests can be derived from the primary legislation of the EU; (2) The Constitutions of the Member States and the fundamental principles of the EU Charter of Fundamentals Rights are not violated, and (3) The activities in question could cause significant damage to society or individuals".

94 Kaiafa-Gbandi, M. Ibid. The Importance of Core Principles of Substantive Criminal Law for a European Criminal Policy Respecting Fundamental Rights and the Rule of Law, 6–33. p. 18.

95 Böse, M.Ibid. The Principle of Proportionality and the Protection of Legal Interests, 35–43. p. 34.

96 Asp, P. Ibid. The Importance of the Principles of Subsidiarity and Coherence in the Development of EU Criminal Law, 44–55. p. 44: "criminal law is a legal area which, by its very nature, is repressive, which (in turn) means that harmonization in this area will – at least in practice – focus on increased repression".

to be the product of a "guilty mind" resulting from "*mens rea*". At a European level this principle results from article 48 of the Charter of Fundamental Rights of the EU.[97] Therefore, the principle of guilt seems to be the one that guided the Commission to require Member States to establish "intent" to criminally sanction insider trading and to provide for criminal liability of legal persons. As already mentioned, the level of culpability required to prove a guilty criminal insider trading varies across the different Member States from "negligence" to "intent". Moreover, some Member States reject the criminal responsibility of legal persons partially because of its incompatibility to their conception of the principle of guilt.[98] Finally, a part of the literature supports that the regime of mens rea and the criminal liability of legal persons should be decided at a national level.[99] Therefore, the dispositions contained in the proposal for Directive relative to criminal liability of legal entities and the degree of culpability (intent) to be held liable may be sensible in practice in some Member States. Furthermore, the EU already made exceptions in the past regarding this aspect in the Convention on the Protection of the European Union's financial interests and accepted that "the intentional nature of an act or omission (…) may be inferred from objective, factual circumstances"[100] (Art. 1§4) and that "each Member States shall take the necessary measures to allow (these persons) to be declared criminally liable in accordance with the principles defined by its national law"[101] (Art. 3).

---

97 Charter of Fundamental Rights of the European Union (OJ C326/391) of 26.10.2012 art. 48: "Everyone who has been charged shall be presumed innocent until proved guilty according to law".

98 Kaiafa-Gbandi, M., 2011. The Importance of Core Principles of Substantive Criminal Law for a European Criminal Policy Respecting Fundamental Rights and the Rule of Law, *European Criminal Law Review* 1, 6–33. p.31. See "Manifesto on European Criminal Policy" ZIS 2009, p. 697 et seq. *available at* www.zis-online.com/dat/artikel/2009_12_383.pdf, accessed 21.7.2014, p. 711: "There are framework decisions that obligate the Member States to impose sanctions on legal person. However, it should be positively noted that as yet it is up to the Member States whether they fulfill this obligation by means of criminal law".

99 Elholm, T.Ibid. The Manifesto on European Criminal Policy in 2011, 86–103. p. 88: "This does not predetermine the answer to the question of whether legal entities can be held criminally liable. There is a decisive difference between guilt of an individual and that of a legal entity. Rules concerning criminal liability of legal entities must thus be elaborated on the basis of criminal law provisions at the national level", p.96: "In some Member States rules on criminal liability for legal persons would not be compatible with their concept of the principle of guilt, forming the basis of their national criminal law system There are framework decisions that obligate the Member States to impose sanctions on legal person. However, it should be positively noted that as yet it is up to the Member States whether they fulfil this obligation by means of criminal law".

100 Convention on the Protection of the European Union's financial interests (OJ 1995 C316) of 27.11.1995 art. 1(4).

101 Convention on the Protection of the European Union's financial interests (OJ 1995 C316) of 27.11.1995 art. 3 "Criminal liability of heads of businesses".

4.2. PRINCIPLES OF SUBSIDIARITY AND COHERENCE

According to the article 5(3) TFEU "the Union shall, in areas that do not fall within its exclusive competence, act only if and in so far as the objectives of the proposed action cannot be sufficiently achieved by the Member States." Stated differently, as far as the national legislator is capable of dealing effectively with a given issue the European legislator should not intervene in criminal matters. This principle insures the protection of the differentiated legal rules and the respect of heterogeneous preferences. As already mentioned these dimensions are of particular importance in criminal matters since they reflect national identities. It is a way to restrict the EU competence and is related to the principle of coherence that states that one shall not, without good reasons, disturb or interfere with the coherence of the national criminal law systems.[102] In the case where instruments dealing with criminal matters are enacted, the article 4(2) TFEU calls for paying a special attention to the coherence of the national criminal law systems, part of the national identities of the Member States. The coherence of the criminal law system relies upon the idea that the entire regime is rooted in historical and cultural national values, particularly sensitive to external influence.[103] This principle is closely related to the notions of democracy, self-governance and State sovereignty. In that respect, it seems that no sufficiently convincing arguments were advanced so far to support the failure of national enforcement of criminal insider trading laws.

The above analysis allows to deduce the following conclusions: criminal law being the stringiest mechanism of control that deeply affects fundamental civil liberties, any initiative in that field of the Commission should therefore be consistent with the principles governing the introduction of substantive criminal rules at EU level. In that respect the Directive on criminal sanctions may be criticised in various aspects. The fact that the Directive was adopted at the same time as the Regulation may also be problematic regarding the principle of proportionality and the principle of *ultima ratio*. The principles of subsidiarity and coherence can be raised as principles supporting the need to have a differentiation of legal rules.

To conclude, the point is not to contest the legitimacy of the EU in criminal matters but to enlighten the importance to restrain the Directive to the strict

102 Asp, P., 2011. The Importance of the Principles of Subsidiarity and Coherence in the Development of EU Criminal Law, *European Criminal Law Review* 1, 44–55. p.46: "The principle of subsidiarity is founded on the idea that society is built from the bottom to the top and not the other way around. This means that the central – or in the case of the EU: the supranational – authorities should fulfil only those tasks that cannot be fulfilled effectively by actions on a decentralized, local or regional, level. In this way one ensures that decisions will be taken as closely to the citizens as is possible having regard to the demands of society".

103 Ibid. p. 44. Elholm, T., 2011. The Manifesto on European Criminal Policy in 2011, *European Criminal Law Review* 1, 86–103. p.91: "criminal law is also a value system, and as such it is a component part of the 'national identities' of the Member states".

minimum in order to facilitate its implementation in a manner that respects civil liberties and citizens preferences. The Treaty of Lisbon mentions the guarantee of the fundamental rights of the citizen as a goal. The Directive should therefore reflect this goal and should be consistent with such guarantee in practice.

Finally, it should be mentioned that Member States are able to oppose any future proposals for amendment of the proposal for a Directive by invoking the emergency clause of article 83(3) TFEU. Indeed, when legislating on substantive criminal law or criminal procedure, Member States can express their opposition and refer to the European Council[104] if they consider that the proposed Directive touches upon fundamental aspects of their national criminal justice system[105], or breach of one of the fundamental principles of criminal law outlined above.

5. CONCLUDING REMARKS

The Directive on criminal sanctions for market abuse has been critically analysed in this paper. The core of the Directive is that insider dealing and market manipulation as defined in have to be criminalised when committed as an intentional offence and that criminal liability of legal entities will have to be provided. Maximum terms of imprisonment are set up. There is currently little evidence that the enforcement of insider trading laws at Member State level would be ineffective, as far as 27 out of the 28 EU Member States have criminal law to back-up insider trading legislation. Hence, the added value of European legislation in this respect is limited. Hence, the mere imposition of criminal sanctions at EU level will of course not guarantee that problems with the effective enforcement of insider trading law, that would currently exist in the Member States, would be solved. Moreover, the Commission refers to a current 'ineffective enforcement' of insider trading law, but there is not much empirical proof that is provided to back this up. If the Commission would refer to the fact that there are few cases, then the problem of course is that merely forcing criminalisation via the EU level will as such not solve that problem. Furthermore, looking at the specific provisions proposed at EU level, the Directive appears criticisable from a qualitative point of view since it is not entirely consistent with the principles governing the introduction of substantive criminal rules at EU level, more particularly the *ultima ratio* principle, the principle of guilt and the principles of subsidiarity and coherence.

Within the scope of this contribution we could only provide a critical analysis of the criminalisation of insider trading at the European level. Our conclusion is

104 COM(2011) 573final.

105 Denmark is not participating in newly adopted measures on substantive criminal law, while the United Kingdom and Ireland only participate in the adoption and application of specific instrument after a decision to "opt" in.

that economic theory casts doubt on whether there is effectively a need of imposing criminal sanctions at European level; the contents of the proposal is moreover to a large extent incompatible with fundamental principles of criminal law. There are, however, other related questions which we could not address. One, highly debated issue in law and economics literature is whether one should prohibit insider trading at all. That is a question which we did on purpose not address for the simple reason that the European Union already took the decision to prohibit insider trading. We hence took that as a given and merely concentrated on the question whether criminalisation at EU level was necessary. However, one could equally pay attention to the more fundamental question whether a criminalisation of insider trading is warranted at all. We already briefly touched upon that issue by pointing at the fact that alternative mechanisms to enforce an insider trading prohibition, like for example private enforcement or the application of administrative sanctions (more particularly administrative fines) may provide appropriate remedies as well. However, we do realise that there may be more to say on the appropriate division of labour between the various enforcement mechanisms and more particularly between administrative enforcement and criminal enforcement. This and other related questions are undoubtedly interesting for further research into this fascinating area.

BIBLIOGRAPHY

Asp, P., 2011. The Importance of the Principles of Subsidiarity and Coherence in the Development of EU Criminal Law, *European Criminal Law Review* 1, 44–55.

Böse, M., 2011. The Principle of Proportionality and the Protection of Legal Interests, *European Criminal Law Review* 1, 35–43.

Choi, S. J., 2001. Assessing Regulatory Responses to Securities Market Globalization, *Theoretical Inquiries in Law* 2, 613–647.

Corstens, G., Pradel, J., 2002. *European Criminal Law*(Kluwer Law International, The Hague).

Elholm, T., 2011. The Manifesto on European Criminal Policy in 2011, *European Criminal Law Review* 1, 86–103.

ESMA, 26.04.2012. *Report: Actual Use of Sanctioning Powers under MAD, ESMA/2012/270*(European Securities and Market Authority, Paris).

Faure, M., 2008. The Continuing Story of Environmental Criminal Law in Europe after 23 October 2007, *European Energy and Environmental Law* 17, 68–75.

Geiger, U., 1998. Harmonization of Securities Disclosure Rules in the Global Market – A Proposal *Fordham Law Review* 66, 1785–1836.

Groenhuijsen, M., Ouwerkerk, J., 2013. *Ultima ration en criteria voor strafbaarstelling in Europees perspectief* (Kluwer, Deventer).

IOSCO, 1998. *IOSCO Report: Causes, Effects and Regulatory Implications of Financial and Economic Turbulence in Emerging Markets* (Emerging Markets Committee of The International Organization of Securities Commissions).

Kaiafa-Gbandi, M., 2011. The Importance of Core Principles of Substantive Criminal Law for a European Criminal Policy Respecting Fundamental Rights and the Rule of Law, *European Criminal Law Review* 1, 6–33

Klip, A., 2012. European Criminal Policy, *European Journal of Crime, Criminal Law and Criminal Justice* 20, 6–7.

Lando, O., 1993. *Die Regeln des Europäischen Vertragsrecht* (Nomos, Baden Baden).

Miettinen, S., 2012. *Criminal Law and Policy in the European Union* (Routledge).

Miglietti, M., 2013. The New EU Criminal Law Competence in Action: The Proposal for a Directive on Criminal Sanctions for Insider Dealing and Market Manipulation, *IES Working Paper 5/2013*, 1–37.

Romano, R., 1985. Law as a Product: Some Pieces of the Incorporation Puzzle, *Journal of Law, Economics and Organization* 1, 225–283.

Siems, M., Nelemans, M., 2012. The Reform of the EU Market Abuse Law: Revolution or Evolution, *The Maastricht Journal of European and Comparative Law* 19, 195–205.

Van den Bergh, R., 2000. Towards an Institutional Legal Framework for Regulatory Competition in Europe, *Kyklos* 53, 435–466.

Van den Bergh, R., Faure, M., 2011. *Critical Issues in the Enforcement of the Anti-Monopoly Law in China: a Law and Economics Perspective* (Edward Elgar, Cheltenham).

Van den Bergh, R., Visscher, L., 2008. *Optimal Enforcement of Safety Law* (Rotterdam).

Van Zeben, J., 2014. *Competence Allocation and Regulatory Functioning. A Study of the European Emission Trading Scheme* (Cambridge University Press).

Visscher, L., 2012. *A Law and Economics View on Harmonization of Procedural Law* (Springer).

Wils, W., 2005. Is Criminalization of EU Competition Law the Answear?, *World Competition* 28, 117–159.

Zhao, L., 2008. *Securities Regulation in the International Environment* (University of Glasgow, Glasgow).

CHAPTER 9
THE CRIMINALISATION OF EU COMPETITION LAW

Sabina ZGAGA

1. INTRODUCTION

European and national competition law prohibits acts restricting competition and thereby defines the limit between the lawful and unlawful acts of competition. According to the legal theory, the primary rules are, defining the required action or the prohibited action.[1] European and national competition law, however, includes also secondary rules,[2] which define the unlawful restriction of competition and sanctions for such conduct. According to the Slovenian Prevention of the Restriction of Competition Act-1 (ZPOmK-1)[3] the unlawful restriction of competition and, thereby violations of primary rules are classified as misdemeanours, for which the undertakings and their responsible persons could be held responsible.[4] Violation of competition law could be classified also as a criminal act, defined by Slovenian national criminal legislation or potentially even European law. Two separate, but also intertwined forms of legal responsibility could therefore arise in the case of the restriction of competition.

This chapter aims to analyse the arguments for regulating and enforcing criminal responsibility in addition to the responsibility for misdemeanours in cases of unlawful restriction of competition in Slovenia and to critically assess current Slovenian legislation. Slovenia namely already defines unlawful restriction of competition as a criminal act in the Criminal Code-1 (KZ-1).[5]

1 M. Pavčnik, *Teorija prava*, GV založba, Ljubljana 2011, p. 94.
2 Ibid., p. 106.
3 Official Gazette RS, No. 36/2008, 40/2009, 26/2011, 87/2011 and 57/2012.
4 Articles 73 and 74.
5 Official Gazette RS, No. 50/2012 (official consolidated version). Other Member States have criminalised competition law as well; United Kingdom, Germany, Ireland The Netherlands, Austria, Estonia, France, Greece, Hungary, Slovakia. See K. Daly, 'Cartels and deterrence-creeping criminalization and the class action boom' (2007) 1 *Bloomberg European business law journal* 1 315, 318.

With this aim, the first part of this paper analyses the legislation of the European Union (hereinafter EU), Constitution of the Republic of Slovenia[6] (hereinafter Constitution) and criminal policy in search of potential supranational, constitutional, and policy arguments in favour of the implementation of criminalisation of competition law.

The next part of the paper focuses on current Slovenian regulation concerning the restriction of competition and certain interesting issues, such as the relation between criminal and misdemeanour responsibility of natural and legal persons, the definition of the perpetrator and accomplices to the criminal act of unlawful restriction of competition[7] and leniency institutes, incorporated in Slovenian criminal procedural and substantive law.

2. IS SLOVENIA OBLIGED TO CRIMINALLY PROSECUTE RESTRICTION OF COMPETITION?

2.1. SUPRANATIONAL REASONS FOR CRIMINALISATION OF RESTRICTION OF COMPETITION

As a member of the EU Slovenia has a duty to implement EU law. In regard to competition, the EU law is of even greater importance, because competition law originates from the EU law, mostly The EC Treaty and subsequently the Council Regulation (EC) 1/2003 of 16 December, 2002 on the implementation of the rules on competition laid down in Articles 81 and 82 of the Treaty (hereinafter the Regulation 1/2003).[8] Moreover, national authorities have jurisdiction only in those competition cases, when the violation of competition has results only in the territory of a Member State, whereas, in other cases the jurisdiction of the EU Commission prevails.[9]

The first argument for incriminating the violations of competition law could, therefore, be sought in the Regulation 1/2003, itself. Certain hints regarding legal responsibility of natural and legal persons could be found. For example, according to article 5 national competition authorities could impose fines, periodic penalty payments, or any other penalty provided for in their national law, but not necessarily of criminal law nature. Furthermore, article 12 provides for the exchange of information in order to impose sanctions on natural persons, but, again, these sanctions are not necessarily criminal. On the contrary, article 23 regulates fines for undertakings and associations and states explicitly that they are *not* of criminal nature. The Regulation 1/2003, the core basis for the

6 Official Gazette Rs, No. 33/1991-I, 42/1997, 66/2000, 24/2003, 69/2004, 68/2006 and 47/2013.
7 Article 225 of KZ-1.
8 [2003] OJ L 1/1.
9 See articles 4 and 5 of the Regulation 1/1/2003 and articles 4, 6, 9 and 11 of ZPOmK-1.

regulation of competition law in the EU, therefore does not demand the criminalisation of competition law, but does not prohibit it either in relation to natural persons.[10]

Although the EU started out as a purely economic and commercial community, it has been quickly gaining criminal law power in the last twenty years.[11] The Treaty on the Functioning of the European Union[12] after the Lisbon Treaty[13], therefore includes a special chapter on judicial cooperation in criminal matters. Regarding substantive criminal law, the powers of EU are based, as in the past, on the principle of harmonisation. Accordingly the EU aims to define minimum mutual standards regarding the definition of a criminal act and criminal sanctions and lets the Member States decide in which way to implement these standards into their national legislation.[14] It is based on the approximation of the laws and regulations of the Member States[15] and not on their unification. This principle should be considered also in connection to the criminalisation of competition law.

The Treaty on the Functioning of the European Union lists also the areas, for which the harmonisation of definitions for criminal acts is possible. These areas are: terrorism, trafficking in human beings and sexual exploitation of women and children, illicit drug trafficking, illicit arms trafficking, money laundering, corruption, counterfeiting of means of payment, computer crime, and organised crime.[16]

The unlawful restriction of violation is not explicitly mentioned among areas for harmonisation of definitions of criminal acts, but there is still a possibility for the jurisdiction of EU. Firstly, violations of competition law could be connected to or subsumed under other areas, which are explicitly in the jurisdiction of the EU,[17] such as money laundering, corruption, or organised crime. Secondly, on the basis of developments in crime, the Council of the EU may adopt a decision identifying other areas of a particularly serious crime with a cross-border dimension resulting from the nature or impact of such offences or from a special need to combat them on a common basis after obtaining consent from the European Parliament.[18]

---

10 W.P.J. Wils, 'Is criminalization of EU competition law the answer?', in: C.D. Ehlermann and I. Atanasiu (eds.), *European Competition Law Annual 2006: Enforcement of Prohibition of Cartels*, Hart Publishing, Oxford, Portland, Oregon 2006 p. 4, 15, 16 and 17.

11 See the content of the third pillar of Amsterdam (1992) and Maastricht (1997) Treaty, the conclusions of the Tampere meeting (1999), Nice Treaty (2001), etc.

12 [2012] OJ C 326.

13 [2007] OJ C 306.

14 Article 82 of The Treaty on the Functioning of the European Union.

15 Ibid.

16 Ibid., article 83.

17 Ibid.

18 Ibid.

It is certainly my opinion that violations of competition law should be considered as serious crimes with a cross-border dimension resulting from the nature or impact of such offences or from a special need to combat them on a common basis, especially due to the importance of the free movement of goods and capital inside the EU. The second reason is the division of jurisdiction between national authorities and the Commission according to Regulation 1/2003. The division of jurisdiction is made upon the differentiation between the national and cross-border effects of the restriction of competition. Consequently it is my opinion that the EU should already adopt regulations with the minimum standards of definitions of relevant criminal acts or at least define more specific legal basis for it. No such directive or framework decision has been adopted yet, though.

Another relevant power of the EU, according to the Treaty on the European Union and the Treaty on the Functioning of the European Union, is the establishment of Eurojust[19] and its potential transformation into the European Public Prosecutor's Office (EPPO).[20] Namely, in order to combat crimes affecting the financial interests of the EU, the Council, by means of regulations adopted in accordance with a special legislative procedure, may establish EPPO from Eurojust.[21] It shall be responsible for investigating, prosecuting, and bringing to judgment, where appropriate in liaison with Europol, the perpetrators of, and accomplices in criminal acts against the financial interests of the EU, as determined by the regulation.[22] Generally, violations of competition law could be subsumed under crimes, which affect the financial interests of the EU and the European Public Prosecutor's Office could have jurisdiction for it.

Despite various drafts on the organisation and powers of the EPPO[23] the Proposal for a Council Regulation on the establishment of the European Public Prosecutor's Office COM(2013) 534 was not drafted until July 2013.[24] This proposal defines the jurisdiction of the EPPO and thereby, the financial interests of the EU as all revenues, expenditures, and assets covered by, acquired through, or due to the EU budget and the budgets of institutions, bodies, offices, and agencies established under the Treaties and budgets managed and monitored by them.[25] The EPPO shall have the exclusive competence to investigate and prosecute criminal acts against the EU's financial interests[26] as provided for under Directive 2013/xx/EU and implemented by national law[27] and other

19 Ibid., article 85.
20 Ibid., article 86.
21 Ibid.
22 Ibid.
23 P. Gorkič, 'Evropski javni tožilec: zdaj gre (zares) zares' (2013) 32 *Pravna praksa* I, II.
24 Ibid.
25 Article 2 of Proposal for a Council Regulation on the establishment of the European Public Prosecutor's Office.
26 Ibid., article 11.
27 Ibid., article 12.

criminal acts, where the acts against financial interests of the EU are inextricably linked with other criminal acts and their joint investigation and prosecution are in the interest of a good administration of justice, under the conditions that the criminal acts are preponderant and other criminal acts are based on identical facts.[28]

The referred to Directive 2013/xx/EU is the Proposal for a Directive of the European Parliament and of the Council on the fight against fraud to the Union's financial interests by means of criminal law, 11 July, 2012 COM (2012) 363 final,[29] which defines the criminal acts against the financial interests of the EU mostly as fraud against financial interests of the EU[30] and fraud related criminal acts affecting the EU's financial interests (including money laundering and corruption).[31]

Although crimes against the financial interests of the EU are currently understood as fraud and fraud related criminal acts, violations of competition law could and should be included in the framework of the substantive criminal law directive and consequently, also the jurisdiction of the EPPO, as the criminal acts, which are inextricably linked with fraud.

Further, according to Article 310 of the Treaty on the Functioning of the European Union, the EU and the Member States shall counter fraud and any other illegal activities affecting the financial interests of the EU.[32] This article is written in a broader manner and does not cover the fraud only. Similarly, according to Article 325, the EU and the Member States shall counter fraud and any other illegal activities affecting the financial interests of the EU through measures, which shall act as a deterrent and be such as to afford effective protection in the Member States, and in all the EU's institutions, bodies, offices, and agencies. Member States shall take the same measures to counter fraud affecting the financial interests of the EU as they take to counter fraud affecting their own financial interests and the European Parliament and the Council shall also adopt the necessary measures in the fields of the prevention of and fight against fraud affecting the financial interests of the EU with a view of effective and equivalent protection in the Member States and in all the Union's institutions, bodies, offices, and agencies.[33]

---

28 Ibid., article 13.

29 L. Kuhl, 'The initiative for a directive on the protection of the EU financial interests by substantive criminal law', (2012) 2 Eucrim, 63, 63.

30 Article 3 of Proposal for a Directive of the European Parliament and of the Council on the fight against fraud to the Union's financial interests by means of criminal law.

31 Ibid., Article 4; L.L. Kuhl, 'The initiative for a directive on the protection of the EU financial interests by substantive criminal law', (2012) 2 Eucrim, 53, 64.

32 Article 310 of Treaty on the Functioning of the European Union.

33 Ibid., Article 325.

Again, although the crimes against the EU financial interest are currently understood as only the fraud and fraud related criminal acts,[34] such as corruption and money laundering. Articles 310 and 325 could and should serve as the legal basis for EPPO's subject jurisdiction and legislative activity in the interest of harmonisation of the EU in the field of violation of competition law. If the EU has a formal legal bases, it should recognise such violations as a threat to its financial interests.

This could be substantiated also by the European Court of Justice (ECJ), Case C-176/03 Commission of the European Communities vs. Council of the European Union[35], in which the ECJ stated that "despite lacking explicit legal basis for adopting criminal legislation for protection of environment and despite the fact that as a general rule, neither criminal law nor the rules of criminal procedure fall within the Community's competence",[36] it does not prevent "the Community legislature, when the application of effective, proportionate and dissuasive criminal penalties by the competent national authorities is an essential measure for combating serious environmental offences, from taking measures which relate to the criminal law of the Member States which it considers necessary in order to ensure that the rules which it lays down on environmental protection are fully effective. That finding is not called into question by the fact that Articles 135 EC and 280(4) EC reserve to the Member States, in the spheres of customs cooperation and the protection of the Community's financial interests respectively, the application of national criminal law and the administration of justice. It is not possible to infer from those provisions that, for the purposes of the implementation of environmental policy, any harmonisation of criminal law, even as limited as that resulting from the framework decision, must be ruled out even where it is necessary in order to ensure the effectiveness of Community law."[37] Accordingly, criminal law measures (including criminalisation of competition law), despite lacking clear legal basis in EU law, could be applied by the EU, when a necessity is recognised for the protection of the vital interests of the EU. This could also be applied to the protection of competition.

---

34 In the same manner the EU Council Framework Decision of 13 June, 2002 on the European Arrest Warrant (2002/584/JHA), which in article 2 lists among criminal acts, for which no double criminality is needed, also fraud and fraud affecting the financial interests of the European Union. However, a European arrest warrant may be issued also for other criminal acts punishable by the law of the issuing Member State by a custodial sentence or a detention order for a maximum period of at least 12 months or, where a sentence has been passed or a detention order has been made, for sentences of at least four months. This could include the Slovenian criminal act of unlawful restriction of competition.

35 < http://eur-lex.europa.eu/LexUriServ/LexUriServ.do?uri=CELEX:62003J0176:EN:HTML >.

36 Case C-176/03 Commission of the European Communities v Council of the European Union, par. 38.

37 Ibid., par. 47–52; G. Hakopan, 'Criminalization of EU competition law enforcement – a possibility after Lisbon?', (2010) 7 *The competition law review* 157, 159.

According to the EU law criminal responsibility of natural persons for violation of competition law is therefore not required, but also not prohibited. The legal basis for criminalisation of competition law of the EU law could be found or, if necessary, formed on the basis of the Lisbon Treaty, as such criminal acts should be considered cross-border crimes that need to be fought with on cross-border basis on one side. Restriction of competition could also be considered criminal acts which harm the financial interests of the EU and could consequently fall within the jurisdiction of the EPPO, if the proposal for the EPPO directive or the substantive criminal law directive regulated it in a such manner.

The main barrier for criminalisation of competition law in the EU is a narrow understanding of the criminal acts, which harm the financial interests of the EU. It is namely limited to EU fraud and fraud related criminal acts,[38] but should be defined in a broader manner as any criminal act, which directly or indirectly harm the financial interests of the EU and at the same time has elements of cross-border crime. Certain competition cases, especially the cross-border ones, should fall within this category.

2.2. THE OBLIGATIONS ARISING FROM THE SLOVENIAN CONSTITUTION

Regulation of free enterprise is regulated also among economic and social relations in the third chapter of the Slovenian Constitution, which is unique in a comparative point of view.[39] The main reason for a regulation of the free enterprise in the Slovenian Constitution lies in the complete change of the economic system in 1991.[40] According to Article 74, free economic initiative is guaranteed and the conditions for establishing commercial organisations shall be established by law. Commercial activities may not be pursued in a manner contrary to the public interest, unfair competition practices and practices which restrict competition in a manner contrary to the law are prohibited.

The Slovenian Constitution, therefore, includes the prohibition of restriction of competition in a manner contrary to the law. The referred to law is the mentioned ZPOmK-1. The primary rules of the Slovenian Constitution (Article 74) and ZPOmK-1, which prohibit certain forms of the restriction of competition (dominant position, concentrations, etc.), should be followed by secondary legal rules, prescribing sanctions for the violation of primary rules. Only then are we

38 K. Daly, 'Cartels and deterrence-creeping criminalization and the class action boom' (2007) 1 *Bloomberg European business law journal* 1 315, 321.

39 L. Šturm (Ed.), *Komentar Ustave Republike Slovenije*. Fakulteta za državne in evropske študije, Ljubljana 2010, p. 713.

40 Ibid., p. 712.

dealing with *lex perfecta* rules,[41] but this does not necessarily infer criminalisation of competition law, since the Slovenian public law recognises two forms of unlawful conduct; criminal acts and misdemeanours.[42]

Again, the criminal responsibility of natural persons for the restriction of competition is therefore possible, but not necessary. Criminal responsibility should be *ultima ratio* according to the general constitutional and criminal law principles. Moreover, according to the principle of proportionality, criminal responsibility should not be regulated, if the responsibility for misdemeanours should suffices for prevention and punishment of the restriction of competition. On the other hand, if responsibility for the misdemeanours does not suffice, criminal responsibility should be introduced, otherwise the constitutional protection of competition is not ensured by the state. The main constitutional issue is therefore the principle of proportionality and the need to find the right balance between effective protection of competition in the form of sanctioning its restriction and protection of free enterprise.

The standard states that, when criminal law protection of competition is necessary and misdemeanour responsibility does not suffice, it could be inferred from the case law of the European Court of Human Rights (hereinafter ECHR) on positive obligations of the states. Namely, in the case of social and economic rights, the government has the obligation to perform certain measures to ensure that specific rights can be enjoyed by individuals. This obligation will demand some help or intervention from the state in order to protect the right.[43]

The Slovenian constitutional law theory also defined Article 74 as a positive obligation type of constitutional right. The state should therefore provide for circumstances, which would enable fulfilment of the principle of competition and implementation of constitutional prohibition of practices which restrict competition in practice and legal systems.[44]

---

41 M. Pavčnik, *Teorija prava*, GV založba, Ljubljana 2011, p. 122.

42 The third form of unlawful conduct comprises of disciplinary infractions, which are restricted within certain organisation.

43 L. Alves, S. A. Gawronski and M. Stupak, 'The positive obligation of states to provide security under the ECHR, the Charter, and the Polish Constitution' <www.google.si/url?sa=t&rct=j&q=&esrc=s&frm=1&source=web&cd=2&ved=0CDAQFjAB&url=http%3A%2F%2Fen.zpc.wpia.uw.edu.pl%2Fwp-content%2Fuploads%2F2010%2F04%2F4.-The-standard-of-the-right-to-security-1.doc&ei=aKFfUqrFCszS4QSjoYC4CA&usg=AFQjCNFKRvCmm4qHIAVESrfPkyqJ3QfjUg&sig2=3IYgx8PgCFsUXabfZExlNw&bvm=bv.54176721,d.bGE> accessed 17.10.2013, p. 3.

44 L. Šturm (Ed.), *Komentar Ustave Republike Slovenije*. Fakulteta za državne in evropske študije, Ljubljana 2010, pp. 716, 719; I. KAUČIČ and F. GRAD, *Ustavna ureditev Slovenije*, GV založba, Ljubljana 2007, p. 148. On the other side, article 74 of the Slovenian Constitution is also a human right, which should be protected by the state from any infringement by the state. In this way, it also has also a negative aspect. L. ŠTURM (Ed.), *Komentar Ustave Republike Slovenije*. Fakulteta za državne in evropske študije, Ljubljana 2010, pp. 713, 714, 719.

The Slovenian state is therefore, obliged to ensure the right to competition in practice by adopting a law, which would define prohibited acts of the restriction of competition (principle of legality, especially *lex certa*) and thereby enable the judicial protection of competition.[45] Absence of such regulation would represent an unconstitutional legal gap.[46]

With an assessment, of whether criminal responsibility is required for the restriction of competition or not, the ECHR's standard of positive obligations should be taken into consideration. At the same time it should be noted that the European Convention for the Protection of Human Rights and Fundamental Freedoms does not include the right to competition unlike the Slovenian Constitution, but mostly civil and political human rights. Regarding the legal values that they protect their importance is greater than the economic right to free competition. Consequently, a stricter standard should be imposed on positive obligations regarding human rights from the European Convention for the Protection of Human Rights and Fundamental Freedoms than on the economic right to free competition. This should be taken into consideration when assessing the content of the positive obligations regarding the right to free competition.

The ECHR found for example in case *X & Y vs. Netherlands*[47] that Article 8 was breached because domestic criminal law did not provide practical and effective protection for a mentally ill child who was sexually assaulted, there may be positive obligations inherent in an effective respect for private or family life and that these obligations may involve the adoption of measures designed to secure respect for private life even in respect to of the relations of individuals between themselves. A state, therefore, may be under positive obligations to ensure that individuals have rights against other individuals.[48] In particular, the court expressed the view that "in the circumstances of the case, the absence of an effective criminal remedy constituted a failure to respect the girl's private life which required measures of effective deterrence. Importantly, civil remedies, which might otherwise be effective, were insufficient to protect her convention interests because they were not without their practical drawbacks. Due to the "fundamental values and essential aspects of private life... at stake" here, effective deterrence, which the court considered to be "indispensable in this

45 Ibid., p. 719.

46 Ibid.

47 Application No. 8978/80, 26/3/1985.

48 L. Alves, S. A. Gawronski and M. Stupak, 'The positive obligation of states to provide security under the ECHR, the Charter, and the Polish Constitution' <www.google.si/url?sa=t&rct=j&q=&esrc=s&frm=1&source=web&cd=2&ved=0CDAQFjAB&url=http%3A%2F%2Fen.zpc.wpia.uw.edu.pl%2Fwp-content%2Fuploads%2F2010%2F04%2F4.-The-standard-of-the-right-to-security-1.doc&ei=aKFfUqrFCszS4QSjoYC4CA&usg=AFQjCNFKRvCmm4qHIAVESrfPkyqJ3QfjUg&sig2=3IYgx8PgCFsUXabfZExlNw&bvm=bv.54176721,d.bGE > accessed 17.10.2013, p. 3; U. Kinkelly, 'Protecting children's rights under the ECHR: the role of positive obligations', (2010) 61 *Northern Ireland* Legal *Quarterly* 245, 258.

area", could only be achieved by criminal law provisions".[49] In certain cases, protection of certain legal values therefore must be accompanied through criminal sanctions.

In regards to certain rights from the European Convention for the Protection of Human Rights and Fundamental Freedoms, the ECHR developed a positive obligation of putting in place a legislative and administrative framework designed to provide effective deterrence against threats to these rights,[50] which in certain cases involves positive obligation in order to penalise and prosecute effectively any relevant act.[51]

As said, these obligations have been developed in connection to the rights from the convention and since it does not include the right to free enterprise, the court has not come up with any such positive obligation in connection to the right to free enterprise. Despite that, the standard of positive obligation should be applied (perhaps in a less strict manner), when deciding, whether the violations of competition law should be defined as a misdemeanour or as a criminal act.

This coincides with the principle of proportionality,[52] especially in regards to the element of necessity of regulation; the measure applied (criminal law sanctions for violations of competition law) must be necessary to achieve the aim (protection of free enterprise and competition) and no other measure (including prescribing the violations as misdemeanours) would suffice.

This brings us to the third potential reason for criminalisation of competition law; criminal policy reasons.

3. CRIMINAL POLICY AS A REASON FOR CRIMINALISATION OF COMPETITION LAW

The majority of the literature concerning the subject of criminalisation of competition law agrees that there is no obligation for criminalisation of competition law in EU law. However, staying on the supranational level the most

---

49 Ibid.

50 H. Tomlin, `Positive obligations under the European Convention on Human Rights` <www.google.si/url?sa=t&rct=j&q=&esrc=s&frm=1&source=web&cd=3&ved=0CD0QFjAC&url=http%3A%2F%2Fwww.adminlaw.org.uk%2Fdocs%2FSC%25202012%2520by%2520Tomlinson%2520QC.docx&ei=sqNfUpijEKiD4AT34oDYCA&usg=AFQjCNGIfphLexyU_SefygKtUvUMLff_-g&sig2=KkJnG4X30J6FFoxN-Tf24g> accessed 17.10.2013, p. 4.

51 Ibid.

52 The principle of proportionality consists of the following elements: there must be a legitimate aim for a measure, the measure must be suitable to achieve the aim (potentially with a requirement of evidence to show it will have that effect), the measure must be necessary to achieve the aim, that there cannot be any less onerous way of doing it and the measure must be reasonable, considering the competing interests of different groups at hand.

frequently mentioned and substantiated arguments for criminalisation of competition level are criminal policy reasons.

Classical sentencing is mentioned in connection to this, such as prevention and retribution, adding to this certain practical reasons. It must be noted however, that the issue discussed in relation to criminal policy has not been the differentiation misdemeanour versus criminal sentences, but the differentiation between fines and prison sentences. The central discussion[53] has been, whether prison sentences should be introduced.[54]

In theory, the most common deterrence and prevention are demanded for regulation of the restriction of competition.[55] Fines, imposed on associations and undertakings involved in restriction of competition are supposedly not efficient enough, since the fines should be high enough, to actually be as efficient and deter the undertaking's ability to pay costly side-effect and forcing them into bankruptcy.[56]

Also, fines are imposed on the associations and undertakings involved and not on the natural persons who actually physically committed the violations. Prison sentences, on the other hand would be imposed on to the perpetrator.[57] Fines are imposed based on the assumption that undertakings will be consequently capable of controlling the natural persons committing the violations. However, certain undertakings might not be capable of such control and fines would not have a direct effect on the perpetrators.[58]

Retribution from the natural person, who is the perpetrator, is also mentioned as a reason for the criminalisation of competition law, due to social harm, caused by the restriction of competition, and due to its immorality.[59]

53 This is also discussed especially in relation to cartels.

54 W.P.J. Wils, 'Is criminalization of EU competition law the answer?', in: C. D. Ehlermann and I. Atanasiu (eds.), *European Competition Law Annual 2006: Enforcement of Prohibition of Cartels*, Hart Publishing, Oxford, Portland, Oregon 2006, p. 1.

55 M. Kocmut, `V keho z direktorji-inkriminacija kartelov`, (2007) 26 *Pravna praksa* 22, 23.

56 W. P J wils, 'Is criminalization of EU competition law the answer?', in: C. D. Ehlermann and I. Atanasiu (eds.), *European Competition Law Annual 2006: Enforcement of Prohibition of Cartels*, Hart Publishing, Oxford, Portland, Oregon 2006 pp. 26, 27, 30, 33; K. Daly, op. cit., p. 315, 316,317; G. Hakopan, 'Criminalization of EU competition law enforcement – a possibility after Lisbon?', (2010) 7 *The competition law review* 157, 157; M. Kocmut, `V keho z direktorji-inkriminacija kartelov`, (2007) 26 *Pravna praksa* 22, 23.

57 W.P.J. Wils, 'Is criminalization of EU competition law the answer?', in: C. D. Ehlermann and I. Atanasiu (eds.), *European Competition Law Annual 2006: Enforcement of Prohibition of Cartels*, Hart Publishing, Oxford, Portland, Oregon 2006, p. 28; K. Daly, 'Cartels and deterrence-creeping criminalization and the class action boom' (2007) 1 *Bloomberg European business law journal* 1 315, 315; M. Kocmut, `V keho z direktorji-inkriminacija kartelov`, (2007) 26 *Pravna praksa* 22, 23.

58 W.P.J. Wils, 'Is criminalization of EU competition law the answer?', in: C. D. Ehlermann and I. Atanasiu (eds.), *European Competition Law Annual 2006: Enforcement of Prohibition of Cartels*, Hart Publishing, Oxford, Portland, Oregon 2006, p. 28.

59 A. Macculloch, `The cartel offence: defining an appropriate `Moral space`, (2012) 8 European competition journal 73, 75–83; W. P J Wils, 'Is criminalization of EU competition law the answer?', in: C. D. Ehlermann and I. Atanasiu (eds.), *European Competition Law Annual*

Despite recognising these arguments, no research has been made in Slovenia yet in order to establish criminal policy grounds for justification of the criminalisation of competition law.

Theory offers a more practical ground for the criminalisation of competition law in EU Member States; namely, prosecutions of competition law violations would be more effective in all Member States, even in those which have already incriminated the restriction of competition, and also in the EU in general. Since the penalty for a criminal act is higher than for a misdemeanour, leniency programmes would be more efficient and whistle-blowers would have more reasons to provide information in misdemeanour and also criminal procedures.[60]

Furthermore, according to Regulation 1/2003 information from one Member State could also be used in another Member State. But the information exchanged can only be used as evidence to impose sanctions on natural persons where the law of the transmitting authority foresees sanctions of a similar kind in relation to an infringement of Article 81 or Article 82 of the Treaty or, in the absence thereof, the information has been collected in a way which respects the same level of protection of the rights of defence of natural persons as provided for under the national rules of the receiving authority. In this case, however, the information exchanged cannot be used by the receiving authority to impose custodial sanctions.[61] It is therefore necessary for successful prosecution of natural persons to ensure the criminalisation of the restriction of competition according to the Regulation 1/2003 throughout the EU Member States.

Moreover, since double criminality is required also for extradition, the criminalisation of competition law in the EU would also enhance the possibilities of extradition across the EU. The effect of this argument has been minimised since the introduction of the European arrest warrant, which does not demand the double criminality. This list, however, does not explicitly include competition violations, for which double criminality is still required.[62]

Last, but not least, the incrimination of competition law should unburden certain Member States, including Slovenia,[63] as more than the current number of

2006: Enforcement of Prohibition of Cartels, Hart Publishing, Oxford, Portland, Oregon 2006, p. 31; M. Kocmut, 'V keho z direktorji-inkriminacija kartelov', (2007) 26 *Pravna praksa* 22, 23.

60 W.P.J. Wils, 'Is criminalization of EU competition law the answer?', in: C. D. Ehlermann and I. Atanasiu (eds.), *European Competition Law Annual 2006: Enforcement of Prohibition of Cartels*, Hart Publishing, Oxford, Portland, Oregon 2006, p. 2 8; M. Kocmut, 'V keho z direktorji-inkriminacija kartelov', (2007) 26 *Pravna praksa* 22, 23.

61 Article 12 of Regulation 1/2003; W. P J WILS, 'Is criminalization of EU competition law the answer?', in: C. D. Ehlermann and I. Atanasiu (eds.), *European Competition Law Annual 2006: Enforcement of Prohibition of Cartels*, Hart Publishing, Oxford, Portland, Oregon 2006, p. 41.

62 Ibid.

63 If there had been any criminal prosecutions of unlawful restriction of competition at all.

Member States would be able to prosecute the relevant criminal acts and no state would create a safe haven from criminal prosecution.[64]

4. STATE OF THE ART CRIMINALISATION OF COMPETITION LAW

As previously mentioned, Slovenian criminal law already includes the criminalisation of competition law. Namely, both criminal codes since the independence have included a chapter of criminal acts against economy and the first criminal act in this chapter is the criminalisation of competition law.

Slovenia was a part of the former Socialist Federal Republic of Yugoslavia (SFRY) before 1991 and reached the international legal status of an independent state in 1991. After the proclamation of the new Constitution (on the 23d of December, 1991) all legal provisions in force at that time stayed in force, except where they were in conflict with human rights and fundamental freedoms. It is interesting to point out that in the field of substantive criminal law, no provision was formally declared in conflict with human rights and fundamental freedoms in the period between the proclamation of the new constitution and the implementation of the new Criminal Code (KZ)[65] in 1995.

Since the previous social and economic order was not based on free enterprise, but on self-regulation, arranged economy and social property,[66] the newly adopted legislation was amended dramatically in regards to these criminal acts. The first criminal act in the chapter of criminal acts against economy was therefore the criminal act of creating monopolistic position, according to which whoever pursued an economic activity, makes an unlawful agreement either restricting another commercial company's participation in the free trade of goods or services or otherwise establishing a monopoly of the commercial company on the relevant market and by coincidence of this agreement, a large property benefit is gained by the commercial company in question or a large property loss[67] is incurred by a third person, shall be sentenced to imprisonment for no more than three years.[68] Despite few amendments to the KZ, in the following years these criminal acts have not been amended in any way until the new KZ-1 was adopted in 2008.

When adopting the KZ in 1994 the commercial legislation had not fully been adopted. This was understood as an obstacle for efficient criminal legislation for the protection of economy. The Protection of Competition Act (ZVK),[69] which

---

64 Ibid., p. 42.
65 Official Gazette RS, No. 95/2004.
66 The Proposal of Criminal Code, p. 63.
67 This represents the amount of fifty average net salaries in Slovenia.
68 Article 231 of KZ.
69 Official Gazette RS, No. 18/1993.

regulated both the prohibition of the restriction of competition and unfair competition, was adopted in 1993, but was later the part concerning the restriction of competition by the Prevention of Restriction of Competition Act (ZPOmK).[70]

The definition of the criminal act of creating a position of monopoly in the KZ was strongly criticised for many reasons.[71] Firstly, it referred only to a monopoly and no other forms of unlawful restriction of competition, and secondly, it criminalised the creation of a monopoly, which was allowed by competition law, and not only its abuse, which was prohibited also in by the ZVK,[72] ZPOmK[73] and ZPOmK-1.[74]

As a result of criminal and competition law, creating a monopoly was allowed by competition law, but breached criminal law. This created a confusing and contradictory situation, contradicting the constitutional principle of rule of law.[75]

The new KZ-1 kept this in the chapter of criminal acts against the economy. The criminal act of abusing a position of monopoly (Article 225), therefore, incriminated anyone who, in pursuing an economic activity contrary to the regulations governing the protection of competition, violates the prohibition of restricting agreements between companies, abuses the dominant position of one or more companies, or creates a forbidden concentration of companies and thus prevents or significantly impedes or distorts competition in the Republic of Slovenia, or in the European Union market, or its significant part, or significantly influences trade between Member States, which results in a large property benefit for such a company or companies, or a large property damage for another company.

The content of this criminal act has been adapted according to the already existing and functioning competition law, the title of the criminal act, however, remained too narrow and referred only to a monopoly, whereas the definition of a criminal act referred to a broader violation of the prohibition of restricting agreements, abuses of dominant position, and to creating a forbidden concentration. The improvement has however been made, according to which the establishing of a monopoly itself was not criminally unlawful.

The criminal act was also amended in relation to sentencing; the sentence was increased and the perpetrator could now be sentenced to prison from six months to five years (instead of up to three years). This changed also the jurisdiction of courts at the first level[76] from district to circuit courts, where lay

70 Official Gazette RS, No. 64/2007.
71 M. Kocmut, `V keho z direktorji-inkriminacija kartelov`, (2007) 26 *Pravna praksa* 22, 24.
72 Article 10 of ZVK; Proposal of Criminal Code-1, commentary to draft Article 225.
73 Article 10 of ZPOmK.
74 Article 9 of ZPOmK-1.
75 Article 2 of Slovenian Constitution.
76 M. Kocmut, `V keho z direktorji-inkriminacija kartelov`, (2007) 26 *Pravna praksa* 22, 24.

assessors take part in the trial as well, despite the criticism that lay judges are not suitable for judging such criminal acts due to the need of specialised knowledge in commercial and economic law.[77] On the other hand, the jurisdiction of circuit courts seems more appropriate, because the criminal procedure in circuit courts (regular criminal procedures) is adapted for investigation and prosecution of more complex criminal acts, such as one from Article 225 of the KZ-1, due to a specially regulated phase of judicial investigation and due to broader legal and practical possibilities of investigations and other measures.[78]

Also, in contradiction to the previous legislation, the KZ-1 defines large property benefit or damage in an absolute manner, as benefit or damage which exceeds 50.000 EUR, which also represents an increase in its severity.

The last amendment to the KZ-1 from 2012[79] also amended this criminal act. Finally, the title of the criminal act was amended according to its definition and content pertaining to the unlawful restriction of competition, which covers not only abuse of dominant position, but also other defined restrictions of competition. Another important amendment was made in regards to leniency. Leniency towards whistle-blowers has strongly been recommended in theory.[80] Accordingly, the amendment introduced the possibility of leniency, according to which the perpetrator who violated the prohibition of the restricting agreements and had declared such an act before it was detected or he knew it had been detected and took part in its investigation and the elimination of consequences and neither compelled others to take part in the restriction of competition nor forced them to continue taking part in the restriction, may be granted a remission of the sentence. This possibility should increase the possibility of using the information in criminal, but also misdemeanour procedure.[81]

Reduction and remission of sentence for competition cases had previously been possible in general on the basis of the KZ-1.[82] But, accordingly, legal basis for remission of sentence must be specifically prescribed, as currently in Article 225, for the court to be able to apply it, whereas the reduction of sentence could have already been applied on the basis of Article 50 of KZ-1, according to which the court may reduce the sentence of the perpetrator if it ascertains that special mitigating circumstances are present, which justify the imposition of a reduced sentence.[83]

---

77 Ibid.

78 Such as the pre-trial detention, tapping, feigned purchase, feigned acceptance, or giving of gifts or feigned acceptance or giving of bribes, undercover operations, etc.

79 Criminal Code-1B (KZ-1B), Official Gazette RS, No. 91/2011.

80 M. Kocmut, 'V keho z direktorji-inkriminacija kartelov', (2007) 26 *Pravna praksa* 22, 24; Proposal of KZ-1B, commentary to Article 225.

81 See also Article 76 of ZPOmK-1.

82 Articles 50–52 of KZ-1.

83 Article 50, paragraph 2 of KZ-1.

Article 294 of the KZ-1 could also be relevant, according to which, a perpetrator of criminal acts in a criminal association who prevents further commission of these acts or discloses information which has a bearing on the investigation and proving of criminal acts that have already been committed, may have his punishment for these acts mitigated, if the unlawful restriction of competition was committed in the framework of criminal association.[84] Previously, remission of sentence was also possible on this basis.[85] This could be relevant, because the restriction of competition is usually executed in the framework of criminal association, due to the nature of this criminal act.

Such amendments of KZ-1 have been stimulated also by the EU Commission's Notice on immunity from fines and reduction of fines in cartel cases, which lays down the framework for rewarding cooperation in the Commission investigation by undertakings which are or have been party to secret cartels affecting the Community,[86] because, by their very nature, secret cartels are often difficult to detect and investigate without the cooperation of undertakings or individuals implicated in them.[87] Despite its validity for Commission cases only, it should be taken into consideration that the supervisory task conferred on the Commission by the Treaty in competition matters encompasses also the duty to pursue a general policy.[88] Therefore, these guidelines could be applied also in national competition procedures[89] and also in criminal procedures as guidance,[90] but at least in the latter case with explicit legal basis.

5. CURRENT ISSUES REGARDING SLOVENIAN CRIMINAL LAW REGULATION

5.1. COMPLICITY

Slovenian criminal legislation had already decided in favour of the criminalisation of competition law twenty years ago. Accordingly, certain criminal law issues are relevant in relation to current Slovenian regulation, firstly, who could be the perpetrator of such criminal act.

The criminal act of the unlawful restriction of competition is regulated in the chapter of criminal acts against the economy. As for most criminal acts from

---

84 Article 294 of KZ-1.
85 In accordance with article 297 of KZ-1.
86 Introduction to the Commission notice on immunity from fines and reduction of fines in cartel cases, paragraph 1.
87 Ibid., paragraph 3.
88 Ibid., paragraph 7.
89 According to Article 76 of ZPOmK-1.
90 According to Article 225 of KZ-1.

this chapter, the physical or direct perpetrator could only be a person, who is pursuing economic activity.[91] This criminal act is therefore *delictum proprium* and cannot be perpetrated by a person, who is not pursuing such activity.[92]

This characteristic influences also the issue of complicity. Aiding abetting and inciting this criminal act could be committed also by someone, who is not pursuing economic activity. A person without involvement in economic activity could therefore still be prosecuted for aiding, abetting, or inciting the unlawful restriction of competition.[93] This also applies to the indirect perpetrator, who was using the direct and physical perpetrator as a tool to commit this criminal act.[94]

A co-perpetrator of this criminal act, however, could again only be someone, who is pursuing economic activity. If a person, who contributed essentially and substantially to the commission of this criminal act, does not have the required characteristic, he or she could only be prosecuted as an aider, abettor, or inciter, but not as the co-perpetrator of unlawful restriction of competition.[95]

5.2. THE RELATIONSHIP BETWEEN A MISDEMEANOUR AND CRIMINAL RESPONSIBILITY

Contrary to the former legislation, the definition of unlawful restriction of competition in KZ-1 explicitly refers to violation of competition law. Namely, KZ-1 as one of the elements of the definition of a criminal act also requires that the violation of the prohibition of restricting agreements between companies, abuse of the dominant position of one or more companies, or creation of a forbidden concentration of companies *is committed contrary to regulations governing the protection of competition*. The legislator therefore responded to the criticism[96] and abandoned previous definition of the criminal act, which was completely independent of relevant definitions of restriction of competition from competition law. Such a lack of consideration caused an intolerable gap between the criminal and competition law definitions.

Contrary to this, the current definition of a criminal act is closely linked to the definition of a violation of competition law and is actually built upon it. The legislator therefore decided to apply a blanket definition of a criminal act,[97] referring the competition law, more specifically to the definition of restriction of

---

91 M. Deisinger, *Kazenski zakonik s komentarjem, posebni del*, GV založba, Ljubljana 2002, p. 469.
92 L. Bavcon et al., *Kazensko pravo, splošni del*, Uradni list, Ljubljana 2013, p. 199.
93 Ibid., p. 349.
94 Ibid., p. 342.
95 Ibid., p. 346.
96 M. Kocmut, 'V keho z direktorji-inkriminacija kartelov', (2007) 26 *Pravna praksa* 22, 24.
97 L. Bavcon et al., *Kazensko pravo, splošni del*, Uradni list, Ljubljana 2013, p. 193. With blanket definition of a criminal act the whole definition of a criminal act could not be found in the

competition according to the ZPOmK-1 and EU Regulation 1/2003. The definition of a criminal act of the unlawful restriction of competition is based upon the definitions of relevant misdemeanours from ZPOmK-1 (contrary to the regulations governing the protection of competition, violates the prohibition of restricting agreements between companies, abuses the dominant position of one or more companies, or creates a forbidden concentration of companies).

This inevitably leads to the question of the relationship between the criminal act of the unlawful restriction of competition from Article 225 of the KZ-1 and the relevant misdemeanours from the ZPOmK-1.

Generally, according to the principle *lex certa* it is desirable that the delineation between criminal acts and misdemeanours and their definitions is clear and precise in the legislation and also in the case law. Lack of the legislator's due diligence, however, could cause a situation in which the same conduct could be subsumed under the definition of a relevant criminal act from the KZ-1 *and* under the definition of a certain misdemeanour, because no clear distinction between the abstract legal definitions of a misdemeanour and a criminal act has been made in legislation.

In such cases a misdemeanour procedure shall not be conducted and sanctions for a misdemeanour shall not be imposed on a perpetrator:

- who in a criminal procedure has already been found guilty of committing a criminal act which the includes elements of misdemeanour;
- against whom the criminal procedure was not instituted following a settlement or procedures according to Article 163 of the Criminal Procedure Act (CPA);[98]
- if he or she has been acquitted by a final judgment for committing a criminal act or
- against whom the criminal procedure has been terminated by a final court decision, the crime report has been dismissed by the state prosecutor, or if the charges have been dismissed.[99]

If the misdemeanour procedure has already been initiated, it shall be suspended until judgment at the end of the criminal procedure has become final.[100] In any case, criminal procedure should prevail.

In case these rules are not respected, KZ-1 provides that a term of imprisonment, a fine, or any other criminal sanction, which the convicted

---

criminal legislation itself, but refers to relevant definitions from other legal acts, which regulate this subject matter.

98 Official Gazette RS, No. 32/2012 and 47/2013.

99 Minor Offences Act (ZP-1), Official Gazette RS, No. 29/2011 and 21/2013. In such case the misdemeanour procedure can only be conducted when the reasons for such a decision do not preclude a misdemeanour procedure.

100 Article 11.a of ZP-1.

person has served for committing a misdemeanour shall be counted as part of the sentence, provided that the elements of the criminal act also constitute a misdemeanour and that the misdemeanour procedure was finalised before the criminal procedure.[101]

The main precondition for establishing the relation between Article 225 of the KZ-1 and relevant misdemeanours from ZPOmK-1 and applying the mentioned rules from the Minor Offences Act and KZ-1, is defining the difference between the relevant definitions in regards to the executing act, the unlawful consequence and the addressee of the relevant provisions (who could be held responsible for the unlawful conduct).

As to the question of, who is held responsible for criminal acts, in regard to criminal responsibility for Article 225 of KZ-1 general rules on complicity for natural persons from Articles 36.a to 41 of KZ-1 should be applied.

On the other hand, ZPOmK-1 in Articles 73 and 74[102] provides a legal basis for the legal responsibility of legal persons, entrepreneurs or an individuals who perform economic activity as well as the responsible (natural) persons of a legal person, or of an entrepreneur and a natural person already controlling at least one undertaking for misdemeanours from ZPOmK-1 (unlawful concentrations, cartels, abuse of dominant position and infringement of the decision of the Slovenian Competition Protection Agency-hereinafter Agency).

The measures from Articles 37, 50, 51, and 53 of ZPOmK-1, based on the decision of the Agency, could be imposed on undertakings, defined as any entity that is engaged in economic activities, regardless of its legal and organisational form and ownership status, including an association of undertakings that is not directly engaged in an economic activity but affects or may affect the behaviour for the market of undertakings.[103]

Leaving legal responsibility of legal persons aside, the responsibility for criminal acts according to KZ-1 and misdemeanours according to Articles 73 and 74 of ZPOmK-1 could overlap firstly in the case of responsibility of natural persons, since both regulations provide for responsibility of natural persons, if the forms of complicity according to KZ-1 overlap with entrepreneurs or individuals who perform economic activity as well as the responsible persons of a legal person or of an entrepreneur and a natural person already controlling at least one undertaking in a concrete case from ZPOmK-1. In such cases the distinction between criminal and misdemeanour responsibility should therefore be based upon the executing act and the defined unlawful consequence of the definitions of criminal act and misdemeanours.

---

101 Article 56 of KZ-1.

102 These are articles which define fines for the unlawful restriction of competition and unlawful concentrations.

103 Article 3 of ZPOmK-1.

The definition of unlawful restriction of competition from Article 225 of KZ-1 therefore includes also a quantative element. Namely, the restriction of competition must result in the prevention, significant impeding, or distortion of competition in the Republic of Slovenia, or in the European Union market, or its significant part, or must significantly influence the trade between Member States in order to represent a criminal act according to Article 225 of KZ-1. This element is, in my opinion, covered also by the relevant elements of unlawful restriction of competition, defined in competition legislation. Namely, the prevention or significant impeding or distortion of competition in Slovenia is defined as the core element of every unlawful restriction of competition in the ZPOmK-1,[104] whereas prevention or significant impeding or distortion competition in the European Union market, or its significant part, or significant influence on trade between Member States could be found in the EU Regulation 1/2003, which also serves as the legal basis for the EU Commission's procedures. Moreover, the distinction between the significant influence inside Member State only and inside the EU or in the trade between Member states is basically the main differentiating element between the two jurisdictions.[105]

Furthermore, the acts of a criminal act and relevant misdemeanours should be analysed. The acts of the criminal act from Article 225 are defined in alternative manner. First alternative act is the violation of the prohibition of restricting agreements between companies. Such an act could also be found in Article 73 of the ZPOmK-1, according to which a certain natural person is fined if he/she acts in contravention of Article 6 of the ZPOmK-1 or Article 81 of the EC Treaty, which both regulate and define exactly the prohibited restricting agreements.[106] Such an act could therefore be subsumed under a misdemeanour according to Article 73 of the ZPOmK-1 or under the criminal act of Article 225 of the KZ-1.

Every act from Article 225 of the KZ-1 must also be accompanied by an objective condition of punishability. Namely, every act should also result in a large property benefit for a company or companies involved, or in a large property damage for another company. Such a precise element could not be found in the ZPOmK-1, but similar quantative element are restrictions of minor importance in the case of restricting agreements from Article 7 of the ZPOmK-1. As mentioned, these conditions are not defined in the same manner, they are similar, but do not overlap completely. In this element (the quantity of property

[104] See Articles 6, 9 and 11 of ZPOmK-1.

[105] Although the proposal of KZ-1 states that the differentiation lies in in prevention or significant impeding or distortion competition. Such opinion is in my opinion incorrect, since the ZPOmK-1 specifically refers to prevention or impeding or distortion of competition also. See Article 1 of the ZPOmK-1 and the Regulation 1/2003.

[106] Article 73, paragraph 1 of ZPOmK-1.

benefit or property damage) the main difference between the relevant criminal act and misdemeanour could, therefore, be hidden.[107]

The second act of a criminal act from Article 225 of the KZ-1, is the abuse of the dominant position of one or more companies. Such an act could also be found in article 73 of the ZPOmK-1, defining a suitable misdemeanour[108] of abusing a dominant position in contravention of Article 9 of the ZPOmK-1 or Article 82 of the EC Treaty.[109] Again, ZPOmK-1 does not include any specific quantative limitation for declaring the misdemeanour of abuse of a dominant position by the Agency, whereas according to the criminal act the unlawful restriction of competition, the executing act must (again) result in large property benefit for involved company or companies, or large property damage for another company.

The last defined act of criminal act of the unlawful restriction of competition is creating a forbidden concentration of companies. Here, in my opinion, the definitions of a criminal act from Article 225 of the KZ-1 and relevant misdemeanours in regard to the unlawful concentrations according to Article 74 of the ZPOmK-1 differ at the most. Relevant definitions of misdemeanours from Article 74 of the ZPOmK-1, namely include failing to notify to the agency a concentration governed by the provisions of the ZPOmK-1, failing to notify it within the time limit referred to in the ZPOmK-1, the breaching of Article 44 of the ZPOmK-1 and implementing rights or obligations arising from the concentration; failing to implement remedies or obligations imposed by a decision declaring the concentration compatible with competition rules; acting in contravention to a decision declaring a concentration incompatible with competition rules or acting in contravention of an enforceable decision issued by the Agency pursuant to Article 53 of the ZPOmK-1.[110] The KZ-1 criminalises the creation of a forbidden concentration, whereas the misdemeanours from ZPOmK-1 define other unlawful acts in relation to this. In the definition of these executing acts, in regards to the unlawful concentration, in my opinion, lies the major difference between the definitions of the KZ-1 and the ZPOmK-1. Not every misdemeanour according to the ZPOmK-1 corresponds to the definition of a criminal act of the unlawful restriction of competition. Contrarily, only graver cases of unlawful restriction and misdemeanours represent a criminal act according to its definition in article 225 of KZ-1 and according to the principles of proportionality and *ultima ratio* of criminal law.

---

107 According to the Proposal of Criminal Code-1 only the worst cases of competition restriction are incriminated.

108 Article 73, paragraph 1 of ZPOmK-1. Other misdemeanours from Article 73 refer to the violations of the Agency's decisions according to Articles 37, 38 and 39 of ZPOmK-1.

109 These two articles both define the abuse of dominant position for national authorities (article 9 of ZPOmK-1) or EU Commission (article 82 of EC Treaty).

110 Article 74 of ZPOmK-1.

In cases, where the definitions of a criminal act from KZ-1 and misdemeanours from ZPOmK-1 overlap, the form of guilt should also be taken into consideration. Namely, according to KZ-1 the perpetrator shall be punished for the criminal act committed through negligence only if the law determines so.[111] Since Article 225 of KZ-1 does not determine so, this criminal act could be committed only intentionally.

On the other hand, according to the Minor Offences Act-1, which defines general rules on guilt for misdemeanours, including the ones, defined in ZPOmK-1, liability for a misdemeanour shall be borne by the perpetrator, who has committed the misdemeanour intentionally or through negligence. Since there is no *lex specialis* regulation in the ZPOmK-1 that a perpetrator shall be liable only for misdemeanours committed intentionally,[112] they are punishable also when committed by negligence. In case of negligence only misdemeanour responsibility is therefore possible.

Since both legal regimes (criminal and competition law) provide legal basis for the responsibility of legal persons, the issue of overlapping legal responsibility of legal persons could also arise.

The criminal responsibility of legal persons is in regulated in Slovenia by the Liability of Legal Persons for Criminal Offences Act,[113] which includes all necessary preconditions for the responsibility of legal persons, relevant sanctions, criminal acts, and special provisions of criminal procedure. The first condition for the responsibility of legal persons for criminal acts is that the relevant criminal act is listed in Article 25, which enumerates criminal acts, for which legal person could be held responsible. Accordingly, Article 225 concerning the unlawful restriction of competition is one of those criminal acts, for which legal person could be criminally responsible.

Additional conditions are regulated also. Generally a legal person could be responsible for this criminal act, if the criminal act committed by the perpetrator was committed in the name of, on behalf of, or in favour of the legal person and if

- the committed criminal act means carrying out an unlawful resolution, order or endorsement of its management or supervisory bodies or
- its management or supervisory bodies influenced the perpetrator or enabled him to commit the criminal act or
- the legal person acquires the unlawfully obtained property benefit or objects obtained through a criminal act or
- its management or supervisory bodies have omitted due supervision of the legality of the actions of employees subordinate to them.[114]

111 Article 27 of KZ-1.

112 Article 9 of ZP-1.

113 Official Gazette RS, No. 98/2004, 65/2008 and 57/2012.

114 Article 4 of Liability of Legal Persons for Criminal Offences Act.

These conditions have to be proven in every case. In my opinion there should be no problem with attributing the criminal act of the unlawful restriction of competition to a legal person, because this criminal act is typically committed in favour of a legal person (certain undertaking) and with which the legal person usually acquires the illegally obtained property benefit.

The differences between the definitions of criminal act and relevant misdemeanours, discussed above with the responsibility of natural persons, should be considered here as well.

Table 2. Relation between criminal and misdemeanour responsibility of natural and legal persons for the unlawful restriction of competition.

Form of responsibility\ person	Misdemeanour responsibility (ZPOmK-1)	Criminal responsibility (criminal legislation)
Responsibility of legal persons	Responsibility for misdemeanours according to the Articles 73 and 74 of ZPOmK-1	Criminal responsibility according to KZ-1 and Liability of Legal Persons for Criminal Offences Act for criminal act of unlawful restriction of competition (Article 225 of KZ-1)
	Any undertaking = any entity that is engaged in economic activities, regardless of its legal and organisational form and ownership status, also an association of undertakings that is not directly engaged in an economic activity but affects or may affect the behaviour on the market of undertakings	Any legal person, except the state and municipalities
Responsibility of natural persons	Responsibility for misdemeanours according to Articles 73 and 74 of ZPOmK-1 entrepreneur or an individual who performs economic activity, responsible person of a legal entity or of an entrepreneur	Criminal responsibility according to KZ-1 for criminal act of unlawful restriction of competition (Article 225 of KZ-1) rules on complicity

5.3. LENIENCY IN CRIMINAL PROCEDURE

Although mostly substantive criminal law issues have been discussed by now, a procedural novelty has been introduced into Slovenian Criminal Procedure Act (ZKP),[115] which could be most useful for prosecuting the criminal act of the unlawful restriction of competition; the plea-bargain[116] and pleading guilty at the pre-trial hearing.[117]

115 Official Gazette RS, No. 91/2011.

116 Articles 450–450.č of ZKP.

117 Ibid., Articles 285a-285f.

If a defendant pleads guilty in a plea-bargain procedure and the agreement is accepted by the court, the agreed sentence is given the defendant. Similarly, if the defendant pleads guilty at the pre-trial hearing and the confession is accepted by court, the trial is omitted and the court imposes a sentence, not higher than the one proposed by the prosecutor.

As the EU Commission mentioned, secret cartels are often difficult to detect and investigate without the cooperation of undertakings or individuals implicated in them.[118] Also, by their nature, there is usually more than one undertaking and natural person involved, which would means that leniency programmes could be effective.

Therefore, for leniency programmes, including substantive institutes such as the remission of sentence on the basis of Article 225 of KZ-1 or other such possibility from KZ-1 and procedural institutes, such as pleading guilty at pre-trial hearing and plea-bargaining could be applied in criminal procedures in regards to the unlawful restriction of competition as well. In such a manner, the prosecution could obtain useful facts and evidence, which could then be applied in criminal procedures against other natural and legal persons.

Although these two procedural institutes are very recent in Slovenian criminal procedure,[119] they have already been widely implemented in practice. The Report of the Office of the State Prosecutor General of the Republic of Slovenia for the year 2012 namely shows that only in the second half of 2012, out of 3.269 pre-trial hearings in 1.199 cases at least one of the defendants pleaded guilty[120] and out of 166 cases of plea-bargaining, the defendant signed the agreement in 140 of the cases.[121] It is true, that considering the number of all convictions (9.296 for the year 2012), 1.199 admissions of guilt do not seem high. However, the total number of all convictions refers to the whole year of 2012, whereas the number 1.199 refers to the period from May 2012 forward only. The report also states that the plea-bargaining appeals mostly to the defendants of graver criminal acts, for which a higher prison sentence is prescribed.[122]

Also, the prosecution has developed a tactic, in which the prosecution tries to find the weakest link among the defendants and begins the plea-bargaining procedure with him, using the information in other procedures.[123]

All these tactics and legal institutes, especially considering the EU Commission's attitude toward leniency programmes and the legal basis for them in the ZPOmK-1, KZ-1 and ZKP, could be successfully applied also in cases of the unlawful restriction of competition.

---

118 Introduction to the Commission notice on immunity from fines and reduction of fines in cartel cases, paragraph 3.
119 They have been implemented only in May 2012.
120 Skupno poročilo o delu državnih tožilstev, p. 30.
121 Ibid.
122 Ibid.
123 K. Šugman Stubbs, op. cit., p. 20–28.

6. CONCLUSIONS

Certain EU Member States have already introduced criminal law sanctions for the unlawful restriction of competition. The EU itself neither includes an explicit or implicit obligation for Member States to criminalise competition law, nor is such conduct criminalised at the EU level.

On the other hand, EU law could be interpreted in such a manner as to enable the implementation of criminal law sanctions for natural persons, beside fines for undertakings, involved in the restriction of competition. For a more explicit and precise legal basis for criminalisation of competition law at the EU level and for the jurisdiction of the EPPO, however, the definition of fraud and fraud related criminal acts should be interpreted and defined in a broader manner. This is in my opinion necessary because the unlawful restriction of competition represents both cross-border crime and crime, which affects the financial interests of the EU and these two forms of crime are in spotlight of the EU criminal justice efforts.

Slovenian legislation recognises misdemeanour and criminal responsibility for unlawful competition restriction. These two forms of legal responsibility could be applied to natural, as well as legal persons by the Agency for misdemeanours, according to the ZPOmK-1 and by courts for the criminal act of the unlawful restriction of competition according to KZ-1. It seems, however, that despite legal basis for the last twenty years, misdemeanour procedure, run by the Agency, is much more frequent and efficient in practice and there are little results in criminal prosecution. In my opinion this could be improved by making good use of the already existing legislation and cooperation between the State Prosecutor's Office and the Agency and not so much by its repeated amendment.

BIBLIOGRAPHY

Macculoch, A., 'The cartel offence: defining an appropriate "Moral space"', (2012) 8 European competition journal, pp. 73–93.

Criminal Code, Official Gazette RS, No. 95/2004 (official consolidated version).

Criminal Code-1, Official Gazette RS, No. 50/2012 (official consolidated version).

Criminal Code-1B, Official Gazette RS, No. 91/2011.

Criminal Procedure Act, Official Gazette RS, No. 32/2012 and 47/2013.

EU Commission: Commission notice on immunity from fines and reduction of fines in cartel cases [2006] OJ C 298.

Hakopan, G., 'Criminalization of EU competition law enforcement – a possibility after Lisbon?', (2010) 7 The competition law review, pp. 157–173.

Kaučič I., and F. Grad, Ustavna ureditev Slovenije, GV založba, Ljubljana 2007.

Daly, K., 'Cartels and deterrence-creeping criminalization and the class action boom' (2007) 1 Bloomberg European business law journal 1, pp. 315–326.

Stubbs, K. Š., 'Plea bargaining: sociološki in psihološki vidiki', Zbornik 4. konference kazenskega prava in kriminologije, GV založba, Ljubljana 2011, pp. 20–28.

Liability of Legal Persons for Criminal Offences Act, Official Gazette RS, No. 98/2004, 65/2008 and 57/2012.

Bavcon, L., et al., Kazensko pravo, splošni del, Uradni list, Ljubljana 2013.

Kuhl, L., 'The initiative for a directive on the protection of the EU financial interests by substantive criminal law', (2012) 2 Eucrim, p. 63–66.

Šturm L., (Ed.), Komentar Ustave Republike Slovenije. Fakulteta za državne in evropske študije, Ljubljana 2010.

Pavčnik, M., Teorija prava, GV založba, Ljubljana 2011.

Minor Offences Act, Official Gazette RS, No. 29/2011 and 21/2013.

Deisinger M.,, Kazenski zakonik s komentarjem, posebni del, GV založba, Ljubljana 2002.

Kocmut, M., `V keho z direktorji-inkriminacija kartelov`, (2007) 26 Pravna praksa 22.

Prevention of Restriction of Competition Act, Official Gazette RS, No. 64/2007 (official consolidated version).

Prevention of Restriction of Competition Act-1, Official Gazette RS, No. 36/2008, 40/2009, 26/2011, 87/2011 and 57/2012.

Gorkič, P., 'Evropski javni tožilec: zdaj gre (zares) zares' (2013) 32 Pravna praksa, pp. II-VI.

Protection of Competition Act, Official Gazette RS, No. 18/1993.

The proposal of Criminal Code, Poročevalec državnega zbora 22/1993.

The proposal of Criminal Code-1.

The proposal of Criminal Code-1B.

Kinkelly U., `Protecting children's rights under the ECHR: the role of positive obligations`, (2010) 61 Northern Ireland Legal Quarterly, pp. 245–261.

Wills W.P. J., 'Is criminalization of EU competition law the answer?', in: C.D. Ehlermann and I. Atanasiu (eds.), European Competition Law Annual 2006: Enforcement of Prohibition of Cartels, Hart Publishing, Oxford, Portland, Oregon 2006.

Tomlin, H., `Positive obligations under the European Convention on Human Rights` <www.google.si/url?sa=t&rct=j&q=&esrc=s&frm=1&source=web&cd=3&ved=0CD0QFjAC&url=http%3A%2F%2Fwww.adminlaw.org.uk%2Fdocs%2FSC%25202012%2520by%2520Tomlinson%2520QC.docx&ei=sqNfUpijEKiD4AT34oDYCA&usg=AFQjCNGIfphLexyU_SefygKtUvUMLff_-g&sig2=KkJnG4X30J6FFoxN-Tf24g> accessed 17.10.2013.

Alves, I., Gawronski, S. A.and Stupak, M., 'The positive obligation of states to provide security under the ECHR, the Charter, and the Polish Constitution' <www.google.si/url?sa=t&rct=j&q=&esrc=s&frm=1&source=web&cd=2&ved=0CDAQFjAB&url=http%3A%2F%2Fen.zpc.wpia.uw.edu.pl%2Fwp-content%2Fuploads%2F2010%2F04%2F4.-The-standard-of-the-right-to-security-1.doc&ei=aKFfUqrFCszS4QSjoYC4CA&usg=AFQjCNFKRvCmm4qHIAVESrfPkyqJ3QfjUg&sig2=3IYgx8PgCFsUXabfZExlNw&bvm=bv.54176721,d.bGE > accessed 17.10.2013.

Vrhovno državno tožilstvo Republike Slovenije: Skupno poročilo o delu državnih tožilstev za leto 2012 <www.dt-rs.si/uploads/porocilo_2012_internet.pdf> (17/10/2013)

CHAPTER 10

CARTEL DETECTION AND COLLUSION SCREENING: AN EMPIRICAL ANALYSIS OF THE LONDON METAL EXCHANGE

Danilo SAMA

In Francia abbiamo seguito le vostre elezioni.
Il capo del governo ha tre reti televisive?'
'Sì'.
'Perché in Francia non si potrebbe, c'è una legge.
Voi non avete la legge antitrust?'
'Sì. Sì e no. Più no che sì'.
Nanni Moretti

1. LIBOR SCANDAL

In 2013, the European Commission imposed an administrative fine of 1.7 billion euro to some of the world's largest banking companies involved in what has been described by the mass media as "Libor Scandal".[1] The record sanction, being the highest ever levied by the officials of Brussels for a cartel infringement, was issued to 8 international financial institutions for participating in illegal agreements relating to interest rate derivatives. As it is common knowledge, interest rate derivatives are financial products, such as futures, options, swaps, which are both employed as insurance tools for managing the risk of interest rate fluctuations and traded worldwide as investment assets by financial intermediaries. The value of these financial derivatives comes from the level of a benchmark interest rate, such as the Euro Interbank Offered Rate (Euribor), which is used for the euro area, or the London Interbank Offered Rate (Libor), which is used for several currencies including the Japanese Yen. In turn, the value of these benchmarks reflects the averaged interest rate at which,

1 Commission Decision of 04.12.2013, *Euro Interest Rate Derivatives*, Case AT.39914; Commission Decision of 04.12.2013, *Yen Interest Rate Derivatives*, Case AT.39861; European *Commission, Antitrust: Commission fines banks € 1.71 billion for participating in cartels in the interest rate derivatives industry*, Press Release, IP/13/1208, 04.12.2013, Brussels, Belgium.

respectively, a selected panel of Eurozone and London banks offer to lend funds in a given currency to other banks on the daily interbank market.

In a nutshell, the cartel aimed at manipulating the pricing process of the Euribor and the Libor, distorting the competition in the underlying trading of interest rate derivatives. Since at least $800 trillion in derivatives, loans, securities and other financial products are tied to the Euribor and the Libor, such was the dimension of the scandal, which *inter alia* has highlighted the urgency of a regulatory reform of the banking sector, the largest one to have been rigged so far.

2. BENFORD'S LAW

A crucial expedient for revealing the "Libor Scandal" has been the leniency program, joined by a member of the cartel at issue providing an active cooperation in the investigation of the Commission in exchange of full immunity. Beyond the success of the cartel settlement procedure and the relevant dimension of the market involved, from a competition policy standpoint, the Libor case offers another interesting food for thought, being an excellent example of how antitrust authorities can employ screening instruments to identify collusive behaviours.

A fascinating technique to detect rigged prices is offered by an odd phenomenon called Benford's Law, otherwise known as First-Digit Law. Although a primordial statement must be attributed to Newcomb (1881),[2] in a 1938 paper, the father of the law, a physicist working at General Electric, recognised the existence of a specific pattern that often occurs in vast datasets.[3] In particular, the law consists in a frequency distribution which describes the probability according to which a number present in a random dataset starts with a certain digit.

Theoretically, if a set of numbers were truly random, each leading digit would appear about 11% of the time. On the contrary, Benford's Law predicts a logarithmic weakly monotonic distribution, according to which the digit 1 occurs as leading digit about 30% of the time, while larger digits occur in that position less and less frequently (cf. Formula 1). In other terms, the leading digits are not distributed evenly, as it would be natural to expect, but following a distribution where 1 is the most frequent and 9 is the less common. The law,

2 S. Newcomb, 'Note on the Frequency of Use of the Different Digits in Natural Numbers' (1881), *American Journal of Mathematics*, Vol. 4, No. 1, The Johns Hopkins University Press, Baltimore, United States, pp. 39–40.

3 F. Benford 'The Law of Anomalous Numbers' (1938), *Proceedings of the American Philosophical Society*, Vol. 78, No. 4, American Philosophical Society, Philadelphia, United States, pp. 551–572.

which has also been generalised to digits beyond the first, tends to be more precise in datasets which exhibit multiple orders of magnitude and for types of values which grow exponentially.

Formula 1. Benford's Law Logarithmic Probability Distribution Function

$$P(d) = \log_{10}(d + 1) - \log_{10}(d) = \log_{10}\left(\frac{d+1}{d}\right) = \log_{10}\left(1 + \frac{1}{d}\right)$$

A brief and intuitive explanation of why the law naturally occurs is that usually we start counting from the digit 1 until the digit 9. It is obvious that if we think to the digits from 1 to 9, we have the same probability that a random number starts with any of these digits. But if we consider a range of numbers, for example from 1 to 20, we count more numbers starting with the digit 1. The same happens if we consider the range of numbers from 1 to 30, where we count many numbers starting with the digit 1, but also many others starting with the digit 2. In any case, what matters is that, in order to have many numbers starting with the digit 9, it is necessary to examine a large dataset. As a result, analysing for instance distributions of numbers related to populations or surfaces, the probability to have a number starting with the digit 1 will be higher than that to have a number with 9 as leading digit. Accordingly, Benford showed that, for several types of distributions, the probability that a number starts with a certain digit tends to be always the same (cf. Figure 1).

Figure 1. Probability Distribution of Leading Digits according to Benford's Law

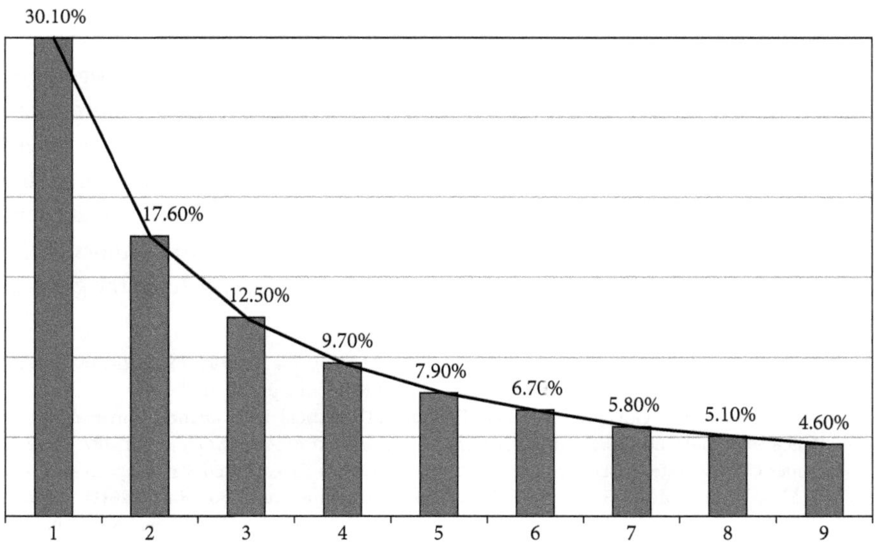

3. LITERATURE REVIEW

The predictive power of Benford's Law has been ascertained valid in several situations normally observable in the real world. Death rates, election votes, financial transitions, government spendings, income distributions, physical and mathematical constants, population numbers and stock prices are just few examples over which the law applies. It is not a case that auditors have successfully employed it to detect frauds and manipulations in accounting data since the 1970s. At that time also Varian (1972)[4] suggested the possibility to use the law to uncover falsifications in socio-economic data collected for public purposes, under the assumption that who aims at rigging datasets tends to provide numbers distributed according to a uniform pattern. Nigrini (1999)[5] as well showed that the law can be exploited for taxation controls, after having tested it with success on real cases of fiscal scams.

Thus, given its regularity, the law can be adopted to test economic data in several cases. Its application is rather straightforward: even though a dataset has been artificially ordered in such a way to preserve randomness, the distribution of the digits will definitely violate the pattern predicted by the law. Within the present framework, in a seminal paper by Abrantes-Metz *et al.* (2011),[6] the authors considered worthwhile to test the theory over Libor data, using the second digit distribution variant of the law. The surprising result was that the benchmark interest rate at issue departed significantly from the Benford's Law pattern over an extended period of time, signalling the possibility of a rate manipulation. As a result, through a quick application of the test, the Libor cartel could have been discovered much time before the opening of the settlement procedure.

In Brähler *et al.* (2011),[7] a Benford's Law test was applied to investigate the quality of macroeconomic data reported by the EU member states to Eurostat in order to comply with the Stability and Growth Pact criteria. Since government statistics are comparable in nature to financial accounting, governments, like firms towards auditors, might be tempted to adjust the national account balances, given the strict obligations to which are subject to. The authors of the study found that the official statistics submitted by Greece registered the greatest

---

4 H.R. Varian, 'Benford's Law (Letters to the Editor)' (1972), *The American Statistician*, Vol. 26, Issue 3, Taylor & Francis Journals, London, United Kingdom, pp. 62–65.

5 M.J. Nigrini, 'I've Got Your Number: How a Mathematical Phenomenon Can Help CPAs Uncover Fraud and Other Irregularities' (1999), *Journal of Accountancy*, Vol. 187, Issue 5, American Institute of Certified Public Accountants, New York, United States, pp. 15–27.

6 R.M. Abrantes-Metz, G. Judge, S. Villas-Boas, 'Tracking the Libor Rate' (2011), *Applied Economics Letters*, Vol. 10, Issue 10, Taylor & Francis Journals, London, United Kingdom, pp. 893–899.

7 G. Brähler, S. Engel, M. Göttsche, B. Rauch, 'Fact and Fiction in EU-Governmental Economic Data' (2011), *German Economic Review*, Vol. 12, Issue 3, John Wiley & Sons, New York, United States, pp. 243–255.

deviation from the expected Benford's Law distribution in comparison to all the other EU countries. The manipulation of financial data by the Greek institutions has officially been certified by the Commission at a later stage.

4. EMPIRICAL ANALYSIS OF THE LONDON METAL EXCHANGE

As well as for the "Libor Scandal", the Wall Street Journal has launched in 2011 an investigation about possible anti-competitive practices on the London Metal Exchange (LME), allegedly resulting in artificially high prices for a category of commodities, above all aluminium, whose hoarding is managed by a group of international banking corporations.[8] In the last years, in fact, the metals industry has been invested by a huge wave of acquisitions by major investment banks of metals warehouses located around the world. According to the allegations, the "too big to fail banks" at issue, being owners of large aluminium warehouses able to hoard massive supply in excess, despite the record levels of production registered since 2011, would have deliberately delayed the market distribution of aluminium products, inflating so its final price and gathering in the meantime exorbitant rents and other fees for the storage operations (cf. Figure 2). As a matter of fact, aluminium is the only commodity for which prompt delivery is not guaranteed, requiring instead its distribution several months. In the past, an analogous supply bottleneck strategy was used by De Beers to obstruct the market clearing and to maintain the price of diamonds extremely high.

The group of bank holding companies owners of the aluminium warehouses has replied to the allegations asserting that it merely follows the guidelines established by the LME (although, it is worth to notice, the investment banks in question are members and shareholders of the LME itself). However, in the United States, three class-action lawsuits were filed in 2013 against the alleged aluminium cartel for its presumed control over the LME. According to the plaintiffs, 5 billion dollars has been the total cost of the cartel at the expense of consumers for the period 2011–2013.[9]

---

8 A. Hotter, T. Shumsky, 'Wall Street Gets Eyed in Metal Squeeze. Some Say Warehousing Inflates Prices' (2011), *The Wall Street Journal*, 17.06.2001, New York, United States.

9 *Master Screens Inc., et al. v. Goldman Sachs Group Inc., et al.*, Case No. 13-CV-00431, United States District Court for the Northern District of Florida, Tallahassee Division; *Superior Extrusion Inc., et al. v. Goldman Sachs Group Inc., et al.*, Case No. 13-CV-13315, United States District Court for the Eastern District of Michigan, Detroit Division; *River Parish Contractors Inc., et al. v. Goldman Sachs Group Inc., et al.*, Case No. 13-CV-05267, United States District Court for the Eastern District of Louisiana, New Orleans Division.

Figure 2. LME Aluminium Price (US$ per Tonne) (2002–2013)

As a result, the main objective of the present paper is to apply Benford's Law to track the daily LME aluminium price over the period 2011–2013, in order to verify possible data manipulations which would suggest the existence of a cartel. We analyze this time period for two basic reasons: firstly, because after the collapse of aluminium prices due to the global financial crisis, 2011 is the year when the commodity at issue began to reach very high prices, apparently not justified by the record levels of production touched; secondly, because the suspect of a possible collusion started to be felt at that time.

For what concerns the application of Benford's Law, since the nominal value of the aluminium price does not change very much over short periods of time, an analysis of the first digit distribution would be meaningless since the pattern predicted by the law would be definitely violated. On the contrary, in Table 2 and 3, as well as in Figure 3 and Figure 4, we can observe how the empirical second digit distribution and in particular the empirical third digit distribution of the LME aluminium price for the period 2002–2013 follow the expected pattern. This confirms the fact that the price spans the nine digit space only if we consider the second and the third digit.

Table 1. Benford's Law Second Digit Test: LME Aluminium (US$ per Tonne) (2002-2013)

Digit	LME Frequency	Benford Rate	LME Rate	Δ
0	226	11.97%	7.48%	-4.49%
1	157	11.39%	5.20%	-6.19%
2	191	10.82%	6.32%	-4.50%
3	447	10.43%	14.80%	4.36%
4	445	10.03%	14.73%	4.70%
5	209	9.67%	6.92%	-2.75%
6	239	9.34%	7.91%	-1.43%
7	377	9.04%	12.48%	3.44%
8	451	8.76%	14.93%	6.17%
9	2	8.50%	9.24%	0.74%
Total	3.021			

Table 2. Benford's Law Third Digit Test: LME Aluminium (US$ per Tonne) (2002-2013)[10]

Digit	LME Frequency	Benford Rate	LME Rate	Δ
0	338	11.97%	11.19%	-0.78%
1	298	11.39%	9.86%	-1.52%
2	294	10.82%	9.73%	-1.09%
3	333	10.43%	11.02%	0.59%
4	313	10.03%	10.36%	0.33%
5	269	9.67%	8.90%	-0.76%
6	291	9.34%	9.63%	0.30%
7	312	9.04%	10.33%	1.29%
8	285	8.76%	9.43%	0.68%
9	288	8.50%	9.53%	1.03%
Total	3.021			

10 In Table 2, Benford's Law second digit rates, rather than third digit ones, are reported since, for the sake of simplicity of computations, we deleted first digits from the entire dataset when we dealt with the third digit distribution. Thus, we can treat third digits as they were second digits. Of course, this expedient does not alter the value of Benford's Law analysis. Furthermore, this allow us to better and equally compare the two LME Aluminium sets of rates, reported in Table 1 and Table 2, respect to Benford's Law one.

Figure 3. Benford's Law Second Digit Test: LME Aluminium (US$ per Tonne) (2002–2013)

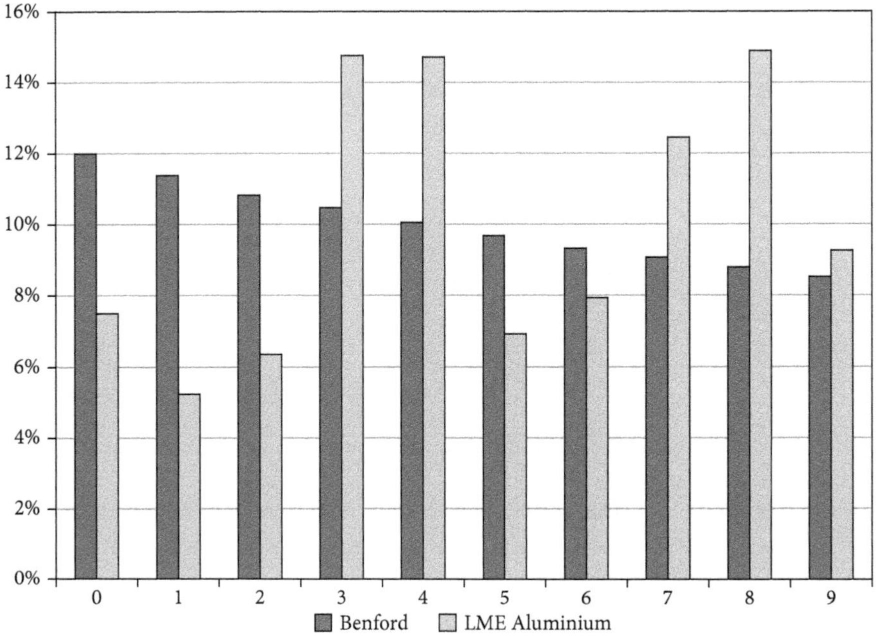

Figure 4. Benford's Law Third Digit Test: LME Aluminium (US$ per Tonne) (2002–2013)

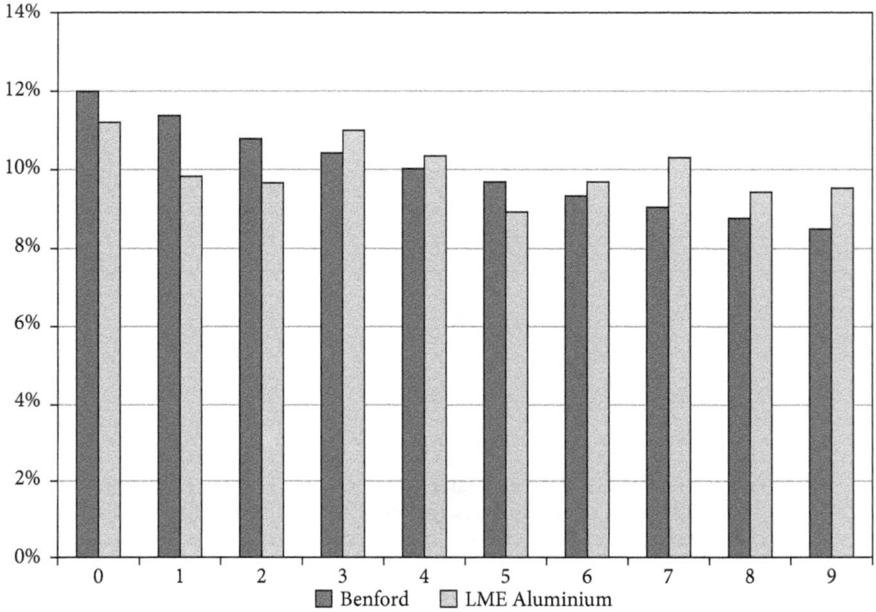

Since our main concern is with the aluminium price trend registered in the last three years, following the methodology adopted to detect the "Libor Scandal", we now proceed to test the closeness to the Benford's Law pattern of the empirical distributions of both the second and third digits of the daily LME aluminium price. Our assessment is based on rolling six month periods, starting from 2011 until 2013. In particular, in Table 3, we present the empirical frequencies of the second digit distribution, whilst in Table 4 we present the empirical frequencies of the third digit distribution. The two tables at issue, given the size, are reported at the end of the current work.

Two are the main results. As for the second digit distribution, we register empirical frequencies which depart significantly from the expected Benford's Law pattern. This raises potential concerns relative to the data integrity of the aluminium price. Only the empirical frequencies of the third digit distribution, which we decided to compute for a more conservative analysis, are in line with the pattern predicted by the law. In this regard, it is important to remind that for the Libor cartel, it was enough to find departures similar to those we found in the empirical second digit distribution of the LME aluminium price to raise alert about possible rigged prices. Furthermore, in the Libor case, several periods of time where Benford's Law was respected were found in any case. Here, instead, at least for the period 2011–2013, the deviation from the expected pattern is constant. Moreover, the deviation of both the second and third digit distributions from the Benford's Law pattern tends to increase over time, reaching the maximum levels in 2013. The opening of an investigation to further examine the aluminium industry, according to the price screen at issue, seems therefore worthwhile.

5. POLICY CONCLUSIONS

In order to detect and fight cartel conducts, the best scenario for competition agencies would be of course the possibility to analyze detailed information on firms' costs and prices, being the price-cost margin a robust indicator of market power. However, information on firms' costs is rarely available. In this context, as pointed out by our analysis of the London Metal Exchange, quick tests such as Benford's Law can only be helpful to inspect markets where price patterns show signs of collusion. Given the budget constraints to which antitrust watchdogs are commonly subject to, a such price screen could be set up, just exploiting the data available, as warning system to identify cases that require the opening of an investigation.

Nevertheless, it is important to underline that Benford's Law, as any other statistical test, cannot be adopted as investigative tool in any circumstance, since not all real data are expected to obey the law at issue. The risk otherwise is to fall into false-positive assessments. In any case, what seems certain is the fact that such a useful instrument, if not employed by competition authorities, will be surely used by firms to further disguise and mystify cartel activities.

BIBLIOGRAPHY

Benford, F., The Law of Anomalous Numbers, (1938) American Philosophical Society, Vol. 78, No. 4, pp. 551–572.

Brahler G., Engel S., Göttsche M., Rauch B., Fact and Fiction in EU-Governmental Economic Data (2011), German Economic Review, Vol. 12, No. 3, John Wiley & Sons, pp. 243–255.

Hotter A., Shumsky T., Wall Street Gets Eyed in Metal Squeeze. Some Say Warehousing Inflates Prices, (17.06.2001) The Wall Street Journal, New York

Newcomb, S., Note on the Frequency of Use of the Different Digits in Natural Numbers, (1881) American Journal of Mathematics, The Johns Hopkins University Press, Vol. 4, No. 1, pp. 39–40.

Varian, H.R., Benford's Law (Letters to the Editor) (1972), The American Statistician, Vol. 26, No. 3, Taylor & Francis Journals, pp. 62–65.

CHAPTER 11

DAMAGES CLAIMS IN THE SPANISH SUGAR CARTEL

Francisco Marcos

Whatever criticisms may be made of a system, which is designed to consolidate a partitioning of national markets by means of national quotas, the effects of which will be examined later, the fact remains that if it leaves in practice a residual field of competition, that field comes within the provisions of the rules of competition.
§ 24 Judgment of 16 December 1975, 40/73 to 48/73, 50/73, 54/73 to 56/73, 111/73, 113/73 and 114/73, Suiker Unie [1975] ECR 1663, 1915

The EU Sugar markets, under the CMO Sugar, are highly conducive to tacit collusion. The geographical separation of markets minimises the need for communication between the firms. A number of possible minor reforms could make the tacit collusion harder to sustain. Free trade would undoubtedly break any tacitly collusive behaviour and bring prices to the level of the world market, such a profound change is not realistic in the short run however.
Swedish Competition Authority, Sweet Fifteen: The Competition on the EU Sugar Markets, Report 7/2002: 88.

1. INTRODUCTION

Until recently private damages claims arising from competition law (EU or domestic) violations have been rare in Spain. The few successful damage claims to date, referred predominantly to violations of Article 102 TFEU (or domestic equivalent).[1] For that reason, the judgments recently delivered by the Spanish Supreme Court awarding € 5 million in damages on the two follow-on actions in the sugar cartel case is of major significance for future antitrust damages claims in Spain.

This chapter considers the relevant considerations made by the Spanish Supreme Court. In particular, it notes the Supreme Court approach as to the

1 See F. Marcos 'Competition Law Private Litigation in the Spanish Courts (1999–2012)' (2013) *Global Competition Litigation Review*, Issue 4: 167–208, 182.

legal force given to public enforcement decisions, the calculation of damages, the Court's approach to the passing-on defence and the standing of indirect purchasers. To position the discussion in context, the article begins with a review of the functioning and singularities of the sugar industry and describes the Spanish Competition Tribunal decision uncovering and sanctioning the sugar cartel.

2. THE SUGAR INDUSTRIES

Certain features of sugar industries make them prone to anti-competitive practices. The raw materials used for sucrose production (sugarcane and sugar beet), are subjected to intense government regulation in many countries.[2] For that reason, the sugar industry competitiveness is heavy burdened by government intervention that may distort business decisions of those involved in

2 Sugar markets are described as *"one of the most subsidised and distorted of all agricultural markets"*, Organization for Economic Cooperation and Development (OECD), *Sugar Policy Reform in the European Union and World Sugar Markets*, 2007, 9. For example, in the EU, since 1967 sugar beet and sugar cane growers are covered by the CAP. Aimed *inter alia* at ensuring *"that the necessary guarantees in respect of employment and standards of living are maintained for Community growers of sugar beet and sugar cane"* EU sugar policy (embodied in the Common Market Organization (CMO) for sugar) includes a price support system, a quota production system, export subsidies and import barriers [see Council Regulation (EEC) nº 1785/81 of 30 June 1981, on the Common organization of the markets in the sugar sector (OJEC L177 of 01.07.1981: 4–31) as amended]. The EU regime was significantly reformed in 2006 to progressively promote the competitiveness and market orientation of the sugar industry (decrease in tariffs, quotas and subsidies), complying with WTO rules, see Council Regulation (EC) nº 318/2006 of 20 February 2006 on the common organization of the markets in the sugar sector (OJEU L58 of 28.02.2006: 1–21). An explanation can be read in European Commission, *The European Sugar Sector: A long-term competitive future*, Sept. 2006. For a brief comment of this reform and its impact in raising the price of sugar see M. Busse & F. Jerosch `Reform of the EU Sugar Market' (2006) *Intereconomics*, March-April: 104–107. Nevertheless, in 2010 European Court of Auditors considered that the reform had a limited impact in increasing competitiveness and efficiency of the industry and did not have the forecasted positive impact in consumer welfare (36% decrease in prices was expected), *Has the reform of the Sugar Market achieved its main objectives?*, Report 6/2010 (available http://eca.europa.eu/portal/pls/portal/docs/1/5996726.PDF visited on 10.01.2015).
The situation is not very different in the U.S. (where regulatory intervention makes the price of sugar in the domestic US market double or treble the world market price), see A.H. Dean 'Artificially Sweetened: An Analysis of the United States Sugar Program', 27 March 2006. *CUREJ: College Undergraduate Research Electronic Journal*, U. of Pennsylvania (available at http://repository.upenn.edu/curej/28, visited on 10.01.2015). See also R.O. Zerbe, 'Monopoly, the Emergence of Oligopoly and the Case of Sugar Refining' (1970) *Journal of Law and Economics*, 13/2: 501–515, 505–607 (*'the most obvious way in which the sugar refining industry has failed to be competitive has been through the intervention of government'*).

production and trade,[3] spreading further the risk of collusion or anti-competitive abuses through all sugar processing and production processes.[4]

Sugar growers and processors are economically interdependent for sugar production, leading to long-term links and contractual engagements among them.[5] Indeed, in comparison to other agricultural products in the Common Agricultural Policy (CAP), it is not the sugar beet which is subject to the majority of the regulatory measures but the processed product (sugar itself), and that gives sugar processors a strong bargaining position vis-à-vis the individual beet growers.[6]

In addition, due to regulation and transportation costs, sugar production and processing markets have a rather limited territorial scope. Indeed, given the existence of substantial entry barriers in the sugar processing market,[7] the sugar processing industries are characterised by national markets with an oligopolistic structure, even monopolistic in some countries.[8]

---

3 On the pervasiveness of protectionist policies in this industry (and how they distort worldwide trade) see D. F. Larson & B. Borrell, 'Sugar policy and reform', *World Bank Policy Research WP* 2602, 2001 (available at http://elibrary.worldbank.org/doi/pdf/10.1596/1813-9450-2602, visited on 10.01.2015). For example, innovation in the sugar industry has been found to be strongly influenced by regulatory changes, see (concerning changes in the EU's CMO for sugar), K. Dillen, M. Demont & E. Tollens, 'European Sugar Policy Reform and Agricultural Innovation' 2008 *Canadian Journal of Agricultural Economics* 56: 533–553.

4 The regulatory distortions present in the EU sugar industries favour anticompetitive behaviour, and removing them would help in tackling it, see N Strand, 'Tacit collusion in the EU Sugar Markets' *Swedish Network for European Studies in Business and Economics (SNEE), WP 204*, 2002 (available at www.snee.org/filer/papers/204.pdf, visited on 20.04.2014) 11 (who argues that sugar price levels 10–20% higher than intervention prices are due to collusion by sugar processing firms). See also Swedish Competition Authority, *Sweet Fifteen: The Competition on the EU Sugar Markets*, 80–88 (available at www.konkurrensverket.se/upload/Filer/Trycksa ker/Rapporter/rap_2002-7.pdf, visited on 10.01.2015).

5 OECD, *Sugar Policy Reform* (*supra* n3) 28. On the tensions and potential conflicts among sugar growers and millers, see Larson & Borrell 'Sugar Policy and Reform' (*supra* n4), 14–15.

6 Swedish Competition Authority, *Sweet Fifteen* (*supra* n5) 57.

7 Apart from the investment costs of building a sugar-processing factory (that cannot be far away from growers as sugar beet or cane need to be processed shorty after harvested to maximize sugar content), which can be substantial [see D Genesove & W P Mullin, 'Testing static oligopoly models: Conduct and cost in the sugar industry, 1890–1914' (1998) *RAND Journal of Economics* 29(2): 355–377, 360–361] there are protectionist interventions and quotas what draw borders in these markets, and make them geographically of national scope. See Strand, 'Tacit collusion in the EU Sugar Markets', 14. This seems to be a frequent feature of international cartels, see M. Levenstrein & V. Y. Suslow, 'Contemporary International Cartels and Developing Countries: Economic Effects and Implications for Competition Policy' (2004) *Antitrust Law Journal* 71: 801–852, 823–824 (*'to use the state as a tool for creating barriers to entry'*).

8 On the high concentration of sugar markets, see OECD, *Sugar Policy Reform* (*supra* n3), 100–101. Although it could well be that some sugar markets are *infra*-national, "*since production quotas in the EU are determined at the Member State Level, it is all too easy without further thought to accept the Member State as the relevant geographical markets*" Swedish Competition Authority, *Sweet Fifteen* (*supra* n5) 42. On one of the few cases where a subnational market was considered by the European Commission, see §§26–31 of Decision of 20 December 2001, IV/M.2530 *Südzucker/Saint Louis Sucre*, OJEU L105 of 24.04.2003, 1–35.

Naturally, sugar markets can be distinguished depending on the use they make of sugar. Sugar in its different varieties (white granulated, liquid and specialty) can be sold to end-consumers, that being a market in itself; however the vast majority of sugar produced is used in other industries. Moreover, there are several sugar-using industries, mainly drink and food processing industries, some of which use sugar as one of their main inputs (in chocolate, biscuit and confectionary industries it accounts for up to 40% cost of final product), but also chemical and pharmaceutical industries.

Besides, several features of sugar as a homogeneous product, and the price-inelastic nature of sugar markets on both the supply and demand sides, together with the concentrated and transparency of the market (through production quotas and intervention prices) facilitates collusion.[9]

Moreover, regarding particularly with the industrial uses of sugar, industrial buyers find themselves in a weak position vis-à-vis producers when bargaining for their sugar supply needs. In many occasions sugar is an input they cannot do without (*ie* it cannot be substituted with other sweetener natural or artificial). Indeed, some evidence points that producers charge their prices following official prices' lists without room for any bargaining (identical discounts being applied).[10] Thus, strong supplier power leads industrial buyers to be dissatisfied with prices paid to producers (perceptions of margins being unreasonably too high) and without alternatives available.[11] Case law and reports in several countries are telling of the anti-competitive risk present in sugar markets (US,[12]

---

9 See Strand, 'Tacit collusion in the EU Sugar Markets' (*supra* n5), 5–6 (average price elasticity of demand is 0.21; '*in seven of fourteen sugar producing Member States, only one producer holds the entire sugar production quota*') and 15 ('*by subsidizing exports and the keeping of stocks the CMO Sugar provides a retaliatory mechanism enabling firms to use the threat of shifting quantities from exports or stocks to sales within the Union*'). See also J. M. Connor, 'The Food and Agricultural Global Cartels of the 1990s: Overview and Update' *Staff paper* 2/2002, Dept. of Agricultural Economics, Purdue University (available at www.agecon.purdue.edu /staff/connor/papers/SP_02_4.asp, visited on 10.01.2015) 7.

10 Swedish Competition Authority, *Sweet Fifteen* (*supra* n5) 58–59.

11 Id., 60–62.

12 See A. S. Eichner, *The Emergence of Oligopoly: Sugar Refining as a case Study* (John Hopkins University Press: Baltimore 1969) and R. Zerbe, 'The American Sugar Refinery Company, 1887–1914: The Story of a Monopoly' (1969) *Journal of Law & Economics* 12(2): 339–375. See U.S. Supreme Court judgment of 30 March 1936, *Sugar Institute, Inc. v. United States*, 297 U.S. 553 (1936) concerning a collusive agreement instrumented through the trade association, commented by J. L. Fly, 'Observations on the Anti-Trust Laws, Economic Theory and the Sugar Institute Decisions I and II' (1936) *Yale Law Journal*, June, 1339–1372 (and December, 228–254). See also, a detailed explanation concerning the information exchange arrangement and its enforcement by D. Genesove & W. P. Mullin, 'The Sugar Institute Learns to Organize Information Exchange', in N. R. Lamoreaux, D. M. G. Raff & P. Temin (eds.), *Learning by Doing in Markets, Firms, and Countries* (1999 University of Chicago Press) 103–144 and D. Genesove & W. P. Mullin, 'Rules, Communication, and Collusion: Narrative Evidence from the Sugar Institute Case' (2001) *American Economic Review* 91(3): 379–398. Given the increasing trend to concentration, it is not surprising that a lot of litigation in the U.S. has taken place in the merger review context, see Judgment of the U.S. Supreme Court of

Colombia,[13] India,[14] Kenya,[15] Korea,[16] Pakistan,[17] South Africa,[18] Zimbabwe)[19] and the EU has not been an exception.[20] Early evidence of collusion was subject

21 January 1895, *United States v. E. C. Knight Co.* ("Sugar Trust case"), 156 U.S. 1 (1895) and Judgment of the U.S. Court of Appeals of the 2nd Circuit of 1 October 1958, *American Crystal Sugar Company v. Cuban-American Sugar Company*, 259 F. 2d 524.

13 See '¿Hay un cartel de azúcar en el país?', Semana, 15 March 2013 (available at www.semana.com/economia/articulo/hay-cartel-del-azucar-pais/337010-3, visited on 10.01.2015). See also J Cortázar-Mora, 'The Colombian Competition Authority modifies the original terms of the opening of proceedings in an investigation of a possible cartel agreement involving twelve sugar mills, two distributors owned by the sugar mills and the trade association that groups them (Sugar cartel investigation)', *Bulletin e-Competitions* April 2013, 52515.

14 Competition Commission of India, Order 30 of November 2011, 1/2010, *In re Sugar Mills* (available at www.cci.gov.in/May2011/OrderOfCommission/SUGAR%20CASE%20NO.%201-2010%2030.Nov%202011.pdf, visited on 10.01.2015).

15 See Kenya Anti-corruption Commission, *Review of the Policy, Legal and Regulatory Framework for the Sugar Sub-Sector in Kenya. A Case Study if Governance Controversies affecting the Sub-Sector*, February 2010 (available at www.eacc.go.ke/docs/sugar-report.pdf, visited 10.01.2015).

16 See S. R. Yun, K. J. Son, I. S. Choi & S. H. Han, 'Korea', in I. K. Gotts (ed), *The Private Enforcement Competition Review* (2002: Law Business Research, London) 259–269. Indeed, in 2007 an informant received 210 million won for information about a sugar cartel, see D. D. Sokol & A. Stephan, 'Prioritizing Cartel Enforcement in Developing World Competition Agencies', in D. D. Sokol, T. K. Cheng & I. Lianos (ed), *Competition Law and Development* (Stanford University Press: 2913) 137–154, 147–148.

17 See Competition Commission of Pakistan, *Enquiry Report on Collusive Practices in the Sugar Industry*, 21 Oct. 2009, S .B. Gilani & S. U. Javed (available at www.cc.gov.pk/images/Downloads/enquiry_reports/enquiry_report_october_2009.pdf visited on 10.01.2015) and *Sectoral Analysis of Sugar Industry with Special Reference to Price Hike*, Syndicate nº 4, S. Zareen, Directorate General of Training and Research (Inland Revenue) Lahore (available at www.dgtrdt.gov.pk/Research/37th_synndicate_%20rports/4.pdf, visited on 10.01.2015).

18 Competition Commission of South Africa 'Should the Competition Commission be bitter about the sugar industry in South Africa?' (2000) *Competition News*, September, 5–6 (available at www.compcom.co.za/assets/Uploads/AttachedFiles/MyDocuments/Dec-00-Newsletter. pdf, visited on 10.01.2015).

19 K. Laschinger, 'End of the road for sugar cartel?', *Finance Week* 8 November 2003, 38.

20 Apart from the Spanish case which motivates this article, concerted practices against TFEU article 101.1 have been found in the British market from 1986 to 1990 [Commission Decision 1999/210/EC of 14 October 1998, Case IV/F-3/33.708-*British Sugar Plc*, Case IV/F-3/33.709-*Tate & Lyle Plc*, Case IV/F-3/33.710-*Napier Brown & Company Ltd*, Case IV/F-3/33.711-*James Budgett Sugars Ltd* (OJUE L76, 22.3.1999, 1–66), mostly confirmed by the Judgments of the General Court of 12 July 2001, T-202/98, T-204/98 and T-207/98, ECR II-2035 and of the Court of Justice of the EU of 29 April 2004, ECR I-4951], in the Belgian and Dutch markets from 1981 to 1989 [Commission Decision of 19 December, Case IV/32.414-*Sugar beet* (OJUE L31, 02.02.1990, 32–45)]. Likewise, the Austrian Bundeswettbewerbsbehörde (BWB) found a cartel formed by Südzucker and Agrana (in which Südzucker holds a stake of about 37.75%) on sugar products in the Austrian market from 2004 to 2008 (BWB/K-191 Zuckerkartell). Finally, the Hungarian Competition Authority (*Gazdasági Versenyhivatal*) investigated a possible cartel operating in the Hungarian sugar industry from 2003 to 2009 involving Agrana Magyarország Értékesítési Kft, Eastern Sugar Cukoripari Zrt, Mátra Cukor Mártavidéki Cukorgyárak Zrt, Magyar Cukorgyártó és Forgalmazó Zrt and Eurosugar SAS but terminated the case in 2012 in part because new legislation adopted permitted cartels of agricultural producers [see www.gvh.hu/en//data/cms998123/sk_2012_12_21_megsz%C3%BCntet%C3%A9s_cukor kartell_a.pdf and A Reger, 'The Hungarian Competition

of the famous *Suiker Unie* case[21] and few months ago the European Commission undertook several inspections at the premises of companies active in the sugar industry in several Member States suspecting of a violation of TFEU article 101 in relation to the supply of white sugar.[22] Recently, the *Bundeskartellamt* has sanctioned a cartel agreement of sugar producers in Germany.[23]

On the other hand, the highly concentrated character of this industry, which makes sugar producers dominant players in their respective markets has also lead to several enforcement actions based on TFEU article 102.[24] The transactions that led to the consolidation of the industry had also prompted merger review proceedings both at EU and national member States level.[25]

Authority puts an end to a long running investigation into a possible cartel infringement by sugar producers' (2012) *e-Competitions*, 52244].

21 See Judgment of 16 December 1975, 40/73 to 48/73, 50/73, 54/73 to 56/73, 111/73, 113/73 and 114/73, *Suiker Unie* [1975] ECR 1663. The EU Court of Justice confirmed most of the holdings by the European Commission in its Decision 73/109/EEC of 2 January 1973, IV/26.918 *European sugar industry* (OJ L140, 26.5.1973, 17–47) which found practices in breach of TFEU articles 101 and 102 in the sugar industry in Belgium, France, Italy, Germany and Holland. See A. Dashwood, G. Diana, H. Laddie & G. I. F. Leigh, 'The Sugar Industry Marathon' (1976) *European Law Review*, 479–499.

22 See 'Antitrust: Commission confirms unannounced inspections in the sugar sector' (available at http://europa.eu/rapid/press-release_MEMO-13-443_en.htm, visited on the 10.01.2015). On 4 February 2014 the investigation was closed due to lack of evidence, see A. White & I. Almeida, 'EU Shuts Sugar Price-Fixing Investigation on Lack of Evidence', *Bloomberg News*, 19 February 2014 (www.bloomberg.com/news/2014-02-19/eu-shuts-sugar-price-fixing-investigation-on-lack-of-evidence.html, visited on the 10.01.2015).

23 See S. Szentesi 'The German Competition Authority finds that the sugar cartel agreement has been implemented under the umbrella of the national industry association (Ofeifer/Südzucker/Nordzucker)' (2014) *e-Competitions* 63959.

24 See Commission Decision 88/518/EEC of 18 July 1988, Case IV 30.178 *Napier Brown – British Sugar* (OJ L 284 of 19.10.1988, 41–59) and Commission Decision of 14 May 1997, Case IV34.621, 35.059/F-3- Irish Sugar, plc. (OJ L258 of 22.09.97, 1–32) concerning discriminatory pricing in the sugar retail and industrial markets of granulated sugar by Irish Sugar (which had market share in Ireland from 1985–1995 above 85–90%), mostly confirmed by Judgment of the General Court (Third Chamber) of 7 October 1999, *Irish Sugar plc v Commission of the EC*, Case T-228/97, ECR 1999 II-02969. Appeal dismissed by ECJ Order of July 10, 2001, Case C-497/99 P. ECR 2001 I-05333. Indeed, recently Napier Brown complained to the UK's OFT that British Sugar has broken competition rules by halting supplies of sugar in contravention of the 1988 Decision (that fined British Sugar and obliged it to honour certain supply conditions). This formal complaint will be dealt with by the (new) CMA, after it took over from the OFT on 1 April 2014.

25 See Commission Decisions of 30 September 1991, IV/M.062-Eridania/ISI, of 20 December 2001, IV/M.2530 *Südzucker/Saint Louis Sucre* (*supra* n8). Merger decisions on this industry have been adopted in every Member State (and there are too many and mostly of little interest to be listed herein) but controversial ones have been those taken in Italy, the Netherlands and Serbia.

3. THE SPANISH SUGAR CARTEL (1995–1996)

The above description of the sugar producing industry is also reflective of the Spanish market, which features the same issues and problems indicated thereto.[26] Indeed, one could well assume that the anticompetitive features present elsewhere may well be more pronounced in the Spanish case.[27]

Following a claim filed by several business associations involved in the confectionery business in Spain, a cartel on the sale of sugar for industrial production organised by the main four manufacturers of sugar (EBRO AGRÍCOLAS, SOCIEDAD GENERAL AZUCARERA, ACOR and AZUCARERAS REUNIDAS) was uncovered and punished by the Spanish competition authorities in 1999.[28]

After an investigation of more than two years, the Defence Competition Tribunal (DCT) found evidence that these four firms had fixed the sugar prices and sale conditions and divided the market geographically among them, in violation of article 1 of the Spanish Competition Act and Article 101 TFEU.[29]

---

26 See the Spanish DCT 1998 report assessing the merger of EBRO and AZUCARERA (report C31/98), two of the firms later found to be involved in the Spanish Cartel. Curiously, in their appeals of the fines imposed by DCT resolution of 15th April 1999 (426/1998), they alleged the nullity of the resolution as it was addresses to two inexistent firms (due to the merger); the National Court (Administrative Ch- Sect.6) judgment of 13 September 2009 rejected this argument.

27 Unearthing the historical origins of the stronger (and many) anticompetitive features of the Spanish sugar industries, see J S McGee, 'Government intervention in the Spanish Sugar Industry' (1964) *Journal of Law & Economics* 7: 121–172, 135 ('*Whenever competition threatened it was throttled by cartels, mergers, and – perhaps most importantly – direct government intervention*'). In the last few years the concentration trend indicated above has further reduced the number producers in the Spanish market. In 2007 the market shares were the following: AZUCARERA EBRO 75%, ACOR 17% and ARJ 8% [See *Defence Competition Service Assessment* Azucarera *Ebro-sugar business of DAI of 22 March 2007*, 15 and Swedish Competition Authority, *Sweet Fifteen (supra* n5*) 51–52*] which also mentioned that ARJ was abandoning the market]. See V Maté, 'Los italianos dejan el azúcar', *El País*, 9 April 2006 (available http://elpais.com/diario/2006/04/09/negocio/1144587816_850215.html, visited on 10.01.2015). Nowadays EBRO is probably monopolist producer in the centre and south of Spain, and has a 75% market share in the North of the country (ACOR holding the remaining 25%).

28 While the enforcement action was taking place, EBRO AGRÍCOLAS merged with SOCIEDAD GENERAL AZUCARERA, further increasing the level of concentration in the industry. The Spanish Government approved the transaction on October 1998 subject to several conditions, which had been recommended by the DCT in its assessment *(supra* n27), see OJ 249 of 17 October 1998, 34461–34462.

29 Article 1 of the Spanish Competition Act is the equivalent of TFEU article 101.1 with not many relevant differences. Although the initial enforcement action involved the producers association (ASOCIACIÓN GENERAL DE FABRICANTES DE AZÚCAR DE ESPAÑA-AGFA) and also considered a potential violation of TFEU article 102 (though an abuse of joint dominant position in the market) none of the two were confirmed in the final decision. The complainants reiterated their abuse of dominance claim in their appeal of the DCT decision in the National Court (Administrative Ch-Sect. 6), though it was rejected by judgment of 3 June 2003.

Looking at the evolution of sugar prices in Spain in 1995 and 1996, the DCT found proof of several collective decisions of raising sugar prices that departed from what could have been expected looking at the intervention prices set within the Common Market Organization/CMO for Sugar (in one case also a price decrease).[30] Sugar market price behaviour in Spain in that period did not reflect changes in the production or input costs, with the four producers mentioned above setting a common base price in a clear and blatant violation of competition law.

Moreover, if that would not have been enough, after inspections in the premises of the companies subject to investigation were conducted, additional written evidence was found of anticompetitive agreements among the four firms and of collective decisions tinkering with sugar market prices, with the producers' agreements and decisions coinciding with the anomalous sugar price changes detected by the DCT.[31] The DCT found evidence of information exchanges among the firms preceding the agreements that lead to the changes in sugar prices, which together with the oligopolistic structure of sugar production in Spain lead to the conclusion that producers had formed a cartel.[32] Of course, cartel members repeatedly argued that their behaviour was justified by the CMO and the CAP, and/or influenced by the restructuring measures of the sugar production industry instigated by the Spanish Ministry of agriculture when Spain entered the EEC in the 1980s', but the DCT (and later the courts) rejected these arguments.[33]

Apart from the price-fixing, the DCT found also proof of market allocation agreements among the four firms, through the 'transfer' of the existing production quotas (due to the sugar CMO) to sugar sale quotas in the market, compensating among themselves for any eventual excesses or deficits, and having all of them the commitment not to serve clients that 'belonged' to other

30 DCT Resolution of 15 April 1999 (426/1998) 90–93. More precisely, there were two rises on February 1995 of 4 pesetas/kg and April 1995 of 4 pesetas/kg, a reduction in price of 2 pesetas/kg in September 1995 and an additional rise of 1 peseta/kg in May 1996.

31 DCT Resolution (*supra* n31) 10–12 and 93–94.

32 In many cases a positive association has been found between industry concentration and likelihood of collusion/ cartel formation, M C Levenstein & V Y Suslow, 'What determines cartel success?' (2006) *Journal of Economic Literature* 44/1: 43–95, 58–61 (the role of the existing industry/trade associations being found also relevant). On the importance of information exchanges among cartel members as means to reinforce cartel discipline, see R. C. Marshall & L. M. Marx, *The Economics of Collusion* (MIT Press 2012): 16–17, 230–32.

33 Much to the contrary, and as recurrent cartels in agricultural goods in Spain (and elsewhere) seem to show, the CAP and CMOs (and/or the equivalents used in other countries) provides a structure (repeated interaction, transparency, artificial-regulatory barriers to entry, etc.) in which collusion seems to be a likely outcome. For an example taken from U.S. experience, see E. Hoffman & G. D. Libecap, 'The Failure of Government Sponsored Cartels and Development of Federal Farm Policy' (1995) *Economic Inquiry* 33: 365–382. Indeed, according to Connor, 'The Food and Agricultural Global Cartels of the 1990s' (*supra* n10) 19 '*The number and size of international cartels in food and agricultural markets far outweighs the cartels discovered in all other markets*'.

cartel members.[34] Additionally, there was evidence of the joint efforts taken by cartel members to prevent and control sugar imports and to limit production to be ensure the effectiveness of price levels agreed.

The enforcement of the price-fixing and the market allocation agreements could be guaranteed by the continuous exchange of detailed production information, sales and forecasts.[35] Through this well organised and support system, cartel members could anticipate and agree beforehand on sugar price changes in the market.[36]

Concerning the harm caused by the cartel, there was evidence of several instances in which customers found out they were paying more than their EU counterparts for their basic sugar inputs (customers making clear their annoyance to cartel members).[37] In addition to already higher sugar prices in the EU due to the CAP (which makes them be twice more expensive than world market prices)[38], prices in Spain used to be higher than rest of EU, and price increases in 1995 and 1996 did not reflect changes in production costs (being 5–10% higher in Spain).[39] The DTC decision showed further evidence of the relevance of sugar as an input in confectioners business, with calculations of the overcharges provoked by the cartel that Spanish confectioners were experiencing in comparison to their French and UK rivals.[40] In the end, the sugar producers were sanctioned with fines totalling € 8.74 million.[41]

---

34 DCT Resolution (*supra* n31) 19–22.

35 DCT Resolution (*supra* n31) 23–25.

36 For more details on the inter-relationships between information, communication and collusion for cartels' stability see J. E. Harrington Jr, 'How do cartels operate?' (2006) *Foundations and Trends in Microeconomics* 2(1): 1–105, 43–72 and M. Levenstein & V. Y. Suslow, 'Cartel Bargaining and Monitoring: The Role of Information Sharing', in Konkurresverket, *The Pros and Cons of Information Sharing* (Swedish Competition Authority: Stockholm 2006), 8–48.

37 DCT Resolution (*supra* n31) 54.

38 OECD, *Sugar Policy Reform* (*supra* n3) 68. Of course, it should be taken into account also that EU market Price support measures also artificially depress world sugar market prices, production and trade; creating further distortions in the sweetener market (id. 44). See also A. Schmitz 'The European Union's high-priced sugar support-regime', in A. Schmitz, T. H. Spreen, W. A. Messina & C. B. Mos (eds), *Sugar and Related Sweetener Markets: International Perspectives* (2002 Wallingford: CAB International) 193–213, 210 (the direct cost to EU consumers of this highly protectionist regime would amount to € 6,500 million per year).

39 DCT Resolution (*supra* n31) 59 (Ebro repeatedly acknowledged a price differential of 2,5–3% but due to Spanish productivity gap).

40 DCT Resolution (*supra* n31) 72–73 and 118 further limiting their suitability to being exported [to which a substantial part (15–45%) of the production was generally aimed].

41 At that time 1,455 million pesetas (€ 8,744,726.119). The case is reported in OECD, *Hard Core Cartels*, 2000, 22 (available www.oecd.org/competition/cartels/2752129.pdf visited on 10.01.2015). The DCT resolution was confirmed in seven separate judgments both by the National Court (four) and by the Supreme Court (three). See National Court Judgements (administrative Ch., Sect.6) of 4 July 2002 (Acor); 13 September 2002 (Ebro); 6 of May 2005 (ARJ) and 3 of June 2003 (complainants). See Supreme Court Judgments (administrative Ch., Sect. 4) of 26 April 2005 (Ebro); of 26 April 2004 (Acor) and of 22 March 2006 (ARJ).

4. DAMAGES CLAIMS IN THE SPANISH SUGAR CARTEL

Apparently, damages caused by the Spanish sugar production cartel exceeded € 25 million.[42] For that reason, once the DCT decision was confirmed by the Supreme Court, some confectioners filed damages claims against Ebro Foods and Acor, the two main cartel members.[43] Confectioners were the main force behind public enforcement and it was natural to expect that they would initiate also private actions aimed at obtaining compensation for the harm caused by the cartel.

For private litigation to begin, together with the DCT resolution, individual confectioner firms presented in court expert economic reports calculating the harm suffered by them in1995 and 1996, while the cartel was in operation. The damages claimed by confectioners amount to the cartel mark-up during that period. Against that defendants opposed that the claimants did not suffer the harm as they would have passed it onto consumers and also that the one-year statute of limitation for this type of claims had lapsed (article 1978.2 of the Spanish Civil Code).[44] Of course, defendants also denied the existence of harm and questioned the damages calculation made by the plaintiffs.

All the court judgments delivered in the case were appealed by the defendants but, at the end, damages awards totalling more than € 5 million were successfully confirmed by the Supreme Court.

These actions have been the most relevant follow-on competition litigation on a cartel case conducted in Spain to date.[45] In practice, there were organised as two different sets of claims, which followed two different proceedings and reached to separate final judgments, depending on the court they were filed -Madrid or Valladolid- (see the sequence of decisions from initial claim to different judgments in Table 1, including damages awarded and rate of success).

---

42 Overall harm estimation from sugar cartel was € 25,2 million see OECD, *Fighting Hard Core Cartels: Harm, Effective Sanctions and Leniency Programs*, 2002, 97 (available at www.oecd.org/competition/cartels/2474442.pdf, visited on 10.01.2015), though no explanation is given of how it is calculated or where this figure comes from.

43 ARJ abandoned the market in 2006 (*supra* n28), and there is no evidence at all that any claim was filed against it.

44 Once the Supreme Court (administrative) confirmed DCT resolution on April 2005, the claimants sent extrajudicial claims to both Acor and Ebro (both in 2005 and 2006) which according to Spanish Law allowed the statute of limitations not to lapse (article 1973 of Spanish Civil Code). For this reason the Madrid judgment of first instance nº 50 of 1 march 2010 rejected this argument.

45 See S. Vande Valle, *Private Antitrust Litigation in the European Union and Japan* (Maklu: Antwerpen 2013) 230 (describing it as one of the leading cases in Europe) and Marcos (2013) *Global Competition Litigation Review (supra* n2) 179.

Table 1. Private Enforcement in the Spanish Sugar Cartel

Valladolid Claim	Date	Damages (€)	Success (%)
Plaintiffs Suit	20 April 2007	Claim of 900,264.66+ interests accrued since suit was filed+ legal expenses	
1st instance (nº 11)	20 February 2009	0 (unsuccessful)	0
Provincial Court (Sect. 4)	9 April 2009[46]	900,264.66+ interests accrued since suit was filed+ legal expenses	100
Supreme Court (Civil Ch.)	8 June 2012	900,264.66+ interests accrued since suit was filed+ legal expenses	100

Madrid Claim	Date	Damages (€)	Success (%)
Plaintiffs Suit	26 April 2007	4,060,119.81+ interest accrued since suit was filed+ legal expenses	
1st instance (nº 50) nº 59/2010	1 March 2010	2,030,059,90 + interest	50 (partial)
Provincial Court (Sect. 8) nº 370/2011	3 October 2011	0 because passing-on occurred	0
Supreme Court (Civil Ch.) nº 651/2013	7 November 2013	4,060,119.81+ interest accrued since suit was filed+ legal expenses	100

In November 2013 the Supreme Court decided the damages claims filed in Madrid by fourteen confectioner firms against Ebro Foods, awarding them more than € 4 million.[47] On the other hand, as it was mentioned before, a similar claim was filed by nine confectioners against Acor in Valladolid,[48] which was finally decided by the Supreme Court on June 2012, condemning Acor to pay more than € 900,000.[49]

46 See P. Perez, 'A Spanish Court provides for the first time ever for compensation of damages caused by a cartel (Sugar Cartel)' (2007) *e-Competitions* 40557.

47 € 4,060,119.81 plus interest accrued since the suit was filed on the 26 of April 2007 and legal expenses. See Supreme Court Judgment of 7 November 2013, *Nestlé et al. v. Ebro Foods* (STS 5819/2013).

48 Four of the claimants coincided with the plaintiffs in the other (Madrid) case: Nestlé, Zahor, Mazapanes Donaire and La Casa.

49 € 900,264.66 plus interests accrued since the suit was filed on the 20 of April 2007 and legal expenses. See Supreme Court Judgment of 8 June 2012, *Galletas Gullón et al. v. ACOR* (STS 5462/2012); referred by P. Pérez, 'The Spanish Supreme Court confirms the Judgment of the Valladolid Provincial Court in the sugar cartel (Nestlé, Gullón, Zahor)' (2012) *e-Competitions* 49040 and further commented by P. Pérez & T. Schreiber, 'Case Comment: Judgment of the

The judgments by the Supreme Court in this case are well founded and cover some legal issues that may be crucial for future damage claims in antitrust cases and which are worth commenting. They touch upon several relevant issues which are also dealt with by the EU Directive on Damages.[50]

5. LESSONS FOR FUTURE PRIVATE CLAIMS

In line with the well-established case law of the European Court of Justice,[51] the Spanish Supreme Court has awarded all the compensation that was claimed by the victims of the sugar cartel. Compensation was awarded on the understanding that the claimants were victims of a tortious action of the defendants: it was their behaviour as participants of the cartel that gave rise to the plaintiffs' cause of action.[52]

On the other hand, the Supreme Court faced some of the typical issues raised on cartel follow-on damages claims, regarding the existence and causal link to the harm caused by the sugar cartel, and also the damages' calculation. In particular, the Supreme Court clarified the link between follow-on private enforcement claims and decisions taken by competition authorities (*infra* §4.1). Additionally it made some relevant considerations concerning the measurement and calculation of damages and the role of expert testimony for that purpose (*infra* §4.2). Finally, it ruled on the passing-on defence opposed by cartel members, which alleged that the plaintiffs (confectioners) had passed-on the cartel overcharge to their customer (*infra* §4.3).

Spanish Supreme Court in ACOR (344/2012) June 8, 2012' (2013) *Global Competition Litigation Review* 1/2013: 37–41.

50 See *Directive 2014/104/EU of the European Parliament and of the Council of 26 November 2014 on certain rules governing actions for damages under national law for infringements of the competition law provisions of the Member States and of the EU* (OJ L 349 of 5.12.2014, 1–19).

51 See EU Court of Justice judgments of 20 September 2001, *Courage v Crehan*, C-453/99 ECR [2001] I-6314 and of 13 July 2006, *Manfredi*, joined cases C-295/04 to C-298/04 ECR [2006] I-6619.

52 Excluding that there was a case of contractual liability/validity, see Legal Ground 12nd of Supreme Court Judgment of 8 June 2012 (*supra* n50). On this alternative, see M.P. Bello, 'Una explicación sobre la posibilidad de alegar responsabilidad contractual en acciones de daños derivados de infracciones de la LDC: A Propósito del caso "Acor"', in J.A. Gómez & A. García (ed), *El derecho mercantil en el umbral del siglo XXI. Libro homenaje al Prof. Dr. Carlos Fernández-Novoa con motivo de su octogésimo cumpleaños* (M. Pons: Madrid 2000) 265–270.

5.1. RELEVANCE FOR PRIVATE ENFORCEMENT OF PRIOR PUBLIC ENFORCEMENT DECISIONS

Follow-on damages claims based on violations of competition law tend to have higher success rates than stand-alone actions,[53] as they benefit from the prior investigations and holdings made by the competition authorities. Binding force of European Commission decisions is set by EU Regulation 1/2003 (article 16) but that is not (yet) the case with the decisions of member States' competition authorities.[54]

In the Spanish sugar cartel case, the private claims followed a prior decision delivered by the DCT, confirmed by review courts, (see *supra* §3) and the final decision by Supreme Court in the civil case includes relevant considerations on the effect prior public enforcement decisions might have in private litigation.[55] For that purpose, the Supreme Court distinguishes the facts and their legal assessment by the competition authorities, from other *dicta* that judgments made in the public enforcement arena related to potential private claims. The rationale which leads Supreme Court ruling in this issue is procedural efficiency and legal certainty (which run against re-litigation of the facts).[56]

Firstly, concerning the factual evidence and their assessment, the Supreme Court clearly holds that, the anti-competitive conduct which was subject to the public enforcement sanctions is at the root of any future compensation claims by the victims and, therefore, all the factual evidence in that regard and concerning its unlawfulness is very useful for private enforcement purposes:

> "*The factual scenario to which the both public and private enforcement relate, as to the existence of a practice restrictive of competition, is the same one, because the private*

53 See Marcos (2013) *Global Competition Litigation Review (supra* n2) 170 (compared to a overall success rate of 26%, follow-on success rate is much higher: 66.7%).

54 Article 9 of the Directive 2014/104/EU (*supra* n51) would change that. See C. Esteva, D. Calisti & L. Haasbeek, 'Towards an Effective Right to Full Compensation: The Proposal for a Directive on Antitrust Damages Actions', *Anuario de la Competencia* 2013: 33–43, 37. This seems not to apply to all Member States, Germany already has codified that the decisions of the Bundeskartellamt (and even of National Competition Authorities of other Member States) are binding the courts, see Sec 33.4 GWB.

55 Given that the Madrid Provincial Court had quashed the plaintiffs' claim ignored several of the findings by the DCT related to the existence of a cartel.

56 Avoiding inconsistency in the application of competition law provisions within public and private enforcement (and the re-litigation of the case), see recital 31 of the Directive 2014/104/EU. It is true, that it extends the binding effect to NCA decisions that may still be under review by courts (something that article 13.2 of the 1989 Spanish Defence Competition Act did not permit, see Third Legal ground, section 4 of Supreme Court Judgment of 7 November 2013), see S. Grassani, 'The Binding Nature of NCA Decisions in Antitrust Follow-on Litigation: Is EU Antitrust Calling For Affirmative Action', (2013) CPI Antitrust Chronicle 5 (*'If competition decisions are to a smaller or larger extend, immune from judicial review on the merits, damages awarded by a civil judge would become the poisonous fruit of the poisonous administrative proceeding they relate to*').

> *claim in the civil jurisdiction is seeking the compensation of damages caused by the cartel whose performance was the subject of the judgment of the administrative jurisdiction that punished the anti-competitive behaviour from the public enforcement perspective*".[57]

Secondly, however, any holding by the public enforcement authorities concerning causation and damages calculation, should be ignored, given the different nature and scope of public and private enforcement. In this regard, the Supreme Court assumes that the cartel punished by the public enforcement authorities led to an overcharge that negatively affected confectioners' costs, raising them, but it rightly considers that the power of public enforcement authorities "*did not reach the issue of the impact of damage by direct buyers to their customers*". It is only in the private enforcement setting by civil courts that it can be decided "*who had suffered injury and exactly how much*".[58]

5.2. DAMAGES' CALCULATION

The calculation of damages caused by anti-competitive actions is one of the most complex issues faced by private competition law claims.[59] Civil judges and courts are frequently criticised for their lack of knowledge and expertise on these matters,[60] though normally parties provide them with expert opinions

---

57 See Third Legal ground, section 5 of Supreme Court Judgment of 7 November 2013 (*supra* n48). Indeed, this is not very different from what the White paper held (European Commission, *White Paper on Damages Actions for Breach of the EC antitrust rules*, COM(2008) 165 of 2 April 2008, 5). See also C Tudor, 'La admisión de la defensa passing-on en el cartel del azúcar' (2012) *Revista de Derecho de la Competencia y Distribución* 11: 277–291, 287–288. The Madrid Provincial Court had considered prices were result of bargaining, which by definition contradicted the decisions by public enforcement activities ('*by holding that the prices were the result of individual bargaining between the defendant and each of the plaintiffs, it frontally contradicts the facts fixed in the judicial review and it does not include any reasoning that may justify such divergence*').

58 Id. In this point the holding by the Supreme Court is ultimately related to the issue of the possible passing-on of cartel overcharge, analysed *infra* §V.3.

59 For an account of the (little) experience on the matter in Spain, see J. Delgado & E. Pérez, 'Economic evidence in private-enforcement competition law in Spain' (2011) *ECLR* 32/10: 507–512. One of the most controversial cases to date was decided by Judgment of Provincial Court of Madrid (Sect. 28) of 25 May 2006, *Conduit Europe v. Telefónica*, see M. Martínez-Granado & G. Siotis, 'Sabotaging Entry: An Estimation of Damages in Directory Enquiry service Market' (2010) *Review of Law & Economics* 6/1: 1–57.

60 See F. Diez, 'Resarcimiento de daños en la aplicación del Derecho antitrust: ¿La gran asignatura pendiente? Análisis de jurisprudencia reciente' in P. Velasco San Pedro et al. (dir.), *La aplicación privada del Derecho de la Competencia* (Lex Nova, Valladolid 2011) 215–228, 228. In this case the judicial arbitrariness that may occur in damage calculation was well seen in the judgment of the Madrid court of first instance of 1 March 2010, which reduced the award to half of the amount claimed by the plaintiff on the "*reasonable basis*" than the defendants' expert had affirmed that in any case, if causality existed, damage could exceed 50% of what the plaintiff was claiming. Critically, when the Supreme Court finally ruled on

supporting the damages they seek. The difficulties raised by this task have pushed the European Commission to adopt a Communication on quantifying the harm in actions for damages based on EU competition law violations accompanied by a Practical Guide.[61]

In this case, at least for the Madrid claim, plaintiffs presented together with their suit a damages' estimate by Nera,[62] which was confronted by a rebuttal of defendants by CompassLexecon,[63] which alleged not only the inexistence of the overcharge claimed, defects in the damages calculation and passing-on of it to the confectioners customers.

On this point, the Spanish Supreme Court makes several relevant considerations on how to measure damages caused by the cartel. The starting point is the "*impossibility of a perfect reproduction of what would have been the situation if there had been no unlawful conduct*".[64] Given the difficulties and problems existing in establishing the proper hypothetical counter-factual or but-for scenario (although in this case strong intervention of sugar prices by CMO should have made calculation of the cartel-free prices simpler), the court sets the threshold of what should be required to the calculation made in the expert reports prepared by the plaintiffs in these cases: that they "*formulate a reasonable and technically sound hypothesis not founded on erroneous and not testable data*".[65] Thus, it is requiring that the experts' report is based on reliable principles and methodology and those are applied to the facts of the case (that need to be sufficient and accurate) to estimate the harm caused by the cartel.[66]

---

the issue considered this outcome to be a '"*Salomonic*" *solution lacking necessary justification*' (Seventh Legal Ground. Section 4 of Supreme Court Judgment of 7 November 2013 *supra* n48).

61 See *Communication from the Commission on quantifying harm in actions for damages based on breaches of Article 101 or 102 of the TFEU*, C(2013) 3440 of 11 June 2013 (Official Journal C167 of 13 June 2013, 19–21) and *Commission Staff Working Document. Practical Guide on Quantifying Harm in Actions for damages based on breaches of Article 101 or 102 of the TFEU*, SWD(2013) 205 (available at http://ec.europa.eu/competition/antitrust/actionsdamages/quantification_guide_en.pdf visited on 10.01.2015).

62 A presentation by the F. Jiménez (at Association of Competition Economist – ACE 2010 Conference, Norwich), who also acted as expert in court, 'Damages in the Sugar cartel in Spain', 12 November 2010 (available at www.competitioneconomics.org/ visited on 10.01.2015).

63 A presentation by N. Watson (also at ACE 2010 Conference, Norwich), who also acted as expert in court, 'The Spanish Sugar Cartel', 12 November 2010 (available at www.competitioneconomics.org/ visited on 10.01.2015).

64 Mirroring §16 of *Practical Guide on Quantifying Harm* (*supra* n61).

65 The Supreme Court is clearly considering the necessary trade-off in damages quantification 'accuracy versus practicality', OECD, *Background Note: Quantification of Harm to Competition by National Courts and Competition Agencies*, DAF/COMP (2011) 25, Nov. 2012, 39–46. At the end, it means, that '*the calculation of damages has to be done on the basis of hypothetical situations that did not occur in reality may justify a greater flexibility in the estimate of damages by the court*' [Seventh Legal Ground, Section 4 of Supreme Court Judgment of 7 November 2013 (*supra* n48)].

66 And also on claimants' standing (see *infra* §V.3) see J. E. Lopatka & W. H. Page, 'Economic Authority and the limits of expertise in antitrust cases' (2005) *Cornell Law Review* 90: 617–703684–693.

On the other hand, the general principle of effective and adequate compensation of damages caused by anti-competitive actions implies that is not enough for the defendant to question the accuracy of the quantification made by the plaintiff, it should justify an alternative better-founded and more plausible calculation.[67]

In assessing the specific calculation made by the plaintiff (in this case to calculate the overcharge by Ebro), the Supreme Court positively considers that the report produced by the plaintiff "*is constructed over correct bases (the existence of a cartel and the concerted prices fixed above those that would result from free competition) and it uses a reasonable method, among the several provided by the economic science and accepted by the courts in other countries, for the calculation of damages caused to plaintiffs, as is to estimate what would have happened if the practice restrictive to competition had not occurred practice by examining the immediately preceding period, taking into consideration prices of sugar in the period immediately before the beginning of the cartel activity, modulating them according to changes in production costs over the performance period that the cartel lasted (specifically, the price of sugar beet, which accounts for 58% of price of sugar production and storage expenses), not taking into account other costs not considered relevant (for their lower incidence in total manufacturing cost of sugar), and comparing the prices charged by the defendant to each plaintiff during the cartel's operation, divided into the four periods following the different concerted price changes*".[68]

The damage calculation by the plaintiffs in this case looked to the *price effects* of the cartel (higher), despite the cartel probably had also major impact in the *quantity* of goods sold (lower).[69] Given that CAP and sugar CMO together with high concentration of the market, price competition would not have been very intense in absence of the cartel, but as no input substitution was feasible for confectioners, their demand for sugar being rather inflexible, they had to pay higher price that they would have had the cartel not existed. Nevertheless, the main reason why the plaintiff calculation probably did not look at the reduction in the consumption was surely that the *quantity effect* was rather felt

67 Moreover, this is very consistent with article 17.1 of the Directive 2014/104/EU (*supra* n51), which requires Member States to "*ensure that the burden and the standard of proof required tor the quantification of harm does not render the exercise of the right to damages practically impossible or excessively difficult*".

68 See Seventh Legal ground, section 2 of Supreme Court Judgment of 7 November 2013 (*supra* n48).

69 For a clear explanation of this distinction, see F. Maier-Rigaud & U. Schwalbe, 'Quantification of antitrust damages' in D. Ashton & D. Henry, *Competition Damage Actions in the EU. Law and Practice* (E. Elgar, Cheltenham-Northampton 2013) 210–262, 214–215, they also point out that '*it is usually easier to demonstrate that a higher price has been paid on units of the good bought in contrast to demonstrating that a certain number of goods were not bought but would have been had the price not increased*', and therefore '*quantity effects have often been neglected*' (id 219). See also D. L. Rubinfield, 'Antitrust Damages' in E. R. Elhauge (ed), *Research Handbook on the Economics of Antitrust Law* (E. Elgar, Cheltenham-Northampton 2012), 378–393, 385.

downstream, by the consumers of sugar-based produced goods (confectionery), who may have bought less of them because of their higher prices as part the cartel overcharge was passed on to them.[70]

In sum, the damage calculation claimed by the plaintiffs included only the cartel mark-up (ie the illegal gain made by cartelists), looking at what competitive prices would have been applicable to their purchases in that period if the conspiracy had not existed. They used for that purpose a *cost-based approach.*[71]

In this case, the main input in the sugar production process is sugar beet (58% of the cost), whose price is strongly influenced by regulation and market intervention through the sugar OCM. Damages calculation looked at the anomalous changes in sugar prices that could not be explained by changes in the costs (see FIGURES 1 and 2 for the graphical representation of damages calculation by plaintiffs' expert). Although, this method may be less reliable in many cases because typically the costs are not independent of the infringement,[72] in this case the operation of sugar OCM and CAP made it independent.

Figure 1. Damage Calculation made by the plaintiff I

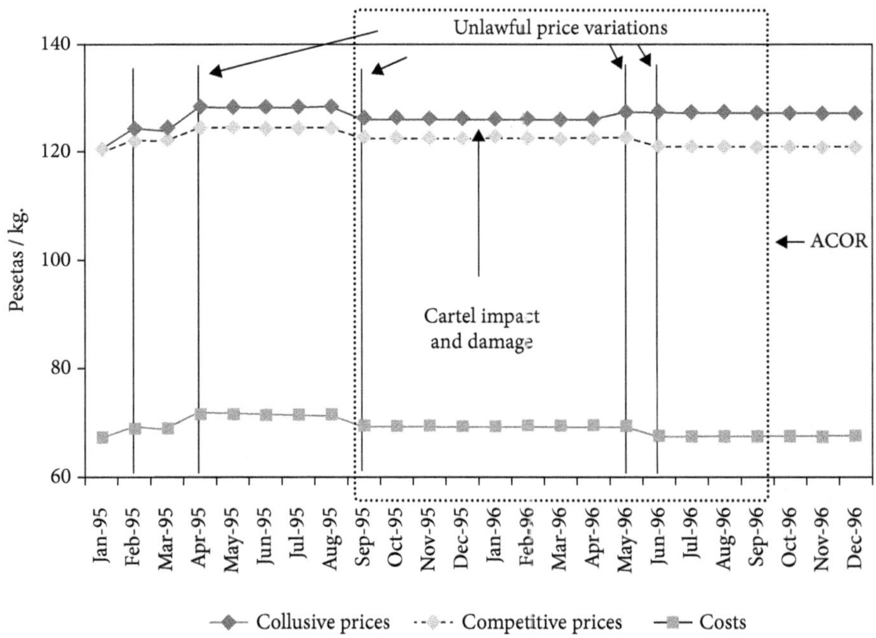

Source: F. Jiménez, 'Damages in the Sugar cartel in Spain' (*supra* n63) 6.

70 See OECD, *Background Note: Quantification of Harm to Competition (supra n65) 26.*

71 OECD, *Background Note: Quantification of Harm to Competition (supra n65)* 36 [*'constructs the but-for price "bottom up" by measuring the relevant costs of the affected product and adding a reasonable profit margin (which would emerge under normal market conditions)'*].

72 R. De Coninck, 'Estimating private antitrust damages', in *Competition Damage Evaluation: A Short State of Play* (Concurrences 3–2010) 4–8, 6.

Figure 2. Damage Calculation made by the plaintiff I – Close-up

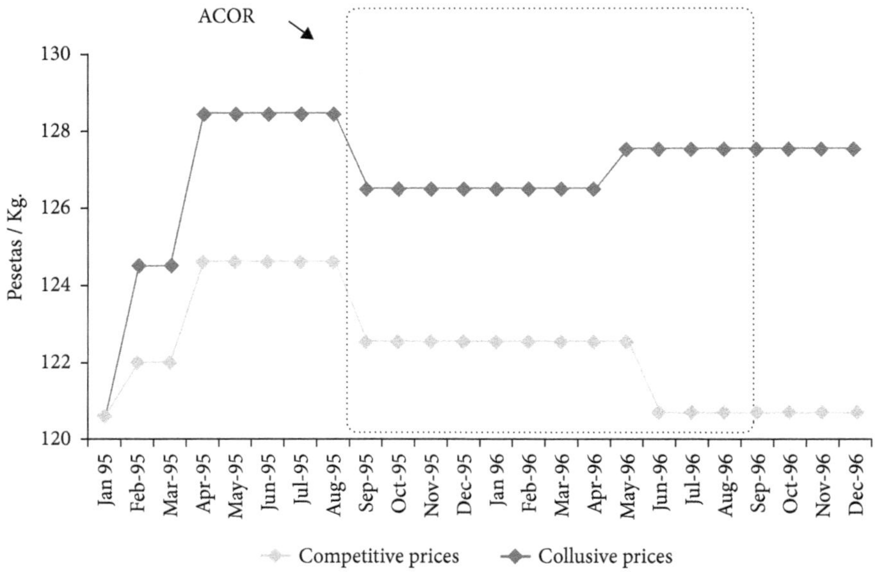

Source: F. Jiménez, 'Damages in the Sugar cartel in Spain' (*supra* n61) 7.

Finally, in order to compensate for the present value of the damages, given that the competition infringement and harm thereby occurred eighteen years ago, interests are included in the award. If that were not the case, inflation would end up radically diminishing the purchasing power of the sum that once was overpaid by victims of the cartel.[73] In this case the Supreme Court included only statutory interest to be applied to the damages claimed by the confectioners, though it does not meet the requirements of Directive 2014/104/EU (article 2).[74] The Supreme Court awards statutory interests from the moment the suit for private damages was brought to court, whilst the Directive affirms it should rather be the occurrence of the harm caused by the infringement (*ie* when the historical damages were incurred). The difference between considering one date or the other is not negligible.[75] In this case, the damages were incurred on 1995–

73 For a recent and comprehensive treatment of this issue, see E. Bueren, K. Hüschelrath & T. Veith, 'Time is Money- How much Money is Time? Interest and Inflation in Competition Law Actions for Damages', *ZEW Discussion Paper nº 14-008, 3* (available http://ftp.zew.de/pub/zew-docs/dp/dp14008.pdf, visited on 10.01.2015).

74 *"Full compensation shall place a person who has suffered harm in the position in which that person would have been had the infringement of competition law not been committed"*. See also recital 12 of Directive 2014/104/EU (*supra* n51) and §20 of *Practical Guide on Quantifying Harm* (*supra* n61).

75 Interest in the € 900,264.66 award is € 208,189.33 (compounded 234,212.99) and it would had been € 802,172.86 (compounded € 1,294,130.00) if the date when the violation started (1 February 1995) were considered. In the € 4,060,119.81 award interest is € 938,916.76 (compounded € 1,056,281.76) but it would have been € 3,617,733.74 (compounded

1996, and that is the date according to the Directive that should be considered in setting the interest, whilst the court in this case set it more than ten years later (20 April 2007).

5.3. THE PASSING-ON DEFENCE

As sugar is an input confectioners use in the manufacturing of their products, defendants opposed that any potential overcharge by the cartel would have been passed-on to the final consumers of the confectionery goods.[76] This defence was also opposed in the U.S. in the massive class action that followed public enforcement actions against the U.S. sugar cartel in the 1970s[77], in that case one of the plaintiffs that was a wholesaler of candy, beverage syrup and other products that claimed damages against the sugar refiners (Stotter) was successful in its claim despite being an indirect purchaser because it bought its products from a firm which was owned by one the cartel members (Amstar).[78]

In the Spanish case the passing-on defence was also used in the public enforcement proceedings to unsuccessfully argue for a reduction of the fine.[79] Moreover, it was this argument that led the Madrid Provincial Court to quash the plaintiffs' claim in 2011[80] and the Supreme Court ruled definitively on the issue in late 2013 (revoking the judgment of the Madrid Provincial Court).

€ 5,836,414.58) if the 1 February 1995 date was considered. These calculations are rough and approximate as more accurate measures would require consideration of different dates where harm was effectively caused (from February 1995 to May 1996) and other information unknown to the author.

76 One of the arguments used by the Ebro in its defence is that the claimants had somehow recognized in their November 1999 filing before the National Court that they had passed-on the cartel overcharge to their customers (but see *infra* n83).

77 See Judgment of 21 October 1976 of US District Court E.D. Pennsylvania, *In re Sugar Industry Antitrust Litigation*, 73 FDR 322 (1976).

78 See Judgment of 3rd Circuit US Court of Appeals of 6 March 1978, *In re Sugar Industry Antitrust Litigation, Stotter & Co., Inc., Appellant, v Amstar Corporation, Borden, Inc., and Its Subsidiaries, Colonial Sugar Company, North American Sugar Industries, Industrial Sugars, Inc., Sugar Refinery of Palm Beach, Inc. (formerly Florida Sugar Refinery, Inc.), Cpc International, Inc, Michigan Sugar Company, National Home Products corporation, the National Sugar Refining Company, Savannah foods and Industries, Inc & Sucrest Corporation, Appellees*, 579 F.2d 13, 18 (1978) ("*True, the price-fixed commodity had been combined with other ingredients to form a different product. But just as the sugar sweetened the candy, the price-fixing enhanced the profits of the candy manufacturer. The situation is the same as if the general contractor which sold the building to the plaintiff in* Illinois Brick *were the manufacturer of the concrete block which went into the structure. In that situation, the concern which the Supreme Court expressed about the proration of overcharge among a number of entities in the chain would not have been present*").

79 By Acor, see National Court (Sect. 6) judgment of 4 July 2002.

80 See Judgment of Provincial Court of Madrid (Sect. 8) of 3 October 2011, *Nestlé et al. v. Ebro* (JUR/2011/386351) and P Pérez, 'The Provincial Court of Madrid accepts the passing-on defence in the sugar cartel' (2011) *e-Competitions* 51098.

On its first decision on the case (in the Valladolid claim), the Supreme Court rejected out of hand the passing-on defence due to lack of proof,[81] on its second judgment (the Madrid claim) the rejection is more elaborate and the construction may have deep implications for competition damages claims in the future in Spain. As the Supreme Court began its argument in more fragile grounds in this case (because the passing-on defence had been estimated by the Provincial Court) its construction on this point tries to be more robust and clear-cut: "*for the claim to be successful not only is needed that there was price collusion causing their artificial rise, but also that such harm was not passed-on by the direct purchasers (who are those that now are claiming) to their clients.*"[82]

Naturally, the starting point was the mark-up in the price of sugar due to the existence and operation of the cartel: compensation for direct purchasers of sugar should be available unless it was proof that they were not those who suffered the harm (*ie* the harm was transferred to their downstream clients).[83]

Although the Spanish Supreme Court expressly referred to US case law excluding the passing-on defence (*Hanover Shoe*)[84] and the broad EU discussion on the issue, it deemed the case to be solved by tort and basic compensation rules in force.[85] It considers admissible to oppose the passing-on defence to a damages claim based on a competition law violation if the harm was transferred downstream "*given that a damages award for a competition law violation is grounded on compensation and that in this area it applies the principle forbidding unjust compensation, it is not reasonable to give damages to whom did not suffer the harm.*"[86]

---

81 See 16th Legal ground of Supreme Court Judgment of 8 June 2012 (*supra* n50), also Fourth Legal ground, section 3 and Fifth Legal ground, section four of Supreme Court Judgment of 7 November 2013 (*supra* n48).

82 See Third Legal ground, section 6 of Supreme Court Judgment of 7 November 2013 (*supra* n48). In this point there is a link to the binding force of public enforcement decisions (*supra* §V.1), the Supreme Court rejects any assessment that in the public enforcement arena could have been made on the issue of "passing-on".

83 Otherwise, there would be overcompensation (or unjust enrichment); so pass-on adjustments on the overcharge would need to be done, see F. Maier-Rigaud, 'Towards a European Directive on Damages Actions' (2014) *Journal of Competition Law & Economics*, advance access, 5–6.

84 Judgment of the US Supreme Court of 17 June 1968, *Hanover Shoe Co v United Shoe Machinery Corp*, 392 US 481 (1968), concerning a claim by a shoemaker to the manufacturer of shoe machinery for monopolization (in which the later opposed the plaintiff had not suffered any injury because it had passed-on any overcharge in the form of higher prices for its shoes).

85 The Supreme Court also mentions EU case law on the exception to the principle of refund of taxes incompatible with EU Law based on an unjust enrichment of the taxable person, EU Court of Justice, Judgments of the Court of 14 January 1997, Grand Chamber, *Société Comateb et al. v Directeur général des douanes et droits indirects*, C-192/95 to C-218/95, 1997 ECR I-00165; of 6 September 2011, Grand Chamber Lady & Kid A/S and Others v Skatteministeriet, C-398/09, 2011 ECR I-7375, and of 17 May 2013 (Seventh Chamber, Alakor Gabonatermelő és Forgalmazó Kft. kontra Nemzeti Adó- és Vámhivatal Észak-alföldi Regionális Adó Főigazgatósága, C-191/12 (not reported).

86 Fifth Legal ground, section 1 of Supreme Court Judgment of 7 November 2013 (*supra* n48).

Nevertheless, the Spanish Supreme Court sets the record straight by imposing on defendants the burden of proving the eventual passing-on (in accordance to article 217.3 of the Spanish Civil Procedure Act),[87] but "*it is not enough to show that the direct purchasers have also raised the price of his products. It is necessary to prove that with such rise he has charged on his clients, he has managed to transfer the harm suffered by the price rise because of the cartel overcharge*". And if it was not clear enough that it was somehow elevating the threshold for the passing-on defence to operate and be effective, it continued -on the negative- if "*the price rise did not managed to transfer all such harm because there had been a sales diminution (due that other competitors did not suffer from the cartel action and had gained some market share, nationally or internationally, to those that did suffer it, or because of the demand contraction due to the rise of prices, etc.) the passing-on defence cannot be accepted or cannot be accepted in its totality*".[88]

The holding of the Spanish Supreme Court fits squarely with article 13 of the Directive, which reads: "*Member States shall ensure that the defendant in an action for damages can invoke as a defence against a claim for damages the fact that the claimant passed on the whole or part of the overcharge resulting from the infringement of competition law*". Note that the Supreme Court is not requiring *whole* passing-on for the defence to be operative,[89] it provides room for the possibility of the defendant proving *partial* passing-on, deferring it to a question of proof. And applying that rule to the case, there was a complete lack of evidence by the defendants on the possible and amount of passing-on (and for that reason the Provincial Court of Madrid Judgment had to be revoked).[90]

87 As article 13 of the Directive 2014/104/EU requires ("*The burden of proving that the overcharge was passed on shall be on the defendant, who may reasonably require disclosure from the claimant or from third parties.*"). On the techniques used for this calculation, see T. Van Dijk & F. Verboven, 'Quantification of Damages', in *Issues in Competition Law and Policy* (ABA Section of Antitrust Law 2008) 3: 2331–2349, 2339–2344.

88 Fifth Legal ground, section 3 of Supreme Court Judgment of 7 November 2013 (*supra* n48).

89 It is true, however, that apparently the force of the argument is put in the whole passing-on defence; the Supreme Court was probably doing so in order to enable the claims to be successful due to the impossibility of compensation to indirect purchasers (confectioners' clients) in case the passing-on defence was accepted. However, Directive 2014/104/EU (*supra* n51) has a solution for that situation in article 14 when it makes easier indirect purchasers' claims in such situations. Looking at the present case, this would have meant that compensation to direct purchasers (confectioners) was due because it would legally be impossible, instead, for indirect purchasers to be compensated. On this point see Esteva, Calisti & Haasbeek, 'Towards an Effective Right to Full Compensation' (*supra* n55) 41 and – critically – Maier-Rigaud, 'Towards a European Directive on Damages Actions' *(supra* n70) 15–16.

90 According to the Supreme Court, the evidence presented by the defendants concerning the amount passing-on was insufficient, not being enough to claim that passing-on existed on the sole basis that the plaintiffs raised the prices of their products, see Fourth Legal ground, section 4 of Supreme Court Judgment of 7 November 2013 (*supra* n48). Commentaries of the case have wondered why defendants did not make efforts to properly argue and proof the passing-on, see O Retortillo, 'Primeros Pasos de los Tribunales Españoles en la Aplicación

Indeed, the Supreme Court decision contains relevant hints for possible procedural and litigation strategies in future cases for both claimants and defendants. Given that whole passing-on will probably never be a plausible scenario (as the mere transfer of the overcharge would not compensate all the harm caused by the cartel), the issue rather turns to the amount of the passing-on.

Furthermore, returning to the sugar cartel, damages calculations might get very complicated: not only it is very difficult that the confectioners had wholly passed to their indirect purchasers the amount of the overcharge[91], but there could also be lost profits due to sales reduction that would not be adequately or effectively compensated.[92]

Given the complex analysis and the evidentiary difficulties that will surely be faced by any defendant in proving the passing-on defence (and specifying the rate of pass-on),[93] the Supreme Court is potentially opening the door to

---

Privada del Derecho de la Competencia. Especial referencia a la reclamación de daños en los casos de cárteles' (2011) *Revista de Competencia y Distribución* 8: 221–232, 232.

91 Concerning whether cuts in subsidies (lower farm and wholesale price) may lead to sugar prices reductions, OECD, *Sugar Policy Reform in the European Union (supra* n3*)*, 40 ["*elements of imperfect competition in downstream sugar using sectors (e.g., industrial users) may lead to some part of producer cuts being absorbed as improved margin and additional profits rather than being passed on to final consumers of refined sugar and sugar contained products*"].

92 And eventually, more speculative damages which would have been caused to those direct purchasers that eventually got priced out of the market, see R. D. Blair; W. H. Page, 'The Role of Economics in Defining Antitrust Injury and Standing', (1996) Managerial and Decision Economics (Special Issue: The Role of Economists in Modern Antitrust),17/2: 127–142, 130 ('*It would seem that they also suffered antitrust injury. This, of course, is correct as an economic matter, but is problematic as a practical matter. [...] The difficulty lies in identifying those who are injured by the deadweight loss. Anyone could claim that he or she would have purchased at the competitive price, but was priced out of the market. Thus, courts are likely to find that the claims of those who refused to purchase at the cartel price are speculative*').

93 Something that is at the basis of why the US Supreme Court excluded this option in 1968, see 392 U.S. 492–493 ('*We are not impressed with the argument that sound laws of economics require recognizing this defense. A wide range of factors influence a company's pricing policies. Normally the impact of a single change in the relevant conditions cannot be measured after the fact; indeed a businessman may be unable to state whether, had one fact been different (a single supply less expensive, general economic conditions more buoyant, or the labor market tighter, for example), he would have chosen a different price. Equally difficult to determine, in the real economic world rather than an economist's hypothetical model, is what effect a change in a company's price will have on its total sales. Finally, costs per unit for a different volume of total sales are hard to estimate. Even if it could be shown that the buyer raised his price in response to, and in the amount of, the overcharge and that his margin of profit and total sales had not thereafter declined, there would remain the nearly insuperable difficulty of demonstrating that the particular plaintiff could not or would not have raised his prices absent the overcharge or maintained the higher price had the overcharge been discontinued. Since establishing the applicability of the passing-on defense would require a convincing showing of each of these virtually unascertainable figures, the task would normally prove insurmountable. On the other hand, it is not unlikely that if the existence of the defense is generally confirmed, antitrust defendants will frequently seek to establish its applicability. Treble-damage actions would often require additional long and complicated proceedings involving massive evidence and complicated theories*') footnote omitted. However, *Hannover Shoe* allowed the passing-on

defendants spending a significant amount of resources in protecting themselves with this tool. That may well overwhelm the courts with complex economic analyses and reduce the effectiveness of private enforcement of competition law (in its compensatory fashion) because if the defence is successful, there would be less potential claims by indirect purchasers.[94] In truth the Supreme Court is merely making clear the rules set by black letter law, it is difficult to hide the unsurpassable difficulties and complexities they introduce for litigants and how negative it may be for the effectiveness of private enforcement of competition law and its compensatory goal.

Overall, one may wonder if *de lege ferenda* it would make more sense to limit standing for claim compensation to those which are better placed and with best incentives to claim damages (or at least do so, if no indirect purchasers do claim).[95] It is obvious that the confectioners have an information advantage in comparison to other potential claimants and that through them it was possible to concentrate a meaningful proportion of the harm (in comparison with the dissemination among final consumers).[96]

6. CONCLUSION

After examining the regulatory background that heavily drags competition in the sugar producing industry, and gives way to frequent anticompetitive behaviour, a prototypical example is examined in the Spanish sugar cartel (1995–1996). Then the paper looks at the € 5 million award for damages caused by the cartel as one of the most relevant developments in private enforcement of competition law in Spain to date. The final decisions on the case by the Spanish Supreme Court include several relevant rulings that will mark civil redress for victims of competition violations in Spain in the future.

---

defence to operate if the defendant could easily prove that the plaintiff was not damaged, see 392 US 494.

94 *'In consequence, those who violate the antitrust laws by price fixing or monopolizing would retain the fruits of their illegality because no one was available who would bring suit against them'*, 392 U.S. 494 (1977).

95 Following, for example, what was advocated in their dissenting opinion by justices Brennan, Marshall and Blackmun to the US Supreme Court judgment of 9 June 1977, *Illinois Brick Co et al v Illinois*, 431 US 720, 748, though clearly this would amount to an asymmetrical treatment in the use of the argument as a shield (by defendants) and as weapon (by indirect purchasers).

96 Those are the reasons justifying the prohibition of the passing-on defence on private litigation for US federal antitrust violations, see *Illinois Brick Co et al v Illinois*, 431 US 720. For a detailed examination of the Supreme Court's ruling in Illinois Brick, based upon the papers of several Supreme Court justices who decided the case, see A. I. Gavil, 'Antitrust Remedy Wars Episode I: Illinois Brick from Inside the Supreme Court' (2005) *St. John's Law Review* 79: 553–624.

The Supreme Court holdings are in line with the new Directive 2014/104/EU of 26 November 2014 on certain rules governing actions for damages under national law for infringements of the competition law provisions of the Member States and of the EU. Firstly, it has clarified the legal force that prior public enforcement decisions by competition authorities as a ground for follow-on private litigation claims. Secondly, it has also spelt out the assessment of expert forensic opinions in court. Finally, it delineated how the conventional civil rules on compensation apply to these claims, leaving room for the passing-on defence to operate if proof enough is provided by the defendants.

BIBLIOGRAPHY

Competition Commission of South Africa, 'Should the Competition Commission be bitter about the sugar industry in South Africa?' 2000, in *Competition News*, September, p. 5–6, visited on 10 January 2015, available at www.compcom.co.za/assets/Uploads/AttachedFiles/MyDocuments/Dec-00-Newsletter. pdf.

De Coninck, R., 'Estimating private antitrust damages' in *Competition Damage Evaluation: A Short State of Play,* Concurrences 3 – 2010, p. 4–8, 6.

Jiménez, F., 'Damages in the Sugar cartel in Spain.' at Association of Competition Economist- ACE 2010 Conference, Norwich, in 12 November 2010. Visited on 10 January 2015, available at www.competitioneconomics.org/

Laschinger, K., 'End of the road for sugar cartel?' Finance, 8 (2003), p. 38.

Watson, N., 'The Spanish Sugar Cartel.' at Association of Competition Economist- ACE 2010 Conference, Norwich, in 12 November 2010. Visited on 10 January 2015, available at www.compe titioneconomics.org/

PART IV

PRELIMINARY RULINGS AND STATE AID CONTROL

CHAPTER 12

STATE AID CASES IN NATIONAL COURTS AND THE EUROPEAN COMMISSION

Arjen MEI

1. INTRODUCTION

Presumably, for national courts' magistrates participating in the present conference and, for that matter, equally for members of any national court as well as the EU courts the substance of state aid cases pertains to the most intriguing and elusive material they ever work with. This may not be very surprising in view of the complexity of state aid regulation as relating to direct control by the European Commission on economic policy measures of Member States, not only those undertaken by central government authorities but also those taken by local and regional bodies, often concerning policies in areas of more or less sensitive interests on which the state aid control may exercise an unexpected impact. Which policy maker would have thought that an Eco tax in Britain[1], a social housing scheme in the Netherlands[2] or nature conservation measures in Germany[3] would come under state aid review, to mention but a few examples.

Looking at the provisions of Articles 107 and 108 of the TFEU, the first impression may be that state aid control is a bilateral matter between the Commission and the Member State under review. This is indeed the main structural feature also reappearing in the implementing provisions of Regulation (EC) no. 659/1999, even after its recent modification by Regulation(EU) no. 734/2013 which qualifies interested market participants as 'market information tools' at the Commission's disposal for purposes of preparing a file. The image is considerably different, however, when looking more closely at the interests of aid

---

1 Case T-210/02, BAA v Commission, on appeal C-487/06P.

2 Case C-567/07, Woningstichting Sint Servatius; also Case T-202/10, Stichting Woonlinie a.o., on appeal C-133/12P and T-202/10RENV pending.

3 Case T-347/09, Germany v Commission.

beneficiaries and their competitors on the market on which they operate. This is where the national courts come into the picture in view of the protection of their legal interests. In this perspective it appears appropriate, first, to highlight the distinct roles of the European Commission and national courts in this area, then, to look somewhat closer at the role of national courts in state aid litigation and, third, to identify instruments of liaison and cooperation between the EU and national levels of shared decision making and judicial review.

2. DISTINCT BUT COMPLEMENTARY ROLES MEET IN THE NOTION OF AID

According to standing case law the implementation of the State aid supervision system is a matter, on the one hand, for the Commission and, on the other, for the national courts. These protagonists of state aid regulation fulfil distinct but complementary roles. It is for the Commission exclusively in the procedures of Article 108 TFEU to assess the compatibility of aid with the internal market within the meaning of Article 107, paragraphs 2 and 3, TFEU. For national courts properly requested to do so, it is to safeguard the rights of individuals in case of infringement of the obligation of the Member States to give prior notice to the Commission of plans to grant aid and of the prohibition to implement the measure before the Commission has assessed its compatibility with the internal market, both following from Article 108, paragraph 3 of the TFEU.[4]

In the low cost carrier case *DHL v. FFH* the Court of Justice reiterates standing case law to the effect that the aim of the system of prior control of state aid is that only aid is implemented that is compatible with the internal market; to that effect the implementation of planned aid is to be deferred until any doubt as to its compatibility is resolved by the Commission's final decision. In the view of the Court the involvement of national courts is the result of the direct effect of the prohibition on implementation on planned aid. While the immediate enforceability of the obligation to stand still referred to in Article 108(3) TFEU extends to all aid implemented without having been notified, national courts must offer to interested individuals the certain prospect that all appropriate conclusions will be drawn from an infringement of that obligation as regards the validity of implementing measures, the recovery of financial support granted in disregard of that obligation and possible interim measures.[5]

The complementary nature of the respective roles of the Commission and national courts resides mainly in the circumstance that neither can exercise the respective competences of the other within its jurisdiction. In particular from

4 Among many other Case C-368/04, Transalpine Ölleitung, par. 36–38, Case C-275/10, Residex, par. 25–27 and Case 284/12, DHL v FFH, par. 26–28.

5 Case C-284/12, fn 5, par. 26, 29–30.

the viewpoint of the individual interests involved, the jurisdiction of the Commission does not appear to be conceived and in any case does not entail sufficient instruments to protect lawful interests of private individuals and eventually redress an unlawful situation. National courts, on the other hand, have no jurisdiction, nor the instruments to intervene in the part of the matter which is to be established at the EU level, *i.e.* the assessment of the compatibility of the measure at stake with the internal market. From this angle, the State aid supervision regime looks like a well-organised multilevel system of EU administration and national judicial protection based on a balanced division of powers.

A particular area where the twain meet, however, is concerned with the complex problem of the notion of an aid. Indeed, on request of a competitor of a (potential) aid beneficiary, a national court may have to assess the legality of a contested measure, e.g. inquiring whether in conformity with the provisions of Article 108, paragraph 3, TFEU, the measure has been properly notified to the Commission or whether it has been implemented in conformity with the obligation to stand still, and if not, to order appropriate relief pending a final decision of the Commission on its compatibility. However, before doing so, it will need to establish whether the contested measure constitutes an aid within the meaning of Article 107, paragraph 1, TFEU. Equally, the Commission will have to establish whether the particular measure before it comes within the scope of the concept of aid in the sense of Article 107, paragraph 1, TFEU, before it proceeds to an assessment of the compatibility of the measure with the internal market. Therefore, in its decisions opening a procedure with a view to a compatibility assessment under Article 108, paragraph 2, TFEU, the Commission usually operates at least a provisional qualification of the measure at issue as an aid.

In view of the complex nature of the concept of an aid, it is of little surprise, then, that a large number of the cases brought in the EU courts, either in direct actions against Commission decisions or in preliminary references by national courts are concerned in the first place with the assessment of whether the required criteria are satisfied, in order for a national measure to qualify as an aid. As a reminder it may be pointed out that Article 107, paragraph 1 TFEU distinguishes four cumulative criteria for the qualification of a measure of a Member State as State aid. The first relates to the association of the aid with the State; the notion of an aid covers any aid granted by a Member State or through State resources in any form whatsoever. Secondly, the measure must distort or threaten to distort competition. Third, the distortion of competition must result from favouring certain undertakings or the production of certain goods, in other words the measure must confer a selective advantage to its beneficiaries. And fourthly, the measure only constitutes State aid in so far as it affects trade between Member States. Moreover, the cumulative application of these criteria rests on the premise that the aid is conferred on an undertaking engaged in the exercise of economic activity on a particular market, as opposed to the exercise of public powers.[6] The legal status of the undertaking, the way in which it is financed and whether it is supposed to generate profits or not, however, are irrelevant in this context.[7]

Each of these elements are the object of more or less developed case law of the EU courts, which cannot be expounded in the scope of the present contribution. A very useful instrument for legal practice, in particular for the purpose of applying the notion of an aid in national courts, will be provided in the Commission Notice on the notion of State aid pursuant to Article 107(1) TFEU, due to be published in the course of 2015.[8] As it is announced, the 50 pages long document clarifies how the Commission understands the concept, in line with existing EU case law and without prejudice to further interpretation by the Court of Justice.

A key issue of the notion of State aid resides in its legal nature which is characterised by vague and broad criteria some of which require complex economic assessments. According to standing case law, State aid is a legal concept which must be interpreted on the basis of objective factors. Therefore, the EU Courts, and for that matter national courts called upon to apply the concept, must carry out a comprehensive review as to whether a measure falls within the scope of Article 107(1) TFEU, having regard both to the specific features of the case and to the economic or technical assessments to be made.[9] At the same time, the judicial review of complex economic or technical assessments is necessarily limited.[10]In particular the concept of economic advantage in the context of the third criterion is illustrative for the rather elusive nature of the judicial review process. It may, on the one hand, require comprehensive review of whether the economic advantage at stake must be assessed on the basis of the so called private investor test, including the appreciation of whether the Member State while using (fiscal) instruments of state power acts as a shareholder of the beneficiary undertaking. On the other hand, judicial review of whether the assessment carried out by the Commission on the basis of the private investor test was appropriate, is necessarily limited in nature.[11] It goes without saying that for the proper application of such a

---

6 Cf Case C-82/01, Aéroports de Paris, par.74.

7 Cf Joined cases C-180–184/98, Pavlov a.o., par.74 and case C-222/04, Cassa di Risparmio, par.122.

8 An equally useful Draft Commission Notice, published for consultation purposes, may already be found on the Commission website.

9 Case C-487/06, BAA v Commission, par. 111.

10 Case C-290/07, Commission v Scott, par. 66.

11 Case C-224/12P, Commission v Kingdom of the Netherlands, ING, DNB, par. 30. See also Case C-124/10P, Commission v EDF, par. 91 *et seq* and Joined Cases C-214/12P, C-215/12P and C-223/12P, Land Burgenland v Commission, par. 91 *et seq*. On the difficulty of distinguishing cases for comprehensive from those for limited review, see my Opinion *In*

complex set of rules and concepts national courts must rely heavily on the case law of the EU courts and the Commission practice.

3. SAFEGUARDING RIGHTS IN NATIONAL COURTS

The division of competences between the Commission and national courts also implies that the legal concepts underlying their respective jurisdictions are diverse. As noted above, the Commission intervenes and has exclusive jurisdiction as regards the appreciation of the *compatibility* of the proposed aid measure with the internal market. National courts, on the other hand, have the task to provide appropriate measures to remedy the *unlawfulness* of the implementation of the aid to the extent that it constitutes an infringement of the obligation to notify and/or to stand still, following from Article 108(3) TFEU. This provision is based on the purpose of ensuring that incompatible aid will never be implemented. The intention being that solely compatible aid may be implemented, the implementation of planned aid is to be deferred until doubt as to its incompatibility is resolved by the Commission's final decision. The idea apparently is that the aid does not remain at the disposal of the recipient until such time as the Commission makes its decision.[12]

In its 2009 Notice on the enforcement of State aid law by national courts the Commission enumerates no less than five remedies which should be available before national courts as against unlawful aid. Interested parties could claim, first, a prohibition of payment of unlawful aid not yet granted; second, recovery of aid unlawfully paid in violation of the obligations to notify and/or to stand still; thirdly, recovery of interest in respect of the period of time the beneficiary has had the sum illegally paid at its disposal, fourthly, damages as a consequence of unlawful aid granted to a competitor and fifthly, appropriate interim measures to block the disposal of unlawful aid.[13] In the leading CELF Case, however, an exception has been provided for the situation where the Commission has adopted a final decision declaring compatible with the internal market an aid implemented contrary to (now) Article 108(3) TFEU. The national court should not be bound to order recovery of such aid, but only payment of interest in respect of the period of unlawfulness.[14]

Search of a Manifest Error: Dutch Complexities between Certainties of the Law and Uncertainties of Economics, EStAL 3/2012, 13–16.

12 Case C-1/09, CELF II, par. 29 *et seq.*

13 Commission Notice on the enforcement of State aid law by national courts (2009/C 85/01), OJ 2009, C 85/1, par. 26 et seq, with further explanation.

14 Case C-199/06, CELF v SIDE. See, however, in contrast with this Grand Chamber judgment, the judgment of the sixth chamber of March 19, 2015 in Case C-672/13, OTP Bank v Magyar Allam, in which it is expressly held that the final decision of the Commission declaring the

The reconstruction under national procedural law of these tasks of national courts as developed in the case law of the Court of Justice and appropriately framed in the Commission's Notice, is not always self-evident, in particular as regards the legal basis of such claims and the question whom to address with which claim.[15] However, some supreme courts have recently taken up these longstanding jurisprudential indications and made major steps in giving them proper effect. In a line of judgments, notably in the low cost carrier cases, lower German courts had shown themselves unwilling to unambiguously draw the consequences of the Court's case law.

In two cases litigation went up to the Bundesgerichtshof which established that the German Civil Code and the Unfair Competition Act offer a sound legal basis for interim relief as well as disclosure proceedings and claims for damages in case of illegal aid, granted in violation of the obligations to notify and to stand still. The Bundesgerichtshof also specified that according to German law contracts purporting the granting of aid would not necessarily be completely null and void, but only in so far as the implied aid extends.[16] Furthermore, it may be inferred from the judgment in the Bicycles case, concerning the complex relationship between EU State aid rules and German procedural law, that in a situation of concurrent proceedings pending at the level of the Commission or the EU Courts, requiring stay of proceedings in the national court, German law offers an appropriate legal basis for provisional payment of disputed sums into a blocked account. This seems fully in line with the Commission Notice and the CELF case law of the Court of Justice.[17]

The Residex case, on reference by the Supreme Court of the Netherlands, is atypical in its peculiarity, to the extent that aid conferred by an administrative body in the form of a guarantee on a loan may not immediately clarify who is the beneficiary, the borrower or the lender or eventually both of them. If the reference did not allow the Court of Justice to solve this intriguing question, it made clear from the outset that the Dutch Supreme Court is equally prepared to interpret the relevant provisions of national law in such a way that it allows for an appropriate legal basis for an infringement of Article 108(3) TFEU to be redressed to the effect of restoring the competitive situation existing prior to the payment of the aid.[18] These cases, and several other for that matter, show that

aid compatible cannot have the effect of regularising *a posteriori* unlawful implementing acts taken in violation of Article 108(3) TFEU.

15 See also Alke Metselaar, Who can invoke State Aid Law before National Judges? That Floating Question of Legal Interest in the Case Law of Dutch Courts, EStAL 2/2014, 250–260.

16 BGH 10 February 2011 in Joined cases ZR 136/09, Flughafen Frankfurt Hahn and ZR 213/08, Flughafen Lübeck.

17 BGH 13 September 2012 in Case III ZB 3/12, EStAL 1/2014, 162, ann. M. Köhler.

18 Case C-275/10, Residex Capital v Gemeente Rotterdam and HR(Supreme Court of the Netherlands) 26 April 2013, no. 08/04343 implementing the Court of Justice's preliminary ruling in C-275/10.

national courts are gradually coming loose of a long uneasy relationship between national procedural law and the requirements flowing from EU state aid law.

At this stage it should be noted that the role of national courts in matters of State aid may be further enhanced by the adoption of a multitude of sector specific instruments and regulatory measures of a general nature providing for policy frameworks and group exemptions, with a view to reduce the need for notification and compatibility assessments under Article 108 by the Commission. As a consequence the role of national courts may extend from safeguarding the rights of individuals in the context of notification and stand still to resolving disputes concerning the application e.g. of the general block exemption and the *de minimis* regulations.[19]

4. LIAISON, COOPERATION AND DELIMITATION

Building on previous informal instruments of cooperation, the 2009 Notice of the Commission on the enforcement of State aid law by national courts offered two forms of support to national courts by the Commission in State aid cases. Firstly, on the basis of the mutual duty of sincere cooperation between the Union and the Member States, at present in Article 4, paragraph 3 TEU, national courts could request the Commission to transmit information relevant to a case pending before them, either concerning a procedure pending before the Commission or concerning Commission decisions and economic data in its possession. Secondly, national courts were invited in the Notice to request the Commission to give an opinion in cases pending before them. According to its Notice the Commission considers this a part of its duty to defend the public interest, not serving any private party interest before the national court in question.[20]

As from the entry into force, in August 2013, of Regulation(EU) no 734/2013[21] these forms of cooperation have been provided with a formal legal basis in a new Article 23a of the Procedural Regulation. Moreover, in an approach similar to its *amicus curiae* role in competition cases under Article 15 Regulation(EC) no 1/2003, a fresh paragraph 2 of Article 23a introduces the power for the Commission to intervene on its own initiative in State aid proceedings before national courts. Written observations may be submitted on the Commission's own initiative. For oral observations, according to the new provision, the Commission needs the permission of the court in question. Unlike Regulation(EC) 1/2003 for competition cases, the Commission's competence to

19 Commission Regulation (EU) No 651/2014 and Commission regulation (EU) No1407/2013 respectively.

20 Notice, fn 14, par. 77 *et seq.*

21 Amending Regulation (EC) no 659/1999 (the Procedural Regulation).

intervene in State aid cases is oriented towards situations 'Where the coherent application of Article 107(1) or Article 108 of the TFEU so requires.'.

Such consideration is undoubtedly apt to boost reservations about this arrangement for intervention of an international administrative authority in national court proceedings, as was the case at the time of its introduction in competition cases. In view of the authoritative position of Commission specialists in often less specifically equipped national courts, the procedural protection of the defence rights of ordinary parties will indeed require special attention in such cases.

This seems all the more important where recent case law underlines the binding nature upon national courts of a provisional qualification of a measure as State aid in a Commission decision opening the formal examination procedure under Article 108(2) TFEU.[22] Admittedly, the Court distinguishes between whether or not the Commission has initiated the formal examination procedure with regard to the measure at issue in the proceedings before the national court. Where the formal procedure has not been opened yet, it may well be for the national court to assess whether the contested measure constitutes an aid and should therefore have been notified.[23] In the case at hand, however, the formal procedure had been opened with regard to a non-notified measure which had been implemented.

The Court considers that the preliminary nature of the opening decision does not mean that the decision lacks legal effects. Irrespective of whether the final decision in the formal procedure confirms or denies the qualification as State aid, the preventive aim of the State aid control system, according to the Court, requires that following the doubt raised in the opening decision as to the aid character of the measure and its compatibility with the internal market, its implementation should be deferred until that doubt is resolved by the Commission's final decision.[24] In the context of the obligation of sincere cooperation on which the system of State aid control is based, national courts must, in particular, refrain from taking decisions which conflict with a decision of the Commission, even if it is provisional. As indicated above[25], national courts are required to adopt all the necessary measures to draw the appropriate conclusions from an infringement of the obligation to suspend the implementation of the aid at issue; to that end, the court continues, national

22 Case C-284/12, DHL v FFH, with several dismissive comments, already on the Opinion of AG Mengozzi: U. Soltesz, *Effet Utile Taken to Extremes: Does an Opening Decision Already Trigger the 'Stand-Still Obligation'?*, EStAL 4/2013, 643–645, Chr. Koenig, *The Judgment in Case C-284/12 under the Socratic Scrutiny of Good Justice*, EStAL 1/2014, 1–3, Ann. L. Ghazarian, *Binding Effect of Opening Decision – Lufthansa AG v FFH*, EStAL 1/2014, 108–114, Ph. Nicolaides, *Are National Courts Becoming an Extension of the Commission?*, EStAL 3/2014, 409–413.

23 Par.34.

24 Par. 37–40.

25 Par.2.

courts may decide to order suspension of the measure in question and recovery of payments already made, but they may also decide to order provisional measures in order to safeguard both the interests of the parties concerned and the effectiveness of the Commission's provisional qualification. It adds that the national court entertaining doubts as regards the state aid character of the measure, may seek clarification from the Commission and/or refer a question to the Court for a preliminary ruling.[26]

In the light of the comments mentioned in footnote 23 it seems appropriate to draw the attention to some eclectic underlying notions. Firstly, it may be underlined that the system of State aid control is based on the fundamental idea of assessment of Member States' aid measures by the Commission as regards their compatibility with the internal market, prior to their implementation. This requires apparently an unconditional obligation to notify. Secondly, in an ideal world, the scope of the notion of an aid under Article 107(1) TFEU and that of the obligation to stand still pursuant to Article 108(3) coincide precisely and completely. In order to make the system work, however, it would appear inevitable that the obligations to notify and to stand still cover not only measures which unquestionably constitute State aid, but also measures which raise doubts as to their aid character. Thirdly, it must be recalled that according to long standing case law the decision initiating the formal examination procedure purports to create autonomous legal effects, in particular to the extent that it leads to suspension of the implementation of the measure at issue following the provisional qualification of the measure as aid, and remaining valid until the end of the formal procedure.[27] It would appear difficult to accept that a decision which is thus binding on the parties, subject to judicial review in the competent EU courts, would not bind national courts, subject to preliminary reference on its validity, provided that such question is admissible in view of the TWD case law. In such perspective, the DHL v FFH judgment is perhaps less surprising than the aforementioned comments imply. Nevertheless, in view of the reference to provisional measures allowing to strike a balance between the interests involved, it may be expected that the legal practice ensuing this judgment will draw heavily on the smooth functioning of proceedings for interim relief, on EU as well as national level.

5. FINAL OBSERVATIONS

The preceding paragraphs show a picture of EU State aid control as an intriguing system of multilevel administration and judicial activity. Interestingly, it is the

---

26 Par 41–43.

27 Cf Case C-312/90, Spain v Commission (Cenemesa), par.12–24 and C-47/91, Italy v Commission (Italgrani), par. 29–30.

very meeting point of the distinct and complementary roles of the Commission and national courts in the application of the notion of State aid that triggers the delimitation of those roles in the DHL v FFH Case. Furthermore, the national courts seem to be picking up their particular role within the framework of each Member State's autonomous, but adapting national procedural system. This development is enhanced by the Commission's policy to the effect of providing for extensive regulatory frameworks and reducing the number of cases dealt with by the Commission. The shift in the activity of the Commission towards a role of amicus curiae in State aid proceedings in national courts, however, will require close scrutiny.

BIBLIOGRAPHY

Alke Metselaar, Who can invoke State Aid Law before National Judges? That Floating Question of Legal Interest in the Case Law of Dutch Courts, EStAL 2/2014, 250–260.

CHAPTER 13
RESCUE AND RESTRUCTURING OF THE STATE AID

Jaka CEPEC

1. INTRODUCTION

The European State Aid rules are part of the overall competition framework, with a goal of ensuring and preserving workable competition in the EU internal market. The State Aid has been a part of EU competition law for several decades, but a combination of legal, economic, and public policy issues, made it sometimes less esteemed, and often neglected by professionals and was consequently for many years considered to be the 'ugly duckling' of EU competition law.[1] The Global economic and financial crisis brought heightened attention to the State Aid rules and the overlooked ugly duckling is changing into a "beautiful swan."[2]

State aid is defined as an advantage in any form whatsoever conferred on a selective basis to undertakings by national public authorities. Article 107(1) of the TFEU defines that any Aid granted by a Member State or through State resources in any form whatsoever[3] which distorts or threatens to distort competition by favouring certain undertakings or the production of certain goods and affects trade among Member States, is incompatible with the Internal Market. The conditions laid down in Article 107(1) of the TFEU are cumulative and thus, for a measure to be qualified as State Aid, all the conditions must be fulfilled simultaneously. Although State Aid and measures with equivalent effect are subject to the general prohibition, the TFEU specifically exempts three categories of aid, which it declares to be "compatible with the internal market."

---

1 Ahlborn C., Berg C., 2004, pp. 41–66.

2 Pesaresi N., Van Hoof M., 2008, p. 1.

3 The ECJ uses a broad view on State Aid and made it clear that the concept of aid does not cover only positive benefits, such as subsidies, but also measures that mitigate the charges an undertaking would normally have to bear, such as the supply of goods or services at a preferential rate, a reduction on social security contributions, or tax exemptions. Craig P., De Burca G., 2011, p. 1088.

These exemptions are (107(2) TFEU): (a) aid having social character granted to individual consumers, provided that such aid is granted without discrimination related to the origin of the products concerned, (b) aid to make good the damage caused by natural disasters or exceptional occurrences and (c) aid granted to the economy of certain areas of the Federal Republic of Germany affected by the division of Germany, in so far as such aid is required in order to compensate for the economic disadvantages caused by that division. Additionally to the three general exemptions mentioned above, paragraph 107(3) TFEU defines further five categories that "may be considered to be compatible with the common market." These are: (1) aid to promote the economic development of areas where the standard of living is abnormally low or where there is serious underemployment, (2) aid to promote the execution of an important project of common European interest or to remedy a serious disturbance in the economy of a Member State, (3) aid to facilitate the development of certain economic activities or of certain economic areas, where such aid does not adversely affect trading conditions to an extent contrary to the common interest; (4) aid to promote culture and heritage conservation where such aid does not affect trading conditions and competition in the Union to an extent that is contrary to the common interest and (5) such other categories of aid as may be specified by decision of the Council on a proposal from the Commission.

The Commission is empowered to decide whether any particular aid falls under one of the five categories and since the TFEU offers no additional elaboration, the Commission has been able to exercise considerable discretion in their interpretation.[4]

The control of state aid is an exclusive and all-encompassing EU competence.[5] It is an area where the Commission enjoys considerable freedom of action, subject only to the scrutiny of the European courts, exercises far-reaching powers, and where its actions have consequences beyond their immediate impact on governments and firms.[6] Generally all new State Aid has to be notified to the Commission "in sufficient time to enable it to submit its comments."[7] State Aid cannot be transacted until the Commission takes a decision. If the Commission takes the view that an aid is not compatible with the TFEU, it can request further information from the member's government concerned. If it still has reservations, the Commission can undertake a more extensive investigation. Depending on the results of its findings, the Commission can decide to approve

4 Kassim H., Lyons B., 2013, p. 2.

5 The European Union (EU) is one of the few jurisdictions in the world that has introduced specific legal provisions for controlling state aid.

6 Kassim H., Lyons B., 2013, p. 2.

7 This has proved to be practically impossible, the more so with 27 members of the EU. As a result, the Commission has issued a number of exemption (especially the block exemptions) and *de minimis* rules, for which notification is not required. Heimler A., Jenny F., 2012, p. 347.

the aid, reduce it or recover it.[8] Article 109 TFEU defines, that "the Council, on a proposal from the Commission and after consulting the European Parliament, may make any appropriate regulations for the application of Articles 107 and 108 and may in particular determine the conditions in which Article 108(3) shall apply and the categories of aid exempted from this procedure." This provision enables the EU to adopt an implementing measure setting out precisely how the Commission is to examine and investigate aids, as well as defining the conditions under which certain categories of aid are exempted from the obligatory notification.[9]

Existing State Aid is kept under constant review by the Commission in cooperation with Member States. If the Commission finds that aid granted is not compatible with the internal market, or that such aid is being misused it can decide at any time, that the aid shall be abolished or altered.[10]

The EU State Aid regulations are extremely broad, as only the pure size of applicable legislation on manufacturing industry and services is a thousand pages long even though it does not include the specific rules applicable to agriculture and fisheries. The EU State Aid provisions can be categorised into: Treaty provisions on state Aid (Articles 107 to 109 TFEU); General procedural rules; Enabling regulations and general block exemption regulation; horizontal rules for State Aid; sector specific rules; specific aid instruments; reference/ discount rates and recovery interest rates; transparency of financial relations between member states and public undertakings; services of general economic interest and finally temporary rules established in response to the economic and financial crisis.[11]

This Chapter presents a short assessment of special rules that govern Rescue and Restructuring State Aid (hereinafter R&R State Aid). The emphasis will be on the newly accepted Guidelines and especially on the question of implementing the general Balancing test rule into the assessment of R&R State Aid.

The structure of the chapter is as follows. In the second subtitle general description of the role and history of special Guidelines for R&R Aid will be presented, followed by an analysis of the implementation of the Balancing test in

---

8 See Article 108 TFEU.

9 Kassim H., Lyons B., 2013, p. 6. See for e.g. the so-called Block Exemption Regulations for State Aid (Enabling Regulation: Council Regulation No 733/2013 of 22 July 2013 amending Regulation (EC) No 994/98 on the application of Articles 92 and 93 of the Treaty establishing the European Community to certain categories of horizontal State aid OJ L204, 31.07.2013; General Block exemption Regulation: Commission Regulation (EU) N°651/2014 of 17 June 2014 declaring certain categories of aid compatible with the internal market in application of Articles 107 and 108 of the Treaty, De minimis aid: Commission Regulation (EC) No 1407/2013 of 18 December 2013 on the application of Articles 107 and 108 of the Treaty on the Functioning of the European Union to de minimis aid; etc.).

10 If the Member State concerned does not comply with this decision within the prescribed time, the Commission or any other interested State may, refer the matter to the Court of Justice of the European Union.

11 For details see EU Rules to state Aid, 2014.

R&R Aid. Subtitle three offers a short critical law and economics overview of the 2014 Guidelines.

2. STATE AID FOR RESCUING AND RESTRUCTURING FIRMS IN DISTRESS

Rescuing and Restructuring State Aid is widely regarded as particularly distortive to the single market as it enables recipients (failing companies) to remain in market, even though under normal conditions they would be forced to exit the market, usually via an insolvency proceeding.[12] This is the essence of competition and it cannot be the norm that companies, which get into difficulties, are or should be rescued by the State.[13] The Commission states in paragraph 6 of the 2014 R&R Guidelines that: "Rescue and restructuring aid are among the most distortive types of State aid. It is well established that successful sectors of the economy witness productivity growth not because all the undertakings present in the market gain in productivity, but rather because the more efficient and technologically advanced undertakings grow at the expense of those that are less efficient or have obsolete products. Exit of less efficient undertakings allows their more efficient competitors to grow and returns assets to the market, where they can be applied to more productive uses. By interfering with this process, rescue and restructuring aid may significantly slow economic growth in the sectors concerned." This means that restructuring should usually be done without State Aid, through agreements with creditors or by means of insolvency or reorganisation proceedings.

Rescue and Restructuring State Aid has direct and indirect negative effects. The direct negative effect is the prevention of insolvency of economically nonviable companies at the expense of its competitors, as this companies, without receiving R&R State Aid would have with certainty exited the market, but now their exit is delayed or altogether prevented.[14]

The indirect negative effects are generated by the mere existence of the R&R aid. Less efficient firms know that the government will rescue them. This creates moral hazard and a willingness to undertake riskier investments.[15]

---

12 Nicolaides P., Kekekelis M., 2004, p. 204.

13 Nicolaides P., Kekelekis M., 2004, p. 205.

14 Maier – Rigaud F., Milde C., 2015.

15 "*Undertakings anticipating that they are likely to be rescued when they run into difficulty may embark upon excessively risky and unsustainable business strategies. In addition, the prospect of rescue and restructuring aid for a given undertaking may artificially reduce its cost of capital, giving it an undue competitive advantage in the marketplace.*" Paragraph 9 of the 2014 R&R State Aid Guidelines.

Correspondingly more efficient firms are discouraged from investing as they know that the government will potentially rescue their competitors.[16]

R&R aid by definition must create a distortion of competition when it is granted. It also slows down the process and thus impedes productivity growth. Even the mere possibility of R&R aid, however, leads to a harmful distortion of investment incentives, encouraging inefficient firms to take more risks, and efficient firms to be less risk taking in respect to investments. The possibility of R&R aid also leads to a lower cost of capital for very large undertakings – who, if one follows the political economy literature, are the most likely recipients of R&R aid – thus stacking the deck against small and medium sized companies (SMEs). Thus, the existence of R&R aid most likely has pervasive distortive effects in the economy even before a single Euro of R&R aid is actually used.[17]

On the other hand, however, as these measures benefit large companies with thousands of employees, there is a strong political incentive for granting them. Keeping a large company alive through restructuring aid, especially if this aid is once and for all, may be justified on grounds of competition because it allows a large competitor to remain in the market, thus keeping industry profit from increasing. Furthermore, since a firm may also become bankrupt because of the existence of restrictive regulations, both in product and in factor markets, restructuring aid may be a way to ease the transition to a more competition-friendly regulatory environment. Finally, under a macroeconomic perspective, avoiding the bankruptcy of a large competitor may help to avoid the disappearance of many small suppliers at the local level, maintaining an employment base often much larger than that of the aided firm. The political pressures in favour of restructuring aid can therefore be quite strong.[18]

The Commission is generally of the opinion that if a firm is not profitable, its exit from the market is an inevitable consequence and Member States should not interfere with this. The reason is that R&R aid supporting unprofitable firms causes the worst competition distortions, because more efficient competitors are adversely discriminated against.[19] R&R State Aid can only be granted if such aid does not go against the common interests of the Community and if the benefits that the aid generate outweigh the costs that it brings.[20] The European Commission has to be especially strict when it assesses rescue or restructuring aid and aid should be allowed only if the overall social benefits from intervention outweigh its costs. "Companies should only be eligible for State aid when they have exhausted all other market options and where such aid is necessary in order to achieve a well-defined objective of common interest. Companies should be

16 Bolsa Feruz M.A., Nicolaides P., 2013, p. 3.
17 Maier-Rigaud F, Milde C., 2015.
18 Heimler A., Jenny F., 2012, p. 358.
19 Grigorian A., Hainova D., Barbova B., 2014, p. 5.
20 British Airways v Commission of the European Communities [1998] E.C.R. II-2405 at [235].

allowed to receive aid under these guidelines only once within 10 years (the 'one time, last time' principle)."[21] It is therefore important to ensure that aid is only allowed under conditions that mitigate its potential harmful effects and promote the effectiveness of public spending.

The Commission additionally stated that "[A]id for restructuring raises particular competition concerns as it can shift an unfair share of the burden of structural adjustment and the attendant social and economic problem onto other producers who are managing without aid and to other Member States. The general principle should therefore be to allow the grant of restructuring aid only in circumstances in which it can be demonstrated that it does not run counter to the Community interest. This will only be possible if strict criteria are met, and if it is certain that any distortions of competition will be offset by the benefits flowing from the firm's survival (in particular, where it is clear that the net effect of redundancies resulting from the firm going out of business, combined with the effects on its suppliers, would exacerbate local, regional or national employment problems or, exceptionally, where the firm's disappearance would result in a monopoly or tight oligopolistic situation) and, where appropriate, there are adequate compensatory measures in favour of competitors."[22]

In order to avoid excessive market distortions, the Commission devised a set of rules which attempt to replicate what the market would have done without the aid, keeping distortions of competition to a minimum, and acting as a deterrent in order to avoiding restructuring in the hope of intervention by the State. These rules are the Community Guidelines for rescuing and restructuring firms in difficulty.[23] Legally speaking, these guidelines are not binding. They are non-obligatory acts, which thoroughly explain the law on state aid, and the criteria under which R&R aid may be granted in derogation from Article 107 TFEU, which generally prohibits state aid. Because these guidelines are issued by the Commission, they reflect the Commission's approach, the future intentions, and the plans can be implied from them. The guidelines on R&R aid for firms in difficulty are especially important, due to their controversial nature that, as previously mentioned, also led to a number of controversial Court decisions.[24]

2.1. RESCUE AND RESTRUCTURING GUIDELINES

Drawing heavily from its experience in dealing with rescue and restructuring State aid cases, the Commission has issued detailed guidelines, to assist Member States to design and notify rescue and restructuring aid schemes that can be

21 Paragraph 8 of 2014 R&R State Aid Guidelines.

22 Paragraph 28 of the 2004 R&R Guidelines.

23 Valle E., Van de Casteele K., 2004, p. 9.

24 Farantouris N, 2009, p. 1.

authorised by the Commission. R&R State aid rules come in question if State Aid is granted to a company in difficulties. A precondition for receiving any R&R Aid is the fact that the undertaking is in difficulty. Difficulty is defined in the Guidelines (Point 20) as:

> A situation, where a company without intervention by the State will almost certainly be condemned to going out of business in the short or medium term. A company is considered to be in difficulty if at least one of the following circumstances occurs:
>
> (a) In the case of a limited liability company, where more than half of its subscribed share capital has disappeared as a result of accumulated losses. This is the case when deduction of accumulated losses from reserves and all other elements generally considered as part of the own funds of the company) leads to a negative cumulative amount that exceeds half of the subscribed share capital;
> (b) In the case of a company where at least some members have unlimited liability for the debt of the company, where more than half of its capital as shown in the company accounts has disappeared as a result of accumulated losses;
> (c) Where the company is subject to collective insolvency proceedings or fulfils the criteria under its domestic law for being placed in collective insolvency proceedings at the request of its creditors;
> (d) in the case of a company that is not an SME, where, for the past two years: I.) the undertaking's book debt to equity ratio has been greater than 7,5 and II.) the undertaking's EBITDA interest coverage ratio has been below 1,0.

The problem of Rescue and Restructuring State Aid was first mentioned in the 1971 in The First Report on Competition Policy.[25] In the 8th Report on Competition Policy in 1978, the Commission for the first time set out the conditions under which such aid would be regarded as compatible with the common market.[26] Due to a vast amount of cases on the issue of R&R aid the Commission issued its first detailed guidelines in 1994. The Guidelines advised Member States on how to design and identify these kinds of aid schemes that can be authorised by the Commission.[27] They were revised in 1997.[28] New Guidelines were adopted in 1999 and in 2004. The 1999 Guidelines were considered very important and successful as they established with certainty the circumstances in which rescue aid is applicable. The Guidelines from 2004 presented an improved and refined version of the 1999 Guidelines. One of its most important contributions was that they clearly gave the conditions that rescue aid must fulfil – namely the reversibility, temporary nature, and short-term economic support.[29] The 2004 guidelines were the basis for almost 200

25 See Anestis P., Mavroghenis S., Drakakaki S., 2004.

26 8th Report on Competition Policy 1978, paragraph 228 and Guidelines on rescue aid communicated by the Commission to the Member States, 24 January 1979.

27 Grigorian A., Hainova D., Barbova B., 2014, p. 5.

28 The 1997 Guidelines added rules for the agricultural sector.

29 Grigorian A., Hainova D., Barbova B., 2014, p. 8.

individual rescue and restructuring cases (granting just under 22 billion EUR in rescue and restructuring aid) over the nearly ten years they were in force, including the restructuring of the PSA group (manufacturer of Peugeot and Citroën), Royal Mail and TV2, of airlines in Austria, Italy, Malta, Cyprus, and the Czech Republic, shipyards in Poland and Croatia, and rail operators in Bulgaria, Greece, and the United Kingdom.[30] They were due to expire after five years but were firstly, due to the global financial and economic crisis, extended until 2012.[31] In 2012 the State aid modernisation initiative was adopted and the Guidelines were further extended until the Commission would adopt new rules. The current R&R State Aid Guidelines were adopted in July 2014.[32]

As already mentioned the financial crisis was one of the reasons that the Commission postponed the revision of the R&R Guidelines. It decided to adopt the Temporary Framework that allowed the Member States to put into place State aid schemes that provide assistance in financing for companies that have had financial difficulties, provided they were not considered to have difficulties (as defined by the R&R Guidelines) on the 1st of July, 2008. The Temporary Framework thus provided temporary relief to companies that were seen as firms in difficulty, and that would normally have to apply to rescue and/or restructuring aid, with the strings attached to that type of aid.[33] The application of the Temporary Framework has had very positive effects. Many companies were able to obtain financing and thus overcome the lack of banks' and financial institutions' financing.

After the acute phase of the crisis, the Commission prepared new R&R Guidelines. The 2014 Guidelines were prepared with the thoughts of many critics of the old Guidelines. The main problems of the 2004 Guidelines were: (a) the unclear definition of "a firm in difficulty", (b) the question of what is considered as own contribution, (c) the issue of appropriate compensatory measures, (d) the problem of compliance with the prior notification rule as the aid is urgent and (d) that the claw back clause should be foreseen as a part of the successful restructuring.[34]

The 2014 Guidelines were prepared to achieve four particular goals: (a) the use of the balancing test, (b) better filters, to ensure that state aid is targeted at cases where it is really needed, (c) a new concept of temporary restructuring

---

30 European Commission, Competition policy brief, new rules on rescue and restructuring aid for industry: the right incentives for innovation and growth, Issue 9, 2014. In the period between 1990 and 2002, the Commission approved the application of rescue and restructuring aid to approximately 120 failing firms, varying from less than 1 million up to more than 20 billion EUR. See Anestis, Mavroghenis, Drakakis, 2004.

31 Kassim H., Lyons B., 2013, p. 12.

32 Community Guidelines on State Aid for Rescuing and Restructuring Firms In Difficulty (2004/C 244/02). The Guidelines are applicable to industry and services except the financial sector.

33 Schütte M., 2012, p. 814.

34 For details see: Schütte M., 2012 or Nicolaides P., Kekekelis M., 2005, p. 205.

support, to simplify the granting of aid for restructuring SMEs while reducing competition distortions, and (d) new requirements for burden sharing, to ensure that a company's investors make a fair contribution to the costs of its restructuring.[35]

The 2014 Guidelines distinguish between rescue aid, restructuring aid, and temporary restructuring support.[36]

Rescue aid is designed to allow firms that are facing imminent collapse to stay in business for long enough to prepare a restructuring plan. Rescue aid is by its nature an urgent and temporary assistance. Its primary objective is to make it possible to keep an ailing undertaking afloat for the short time needed to work out a restructuring or liquidation plan. The general principle is that rescue aid makes it possible to provide temporary support to an undertaking facing a serious deterioration of its financial situation, involving an acute liquidity crisis or technical insolvency. Such temporary support should allow time to analyse the circumstances which gave rise to the difficulties and to develop an appropriate plan to remedy those difficulties.[37] It must be in the form of liquidity support (loans or loans guarantees) and has a maximum duration of six months. If further public support is needed after that, it must be in the form of restructuring aid.

Restructuring aid often involves more permanent assistance and must restore the long-term viability of the beneficiary on the basis of a feasible, coherent, and far-reaching restructuring plan, while at the same time allowing for adequate contribution and burden sharing and limiting the potential distortions of competition.[38] The Member State concerned must submit to the Commission, a feasible, coherent, and far-reaching restructuring plan that will, within a reasonable timescale and on the basis of realistic assumptions as to future operating conditions that should exclude any further State aid not covered by the restructuring plan, restore the beneficiary's long-term viability.[39] The restructuring period should be as short as possible and the it involves one or more elements. It especially involves the reorganisation and rationalisation of the beneficiary's activities on to a more efficient basis, typically involving a withdrawal from loss-making activities; restructuring of existing activities that

---

35 European Commission, 2014.

36 The Guidelines apply to all undertakings in difficulty, except to those operating in the coal sector (19) or the steel sector (20) and those covered by specific rules for financial institutions.

37 Paragraph 26 of the 2014 Guidelines.

38 Paragraph 27 of the 2014 Guidelines.

39 The restructuring plan must identify the causes of the beneficiary's difficulties and the beneficiary's own weaknesses, and outline how the proposed restructuring measures will remedy the beneficiary's underlying problems. For more details, see Paragraphs 45–52 of the 2014 Guidelines.

can be made competitive again and, if possible, diversification towards new and viable activities. It typically also involves financial restructuring in the form of capital injections by new or existing shareholders and debt reduction by existing creditors. The granting of the aid must therefore be conditional on the implementation of the restructuring plan.

The final objective of restructuring aid is the restoration of the profitability of the firm. Therefore the Commission maintains that it will approve the aid only if the member state can show that there is a high probability that the aid will succeed in bringing the firm back into profit.[40]

To approve restructuring aid, the Commission needs to be satisfied that: (a) the restructuring plan can be expected to bring the firm back to long-term viability without further public support, (b) the firm will bear a sufficient proportion of the cost of its restructuring, and (c) the plan provides for adequate measures, such as asset sales or capacity reductions, to keep the competition distortions caused by the aid to a minimum.[41]

Temporary restructuring support is liquidity assistance is designed to support the restructuring of an undertaking by providing the conditions needed for the beneficiary to design and implement the appropriate action in order to restore its long-term viability. Temporary restructuring support is a kind of prolonged rescue aid that enables restructuring without the restructuring state aid support. It consists of aid in the form of loans or loan guarantees which should be restricted to the amount needed to keep the beneficiary in business for the duration of the support period. The duration of the support may not exceed 18 months. The main advantage of the temporary restructuring support is the requirement for a simplified restructuring plan instead of the full one which is obligatory for the restructuring aid. Temporary restructuring support may only be granted to SMEs and smaller State-owned undertakings.[42] Temporary restructuring support may also be granted to undertakings that are not in difficulty but are facing acute liquidity needs due to exceptional and unforeseen circumstances.

2.2. THE BALANCING TEST IN R&R STATE AID

One of the most important changes compared to previous versions of the R&R Guidelines is the introduction of the balancing test, as originally set out in the common principles for the assessment of State aid ("Common Principles"), in the consideration if an R&R State Aid should be granted or not. The balancing

40 Heimler A., Jenny F., 2012, p. 359.
41 European Commission, 2014.
42 Paragraph 28 of the 2014 Guidelines.

test requires that R&R aid must first aim at an objective of common interest. Second, it must be well designed to deliver the objective of common interest, which in particular means that it must be the least distortive aid instrument, have an incentive effect, and be proportional. Third and finally, the positive effects of R&R aid in terms of delivering the objective of common interest must outweigh the negative effects of the aid in terms of distortions of competition. Only after all three criteria are achieved is R&R aid justified under the balancing test, and thus, presumably, legal under EU State aid rules.[43]

The general balancing test as set out in the Common Principles involves the following steps:[44]

1. Is the aid measure aimed at a well-defined objective of common interest?
2. Is the aid well designed to deliver the objective of common interest i.e. does the proposed aid address the market failure or other objectives?
   (a) Is the aid an appropriate policy instrument to address the policy objective concerned?
   (b) Is there an incentive effect, i.e. does the aid change the behaviour of the aid recipient?
   (c) Is the aid measure proportionate to the problem tackled, i.e. could the same change in behaviour not be obtained with less aid?
3. Are the distortions of competition and effect on trade limited, so that the overall balance is positive?

The corresponding balancing test in the context of R&R aid is expressed in paragraphs 38 and 39 of the R&R Guidelines and will be explained in detail in the next paragraphs. For an R&R State Aid to be compatible with the internal market, all of the following seven criteria must be met.

2.2.1. Contribution to a Well-defined Objective of Common Interest

State aid has to be aimed at a well-defined objective of common interest in accordance with Article 107(3) of the Treaty. State Aid can be justified only if clear evidence can be provided that the aid aims to prevent social hardship or addresses market failure by restoring the long-term viability of the undertaking. This means that an aid aimed to merely prevent an undertaking from exiting the market does not constitute a sufficient justification for aid.[45] Social hardship

43 Maier-Rigaud F, Milde C., 2015.

44 See paragraph 9 of the Common Principles for an Economic Assessment of the Compatibility of State Aid under Article 87(3).

45 The Commission stresses the importance of the market exit to the process of productivity growth.

can be demonstrated more or less only through unemployment rates.[46] As economic and social cohesion is a priority objective of the European Union, the Commission will take the needs of regional development into account when assessing restructuring aid in assisted areas, but merely "the fact that an ailing undertaking is located in an assisted area does not, however, justify a permissive approach to aid for restructuring."[47]

Following situations are considered market failure: (a) risk of disruption to an important service which is hard to replicate and where it would be difficult for any competitor simply to step in; (b) the exit of an undertaking with an important systemic role in a particular region or sector would have potential negative consequences, (c) the failure or adverse incentives of credit markets would push an otherwise viable undertaking into bankruptcy, (d) the exit of the undertaking concerned from the market would lead to an irremediable loss of important technical knowledge or expertise or (e) similar situations of severe hardship duly substantiated by the Member State concerned would arise.[48]

2.2.2. The Need for State Intervention

State Aid must be targeted towards a situation where aid can bring about a material improvement that the market cannot deliver by itself (for example by remedying a market failure or addressing an equity or cohesion concern). This means that Aid can be granted only if the market itself cannot deliver a similar result, as the financial troubles are a result of a market failure or the market solutions are not feasible but aid is needed to address the question of social hardship. As a consequence, Member States must provide a comparison with a credible alternative scenario not involving State aid, demonstrating how the relevant objective or objectives would not be attained, or would be attained to a lesser degree, in the case of that alternative scenario (the so called counterfactual analysis).

2.2.3. Appropriateness of the Aid Measure

An aid measure will not be considered compatible if other, less distortive measures allow the same objective to be achieved. In the case of rescue aid, aid can only consist of temporary liquidity support in the form of loan guarantees or loans. In the case of restructuring aid, Member States are free to choose the form

---

46 The unemployment rate in the region concerned must be either higher than the EU average persistent and accompanied by difficulty in creating new employment in the region or regions concerned, or higher than the national average, persistent and accompanied by difficulty in creating new employment in the region concerned.

47 Paragraph 97 of the 2014 R&R Guidelines.

48 Paragraph 44 of the 2014 R&R Guidelines.

of the aid, but they should ensure that the chosen instrument is appropriate to the addressed issue.[49]

2.2.4. Incentive Effect

Member States must show that in the absence of aid, the beneficiary would have been restructured, sold, or wound up in a way that would not have achieved the objective of common interest.

2.2.5. Proportionality of the Aid

The proportionality of State aid is one of the central issues of the 2014 R&R State Aid Guidelines. The basic principle is that the aid must not exceed the strict minimum needed to achieve the objective of common interest. In the case of rescue aid, the amount has to be limited to the amount needed to keep the beneficiary in business for six months.

The proportionality of restructuring state aid is defined as the absolute minimum amounts and intensity of restructuring aid necessary, in order to enable restructuring to be undertaken, in light of the existing financial resources of the beneficiary, its shareholders or the business group to which it belongs. Special focus is given on the question of adequate (sufficient) own contribution and burden sharing.

State Aid can only be granted if the beneficiary can provide a significant contribution to the restructuring costs either from its own resources or from its shareholders, creditors, or new investors. Its own contribution should be comparable to the aid granted in terms of effects on the solvency or liquidity position of the beneficiary.[50] Its own contribution will normally be considered adequate, if it amounts to at least 50% of the restructuring costs. In exceptional circumstances and in cases of particular hardship, which must be demonstrated by the Member State, the Commission may accept a contribution that does not reach 50% of the restructuring costs, provided that the amount of that contribution remains significant.[51]

State aid can only be granted if existing shareholders (investors) bear an adequate share of the burden. Adequate burden sharing will normally mean that

---

49 In the case of solvency problems, increasing assets through recapitalization might be appropriate, whereas in a situation where the problems mainly relate to liquidity, assistance through loans or loan guarantees might be sufficient.

50 For example, where the aid to be granted enhances the beneficiary's equity position, the own contribution should similarly include measures that are equity-enhancing, such as raising fresh equity from incumbent shareholders, the write-down of existing debt and capital notes or the conversion of existing debt to equity, or the raising of new external equity on market terms.

51 Paragraph 64 of 2014 R&R Guidelines.

incumbent shareholders and, where necessary, subordinated creditors, must absorb losses in full.[52] Therefore, State intervention should only take place after losses have been fully accounted for and attributed to the existing shareholders and subordinated debt holders. Adequate burden sharing will also mean that any State aid that enhances the beneficiary's equity position should also be granted on terms that afford the State a reasonable share of future gains in value of the beneficiary, in view of the amount of State equity injected in comparison to the remaining equity of the company after losses have been accounted for.[53]

2.2.6. Avoidance of Undue Negative Effects on Competition and Trade between Member States

The negative effects of aid must be sufficiently limited, so that the overall balance of the measure is positive. The negative effect is limited with the "one time, last time" principle and with measures to limit distortions of competition.

To reduce moral hazard, such as excessive risk-taking incentives and potential competitive distortions, aid should be granted only once (the so called "one time, last time" principle). This rule is a bit softened, as State Aid to a specific beneficiaries is limited to once every 10 years: "Commission will not grant new state aid for rescue and restructuring before 10 years have elapsed since the aid was granted or implementation of the restructuring plan was halted (whichever occurred the latest)."[54]

Measures to limit distortions of competition can take several forms and are divided into following measures: (a) structural, (b) behavioural[55], and (c) market opening measures.

Structural measures are the most common (standard) measures and consist mainly of divestments and the reduction of business activities.[56] This means that beneficiaries may be required to divest assets, reduce capacity, or market presence. Divestments, write-offs, and closure of loss-making activities which would at any rate be necessary to restore long-term viability, will generally not be considered sufficient.[57]

---

52 Subordinated creditors should contribute to the absorption of losses either via conversion into equity or write-down of the principal of the relevant instruments.

53 See Paragraph 67 of 2014 R&R Guidelines.

54 Paragraph 72 of 2014 R&R Guidelines enables certain exceptions of the general rules of the one time last time principle.

55 Behavioural measures must be applied in all cases in order to avoid undermining the effects of structural measures.

56 Such measures should take place, in particular, in the market or markets where the beneficiary will have a significant market position after restructuring, in particular those where there is significant excess capacity.

57 Measures that limit distortions of competition should not lead to deterioration in the structure of the market. Structural measures should therefore normally take the form of

Behavioural measures aim to ensure that aid is used only to finance the restoration of long-term viability and that it is not abused to prolong serious and persistent market structure distortions or to shield the beneficiary from healthy competition. Beneficiaries must be required to refrain from acquiring shares in any company during the restructuring period, except where indispensable to ensure the long-term viability of the beneficiary and are required to refrain from publicising State support as a competitive advantage when marketing their products and services.

Market opening measures are aimed at promoting more open, sound, and competitive markets, for instance by favouring entry and exit. They commitments may be given to the Member State concerning or directly to the beneficiary. Commitments can, in particular, include measures to open up certain markets directly or indirectly linked to the beneficiary's activities to other Union operators. Such initiatives may replace other measures in order to limit distortions of competition that would normally be required of the beneficiary.

2.2.7. *Transparency of Aid*

Transparency means that all stakeholders and the public must have easy access to all relevant acts and pertinent information about the aid awarded. Member states must therefore publish: (a) the full text of approved aid scheme; (b) the identity of the granting authority, and (c) the identity of individual beneficiaries.[58]

3. SPECIAL RULES FOR AID SCHEMES FOR SMALLER AID AMOUNTS AND BENEFICIARIES (AID FOR SME)

As the Commission considers R&R State aid for Small and Medium Sized firms (SMEs) has a more limited potential for a significant distortion of competition, because of the small size of the aid amounts and the beneficiaries at stake, the Commission has prepared a separate set of rules (special, more flexible rules) for granting R&R State aid to SMEs. Member States can prepare special aid schemes

divestments on a going concern basis of viable stand-alone businesses that, if operated by a suitable purchaser, can compete effectively in the long term. Where it appears that it may be difficult to find a buyer for the assets which a beneficiary proposes to divest, it will be required, as soon as it becomes aware of such difficulties, to identify alternative divestments or measures to be taken in relation to the market or markets concerned if the primary divestment fails.

58 The requirements to the public the mentioned data can be waived with respect to individual aid awards bellow 500.000 EUR.

for granting State Aid to SMEs. The total amount of aid granted to any one company may not be more than 10 million EUR. Additional to rescue and restructuring aid, SMEs can also apply for temporary restructuring support aid.

Even though SMEs must generally meet all described criteria (conditions) for granting state aid the Commission considers that it is appropriate to provide simplified conditions in certain respects, to enable Member States to apply those conditions without further reference to the Commission. The idea is to reduce the burden on SMEs and smaller State-owned undertakings, of providing the information required for granting aid.

For granting aid under schemes prepared by a Member State, it is sufficient for a Member State to determine that the failure of the beneficiary would likely involve social hardship or a market failure, in particular that: (a) the exit of an innovative SME or an SME with high growth potential would have potential negative consequences; (b) the exit of an undertaking with extensive links to other local or regional undertakings, particularly other SMEs, would have potential negative consequences;(c) the failure or adverse incentives of credit markets would push an otherwise viable undertaking into bankruptcy; or (d) similar situations of hardship duly substantiated by the beneficiary would arise.[59]

In the case of Medium-sized companies, its own contribution is considered to be adequate if it amounts to at least 40 percent of the restructuring cost and in the case of small enterprises it must amount to at least 25 percent. The "one time, last time" principle must be fully respected, but measures to limit distortions of competition can be disregarded.

Once a scheme has been approved by the Commission, grants of aid to individual companies do not need to be authorised in advance, provided they meet the conditions of the scheme. The New Guidelines make it clear that schemes are the best way to grant aid to SMEs.[60]

4. CRITICAL LAW AND ECONOMICS OVERVIEW

Using the general balancing test, Maier-Rigaud and Milde made a critical law and economics assessment of the 2014 R&R Guidelines.[61] They argue that even though the aid measures two well-designed objective of common interest namely: disparities caused by a severe market failure and social cohesion, R&R Aid, apart from exceptional cases, does not meet the main two criteria, namely the Aid is not well designed to deliver the objective of common interest and the

59 Paragraph 107 of the 2014 R&R Guidelines.
60 Greenber Traurin, LLP, 2014.
61 Maier-Rigaud F., Milde C., 2015.

distortions of competition is in the vast majority of cases larger than the positive effects of R&R Aid.

R&R State Aid can, by definition, not be aimed at the correction of a market failure. On the one hand it's hard to imagine that a severe market failure could possibly be the origin of the difficulties of a single company. A severe market failure means that the whole segment of the economy should/would be in distress. But if, for argument's sake, we neglect this argument, we can also see that with a one-time disbursement of funds, R&R aid is not suitable to address any market failure that, by its very, nature must be due to a systematic or structural characteristic of the market and thus would require a permanent structural intervention to be corrected. Market failures as a candidate for an objective of common interest to justify R&R aid thus have to be ruled out.[62]

Secondly, R&R State Aid can also be granted for the reason of social cohesion (prevention of an increase of unemployment in regions with above average unemployment). State Aid given to a company would without a doubt, in the short run, prevent or reduce an increase in unemployment it that region. But if the sole purpose of the Aid is to help the unemployment of a disadvantaged region, obviously, regional aid, which is specifically designed to address disadvantaged regions, would be a more suitable instrument to address this issue.[63] Maier – Rigaud and Milde are arguing that R&R State Aid can, however, be best suited to prevent an immediate increase in unemployment in the disadvantaged region. Thus R&R aid may be considered an appropriate policy instrument to achieve the objective of preventing an increase in unemployment and its negative social consequences in a particular region.[64]

Maier – Rigaud and Milde are also arguing that rather than subsidising an inefficient firm, the more targeted and, arguably, more efficient aid is in reducing social hardship, would be direct aid to the affected on employees and their families. Such aid could include retraining and relocation grants. This would avoid the unnecessary and clearly unwarranted side effect of R&R aid that part if not most of it would benefit investors located outside of the disadvantaged region.[65]

62 Maier-Rigaud F., Milde C., 2015.

63 Regional aid also contains aid tools, such as aid that solely affects the location decision for an investment in the same relevant geographic market, that are clearly less distortive than R&R aid, and aid tools, such as operating aid, which may be better suited to address long-term regional disadvantages. Maier-Rigaud F., Milde C., 2015.

64 Ibid. They also argue that: "*in this respect a strong argument can be made that R&R aid, again by design, is not proportional, as a large part, if not most, of the aid will benefit, i.e. bail out, investors who are typically located outside of the disadvantaged region. Arguably, instead of subsidizing an inefficient undertaking, the same amount of aid would be better invested in supporting affected employees of the failing undertaking with retraining and relocation grants, e.g. from the European Social Fund.*"

65 Maier-Rigaud F., Milde C., 2015.

As already mentioned, State Aid can only be allowed if the positive effects outweighs the negative effects. R&R State aid can potentially be an appropriate tool in the prevention or reduction of the increase of unemployment in a disadvantaged region. In that case, the larger the benefit of the R&R aid is in terms of employees "saved", the larger the distortion of competition is, by keeping the undertaking alive. Furthermore, the Commission noted in the 2014 Guidelines that: "the fact that an ailing undertaking is located in an assisted area does not, however, justify a permissive approach to aid for restructuring: in the medium to long term it does not help a region to prop up companies artificially. Furthermore, in order to promote regional development it is in the region's own best interests to apply its resources in such a way as to rapidly develop activities that are viable and sustainable."[66] Consequently, this means that the balancing of the severe and pervasive harm of R&R aid in general and in any specific case on the one hand and the doubtful appropriateness of R&R aid as a policy tool for a rather narrow objective of common interest on the other hand do not "survive" the balancing test and should therefore reasonably lead to the prohibition of R&R aid in this case.

Given the stark contrast between clear and severe negative effects on the one hand and clear doubts on whether R&R aid is a well-designed instrument in this specific case where it is a candidate policy instrument at all on the other hand, it does not seem reasonable conclusion that positive effects of the aid outweigh the negative ones. Nevertheless, this conclusion can be drawn when attaching very high weight to the prevention of unemployment and very low weight to the specific and general distortions of competition, so that a positive outcome of the balancing test cannot be logically excluded.[67]

Maier – Rigaud and Milde additionally show, that regarding the objective of preventing the interruption of the provision of an SGEI, it could be argued that R&R aid passes the balancing test only in cases of SGEIs. This is due to the fact that SGEI, by definition, are goods and services that are not provided by "the market" so that there is no distortion of competition in any market by granting (additional) public funds in the form of R&R aid. At the same time, the provision of SGEI is the objective of common interest itself, the contribution to an objective of common interest trivially outweighs the non-existent distortions of competition. Even in this context, however, it is doubtful whether R&R aid is the most appropriate policy tool. If the provision of an SGEI is in peril due to an undertaking in difficulty, the obvious solution would be to either raise the compensation for the SGEI provider or to look for another undertaking better able to provide the SGEI.[68]

---

66 Paragraph 97 of the 2014 R&R Guidelines.

67 Maier-Rigaud F., Milde C., 2015.

68 Maier-Rigaud F., Milde C., 2015.

Additionally, negative arguments towards R&R Stata Aid can also be drawn from empirical research. A number of studies have already assessed the effectiveness of rescue and restructuring aid by investigating whether the aid has been successful in ensuring the long-term viability of the aid recipient companies. Their findings are, at best, mixed. A significant proportion of the aid beneficiaries have not managed to escape bankruptcy. The reasons for this failure of aid in preventing bankruptcy are not known. Perhaps the aid was granted too late. Or perhaps the aid recipients were already in such dire condition that no aid could have helped them.[69]

A study conducted by Chindooroy, Muller, and Notaro in 2007 showed, that about one half of companies that received the rescue aid did not survive. Failure among companies that received restructuring aid was about 20 percent. They conclude that the probability of success is related more too some key characteristics of aid-receiving firms, of the sector to which they belong and/or the type of difficulty they encountered and less to the policy framework of rescue and restructuring State aid.[70] A similar research done previously by the London Economics in 2005 showed that out of 69 companies, 22 folded and 47 survived. The mortality rate of aid-receiving companies was particularly high in the case of companies that received only rescue aid. The overall performance of the companies having received rescue and/or restructuring State aid was generally positive, both in absolute terms and relative to the performance of the comparator companies as about half of the aid-receiving companies, by 2002, had actually increased their levels of employment since first receiving State aid, relative to their comparators.[71]

On the other hand, empirical research done by Nulsch in 2014 indicates that: "Firms which received R&R aid seem to have a higher probability to survive than firms in comparable difficulties were the Commission denied the payment of aid. Yet, the governmental support was in that respect effective as supported firms seem to have a higher probability to survive than firms was such support has been denied. The study has also shown that long-term restructuring; a transition background and older firms have a higher probability to survive after having received state aid than their counterparts. Smaller firms tend to have a higher chance to survive than larger firms, yet the statistical evidence is not as strong as for the other variables."[72]

---

69 Bolsa Feruz M.A., Nicolaides P., 2013, p. 1.

70 See for details Chindooroy R., Muller P. and Notaro G., 2007.

71 See for details: London Economics, 2005.

72 Nulsch, 2014, p. 25.

5. CONCLUSION

The chapter present an overview of the Rescue and Restructuring State Aid Guidelines with an emphasis on the criteria that must be met for R&R State Aid to be in compliance with the TFEU rules on competition law. As a part of the after crisis modernisation of the Commission's State Aid modernisation program, the Commission issued new and revised Guidelines on Rescue and Restructuring State Aid in 2014. The adoption of the new Guidelines is meant to significantly change the EU rules applicable to state aid for undertakings. The Commission will be accorded more power in deciding whether, and on what conditions EU Member States can grant this type of aid.

The 2014 Guidelines have evolved and are becoming more comprehensive and are being constantly adjusted to clarify the concepts, which have remained unclear in the previous guidelines. The Guidelines have also given much more attention to the SMEs, including the newly integrated temporary restructuring support.[73]

Four major novelties of the 2014 Guidelines are: (a) the use of the balancing test, (b) filters designed to check that aid, in a given case, is truly in the public interest, (c) the temporary restructuring support for SMEs, and (d) burden sharing and own contribution demands.

The main, practical implication of the New Guidelines consists of making it more difficult for companies to be eligible for rescue and restructuring aid and to comply with the compatibility criteria for Commission approval. According to Maier – Rigaud and Milde, if the economic principles set out in the New Guidelines are taken seriously, the balancing test is so harsh, that the New Guidelines ultimately mean nothing less than the abolition of R&R aid in practice, since by design, R&R aid cannot contribute to an objective of common interest in any way, except in two, very specific situations. These two specific situations are R&R aid as a special case of regional aid, in order to prevent immediate loss of employment or as a way to correct a problem in the provision of SGEI. They conclude, that given the explicitly recognised, severely harmful effects of R&R aid and the explicitly recognised existence of bankruptcy and insolvency proceedings that allow market economy actors to identify viable undertakings and productive assets and to keep them in or return them to the market, the question is why the Commission did not flat-out prohibit R&R aid entirely with the revision of the R&R Guidelines.[74]

---

73 Grigorian A., Hainova-Blagovesta Barbova D., 2014.

74 Maier-Rigaud F. and Milde C., 2015.

BIBLIOGRAPHY

Ahlborn C., Berg C., Can state aid control learn from antitrust? The need for a greater role for competition analysis under the state aid rules, In Biondi A., Eeckhout P., Flynn J. (eds), *The law of state aid in the European Union*, Oxford University Press, Oxford, (2004), pp. 41–66.

Anestis P., Mavroghenesis S., Drakakaki S., Rescue and Restructuring Aid: A Brief Assessment of the Principal Provisions of The Guidelines, *European State Aid Law Quarterly*, 1, 2004, pp. 27–34.

Biondi A., Righini E., An Evolutionary Theory of EU State Aid Control, *Legal Studies Research Paper Series: Paper No. 2014–41*, King's College London Dickson Poon School of Law.

Blauberg M., Compliance with rules of negative integration: European state aid control in the new member states, *Journal of European Public Policy*, 16(7), 2009, pp. 1030-1046.

Bolsa Feruz M.A., Nicolaides P., The Economics of State Aid for the Rescue and Restructuring of Firms in Difficulty: Theoretical Considerations, Empirical Analysis and Proposals for Reform, Department of European Economic Studies, *Bruges European Economic Research Paper No* 27, 2013.

Chindooroy R., Muller P., Notaro G., Company survival following rescue and restructuring State aid, *European Journal of Law and Economics*, 24(2), 2007, pp. 165-186.

Craig P., de Bùrca, G. EU Law, *Text, Cases and Materials*, Fourth Edition, Oxford University Press, Oxford, 2011.

European Commission, The effects of temporary State aid rules adopted in the context of the financial and economic crisis, Commission Staff Working Paper, 2011.

European Commission, *EU Competition Law, Rules Applicable to State Aid*, Situation as at 15 April 2014, Luxembourg, Office for Oficial Publications of the European Union, 2014.

Farantouris N.E., Firms in difficulty and state aids: a compatibility analysis, *European Competition Law Review*, 30 (10), 2009, p. 494–504.

Greenber Traurin, LLP, European Union Guidelines on State Aid for Rescuing and Restructuring Non-Financial Undertakings in Difficulty, *The National Law Review*, posted on 17. December, 2014.

Grigorian A., Hainova D., Barbova B., 2014, *The Past, Present and Future of the Rescue and Restructuring Guidelines for Undertakings in Difficulty, State Aid & Public Procurement in the European Union*, IER 4014.

Heimler A., Jenny F., The limitations of European Union control of State Aid, *Oxford Review of Economic Policy*, 28(2), 2012, pp. 347-367.

Kassim H., Lyons B., The New Political Economy of EU State Aid Policy, *Journal of Industry, Competition and Trade* 13(1), 2013, pp. 1–21.

London Economics, *Ex-Post Evaluation of the Impact of Rescue and Restructuring Aid on the international Competitiveness of the Sector(s) affected by Such Aid*, European Commission, Enterprise and Industry Directorate-General, Brussels, 2005.

Maier-Rigaud F., Milde C., The Rescue & Restructuring Aid Guidelines of the European Commission – An economic point of view, *SSRN Working paper, February 2015.*

Nicolaides P., Kekekesil M., An Economic Analysis of EC Guidelines on State Aid for the Rescue and Restructuring of Companies in Difficulty, *Intereconomics*, 39(4), 2004, pp. 204-212.

Nicolaides P., Kekekelis M., When do Firms in Trouble Escape from State Aid Rules?, *European State Aid Law Quarterly* 1, 2005, pp. 17-25.

Nulsch N., Is Subsidizing Companies in Difficulties an Optimal Policy? An Empirical Study on the Effectiveness of State Aid in the European Union, Halle Institute for Economic Research, *IWH Discussion Papers, No. 9/2014.*

Pesaresi N., Van Hoof M., State Aid control; an introduction, In: Mederer W., Pesaresi N., Van Hoof M., *EU Competition Law*, Vol. IV, Leuven: Claeys & Casteels, 2008, p. 1.

Schutte M., Revising the Rescue and Restructuring Aid Guidelines for the Real Economy – A Practitioner's Wishlist, *EStAL*, 4, 2012, pp. 813-819.

Valle E., Van De Casteele K., Revision of the Rescue and Restructuring Guidelines: A Crackdown?, *European State Aid Law Quarterly* 1, 2014, pp. 9-15.

CHAPTER 14

EU ACCESSION PROCESS, JUDICIAL REVIEW AND STATE AID IN TURKISH COMPETITION LAW

Ayşe Gül Kökkılınç

1. INTRODUCTION

Turkey was recognised as a candidate country for joining the European Union during the Helsinki European Council held on December 10–11, 1999. Competition Policy is one of the titles of the chapters belonging to the negotiations of the accession, which began between Turkey and the EU as of October 3, 2005, following the decision of the European Council dated of December 17, 1994. It is required that Turkey, as well as, all other candidate countries, should create a balance with the *acquis communautaire, in* relation to competition. The competition *acquis* covers both anti-trust and state aid controlled policies. It includes rules and procedures to counteract anti-competitive behaviour by companies, to scrutinise mergers between undertakings, and governments from granting state aid, that would distort competition in the internal market.

The competition *acquis* is, to a large extent, linked to the obligations arising from the Customs Union between the EU and Turkey. The obligations placed on Turkey by the Article 16 of the Association Agreement, known as the Ankara Agreement, which formed an association relationship between the EEC and Turkey and envisaged a progressive establishment of Customs Union (signed on October 12, 1963 and entered into force on December 1, 1964) that specifies the principles in the provisions of the Treaty of Rome, concerning competition taxation and the approximation of laws be made applicable in the association relationship. The Customs Union between the EU and Turkey, which was put into effect on January 1, 1996, was based on the Association Council Decision made in March and has an effect on the adoption of the competition rules. According to Article 39, regulated under the Section heading "Competition of the Customs Union Decision" numbered 1/95, concerning the completion of the

Customs Union between Turkey and the Community, Turkey shall ensure that its legislation in the field of competition rules is made compatible with that of the European Community and it is applied effectively. In this context, Turkey should adopt a law which contains the rules concerning the prohibited behaviour of undertakings within the framework laid down in the EC Treaty and establish a competition authority which would apply the rules effectively within one year after the Customs Union was entered into force and should also ensure it is applied to the block exemption rules which are in force in the Community, as well as, the case-law developed by EC authorities within the same period.

Turkey enacted the Act on the Protection of Competition No: 4054 in 1994 before the Customs Union was entered into force. The Act on the Protection of Competition No:4054, was adopted by the Turkish National Grand Assembly on October 7, 1994 and entered into force after being published in the Official Gazette on October 13, 1994. In preparation of the Draft Act, the US, British, and EU rules were taken into consideration. The Turkish Competition Authority (TCA) was establishment within 8 months and was announced to the public through a Communiqué published on November 5, 1997, as per the Provisional Article 2 of the Act and started to take into account the applications made therein.[1]

The accession negotiations started with Turkey on October 3, 2005. During the screening meetings which were held in Brussels on November 8–9, 2005 and December 1–2, 2005.Basically the subject matter was centred on anti-trust rules, undertakings having exclusive and special rights, public monopolies, and supervision of state aid had been were envisioned under the Competition Policy chapter which corresponds to the 8th among 35 titles. The competition *acquis* covers both anti-trust and state aid control policies. It includes rules and procedures counter act anti-competitive behaviour by companies, to scrutinise mergers between undertakings, and governments from granting state aid, which would distort competition in internal market. Generally, the competition rules are directly applicable in the entire EU and Member States must co-operate fully with the Commission in enforcing them. The Competition Policy is one of the chapters where the European Commission assesses whether or not Turkey possesses the ability to assume the obligations for membership in regular reports on Turkey's progress towards accession.[2] As it is emphasised in the National Program of 2001, Turkey's final objective is to ensure "workable competition" within the markets for goods and services, and to establish a culture of competition as well as a stable and properly functioning competition policy in Turkey.[3]

---

1 2001 Year NPAA, (National Program fort he Adoption of Acquis) www.abgs.gov.tr/index.php?p=195&l=2. Accessed Date: 13.04.2014.

2 European Union Process, In General. www.rekabet.gov.tr/default.aspx?nsw=SiqkAswzJcVjtgIWvGsz8A==-SgKWD+pQItw=&nm=313, date Accessed:13.04.2014.

3 2001 Year NPAA, www.abgs.gov.tr/index.php?p=195&l=2. accessed date: 13.04.2014.

2. ANTI-TRUST RULES

Anti-trust rules are regulated by Act No: 4054 on the Protection of Competition. The Act includes rules and procedures to fight anti-competitive behaviour by companies and to scrutinise mergers between undertakings. The adoption of the Act on the Protection of Competition is based on the "Economic Provisions" of the Constitution of the Republic of Turkey concerning the supervision of markets and the regulation of foreign trade. Article 167 of the Constitution of the Republic of Turkey places a duty and a responsibility on the state to take measures to ensure and promote the sound and orderly functioning of the markets for money credit, capital, goods, and services and to prevent the formation of monopolies and cartels in the markets, emerging through practice or agreement. The environment created by the new economic model adopted in Turkey in the 1980s affected the regulation of Article 167 of the Constitution that placed an explicit duty on the State regarding the prevention of monopolisation and cartel formation in the markets. It is stated in the General Preamble of the Act that the economic system in the country is the market economy and competition constitutes the basic central component of the economic policy, which is implemented in order to ensure and protect the functioning of market economies. In order to create sound markets, encourage entrepreneurs, ensure efficient allocation, and use the limited sources of the country in the most productive way, the Act on Protection of Competition, which is compulsory as a constitutional directive, has been prepared.[4]

The purpose of the Act is to prevent agreements, decisions and practices preventing, distorting, or restricting competition in the market, and the abuse of dominance by the undertakings dominance in the market, and to ensure the protection of competition by performing the necessary regulations and supervisions to this end. The Act on the Protection of Competition No 4054, is designed to ensure the protection of competition through the necessary regulation, supervision, and prevention of abuse of dominant position by those undertakings which are dominant in the market, and of the agreements, decisions, and concerted practices which prevent, restrict, or distort competition within the markets in the Republic of Turkey. All agreements, decisions, and practices preventing, distorting, or restricting competition in the markets of the Republic of Turkey, and the abuse of the dominance by the undertakings dominant in the market, and any kind of legal transactions and behaviour having the nature of mergers and acquisitions, which will decrease competition to a significant extent, are within the scope of the Act.[5] As a consequence of the

4 General Preamble of the Act. www.rekabet.gov.tr/default.aspx?nsw=SiqkAswzJcVjtgIWvGsz8A==-SgKWD+pQItw=&nm=313, date accessed: 13.04.2014.

5 The Act on Protection of Competition, www.rekabet.gov.tr/default.aspx?nsw=SiqkAswzJcVjtgIWvGsz8A==-SgKWD+pQItw=&nm=313, date accessed: 13.04.2014.

system being called "effect theory" in the Act, those undertakings whose headquarters are outside the borders of the Republic of Turkey, but who operate in Turkey also fall within the scope of the Act. It is emphasised in the grounds of Article,1 regulating the purpose of the Act that the competition in a market economy not only ensures effective utilisation of the resources, but also causes a fall in prices of the competing products and causes those undertakings which want to have a larger share in the market to increase the quality of their products and to use new technologies in production. On the other hand, the fall in prices and a rise in social benefits by protecting the whole society, that is, the consumers. For these reasons, the purpose of the Act is for the State to ensure protection through the necessary legal arrangements.

Within the framework of the commitments arising from Article 41 of Association Council Decision No 1/95, the Act on Competition stipulates that the rules of competition shall apply to undertakings from both the public and the private sectors. However, TCA has exclusive competence to enforce anti-trust rules, it has not been able to intervene in distortions of competition which arises from the provisions of the other legislation pertaining to public undertakings entitled to special or exclusive rights.[6]

2.1. CARTELS AND OTHER AGREEMENTS LIMITING COMPETITION

Agreements and concerted practices between undertakings, decisions, and practices of associations of undertakings, which have as their objective, effect, or likely effect, the prevention, distortion, or restriction of competition directly or indirectly in a particular market for goods or services are illegal and prohibited under Article 4 of the Act on Protection of Competition. Article 4 is in parallel with Article 81 of the Rome Treaty with some minor exceptions.[7] In the article concerned, examples regarding violations are provided in six paragraphs: price fixing, market sharing, agreements on quantitative restraints, etc. Such cases are, in particular as follows; (i) Fixing the purchase or sale price of goods, or services price of goods or services, elements such as cost and profit which form the price, and any terms of purchase or sale (ii) Portioning markets for goods or services, and sharing or controlling all kinds of market resources or elements (iii) Controlling the amount of supply and demand in relation to goods or services, or determining them outside the market (iv) Complicating or restricting the activities of competing undertakings, or excluding undertakings operating in

6 Grounds for the Articles, www.rekabet.gov.tr/default.aspx?nsw=SiqkAswzJcVjtgIWvGsz8A==-SgKWD+pQItw=&nm=313, date accessed: 13.04.2014.

7 2001 Year NPAA. Official Gazette Dated 24 March 2001 No. 24352 (Turkish) www.abgs.gov.tr/index.php?p=195&l=2.

the market by boycotts or other behaviour, or preventing potential new entrants to the market (v) Except in exclusive dealing, applying different terms to persons with equal status for equal rights, obligations, and acts (vi) Contrary to the nature of the agreement or commercial usages, obliging to purchase other goods and services together with a good or service, or trying a good or service, or tying a good or service demanded by purchasers acting as intermediary undertakings to the condition of displaying another good or service by the purchaser, or putting forward terms as to the resupply of a good or service supplied.

For the purposes of the article, the term agreement is used to refer to all kinds of compromises or deals in which the parties feel bound, even if these do not meet the conditions of validity in regards to the Civil Law. Even if the existence of an agreement between the parties cannot be established, direct and indirect relations between the undertakings that replaced their own independent activities and ensure a coordination and practical cooperation are prohibited if they lead to the same result. Thus it is intended to prevent the undertakings from legitimising acts limiting competition via fraudulent means. Agreements restricting competition may be in the form of vertical and horizontal agreements. Agreements made within the same level are called horizontal agreements and it is accepted that these agreements have competition distorting effects.

In cases where the existence of an agreement cannot be proved, that the price changes in the market or the balance of demand and supply, or the operational areas of undertakings are similar to those markets where competition is prevented, distorted, or restricted constitutes the assumptions that the undertakings are engaged in concerted practices. Each of the parties may relieve itself of the responsibility by proving it has not engage in concerted practice, provided that it is based on economic and rational facts. As it is stated in the article, in a legal regime where agreements restricting competition are prohibited, they are generally made in secret and proving their existence is quite different and sometimes even impossible; therefore in these cases the assumption that the undertakings engaged in concerted practice are accepted and the burden of proof is passed on to the relevant undertakings.

If agreements, concerted practices, or decisions of an association of undertakings limiting competition have positive effects on the economy and if these positive effects are not reflected on the consumer and stay as firm profits, the exemption will not be implemented. The Turkish Competition Authority may decide to exempt agreements, concerted practices, and decisions that were ensuring new developments and improvements, or technical development in the production or distribution of goods and the provision of services: benefitting the consumer; not eliminating competition in a significant part of the relevant market and not limiting competition more than what is compulsory for achieving the goals set out with the abovementioned provisions, from the application of the act. Only those competition limitations which are necessary and compulsory for achieving the beneficial effect will be granted exemption. It is such that, with these limitations, competition must not be eliminated in a significant part of the relevant product market. In order to ensure that such agreements may be concluded and the consequent net comparative benefit expected from them may be gained, agreements restricting competition are exempt from the prohibitive provision of the Art.4 of the Act aimed at anti-competitive agreements. However exemption decisions will be given for a certain period and will be renewable if the specified conditions exist. Thus it will be given to the Board with the power to monitor the changes that may emerge or the developments that may cause a restriction in competition within the relevant market, after the exemption decision has been taken.

It is granted a block exemption if a communiqué from the Turkish Competition Authority is given to the group agreements which carry the conditions mentioned that benefit from the exemption and do not require separate notification. Individual exemption evaluations are intended for agreements which do not fall under the scope of block exemptions and do not require the notification of the Competition Board. In the first Regular Progress Report, prepared by the Commission in 1998, it is stated that Turkey had already complied with some of its obligations in regards to ensuring the competition rules with Community law but it was required to be done in relation to block exemptions, complying with the Community legislation and above all, effective implementation of competition law.[8] In this respect, the Turkish Competition Authority issued communiqués[9] and guidelines.[10] As it is emphasised in

8 Regular Report From The Commission on Turkey's Progress Towards Accession, 1998. www.abgs.gov.tr/files/AB_Iliskileri/Tur_En_Realitons/Progress/Turkey_Progress_Report_1998.pdf. p. 33.

9 *Block Exemption Communiqué concerning Vertical Agreements, (2002/2); Block Exemption Communiqué concerning Research and Development Agreements, (2003/2); Block Exemption Communiqué concerning Vertical Agreements and Concerted Practices in the Motor Vehicles Sector (2005/4) Block Exemption Communiqué concerning Technology Transfer Agreements (2008/2) Block Exemption Communiqué concerning Insurance Sector (2008/3); Block Exemption Communiqué on the Procedures and Principles to be Pursued in Pre Notifications and Authorization Applications to be Filed with the Competition Authority in order for Acquisitions Via Privatization to become Legally Valid (2013/2); Block Exemption Communiqué on Specialization Agreements (2013/3).*

10 *Guidelines on the Explanation of the Block Exemption communiqué concerning Vertical Agreements and Concerted Practices in the motor Vehicles Sector (2006); Guidelines on the Voluntary Notification of Agreements, Concerted Practices and Decisions of associations of Undertakings (2006); Guidelines on Certain Contract Manufacturing Agreements between Non- Competitors (2008); Guidelines on the Application of Articles 4 and 5 of the Act no 4054 on the Protection of Competition to Technology Transfer Agreements (2009); Guidelines on the vertical agreements (2009) Guidelines on the General Principles of Exemption (2013); Guidelines on the Explanation of the Regulation on Active Cooperation for Detecting Cartels (2013); Guidelines on the Horizontal Cooperation Agreements (2013); Guidelines on the Assessment of Horizontal Mergers (2013); Guidelines on the Assessment of Non-horizontal Mergers(2013); Guidelines on the Transactions Regarding Mergers and the Notion of Control(2013).*

2001Regular Progress Report, Turkey had further aligned its legislative framework in the area of anti-trust policy in order to conform to the Community acquis and the obligations of the Customs Union Agreement, and adapted to a considerable degree, the secondary regulation, in particular the area of block exemption regulations.[11] Concerning the antitrust rules, the TCA implemented legislation concerning block exemption on R&D agreements in 2003. This communiqué aimed to clarify the application of competition rules for undertakings carrying out joint R&D activities and encouraging co-operation between undertakings in this field. The adoption of block exemption regulation by R&D agreements was evaluated as a positive step by the Commission. Newly implementing legislation, modernised rules on vertical restraints and simplified procedures in conformity with the principles laid down by the acquis have been adopted. Pursuant to this legislation, the TCA annulled the implementation of separate block exemptions on exclusive distribution, exclusive purchasing, motor vehicle, and franchising agreements. The TCA also published the Guidelines on the Application of Block Exemption on Vertical Agreements. Issues such as selective distribution, agreements between competitors, agreements involving intellectual property rights, and agency agreements are also addressed in the Guidelines.[12]

2.2. ABUSE OF DOMINANT POSITION

Under Art.6 of the Act on Protection of Competition, it is prohibited for undertakings that obtain dominant position in the market to abuse their position to restrict, prevent, or distort competition in the country or use their position in a way which would cause these effects. The abuse, by one or more undertakings, of their dominant position in a market of goods or services within the whole or a part of the country on their own or through agreements with others or through concerted practices, is illegal and prohibited. Abusive cases particularly involve; (i) preventing directly or indirectly, another undertaking from entering into the area of commercial activity, or actions aimed at complicating the activities of competitors in the market (ii) making direct or indirect discrimination by offering different terms to purchasers with equal status and equal rights, obligations, and acts (iii) purchasing another good or service, or trying a good or service demanded by purchasers acting as intermediary to the condition of displaying another good or service by the purchaser, or imposing limitations with regard to the terms of purchase and sale

11 Www.abgs.gov.tr/files/AB_Iliskileri/Tur_En_Realitons/Progress/Turkey_Progress_Report_2001.pdf.

12 Www.abgs.gov.tr/files/AB_Iliskileri/Tur_En_Realitons/Progress/Turkey_Progress_Report_2003.pdf.

in case or resale, such as not selling a purchased good below a particular price (iv) actions which aim at distorting competitive conditions in another market for goods or services by means of exploiting financial, technological, and commercial advantages created by dominance in a particular market (v) restricting production, marketing and technical development to the prejudice of consumers.

In terms of competition law, an undertaking's growth through its internal dynamics and obtaining dominant position in various sectors is not objectionable. In some cases the undertaking may gain a dominant position due to protection provided by law, as industrial and trade property rights grant such protection. The use of these must in no way serve the purpose of eliminating competition.

2.3. MERGERS AND ACQUISITIONS

Merger by one or more undertakings or acquisition by an undertaking or person from another undertaking, except by way of inheritance, of its assets, all or a part of its partnership shares, or of means which confer the power to hold a managerial right, with view to creating a dominant position or strengthening its/their dominant position, which would result in significant lessening of competition in a market for goods or services within the whole or a part of country, is illegal and prohibited. Mergers and acquisition transactions which pose the risk of decreasing the competition in the market by creating or strengthening a dominant position and those which increase prices for customers, decrease variety, and undermine innovation are prohibited under Article 7 of the Act on Protection of Competition.

In Article 7 of the Act, it is ruled that mergers and acquisitions will be prohibited in the case of a dominant position or strengthening of the dominant positions of more than one undertaking in such a way as to significantly decrease competition in the market. The point to be noted here is the fact that growth of undertakings outside of their own integral dynamics is under control. In fact, while dominant position is not a cause for prohibition in Art.6; this article prohibits undertakings from obtaining a dominant position by mergers and acquisitions, in such a way as to significantly decrease competition. It is an accepted fact that obtaining a dominant position through mergers or acquisitions causes a larger distortion in the competitive regime than the undertaking's obtaining a dominant position through growth with its own internal dynamics. Article 7 of the Act includes parallel arrangements with EU Regulation on Mergers No 4064/89/EEC.[13]

---

13 2001 Year NPAA. Official Gazette Dated 24 March 2001 No. 24352 (Turkish) www.abgs.gov.tr/index.php?p=195&l=2.

The Board shall declare, via communiqués, the types of mergers and acquisitions which have to be notified to the Board and for which permission has to be obtained, in order for them to become legally valid. As a rule, there is no obligation to obtain permission from the Board for the merger and acquisition transactions to be valid. In other words, merger and acquisition transactions will be valid without the permission of the board. However, there are exceptions to this rule. Invalidating mergers and acquisitions that violate this Act after they gain validity do cause some problems. For this reason, the Board has been granted the right to issue communiqués concerning which types of mergers and acquisitions must obtain permission before gaining validity. In accordance with Article 7 of the Act no 4054 and the Communiqué Concerning the Mergers and Acquisitions Calling for the Authorisation of the Competition Board, No: 2010/4 (Communiqué no 2010/4) issued in order to establish the principles and procedures for the application of this article, requires that mergers and acquisitions which lead to permanent changes in the control and which exceed certain turnover thresholds, be presented to the Competition Board in order to become legally valid. The Competition Authority also published Guidelines on Transactions Regarding Mergers and the Notion of Control (2013 Progress Report).

In determining whether or not a merger/acquisition falls under Article 7 of the Act, the concept of control is taken into account. Control may be acquired through rights, contracts or other instruments which grant the power to exercise decisive influence – de facto or de jure – over an undertaking. Hence, only those mergers/acquisitions involving a permanent change in control are considered under Article 7. In other words, a merger of undertakings which are within the same economic entity, which are controlled by the same persons or undertakings, or an acquisition taking place between these undertakings that does not lead to a change in control do not fall under Article 7.

In regards to mergers/acquisitions which result in a change of control, turnover thresholds have been determined by the Communiqué on the Mergers and Acquisitions Calling for the Authorisation of the Competition Board (Communiqué No. 2010/4). Mergers and acquisitions by undertakings whose turnovers in the relevant market are above the specified thresholds can only be legally valid following the authorisation of the Competition Board. Within this framework, as a rule, an application must be made to the Competition Authority for authorisation of the merger/acquisition transactions, which involve a change in control and which exceed the thresholds laid out in the Communiqué no 2010/4.

The Board is notified of a merger or acquisition agreement falling under article 7. The Board is, as a result of a preliminary examination to be performed by it within fifteen days, obliged to permit the merger or acquisition transaction, or if it decides to deal with this transaction under final examination, it is obliged to duly notify, with its preliminary objection letter, those concerned in the matter of the merger or acquisition transaction are suspended and cannot be put into practice until the final decision, together with other measures deemed necessary by it. In this case, the provisions of articles 40–59 of this Act shall be applicable. Where the Board does not respond to or take any action for the application as to a merger or acquisition within due time, merger or acquisition agreements shall take effect and become legally valid after 30 days from the date of the notification (Art. 10).

Where a merger and acquisition transaction whose notification to the Board is compulsory, the Board is not notified the Board shall deal with the merger or acquisition under examination on its own initiative, when it is informed about the transaction anyway. As a result of the examination; it allows the merger or acquisition in case it decides that the merger or acquisition does not fall under the first paragraph of article 7, but imposes fines on those concerned due to their failure to notify. In case it decides that the merger or acquisition falls under the first paragraph of article 7, it decides that the merger or acquisition transaction be terminated, together with fines; all *de facto* situations committed contrary to the law be eliminated; any shares or assets seized be returned, if possible, to their former owners, whose terms and duration shall be determined by the Board, or if not possible, they are assigned and transferred to third parties; the acquiring persons may by no means participate in the management of undertakings acquired during the period until these are assigned to their former owners or third parties, and that other measures deemed necessary be taken (Art. 11).

3. COMPETITION AUTHORITY

The Competition Authority (TCA) was established in 1997, in order to observe the implementation of the Act on Protection of Competition and to fulfil the duties assigned to it by the Act. The main goal of the Competition Authority, which is charged with enforcing the Act, is to ensure the formation and development of markets for goods and services in a free and sound competitive environment and to prevent any threats to the competitive process in the markets. Within that framework, The Competition Authority, (i) penalises undertakings which distort or prevent competition in the market, through examination and investigation processes subject to detailed regulation (ii) grants exemption to and prepares secondary regulations for agreements which are in conflict with competition rules but are beneficial to the economy and the consumers (iii) prevents monopolisation within the market by examining mergers, acquisitions, and joint ventures over a certain threshold (iv) in the privatisation stage, examines the transfer of public undertakings to the private sector, and through privatisation, reduces the effects of the state on the economy while preventing monopolisation within the markets by sending opinions on various acts and regulations, which would negatively affect or restrict competition in the markets, to government institutions and any organisations concerned.[14]

The Authority, having a public legal personality and administrative and financial autonomy, is independent in fulfilling its duties. No organ, authority, or person may give commands or orders to influence the final decision of the Authority. Within the amendment made by the Decree Law No: 661 of November 2, 2011, the Competition Authority became the related institution of the Ministry of Customs and Trade.

The organisation of the Competition Authority consists of the Competition Board, Presidency, and Service Units. The Competition Board is the decision-making body of the Authority and consists of seven members including a Chairman and Deputy Chairman. The members are appointed by the Council of Ministers from among the two candidates apiece, to be nominated from inside or outside the following institutions for each vacant membership: three members from the Ministry of Customs and Trade, one member from the Ministry of Development, one member from the Turkish Union of Chambers and Commodity Exchanges, and one member from among the two candidates apiece, to be nominated by the Supreme Court and the Appeals and Council of State from inside their own institutions. One of the members from the Ministry of Customs and Trade quota is appointed from among the Authority personnel. The Council of Ministers appoints the Chairman and the Deputy Chairman from among Board members.[15]

---

14 Turkish Competition Authority, www.rekabet.gov.tr/default.aspx?nsw=SSepy8CY9Ozs1cKhr lS9pg==-SgKWD+pQItw=&nm=191, date accessed:13.04.2014.

15 *The Chairman and the members of the Board shall be appointed from among those who had a four-year education in law, economics, engineering, management, or finance, either at home or abroad, possesses a sufficient degree of professional knowledge and experience, and have worked in the public or private sector for at least 10 years, in line with their professions. Furthermore, it is compulsory that the members bear the qualifications mentioned in the Art.48. paragraph (A) sub-paragraphs 1,4,5,6,and 7 of the Civil Servants Act No.657. The term of the office of the Chairman, Deputy Chairman, and members of the Board is six years. A member whose term has expired is eligible for re-selection. One third of the members of the Board are renewed every two years. During renewal, numbers and ratio in the provisions concerning the organization of the Board are taken into account. Should the chairmanship and the memberships be vacated before the expiration of the term of office due to any reason other than renewal selection an appointment is carried out within one month for the vacated seats. The one appointed in such a case completes the term of the person she/he replaces.*
President of the Board or Board members may not be removed from office for any reason before the completion of their term of office. However, the President of the Board or Board members may be relieved of their duties in case they are found, by Board decision to no longer have the qualifications necessary for appointment of to be in violation of Art.25 of the Act, or in case they are found guilty, by court decision, of committing a crime related to the duties entrusted by the Act.
The offices of the Chairman and members of the Board may not undertake any official or private mission, engage in commerce, be shareholders in partnerships, unless is based on a

The Presidency which consists of the Chairman of the Board, Deputy Chairman, and Vice Presidents of the Board are authorised to appoint the personnel of the institution except for the Vice Presidents and the Chief Legal Advisor, without taking the approval of the Competition Board. The Decree Law issued in 2011 changed the rules for the appointment of its chairman and deputy chairman, which adds to concerns about the TCA's ability to preserve its independence, triggered in 2011 by a decree authorising the competent minister to monitor and inspect the activities of the TCA.[16]

The Competition Authority is an independent authority, but it was reported recently the governmental efforts to establish a uniform organisational structure for all independent regulatory authorities by adopting framework legislation, raises concerns about potential political intervention in the operations of the Competition Authority.[17] However, as it is stated in the last Regular Progress Reports, the Competition Authority continued to uphold a satisfactory level of administrative and operational independence. The Authority's overall administrative capacity remains high.[18]

The Competition Authority has a sufficient administrative capacity to ensure antitrust enforcement and merger control. Although this Authority has exclusive competence to enforce anti-trust rules, it was criticised for not being able to intervene in distortions of competition which arise from other legislation containing anti-competitive provisions. The Competition Authority's competence over undertakings is therefore seriously restricted by such legislation.[19] Due to incomplete legal alignment, the Competition Authority does not enjoy the appropriate powers and competence to effectively apply competition law to public enterprises, state monopolies and companies having special rights. There is a need to empower the Competition Authority to

special Act. The Chairman and the members of the Board are, prior assuming office, obliged to dispose of all kinds of securities in their possession within the meaning of the capital market legislation, apart from securities issued by the Treasury in connection with borrowing, by means of selling or transferring them to persons other than their kin by marriage up to the second degree. Those members who do not conform with this provision within 30 days shall be deemed to have resigned from membership. Positions in associations and foundations which aim at social assistance and education, and partnership in non-profit cooperatives fall outside this provision. The members and staff of the Board may not disclose and use in their own or others' interests the confidential information as to the Authority and trade secrets of undertakings and associations of undertakings that they learned during the implementation of this Act, even if they left their office.

16 Www.abgs.gov.tr/files/tr_rapport_2012_en.pdf.

17 Regular Progress Report For Turkey Prepared By The Commission, 2004. www.abgs.gov.tr/files/AB_Iliskileri/Tur_En_Realitons/Progress/Turkey_Progress_Report_2004.pdf.

18 Regular Progress Reports For Turkey Prepared By The Commission (2009. 2011,2013), www.abgs.gov.tr/files/AB_Iliskileri/Tur_En_Realitons/Progress/turkey_progress_report_2009.pdf.: www.abgs.gov.tr/files/AB_Iliskileri/AdaylikSureci/IlerlemeRaporlari/tr_rapport_2011_en.pdf, www.abgs.gov.tr/files/tr_rapport_2012_en.pdf.

19 Www.abgs.gov.tr/files/AB_Iliskileri/Tur_En_Realitons/Progress/Turkey_Progress_Report_2005.pdf.

intervene effectively in cases of competition infringements by public enterprises, state monopolies, and companies having special rights. Furthermore, a large number of specific sectorial laws, in particular granting special and exclusive rights on services, contradict the Act and de facto prevent the Competition Authority from enforcing the Competition Act. The Competition Authority should interpret the definition of undertakings in a broader way in cases involving public entities and more frequently use its ex officio competence to apply the competition provisions to the publicly controlled sectors.[20]

The Competition Authority continued to strengthen its enforcement record and capacity by making amendments within the scope of restricting the institution and adopting a number of decisions regarding the distortion of competition. Within the framework of a restructuring process, a separate unit is set up regarding the decisions that will enable the accomplishment of objectives, such as ensuring uniformity of the Competition Board's decisions. In this respect, it is important that a separate unit has been established regarding competition advocacy for raising public awareness on the merits of competition.[21]

4. FINES

The TCA, either upon a complaint or on its own initiative, decides to initiate a direct investigation or make a preliminary research to clarify whether or not an investigation on undertakings violating competition is required. Administrative fines are regulated under the 3rd Chapter of the Act. If the Board verifies any infringement of Article 4 or 6 of the Act at the end of the investigation, it may decide to impose an administrative fine on the undertakings or associations of undertakings violating the rules of competition per Article 16 of the Act.

Two types of fines are provided for in Article 16 of the Protection of Competition Act. Acts specified in the first paragraph are minor or more procedural acts, in comparison to the second paragraph. The second paragraph on the other hand provides substantial acts. Acts punished with fines might have been committed intentionally or in negligence. Among the cases that a) False or misleading information or documents are provided in exemption and negative clearance applications and in authorisation applications for mergers and

20 Www.abgs.gov.tr/files/AB_Iliskileri/Tur_En_Realitons/Progress/Turkey_Progress_Report_2002.pdf.

21 *"In 2012, within the scope of the importance that it attaches to the activities on disseminating the competition culture, the Authority published three different reports as part of its competition advocacy duty. The first one of these reports lays down the regulatory barriers and other barriers to competition in 11 industrial sectors whereas the others contain detailed research studies regarding the Fast moving Consumer Goods Retail Sector and the Natural Gas Sector."*, www.abgs.gov.tr/files/tr_rapport_2012_en.pdf.

acquisitions, b) Mergers and acquisitions that are subject to authorisation are realised without the authorisation of the Board, c) In implementation of articles 14 and 15 of the Act, incomplete, false, or misleading information or documents are provided, or information or documents are not provided within the determined duration at all, d) On-the-spot inspection is hindered or complicated; the Board shall impose on natural and legal persons having the nature of an undertaking and on associations of undertakings or members of such associations an administrative fine by one in a thousand of the annual gross revenues of undertakings and associations of undertakings or members of such associations which generate by the end of the financial year preceding the decision, or which generate by the end of the financial year closest to the date of the decision if it would not be possible to calculate it and which would be determined by the Board for those mentioned in sub-paragraphs (a), (b) and (c), and by five in one thousand of their gross revenues to be calculated in the same manner for those mentioned in sub-paragraph (d). However, the penalty to be determined pursuant to this principle cannot be less than ten thousand Turkish Liras. Pursuant to sub-paragraph (b) of this paragraph, an administrative fine is imposed to either of the parties in merger transactions and only to the acquirer in acquisition transactions.

The realisation of on-the-spot inspection with a court decision shall not hinder the application of an administrative fine provided for in this Act in relation to the hindrance and complication of on-the-spot inspection. To those who exhibit behaviour prohibited in articles 4, 6, and 7 of this Act, an administrative fine shall be imposed up to ten percent of the annual gross revenue of the undertakings and associations of undertakings or members of such associations, generated by the end of the financial year preceding the decision, or which is generated by the end of the financial year closest to the date of the decision if it is not possible to calculate it and would be determined by the Board. In the case of administrative fines mentioned in paragraph three are imposed on undertakings or associations of undertakings, an administrative fine up to five percent of the penalty imposed on the undertaking or association of undertakings shall be imposed on managers or employees of the undertaking or association of undertakings who are determined to have a decisive influence in the infringement.

When deciding on an administrative fine pursuant to paragraph three, the Board shall take into consideration issues such as the repetition of infringement, its duration, market power of undertakings or associations of undertakings, their decisive influence in the realisation of infringement, whether they comply with the commitments given, whether they assist with the examination, and the severity of damage that takes place or is likely to take place, within the context of article 17 paragraph two of the Faults Act dated 30/3/2005 and numbered 5326.

The undertakings or associations of undertakings or their managers and employees making an active cooperation with the Authority for the purpose of revealing contrariness to the Act, penalties mentioned in paragraphs three and four may not be imposed or reductions may be made in penalties to be imposed pursuant to such paragraphs taking into consideration the quality, efficiency, and timing of cooperation and by means of demonstrating its grounds explicitly. Issues taken into consideration in fixing administrative fines to be imposed pursuant to this article, terms for immunity from or reduction of fines in case of cooperation, and procedures and principles in relation to cooperation shall be determined by regulations to be issued by the Board.

Provided that the penalties mentioned in article 16, paragraph one, are reserved, the Board shall, for each day, impose on undertakings and associations of undertakings a proportional administrative fine of five in ten thousand annual gross revenues of the relevant undertakings and associations of undertakings and/or members of such associations which generate by the end of the financial year preceding the decision, or which generate by the end of the financial year closest to the date of the decision if it is not possible to calculate it and which would be determined by the Board in the event of a) Obligations introduced or commitments made by a final decision or interim measure decision are not complied with, b) On-the-spot inspection is hindered or complicated c) In implementation of articles 14 and 15 of the Act, information or document requested is not provided within the duration determined.

Pursuant to paragraph one sub-paragraphs (a) and (c), administrative fines can be imposed at the end of the duration given for complying with the obligations in the decisions mentioned in these sub-paragraphs. The administrative fine related to the act in sub-paragraph (a) can be imposed from the day following the notice of this decision if any duration has not been determined in the decision where an obligation is introduced and the administrative fine related to the acts in sub-paragraph (b) can be imposed from the day (Article 17). In order for the Board to be able to put the decisions and measures into practice, there is a need for another coercive power than those provided for in article 16. This must be such coercion that the undertaking sees a benefit in conforming to this decision and measure without delay. The best method of ensuring this is to apply a fine for each passing day without the decision or the measure being conformed to. In doing so, undertakings will be incentivised towards meeting the decisions without delay.

In 2008, important amendments were made in Article 16 of the Act and the Turkish Competition authority was forced to adopt regulations in relation to fines and leniency and a provision providing a legal basis for leniency was adopted. Turkish Competition Law in the new rules provided effective tools such as leniency and sanctions against individuals as well as a more transparent policy in relation to fines.[22] Under Art.16 (7) of the Act on Protection of

22 GUNDUZ Harun, "*Fines in Turkish Competition Law: Has the Lottery Ended?*" Rekabet Dergisi/ Competition Journal, Vol: 13 Number:4,October 2012, p. 59–60.

Competition[23] "to those the undertakings or associations of undertakings or their managers and employees making an active cooperation with the authority for purposes of revealing contrariness to the Act, penalties mentioned in paragraphs three and four may not be imposed or reductions may be made in penalties to be imposed pursuant to such paragraphs taking into consideration the quality, efficiency and timing of cooperation and by means of demonstrating its grounds explicitly".

After the amendments of the Act which were made to improve law enforcement capacity of the Act; in 2012 Turkish Competition Authority adopted two regulations which aim to provide principles and procedures relating to the setting of fines and leniency.[24] These regulations concerned the fines for cartels and on immunity from and the reduction of fines in cartel cases where undertakings cooperate with competition authority. A special unit was established within the authority to implement the leniency regulation and respond to requests for information from those wishing to benefit from it.[25] Through these regulations, the Turkish Competition Authority aimed to provide a new regulatory framework for its enforcement policy in line with the ongoing process in order to align Turkish Competition Law more closely with EU Law.[26] According to the provisions of Regulation on Fines to Apply in Cases of Agreements and Concerted Practices and Decisions Limiting Competition and Abuse of Dominant Position[27] in case where the undertakings or association of undertakings that engaged in other violations admit their violations and active cooperation; the fine shall be reduced by one sixth to one fourth. Under Article 5 of the Active Cooperation and Leniency Regulation, the undertakings who submit the information and evidence and meet the conditions stated in Article 6 of the Regulation, but which are not covered by the provision related to immunity from fines shall benefit from a reduction of fines. In this framework (i) the fine to be imposed to the first undertaking shall be reduced by one-third to one-half (ii) the fine to be imposed to the second undertaking shall be reduced by one fourth to one-third (iii) the fines to be imposed to other undertakings shall be reduced by one sixth to one-fourth.[28]

---

23 Amended Article: Date: 23.1.2008-Law No: 5728/Article 472.

24 Aygün Esin, *"Cartel Settlements. General Features, Recent Developments in the European Commission's Practices and Implications For Turkey"*, Rekabet Dergisi/Competition Journal, Vol:14, Number:2, April, 2012, p. 29.

25 Www.abgs.gov.tr/files/AB_Iliskileri/Tur_En_Realitons/Progress/turkey_progress_report_2009.pdf.

26 Elçi ELa, *"Leniency Programs: Features, Components and How They Appear in EU and TURKEY"* Rekabet Dergisi/ Competition Journal, Vol: 12 Number:2, April 2011, p. 28.

27 Published in Official Gazette, Dated 15.09.2012 Numbered 27142.

28 Aygün *"Cartel Settlements"*, p. 30.

5. JUDICIAL REVIEW OF DECISIONS MADE BY THE COMPETITION BOARD

The final decisions of the Board are under jurisdictional review. As their administrative nature is more dominant, the Council of State has jurisdiction over the decisions of the Board. A provision stating that fines shall not be paid until they are finalised is added to the draft and it is partially separated from the principles of Administrative Law. However, in cases where parties apply to the court, the Board's decisions are subjected to jurisdictional review and parties are prevented from experiencing losses. Moreover, decisions are subjected to provisions of the Act on the Procedure for the Collection of Public Receivables in order to assure the collection of fines. It is emphasised that the fines in articles 16 and 17 are not penalties in the sense of criminal code, but are administrative sanctions.

Concerning the administrative capacity, the inspection powers of the TCA have been reinforced. The TCA can now perform on-the-spot inspections, with the court order, to obtain information and documents from companies which are being investigated.[29] The decisions of the TCA become effective after the publication on the internet page of the TCA in such a way as to not disclose the trade secrets of the parties. Before an was amendment made to Article 53 (1) of the Act on Protection of Competition[30] the TCA was required to issue its decisions in the Official Gazette.[31] With the amendment made to Article 53 (1) of the Act on Protection of Competition the phrase of "after finalisation" included in the first paragraph has been eliminated.[32]

In 2008, the amendment made with Law No: 5728 changed the judicial authority for appeals against the Board's decisions. According to the amended Article 55 (1) of the Act on Protection of Competition, suits shall be filed against administrative sanctions before the competent administrative courts instead of the Council of State.[33] All types of suits filed against Board decisions shall be taken as a priority matter. The right to appeal of Council of State against the decisions of the administrative courts remained. According to Article 55 (2) of the Act amended with Law No. 5728, appealing against decisions of the Board shall not cease the implementation of decisions, and the follow up and collection of administrative fines. Appealing against decisions of the Board shall not cease

29 Www.abgs.gov.tr/files/AB_Iliskileri/Tur_En_Realitons/Progress/Turkey_Progress_Report_2003.pdf.

30 Amended phrase: Date: 17.09.2004-Law No: 5234/Article 29 "The phrase of " in the Official Gazette" included in this paragraph has been amended and it has been inserted in the text".

31 Www.abgs.gov.tr/files/AB_Iliskileri/Tur_En_Realitons/Progress/Turkey_Progress_Report_2005.pdf.

32 Annulled phrase: Date: 01.08.2003- Law No: 4971/ Article25.

33 Amended Article: 23.1.2008–5728/Article 474).

the implementation of decisions, and the follow up and collection of administrative fines.[34]

In 2003 Parliament adopted a law amending the Act on Protection of Competition which allows fines imposed by the TCA to be collected immediately without waiting for the Council of State (Supreme Administrative Court) to rule on appeals. This provision allows a more effective implementation of the TCA's decisions. Before the amendment was made, in the event of an appeal, the Act did not allow fines to be collected until the Council of State had made its decision. As it was stated in 2002 Regular Progress Report, slow processing of appeals against the TCA by the Council of State (Supreme Administrative Court) delays effective implementation of competition rules. The implementation of administrative fines in order to ensure compliance with competition rules and procedures, should not act as a deterrent due to high inflation. The other amended provision of the envisaged was all the fines collected to be paid to Treasury[35] and TCA might no longer retain 25% of fines imposed.[36] This provision removed the risk of a conflict of interest.[37]

The Private Law consequences of limiting competition are regulated in Section 5 of the Act. According to the Article 56 of the Act, any agreements or decisions of undertakings, contrary to Article 4 of the Act are invalid. The performance acts arising out of such agreements and decisions may not be requested. In the event of a request for reclamation due to the invalidity of the previous acts fulfilled, the return obligation of the parties is subject to Article 77–79 (Article 63–64) of the Turkish Code of Obligations. The unjust enrichment provision of (previous Article 65) the Code of Obligations is not applicable to disputes arising from the Act.

Under the Article 57 of the Act on Protection of Competition concerning the right to compensation, anyone who prevents, distorts, or restricts competition via practices, decisions, contracts, or agreements contrary to the Act, or abuses his dominant position in a particular market for goods and services, is obliged to compensate for any damages. If the damage has resulted from the behaviour of more than one person, they are responsible for the damage jointly. Those who suffer as a result of the prevention, distortion, or restriction of competition, may claim as damages the difference between the cost they paid and the cost they would have paid if competition had not been limited. Competing undertakings affected between the cost that was paid and the cost they would have paid if competition had not been limited. Competing undertakings affected by the

34 Www.abgs.gov.tr/files/tr_rapport_2012_en.pdf.

35 Revenues belonging to the Authority are collected in an account to be opened in the Central Bank of the Republic of Turkey or a state bank. (Annulled last sentence: Date: 01.08.2003-Law No: 4971/Article 25-B.

36 Annulled Art.39(b) Date: 01.08.2003-Law No: 4971/Article 25-B.

37 Www.abgs.gov.tr/files/AB_Iliskileri/Tur_En_Realitons/Progress/Turkey_Progress_Report_2002.pdf.

limitation of competition may request that all of their damages are compensated for, by the undertaking or undertakings that limited competition. In determining the damage, all profits expected to be gained by the injured undertakings are calculated by taking into account the balance sheets of previous years as well. If the resulting damage arises from an agreement or decision of the parties, or from cases involving gross negligence, the judge may, upon the request of the injured, award compensation by three fold of the material damage incurred or of the profits gained or likely to be gained by those who caused the damage (Article 58).

Should the injured submit to the jurisdictional bodies proofs such as the actual portioning of markets, stability observed in the market price for a quite a long time, the price increase within close intervals by the undertakings operating in the market, which give the impression of the existence of an agreement, or the distortion of competition in the market, then the burden of proof falls on the defendants to prove that the undertakings were not engaged in concerted practice. The existence of agreements, decisions, and practices limiting competition may be proved by any kind of evidence (Article 59).

6. CONCLUSION

As it is stated under the National Programme for the Adoption of the Acquis, Turkish Competition Law is to a great extent, parallel to Competition Law of the EU. Turkey aligned its legislative framework in the area of antitrust policy in order to conform to Community acquis and the obligations of the Customs Union. The Act on Protection of Competition is largely modelled on the main principles of the Treaty of Rome.

Harmonisation with the anti-trust *acquis* is well underway. Alignment in the field of anti-trust and merger control is advanced. As it is repeatedly confirmed by EU Institutions, Turkey's level of alignment in the field of anti-trust and mergers is high. The Law on Protection of Competition and the regulation on mergers and acquisitions reflect the main principles of community rules. The level of enforcement by the TCA continues to be satisfactory.[38] In 2013 TCA adopted several new guidelines including horizontal cooperation agreements and assessments of mergers. However, it is stated that the banking mergers and acquisitions resulting combined sectorial markets share below 20% remaining outside the scope of the Act.[39]

Anti-trust and merger control rules are largely aligned and enforced effectively. Turkey is expected to align with on the horizontal cooperation agreements, *de minimis* rules as well as public undertakings and undertakings

---

38 2006.

39 2013.

enjoying exclusive and special rights.[40] Within the framework of the commitments arising from Article 41 of Association Council Decision No 1/95, the Act on Competition stipulates that the rules of competition shall apply to undertakings from both the public and the private sectors. Nevertheless, the provisions pertaining to public undertakings to which special or exclusive rights have been granted should be revised to ensure full alignment with Article 41. The authority to amend the laws of undertakings vested with special rights has been given solely to such undertakings or to the ministries. The Competition Authority has stated its opinions on whether or not the amendments made are in compliance with the rules of competition. The TCA did not have the appropriate powers and competence to effectively apply competition law to public enterprises, state monopolies, and companies having special rights. There is a need to empower the TCA to intervene effectively against competition infringements by public enterprises, state monopolies, and companies with special rights. Public authorities responsible for sectorial legislation should completely align with the *acquis* as a matter of priority. Although the TCA has exclusive competence to enforce anti-trust rules, it has not been able to intervene in distortions of competition which arise from other legislation and a comprehensive review of this state of play should be initiated urgently. The TCA's remarks concerning drafts of all types of legislation which may have an impact on competition are often not taken into account. The commitment by all public and legislative authorities to remove and avoid legal barriers to competition should be ensured. The sector regulatory authorities such as the Energy Market Regulatory Authority, the Telecommunication Authority, the Banking Regulatory, and Supervision Authority do not ensure efficient cooperation and use of consultation mechanisms with the TCA in order to prevent any competition distortions in their respective regulated markets yet.[41] No development can be recorded in regard to the alignment of rules concerning public undertakings and undertakings having exclusive and special rights. Turkey needs to ensure transparency of the financial relationships between public authorities and public undertakings.

The TCA enforces anti-trust rules effectively with a satisfactory level of independence. The TCA's overall administrative capacity is high. The TCA displayed a satisfactory level of administrative and operational independence and a commitment to high-level training for its staff.[42] As it is confirmed repeatedly in the Regular Progress Reports, the Competition Authority continued to uphold a satisfactory level of administrative and operational independence. The Competition Authority's overall administrative capacity

40 2011, 2012, 2013.

41 Www.abgs.gov.tr/files/AB_Iliskileri/Tur_En_Realitons/Progress/Turkey_Progress_Report_2005.pdf.

42 Www.abgs.gov.tr/files/AB_Iliskileri/AdaylikSureci/IlerlemeRaporlari/tr_rapport_2011_en.pdf.

remains advanced. The Competition Authority continues to strengthen its enforcement record and capacity by adopting a number of decisions regarding the distortion of competition. In this respect, the Authority published communiqués and guidelines in 2013. However, as it is stated in the Progress Report prepared by Turkey[43] in addition to these regulations, Turkish Competition Authority prepared a Draft Law Amending the Act on Protection of Competition by taking into account the EU competition rules as well. This Draft Law also covers a number of provisions expected by the European Commission to be aligned with the EU *acquis* and expressed in previous Progress Reports.

In the area of state aid, the legislation on state aid monitoring is not conformed to *acquis.* As it is repeatedly stated in the regular progress reports, this is the major factor in the delay of the adoption of an Association Council decision on the implementation of competition rules, despite the fact that Turkey is committed under the Customs Union to align and set up a state aid monitoring authority.[44] This is hindering the implementation of competition rules, resulting in potential competition infringements in markets via the allocation of public resources. Besides, the absence of reporting of state aids based on the EU standards reduces the transparency of financial transactions between the stage and undertakings.[45]

The legislation implementing the State Aid Law has been prepared, and was originally scheduled to be enacted by the end of September, 2011. However, a decree issued in November, 2011, extended this deadline to the end of June, 2013. Moreover, a significant incentives package, superseding the 2009 stimulus package, was published on June 19, 2012. This new package, together with the free zones regime, remains one of several schemes in need of alignment with Customs Union rules. The State Aid Authority still needs to establish a formal State aid inventory and a plan for aligning all State aid schemes with the acquis.[46] An important difference between the legislation of Turkey and that of the EU is that, in accordance with the current Turkish legislation, the Competition Authority, unlike the European Union Commission, is not the authorised body to supervise state aid.[47] Following the adoption of State Aid Law, The Board of the State Aid Monitoring Authority has been appointed and competent staff has been transferred from the Treasury. However, further efforts are still required in

---

43 Progress Reports Prepared by Turkey. www.abgs.gov.tr/files/AB_Iliskileri/AdaylikSureci/IlerlemeRaporlari/2013_tr_progress_report.pdf.

44 Regular Progress Reports prepared by the Commission, www.abgs.gov.tr/files/AB_Iliskileri/Tur_En_Realitons/Progress/turkey_progress_report_.

45 Regular Progress Reports prepared by the Commission, 2003,2004,2005, www.abgs.gov.tr/files/AB_Iliskileri/Tur_En_Realitons/Progress/turkey_progress_report_.

46 Www.abgs.gov.tr/files/tr_rapport_2012_en.pdf, www.abgs.gov.tr/files/AB_Iliskileri/AdaylikSureci/IlerlemeRaporlari/tr_rapport_2011_en.pdf.

47 NPAA 2001. Official Gazette Dated 24 March 2001 No. 24352(Turkish) www.abgs.gov.tr/index.php?p=195&l=2.

the area of alignment for existing State Aid schemes. The state aid law remains ineffective in the absence of implementation of legislation.[48] The entry into force of legislation implemented into state aid law was postponed for a second time. The State Aid Monitoring Authority still needs to establish a formal state aid inventory. It is also expected to create a plan for aligning all state schemes with the *acquis*.[49]

BIBLIOGRAPHY

Aygun, E., *'Cartel Settlements. General Features, Recent Developments in the European Commission's Practices and Implications For Turkey'*, Rekabet Dergisi/Competition Journal, Vol:14, Number: 2, April, 2012, p. 29, 30.

Elçi, E., *'Leniency Programs: Features, Components and How They Appear in EU and TURKEY'* Rekabet Dergisi/ Competition Journal, Vol. 12 Number: 2, April 2011, p. 28.

Gunduz H., *'Fines in Turkish Competition Law: Has the Lottery Ended?'* Rekabet Dergisi/ Competition Journal, Vol. 13 Number: 4, October 2012, p. 59–60.

48 Www.abgs.gov.tr/files/tr_rapport_2012_en.pdf, www.abgs.gov.tr/files/AB_Iliskileri/Adaylik Sureci/IlerlemeRaporlari/tr_rapport_2011_en.pdf.

49 Www.abgs.gov.tr/files/2013%20ilerleme%20raporu/tr_rapport_2013_en.pdf.

PART V

ECONOMIC EVIDENCE, ENFORCEMENT PROBLEMS AND NATIONAL COURTS

CHAPTER 15

GOOGLE, COMPETITION POLICY AND THE OWL OF MINERVA

Rosamaria Bitetti

1. CAN THE OWL OF MINERVA SPREAD ITS WINGS AND FLY?

With a powerful metaphor, philosopher Hegel described philosophy as the Owl of Minerva, which "only when the dusk starts to fall does it spread its wings and fly".[1] Philosophy comes only at the end of the day, as a descriptive reflection on what happened, and Hegel's owl cannot reverse the motion of the stars and stop the twilight. Economics is the philosophy of modern competition policy: economic theory, competition policy and competition law are inextricably intertwined. Ever since competition law came into existence, the economic theory of competition has exercised its influence upon it. Rules change as, and when, the underlying economic theory changes. As time went by, different paradigms (Neoclassical, Harvard, Chicago, Game theory) informed antitrust enforcement.[2] Competition policy changes because the definition of competition, the way it works and how it can be promoted are not univocal and eternal tenets in the economic science.

Pretty much like Hegel's owl of Minerva, they rather followed changes in economic history and society. For instance, the theory of perfect competition is clearly modelled after the agricultural market, which was easier to observe when the competition was described as emerging among atomistic producers of homogeneous goods. Features of specific markets observed by economists in a given historical period did shape the content of an otherwise vague concept such as barriers to entry: economies of scale reflect the importance of the efficient plant size in classic manufacturing industries; capital investments reflect the historical scarcity of these assets before the improvement of legal tools to raise capital; the idea that aggressive advertising can be a limit to competition is

1 Hegel 1821.

2 Kovacic 1992.

linked to the emergence of traditional media such as newspapers and television, which created a limited number of powerful channels to reach consumers. Much of the reflection about distribution agreements, tying and bundling came of course after the emergence of department stores and distribution networks.

But unlike the owl of Minerva, which can only come to the scene too late to give instructions about how the world ought to be, economic theory does affect economic relations by informing competition law. Our owl can actually change the motions of the stars and stop the twilight, for good or for bad. Thus, it is of the utmost importance to be sure that it flies, to follow the metaphor, in the right direction and at the right time: this is the purpose of this paper. I will analyze the main trends in the new economy of internet-based transactions, trends that are demoting the explanatory power of economic models traditionally describing unilateral conducts. I will try to ascertain whether a specific innovation in economic theory, namely behavioural economics, can actually inform antitrust with new and more useful models to assess whether an abuse has occurred. This comparison will be carried through the lens of a real, and representative, case study: Google and its current troubles with antitrust authorities all over the world.

The Google saga is an important experiment to assess whether antitrust investigations incur in mistakes when the underlying monopoly models are not revised to accommodate digital economic postulates, and whether behavioural economics can cast a light and help avoiding those mistakes. Mistakes that are especially dangerous when they might result in reduced innovation and, as such, competition. The Google saga is thus an unavoidable issue when discussing antitrust, pretty much as ten years ago it was impossible to discuss competition policy without talking about Microsoft.

A few years later we can already enjoy some of the benefit of hindsight: our reflection can fly after economic events and learn something in perspective. The Redmond Giant is, today, far less dangerous for competition authorities, but in reducing Microsoft's market power the role antitrust, though aggressive, was only marginal. Real competition came from outside the channels of competition that were taken into account at the time of the Microsoft processes. Indeed, competition remedies were quite inefficient – as I will discuss further on. Competition comes from the rise of open source software, the shift to cloud computing as a further step in the process of dematerialization of digital economy, and, of course, the rise of Google. As a result, Microsoft is now only a marginal concern for competition, and it is even a plaintiff against Google.

The opportunity of looking back, like Hegel's owl, at the Microsoft cases should give us some perspective on the ephemeral nature of monopoly and other competition models in highly innovative contests, and somehow a heritage of economic analysis that passed the test of time. I will use the Google case to test whether a further set of theoretical tools, less known at the time of Microsoft, but increasingly popular today: behavioural economics. Never like today competition issues deal with markets with a high rate of innovation: if these economic models are meant to be policy relevant, they must be able to provide useful insights in a case that is meant to be the new cornerstone of competition policy. Just as it happened at the time of Microsoft, the antitrust, law and economics academic community is today devoting an uncountable amount of bytes typing its analysis of every angle in the Google cases.

Surprisingly, though, there is very little literature that explicitly uses behavioural economics to assess the strength and the scope of the abuse allegations. After reviewing some key features of competition in the age of internet, I will go back to this point and try to incorporate behavioural economics into the analysis of this paradigmatic saga.

2. THE NEW ECONOMY: DID THE DUSK BEGIN TO FALL?

Or, did contemporary economics elaborate useful models and doctrines for antitrust enforcement in the new era? The first problematisation of the relationship between antitrust and the new economy can be traced back to Richard Posner.[3] He defined the new economy as the union of three sectors, manufacturers of computer software, internet-based businesses, and communications services and equipment meant to support the first two markets – and while a lot changed since 2000, this definition still applies if we take into proper account the fact that the bulk of innovation and market growth happened in the second of the two markets, which is where nowadays the antitrust debate is discussed. Back at the time, Posner argued that there was no real problem in applying antitrust models to the new economy, since "antitrust doctrine is supple enough, and its commitment to economic rationality strong enough, to take in stride the competitive issues presented by the new economy" – but he also quite prophetically added that "the real problem lies on the institutional side: the enforcement agencies and the courts do not have adequate technical resources, and do not move fast enough, to cope effectively with a very complex business sector that changes very rapidly". For this reason, he claimed for a cautionary approach to antitrust enforcement in the new economy.

Twelve years later, he was right: enforcement agencies have been far from cautious and extremely active in the new economy. Manne and Wright explain this tech-activism with a sort of career incentive-driven cultural prejudice against innovative practices that are hard to understand, and thus more easily interpreted as abusive, by economists and enforcers.[4]

3 Posner 2000.
4 Manne & Wright 2010.

And another important shift from Posner's time is the fact that 2010s antitrust doctrine (and regulation in general) is no longer committed to economic rationality, but it is now modelled after what Russell Korobin names "regulatory agnosticism": influenced by behavioural economics, it deviated from the assumption of rationality and the possibility of relying on revealed preferences to analyze economic outcomes (we will see this aspect in the next section). As a result, the debate about effectiveness of antitrust in the new economy is far from dead and very important.[5]

Internet and communication technologies are driving a new economic revolution, whose incredible extent, probably, we are only beginning to appreciate, and whose effects, definitely, we are just beginning to understand. I can only attempt at an overview of the most significant features of these phenomena, without any conceit of a completeness which is far from the scope of this paper and, probably, of current state of economic knowledge.

The first and more obvious feature of the new economy is the incredible amount of information that computer-mediated transactions have made possible to create and share in the economic system. One of the first consequences of the increased rate of knowledge transmission in society is the creation of new and innovative products at a pace that humans never experienced before. But knowledge and product innovations are just an aspect of the internet revolution. Indeed, the dramatic fall of the cost of information made a great deal of business innovation: Hal Varian highlights the possibility of creating new and more efficient contracts due to the fact that more and more aspects of economic transactions became observable and thus apt to monitoring. The whole online advertising world, which lies at the heart of current debates, is a perfect example of this revolution: now an advertiser can actually monitor how many people look at their ad – or even better, click through it. The reduction of uncertainty about the return of investments in advertisement creates *ex ante* incentives to entering into the contract. As a result, online advertisement became more effective and more spread.[6]

The increased amount of real-time information about transactions makes it possible to know more about people's preferences, build small to medium scale experimental business models and test them on the marketplace, rather than rely on, no matter how authoritative and expensive, opinions from managers and experts.

Business model experimentation is another fundamental, though less obvious feature of the new economy. Experimentation is not only easier now, but it is also necessary in order to cope with the high level of competition and the specific features of digital goods.

---

5 Korobin 2011.

6 Varian 2010.

ICTs, together with the progressive fall of shipment costs created a unified marketplace in which incumbent businesses and new entrants can offer their services to a much larger market than ever. They can reach new customers through websites, find investors and commercial partners far away from home in a worldwide cooperation.

Worldwide cooperation is made increasingly easier by the fact that ICTs allow for a radical decentralisation of physical, human and social capital inputs with cloud computing.[7] Also, significant upfront capital investments such as data storage, generic components, applications, can be now acquired off the shelves from platform services – turning fixed into variable costs, and decreasing this variable cost at an incredible rate.

The other force behind the need of business model experimentation – and behind the whole new economics – is the function of production of digital goods, which is characterised by "radical scale economies", meaning that almost all production costs are upfront, while the marginal cost of reproduction is close to zero. As a result, also the price that can be charged is often close to zero. Which calls for a big business problem: how to recoup the initial investment and hopefully get some profits? This is a relatively new problem entrepreneurs have to cope with: they don't only have to imagine a product that can please their customers, but they also have to figure out how to make them (or someone else) pay for it. The first years of the new economies – in which we are still living – are a tumultuous magma of business model experimentation.

One of the new economy business models relies on customisation and personalisation of goods: since incredible amounts of information about customers preferences are now available, and the marketplace is so large that entrepreneurs can reach millions of potential customers by focusing on the long tail of the demand function, they can make their products targeted for special customers hoping that they will buy that product that so much reflects their unique mix of preferences. Paradoxically, then, consumer welfare is increased by the fact that the market is offering them customised goods. Goods that are less and less substitutable, no longer being one-size-fits-all. Also, businesses can rely on the information they have to perfectly discriminate, and charge each buyer according to his willingness to pay.[8]

An extreme version of this strategy is the Freemium model, by which a product or service is provided free of charge to most of its users, but a premium is charged for advanced features, functionalities, or related products and services. The provision of a good, free of charge, helps the entrepreneur to make his product visible to a very large customer base, to subsequently fish a limited group of people willing to pay for his premium service.

---

7 Benkler 2010.

8 In a contest with low barriers to entry, this will generate optimal amount sold and competition will shift all the surplus to the customer see Varian 2005, pp. 1-46.

Alternatively, if an entrepreneur cannot find premium customers, he can focus on a more traditional business model: advertisement. The producer allows the advertisers to pay for its service to other customers, who pay back for the service provided, rather than with money, with their attention to advertisements or "eyeballs", as it has become commonly known.

In both cases, the entrepreneur is building his business on cross-subsidisation, by letting a subset of its customers pay for the others – a model that it is often defined as a two-sided market.[9] The cross-subsidisation can happen between premium users, covering the cost of providing the service also for free users, or between buyers of advertisement space covering the costs of providing the digital product to all the consumers. And in both cases, there are important economies of scale: the larger is the customer base, the more likely is that the entrepreneur will find long tail, willing to pay customers. The more popular the digital goods become – and popularity in the new information economy is an observable and quantifiable phenomenon – the more advertisers will be willing to buy from the entrepreneur. If the service provider fails to reach a significant dimension, he will not be able to enjoy these scale economies.

Two considerations follow from this complex system. First, that the entrepreneur has a greater incentive to innovate its own product or products (free version and premium, as well as digital service in itself and advertisement). Advanced features and increased functionality are an important feature of the new economy: that is because the provider of a digital good or service has to compete, other than with other providers, with himself. He needs to improve its basic products in order to obtain the larger customer base possible, and as a consequence, the potential buyers of its ancillary advertisement services. But he needs to improve his premium services in order to motivate the premium buyer – and after a while he can pass on to the basic service the additional features, once he finds better ones for premium users. Self-competition results in a self-enforcing contract between the producer and its discriminated customers: if he tries to acquire premium users by degrading the quality of its free services instead than by improving its premium ones, he will lose customer base, therefore popularity and advertisers. If he tries to charge a price too high to both advertisers and premium users, they will not be willing to subsidise the other users. It should be noted that self-competition as a disciplining and innovative force also works in markets for digital but not completely immaterial goods such as software or electronics. Since these goods are not perishable, a provider needs to compete with its previous release, and he can do it only by adding new functionalities and features.[10]

The second consideration which follows the importance of popularity in these business models is that the digital market will see the emergence of either

9 Katz and Shapiro 1986.

10 McKenzie & Lee 2001.

providers that will focus on a (not so) small market niche of potential customers with peculiar demand or providers that will try to build the largest possible network of customers, resulting in "winner-take-all" (or most) of the market.[11]

This is also explained by using the concept of network economies: the fact that when one product become popular, and its market share increases, the value of the product to consumers increases because they value the fact that other people are using the same product – a network externality. Consumers utility from the goods is then partially derived from the characteristics of the good itself, and partially from the fact that is mostly used and from the expectation that it will be used by more and more people in the future. This characteristic lead many observers to suggest that, since people do not incorporate in their utility function only the intrinsic value (sic!) of the good, but also the diffusion or expected diffusion of the product, they will end up selecting as dominant a provider of a good that is not the best, but it simply is (or it is expected to be) the most popular. And the network externality idea leans to the problem of lock-in[12], which is actually a borderline concept between traditional and behavioural economics, since the latter plays a great emphasis on path dependency and consumer inertia.

And while there is a lot of theoretical controversy on the concept of lock-in both in the offline and the digital world[13], in the latter we can see an incredible rate of obsolescence of dominant positions. We already mentioned Microsoft; in the 2000s Posner's article, the first example that comes to his mind is AOL. AOL and Microsoft, pretty much like AltaVista, Yahoo!, BlackBerry, Nokia, MySpace, enjoyed for a limited period a customer base as large as to look likely to be able to lock customers in, but then they quickly become obsolete and not antitrust-scary anymore.

New powerful players entered the game: Google, to begin with. But also Facebook provides a good example of the extent of transformations in the digital economy: when it was founded, in 2004, the most popular brand on the Internet was Microsoft's MSN – Google itself only scored fifth. The most authoritative encyclopedia was Encyclopedia.com. In 2012, Facebook had more users than the whole Internet in 2004.[14]

Paraphrasing Adam Thierer, the age of the tech titans takes place in the land of Schumpeterian 'creative destruction', where "innovative risk-takers are constantly shaking things up and displacing yesterday's lumbering, lethargic giants. In markets built largely upon binary code, the pace and nature of change has become hyper-Schumpeterian: unrelenting and utterly unpredictable".[15]

11 Frank & Cook 1995.
12 David 1985.
13 Liebowitz & Margolis 1990, 2001.
14 Garber 2012.
15 Thierer 2011.

This fierce competition among technologies and networks is once again possible because the new economy has no frontiers, and new entrants can come from anywhere, gathering investments from everywhere, and creating innovation from knowledge and tools that are more and more spread in society. It also depends from the production function of digital goods, whose input are immaterial and thus whose supply can be quickly expanded in order to compete with dominant providers that are falling behind with innovation or charging prices too high.

In front of the radical transformations happening in the economic reality at the time of the internet, looks like the owl of economic theory has left its nest too early and, blinded by the daylight, doesn't really know in which direction to fly. Since Posner's call for caution in antitrust enforcement was left unanswered, we should look further to see if the conceptual tools retrieved from last centuries economics are still holding and whether they can accommodate digital postulates. If, alternatively, we do not have economic models strong enough to analyze economic phenomena that are happening for the first time in an economy stormed by technological transformations, we should back the call for caution, wait for the dusk to fall and for the owl to see again.

3. THE BREEZE OF BEHAVIOURAL ANTITRUST

Following the Hegel's owl metaphor, behavioural economics is like a new breeze, growing stronger and suggesting our owl in which direction to fly. Over the last fifteen years, behavioural economics, i.e. the use of psychology to reconsider the homo œconomicus paradigm has become a popular field of study in law and economics. Broadly articulated for the first time in Cass Sunstein and Richard Thaler's call for so-called "libertarian paternalism"[16] and again in their book *Nudge*[17], behavioural law and economics has become very influential in regulation[18], suggesting to design regulatory interventions taking into account the evidence of systematic irrational deviations from the neoclassical theory of behaviour and to incorporate little "nudges" that can "steer people in directions that will promote their welfare but will not prescribe or proscribe any particular choices" and thus improve consumer choice. More recently, several commentators have argued in favour or against of incorporating of behavioural economics within antitrust law.[19]

16 Sunstein & Thaler 2003.

17 Sunstein & Thaler 2008.

18 Cass Sunstein has been appointed Administrator of the Office of Information and Regulatory Affairs in the US, Richard Thaler has been involved in the creation of a unit in the British regulatory unit in order to incorporate the principles of Nudge into public policy. The US Consumer Financial Protection Bureau represents the clearest example of behavioural law and economics influence in regulation.

19 Reeves & Stucke, 2010; Stucke, 2007; Tor & Rinner 2009; Wright & Stone 2010.

Advocates of behaviourally informed competition policy argue that economics, and antitrust in particular, have insofar "worship[ed] at the shrine of rationality".[20] Most of economics and regulation models are indeed built on the assumption that individuals and firms maximise the achievement of their goals.[21] Recent economic literature, on the other hand, has increasingly focused on systematic mistakes (biases) that people make while taking their decisions: in other words, their revealed preferences are no longer a good economic instrument, because "in some cases *individuals make inferior decisions in terms of their own welfare* -- decisions that they would change if they had complete information, unlimited cognitive abilities, and no lack of willpower."[22]

Behavioral economics criticises most of the assumptions behind the standard economic model[23], and tries to build a new model of human behaviour drawing from the results of psychological experiments and surveys. It brings then the promise of a more realistic model of how consumers, firms and regulators act in the marketplace, which should bring about important consequences in the field of antitrust enforcement.

I will not try to address here the methodological and substantial concerns regarding the findings of behavioural economics and its (lack of a) model of human choice. I will rather have an "after win" approach and answer to the popular call for behaviourally informed competition policy. I will try to establish if antitrust can take into account biases in the behaviour of market actors such as consumers and firms (or better, their managers or entrepreneurs) and build better instruments to reconstruct an offense and propose a more effective remedy.

While the behavioural antitrust literature continues to grow – and reaches the ears of regulators, politicians and antitrust enforcers[24], some authors are reasonably sceptical about the fact that behavioural economics is advanced and consistent enough to be applied in market regulation without slipper in arbitrariness.[25] Others have argued with some success that contemporary

20 Leslie 2010.

21 It should be noted that in sophisticated economic approaches, this assumption does not entail any value judgment about the optimality or desirability or quality of goals that economic actors pursue, but it rather implies a procedural rationality that falls from the logical necessity of choosing, among scarce means, those that the actor believes to be more appropriate to reach his goals – no matter how sub-optimal, undesirable or plainly wrong those goals might be. See e.g. Mises 1949.

22 Sunstein and Thaler, 2008, p. 1161.

23 Specifically, it criticizes the assumption behind the concept of preferences: standard microeconomics requires that preferences adhere to the assumptions of completeness, reflexivity, transitivity, continuity, strong monotonicity, non-satiation, and convexity. These are the conditions for the utility function, upon which the economic actor makes his choices, to exist and be quasi-concave. See e.g. MasColell et al. 1995.

24 Rosch 2010.

25 Whitman and Rizzo 2007; Wright & Stone 2010.

antitrust has, especially in Europe, already incorporated behavioural concerns.[26] But, in general, the law and economics community seems, at most, convinced that the behavioural demolition of market actors' rationality can justify a different, and most likely more energetic antitrust approach.

But surprisingly enough there is very little use of behavioural economics in the analysis of the Google case. This comes at odds with the general claim that behavioural economics is a new and more fecund paradigm in economics and that should be used more in antitrust analysis. If a paradigm, no matter how popular in the academic community, does not provide useful analytical tools to deal with what is probably the biggest challenge in economic analysis of antitrust of our times, might it not be the case that it is not that new and useful at all? Leaving this scepticism aside, I will try to take behavioural economics seriously and incorporate it in my analysis of the issue.

4. GOOGLE, A TALE OF A VIRTUOUS MONOPOLIST?

Once upon a time, there was a small, innovative company, founded by two nerd students at Stanford, that delivered an incredibly innovative search experience, found a path-breaking business model, challenged and defeated giant monopolists of his early times, and become quite big. In the process, it kept innovating and offering more and more features and products – most of which were considered incredible solutions both by technology analysts and by customers, who kept using them. Many others just did not take off and were discarded – and kept experimenting and improving with its core business: search. As a result, it became the target of antitrust authorities from all over the world.

Google core business is internet search, and it has been an incredible product innovator[27], sorting out in 1996 a sophisticated algorithm to interpret people's inquiry, filter results and rank them according to their relevancy – back in the prehistoric times of search, it was mostly done by human power. In 1998 Google revolutionised the concept of relevancy building it on links and off-the-page criteria used as votes from other web users, instead that just relying on frequency of words and location (on-the-page criteria).

This allowed for much better search results, but the innovation wasn't over, ad a second major improvement in the search started in 2007, when Google launched its Universal search: mixing different results such as pages, simple

26 Petit & Neyrinck 2010.

27 The history of technological innovations in the search engine market is retrieved from a series of articles published in the sectoral blog *Searchengineland.com* by Danny Sullivan 2007, 2008, 2012.

information like time and weather, maps and other "relevant" answers into its result page. These are considered vertical search results as opposed to general results because, they retrieve results for a query, e.g. "pizza", only in images or addresses, or pizzerias. Integration of vertical searches results improve the Google's user experience, but only as long as the answers are the right, i.e. more relevant, ones.

In 2008 Google started experimenting new ways to better retrieve individually relevant results with Google Personalised search, that takes into account customers search history to deliver results more relevant to them (if I type Google, it will most likely return to me articles about Google's antitrust troubles), and launching in 2012 the Search Plus Your World feature. Assuming you can learn something about what a web user is asking for in a search query from what he and his friend liked and shared before, the result incorporates preferences retrieved from Google own social network, Google plus.

In 2012 Google launched its Knowledge Graph, that provides a box with popular facts about people, places and things alongside links to other content, revolutionising once again the search process, which will now work with logical entities in addition to web pages.

But that was not enough. In these years, Google launched hundreds of other products: some of them become extremely popular, like Gmail, Google Maps or its mobile operating system, Android. Some others were popular for a while then become obsolete, like Blogger. Some remained unknown for most of the population but used by fringe users (like Ngram Viewer for searching trends in academic publications, or Google Refine, used to clean up messy data-sets). Some other products, while meant for the general public, failed miserably to reach customers and were shut down, like Google Buzz, Google Waves and Knol (the first two are social sharing platforms, while the latter was an alternative to wiki platform for user-generated encyclopedia). As a result of this continuous innovation, Google become the dominant search engine of the new economy.

Google was also an incredible innovator in business models: it decided to base all its revenue on advertising, against the current trend of allowing for paid results in the organic searches. And since in computer-mediated transactions it is possible to make observable aspects of a contract that used to be unobservable, it started charging advertisers only for effective clicks. It also created a sophisticated auction system to allocate the space for ads, taking into account both the relevance of the page, through the quality score, and the advertisers willingness to pay. Since Google offered a more measurable and effective form of advertising, not only did it become the larger provider of search advertisement, but it also pushed this form of advertising (as opposed to display advertising, like pop ups and banners) to be the most important in the internet world.

But this is a tale of a virtuous monopolist that, no matter how virtuously, became a monopolist nonetheless: "it fills all the criteria for tracing brave risk-taking, innovation, economic growth (...), but could at the same time threaten the market's development".[28] This is also the tale of the unsolved conflict between static and dynamic competition in antitrust, which is exacerbated in the new economy because of the pace of innovation: if an innovation, that delivers a huge benefit to consumers, falls in the categories of abuse according to traditional economic models, antitrust falls in a logical short-circuit.

In 2010, pushed by complaints filed by several competitors, the European Commission started a formal investigation against Google. While still *in fieri*, the EU case give us a good framework to analyze the Google saga – also because it covers the same main criticism raised by other competition authorities, such as the FTC investigation launched in June 2011 on similar issues.

According to the Commission press release, four are the main conducts that might be found as abusive: first, whether "Google has abused a dominant market position in online search by allegedly lowering the ranking of unpaid search results of competing services which are specialised in providing users with specific online content such as price comparisons (so-called vertical search services) and by according preferential placement to the results of its own vertical search services in order to shut out competing services".[29] This issue can be framed, in general, as a foreclosure abuse, and it is specifically assimilable to the instances of abusive bundling and, in extreme, to refusal to supply. But this issue went far beyond the scope of antitrust to symptomise a more general concern about Google's ability to manipulate search results and thus manipulate the access to world information.[30]

Secondly, in order to better define the foreclosure abuse, the Commission declared that was also going to investigate "allegations that Google imposes exclusivity obligations on advertising partners, preventing them from placing certain types of competing ads on their web sites", and "suspected restrictions on the portability of online advertising campaign data to competing online advertising platforms", which can be conformed as a more or less graduate form of exclusive agreements.[31]

Finally, the Commission declared to investigate "into allegations that Google lowered the 'Quality Score' for sponsored links of competing vertical search services. The Quality Score is one of the factors that determine the price paid to Google by advertisers": this abuse is more related to a less used case-law of the exploitative abuses.

28 Pardolesi & Arnaudo 2010, p. 10.
29 European Commission 2010.
30 Pasquale & Bracha 2008; Vaidhyanathan, 2011; Auletta 2009.
31 Exclusive dealing agreement are a form of abuse instrumental to foreclosure. Compared to other issues raised, they have to be evaluated on a case by case standard, considering specific factors such as duration, exclusivity and automatic renewal clauses – information that will not be in the public domain until the procedure is closed. As such, we need to postpone the analysis of these abuse allegations.

Instead of formally concluding the investigation with a Statement of Objections, in May 2012 the EU Commission asked Google to propose remedies to address some of the issues that were originally included in the investigation, and in particular: a. preferential treatment of its own vertical search products over competing ones; b. the aggregation and integration in search results of original material from the websites of its competitors such as review[32]; c. exclusive arrangements with advertising partners and d. restriction on the portability of data from online search advertising campaign.[33]

And while the formal investigation is not over with the request of commitments, this solution tells us something. First of all, that the EU Commission is somehow more cautious than it had been before in addressing competition issues related to this "virtuous monopolist". The commitments requested from the Commission are interesting for what they ask, but also for what they do not ask: in the final version, the issue of the Quality score as a price setting instrument is not mentioned, meaning either that the Commission decided to avoid the slippery path of an exploitative abuse, which entails interfering with prices setting, or that it is open to a cooperative solution.

Finally, this choice from the Commission can also be interpreted as an admission of the lack of remedial solutions consistent and efficient enough to be imposed – which is in line with recent literature on search neutrality[34] – and thus the choice to resort to co-regulation to find a more flexible solution.

There's a lot on the antitrust table in the tale of Google, which will give us the chance to test both traditional and behavioural economic models in addressing the competition concerns in order to see where there are troubles in using those models to address the magmatic, innovative realm of the new economy.

5. THE TROUBLE WITH DOMINANCE

The first problem in defining a single firm conduct as abusive is the assessment of dominance. This is a twofold process: first, the competition authority needs to define the relevant market, and second it has to prove that the undertaking has some degree of market power. Market power is defined by which is built upon three key variables: the market position of the dominant undertaking and its competitors; the constraints imposed by the credible threat of future expansion by actual competitors or entry by potential competitors; the constraints imposed by the bargaining strength of the undertaking's customers.[35]

32 This issue, though concerns much more intellectual property rights violations or, at best, unfair trade practices – as such, is no relevant to our analysis and I just mention it for sake of completeness.

33 Almunia 2012.

34 See e.g. Ammori & Pelican 2012.

35 European Commission 2009, pp. 9–12.

Google is certainly big and the most popular search engine: but is size enough to consider it dominant? The internet is delivering new and new good any day, whose degree of substitution and complementarity is very hard to assess. In addition, the new economy is built on non-traditional business models that mix together two markets in order to allow for cross-subsidisation among different groups of consumers or buyers of two different goods. Also, the level of competition among alternative means to reach a certain end is quite important – so competition doesn't happen among homogeneous goods, but rather comes from very different ones.

For instance, if I want to buy a camera, I can go on Google and search for camera, or I can just type the EBay or other sellers' address on my browser bar. This alternative ways to reach a seller are not counted in the relevant market, because are not part of search inquiries. Still, they are in the realm of alternatives. So, what is Google selling, exactly? It is selling a. organic search results, for free; b. several other digital products, mostly for free, and c. operating systems, in a market that is mostly outside the scope of our analysis. But its core source of revenues is d. advertising, and specifically, search advertising, which is the relevant market for the antitrust controversies we are discussing. Of course, though, indirectly Google gets revenues also from a. (and b.), because it creates the scale of the customer base that will attract buyers of d. Now, neither the market of search and the market for online advertising are easy to define, because it is not easy to list and compare all the possible substitute goods. Provided that both general search and advertisement are meant as an instrument to lower the cost of information[36], first of all, they are substitutable among each other. A clear manifestation of this is the proliferation of Search Engine Optimisation (SEO) marketing professionals: a firm can decide to invest its marketing resources in paid advertisement on Google, or in SEO and improve its ranking in the organic results. As a mean to reach information, no matter how important, search engines are not the only possible instrument: people can just remember the address, or reach websites through suggestion from friends in their social network. All these are substitute for Google queries.

As a mean to reach customers, search advertising also competes with other forms of online advertisement, such as display advertising, which accounts for 45% of all online advertisement or viral advertisements, which require artistic and marketing expenses instead of paying for a visible spot. Even more: search advertising competes with offline advertising, since there is a sort of cross-elasticity between online and offline marketing expenditures.

It is often argued that other forms of advertising are not substitutes of search advertisement because only the latter allows for a profilation of the potential client. First of all, this is not historically true: targeting the right customer has

[36] Stigler 1983, as reported, together with most useful insights to analyze the Google case, in Manne & Wright 2011.

always been the goal of advertisement. Indeed, ads run on Vanity Fair are different from those run on Sports week, and TV advertisers buy time-slots during shows that can interest viewer whose profile fits the buyer of their products. And this is even less true in the online world, where also the display advertising is getting more and more personalised.

The task of assessing the relevant market in the new economy is even more complicated by the fact that often digital goods are priced at zero or close to zero. Traditionally, competition authorities rely on price variation to define whether a good is a substitute and shall thus be included in the relevant market with the Small but Significant Non-transitory increase in Price (SSNIP) test – which measures how much consumer will switch to an alternative when the allegedly dominant firm increases its price. Of course, when the price of a digital good is zero, like in the search market, it is harder for antitrust enforcers to analyze consumers behaviours.

Unfortunately, behavioural economics cannot give us better indications in this field: in the behavioural model of choice, people might be influenced by the endowment effect or other heuristics and perceive goods that they already use, or that are dominant in the markets, as standing alone and not competing with alternatives. How strong are these effects? In normal markets, idiosyncratic preferences are incorporated, and made measurable, by the SSNIP test and the residual demand elasticity – so that, even if the behavioural findings correctly describe human behaviours, they have no practical use. But when it comes to digital goods, priced zero, it is impossible to estimate these effects and thus any antitrust analysis built on behavioural assumption will simply rely on opinions and perceptions. Maybe these effects can be quantified through surveys and interviews, but even if we can avoid the distortionary effect, suggested by behavioural economics, of the way the survey is framed, we are switching from a measurement based on revealed preferences to one based on stated preferences. And if people are biased when making their market choices – whose consequences are doomed to bare in terms of ex post dissatisfaction about their purchase – there is no reason to assume that those cognitive forces will not play against them also when they reply to a survey, when they do not have any incentive to overcome cognitive shortcuts because there is no sanction for their actions.

Once the market is defined, and we have seen how hard it is in this case, we should be able to assess the dominance in that market. Historically, the most important surrogate for a firm market dominance has been its share of the industry (the relevant market) total output in a given year, because of a correlation between market share and market power, or the ability to deviate from marginal cost pricing.[37] Now, this correlation is built on the assumption that the larger the share of the output produced by the firm, the higher its ability of reducing the quantity produced and, as such, to raise the price. But this

[37] Hovenkamp 1999.

correlation doesn't hold that much in the new economy for two sets of reasons: first, that digital good have marginal cost of production close to zero, so it easy for competitors who retain a small market share, to instantly increase their production as soon as the monopolist start abusing his power.[38]

Google now operates 80% of global search queries – which raises to 95% in Europe, but falls to 74% in the US or to 49% in China[39] – and it is considered the gateway to the world's knowledge. But paradoxically, if tomorrow was suddenly shut down all of its market shares would be immediately taken over by its competitors and the knowledge of the world will still be accessible, even with some minor quality problems. As such, the advertisers that are now using Google to promote their goods, could instantly use other means. Out of the paradox, this means that if Google increases its prices or lowers its quality – in other words, if stops innovating itself – its market shares can be to a large extent covered by someone else.

The other aspect that lowers the significance of the correlation between market share and market power is the very nature of competition in the new economy: a competition that may come from everywhere, since geographical distances are no more an issue in defining the relevant market.

Which brings us to the second element of the assessment of dominance: the "credible threat" of future expansion by actual competitors or entry by potential competitors. While we have insofar observed that the new economy, by increasing worldwide cooperation and competition, makes the threat of competition stronger, behavioural economics suggests that this might not be the case. The concept of "credible threat" is very much passable of behavioural interpretations, since it relies a lot on firm expectations that, as we have learned by now, are not always rational.

In addition, also the competitors' willingness to enter the market might be plagued by irrationality: on one hand, because of the endowment effect and risk aversion, "a new entrant will prefer to spend resources, and secure gains, on its existing market, rather than to enter a new market, where gains are potentially higher, but haphazard"[40] – a claim that sounds far from realistic in the digital world where the rate of creation of new goods, new services and new markets is extremely high.

On the other hand, though, behavioural insights might also suggest that "firms often enter markets that are protected by high barriers. To start, decision-makers often tend to be overconfident, by virtue of optimism and desirability biases. Those individuals typically underestimate basic economic facts which run contrary to their projects, and overestimate the intrinsic value of their purported plans. In such settings, of course, entry may fail, but the threat of

38 McKenzie & Lee 2001.

39 Data retrieved from www.netmarketshare.com/, referring to the period 2012 Q2.

40 Petit & Neyrinck, 2010, p. 7.

irrational entry will discipline the incumbent firm".[41] But if the conclusions that we can draw from behavioural analysis are contradictory, it is hard to see any practical use for antitrust.

In one of the very few papers using behavioural instruments to analyze the Google case, Stucke theorises trial-and-error learning as an entry barrier in the search engine market: "if firms and consumers have biases and heuristics is learning as an entry barrier, namely, companies to effectively compete need a minimum level of trial-and-error feedback. Firms can have imperfect knowledge about current and future consumer preferences, a blurred and changing understanding of their goals and preferences, and a limited repertoire of actions to cope with whatever problems they face. Consumers have changing and, at times, inconsistent preferences".[42]

But this behavioural twist doesn't add much at the traditional description of the market process as a discovery procedure, in which entrepreneurs try different strategies and solution to better please their customers[43]: the fact that they have more experience (or, learning economies), doesn't prevent other entrepreneurs to try different solutions and strategies. To some extent, Stucke is deriving simply the barrier to entry from the market share, assuming that there are economies of scale in the search engine market, and while there are certainly learning economies coming from the amount of search performed[44], it is not necessarily true that this are related to the market share. In fact, quality depends on the absolute number of queries managed, not the relative one: and as such, even if Google's competitors now retain a much smaller market share, they still are handling a very large number of queries.

Considering the expansion of the total number of queries, this is most likely larger than the number of queries that Google was able to crunch when it entered the market and then become dominant, just because in the trial-and-error market process Google discovered the best way to provide an answer to those queries.

If barriers to entry and credible threats are a much more blended concept in the new economy, a greater emphasis, in the assessment of dominance, should be placed on the third force, the constraints imposed by the bargaining strength of the undertaking's customers. Which brings us back to the consumer role in the economy: a topic about which behavioural economics has said a lot, but probably too much to be useful in antitrust analysis. If indeed we accept the limited knowledge, limited willpower and limited self-interest vision of the consumer, we should assume that he has never any bargaining power – and even when he's got some, we cannot really rely on the way he uses it, because his choices are revealing, rather than his true preferences, his biases.

41 Petit & Neyrinck, 2010, p. 7.
42 Stucke 2011, pp. 9–10.
43 Kirzner 1997.
44 Luchetta 2013.

I believe this is a fundamental point in the discussion about antitrust in the new economy: never like today, we have alternative products or means to reach what we want. Most of them are also for free, switching costs are quite low. In Google's own worlds, the biggest constraint is the fact that "competition is just a click away"[45]: Google's user can use another engine at any time, without even typing a web address (they can just Google it).

If we use behavioural analysis, we can say the lack of switching is merely due to their inertia. Or, the popularity of a search engine cannot be explained in terms of its technological superiority, but rather by herding behaviours.[46] As a result, they end up locked in an inferior technology, or remain loyal to a monopolist even when it sells inferior products.[47]

Of course, these explanations be as good as any other, once we decide to cross the border of psychology and not to rely on revealed preferences anymore. But what I will argue is that these biases, and especially cognitive biases, do hold much better in the traditional economy than in the internet one. Indeed, consumers have never been so much empowered with choice as in the new economy of information: a global marketplace, technological competition, cheapest cost of information in the story of mankind, and tools to compare alternatives freely available on the internet.

Before of any economic choice, a consumer can easily compare its options from the comfort of his armchair, without the pressure of the personal relation with the seller (a pressure that has been recognised by behavioural economics when informed consumer protection regulation prescribing longer cooling off periods for door-to-door selling). He can read on line reviews or, if he is really lazy, watch video-reviews, which are booming on the internet. Customers can voice their dissent and dissatisfaction writing reviews that will reach many more people that it was ever conceivable before the internet. When the cost of information and communication is so low, each customer might easily become a sophisticated buyer and react to anticompetitive behaviours from the monopolist. Focusing on behavioural biases might push out of sight this important aspect of the new economy.

In the end, it does seem fair to conclude that it is much harder to prove dominance in the new economy because traditional economic models do not completely grasp the complexity of competition and business models. And that behavioural economics cannot equip us with better instruments to asses it. But setting aside these perplexities, I am going to assume the dominance of Google in the next section, in order to assess how dangerous are the specific abuses.

---

45 Kovacevich 2009.

46 Stucke 2011, pp. 9–10.

47 On this specific point, though, I'm also unconvinced that the lock in applies to a brand (Google) as well as for a technology (search engines).

6. THE TROUBLE WITH ABUSES

The assumption that the relevant market is defined properly, and subsequently, that the market share and market power of the dominant firm are substantial is especially important considering the EU special responsibility doctrine, i.e. that if a firm has a dominant position[48] then it has "a special responsibility not to allow its conduct to impair competition on the common market"[49], which is to say that some behaviours, such as tying, refusal to supply, exclusive agreements that would be allowed below a certain market share are not acceptable anymore. Or better, the monopolist can still play an efficiency defence, according to the Enforcement Guidelines from the EC Commission.[50]

The dominant undertaking can explain that there are pro-competitive aspects of its conduct and that he is passing on to the consumer part of the efficiencies – but it will be harder to balance the efficiency effects with the foreclosure effects.[51]

In our case, because of its alleged dominance, Google can be charged of illegal bundling or refusal to supply even though a preferential treatment is a common feature of the industry – and as such, done also by Google's competitors that filed a complaint before the European Commission or the FTC.

But this happens because adding additional features to your own products is, rather than an abusive tying, a normal feature of the digital marketplace.

This issue, indeed, can be addressed as a tying case or, in a more extreme version, as an denial to supply an essential facility case, and while we still don't know how the competition authorities will deal with both, we can use the case to examine how strong these economic model holds in the new economy.

7. REFUSAL TO SUPPLY

The refusal to supply argument is extremely popular among critics of Google and supporters of search neutrality: not surprisingly, since the essential facility narrative is quite powerful. After all, Google manages the majority of searches, and if your website does not appear in Google results, it basically doesn't exist in the digital marketplace. Vertical search engines, whose placement in organic results was lowered by the change in Google's algorithm saw their traffic fall dramatically overnight.[52] But is it enough to qualify Google as an essential

48 The lowest market share used to assume dominance was 39.7%in the BA/Virgin case of 2004.

49 Industrie Michelin v Commission of the European Communities, Case 322/81, 1883.

50 European Commission 2009, pp. 28–31.

51 European Commission 2009, p. 30.

52 Foundem's Google Story, August 2009, Searchneutrality.org.

facility? The essential facility doctrine is indeed quite controversial in economic analysis and in antitrust enforcement[53], because it lowers the ex ante incentives to invest in an efficient platform. This is particularly important in the new economy, where the ability of building a large network – or simply a large customer base – is often the best business solution to deal with the close to zero marginal price of digital goods.

In the specific case, moreover, it is very hard to assess if Google is an essential facility because, as we mentioned before, it is very hard to define the relevant market: Google is actually dominant only if we assume that Internet (unpaid) search is not competing with other instruments to reach users' attention[54], but we argued that this is not the case. If Google is not an essential, but just a very effective facility, there is no reason to share the benefits of its efficiency with Google's competitors instead than with its customers. Because configuring some sort of duty to supply Google's platform to its competitors – even if this stretch of the special responsibility doctrine is acceptable – comes at an high price: that of lowering Google's ability of doing its own job, which is, exactly, to discriminate between websites relevant to the user's query and websites that are not. A job that Google is already required to perform at best: otherwise "competition is just a click away" and Google will lose its customer base. We can even extend this reasoning to state that if there is a demand for neutrality in the market, Google will provide it – but behavioural economist will argue, against it, that cognitive heuristics and network effects can prevent users to use their countervailing power against the monopolist, and they might end up locked in the monopolistic status quo. This depiction of human choice goes back to the unsolved issue we raised before of the role of the information-empowered consumer in the new economy. But it is also build on the assumption that network effects, that Google platform allegedly enjoys, are either externalities that might bring to market failures, or some form of consumer's bias due to lock-in effects, as we discussed earlier.

Indeed, Write and Manne effectively argued that Google does not enjoys these network effects. In the search market, there is not increased utility for a user derived from the number of other users – except, maybe, from the fact that by handling a larger number of queries, Google can perform better result: but this is rather a demand-side economy of scale than a network externality. Advertisers do not increase their utility by the number of other advertisers who join the network – quite the opposite, because increased demand will increase the price. Additionally, the increased utility they enjoy by the increased number of search users is internalised by the price – click sensitive – they pay to Google: technological innovation and the information availability made Google able to

53 Although much more so in the US after the Trinko case than in Europe after the Microsoft (Server) case.

54 Manne & Wright 2011.

perfectly internalise what could have been a network externality, leaning to a market failure.[55]

If the lack of search neutrality is not a market failure, then the problem of Google's power to discriminate resulting in a danger for the internet world should not be address with competition law. A similar point is made also by Frank Pasquale, who co-authored the first and most influential article addressing the problem of search neutrality, when he writes "Federal Search Commission, like many other parts of the search engine accountability literature, tried too hard to shoehorn a wide variety of social concerns about search engines into the economic language of antitrust policy exclusive agreements".[56] Whether this problem can be addressed with other forms of regulation, is another interesting, and debatable issue, but it is outside the scope of our analysis.

The core business of competition law is, indeed, competition and addressing a specific subset of market failures related to the monopoly problem not to solve other regulatory issue such as plurality. Competition policy has been often stretched up, especially in Europe, to cope with other goals in a multi-valued approach, but this approach has not been regarded as successful and has been discarded by the European Commission.[57] Using a controversial economic model, the essential facility doctrine, to pursue a non-economic goal inside competition law is a strategy as far as possible from the cautious approach Posner suggested in the complex and fast evolving world of the new economy.

8. TYING OR BUNDLING

Alternatively, we can construct the preferential treatment of Google's own services as a form of bundling. We can consider Google Universal Search, i.e. the fact that it integrates its own products such as Maps, Shopping or Google Plus profiles results of important people in its search results, as a tying that the search engine uses to leverage its own products against those offered by competing vertical search engines. Also, Search Plus Your World can be seen as a way to leverage Google's social network, Plus, by linking it to its broadly appreciated organic search services in order to compete with much more popular social networks such as Facebook, Twitter or Tumblr.

Let's start by disclosing that the leverage theory is a quite old and criticised economic model, as the Chicago School argued. It is erroneous to claim that a monopolist can artificially increase its profits in a competitive or partially

55 Write & Manne 2011.
56 Pasquale 2010, p. 402.
57 Pardolesi 2005.

competitive market.[58] Still, this theory is quite alive in antitrust enforcement, and partly so because of behavioural concerns[59]: behavioural economics tends to emphasise the extent of the bundling ability of a monopolist because of consumer biases, because "even small switching costs can have significant effects on consumer behaviour in the presence of consumer inertia, endowment effects, and default bias. This can, in turn, make foreclosure more likely to occur through tying and bundling".[60] A clear exemplification of this reasoning is the 2004 and 2007 European Commission Vs Microsoft cases, in which the Microsoft was charged of illegally tying, respectively, Window Media Player and Internet Explorer by integrating these features into its operating system, even though they were added for free and it was easy to access alternative products – mostly for free – in the marketplace, because of the leveraging power of the default option.

Instead of discussing whether consumers are really biased by defaults when deciding not to switch to a competitor – instead of simply enjoying the additional feature offered for free, we should try to understand if this theoretical tool is more or less apt to interpret the competitive process in the new economy.

First of all, as we mentioned before, integrating new features and options is a natural trait of the digital marketplace. And this is due precisely to competition: producers of digital goods that are not perishable – like operating systems – have to compete with themselves, and add new features in order to motivate the customer to buy the new version of their product. Producers of perishable digital goods – like search queries – are in a self-enforcing contract relation with their customers, either when they use a Freemium business model or when they have to build, and keep, a free customer base large enough to motivate advertisers to pay for reaching it.

Generally speaking, it is reasonable to assume a market demand for multi-tasking products, or at least for interoperability among different tools: for instance, internet users appreciate the ability to search through their emails and online documents, and search the web from their email box or a social network page. As a result, the line between complementary products and additional features get blurred and it is hard to tell when the monopolist is bundling a different good instead of adding an additional feature.

Let's take a look at bundling of Google Plus in Google's homepage and in Gmail[61], and the integration of Google Plus social preferences in Google's

58 Bork 1978.

59 Even before the rise of behavioural economics, "competition law captures anticompetitive bundling strategies which go well beyond conventional economic theory" Petit & Neyrinck 2010. p. 24.

60 Benett & al. 2010, p. 121.

61 Gmail, while quite popular, cannot really be considered dominant in the market for email clients, because it competes with all the alternative email providers and off-line email clients.

general algorithm for search relevancy. Is it an illegal bundling, or just a way to fight obsolescence when the market for search engines might, in the future, be more and more influenced by social networks? When most of the information on people's preference is created in social networks that are, to some extent, closed systems that Google cannot (or cannot perfectly) access for crawling information[62], the only possible way for Google to be competitive is to make, instead of buy, this vital input for its future services. Vital exactly because of competition, since Google's competitor Bing, for instance, has a privileged accessed to Facebook's information about social preference thanks to a search agreement with the web larger social network, which also might enter the search engine market in the future. The least we can say, is that pro-competitive effects of this bundling must be weighed against the foreclosure effects of tying.

An economic theory that overestimate the leverage effects and does not account for an important feature of the innovation in the digital marketplace is less useful than one that does understand it. So, behavioural enrichments of the leverage theory are not fruitful in the new economy. Also because here we can learn a bit from the Hegel's owl, look back at the relatively brief history of the new economy and learn from that little dusk that has fallen insofar. Think about the Microsoft failure to leverage Window Media Player or Internet Explorer: both attempts were defeated not by an antitrust remedy – which proved to be largely ineffective, as we will discuss later – but rather by the rise of highly innovative competitors such as ITunes, Firefox and Chrome.

The very history of Google is full of failures to leverage its products. Knol was launched in 2008 as an alternative to Wikipedia's platform for a peer encyclopedia: it was shut down in 2012 due to lack of success. Google Buzz and Google waves were two attempts at entering the social networking and micro blogging markets: they were launched with great enthusiasm and marketing investments from the Mountain View, never really took off and were discontinued respectively, in 2011 and 2012. Google Buzz, particularly, was added as default to Gmail's functionalities and, at least in the initial phase, it was not possible to opt out, configuring a truly coercive bundling: the internet marketplace immediately reacted with polemics about this business practice, that was corrected in a prompt way: this little digression shall teach us something about the actual role of the customer in constraining market power in the new economy.

Conversely, other products such as Gmail and Google Maps quickly gained market shares and become among the most popular products of the company.

62 Amit Singhal, who oversees Google's ranking algorithms declared "Facebook and Twitter and other services, basically, their terms of service don't allow us to crawl them deeply and store things. Google+ is the only [network] that provides such a persistent service" in an interview to SearchEngineLand.com, available at http://searchengineland.com/googles-results-get-more-personal-with-search-plus-your-world-107285.

The main difference among the two sets of products might be the degree of innovation delivered by Gmail and Google maps, as recognised by tech experts – if this is true, we can conclude that in the digital market place these products reached their success because they really delivered new services to the customer, and not because of the leverage power. But we can also argue that also Knol, Google Buzz and Wave were innovative, or at least as innovative as their competitors in technical terms. Still, they failed to please the consumer. It might be because they were, simply not good enough, but it might also be because consumers have idiosyncratic preferences for other, less efficient, products, are biased in favour of the *status quo* or whatever non rational explanation behaviourists can give us. This simply means that psychological biases work both in favour and against the monopolist, and we cannot rely on them to sustain the leverage theory.

9. THE TROUBLE WITH REMEDIES

In the last section we assume, against what we discussed in the previous paragraphs, that Google is dominant and that its conducts are indeed abusive, and we accept the argument that its innovative way of delivering search results, while increasing the quality of services provided to both consumers and advertisers, still harms them in the long term because it decreases competition by foreclosing the market to its competitors. We are still in the troublesome position of trying to find remedies that will improve, the current situation.

Probably, also competition authorities are a bit lost here: as we can interpret the lack of a precise request from the European Commission and the reliance, instead, on the request of commitments from Google. Since the new economy is characterised by a great complexity of business models, integration of products and sophisticate technological knowledge, it is even more complex for antitrust enforcers to overcome information asymmetries and draft regulatory or structural remedies.

Traditional antitrust remedies, such as fines have certainly a deterrence effect, but they might arrive too late, when the monopolist has already created a large customer base thanks to his abusive conducts – and considering the network effects in the internet-based economy, they might not affect the dominant position anymore.

We can take behavioural allegation seriously about how imperfections in people's choice exacerbate their lock in the monopolist technology – in our case: people do not switch to competitors even though Google, by favouring its own results, does not meet to their demand for neutrality because they are locked in by their status quo bias. Still, it doesn't mean that regulators can find the right technological solution to perform and display searches with perfect equilibrium between relevancy, neutrality and business sustainability. Pretty much like in the general debate about standard lock in, it is hard to believe than the most efficient standard can be chosen outside of a market process.[63]

Here, behavioural economics comes with a quite practical and elegant solution: rather than imposing a restriction, better to gently "nudge" consumers by changing a default rule. The problem with nudge-based regulation instead of coercive one is exactly that people are still free to chose and opt out the regulatory default for the previous one that the regulatory intervention is trying to change. But if, as behavioural antitrust defendants claim, we cannot rely on people's preferences regarding a certain choice – since they are originally biased – why should we draft a regulation that allows for opt out, and let them switch back to the previous, allegedly inefficient, situation? The behavioural remedy risks to be ineffective, in the eye of its proponent, to unlock the consumers. Arguably, regulatory interventions inspired by behavioural economics will necessarily encounter only modest results at meeting their goals because of their very structure: by not imposing any particular outcome, they still rely on consumers' preferences. But consumers can always choose not to react to the nudge, and be consistent with their allegedly biased preference. This could lead to potential slippery slopes when at least some decision-makers may view the (apparent) failure of one intervention as justification for further, more intrusive intervention.

We have a quite recent case to test the effectiveness of these proposal: in December 2009, the Commission closed its investigation about abusive tying of Internet Explorer by accepting legally binding commitments from Microsoft. Since March 2010 and for five years, Microsoft will offer to the European consumers a ballot screen enabling users of Windows to choose which of its competitors' web browser(s) they want to install in addition to, or instead of, Internet Explorer. This remedy was clearly inspired by behavioural insights: a regulatory intervention that doesn't impose a restriction (e.g. unbundling Internet Explorer) but rather changes a default rule (demand the customer to initially make a pre-selection between a range of competing web browsers). Two years later, we can actually see that IE's market share fell from 45.32% to 28.5%. But it is due to the ballot screen? Let's take a look at the trend:

63 Cowen & Crampton 2002.

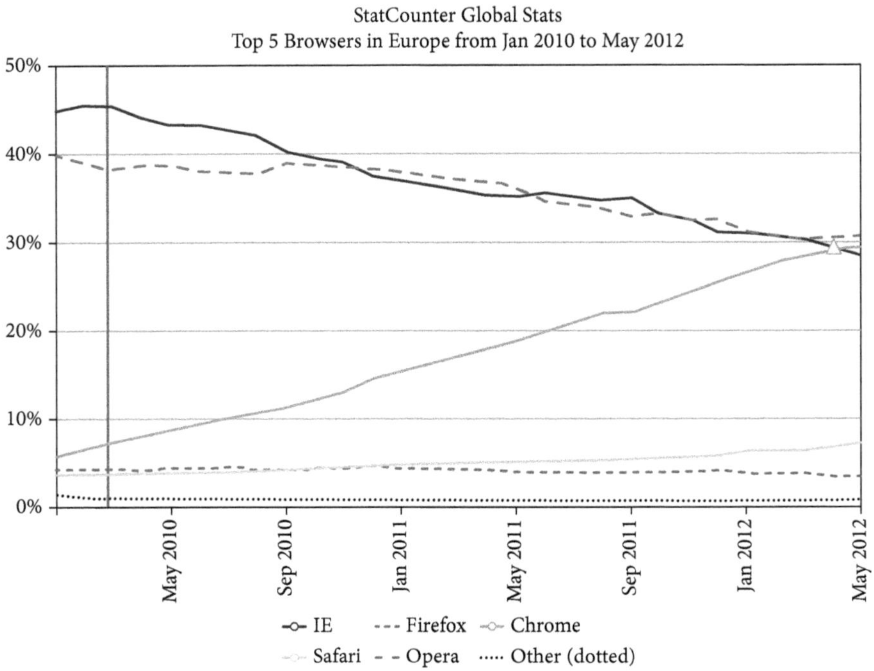

There is actually no particular dip in correspondence of the initial months of the Ballot Choice' implementation (the red line). Rather, IE's quota started to drastically fall when Chrome, delivering a new and faster Internet experience started eroding IE's market quote (together with Mozilla, whose trend is less drastic). And comparing browser's market trends in EU and worldwide, there is no significant difference between the "de-biased" choices of European consumers and those from the rest of the world, who did not enjoy the antitrust nudge. This is consistent with our criticism of the behaviourally inspired remedies, but also with the idea that competition, in the new economy, comes more from innovation than from regulatory authorities.

And while the opt-out default changing regulation is less dangerous than traditional command and control ones, it certainly doesn't come without a price. In the IE case, soon after the Ballot Choice portal was launched, some smaller competitors (so called second-tier browsers because were not immediately visible in the box) appealed to the EU Commission for a better placement.

This result is consistent with more classical economic theory: often, state regulation freezes competition, by enforcing the state of the market. A new, innovative browser will find it harder to penetrate the market, since this regulatory intervention translated the browser choice in a choice between available browser. Had this happened at the time of the 2002 US Internet Explorer Case, the customer would have probably been left with a more balanced division of market shares between Netscape and Explorer, but without Firefox or Chrome and the great deal of innovation they brought into the browser market.

Even with its imperfection, this solution still looks like the most viable as a conclusion of the Google saga. It would be easily applied to the alleged tying by defaults of the Google search engine to Google Chrome, but it looks like it is not necessary at all: new installations of Chrome already pop-up to first time users the suggestion that they can change their default search engine. And Google drafted the nudge better than the regulator: it simply suggests to go looking for alternative search engines instead than providing a defined set of alternatives which might freeze innovation.

It is hard, but not inconceivable, to imagine how to apply this regulatory technique to the search engine market: for instance, the default landing page for a query might display only organic and paid results, while a richer and sophisticated search experience, including Universal Search and Knowledge graph results, could be displayed on demand. Regulators can ask Google to provide Personalised search and Search Plus Your World results only to users who opt-in for this system – which is now the default.

Of course, this will turn back the time of innovation respectively to 1998 and 2007: it will basically ask to Google to compete less on improving innovating its products. It will raise Google's costs in acquiring social generated information to build the personalised search of the future. It will hamper its complex business model by damaging some users, who can easily switch to Google's competitors. Competitors which, not burdened by any special responsibility, are still able to use the full power of innovation.

The 1998 or 2007 antitrust-friendly version of Google will give more space to vertical engines and alternative providers of information, but we shall remember that competition law is not meant to protect competitors, but either the competitive process or the consumers. As for the competitive process, the traditional justification for preventing foreclosure – which is: harming competitors – is that it reduces future consumer welfare by reducing its future options. But this idea risks to miss the fact that, in the new economy most of the consumer options come from innovation and fierce competition – fierce exactly because new entrants have to compete with virtuous, innovative monopolies. A competition policy based on economic models that force monopolists to compete less instead of more does not solve antitrust's inner conflict with innovation is probably counterproductive in the new economy.

Still, proponents of behavioural remedies have some success in arguing that "nudge" solutions and changing defaults are the less dangerous approach: they will accommodate antitrust concerns about increasing consumer choice and thus consumer welfare, and at the same time leave to people the freedom of switching back to the normal outcome of the market process. But what if people really want the innovations that Google delivered insofar, and they do really appreciate the fact that it can actually match better their preferences?

They will switch back to the original version of Google, and the remedy will be largely ineffective, as it was in the Explorer case. But it will came at a higher cost for the consumer, who now has to opt-in in order to reap the full benefits of innovation, since the regulatory default option has a lower quality than the market one: quite paradoxical if we assume that the whole purpose of antitrust is to protect consumer welfare.

10. CONCLUSIONS

After a long flight in the daylight of fast changing new economy, our owl is still lost.

The Google case was our *experimentum crucis* to assess whether traditional economic models or behavioural ones are able to solve the inner conflict between innovation and antitrust. Competition policy, to be considered effective, needs to deliver benefits to consumers. But when most of the benefits for consumers comes from innovation, and regulatory models are not able to account for it, antitrust risks to delay, rather than increase, innovation and benefits to consumers: as such, those models need to be rethought. Behavioral economics, though, doesn't seem to be the paradigmatic shift we need to address this concern – it rather looks like a paradigm even less able to understand innovation. It does not provide us with tools to better assess dominance, nor to analyze single abuses. It can yes suggest viable remedies, but with the caveat that most of the value of behavioural remedies comes from the fact that they are going to be largely ineffective – even though they will still impose a cost on consumers.

We should be aware that a competition policy informed by weak economic models can stop the movement of innovation, maybe we shall accept that, at least until the night has fallen and we can better understand the new economy, we should have a cautionary approach to competition law.

BIBLIOGRAPHY

Ammori, Marvin and Pelican, Luke, "Proposed Remedies for Search Bias: 'Search Neutrality' and Other Proposals in the Google Inquiry", *Journal of Internet Law*, May 14, 2012. Available at SSRN: http://ssrn.com/abstract=2058159.

Auletta, Ken, *Googled: The End of the World as We Know It*. New York: Penguin, 2009.

Benett, M., J. Fingleton, A. Fletcher, L. Hurley and D. Ruck, "What Does Behavioral Economics Mean for Competition Policy?", *Competition Policy International*, Spring 2010, vol. 6, n° 1, p. 121.

Benkler, Yochai, "Decentralization, Freedom to operate & Human Sociality" in: Berin Szoka and Adam Marcus (eds) *The next Digital Decade: Essays on the Future of the Internet.* Washington D.C.: TechFreedom, 2010, pp. 257–272.

Bork, Robert H., *The antitrust paradox: a policy at war with itself.* New York: Basic Books, 1978.

Cowen, Tyler and Eric Crampton, *Market Failure or Success: The New Debate.* Oakland, CA: The Independent Institute, 2002.

David, Paul A., "Clio and the economics of QWERTY", *American Economic Review* 1985, 75: 332–337.

European Commission, *Commission probes allegations of antitrust violations by Google,* Press release IP/10/1624. 30 November 2010 http://europa.eu/rapid/pressReleasesAction.do?reference=SPEECH/12/372&format=HTML&aged=0&language=EN.

European Commission, *Guidance on the Commission's enforcement priorities in applying Article 82 of the EC Treaty to abusive exclusionary conduct by dominant undertakings,* OJ, C 45, 24 Feb 2009.

Frank, Robert H., and Philip J. Cook, *The winner-take-all society.* New York: Free Press, 1995.

Garber, Megan, "The Internet at the Dawn of Facebook" *The Atlantic,* 17 May 2012. Available at www.theatlantic.com/technology/archive/2012/05/the-internet-at-the-dawn-of-facebook/257342/.

Hegel, Georg Wilhelm Friedrich, *Philosophy of right,* 1821. Trans. HB Nisbet, ed. AW Wood (Cambridge: 1998).

Hovenkamp, Herbert, *Federal Antitrust Policy: The Law of Competition and Its Practice.* St. Paul, MN: West, 1999.

Joaquín Almunia, "Competition Policy Statement of VP Almunia on the Google antitrust investigation", SPEECH/12/372 21 May 2012 http://europa.eu/rapid/pressReleasesAction.do?reference=SPEECH%2F12%2F372&format=HTML&aged=0&language=EN&guiLanguage=en.

Katz, M. and C. Shapiro (1986), "Technology Adoption in the Presence of Network Externalities" *Journal of Political Economy,* Vol. 94, No. 4, pp. 822–841.

Kirzner, Israel M., "Entrepreneurial Discovery and the Competitive Market Process", *Journal of Economic Literature,* Vol. 35, No. 1 March 1997, pp. 60–85.

Korobkin, Russell B., "What Comes After Victory for Behavioral Law and Economics?" *UCLA School of Law, Law-Econ Research Paper* No. 11–10, 2011. Available at SSRN: http://ssrn.com/abstract=1787070.

Kovacevich, Adam "Google's Approach to Competition", *Google Policy Blog* May 8, 2009, http://googlepublicpolicy.blogspot.com/2009/05/googles-approach-tocompetition.html.

Kovacic, William E., "The Influence of Economics on Antitrust" *Law, Economic Inquiry,* 1992, vol. 30, issue 2, p. 294–306

Leslie, Christopher R., "Rationality Analysis in Antitrust", *University of Pennsylvania Law Review,* Vol. 158, No. 2, 2010; Available at SSRN: http://ssrn.com/abstract=1557850

Liebowitz, Stan J. and Stephen Margolis, "The Fable of the Keys" *Journal of Law and Economics,* 1990 22: 1–26.

Liebowitz, Stan J. and Stephen Margolis, *Winners, losers & Microsoft: competition and antitrust in high technology (Rev. ed.)* Oakland, Calif.: Independent Institute, 2001.

Luchetta, Giacomo, "Is the Google platform a Two-Sided Market?, Jnl of Competition Law & Economics (2014) 10 (1): 185–207 first published online September 12, 2013 doi:10.1093/joclec/nht026.

Manne, Geoffrey A. and Wright, Joshua D., "Google and the Limits of Antitrust: The Case Against the Antitrust Case Against Google", *Harvard Journal of Law and Public Policy*, Vol. 34, No. 1, Winter 2011. Available at SSRN: http://ssrn.com/abstract=1577556.

Manne, Geoffrey A. and Wright, Joshua D., "Innovation and the Limits of Antitrust", *Journal of Competition Law and Economics*, March 2010 Vol. 6, Issue 1, pp. 153–202, 2010. Available at SSRN: http://ssrn.com/abstract=1578762.

MasColell, A., M. Whinston and J. Gree, *Microeconomic Theory*, Oxford: Oxford University Press, 1995.

McKenzie, Richard B. and Dwight R. Lee, "How digital economics revises antitrust thinking" *The Antitrust Bulletin*, 36 Summer 2001, 253–98.

Mises Ludwig, *Human Action: A Treatise on Economics*. New Haven: Yale University Press, 1949.

Pardolesi, Roberto and Arnaudo, Luca, "Single-Firm Conduct: A Discipline in Search of Itself (Try with Google?)", *LE Lab working paper*, January 25, 2010. Available at SSRN: http://ssrn.com/abstract=1541928, p. 10.

Pardolesi, Roberto, Modernization: the "new mantra" of Trans-Atlantic competition law, speech at Harvard University on February 11, 2005, Available at www.law-economics.net/public/Boston%20speech%20revised%2007–02.pdf.

Pasquale, Frank, "Dominant Search Engines: An Essential Cultural & Political Facility" in: Berin Szoka and Adam Marcus (eds) *The next Digital Decade: Essays on the Future of the Internet*. Washington D.C.: TechFreedom, 2010, p. 402.

Pasquale, Frank A. and Bracha, Oren, "Federal Search Commission? Access, Fairness and Accountability in the Law of Search", *Cornell Law Review*, September 2008. Available at SSRN: http://ssrn.com/abstract=1002453.

Petit, Nicolas and Neyrinck, Norman, "Behavioral Economics and Abuse of Dominance: A Proposed Alternative Reading of the Article 102 TFEU Case-Law", *College of Europe GCLC Working Paper* No. 02 2010.

Posner, Richard A., "Antitrust in the New Economy", *University of Chicago Law & Economics, Olin Working Paper* No. 106. November 2000 Available at SSRN: http://ssrn.com/abstract=249316.

Reeves, Amanda P. and Stucke, Maurice E., "Behavioral Antitrust", *Indiana Law Journal*, Vol. 86, 2010; Available at SSRN: http://ssrn.com/abstract=1582720.

Rosch, J. Thomas (Commissioner, Federal Trade Commission) "Behavioral Economics: Observations Regarding Issues That Lie Ahead", *Remarks before the Vienna Competition Conference*, Austria, June 9, 2010. Available at http://ftc.gov/speeches/rosch/100609viennaremarks.pdf.

Stigler, George, *The Organization of Industry*. Chicago: University of Chicago, 1983.

Stucke, Maurice E., "Behavioral Antitrust and Monopolization", *Journal of Competition Law and Economics*, November 17, 2011; Available at SSRN: http://ssrn.com/abstract=1961327.

Stucke, Maurice E., "Behavioral Economists at the Gate: Antitrust in the 21st Century" *Loyola University Chicago Law Journal*, Vol. 38, 2007; Available at SSRN: http://ssrn.com/abstract=981530.

Sunstein, Cass R. and Thaler, Richard H., "Libertarian Paternalism Is Not An Oxymoron" *University of Chicago Law Review* 70 (4), (2003): 1159–1202.

Thaler, Richard H., and Cass R. Sunstein. *Nudge. Improving Decisions about Health, Wealth, and Happiness.* New Haven, CT: Yale UP, 2008.

Thierer, Adam. "Of 'Tech Titans' and Schumpeter's Vision", *Forbes*, 22 Aug. 2011. www.forbes.com/sites/adamthierer/2011/08/22/of-tech-titans-and-schumpeters-vision/2/.

Tor, Avishalom and Rinner, William J., "Behavioral Antitrust: A New Approach to the Rule of Reason after Leegin", *University of Haifa Faculty of Law Legal Studies Research Paper Series*, December 1, 2009. Available at SSRN: http://ssrn.com/abstract=1522948.

Vaidhyanathan, Siva. *The Googlization of Everything: (and Why We Should Worry).* Berkeley: University of California, 2011.

Varian, Hal R., "Computer-Mediated Transactions" in: Berin Szoka and Adam Marcus (eds) *The next Digital Decade: Essays on the Future of the Internet.* Washington D.C.: TechFreedom, 2010. 239–257.

Varian, Hal R., "Competition and Market Power" in: Farrel, Joseph, Carl Shapiro and Hal R. Varian (eds), *The Economics of Information Technology: an Introduction.* Cambridge: Cambridge Univ. Press. 2005. 1–46.

Whitman, Douglas Glen and Mario Rizzo, "Paternalist Slopes", *NYU Journal of Law & Liberty*, 2007.

Wright, Joshua D. and Stone, Judd E., "Misbehavioral Economics: The Case Against Behavioral Antitrust", *Cardozo Law Review*, Vol. 33, No. 4, 2012, pp. 1517–1533. Available at SSRN: http://ssrn.com/abstract=1686389.

CHAPTER 16

THE INTERACTION BETWEEN EU REGULATORY IMPLANTS AND THE EXISTING CROATIAN LEGAL ORDER IN COMPETITION LAW

Jasminka PECOTIĆ KAUFMAN and Vlatka BUTORAC MALNAR

1. INTRODUCTION

It is a well-known fact that the major jurisdictions in the world, and most notably the USA and the EU, act as leaders in the world's ideological convergence, reshaping many smaller nations' economic, political, and cultural climate according to its own image. Without having philosophical arguments on the desirability of such processes, it can be stated that they were and remain a success. For many years we have been witnessing the European enlargement project – the integration of former transitional countries into the economic and political union of western market economies. This very demanding project and the most desired goal for candidate and accession countries was performed mostly through the implementation of EU rules into the local legal systems not tailored to local problems, and what is more, it is often not compatible with the local institutional framework. The implementation of laws is rarely an issue, as it is often done by way of pure translation of foreign rules;[1] however, problems tend to occur at the enforcement stage. Adopting foreign legal solutions is always a sensitive question as it requires not only the adjustment of legal rules, but also the development of institutions, substantive capacity building and sometimes major changes in values and thinking.

One of the most noticeable areas in this regard is the competition law regime, as it plays a central role in the protection and effectiveness of the European market. Today few would contest the necessity for convergence of competition

1 For details on legal theory on transplants as an exercise of translation see ER Saldarriaga, 'Comments on Panel III Hybrid cultures: borrowings and imposition' (2008), 77 Rev. Jur. U.P.R. 433.

law regimes in Europe, as processes are essential for the proper functioning of its market. With this in mind, the right question is not whether convergence is a necessary and legitimate aim, but rather what are the problems in achieving this aim and what is the level of success in the accession countries.

The authors will attempt to illustrate the difficulties in harmonising competition laws and their enforcement in the case of Croatia, a country which has undergone a number of substantial changes in the area of competition law over the last decade, in order to fully comply with the harmonising obligation and render effective thereby implemented rules.

In order to address this topic properly, the discussion is placed within a broader theoretical context, i.e. within the theory of legal transplants. We put forward a general argument, claiming that the efficiency of legal transplants (institutional and substantive alike) is affected by the relationship between existing rules and institutions of the recipient legal order with the imported ones.

Such interactions obstruct the likelihood of a blue-print transfer of rules and institutions across countries. We believe this to be the key problem of competition law development in Croatia. This argument is supported with a thorough analysis of the Croatian institutional setting for the enforcement of competition rules, followed by an analysis of substantive competition law development in Croatia. We conclude that while today Croatian competition rules are aligned with the EU rules and the institutional framework is functional, two important questions remain: first, how to integrate the Competition Agency as an independent administrative body into the Croatian legal order; and second, are the substantive rules implemented by through the application of SAA, which is legitimately applicable to purely domestic cases.

Both issues could appear to be of a purely theoretical value, as Croatian obligations towards the EU seem to have overpassed any national considerations so long as the implemented substantive, procedural, and institutional regime is operative. However, as Professor Smerdel, one of Croatian's constitutional founding fathers stated recently, uncritical and eager implementation of foreign rules might in the long run, cause serious 'collateral damage to the protection of constitutional rights in proceedings before independent agencies',[2] and thus it seems appropriate to address the above mentioned issues.

2. BACKGROUND

When approaching the issue of legal harmonisation in the context of the EU, one has to touch upon the effects of the process of legal transplantation. The term

---

2 B. Smerdel, 'Platypus reconsidered: How to Integrate Independent Regulators into the Croatian Constitutional Order', in Nada Bodiroga-Vukobrat and others (eds.), *Regulatory Agencies in the Tension Between Law and Economics*, Verlag Dr. Kovač, Hamburg, 2012, 14.

"legal transplantation" denotes efforts to transmit legal norms and institutions from one setting to another'[3] and there is nothing exceptional about it.[4] Legal transplants are not 'isolated occurrences, despite the economic, social, political, and cultural barriers that separate the world's legal systems'.[5] Even though these differences tend to influence strongly the success of legal transplants in host countries, the latter remain to be a wide spread means of legal change.

While some authors tend to believe that legal transplants are impossible 'on the basis of the assumption that law as a social construct cannot remain the same, once it is dislocated',[6] others believe that they are possible through the process of 'cultural adaptation as the necessary counterpart of the transplantation process'.[7]

In that light, recently Bömer stated 'There are no foreign laws or institutions that can be copied, borrowed, or transplanted because every copy, transplant, or borrowing is the reading of an original text that becomes a completely new and original text when read and interpreted by the reader'.[8]

Although generally true, this contention can be refuted in the context of the EU. In fact, this is not an imminent problem in the EU harmonisation process

---

3 Tel Aviv University, The Buchmann Faculty of Law, 'Histories of legal transplantations: Introduction' (2009) 10 Theo Inq L. 299, 299.

4 It is beyond this paper to give a detailed overview of the theories of legal transplants, for more see eg O. Kahn-Freund, 'On Use And Misuse Of Comparative Law' (1974) 37 Mod. L. Rev. 1; A. Watson, *Legal transplants: An Approach to Comparative Law* (2nd edn., University of Georgia Press 1993); P.H. Brietzke, 'Designing the Legal Frameworks for Markets in Eastern Europe' (1994) 7 Transnat'l Law 35; U. Mattei, 'Efficiency in Legal Transplants: An Essay in Comparative Law and Economics' (1994) 4 Int'l Rev. L. & Econ. 3; G. Ajani, 'By Chance And Prestige: Legal Transplants In Russia And Eastern Europe' (1995) 43 Am. J. Comp. L. 93; L Lessig, 'Understanding Changed Readings: Fidelity And Theory' (1995) 47 Stan. L. R. 395; LA Mistelis, 'Regulatory Aspects: Globalization, Harmonization, Legal Transplants, And Law Reform – Some Fundamental Observations' (2000) 34 Int'l Law 1055; PG Monateri, 'The Weak Law: Contaminations and Legal Cultures' (2003) 13 Transnat'l L. & Contemp. Probs. 575; D Berkowitz, K Pistor, JF Richard, 'The Transplant Effect' (2003) 51 Am. J. Comp. L. 163; P Legrand, 'Comparative Legal studies and the Matter of Authenticity' (2006) 1 J. Comp. L. 365; M Brömer, 'The Use Of Foreign Law As Strategy To Build Constitutional And Democratic Authority' (2008) 77 Rev. Jur. U.P.R. 411; ER Saldarriaga, 'Comments on Panel III Hybrid cultures: borrowings and impositions' (2008) 77 Rev. Jur. U.P.R. 433; M Graziadei, 'Legal Transplants And The Frontiers Of Legal Knowledge' (2009)10 Theo Inq L 723; A Likhovski, 'Argonauts of eastern Mediterranean: Legal transplants and Signaling' (2009) 10 Theo Inq L 619.

5 M. Graziadei, 'Legal Transplants And The Frontiers Of Legal Knowledge' (2009) 10 Theo Inq L723, 723.

6 Ibid at 728 citing P. Legrand, 'The Impossibility Of Legal Transplants' (1997) 4 Maast J Eur & Comp L. 111.

7 Ibid at 728 citing D. Nelken and J. Feest (eds), *Adapting Legal Culture* (Hart Publishing 2001).

8 M Brömer, 'The Use Of Foreign Law As Strategy To Build Constitutional And Democratic Authority'(2008) 77 Rev. Jur. U.P.R. 411 as reproduced by ER Saldarriaga, 'Comments of Panel III Hybrid Legal cultures: Borrowings and impositions' (2008) 77 Rev. Jur. U.P.R. 433, 436.

since the EU requires not only the import of basic rules, but all interpretative tools developed by the EU institutions as well. This is a very special feature of the EU harmonisation process as it recognises the importance of interpretation in achieving full convergence. However, the translation effect still plays an important role in achieving the much desired blue print effect of the imported EU rules. This issue goes beyond the accession countries, as it affects all member states of the EU. If one accepts the proposition of the impossibility of linguistic universalism, than this issue will remain one of the most important obstacles to the EU harmonisation project, and thus deserves further analysis, which is beyond the scope of this paper.

Irrespectively of how one theoretically approaches the issue of legal transplants, as inherently linked to the society in which they operate,[9] or completely independent from it,[10] affected substantially by the translation process or not, what can be traced as a common ground is that there are no blue print transfers of rules or institutions across countries. This is an important conclusion in light of the EU harmonisation process, as it aspires to achieve a blue print effect of its rules in the accession countries.

In modern history, the process of legal borrowings and impositions can be observed in Central and Eastern European countries during their transition from centralised to market economies. The scope of legal reforms during this period has been linked to a legislative tornado with mixed results,[11] particularly in countries aspiring to join the EU.

Kovacic rightly observed that 'to create a legal infrastructure for a market economy, a formerly communist or socialist country may need to adopt a wide array of new laws, including measures governing administrative practice and procedure, banking, bankruptcy, business associations, contracts, customs, environmental protection, insurance, intellectual property, judicial reform, labour, privatisation, product liability, property, securities, taxation, and trade'.[12] However, competition policy, perceived to be the cornerstone of market economy, was one of the most important policies to be implemented.

Most accession countries implemented some form of competition legislation and institutional framework for its application even before the formal beginning of the accession process. These antimonopoly laws were designed to create, develop, and protect competition during the transition from a socialist to a

9 O. Kahn-Freund, 'On Use And Misuse Of Comparative Law' (1974) 37 Mod. L. Rev. 1.

10 A. Watson, *Legal transplants: An Approach to Comparative Law* (2nd edn., University of Georgia Press 1993).

11 D Berkowitz, K Pistor, JF Richard, 'The Transplant Effect' (2003) 51 Am. J. Comp. L. 163, 164.

12 WE Kovacic, 'Designing and Implementing Competition and Consumer Protection Reforms in Transitional Economies: Perspectives from Mongolia, Nepal, Ukraine and Zimbabwe' (1994–1995) 44 DePaul L. Rev. 1197, 1213.

market-based economy.[13] However, it was not long before such rules had to be changed, as the EU required them to apply the totality of EC competition rules (including all the interpretative tools developed by EU institutions) in all cases which would affect trade between the respective country and the EU.[14] This is how the massive importation of EU competition rules into national legal systems commenced.

It was a beneficial process, as it allowed former central oriented economies to quickly overhaul their somewhat rudimental, statutory laws, regulating the new market economy. However, there was little room for tailoring imported rules to specific needs.[15]

Competition policy was soon designed without accounting for initial conditions that will determine the effects of competition law enforcement.[16] The rapid development of laws, the extensiveness and sophistication of imported rules were so overwhelming that national legislators instead of 'reinventing the wheel' for national purposes, relied on EU competition rules in a purely domestic context, achieving questionable results in terms of the economic development. At least that was the case for Croatia. Furthermore, such legislative approaches raised serious constitutional concerns in terms of direct application of foreign rules to purely domestic cases.

Additional issues stemmed from the inefficiency of the new enforcers, institutions whose fundamental prerequisite was to be their independence. '[A]vailable evidence from formerly socialist countries suggests that the enforcement of transplanted law is often problematic. Weak legal institutions have been singled out as the key impediment to future growth and development in these countries'.[17] It comes as no surprise that the latter has dramatically affected the efficiency of imported competition rules in Croatia as well.

Most of the scholarship analyses the viability of the transplantation process from the point of view of social, cultural and linguistic influence on what has

---

13 C. Brezinski, 'Competition And Antitrust Law In Central Europe: Poland, The Czech Republic, Slovakia, And Hungary' (1993–1994) 15 Mich. J. Int'l L. 1129, 1132.

14 Europe Agreements expressly require that any practices contrary to the competition rules be 'assessed on the basis of criteria arising from the application of the EC rules of the EC Treaty.'

15 'With respect to the CEECs, the European Union chose a course of unilateralist harmonization. This route had two serious downsides: (1) the CEECs lost their freedom to choose and tailor competition law to their needs; and (2) parts of EC competition law are probably not optimal for CEEC needs. The choice had one major advantage; the nations have developed a much greater commitment to competition policy than would probably otherwise have been the case'. EM. Fox, 'The Central European Nations and the EU Waiting Room--Why Must the Central European Nations Adopt the Competition Law of The European Union?' (1997–1998) 23 Brook. J. Int'l L. 351, 363.

16 On the importance of initial conditions for the efficiency of enforcement see W.E. Kovacic, 'Institutional Foundations for Economic Legal Reform in Transition Economies: the Case of Competition Policy and Antitrust Enforcement' (2001) 77 Chi.-Kent L. Rev. 265, 309.

17 D. Berkowitz, J.F. Richard, K. Pistor, 'Economic Development, Legality, And The Transplant Effect' (2003) 47 Eur. Econ. Rev. 1, 2, available at http://siteresources.worldbank.org/INTLAWJUSTINST/Resources/pistor-transplants.pdf.

been imported. Not contesting the importance of such influences, the authors try to put forward an additional dimension to the debate, namely the influence of the receiving legal order, meaning the totality of existing laws, regulations, and institutions of the effectiveness of imported rules.

In this respect, Croatia may serve as a good example. What can be observed in Croatia is a decade of institutional and substantive law development, manifested by the intricate interplay between the new rules and institutions and the existing ones, proving that each legal order operates as a single whole. Whatever is imported – be it rules, legal concepts or institutions – it cannot function on its own. It necessarily operates within a predetermined structure of existing regulations and institutions, which in turn affects substantively the success of the transplantation and more often than not, raises constitutional concerns.

3. THE EARLY DEVELOPMENT OF THE INSTITUTIONAL SETTING

Free market competition became a constitutional category in Croatia with the very first version of the Croatian Constitution in 1990.[18] However, it was only in 1995 that the first set of rules in the area of competition law was adopted.

In most transitional countries competition rules were adopted somewhere between 1990 and 1993. The reason for such a late enactment of competition regulation in Croatia is twofold: on one hand the legislator was of the opinion that competition rules ought to be the 'crown' of the all economic legislation, and thus should be the last enacted, and on the other hand there were technical problems most notably in the definition of the term 'concentration' as it required a previous definition of basic terms in the Company's Act.[19]

Although the first competition Act in Croatia was adopted in 1995, its enforcement began in 1997 with the appointment of the first director of the Croatian Competition Agency. The enactment of the earliest Competition Act and the establishment of the Agency were unrelated to the EU accession process which started only in 2001 with the conclusion of the Stabilisation and Association Agreement between Croatia and the EU.

The Act of 1995 already included basic EU rules, namely former Articles 81 and 82 of the TEC (now articles 101 and 102 of the TFEU), whereas the rest of the Act combined solutions recognised by German and French competition

---

18 Article 49 (1) and (2) of the Constitution of the Republic of Croatia, Narodne novine 41/2001 reads as follows: 'Free enterprise and free markets shall form the foundation of the economic system of the Republic of Croatia. The state shall ensure all entrepreneurs equal legal status on the market. The abuse of monopolies, as defined by law, shall be forbidden.'

19 M. Cerovac, 'Novi Zakon o zaštiti tržišnog natjecanja' (2003) 9 Hrvatska pravna revija, 44.

laws.[20] This was part of a voluntary convergence initiated as a preparation for the formal accession process to the EU.[21]

Since the regulatory purpose of the EU and Croatian rules were aligned, upgrading substantive legal rules did not create major problems. In time, the domestic lawmaker expanded substantively the national body of law by borrowing EU legislative solutions. The problem, however, was the institutional framework.

'Many modern law reform programs, including competition policy projects, have tended to begin by creating the conceptually ideal legal regime on the assumption that political and administrative constraints that will influence the application of the law can be resolved later'.[22] Croatia is no exception to this trend. It appears that Croatia introduced elaborated substantive rules before it had created functional ground work for their application. However, institutional limitations must not be disregarded in the process of harmonisation of substantive rules,[23] as competition systems have come to realise 'a body of competition law is only as good as the institutions entrusted with their implementation.'[24] 'In fact, empirical analysis suggests that there is little correlation between the level of legal protection afforded by statutes on one hand and measures for the effectiveness of legal institutions on the other'.[25]

PROBLEMS WITH THE INDEPENDENCE OF THE COMPETITION AGENCY'S AND LIMITATION OF ITS POWERS

Making a formal decision on the establishment of the Competition Agency through the 1995 Competition Act did not suffice for its proper functioning. The Agency was understaffed and its composition did not guarantee its declared independence.

20 Ibid.

21 More on effects of voluntary harmonization see D. Evans, 'Voluntary Harmonisation In Integration Between The European Community And Eastern Europe' (1997) 22 (3) EL Rev. 201–220.

22 W.E. Kovacic, 'Institutional Foundations for Economic Legal Reform in Transition Economies: the Case of Competition Policy and Antitrust Enforcement' (2001) 77 Chi.-Kent L. Rev. 265, 315.

23 M.S. Gal, 'When the Going Gets Tight: Institutional Solutions When Antitrust Enforcement Resources Are Scarse'(2010) 41 Loy. U. Chi. L. J. 417, 439.

24 W.E. Kovacic; D. Eversley, An Assessment Of Institutional Machinery: Methods Used In Competition Agencies And What Worked For Them International Competition Network, Competition Policy Implementation Working Group, Subgroup 2 on Experiences on Younger Agencies, available at <www.internationalcompetitionnetwork.org> accessed 18 June 2013.

25 D. Berkowitz, K. Pistor, J.F. Richard, 'The Transplant Effect' (2003) 51 Am. J. Comp. L. 163, 164.

The 1995 Act, provided that the only body of the Agency is to be the Director. The responsible decision-making body was the 'Advisory board' whose members were elected from the recognised specialists in the area. Members of the advisory board, who were not employees of the Agency, were elected by the government on the proposal of the Director of the Agency for a mandate of 4 years and were remunerated for their work. Such composition was prone to political influences through the appointment procedure and influences of market stakeholders who tried to get access to the decision making body or influence the decision making process though lobbying.

Additional issues stemmed from the fact that, the 1995 Act had a major lack of procedural rules. For that reason, the Agency had to act according to the rules of the General Administrative Procedure Act.[26] These rules proved to be outdated and much too rigid for sophisticated competition cases and the required expedience of the Agency's decision-making process.[27]

An additional problem was posed by the existence of article 266 of the same General Administrative Procedure Act, which read as follows:

> An enforceable order may be revoked if necessary to avert any serious and immediate danger to the life and health of people, public safety, public peace and order or public morals, *or to eliminate any economic disturbances*, if the said cannot be successfully averted or eliminated by other means that would impinge upon the acquired rights to a lesser extent. An order may be partially revoked, to the extent necessary to avert danger or protect the said general public interests.[28]

The authority to make such decision rested with the Government only in cases where there was no other competent body within the state administration.[29] Being an agency independent from the state administration, there was no supervising body, and thus because of art. 264 of the General Administrative Procedure Act, such authority was given to the Government.[30]

Accordingly, in exceptional circumstances, the Government of the Republic of Croatia had the authority to abolish administrative decisions including the decisions rendered by the Croatian Competition authority.

---

26 Zakon o općem upravnom postupku, Narodne novine 53/92, 103/96.

27 M. Cerovac, 'Novi Zakon o zaštiti tržišnog natjecanja' (2003) 9 Hrvatska pravna revija, 44.

28 General Administrative Procedure Act, art 266 (emphasis added).

29 Article 266 (2) read: 'If an order was adopted by a first-instance agency, the order may be revoked by the first-instance agency itself, within the meaning of §(1) of this article, and if such agency does not do that, by a second-instance agency. If the second-instance agency does not exist, the order shall be revoked by the ministry or other republican administrative agency having jurisdiction over the administrative matter in controversy. If a second-instance agency with jurisdiction cannot be determined, article 264, §(1) of this Act shall be applied.'

30 Article 264 (1) read: '[...] If the agency competent for a specific administrative matter cannot be determined or if the second-instance order was adopted by the ministry or any other republican state administrative agency, the Government of the Republic of Croatia is competent to annul or revoke the order.'

Finally, one of the biggest enforcement problems proved to be the limitation of the Competition Agency's powers to sanction undertakings in the case of finding competition law infringements.[31] This problem continued to persist until the enactment of the current Competition Act of 2010. A detailed explanation of this problem is given within the next chapter.

4. COMPETITION ACT 2003

The first major overhaul of the competition legislation, accompanied by a large number of adjoining regulations on specific issues, was finished in 2003 when the new Competition Act came into force. This Act was the direct result of the obligations undertaken by the Stabilisation and Association Agreement.

Recognising deficiencies of the institutional framework, the new Competition Act improved substantially the rules on the composition and authorities of the Competition Agency. The managing body became the five-member Competition Council, one of which is the President. Likewise, rules regarding the independence and expertise of the Council members, as well as new procedural rules, better adapted to the Agency's decision-making process, were welcomed.

Article 31 stated that members of the Competition Council may be appointed provided that they meet the criteria of being a citizen of the Republic of Croatia who holds a university degree, has ten years of work experience in the professional field concerned, i.e. having specific knowledge in the field of competition law, company law, commercial law, finances and accountancy, microeconomics and other related areas of law and economics. Moreover, the President and the members of the Council may not be state officials, persons who perform duties in any administrative body of a political party, members of supervisory boards and executive bodies of undertakings, or members in any kind of associations of legal or natural persons, which could lead to a conflict of interest.

However, two aspects remained unchanged – article 266 of the General Administrative Procedure Act, which was found to be a major threat to the Agency's independence,[32] and the lack of the Agency's authority to impose fines for breaches of competition law.

31 It appears that the Croatian problem regarding sanctioning was an isolated case in Europe. To the best of our knowledge other European countries found competition law infringements to be either criminal offences or offences *sui generis*, enabling the competent bodies to vest the independent competition agency with the authority to sanction undertakings upon finding competition law infringement. See Croatian preparatory notes of the Competition Act (Prijedlog Zakona o zaštiti tržišnog natjecanja, s konačnim prijedlogom zakona), available at https://infodok.sabor.hr>, accessed 18 June 2013.

32 Commission, Screening Report Croatia 2006 COM (2006), ch 8 states: 'The Competition Act of 2003 requires further alignment. In addition to the need for general fine-tuning of the provisions, a single competition regime still needs to be created to ensure that the

4.1. ARTICLE 266 OF THE GENERAL ADMINISTRATION PROCEDURE ACT

While the issue of the Agency's authority could have been solved by the Competition Act, changing Article 266 required changes to the General Administrative Procedure Act.

However, at the time there was no political drive to change an act that covered the procedures of all administrative bodies. If this was to be undertaken, it would have been done within a general reform of the administrative procedure, article 266 being of minor importance in that regard.

Furthermore, the named rule was not about controlling the Agency's decisions. In fact, the General Administrative Procedure Act, containing the disputed rule, was enacted prior to the establishment of the Agency and the enactment of the first Competition Act. In this light, its purpose was not to institute a governmental control over the Agency, thereby hampering its independence; rather it was aimed at protecting the general public from administrative decisions which might endanger their safety. This is evident in the fact that article 266 has actually never been invoked against the decisions of the Agency.

The abstract normative threat to the independence of the Agency may be seen as a collateral downside of the transplantation process. Declaring the independence of the Agency from any kind of political control cannot be done by way of a specialised legislation. The latter does not suffice, because the nature of law is such that no legislation, no matter how specific, exists in a legal vacuum. A complex interaction of a variety of laws always comes into play. This is an important issue when contemplating the importation of foreign rules.

When the situation was optimal, the reform of general administrative procedure took place. The Croatian Parliament enacted the new General Administrative Procedure Act[33] which came into force in 2010, thereby abolishing the contested rule 266.[34]

The above raised considerations had to conclude that enacting specific, foreign originating laws could not be an isolated occurrence, i.e. an individual act of enactment; instead it requires an adaptation of all related legislation. With this in mind, transplantation account for a long process involving the growth of the entire legal order. New ideas and rules can grow only as fast as the legal order itself progresses. Before the two are synchronised, their dichotomy will burden the enforcement process.

Competition Act applies to all sectors, particularly banking and telecommunications. As regards article 226 of the General Administrative Procedures Act, the Government's power to overturn decisions has to cease to be applied altogether.'

33 Zakon o općem upravnom postupku, Narodne novine 47/09.

34 The idea behind the former 266 rule can be traced in the new General Administrative Procedure act as well, however, not in cases of economic disturbances.

4.2. LIMITATION OF SANCTIONING POWERS OF THE COMPETITION AGENCY – INVOLVEMENT OF THE MISDEMEANOUR COURTS

A somewhat similar situation can be found in what was then the lack of the Competition Agency's power to sanction undertakings for competition law infringements. Such authority rested with misdemeanour courts, as breaches of competition rules were characterised as misdemeanour offences by the Competition Act.

In Croatia, misdemeanour offences are subject to a special act, the Misdemeanour Act,[35] which proscribes procedures and competent bodies for handling such cases. Under the Misdemeanour Act, only misdemeanour courts and state administrative bodies are competent in deciding on such offences.

In fact, article 78 of the named Act proscribed that the fine or other sanctions for a misdemeanour offence can impose on offenders only by the competent misdemeanour court and the competent state administration body conducting the misdemeanour proceeding according to the Misdemeanour Act. However, the Competition Agency was established as a legal person with public authorities entirely independent from the state administration and therefore it did not fit into the classical state administration system.[36] Consequently, it could not have been vested with the right to conduct misdemeanour procedure and to impose the legally proscribed sanctions.

It is unclear why the Croatian lawmaker decided to limit the Agency's powers to such an extent. It seems possible that this was the result of the unawareness of practical implications of such limitation or the novelty of independent agencies as legal subjects in the Croatian public sector.[37]

In fact, this previously unknown institutional concept in Croatia was, and remains to be uncovered by the Constitution, not provided for with any systemic statute nor regulated by any general law.[38] Moreover, one cannot construct a valid legal argument as to why the Agency did not have such a crucial power for the efficient enforcement of competition rules for so many years, as there would have been no legal restrictions in that regard were the violations of competition rules characterised as offences *sui generis*.

It appears to be a rather unfortunate result of an *impromptu* implementation of foreign rules and institutions originating from different social and legal surroundings, into the domestic legal order.

---

35 Zakon o prekršajima, Narodne novine 88/02.

36 S. Barić, D. Đerđa, 'Issues Related to the Statutory Regime of Regulatory Agencies in the Republic of Croatia', in N. Bodiroga-Vukobrat and others (eds), *Regulatory Agencies In The Tension Between Law And Economics*, (Verlag Dr. Kovač, Hamburg, 2012), 47.

37 Ibid 45.

38 Ibid.

Regrettably, since 1991, a number of independent and regulatory institutions were established on an *ad hoc* basis, without considering the overall functioning of the existing legal order.[39] When it comes to the Competition Agency in particular, it was not taken into account that restricting its powers of enforcement would inevitably call for the involvement of another institution.

As emphasised, each legal order operates as a single entity, whereas it is to be expected that new institutions, rules, and procedures will, to a certain extent, become intertwined with the existing ones. However, it appears that the Croatian lawmaker was unaware to what degree such entanglement would hamper the overall enforcement of competition rules and the independence of the Agency.

The 2003 Competition Act, did not allow for appeals against the Agency's decisions. Instead, the injured party could have initiated an administrative dispute before the Administrative Court of the Republic of Croatia.[40] This was supposed to be the only judicial control over the Agency's decisions.

However, this control had one major legal drawback – the Administrative court was not a full jurisdiction court and, accordingly, had stern restraints on the fact-finding procedure and power to decide on the merits of the case. This was allowed only in exceptional circumstances.

Act on Administrative Disputes, Article 39 (1) proscribed the following: 'The court shall decide the dispute, as a rule, on the basis of the facts established in the administrative proceedings (…)'.[41]

The powers to determine independently the facts of cases brought before it and conduct an oral hearing for that purposes, was restricted to the following exceptional circumstances:

> "If the annulment of the challenged administrative act and a reopening of proceedings before the competent body, would cause the plaintiff harm which would be difficult to rectify, or if on the basis of public documents or other evidence in the case files it is clear that the facts of the case differ from those established in the administrative proceedings, or if in the same dispute an administrative act has already been annulled, and the competent body did not act completely in accordance

39 Since 1991 a number of bodies have been established in Croatia such as the Agency for Supervision of Pension Funds and Insurance Companies, The Croatian Food Agency, The Croatian Agency for Small Businesses, The Agency for Coastal Liner Shipping, The Croatian Compulsory Oil Stock Agency, The Agency for Real Estates Transactions and Intermediation, The Environment Agency, The Education and Teacher Training Agency, The Croatian Accreditation Agency, The Agency for Vocational Education, The Agency for Science and Higher Education, and The Agency for Adult Education.

40 The Administrative Court of the Republic of Croatia was established in 1977.

41 Zakon o upravnim sporovima, Narodne novine 53/91, 9/92, 77/92, article 39 (1).

> with the judgement, the court may itself establish the facts of the case and render a judgement, or a ruling on the basis of the facts established in this way.[42]
> When the court finds that a contested administrative deed has to be annulled, it may adjudicate on the administrative matter by a judgement if the nature of things allows and if the information from the procedure provides a reliable basis. Such judgement replaces the annulled deed in all respects."[43]

Although the wording of the latter article does not suggest that deciding on the merits of the case should be allowed only in exceptional circumstances under which the independent fact-finding procedure is allowed, this is how the judges and academics interpreted this provision. This is evident by the fact that, over the last two decades there have been almost no judgements which adjudicated the administrative matter.[44]

Thus, as a rule, in cases where legal mistakes were found, the Administrative Court annulled the reviewed decision and returned the case back to the competent administrative body. Since the establishment of the Agency and commencement of its proceedings, the Administrative Court has never decided on the merits of a competition case brought before it, hence its reviewing powers and the manner in which they were exercised were exceedingly narrow.

The right to judicial control did not postpone the determination and execution of the appropriate legal sanction. Consequently, upon finding competition law infringement, the Agency (not having the power to impose fines itself) regularly made a claim to the competent misdemeanour court to start the minor offence proceedings against the undertaking concerned and the responsible person of the respective undertaking.

The rules of misdemeanour procedure are of inquisitorial nature, meaning that the misdemeanour courts have the authority to once again establish the very act of violation of competition rules before proclaiming a legal fine. Misdemeanour courts were thus *de facto* empowered to act as inexperienced and non-expert second instance of unintended judicial control over the legality of the Agency's decisions.

In addition, competition law judgments rendered by the misdemeanour courts were subject to appeal before the High Misdemeanour Court. Consequently, there was an additional instance of judicial control over the Agency's decisions.

---

42 Ibid, art 39 (2).

43 Ibid, art 42 (3).

44 See P. Krijan, *Komentar Zakona o upravnim sporovima sa sudskom praksom* (Informator 2001), 195.

Ironically, misdemeanour courts, which were only supposed to serve the practical function of imposing legal fines, had the power to decide the merits of the case. As a consequence, their powers to control the Agency's decision were much wider than the powers of the Administrative Court – the only court originally meant to act as the Agency's controller. This was the result of a complex institutional interplay and the interaction of laws and procedures applied by the institutions involved. This interaction made quite a mess in resolving competition law cases, while undermining the independence of the Agency.

In practice, the misdemeanour courts did not exercise their powers to the full extent, mostly because misdemeanour judges were quite reluctant to enter into specific and expert arguments, and in most cases they stayed proceedings until the Administrative Court made a ruling on the Agency's decision, proclaiming it to be a preliminary point of law.[45] The result was that in some cases, by the time such decisions became legally valid, the statute of limitations would expire and no fine could have been imposed, anyway. In cases in which they actually did fine the responsible undertakings, such fines were so low that they did not correspond to the degree of infringement nor did such fines deter the undertakings from similar behaviours in the future.

In fact, Misdemeanour courts were for this purpose lavishly applying the general rule of criminal law on immunity from fines and the reduction of fines, and thereby perversely distorting the efficient prosecution of undertakings that breach competition rules.[46] The system was inefficient to such a degree that undertakings could have actually weighted the costs of a possible fine against potential profits arising from violations of competition rules.

This is evident from the numbers. Between 2004 and 2008, the Agency found over a hundred infringements of competition law, most of them being hard-core infringements for which the Competition Act envisages fines of up to 10% of the overall yearly turnover, and yet in the same period misdemeanour courts imposed overall fines of only 1 mil. HRK (approximately 130.000 EUR).[47] Neither capacity building of the Competition agency, nor improvement of substantive rules could have ever overcome such a huge enforcement obstacle. Drastic changes of law were required.

45 Croatian Parliament, Croatian Preparatory Notes of the Competition Act (Prijedlog zakona zaštiti tržišnog natjecanja, s konačnim prijedlogom zakona), available at <https://infodok.sabor.hr>, accessed 18 June 2013.

46 D. Mlikotin Tomić, J. Pecotić Kaufman, 'Evolution of Cartel Practice in Croatia', available at <http://bib.irb.hr/datoteka/390283.evolution_of_cartel_practice_in_Croatia.pdf>, accessed 18 June 2013, 2.

47 Croatian Parliament, Croatian preparatory notes of the Competition Act, (Prijedlog zakona zaštiti tržišnog natjecanja, s konačnim prijedlogom zakona), available at <https://infodok.sabor.hr>, accessed 18 June 2013.

5. NEW INSTITUTIONAL SETTING AND OPEN ISSUES

In 2010 the new Competition Act came into force.[48] This latest revision of competition rules brought about major changes, in particular the introduction of the leniency programme and the power of the Competition Agency to directly fine undertakings for breaches of competition rules.

Misdemeanour Courts are thus no longer involved in the enforcement process. This was a completely novel concept in the Croatian legal order. The Competition Agency is the only institution outside the state administration system that has such powers (both to fine and waive fines *via* misdemeanour procedure).

This has been achieved by treating competition law violations as offences *sui generis* in the new Competition Act, bypassing the jurisdictional provisions of the Misdemeanour Act, while simultaneously granting the Agency the right to conduct the procedure as proscribed by the Misdemeanour Act.[49]

As controversial as it may sound, this was the only means of enabling the Agency to acquiring new enforcement power without distorting the rules on the delegation of powers. However, the new Competition Act has precautionary introduced a rule under which the initiation of the administrative dispute against a decision of the Agency postpones the execution of the fine imposed by it until the judgement of the competent administrative court becomes legally valid. This is an exception to the general rule providing that a complaint does not prevent the enforcement of an administrative deed against which was submitted.[50]

At the moment, there is no other Croatian act proscribing such an effect of a complaint upon the execution of an individual decision rendered by public bodies.[51] Widening the powers of the Agency on one side, while on the other, the lawmaker has once again opted for a rule that might hinder the full efficiency of competition law enforcement.

Furthermore, as of January 2012 a new Act on Administrative Disputes is in force.[52] The new law introduced changes that may directly affect the quality of the judicial control over Agency's decisions.

Instead of a single Administrative Court of the Republic of Croatia, there are now 4 administrative courts having different territorial jurisdiction, each being a full jurisdiction court. In other words, administrative courts are now obliged to

48 Zakon o zaštiti tržišnog natjecanja, Narodne novine 79/09.
49 To the best of our knowledge these are the only *sui generis* offences in Croatia.
50 Act on Administrative Disputes 53/91, 9/92, 77/92, art 26.
51 D. Đerđa, M. Šikić, *Komentar zakona o upravnim sporovima* (Novi Informator 2012) 175.
52 Zakon o upravnim sporovima, Narodne novine 20/2010.

decide on the merits of the case based on an independent fact-finding procedure, whenever the filing party makes such a requirement.[53]

Furthermore, administrative disputes are no longer one-instance proceedings. Judgements rendered by misdemeanour courts can be appealed to the newly established High Administrative Court of the Republic of Croatia. The new organisational structure and reviewing powers have the potential of meaningfully improving the judicial control over the Agency's decisions. However, it is yet to be seen as to whether these changes will indeed render the enforcement of competition rules substantially more efficient.

The newly acquired powers of the administrative courts bring about a lot of responsibility, whereas there should be no deficiency of expert human resources. Nevertheless, at the moment administrative courts do not possess a sufficient number of qualified judges to scrutinise and overturn the decisions of the Agency.

It is important to stress that the right and obligation of administrative judges to decide on merits of a case is not limited to competition cases. Instead, it extends to all areas of administrative procedure. This means that the judges will have to switch from one specialised area to another. One can hardly expect the judges to be proficient in all areas. The lack of specific knowledge will inevitably affect the quality of judicial control. It would have been much wiser had the legislator decided to form specialised departments for particular issues, especially for interdisciplinary areas such as competition law. And yet it did not opt for such an organisational structure. The operation of legal order, although this time through some other types of considerations seems to have once again endangered the effectiveness of enforcement.

Furthermore, the Agency is financed through the state budget, which is subject to deep financial constraints. The most evoked political motto over the past 5 years has been the 'tightening of the belt'. The state is under an imperative to dramatically cut its expenses. This in turn implies no increase of funds for the Competition Agency.

Financial resources are not sufficient to meet the burden of proof required by EU rules. The latter point is not to be disregarded, as in such circumstances, the competent bodies may either pursue fewer cases, or take the risk of misapplying imported rules and hence endanger the process of transplantation or even worse, render erroneous decisions which would compromise the very essence of the competition policy.

The influence of scarce enforcement resources (both financial and human) on optimal institutional design has been recently researched by Gal, who suggested

53 Article 31 of the new Act on Administrative Disputes proscribes that the court may decide only within the limits of the claim.

that instead of tailoring institutional structures to ready-made rules, for small and developing countries, it might be wiser to do the opposite, i.e. to adjust substantive rules to fit the institutional endowment restrictions.[54]

As sound as this suggestion might be, once the process of creating substantive rules has been finished, it is difficult, though not impossible, to undertake this process. One important move in that direction can be found in the new Croatian rule on merger notifications.

The new Competition Act imposes the notification obligation to merging parties who reach a certain turnover threshold, but only where at least one of the parties has its seat and/or subsidiary in the Republic of Croatia.[55] The latter requirement might reduce the costs of merger reviews, as there will be far less cases of merger notifications. Consequently, the existing resources can be redirected towards more serious competition law concerns, particularly cartel investigations.

In this respect much more could have been done in the national competition law context. Croatia has never been forced to blueprint EU laws in the entirely national context. And yet, this is the result of a free-ride approach to competition law the consequences of which might transpire in the near future.

Finally, even if all of the above considerations are successfully overcome, the Competition Agency has to outlast the pressures of constitutionalists claiming that independent and, in particular, regulatory agencies do not fit our constitutional order, arguing that wide-ranged authorities attributed to agencies in general make them incoherent with the classical model of power separation pursuant to the Croatian constitution.[56]

This is an on-going debate[57] calling for a general regulation of independent and regulatory agencies with precise rules governing their structure and powers.

---

54 M.S. Gal, 'When the Going Gets Tight: Institutional Solutions When Antitrust Enforcement Resources Are Scarse' (2010) 41 Loy. U. Chi. L. J. 417, 439.

55 Competition Act 2009, art 17.

56 S. Barić, D. Đerđa, *Komentar zakona o upravnim sporovima* (Novi Informator 2012) 347.

57 See eg B. Smerdel, 'Regulatorne agencije' (2006) Informator 1, 1–3; S. Ivanda, 'Agencija kao novi ustrojbeni oblici pravnih osoba u djelatnostima javnog sektora' [2007] Pravni vjesnik 195, 195–215; I. Koprić, A. Musa, V. Đulabić, 'Europski standardi regulacije službi of općeg interesa: kvazi nezavisna regulacijska tijela u izgradnji modernog kapitalizma' [2008] Hrvatska i komparativna javna uprava, 647, 647–688; A. Musa, 'Regulacija i neovisna regulatorna tijela u suvremenom društvu' [2008] Država i uprava, 65, 65–80; F. Staničić, 'Pravna narav regulatornih agencija u RH' [2010] Pravo u gospodarstvu 1341; S. Barić, D. Đerđa, 'Zakonsko uređenje regulatornih agencija u RH' [2010] Informator No. 5908, 2, 2–8, J. Džinić, 'Regulacijska tijela i regulacija: neki problemi u pogledu (ne) donošenja uredbi za izvršenje zakona' [2011] Hrvatska i komparativna javna uprava, 651, 651–679; A. Musa, I. Koprić, 'What Kind Of Agencification In Croatia? Trends And Future Directions' [2011] Transylvanian Review of Administrative Sciences, Special issue, 33, 33–53; S. Barić, D. Đerđa, 'Issues Related to the Statutory Regime of Regulatory Agencies in the Republic of Croatia', in N. Bodiroga-Vukobrat and others (eds), *Regulatory Agencies In The Tension Between Law And Economics* (Verlag Dr. Kovač 2012) 45–66; B. Smerdel, 'Platypus reconsidered: How to

However the authors deem that it is far too late for the enactment of such a general law, as it will be almost impossible to capture all types of agencies already established and functioning in Croatia in a structured and coherent manner. New rules bear a risk of destabilising the existent and fragile institutional structure and causing greater confusion.

Had this been done long ago, prior to the establishment of the first agency, most of the problems affecting their operation could have been avoided. This testifies to the inappropriateness of haste institutional transplantations and problems that follow in countries that have not sufficiently developed the existing legal order to be successful recipients.

6. DEVELOPMENT OF SUBSTANTIVE COMPETITION LAW RULES

When it comes to the transplantation of substantive competition law rules into the Croatian legal order, the situation was not as problematic as the one just described in the institutional context. Nevertheless, one issue marked the development process i.e. the legitimacy of the application of EU substantive competition rules and interpretative tools developed by EU institutions to purely domestic cases.

This is an issue about to be resolved, as Croatia will enter the EU, meaning the constitutional amendments providing for, *inter alia*, the duty to interpret national law in accordance with EU law will come into force.

In fact, in 2010, the Croatian Parliament adopted a major constitutional amendment envisaged to come into force on July 1, 2013, consisting of an entire chapter regulating the status of the European Union Law in the national legal order. New Chapter VIII entitled 'European Union' contains, *inter alia*, a provision (article 145) proscribing the following:

> (1) The exercise of the rights ensuing from the European Union *acquis communautaire* shall be made equal to the exercise of rights under Croatian Law; (2) All legal acts and decisions accepted by the Republic of Croatia in European Union institutions shall be applied in the Republic of Croatian in accordance with the European Union *acquis communautaire*; (3) Croatian courts shall protect subjective rights based on the European Union *acquis communautaire*; (4) Governmental

---

Integrate Independent Regulators into the Croatian Constitutional Order' in N. Bodiroga-Vukobrat and others (eds), *Regulatory Agencies in the Tension Between Law and Economics* (Verlag Dr. Kovač 2012) 11–24.

agencies, bodies of local and regional self-government and legal persons vested with public authority shall apply European Union law directly.

Still, it is interesting to look into the Croatian competition law development as it reiterates the proposition of transferring specific rules is not possible until the entire legal order is accommodated to accept the application of such rules.

Recently Professor Rodin advanced the opinion that article 145 (2) of the Croatian Constitution 'conceals the actual scope of the obligation which extends not only to the self-referential duty to apply EU law, but also *a duty to interpret and apply national law in accordance with it*.[58] Should indeed this interpretation be embraced by the Croatian courts, there would be no more constitutional concerns regarding the application of EU rules to purely domestic cases. At the moment, however, this continues to be an important legal consideration.

As anticipated, the insistent interference of the existing rules operating within the recipient legal order obstructs the proper functioning of legal transplants. Hence, the efficiency of integrated rules and ideas goes hand in hand with the development of the entire legal order. In the case of the transported substantive competition rules, the problems in Croatia originated from apparently conflicting exercise of rights and obligations arising out of the Stabilisation and Association Agreement and the Constitution of the Republic of Croatia.

The Stabilisation and Association Agreement between Croatia, the European Communities, and the Member States (further as SAA) marked the beginning of a contractual relationship between the parties by establishing 'an association', thus paving the way for the future *rapprochement*.[59]

The SAA was signed on 29 October, 2001 in Luxembourg. Just like the Europe Agreements, the SAA is a mixed agreement, which means that some of its provisions belonged to what was previously referred to as 'Community *acquis*' (first pillar), and some of its provisions belonged to the second and third pillar. This meant that the entry into force of the entire SAA was dependent on the ratification process which was expected to take some time (the SAA came into force in its entirety on February 1, 2005). The first pillar provisions of the SAA were singled out in another international agreement: the Interim Agreement on Trade and Other Trade Related Issues (IA) concluded on November 29, 2001 between Croatia and Community. The IA entered into force on March 1, 2002.

---

58 Constitution of the Republic of Croatia, Narodne novine 85/10 (consolidated text), art 145. See S. Rodin, 'Croatian Constitution And Internal Market Of The European Union', in *Collection Of Papers: Tackling Constitutional Challenges On The Road To The European Union: Perspectives From South-East European Accession Countries* (Zenith Association and Konrad Adenauer Stiftung, Skopje 2012), 26 – 47 (emphasis added).

59 Stabilisation and Association Agreement between the European Communities and their Member States, of the one part, and the Republic of Croatia, of the other part [2005] OJ L26/1 (SAA).

After the SAA came into force in 2005 the IA ceased to be applicable. In spite of all difficulties encountered, this has ultimately become a success story for Croatia which is due to joining the EU on 1 July, 2013.[60]

Very much like Europe Agreements, the SAA contains two types of provisions crucial for transplanting EU competition rules into the domestic legal system prior to the accession. The first one – article 69 – relates to 'the approximation of Croatia's existing legislation to that of the Community' with the obligation to 'endeavour to ensure that its existing laws and future legislation will be gradually made compatible with the Community *acquis*',[61] while the second one – article 70 – provides for the obligation of Croatian competition authorities to apply EU criteria in cross-border competition cases.[62]

On the grounds of article 69 SAA the first wave of 'approximation' of existing legislation took place with the enactment of a thoroughly revised Competition Act in 2003. Much of the black letter rules contained in this Act were Croatian translations of the EU basic competition law provisions.

The second wave of approximation took place in 2009, once again with the enactment of a new Competition Act, which introduced *inter alia*, direct fining powers of the Competition Agency, the leniency programme etc. Many provisions of the Competition Act are very similar if not identical to the EU rules. The same can be said for many Member States, most notably countries that joined the EU in 2004.[63]

There was nothing controversial about article 69 of the SAA. It served as a legal basis for the formal transplantation process of much needed substantive competition rules into the domestic legal order.

However, the second provision – article 70 SAA – calling for the application of interpretative instruments developed by the EU institutions, proved to have a stray influence on the way competition rules were to be enforced in Croatia. This provision instigated a voluntary and comprehensive acceptance of EU rules,[64] however, much too wide in the eyes of many as it raised constitutional concerns.

---

60 See Treaty on Accession of Croatia [2012] OJ L112/10. Croatia applied for EU membership on 21 February, 2003, and in June 2004 European Council confirmed its candidate country status. Accession negotiations were launched on 3 October, 2005.

61 SAA, art 69 para 1. See also SAA, art 69 para 2: 'This approximation will start on the date of signing of the Agreement, and will gradually extend to all the elements of the Community acquis referred to in this Agreement (...) In particular, at an early stage, it will focus on fundamental elements of the Internal Market *acquis* as well as on other trade-related areas, on the basis of a programme to be agreed between the Commission of the European Communities and Croatia (...)'.

62 SAA, art 70.

63 For example, Estonian antitrust laws are almost identical to the laws of the European Union, often even in their wording. See J. Thielert, M.P. Schinkel, 'Estonia's competition policy: a critical evaluation towards EU accession' (2003) 24(4) E.C.L.R. 165, 165–175.

64 The same process took place in CEECs under Europe Agreements. Many CEECs authors have expressed the positive attitude towards transplanting EU law concepts. See eg T Skoczny,

According to article 70 SAA restrictive agreements, abuses of dominant position and illegal state aids were pronounced as 'incompatible with the proper functioning of the Agreement',[65] provided 'they may affect trade between the Community and Croatia.' The cross-border effect criterion from Article 70 SAA is the same cross-border criterion as laid out in Articles 101 and 102 TFEU. This criterion is used to draw a line between application of EU law and the law of a Member State. If no cross-border effect can be established, domestic competition rules apply to a restrictive agreement or an abuse of dominant position.

Moreover, any conduct in breach of article 70 SAA was to be assessed on the basis of 'criteria arising from the application of the competition rules applicable in the Community, in particular from Articles 81, 82, 86, and 87 TEC and interpretative instruments adopted by the Community institutions'.[66] Clearly, the first leg of the provision listed three modes of illicit conduct by undertakings in the market, and the second leg of the provision enumerated the sources of applicable law.

Most likely, problems would have been less significant had the Croatian Competition Agency limited itself to the application of EU rules, criteria, and interpretative tools only to cases affecting trade between the EU and Croatia. That would have rendered a more faithful exercising of rights and obligations arising out of the SAA. However, this has not been the case.

The totality of EU competition law (including all criteria and interpretative tools) was given direct effect. In other words, EU competition law was and remains to be, regularly applied by the Croatian Competition Agency in its decision-making practice, i.e. whether it affects trade between the EU and Croatia or not. In almost each substantive decision of the Agency, relevant EU legislation or ECJ case law is invoked.[67]

However, there is nothing surprising about it. Initially, competition rules were as novel as the market economy, itself. There was no prior experience, case-law, guidelines, economic concepts were novel, there was no competition culture

---

'Harmonising Polish Antimonopoly Law with EC Competition Rules' (1997) 1 YB Polish EurS, 89, who notes that 'the voluntary acceptance of judicial standards of EC law would quicken the pace of modernisation of Polish competition law and raise the level of clarity of the competition rules, being an important part of „framework conditions" for economic activity'. See also J Sarai, 'Hungarian Competition law – developments in the last decade and follow-up' (2007) Revue Lamy de la Concurrence: 'The Hungarian legislators have always been of the opinion that a close harmonisation of the national competition law to the EC norms is necessary'.

65 SAA, art 70 para 1.

66 SAA, art 70 para 2. Unlike Europe Agreements there is no provision mandating that the implementing rules be adopted by the (Stabilisation and Association) Council.

67 See for example case *AZTN v Tisak d.d. and Distri-Press d.o.o.* [2007] Narodne novine 6/08 (abuse of dominant position, decision of the Competition Agency of 15 October, 2007, further as *Tisak d.d. case*) where case law of the ECJ was cited to explain why the conduct at hand was abusive (following ECJ cases were referred to: Michelin, Irish Sugar, British Airways).

and experts in the field were few, if any. Because these initial conditions were not taken into account at the time of importing the complex competition rules, the Croatian Competition Agency had no other choice but to rely on the experiences of the EU. Furthermore, there is an inherent logic in interpreting imported rules in the spirit originally attributed to them.

Yet, the Croatian Constitution, very much like all European constitutions, treasures the principle of the rule of law. The basic demand of this principle is the application of general laws which are known in advance and are applicable to all persons equally,[68] with an emphasis of ensuring legal certainty and predictability of action of state institutions. Accordingly, the Croatian constitution does not permit direct application of foreign legal rules.

Simultaneously, the Constitution of the Republic of Croatia proscribes that all ratified international agreements form an integral part of the Croatian legal order and are above national laws in the structure of legal hierarchy. Accordingly, by the exercising the same principle (the rule of law), any national law which would be contrary to a ratified international contract would be unconstitutional.

Now, the SAA, quite uniquely, requires the approximation of laws and in competition cases specifically, the direct application of primary EU competition rules contained therein, as well as the application of EU criteria and interpretative tools not contained therein. Therefore, SAA can be seen as a very specific form of agreement, much wider in scope from traditional international agreements, which brought about a conflicting effect of the same constitutional principle.

On one hand, it is unconstitutional to directly apply foreign rules whose content is not known in advance, and on the other hand, obligations undertaken by the SAA, requiring the application criteria and interpretative tools that are not known in advance, are to be observed.

It was very difficult to strike a balance between demands of interpretation and application of SAA with the demands of interpretation and application of traditional international law contracts in the constitutional context.[69] In light of these considerations, the most important question to be answered was whether EU competition rules were being applied as a source of law, involving an unconstitutional direct application of foreign rules, or only as an auxiliary means of interpretation justified by the application of the SAA.

---

68 S. Barić, 'Predklinički problem hrvatskog konstitucionalizma:dvojbeno funkcioniranje vladavine prava u formalnom smislu', [2012] Ustavi i demokracija: strani utjecaji i domaći odgovori: okrugli stol održan 7. prosinca 2011 u palači Akademije u Zagrebu 249, 251.

69 S. Rodin, 'Sporazum o stabilizaciji i pridruživanju u pravnom poretku Europke Zajednice i Republike Hrvatske' in D. Hrabar and Irena Majstorović (eds), *Zbornik Pravnog fakulteta u Zagrebu* (Pravni fakultet, 2003), 591–613. This is a very interesting article arguing that that the SAA should be interpreted and applied in light of the *'acquis communautaire'*.

7. EU COMPETITION RULES: A SOURCE OF LAW OR AN AUXILIARY MEANS OF INTERPRETATION

The Competition Act of 2003 contained a provision, article 35, which read as follows:

> In the assessment of different forms of prevention, restriction, or distortion of competition, that may affect trade between the Republic of Croatia and the European Communities, the Council shall in accordance with article 70 of the Stabilization and Association Agreement [...] accordingly apply the criteria arising from the correct application of the rules regulating competition in the European Communities.[70]

The Agency tried to justify its application of EU competition rules on the grounds of this article. Strictly speaking, it was not necessary to insert in the Competition Act a provision calling for the application of EU rules since the SAA, being an international agreement and thus an integral part of the Croatian legal order, would have been applicable anyway. However, from a practical point of view it was probably regarded useful to have such a provision incorporated in the main act governing this area. This provision however, far from being practical, instigated fierce reactions of undertakings that were found to have infringed Croatian competition rules.

7.1. CASE *PLIVA D.D./INFAI-NMR*

The application of EU rules first became contentious in Pliva d.d./INFAI-NMR GmbH case.[71] In this case the Competition Agency declared, on the basis of EU criteria governing vertical agreements, that several provisions of an exclusive distribution agreement were null and void.

The Competition Act in force at that time contained no detailed rules on the assessment of exclusive distribution agreements, the Agency decided to apply EU rules on vertical agreements. Pliva d.d., a major pharmaceutical company in Croatia, challenged this ruling before the Administrative Court of the Republic of Croatia. It argued that EU provisions on vertical agreements could not have been applied by the Agency because those rules regulated competition within the common market, i.e. within the European Union which is an association of states not including the Republic of Croatia.

70 Competition Act 2003, art 35 para 3.

71 [2003] UP/I 030-02/2002-01/44 urbroj: 580-02-03-17-04 decision of the Competition Agency from 13 February 2003.

Moreover, it brought forward the argument that article 35 IA and article 70 SAA could not have been interpreted as giving rise to an obligation (nor a power) of competent authorities in Croatia to directly apply EU rules, but could have only been interpreted as an obligation of Croatia, as a signatory of those international agreements, to align its legislation in the area of competition law with the EU law.

The Administrative Court accepted the arguments of Pliva and squashed the decision of the Agency.[72] It started by holding that, pursuant to the Croatian Constitution, international agreements in force were to be seen as part of the internal legal order of the Republic of Croatia and were thus above domestic laws. Therefore, IA and SAA as international agreements could have been applied to such a case. However, EU criteria, standards and interpretative instruments as invoked by the Agency, which have not been part of the international agreements themselves, or which have not been taken over and published as part of a Croatian law could not have been used as a source of law.

7.2. CASE *P.Z. AUTO*

Only several days after the decision of the Agency in the Pliva/Infai case, the same issue came up in another pending case before the Administrative Court. In this case, the Agency found that P.Z. Auto, a general importer of VW cars for Croatia, abused its dominant position.[73] At the time there were no domestic rules on motor vehicles distribution, so the Agency applied EU criteria regarding selective distribution of motor vehicles.

Another issue relevant in this case was raised by the fact that the scrutinised agreement was both concluded and rescinded before IA and SAA had come into force.

In its appeal to the Administrative Court, P.Z. Auto argued that IA and SAA could not have been applied retroactively since article 140 of the Croatian Constitution provided that international agreements must be in force in order to be regarded as a constituent part of the internal legal order.

Furthermore, it was argued that EU instruments could not have been applied to the case at hand as no official translations were available, nor were these instruments officially published.

Unlike in the Pliva/Infai appeal case, the Administrative Court held that the Agency had not erred in its application of substantive rules by applying criteria developed under EU law.[74] On the contrary, it held that the Agency was authorised to apply EU rules on the basis of article 70 and 130 SAA.

---

72 *Pliva d.d. Zagreb v AZTN* [2006] Narodne novine No 16/07 decision of the Administrative Court from 26 October, 2006, Us-5438/2003-7.

73 [2003] Narodne novine 19/2003 UP/I-030-02/2002-01/60, Urbroj: 580-02-02-10-4, decision of the Agency from 19 February, 2003.

74 *P.Z. v AZTN* [2006] Narodne novine 29/07 Us-4832/2003-6 decision of the Administrative Court from 9 November, 2006.

In regards to the issue of temporal application of the IA and SAA, the Administrative Court held that the fact that the contentious contractual relationship was concluded before the IA and SAA came into force, did not mean that they were not applicable to the case at hand. The court reasoned that the goal of those international agreements was to eliminate any agreements, i.e. any potential legal relationships which restrict free competition in the market.

The two conflicting judgments of the Administrative Court came out within two weeks. The one adjudicating that the EU criteria were unjustifiably applied as a source of law since they are not part of the relevant international agreements nor of any domestic legislation[75] and the ruling that the EU criteria were being used as an auxiliary means of interpretation and as such may have been applied on the grounds of the SAA.[76]

The Constitutional Court got the opportunity to deal with this issue after P.Z. Auto came forward arguing that the application of EU rules was unconstitutional on the ground that IA and SAA were applied retroactively. Furthermore, referring to the decision of the Administrative Court in the Pliva/Infai case, P.Z. Auto argued that while article 140 of the Croatian Constitution allowed the application of these international agreements, it did not allow the application of the EU criteria and interpretative instruments which were not part of those agreements and which were not promulgated as Croatian laws.

The Constitutional Court rejected such reasoning. It held that the Agency and the Administrative Court had the right to apply the provisions of SAA and IA, provided that the appraisal of the conduct of undertakings which were assessed took place when those agreements were in force,[77] thereby solving in general terms, the issue of temporal application of the IA and SAA. Since, in the case at hand, these international agreements were not in force, the Constitutional Court held that the relevant authorities applied them merely as 'an auxiliary means of interpretation' of domestic rules.

Such a practice of filling the *lacunae* was, as the Court held, consistent with the 'spirit of the national law' and 'was not contrary to the explicit solutions of the Competition Act'.[78] The Court noted that the competent authorities are in obligation to apply criteria which arise from the application of EU competition rules and from interpretative instruments adopted by EU institutions, since the SAA contains an obligation not only to apply relevant domestic law but also to take account of the relevant EU law.

---

75 *Pliva d.d. Zagreb v AZTN* [2006] Narodne novine, Nc 16/07 decision of the Administrative Court from 26 October 2006, Us-5438/2003-7.

76 *P.Z. v AZTN* [2006] Narodne novine 29/07 Us-4832/2003-6 decision of the Administrative Court from 9 November, 2006.

77 *P.Z.A. d.o.o. V.G.*, [2008] Narodne novine 25/08 decision of the Constitutional Court from 13 February, 2008, U-III/1410/2007.

78 Ibid.

This is not an unusual position. Even prior to their accession, courts in the CEECs held that EC rules may serve as an inspiration when applying domestic competition rules. For instance, the Czech Republic High Court confirmed this proposition in the matter of *Skoda automobilová, a.s.* (judgment of November 14, 1996) that, although the judgments of the European Court of Justice and decisions of the Commission are not binding to the Office and do not constitute precedents for the decision-making in the relevant matters, such decisions serve as an important source of information and inspiration which is helpful in the application and enforcement of competition principles.

The Czech Republic High Court stated the following:

> (...) the Competition Act adopted the basic ideas of the Treaty of Rome which is an absolute necessity with a view to the harmonisation of law. The defendant (*i.e.* the Office) is not at fault if it strives to apply the law in a manner compatible with the practice of the E.C. Court of Justice (or the Commission).[79]

Skoda filed a constitutional complaint against the High Court judgment, seeking annulment of the judgment and arguing, *inter alia*, that in its interpretation of the abuse of dominance on the part of Skoda, the Office relied on article 82 of the Treaty of Rome.

According to the findings of the Constitutional Court, an interpretation drawing on the competition rules set forth by the Treaty of Rome cannot be deemed anti-constitutional. The Treaty of Rome is based on the same values and principles as the Constitutional Order of the Czech Republic.[80]

Coming back to the Croatian Constitutional Court's decision, in the case P.Z. Auto, the Court further observed that article 70 para 2 SAA and article 35 para 2 IA must be seen in the context of the obligation of Croatia to align its legislation with EU *acquis*. When applying domestic legal rules that were aligned with the *acquis*, national authorities must apply them 'as they are applied in the EU' and 'consistent with the meaning and the spirit of rules with which the alignment was done'.[81] However, the Court emphasised that this does not mean that EU law was being formally introduced into the Croatian legal system through the SAA

79 Finding of the Constitutional Court of May 29, 1997. See T. Fiala, 'The new Competition Act in the Czech Republic' (2002) 23 (8) E.C.L.R. 400, 400–406.

80 Ibid.

81 Recently the European Court of Justice confirmed it had jurisdiction to hear preliminary reference cases in which interpretation of a domestic provision mirroring article 101 TFEU was requested by the national court. In case *Allianz Hungária Biztosító Zrt. and Others* the Court held that, although the agreements at issue did not have an impact on intra-Community trade, it was 'clearly in the interest of the European Union that, in order to forestall future differences of interpretation, provisions or concepts taken from European Union law should be interpreted uniformly, irrespective of the circumstances in which they are to apply' (Case C-32/11 *Allianz Hungária Biztosító Zrt. and Others v Gazdasági Versenyhivatal* [2013] ECR I - 0000, para 20).

provisions. The EU criteria, standards, and interpretative instruments were not applicable as 'a primary source of law but as an auxiliary means of interpretation'.[82]

However, even after this decision, it took some time to settle the case law of the Administrative Court.[83] Eventually, the decision of the Constitutional Court in case P.Z. Auto started to be invoked as settled case-law in order to justify the application of EU rules.[84]

The Croatian constitutional court's decision clearly shows how in the competition law context, the borderline between the application of EU rules as a source of law and as a purely interpretative tool is rather thin. Although we agree, there is one point of disagreement – the Constitutional court failed to address explicitly the cross border criterion for the application of the EU law. Seen from this perspective, the application of the SAA remains to be unsolved in a purely domestic context. By omitting to decide on this issue, only a year later a new conflicting legal interaction occurred. This time the relationship between the SAA and the new Competition Act posed difficulties.

8. THE APPLICATION OF EU COMPETITION LAW: COMPETITION ACT 2009

It appeared that the contemplated issue would become obsolete after the adoption of the Competition Act 2009, as it was meant to codify findings of the named constitutional decision. However, this was done in a legally questionable

82 After the Constitutional Court in P.Z. Auto case ruled in favour of the Competition Agency a new decision was adopted by the Agency in Pliva/Infai case, which invoked the decision of the Constitutional Court to confirm its right to apply EU rules. See *Pliva d.d. and INFAI-NMR GmbH* [2008] Narodne novine 20/08 decision of the Competition Agency of 3 April 2008.

83 In a state aid case, the Administrative Court quashed the decision of the Agency which applied EU rules as a source of law. See case *Varteks d.d.*, decision of the Competition Agency of 4 April 2007 UP/I 430-01/2004-01/42, urbroj: 580-03-07-17-24; *Varteks d.d. v AZTN*,, Narodne novine 12/11, decision of the Administrative Court Us-5362/2007-10 from 03 November 2010. Although the P.Z. Auto decision of the Constitutional Court was adopted more than two years ago (13 February, 2008), the Administrative Court (obviously relying on its previous rulings) held that EU rules which were not part of the IA or SAA nor promulgated as domestic legislation, could not stand as sources of law. The Agency reacted by adopting a new decision which invoked the ruling of the Constitutional Court in the case of P.Z. Auto which indeed held that it was an obligation of the Agency to take account of the EU rules, using them merely as interpretative instruments to interpret Croatian rules. See *Varteks d.d.* UP/I 430-01/2004-01/042, decision of the Competition Agency from 19 May, 2011.

84 In the *Tisak d.d. case* (see *n* 68) the Agency used case law of the ECJ as relevant to explain why the conduct at hand was abusive (Michelin, Irish Sugar, British Airways). This time the Administrative Court was quick to accept the position of the Agency as correct, noting that EU case law was an important interpretative instrument for application of Croatian rules (*Tisak d.d. v AZTN* [2010] Narodne novine 93/10 judgment of the Administrative Court, Us-12775/2007-5 from 06 May, 2010). In the same case the Constitutional Court confirmed its ruling in P.Z. Auto case by affirming the right of the Agency to apply EU rules (*Tisak d.d.* [2011] Narodne novine 28/11 decision of the Constitutional Court U-III/4082/2010 from 17 February, 2011).

manner as the normative expression of the Constitutional Court's finding contained in the new Competition Act unsuccessfully strived to widen the scope of the SAA, thus causing an even greater confusion.

Namely, from the Competition Act 2003 to the Competition Act 2009 the provision justifying the application of the totality of EU rules had been changed only slightly in wording, but arguably quite significantly in its legal implications. In the Competition Act 2009, article 74 reads as follows:

In application of this Act, particularly in the case of legal voids and uncertainties relating to the interpretation of competition rules, in accordance with article 70 of the Stabilization and Association Agreement between the Republic of Croatia and the European Communities and their Member States (...), criteria arising from the application of the competition rules applicable in the European Community shall be accordingly applied.[85]

The similarities and dissimilarities between the two Competition Acts in regards to the provision 'implementing' article 70 SAA can be summarised as follows:

Table 1

Article 35 para 3 Competition Act 2003	Article 74 Competition Act 2009
in accordance with article 70 SAA	
in the assessment of different forms of prevention, restriction or distortion of competition, that may affect trade between the Republic of Croatia and the European Communities	in the application of this Act, particularly in the case of legal voids and uncertainties relating to the interpretation of competition rules
The Agency shall accordingly apply the criteria arising from the application of EU competition rules	

Both provisions invoke article 70 SAA and partly copy the SAA wording (i.e. application of the criteria arising from EU competition rules). However, while the Competition Act 2003 referred to the application of EU rules to situations that may affect trade between Croatia and EU, obviously borrowing its wording from the SAA, the Competition Act 2009 makes a shift from the SAA with the presumed intention to broaden the scope of application of EU rules.

By omitting to mention the 'effect on trade between the EU and Croatia', the provision extends the application of EU rules and instruments to purely domestic cases. Furthermore, by including the words 'in application of this Act' the provision attracts under the umbrella of EU rules not only restrictive agreements and abuse of dominant position as proscribed by the SAA, but merger control as well, since provisions on merger control are part of the

[85] Competition Act 2009, art 74.

Competition Act. Finally, the provision proscribes that EU rules are to be applicable 'particularly in the case of legal voids and uncertainties relating to the interpretation of competition rules'.

We believe that article 74 suffers from major legal drafting deficiencies resulting from a somewhat inept effort to accommodate the obligations undertaken by article 70 of the SAA and simultaneously, the need to overpass any inconsistencies, or legal *lacunas* in purely domestic cases, including mergers.

It appears that the Competition Act of 2009 intended to permit explicitly the application of EU rules to all competition cases. All the same, the Competition Act of 2009 could not avoid referring to article 70 SAA, because this is the only legal basis for the application of EU rules. However, the SAA clearly enables the application of EU rules only to agreements and abuse of dominant position in situations with a cross-border effect on trade. Consequently, it would not be acceptable to interpret this domestic provision as widening its scope. It is article 70 SAA that defines its own limits. Therefore, we find the disputed provision of the Competition Act of 2009 to be inherently inconsistent. On the one hand, it invokes the provision of the SAA, while on the other, it tries to overcome it.

It may be asked what leads us to deduce that the intention of the article 74 of Competition Act of 2009 was to broaden the scope of application of EU criteria. As already emphasised, it is a regular practice of the Competition Agency to invoke precisely this provision in merger cases as a legal ground for the application of EU criteria (and previously article 35 para 3 of the Competition Act of 2003).

Furthermore, in its decisions on restrictive agreements and abuse of dominant position, the Competition Agency makes no assessment of cross-border effect, nor does it at all mention the effect on trade criterion.[86] This leads to a conclusion that the disputed provision was indeed meant to broaden the scope of the SAA.

It was perhaps the view of the Constitutional Court, or more likely the misinterpretation thereof, which inspired the wording of article 74 of the Competition Act of 2009. The Constitutional Court's decision seems to have been understood as generally demanding that any 'domestic legislation which

86 This seems to have changed lately. In a state aid case the Competition Agency found no state aid since there was no cross-border effect on trade between Croatia and the EU (Ministry of Maritime Affairs, Transport and Infrastructure granted to HŽ Infrastruktura, a state company, state guarantee for a loan with a commercial bank; upon notification by the grantor of aid the Competition Agency decided that the guarantee was not to be regarded as state aid, since HŽ Infrastruktura was active on a non-liberalised market, thus the state guarantee had no effect on trade between Croatia and the EU), <www.aztn.hr/article/1223/jamstvo-hz-infrastrukturi-i-opcoj-bolnici-pula-nije-potpora > (accessed 1 February 2013).

was aligned to the *acquis*' must be applied, taking into account 'the meaning and spirit' of EU rules. Since domestic rules on merger control have been aligned (to a large extent) with EU rules, it could be argued that the Competition Agency in individual cases would be obliged to apply them as it is done in the Union, observing the meaning and spirit of EU rules. Nonetheless, in our opinion it remains doubtful whether article 74 of the Competition Act can be seen as the appropriate legal basis for the application of EU rules in merger cases and cases without a cross-border effect.

9. CONCLUSIONS

Even prior to Croatian's EU accession, EU competition rules left a significant mark on how competition law was enforced in Croatia. At first, due to a lack of regulation, EU rules were abundantly used by the Competition Agency in order to reach decisions in individual cases. However, the reliance on EU law continued even after extensive rewriting of the Competition Act in 2003 and 2009, which were aligned ever more to the *acquis*. Since EU rules were consistently being applied both to cases with a cross-border element as well as to cases where the effect on trade between Croatia and the EU was less obvious, it may be noted that Croatia has for many years (at least in regards to the area of competition law) and to a great extent, already been a part of the EU legal order.

In fact, the turning point has been the entry into force of the Interim Agreement which made possible the coming into force of article 70 SAA, which in turn, provided for the application of EU competition law in Croatia. After initial challenges, the practice of applying EU rules became stable after the Constitutional Court's decision to approve the practice of the Competition Agency in relying on EU law by qualifying EU rules as 'an auxiliary means of interpretation'. Clearly the Court could not have ruled that the *acquis* was to be applied as a source of law, as Croatia was still going through the pre-accession process and EU law was treated as a foreign legal order. However, one has to wonder whether *de facto* there is a difference, especially looking at the way EU rules were treated in the decision-making practice of the Competition Agency, in the application of EU rules as a source of law as opposed to EU rules as an auxiliary means of interpretation.

CHAPTER 17

EMPIRIC ASSESSMENT OF THE ROLE OF ECONOMIC ANALYSIS IN RUSSIAN COMPETITION LAW

Anastasia SHASTITKO

1. INTRODUCTION

Antitrust regulation is one of the legal spheres where law enforcement should be based on the principles of economic theory. Thus antimonopoly policy is the meeting point of economics and law. It entails new approaches to antitrust cases for either disciplines or conflicts caused by disagreements on the diverse methods. The main difference between economic and legal approaches is that the former is inclined to be more flexible norms while the latter prefers bright-line rules.

This work, which touches upon the question of whether economic theory could guide antimonopoly policy, studies the element of antimonopoly law enforcement known as an economic analysis of the market. Its logic comes from economic theory. Economic analysis is used to qualify market conditions and market positions of the economic entities. It makes an investigation of each antitrust case more individual and increases its accuracy. It also leads to more flexible antitrust law enforcement because the qualification of the behaviour of economic entities became dependent on the qualification of their market positions and market conditions in general.

The main objective of this chapter is to estimate the role of economic analysis in litigations where companies appeal the decisions of antitrust authorities. Two types of infringes were considered: abuse of dominant position (article 10 of the Federal Law No. 135- FZ "On the Protection of Competition") and agreements restricting competition (article 11 of the Federal Law No. 135- FZ "On the Protection of Competition"). As it was mentioned above, to qualify the behaviour of economic entities it is necessary to qualify their market positions and market conditions. For this purpose economic analysis is applied according to the special Order "On a process of market competition level analysis" that consists of the following elements:

- time interval
- product market
- geographic market
- composition of market (economic entities)
- market volume and companies' shares on it
- market concentration level
- entry barriers
- market competition level.

The chapter estimates the influence of an economic analysis application in litigation on its outcome and its durability and reveals factors that form the demand for economic analysis by antitrust authorities. The study has the following hypotheses. The first hypothesis is that economic analysis could influence a litigation outcome, in particular, that it could increase the probability of an antitrust authority winning a case. On the one hand, the antitrust authority of Russia, especially its central government has some advantages (financial and administrative) concerning the question of an economic analysis application. This could be the reason that in any case in the sample of this study companies did not initiate an economic analysis application. On the other hand, large companies usually have enough resources to provide an economic analysis. In this case the capabilities of companies and antitrust authorities, especially on the regional level (departments of antitrust authority) are at least equal. In this case the fact that an antitrust authority usually initiates an economic analysis application could mean that an antitrust authority, but not companies, treat it as a powerful argument in litigation that determines the underlined hypothesis.

Next, the appearance of The Order "On the process of market competition level analysis" and its application in lawsuits are the evidences of expansion of the *rule of reason*. The general understanding of economic analysis necessity could cause the appearance of the Order while the intensity of its application shows to what extent the Russian antitrust authority is ready for new approaches. Economic analysis is potentially very powerful argument either for the defence or for the prosecution, but the Russian antitrust authority is usually inclined to control the execution of formal rules. As far as an application of economic analysis, in addition to objective reasons, could be caused by the Law "On the Protection of Competition" that prescribes use of it in cases under article 10 (abuse of dominant position) but does not do so for article 11 (agreements restricting competition), the hypothesis is that the probability of economic analysis being used is higher for cases instituted under article 10 than for cases instituted under article 11.

The last hypothesis is that economic analysis increases durability of a case and creates additional costs. According to some scholars, economic analysis makes cases more cumbersome and increases their duration. It leads to additional costs caused by a list of required documents, which should be presented in litigation or by an expert.

The investigation is focused on litigations. Consequently an observation in the empiric part of this research is a case of an appellate court. It has a list of characteristics. These characteristics have a significant effect on the litigation outcome, its durability, and the demand for economic analysis was revealed.

The second part of this work reviews the articles that treat the problem of collaboration between economics and law in general and the role of economic analysis in particular. The third part presents the database that was formed especially for this research. The database was compared with a general sample to assess the representatively of the empiric results. The analysis of the general sample revealed some trends in Russian antitrust in the last few years. The forth part contains the econometric analysis used to test the underlined hypothesis. The conclusion summarises the results of the analysis and its limitations.

2. REVIEW OF PROBLEM

The majority of researchers that point out the problem of collaboration between economics and law pertaining to antitrust law enforcement consider applied methods of economic theory, for example, the possibility to analyze the behaviour of economic agents using structural models. Usually they provide a theoretical analysis of the advantages and disadvantages of these approaches and the consequences of their application. Most of the authors concur in expansion of the role of economics in antitrust law enforcement as a development trend of antimonopoly policy. The consequences of this development are the subject of vast amount studies.

Scholars agree that economics is essential for antitrust law enforcement.[1] The role of market analysis in litigations is increasing; the so-called *rule of reason* is becoming more preferable. It makes an investigation of each case more individual, considering the circumstances.

Both the US and the EU have chosen to develop antitrust policies development with an increasing role of economics. This choice could be explained by globalisation or antitrust law convergence[2] or by the advantages of a flexible approach based on economic analysis. The trump card of this approach is that it let to take into account factors missing by bright-line rules. '... *life is*

1 Muris 2003; Schinkel et al. 2004.
2 Hwang Lee 2004.

normally to complex for absolute rules'.[3] For antitrust law enforcement it means that if antitrust policy is purely based on bright-line rules, some social benefits could be lost. The flexible approach demands the analysis of benefits and costs of the behaviour of economic entities. For instance, on the one hand a merge of two firms could increase the probability of abuse of dominant position, but on the other hand it could reduce transaction and production costs, improving efficiency of production. Or, for example, a company could be accused not only in too high price level but also in too low one (predatory pricing). In this case an antitrust authority should compare the short-run benefits of consumers caused by low prices and their long-run costs that could be caused by decrease in competition level after the exit of some firms from a market due to their negative profits.

The *rule of reason* let to reduce welfare losses that could occur in case of formal application of bright-line rules, for example, if a merge of two firms is prohibited while it could dramatically increase efficiency of production or decrease transaction costs. Thus the *rule of reason* decreases the probability of a type one error, when innocents are accused, or when a merger with a positive effect that overweighs a negative one is prohibited. On the other hand the opponents of an approach based on economic analysis argue that it creates loopholes for unconscientious firms and increases the probability of a type two error that is to acquit infringers or to permit a merger with a negative effect that overweighs a positive one.[4]

One of the characteristics of an approach based on principles of the economic theory is that it often resorts to quantitative methods. There is no consensus among scholars according to appropriateness of these methods for law enforcement. The proponents of quantitative methods contend for their objectivity that could decrease the uncertainty of antitrust law enforcement, increase its transparency and curb the despotism of antitrust authority.[5] The opponents of these methods on the contrary argue that they increase the uncertainty.[6] Results and conclusions obtained form quantitative methods depend on advanced hypotheses, available data and chosen yardsticks. Hence two different models could give two contradictory results.

Finally economic analysis itself is also criticised. The first argument is that its application could lead to additional costs caused by a list of required documents that should be presented in litigation or by an expert engagement.[7] The second argument is that economic analysis enlarges a petition docket, and under limited time it creates pressure and could affect a decision-making process. Courts prefer administrable rules, because they minimise litigation costs. A decision

---

3 Breyer 2009.
4 Christiansen 2005.
5 Drauz 2002.
6 Christiansen 2005.
7 Christiansen 2005.

based on bright-line rules is less contradictive and hence clearer for the public at large.[8]

Comparatively few empirical analyses on this problem were performed. This paper presents the empirical analysis of the role of economic analysis in lawsuits, where infringements of antitrust law are judged.

The publication of Schinkel, Carree and Gunster (2004) also provides the empirical analysis of litigations on infringements of antitrust law (abuse of dominant position and agreements restricting competition, article 81 and article 82 of the European Commission Treaty). The authors have used the official records on all published antitrust decisions by the antitrust authorities of the US and the EU as well as the decisions of appellate courts. They have constructed the list of characteristics of each case, for example, their duration and the level of imposed fines. The main objective of this work was to reveal some trends of competition policy development. According to the obtained results the number of appellations rises with the complexity of cases, and the level of complexity is inversely proportional to the likelihood that decision will be annulled. Economic rationales increase the probability of companies to make out a case.

It is worth to mention that this analysis was improved in several years.[9] The authors revealed reduction in the number of annulled decisions and rise in the number of complex cases where none of two parties (antitrust authorities and companies) receives a full legal victory. It was also determined that large a petition docket does not necessary lead to high duration of a decision-making process.

The key differences between this work and the works of Schinkel, Carree and Gunster (2004, 2008) are the following. First of all its analysis concerns the antitrust policy of Russia. Secondly, its empirical part considers factors that could influence an outcome of litigation and its durability paying more attention to economic rationales.

Economic rationales in Russian litigations are based on The Order No. 108 "On the process of market competition level analysis" which entered into force on 25 April 2006 or its new version The Order No. 220 "On the process of market competition level analysis", which entered into force on 28 April 2010. Rate and efficiency of the usage of these orders determine the role of economic analysis in Russian antitrust.

The research of Avdasheva and Shastitko A.E. (2011) provides the investigation that concerns the scale of an economic analysis application in Russia. The authors revealed the demand for each element of economic analysis and the most popular methods of the analysis. They showed that parties in

8 Breyer 2009.
9 Schinkel et al. 2008.

litigation prefer to use concentration level to determine market competition level, while entry barriers are rarely investigated. The following phenomenon is underlined in this work. The Russian antitrust authorities including courts are inclined to enforce antitrust law literally, ignoring circumstances. As a result, efforts of parties in litigations shift to formal control for compliance of conduct and position of market participants with law. In this case economic analysis is hardly useful. It is the evidence of underdevelopment of the *rule of reason* approach in Russian antitrust.

The next research[10] also considers rate and efficiency of the usage of economic analysis in Russian antitrust, in particular in litigations under article 10 (abuse of dominant position) and article 11 (agreements restricting competition) of the Federal Law No. 135- FZ "On the Protection of Competition". This investigation was based on the sample, consisted of those decisions by the antitrust authority of Russia to which an appeal was lodged. In each case of the sample economic analysis was used. The special attention was paid on the elements of economic analysis (time interval, product market, etc.) The correlation analysis, carried out on the available data, revealed that the number of elements used does not increase durability of a case, and some of them even tend to decrease it. In contrast to this article the research of Kurdin and Shastitko A.A. (2013) does not concern the effect of an economic analysis application on a litigation outcome, because its sample does not contain cases without economic analysis. However it provides some evidence that if companies contest economic analysis presented by an antitrust authority it increases their probability to win a case.

This work offers the empirical analysis based on the enlarged sample that includes cases without economic analysis. This gives an opportunity to reveal factors that affect a decision-making process of appellate courts, durability of litigation and the demand for economic analysis.

3. DATABASE

3.1. DESCRIPTION

The database of the empirical analysis was collected form official records on published decisions by the Supreme Court of Arbitration of the Russian Federation (http://arbitr.ru/) on appellate decisions of antitrust authorities. It consists of 149 cases of antitrust law infringements for the period from 2007 until 2011 and includes cases under article 10 (abuse of dominant position) and article 11 (agreements restricting competition) of The Federal Law No. 135-FZ,

10 Kurdin and Shastitko A.A. 2013.

"On the Protection of Competition". Cases with economic analysis constitute 35% of the sample.

Most of variables in the analysis are dummies. It is the result of transformation of the qualitative information, contained in published decisions, into the quantitative information for empirical analysis. Each variable is a key figure of a case. The full list of variables is presented below.

- Economic analysis (1, if it was used);
- Article – 10 or 11 (1, if article 11);
- Durability of a case;
- Decision of appeals court – in favour of a company or in favour of an antitrust authority (1, if in favour of a company);
- Instances (there are four instances of the Appellate Court in Russia);
- Market type – goods market or service market; financial market is considered as a part of service market (1, if goods market);
- Expert (1, if he was engaged);
- Natural monopoly (1, if company is);
- Region – whether region where a case was considered is developed (1, if it is);
- Company contests economic analysis (1, if company contests not only the qualification of behaviour but also the qualification of position).

Economic analysis as it was mentioned above consists of the following elements: time interval, product market, geographic market, composition of market, market volume and companies' shares on it, concentration level, entry barriers and finally market competition level. To apply economic analysis either all of the elements could be used or just some of them.

It is impossible to qualify the market position of economic entity without identification of product and geographic markets. That is why all cases with economic analysis in the sample contain these two elements. It is necessary to determine market volume and market composition to calculate companies' shares. Hence these three elements are used always together. Usually economic analysis in litigation is provided by an antitrust authority (all cases of the sample), while companies contest some of its elements, the whole analysis or do not contest it at all. The graph below is based on the 52 cases of the sample, where economic analysis was used and presents the demand for its elements (see Appendix, Table 1).

Graph 1. Demand for the elements of economic analysis

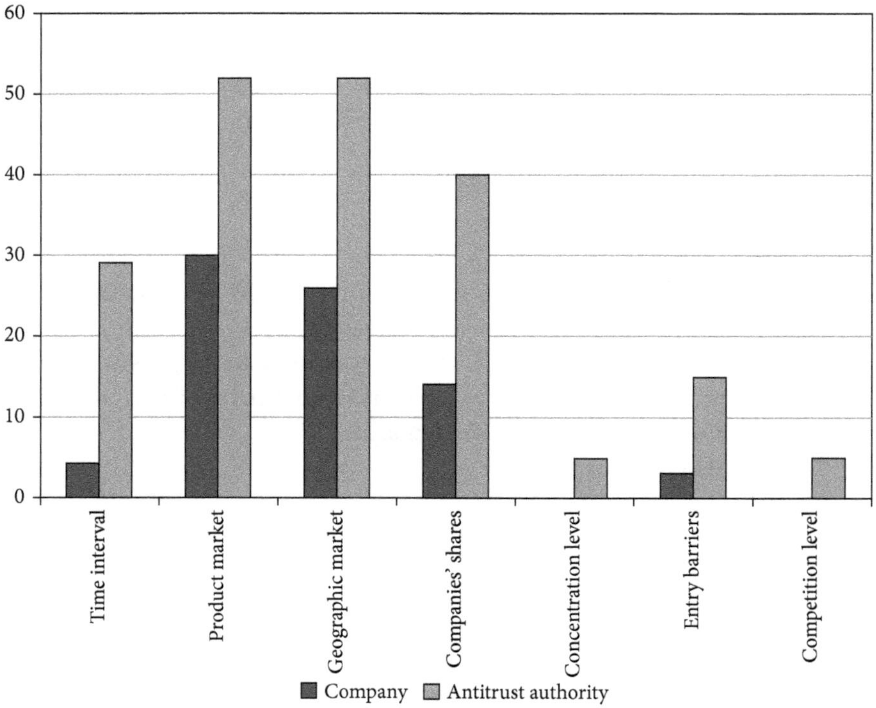

Source: http://arbitr.ru/

The most popular element of economic analysis after product and geographic markets is companies' shares. As it was mentioned above, product and geographic markets are automatically identified and it could be noticed that companies also contest these elements the most frequently. Entry barriers were determined three times more often than concentration level during the period under investigation. It could mean that the antitrust authority of Russia tends to control market contestability instead of its competition level.

The antitrust authority of Russia has 82 departments and 32 of them appear in the sample. Each department corresponds with the region of Russian Federation. For this analysis developed region is assumed to be a region from the first half of the socio-economic development rating (see Appendix, Table 2).

The table below offers some statistics of the sample. It shows that cases under article 10 dominate. Economic analysis was applied in more than one third of cases. The number of cases with natural monopolies is relatively small. There are slightly more cases with decisions by appellate courts in favour of an antitrust authority. In average a case held more than two out of four instances. It is worth to mention that among the 52 cases where economic analysis was used only three cases held one instance and other 49 cases achieved the third instance.

Table 1. Sample statistics

	Number of cases	Share in sample
Article 11	37	25%
Goods market	64	43%
Economic analysis	52	35%
Natural monopoly	16	10,7%
Decision in favour of a company	61	43%
Average durability of a case	14 months	
Average number of instances	3	

Source: http://arbitr.ru/

3.2. COMPARISON OF THE SAMPLE AND THE GENERAL SAMPLE

According to the official statistics the number of considered applications under article 10 by the antitrust authority of Russia rose by 67% from 2007 until 2011. The share of instituted legal procedures fall by 25% during this period, while the share of cases where antitrust authority revealed infringements increased by 27,7% and the share of appealed decisions by 4,7%. The share of annulled decisions decreased by 49% during this period. This statistics shows that the antitrust authority of Russia is enhancing its activity. Increase in the share of cases where antitrust authority revealed infringements could by caused by decrease in the number of instituted legal procedures that means that an antitrust authority tends to eliminate unpromising cases on a earlier stage of investigation. Decrease in the share of annulled decisions could be the evidence of increasing efficiency of an antitrust authority.

The situation for article 11 is slightly different. The number of considered applications here increased by 88%, while the share of instituted legal procedures by 133% and the share of cases, where antitrust authority revealed infringements by 38%. It confirms the conclusion about the enhancing activity of the Russia's antitrust authority. However in comparison to article 10, the share of appealed decisions significantly rose by 57% and the share of annulled decisions by 64%. It could be the evidence that companies' position in cases under article 11 is improving.

To make a conclusion about representativity of the sample the latter should be compared with the general sample. The sample consists of 149 observations that is 2,8% of the general sample. There are 37 cases under article 11 and 112 cases under article 10 in the sample that are 4% and 2,5% of the general sample correspondingly. The share of cases under article 11 in the sample is 25% that is by 10% more than in the general sample. The table below presents the statistics of decisions by appellate courts in the sample and in the general sample.

Table 2. Share of decisions in favour of companies

Share of decisions in favour of companies	In sample	In general sample
Under article 10 (abuse of dominant position)	43.75%	15.6%
Under article 11 (agreements restricting competition)	32%	19%
Under both articles	41%	16%

Source: http://arbitr.ru/

According to this table the sample is biased. The share of cases under article 10 where a decision was pronounced in favour of a company is almost three times higher in the sample than in the general sample. The biasness of the sample for article 11 is less dramatic but still significant. This fact should be taken into account during the interpretation of the regressions outcomes. It means that coefficients of variables that significantly increase the probability of companies to make out a case could be overestimated.

The reason for this bias lies behind a method of the sample construction. The source of data is the official site of the Supreme Court of Arbitration of the Russian Federation. It means that the biasness is caused by the selective criteria for courts' decisions to be published on this site.

4. ECONOMETRIC ANALYSIS

The econometric analysis consists of three models. The first model represents a decision-making process of appellate courts and reveals the role of economic rationales in this process. This model tests the hypothesis that economic analysis is a powerful argument and increases the probability of antitrust authority to make out a case.

The model is based on the Probit technique and corresponds to the following equation.

$$p1\ (x) = P_1(Y = 1/X = x) = \Phi\ (X^T\beta),$$

where $p1$ is the probability that company makes out a case, X is a set of independent variables.

Table 3. Outcomes of the regression with decision of an appellate court as a dependent variable

Dependent variable	Independent variable	Coefficient	Marginal probability effect
Decision of appellate court	Economic analysis	-0,49** (0,23)	-0,19
	Article 11	-0,4* (0,25)	-0,16
	Constant	0,03 (0,15)	0,01

$R_{pseudo}^2 = 0,03$
**-coefficient is significant at 5% level
*-coefficient is significant at 10% level
(standard errors in parentis)

To test the first hypothesis the following variables were regressed: economic analysis (1, if it was used), article – 10 or 11 (1, if article 11), market type – goods or service market (1, if goods market), expert (1, if he was engaged), natural monopoly (1, if company is), region (1, if it is developed), company contest (1, if not only the qualification of behaviour, but also the qualification of position) (see Appendix, Table 3, model 1). The table above represents two variables that affect a litigation outcome (see Appendix, Table 3, model 2). The majority of cases where decisions were held in favour of companies were instituted under article 10. It could mean either that the position of companies is stronger in cases under this article or that antitrust authority is inclined to wild inquisitions of companies in abuse of dominant position. The analysis of the general sample revealed that the number of annulled decisions under article 10 decreased while the number of annulled decisions under article 11 increased. It could mean that there were more annulled decisions under article 10 during the period under review, but there is a decline trend. However it is worth to remind that the sample is biased for article 10 more than for article 11 that could cause this result.

According to the obtained results economic analysis is a significant argument in litigation. It improves the position of an antitrust authority and increases its probability to win a case that confirms advanced hypothesis. The share of decision in favour of companies in the sample is significantly higher than in the general sample. It means that in reality the role of economic analysis could be even more important.

Economic analysis is an endogenous variable. The Housman test that was applied to check the regression for the endogeneity problem (see Appendix, Table 3, model 3) showed that the regression does not suffer form this problem and hence its results are relevant.

The second model was employed to investigate the demand for economic analysis by an antitrust authority and verify the hypothesis that economic analysis is usually used by formal reasons.

This model is also based on the Probit technique and corresponds to the following equation.

$$p2\,(x) = P_1\,(Y = 1/X = x) = \Phi\,(X^T\beta),$$

where *p2* is the probability that economic analysis will be used, *Z* is a set of independent variables.

Table 4. Outcomes of the regression with economic analysis as a dependent variable

Dependent variable	Independent variable	Coefficient	Marginal probability effect
Economic analysis	Goods market	0,85*** (0,22)	0,31
	Article 11	-0,74*** (0,29)	-0,27
	Constant	-0,63*** (0,16)	0,23

$R_{pseudo}^2 = 0{,}11$
***-coefficient is significant at 1% level
(standard errors in parentis)

To test the second hypothesis the following variables were regressed: article – 10 or 11 (1, if article 11), market type (1, if goods market), expert (1, if he was engaged), natural monopoly (1, if company is), region (1, if it is developed) (see Appendix, Table 4, model 4). The table above contains the results of the model that revealed that the demand for economic analysis by an antitrust authority depends on market type and article (see Appendix, Table 4, model 5). Economic analysis is mostly applied on goods markets. The point is that the majority of service markets in the sample is a communication service, and for this type of markets it necessary to apply a specific approach with different economic analysis. Thus economic analysis is difficult to apply on these markets and hence it is used rarely.

The demand for economic analysis is higher for cases under article 10. It means that economic analysis in Russian antitrust is used by formal reasons, according to law, but not by objective reasons, according to its power in litigation. It confirms the mentioned supposition.

The third model tests the hypothesis that economic analysis increases durability of a case. Durability of a case could be interpreted as a proxy for litigation costs, because the longer is a case the higher is its costs.

This model is based on the OLS technique and corresponds to the following equation.

$Y = \varphi + \omega W + \vartheta,$

where Y is the durability of a case, W is a set of independent variables, ϑ is random error.

To test the last hypothesis the following independent variables were regressed: economic analysis (1,if it was used), article – 10 or 11 (1, if article 11), instances (out of four), expert (1, if he was engaged), natural monopoly (1, it company is), region (1, if developed), company contest (1, if not only the qualification of behaviour, but also the qualification of position) (see Appendix, Table 5, model 6). The Breusch-Pagan test revealed heteroscedasticity problem of the obtained regression (see Appendix, Table 5, model 7); hence White standard errors were employed. The table below represents the final version of the model (see Appendix, Table 5, model 8). The Ramsey test showed that the model does not suffer from an omitted variables problem (see Appendix, Table 5, model 8).

Table 5. Outcomes of the regression with durability of a case as a dependent variable

Dependent variable	Independent variable	Coefficient
Durability of a case	Instances	3,45*** (0,44)
	Goods market	5,15*** (1,26)
	Economic analysis	4,44*** (1,47)
	Constant	1,55 (1,18)

$R2 = 0,4$
***-coefficient is significant at 1% level
*-coefficient is significant at 10% level
(standard errors in parentis)

The number of instances held by a case has a predictable positive effect on its durability. Cases about goods markets last significantly longer than cases about service market. It could be caused by the fact that an economic analysis is usually applied to goods markets but the model was tested for the endogeneity problem, which was found to be absent (see Appendix, Table 5, model 9). Hence the reason is different, and this question remains open.

The role of economic analysis proved to be significant; litigations become longer when it is used. It gives some evidence in favour of mentioned hypothesis that an economic analysis application leads to additional costs.

To conclude, the models were tested for a multicollinearity problem. The test revealed that there is no such problem (see Appendix, Tables 3–5). Finally it is worth mentioning that the Probit models could have overestimated coefficients, because there were less than 500 observations in the sample.

5. CONCLUSION

The results obtained provide the evidence in favour of the mentioned suppositions. Firstly, the investigation confirms that an economic analysis increases the durability of cases. However this evidence is not enough to conclude that the usage of economic analysis leads to higher social costs. The benefits and costs of its application should be weighted in order to analyze the effect on social welfare. Secondly, it was shown that economic analysis is an important argument in litigation and that it increases the probability of antitrust authority to make out a case. Thus if a decision about application of economic analysis is based on its weight in litigation, its application should be extended. But the antitrust authority of Russia seems to underestimate the role an economic analysis could play in litigation. The investigation of the demand for economic analysis revealed that it is used mostly in cases under article 10 (abuse of dominant position). Hence an antitrust authority is more likely to be obliged to use an economic analysis than be aware of its real power.

The sample of the analysis is biased, thus the obtained results cannot completely reflect reality. This fact should be taken into account during their interpretation. For example, there are significantly more decisions in favour of companies in the sample than in the general sample. This means that in reality, economic analysis could be an even more powerful argument for antitrust authorities than the investigation revealed.

Extending the time interval of the analysis and hence enlarging the sample could improve this research. It could help solve the problem of biasness and increase the quality of the econometric results. In addition it takes into account some changes in the Russian antitrust law (in the Federal Law No. 135- FZ "On the Protection of Competition", in the Order № 220 "On a process of market competition level analysis" in comparison to its previous version and in the system of sanctions).

BIBLIOGRAPHY

Avdasheva, S., Shastitko A.E., 'Economic analysis in the cases of competition law infringements' (2011) (*Voprosy economiki)*, 2, pp. 122–139.

Breyer S., 'Economic reasoning and judicial review' (2009) (*Economic Journal)*, 119, pp. 123–135.

Drauz, G., 'A View from Inside the Merger Task Force: Comments on "Reforming European Merger Review: Targeting Problem Areas in Policy Outcomes"' (2002) (*Journal of Industry, Competition and Trade)*, 2(4), pp. 391–399.

George E.T., Epstein L., 'On the Nature of Supreme Court Decision Making' (1992) (*The American Political Science Review)*, 86(2), pp. 323–337.

Kurdin, A., Shastitko, A.A., 'Economic analysis application in antitrust litigations: empiric analysis' (2011) (*Journal Economicheskaya politica)*, 4, pp. 91–111.

Lee, H., 'Influencing a global agenda: Application of the modernization of European competition law for the WTO' (2004) (*Erasmus Law and Economics Review)*, 1, 2, pp. 111–141.

Muris, T.J., 'Improving the economic foundations of competition policy' (2003) (*Geo. Mason L. Rev.*), 12(1).

The Federal Law No. 135-FZ, "On the Protection of Competition", which entered into force on 26 October, 2006.

The Order No. 220 "On the process of market competition level analysis", which was entered into force on 28 April, 2010.

The Order No. 108 "On the process of market competition level analysis", which was entered into force on 28 April, 2006.

www.arbitr.ru – The Supreme Court of Arbitration of the Russian Federation

http://riarating.ru/infografika/20120702/610227291.html – RIA "News"

APPENDIX

Table 1. Demand for the elements of economic analysis

Elements of economic analysis	Company	Antitrust authority
Time interval	4	29
Product market	30	52
Geographic market	26	52
Companies' shares	14	40
Concentration level	0	5
Entry barriers	3	15
Competition level	0	5

Table 2. Rating of the regions presented in the sample on 2011

№	Region	Rating according to the economic and social development for 2011
1	Moscow	1
2	St-Petersburg	2
3	Tumenskaya oblast'	4
4	Sverdlovskaya oblast'	7
5	Krasnoyarskiy krahy	8
6	Respublica Tatarstan	9
7	Krasnodarskiy krahy	13
8	Permskiy krahy	14
9	Samarskaya oblast'	15
10	Kemerovskaya oblast'	17
11	Nizhegorodskaya oblast'	18
12	Chelyabinskaya oblast'	19
13	Rostovskaya oblast'	21
14	Respublica Komi	22
15	Irkutskaya oblast'	24
16	Novosibirskaya oblast'	25
17	Voronezhskaya oblast'	32
18	Vladimirskaya oblast'	34
19	Volgogradskaya oblast'	35
20	Udmurtskaya respublica	39
21	Vologodskaya oblast'	40
22	Arhangelskaya oblast'	41
23	Saratovskaya oblast'	42
24	Kaliningradskaya oblast'	45
25	Novgorodskayz oblast'	52
26	Ryazanskaya oblast'	53
27	Penzenskaya oblast'	59
28	Astrahanskaya oblast'	64
29	Kurganskaya oblast	66
30	Ivanovskaya oblast'	70
31	Respublika Mariy El	72
32	Respublica Altay	80

Source: RIA "News" (http://riarating.ru/infografika/20120702/610227291.html)

Table 3. The results of the first model

Sample size	149		
Dependent variable	Decision by appeals court (1, if in favour of a company)		
Independent variables	**Model 1**	**Model 2**	**Model 3**
Constant	0,08 (0,36)	0,03 (0,15)	0,1(0,18)
Economic analysis	−0,6 (0,37)	−0,49**(0,23)	−0,4(0,27)
Article (1, if Article 11)	−0,37 (0,27)	−0,41*(0,25)	−0,44*(0,26)
Market type (1, if goods market)	−0,05(0,24)	–	–
Expert	0,29(0,55)	–	–
Natural monopoly	0,02(0,3)	–	–
Region (1, if developed)	−0,05(0,34)	–	–
Company contests economic analysis	0,15(0,42)	–	–
Residuals of the reduced form equation with economic analysis as a dependent variable, market type and article as independent variables	–	–	−0,44(0,74)
R^2	3%	3%	3%
Multicollinearity	–	no	–
Hausman test (Ho: no endogeneity problem)	–	–	Pr>chi2 = 0.55

**-coefficient is significant at 5% level
*-coefficient is significant at 10% level
(standard errors in parentis)

Table 4. The results of the second model

Sample size	149	
Dependent variable	Economic analysis	
Independent variables	**Model 4**	**Model 5**
Constant	−0,9(0,35)	−0,63***(0,16)
Market type (1, if goods market)	0,75***(0,24)	0,85***(0,22)
Article (1, if Article 11)	−0,79***(0,3)	−0,74***(0,29)
Expert	0,38(0,57)	–
Natural monopoly	−0,38(0,33)	–
Region (1, if developed)	−0,49(0,35)	–
R^2	13%	11%
Multicollinearity	–	no

***-coefficient is significant at 1% level
(standard errors in parentis)

Table 5. The results of the third model

Sample size	149			
Dependent variable	Durability of a case			
Independent variables	**Model 6**	**Model 7**	**Model 8**	**Model 9**
Constant	–1,18(2,5)	1,56 (1,65)	1,55(1,18)	1,56(1,65)
Instances	3,62***(0,62)	3,45*** (0,6)	3,45***(0,44)	3,48***(0,64)
Expert	–4,64(2,99)	–5,13* (2,9)	–	–
Market type (1, if goods market)	4,77***(1,27)	5,4*** (1,2)	5,15***(1,26)	5,16***(1,22)
Economic analysis	2,72(1,88)	4,64*** (1,26)	4,44***(1,47)	4,57***(1,49)
Article (1, if Article 11)	1,25(1,48)	–	–	–
Natural monopoly	–1,24(1,62)	–	–	–
Region (1, if developed)	2,64(1,79)	–	–	–
Company contests economic analysis	3,41(2,14)	–	–	–
Residuals of the reduced form equation with economic analysis as a dependent variable, instances, market type and article as independent variables	–	–	–	–0,67(4,06)
R2	44%	41%	40%	40%
Breusch-Pagan test (Ho: no heteroscedasticity)	–	Pr>Chi2= 0,0001	–	–
Ramsey test (Ho: no omitted variables)	–	–	Pr>F = 0.5905	–
Multicollinearity	–	–	no	–
Hausman test (Ho: no endogeneity problem)	–	–	–	Pr>F = 0.87

***-coefficient is significant at 1% level
*-coefficient is significant at 10% level
(standard errors in parentis)

CHAPTER 18

CHALLENGES OF PRIVATE ENFORCEMENT OF ANTITRUST IN SLOVENIA

Ana Vlahek

1. INTRODUCTION

In recent years, the number of cases in which plaintiffs are seeking compensatory damages caused by anticompetitive behaviour and other forms of relief has been rising in Slovenia facing the courts, businesses and their representatives, to some extent even national competition authorities with novel and complex issues of antitrust private enforcement. Private enforcement of antitrust in Slovenia is still in its initial stage with the majority of cases still pending with the courts. It is thus yet to be seen how qualified are the judges in tackling antitrust cases.

The paper analyses focal elements of current regulation of private enforcement of antitrust in Slovenia. It focuses on relevant European legal framework, in particular on the new Directive 2014/104 and its *travaux préparatoires*, as well as on relevant national legislation. Article 62 of the Prevention of Restriction of Competition Act of 2008 (PRCA-1)[1] setting down some specific rules as regards antitrust damages lawsuits, and other, more general pieces of Slovenian legislation relevant in proceedings of private

---

[1] Sl. *Zakon o preprečevanju omejevanja konkurence* (*ZPOmK-1*), Official Gazette RS, No. 36/2008, with further amendments. English version of the Act is available at: <www.varstvo-konkurence.si/fileadmin/varstvo-konkurence.si/pageuploads/ZPOMK-1-EN_consolidated_2013.pdf> (13 July 2015) (*nota bene*: the text is a consolidated version of the original text of 2008 and its 2009, 2011, 2012, and 2013 amendments, but not of its latest amendment of 2014). PRCA of 2008 replaced the eponymous act of 1999 (PRCA; Sl. *Zakon o preprečevanju omejevanja konkurence (ZPOmK)*, Official Gazette RS, No. 64/07, with further amendments). Before the PRCA of 1999 entered into force, Slovenian competition law was regulated in the Protection of Competition Act of 1993 (PCO; Sl. *Zakon o varstvu konkurence (ZVK)*, Official Gazette RS, No. 18/93). For further details as to these acts, see *Zabel et al.: PCA of 1993 Commentary*; *Galič et al.: PRCA Commentary*; *Grilc et al.: PRCA-1 Commentary*; *Fatur & Podobnik: Competition Law in Western Europe and USA: Slovenia*); *Grilc & Podobnik: Das Wettbewerbsrecht in Slowenien*.

enforcement of antitrust are also presented and are assessed through the prism of the new directive. Further, the paper elaborates on the *status quo* of private enforcement of European and national antitrust in Slovenia and tries to find reasons for its inefficiency. Relevant follow-on and stand-alone private lawsuits that are or were pending before Slovenian courts that are analysed in the final chapter, also mirror the challenges of Slovenian judiciary in private antitrust enforcement proceedings.

2. REGULATION OF PRIVATE ENFORCEMENT OF ANTITRUST IN SLOVENIA

2.1. JURISDICTION IN ANTITRUST PRIVATE ENFORCEMENT CASES

The presently valid act regulating competition law in Slovenia, i.e. the PRCA-1, does not set out any specific rules on jurisdiction in antitrust private enforcement cases. General rules of the Civil Procedure Act (CPrA)[2] therefore apply.

According to the CPrA, jurisdiction in first-instance civil and commercial cases in Slovenia is divided between local and district courts based on various criteria.[3] In general, local courts have jurisdiction in those cases where the disputed value does not exceed EUR 20.000, whereas district courts hear the cases where the disputed value exceeds EUR 20.000.[4] However, in certain matters, jurisdiction is divided regardless of the disputed value. For example, district courts have exclusive jurisdiction in commercial cases (save in those concerning easements and real encumbrances, lease or tenancy relations, and disturbance of possession where local courts always hear the cases), in disputes

2 Sl. *Zakon o pravdnem postopku (ZPP)*, Official Gazette RS, No. 26/99, with further amendments. For further details as to the act, see *Ude et al.: CPrA Commentary.*

3 It is to be noted that there are no specialized civil or commercial courts in Slovenia, only specialized divisions for civil and commercial cases are organized within larger district courts, high courts as well as the Supreme Court of RS. First instance cases before local and (mostly also before) district courts are held before a single judge which is currently also the case in cases of private enforcement of competition (the 2008 CPrA amendment annulled Article 34 of the CPrA which set out that cases relating to "protection of competition" are always assessed by a panel of judges). High courts having (*inter alia*) supervisory jurisdiction over local and district courts, hear the cases in panels of three judges, while the Supreme Court as the third instance court (assessing cases in extraordinary remedy proceedings, limited to questions of substantive law and of serious breaches of procedure) hears the cases in panels of three or five judges. In some cases within the jurisdiction of the high courts, a sole judge issues decisions, while in some cases within jurisdiction of the Supreme Court, a panel of seven judges issues decisions. For further details, see the relevant provisions of the CPrA and the Courts Act (Sl. *Zakon o sodiščih (ZS)*, Official Gazette RS, No. 19/94, with further amendments). See also *Galič: Civil Procedure, Slovenia*, p. 183.

4 Articles 30 and 32 of the CPrA.

arising from bankruptcy proceedings, as well as in matters concerning "protection of competition".[5]

Commercial cases to which a specific set of rules of the CPrA applies,[6] are those cases where both parties are registered commercial companies or institutes, co-operatives, local communities or the state, irrespective of whether a dispute between them results from pursuing their commercial activity.[7] Litigations between one of these persons and a natural person who is a registered proprietor of a business (the so-called sole trader), as well as litigations between two sole traders are, however, deemed commercial only if the dispute has arisen within their commercial activity. Certain types of disputes, such as disputes between partners, partners and commercial companies, commercial companies and their management, disputes arising out of contracts on concession, disputes relating to bankruptcy, patents, trademarks as well as disputes concerning "protection of competition", are always deemed commercial regardless of a party's status.[8]

As in competition law cases usually two commercial entities will be in dispute (e.g., one telecommunications operator will be claiming damages from another operator having dominant position on the relevant market arguing that the defendant had breached European or/and Slovenian antitrust) thus making the dispute commercial, a district court will have jurisdiction and specific set of rules of the CPrA on proceedings in commercial matters will apply. The disputed value in such cases will also most plausibly exceed EUR 20.000 triggering the jurisdiction of district courts. Until the date of completion of this paper, all competition law cases in Slovenia have been commercial. Even regardless of the disputed value and of the type of dispute (be it civil or commercial) cases of private enforcement of antitrust would surely be characterised as matters concerning "protection of competition" thus automatically switching jurisdiction to district courts, as well as activating specific provisions of the CPrA regulating commercial disputes. Thus, also in actions with smaller claims (i.e. those where the disputed value does not exceed EUR 20.000) in non-commercial disputes (e.g. in damages actions between a consumer and his or her operator who had abused its dominant position), district courts applying procedural rules in commercial matters would have jurisdiction. Due to the potential complexity of competition law-related issues (even in cases of follow-on private actions) and the need to apply competition law and other legal rules relevant within the sphere of enforcement of competition law uniformly, giving jurisdiction to district courts in all cases of antitrust private enforcement is undoubtedly reasonable. In contrast with some other legal areas, such as

5 *Ibid.*
6 I.e., Articles 480–497 of the CPrA.
7 Article 481 of the CPrA.
8 Article 482 of the CPrA.

intellectual property where only the District Court in Ljubljana has jurisdiction at first instance, there is, however, unfortunately no specialised court in Slovenia assessing competition law issues. I would petition for such regulation coupled with a demand for guaranteeing that only judges proficient in competition law are appointed to assess competition law cases. This is in particular important in the initial stage of handling antitrust damages and other antitrust related civil and commercial cases before Slovenian courts when private enforcement of antitrust is only evolving. The reasonableness of the rule in force prior to the 2008 CPrA amendment setting out that cases of "protection of competition" are handled by a panel of judges, not by a single judge, could also be assessed and the rule, if found appropriate, reintroduced.

The CPrA does not regulate disputes concerning "protection of competition" in a specific chapter. It does, however, state with regard to certain rules that they are or are not to be applied to disputes relating to "protection of competition". Such disputes can, for example, never be characterised as small claims disputes.[9] Further, the following special rules of the CPrA on commercial disputes[10] apply also to disputes relating to "protection of competition":[11] in commercial litigation concerning the determination of existence or non-existence of a contract, or the performance of contractual obligation or cancellation of a contract, or the right to damages sustained due to breach of contractual obligations, the territorial jurisdiction is vested, in addition to the court of general jurisdiction,[12] also in the court on the territory of which the defendant should have rendered the performance stipulated by the contract;[13] in cases of urgency, the court may schedule the hearing immediately after the preliminary examination of the statement of claims, and it may do so by way of telephone, telegraph or other means of telecommunications;[14] when after receiving the defence plea the court establishes that the facts are not disputed between the parties, and that no other obstacle hinders the court to render the award, it may do so without holding a

9 Article 444 of the CPrA. Articles 442–458 of the CPrA regulating small claims disputes therefore do not apply to cases of protection of competition.

10 Articles 480–497 of the CPrA.

11 Article 483 of the CPrA.

12 In disputes against legal persons, the general territorial jurisdiction is vested in the court on the territory where the legal person has its registered office (according to Article 48 of the CPrA, in the event of doubt, the registered office is deemed to be the place where the management of the legal person is located). In some cases, however, rules on special territorial jurisdiction apply (Articles 49–65 of the CPrA). For example, if the same action is brought against several persons who are under territorial jurisdiction of several courts, the territorial jurisdiction shall be vested in the court of territorial jurisdiction over one of the co-defendants (Articles 35–38 of the CPrA). Further, the territorial jurisdiction to decide upon tort liability is vested, in addition to the court of general territorial jurisdiction, also in the court on the territory of which the tort has been committed, as well as in the court on the territory of which the damage has occurred.

13 Article 485 of the CPrA.

14 Article 487 of the CPr.

hearing;[15] the extraordinary remedy of revision is not admissible in commercial litigation unless the amount in dispute with respect to the contested part of the judgment exceeds EUR 200.000;[16] the parties to a commercial litigation may not produce oral statements on the record outside the hearing;[17] etc. Outside these special provisions of the CPrA,[18] general provisions of the CPrA are to be applied.[19]

2.2. LEGAL STANDING IN ANTITRUST PRIVATE ENFORCEMENT CASES

The PRCA or any other piece of legislation in Slovenia does not regulate who has legal standing in antitrust private enforcement cases. General rules of the CPrA therefore apply. According to the CPrA, any natural or juridical person (as well as anyone else if provided so by the law) has standing to file a claim with the court.[20] An action may be filed by a person who asserts that he or she personally suffered a direct violation of his or her rights.[21] For an action to be admissible (as a matter of procedural law), it is not necessary to prove that the rights of a plaintiff were violated, but it is necessary to assert such a violation.[22] A plaintiff must also possess a legal interest for the action[23] which is admissible only if a plaintiff seeks to protect his or her own (asserted) rights and not the rights of a certain third person.[24] Thus, there are, as a rule, no popular actions (*actio popularis*) and no class actions available under Slovenian law.[25] However, a statute can provide for a possibility to file an action, the object of which is not a protection of rights of the plaintiff but of a certain third person or of an

15 Article 488 of the CPrA.

16 Article 490 of the CPrA.

17 Article 494 of the CPrA.

18 As of 2008, Article 34 of the CPrA (providing that cases relating to "protection of competition" are always assessed by a panel of judges, never by a single judge to whom the cases are otherwise assigned at local courts as well as in the majority of district courts proceedings) and Article 367 of the CPrA (listing the cases of "protection of competition" among the cases where revision by the Supreme Court of RS is always allowed; as before 2008, revision was always possible in cases of "protection of competition", Article 490 of the CPrA was irrelevant with this regard) which were also "protection of competition" specific, are no longer in force.

19 For more details on Slovenian civil procedure, see *Galič: Civil Procedure, Slovenia*.

20 See Articles 76 – 85 of the CPrA. *Galič: Civil Procedure, Slovenia*, p. 96.

21 *Galič: Civil Procedure, Slovenia*, p. 96.

22 *Ibid.*

23 The declaratory action is the only kind of action where a claimant must expressly satisfy the court that there exists a legal interest for the action (Article 181 of the CPrA). With regard to actions for performance and constitutive actions, the existence of legal interest is presumed. However, this presumption is rebuttable. *Galič: Civil Procedure, Slovenia*, p. 98.

24 *Galič: Civil Procedure, Slovenia*, p. 96.

25 *Ibid.*

unidentified circle of persons.[26] For example, in the context of environmental protection, anyone can file an action for a cessation of certain acts, which impose imminent harm to the environment, whereby it is not obligatory for the plaintiff to assert any personal interest.[27] Similar is also true for the request for a removal of a source of danger threatening to cause larger harm to the plaintiff or to an unidentified number of persons, and for the request to refrain from activities causing disturbance or damages risk if these cannot be prevented by other appropriate means.[28] Furthermore, according to the Consumer Protection Act,[29] an organisation for the protection of consumers may file an action for: (1) declaration that certain general contract terms, which a trader used in contracts, already entered with consumers, are null and void;[30] and (2) for a cessation of applying these general contract terms in future contracts.[31] Similar representative actions are available also within environmental protection.[32] Apart from these specifically regulated *actiones popularis* and representative actions, joinder of parties where several persons may under specific circumstances sue or be sued by the same action as co-litigants, is available under the CPrA.[33] As of October 2008, model case procedure is also available under Slovenian civil procedure regulation enabling the courts to deal with a large number of claims in a connected manner and thereby speed up the proceedings.[34]

Class actions within competition law have to date not been possible in Slovenia. The previously mentioned declaratory and condemnatory (obliging to omission) representative actions filed by organisations for the protection of

26 *Ibid.*

27 *Ibid.*, pp. 96–97. For further details, see also *Damjan: Množični zahtevki zaradi posegov v zdravo življenjsko okolje*, pp. 263–264. This form of *actio popularis* is regulated in the Environmental Protection Act (EPA; Sl. *Zakon o varstvu okolja (ZVO-1)*), Official Gazette RS, No. 41/04, with further amendments.

28 Article 133/1 of the Code of Obligations (CO; Sl. *Obligacijski zakonik (OZ)*), Official Gazette RS, No. 83/2001, with further amendments.

29 CPA; Sl. *Zakon o varstvu potrošnikov (ZVPot)*, Official Gazette RS, No. 20/98, with further amendments.

30 Articles 74, 74.a and 75 of the CPA.

31 Article 76 of the CPA. So far, no such representative actions have been filed. For further details, see *Galič: Civil Procedure, Slovenia*, pp. 96 – 97; *Galič: Skupinske tožbe na področju potrošniškega prava.*

32 Article 14 of the EPA. See *Damjan: Množični zahtevki zaradi posegov v zdravo življenjsko okolje*, pp. 265–266.

33 If, in respect of the cause of action, they form a legal community; or if their rights or obligations are based upon the same factual and legal ground; or if they are joint and several debtors or creditors. If claims of different persons are based only on a similar factual and legal ground, they can act as co-litigants only if the same court has the subject matter and territorial jurisdiction over each of the claims and each of the defendants (Article 191 of the CPrA). *Galič: Civil Procedure, Slovenia*, p. 102. For further details on the so-called ordinary, uniform, and necessary co-litigants, see *Galič: Civil Procedure, Slovenia*, p. 102.

34 Article 279.b of the CPrA. For further details, see *Damjan: Množični zahtevki zaradi posegov v zdravo življenjsko okolje*, pp. 262–263; *Betetto: Vzorčni postopek.*

consumers are not particularly relevant for collective private enforcement of antitrust. It is, however, yet to be seen if and how the Slovenian legislator will broaden the possibilities for collective redress after the (non-binding) Recommendation on collective redress was issued by the European Commission in June 2013.[35]

In Slovenian cases of private enforcement of antitrust, competitors are in practice those filing actions while consumers have to date to my knowledge not yet instituted any proceedings. The consumers in Slovenia rarely seek court assistance in enforcing their rights as this is often way too expensive and time-consuming having regard to small claims that are usually at stake in such cases. For these reasons, two group out-of-court activities have taken place in the recent years aiming at forcing the (alleged) infringers to refund the overcharges paid on the basis of their restrictive practices. The first such activity was launched in 2009 relating to the resounding "electricity cartel" after the Supreme Court of RS (almost entirely) dismissed the actions against the decision of the Competition Protection Office of RS (CPO; now Public Agency of RS for the Protection of Competition (PAPC))[36] finding that four Slovenian electricity undertakings concerted their electricity prices.[37] The case was a massive breakthrough of antitrust importance in Slovenia as it had direct impact on almost every Slovenian household and business. After the judgements were issued, a Society for the refund of electricity overcharges[38] was established that campaigned for the follow-on private enforcement in order to give effect to the judgment in every-day life. Tens of thousands of consumers in Slovenia joined the society which was assisted by a law office and a couple of volunteers.[39] Under pressure from the Society and the media, the undertakings have decided to refund a certain amount of the overcharges before any suits were filed with the courts. The other out-of-court grouping of consumers is currently under way

35 Commission Recommendation of 11 June 2013 on common principles for injunctive and compensatory collective redress mechanisms in the Member States concerning violations of rights granted under Union Law (2013/396/EU). See *Vlahek: Kolektivno varstvo v EU.*

36 The Agency is the institution principally responsible for the enforcement of competition policy in the Republic of Slovenia as of 1 January 2013. Before that, this task was entrusted to the CPO which was established in 1994 as a public body organized within the Ministry for Economic Relations and Development. Calls for greater independence of the CPO (echoing also from the OECD) have led to a reorganization of the office into an agency. The previous status of the Slovenian competition authority as the executive body in the framework of the ministry has been elevated to the status of an independent and autonomous public agency established by the Republic of Slovenia. The 2011 and 2012 amendments of the PRCA-1 established and regulated *a novo* the PAPC replacing the CPO.

37 Decisions Nos. U 5/2008, U 2/2008, U 9/2008, U 4/2008, and U 6/2008 of 30 June 2009, reviewing the CPO's decision No. 306-168/2007-57 of 6 August 2008.

38 Later renamed Society for the Rule of Law (<www.dzp.si> (13 July 2015)).

39 The society obtained over 70.000 authorizations from the citizens to address to the undertakings the claims in their names for refund of the overcharges (amounting to approx. EUR 30-300 per household). A law office was also engaged in the project in case actions had to be filed with the court.

under the organisation of the Slovene Consumers' Association[40] with regard to the sums paid by the customers of Telekom Slovenije d.d. as a consequence of tying/bundling of ISDN and ADSL telecommunications services. The CPO held in March 2008 that Telekom Slovenije d.d.'s abusive practices as regards unjustifiable technological tying/bundling of ISDN and ADSL constitute an abuse of dominant position.[41] In November 2009, the Administrative Court reviewing the CPO's decision found procedural errors in the decision and sent it back to the CPO for re-examination. In the new proceedings, the PAPC adopted a decision in 2013[42] finding anti-competitive conduct on the part of Telekom Slovenije d.d. from December 2002 to September 2005 (i.e. for a shorter period as determined in the first CPO's decision).

Telekom Slovenije d.d. filed a lawsuit against the PAPC with the Administrative Court of RS requesting that the PAPC's decision is annulled. In January 2015, the Administrative Court of RS dismissed the action (at that moment, the decision of the PAPC became final)[43] and Telekom Slovenije d.d. decided to file a revision with the Supreme Court of RS where the case is currently pending. Having regard to the fact that the limitation period with regard to these repayments may soon run out (stressing that it is not clear how the rules on limitation (referring obviously to the rules of the PRCA-1 on suspension of limitation of antitrust damages claims and their temporal application) are to be applied in antitrust cases),[44] the Slovene Consumers' Association has publicly requested Telekom Slovenije d.d. to repay each of their customers a sum of EUR 105,20 (mirroring approx. the sum paid for the ISDN as determined by the PAPC in its decision) or to promise in a notarial statement that it will refund the customers the amounts paid for and/or because of the ISDN in case the Supreme Court of RS rules in favour of the PAPC. Telekom Slovenije d.d. answered that as the case is still pending with the courts, no out-of-court settlements or other agreements are possible. The Slovenian government who was also requested to intervene and force Telekom Slovenije d.d. to submit its statement, has allegedly not responded.[45] The association has thus drafted lawsuits against Telekom Slovenije d.d. and has invited all interested consumers to become members of the association and thereby receive assistance and guidance as to filing their individual lawsuits against Telekom Slovenije d.d.

---

40 Sl. *Zveza potrošnikov Slovenije (ZPS)*, a non-governmental organization established in 1990 whose task is to protect and represent consumer interests.

41 Decision No. 3072-2/2004-81 of 31 March 2008. The proceedings before the CPO started in October 2004.

42 Decision No. 3072-2/2004-132 of 25 October 2013.

43 <www.varstvo-konkurence.si/medijsko-sredisce/novica/?tx_ttnews%5BbackPid%5D=1438&tx_ttnews%5Btt_news%5D=5355&cHash=06f658eff0250c050fe3e0513cffe022> (13 July 2015).

44 See *supra* chapter III 1 (ix).

45 <https://www.zps.si/index.php/nasveti-in-zakonodaja-topmenu-235/mobilniki-tv-splet/7300-> (13 July 2015).

Some lawyers and law offices have also offered legal assistance to consumers in advancing with their claims against Telekom Slovenije d.d.

3. CIVIL LAW SANCTIONS FOR ANTITRUST BREACHES

3.1. DAMAGES FOR BREACHES OF EUROPEAN AND/OR SLOVENIAN ANTITRUST

The Protection of Competition Act of 1993 (PCA) as well as the (no longer valid) Prevention of Restriction of Competition Act of 1999 (PRCA) did not provide for any specific instruments to alleviate private enforcement of competition law in Slovenia. They merely stated that anyone sustaining a loss as a consequence of competition law infringement could seek damages in accordance with the general rules of obligations.[46]

The PRCA-1 of 2008 has broadened its traditional administrative scope by including a new Article 62 regulating some of the core aspects of damages claims within private enforcement of antitrust. When drafting the PRCA-1 of 2008, the Slovenian legislator had been inspired by the CJEU's case-law as well as by the European Commission's activities aiming at fostering private enforcement of antitrust in the Member States. Although at that time no binding secondary legislation of the EU existed regulating antitrust damages actions, the drafters of the PRCA-1 had already modelled the Slovenian regime upon the planned future European regulation of antitrust damages claims enshrined, *inter alia*, in the European Commission's White Paper of April 2008 on damages actions for breach of EU antitrust rules.[47]

Article 62/1 of the PRCA-1 states that anyone who intentionally or negligently breaches Articles 6 or 9 of the PRCA-1 or Articles 101 or 102 TFEU, is liable for damages resulting from such breach. Article 62/2 of the PRCA-1 provides for a binding effect of a final PAPC's or European Commission's decision finding a breach of Slovenian or European antitrust, whereby this rule does not prevent Slovenian courts to apply Article 267 TFEU. Article 62/3 of the PRCA-1 states that during the administrative proceedings before the SCPA or the European Commission, the limitation is suspended until the finality of the proceedings. Article 62/4 obliges Slovenian courts to inform the PAPC of every action

46 Article 27 of PCA of 1993, and Article 44 of the PRCA of 1999. Until 1 January 2002 when the CO came into force, rules on damages applicable in Slovenia were set out in the Yugoslav Law of Obligations of 1978, Official Gazette of SFRJ, No. 29/78, with further amendments.

47 White paper on damages actions for breach of the EC antitrust rules, COM(2008) 165 final. An overview of EU antitrust damages regulation is presented in *Vlahek: Oris odškodnin....*

requesting damages for breaches of Slovenian or European antitrust and is to be read together with Article 63 of the PRCA-1 that sets out the general regime of cooperation between the courts on the one hand and the PAPC and the European Commission on the other

Apart from the case-law of the CJEU (e.g. *Courage and Crehan* of 2001,[48] *Manfredi* of 2006,[49] *City Motors* of 2007,[50] *X BV* of 2009,[51] *Pfleiderer* of 2011[52] and *Donau Chemie* of 2013,[53] *Otis* of 2012,[54] *Kone* of 2013[55]) setting out some basic principles of private enforcement of European antitrust, and some general and more or less declarative statements on the importance of private enforcement within the EU entailed, for example, in Regulation 1/2003,[56] no detailed and systematic legislation on antitrust damages actions has been drafted within the EU until recently. A Directive on rules governing damages actions for infringements of European antitrust was drafted by the European Commission in 2009. It was, however, faced with strong opposition (in particular due to its provisions on collective redress) and supposedly therefore withdrawn from the debate. A new Directive on certain rules governing actions for damages under national law for infringements of the competition law provisions of the Member

48 C-453/99 *Courage Ltd v Bernard Crehan and Bernard Crehan v Courage Ltd and Others.* In its ruling, the CJEU (ECJ at the time) confirmed undoubtedly for the first time that damages may be claimed for breaches of European antitrust, and explained that parties to anticompetitive agreements, too, may under specific circumstances claim damages.

49 C-295/04 *Vincenzo Manfredi v Lloyd Adriatico Assicurazioni SpA*, C-296/04 *Antonio Cannito v Fondiaria Sai* SpA, C-297/04 *Nicolò Tricarico v Assitalia Sp*, and C-298/04 *Pasqualina Murgolo v Assitalia SpA*. In its ruling, the CJEU (ECJ at that time) interpreted the *status quo* of European regulation of antitrust damages claims and set out the prerequisites for regulation of certain relevant issues by the Member States.

50 C-421/05 *City Motors Groep NV v Citroën Belux NV* where the CJEU (ECJ at that time) confirmed its findings in *Courage and Crehan* and *Manfredi.*

51 C-429/07 *Inspecteur van de Belastingdienst v. X BV* where the CJEU (ECJ at the time) interpreted the European Commission's amicus curiae cooperation with national courts as laid down in Article 15/3 of Regulation 1/2003. For further details, see *Vlahek: Amicus curiae....*

52 C-360/09 *Pfleiderer AG v Bundeskartellamt* where the CJEU has interpreted how the national courts are to tackle with the issue of access of private enforcement plaintiffs to leniency documentation.

53 C-536/11 *Bundeswettbewerbsbehörde v Donau Chemie AG and others* also dealing with access to leniency documentation by plaintiffs in damages actions.

54 C-199/11 *Europese Gemeenschap v. Otis NV and others* where the CJEU has ruled on the question whether the European Commission may represent the EU in private damages actions against the undertakings which were found in breach of EU competition law established by the Commission.

55 C-557/12 *Kone AG, Otis GmbH, Schindler Aufzüge und Fahrtreppen GmbH, Schindler Liegenschaftsverwaltung GmbH, ThyssenKrupp Aufzüge GmbH v ÖBB-Infrastruktur AG*, where the CJEU has stated that national legislation excluding liability of members of a cartel for the so-called umbrella effects in the form of higher prices set by cartelists' competitors, is not in line with EU law.

56 Council Regulation (EC) No 1/2003 of 16 December 2002 on the implementation of the rules on competition laid down in Articles 81 and 82 of the Treaty (Text with EEA relevance), OJ L 1, 4.1.2003, p. 1–25 See, for example, paragraph 7 of the Preamble of the regulation.

States and of the European Union was drafted by the Commission in June 2013[57] and was forwarded to the European Parliament and the Council in adoption. The new Directive 2014/104 was adopted on 26 November 2014.[58] It entered into force on 25 December 2014. Its implementation deadline is set to 27 December 2016.[59]

It should be noted that the title of the directive (as well as the definition provided in point 1 of Article 2 of the directive) is somewhat misleading as it suggests that the directive applies also to actions for breaches of (purely) national antitrust. Paragraph 10 of the preamble to the directive as well as point 3 of Article 2 of the directive clarify that the term "national competition law" refers only to cases where the infringement also has an effect on trade between the Member States, as in this case European antitrust is to be applied next to national antitrust as required by Article 3 of Regulation 1/2003.[60] The directive does therefore not set out rules also as regards enforcement of purely national antitrust. It would nevertheless be reasonable if the Slovenian legislator aligns rules (at least those that are regulated in the directive) on actions for damages for breaches of national antitrust with those on actions for damages for breaches of EU antitrust.

With regard to the rest of the rules which are still governed by national law (regarding breaches of EU antitrust and of national antitrust), the directive requires the Member States to respect the principles of effectiveness and equivalence.[61] Until the new directive is implemented into Slovenian law (hopefully not merely the copy-paste way), the existing provisions of national law will complement the existent European regime as regards damages actions in cases of breaches of Articles 101 or 102 TFEU. With regard to breaches of Slovenian antitrust, only Slovenian law applies (although the concepts of EU law

57 Proposal for a Directive of the European Parliament and of the Council on certain rules governing actions for damages under national law for infringements of the competition law provisions of the Member States and of the European Union (Text with EEA relevance), COM(2013) 404 final, available at (in English): <http://eur-lex.europa.eu/LexUriServ/LexUriServ.do?uri=COM:2013:0404:FIN:EN:PDF> (13 July 2015).

58 Directive 2014/104/EU of the European Parliament and of the Council of 26 November 2014 on certain rules governing actions for damages under national law for infringements of the competition law provisions of the Member States and of the European Union (Text with EEA relevance), OJ L 349, 5.12.2014, p. 1–19; available at (in English): http://eur-lex.europa.eu/legal-content/EN/TXT/PDF/?uri=CELEX:32014L0104&from=EN (13 July 2015).

59 Article 22 of the directive sets out important rules as to temporal application of national legislation implementing the directive.

60 The PRCA-1 regulates the so-called unified proceedings of Slovenian competition authority, i.e. proceedings held applying simultaneously Articles 6 of PRCA-1 and 101 TFEU or Articles 9 of PRCA-1 and 102 TFEU. For further details, see *Vlahek* in *Grilc et al.: PRCA-1 Commentary*, pp. 84 – 87, and *Bratina* in *Grilc et al.: PRCA-1 Commentary*, pp. 287 – 289.

61 Article 4 of the directive. These principles were emphasized already in the CJEU's preliminary rulings, for example, in the *Manfredi* judgement (C-295/04 *Vincenzo Manfredi v Lloyd Adriatico Assicurazioni SpA*, C-296/04 *Antonio Cannito v Fondiaria Sai* SpA, C-297/04 *Nicolò Tricarico v Assitalia Sp*, and C-298/04 *Pasqualina Murgolo v Assitalia SpA*).

are of importance to purely national cases as well, since Slovenian competition law is to a great extent transcribed from European competition law). With respect to all those issues of antitrust damages actions not covered by EU law and/or by Article 62 of the PRCA-1, general provisions of the CO on damages apply.[62]

The directive addresses the following issues: full compensation principle (Chapter I, Articles 1/1 and 3); disclosure of evidence (Chapter II, Articles 5–8); effect of national competition authorities' decisions in private lawsuits (Chapter III, Article 9); limitation periods (Chapter III, Article 10); joint and several liability of infringers (Chapter III, Article 11); passing-on (Chapter IV, Articles 12–16); quantification of harm and rebuttable presumption that cartels cause harm (Chapter V, Article 17); consensual dispute resolution (Chapter VI, Articles 18–19).

3.2. FULL COMPENSATION AND SINGLE DAMAGES

Under Slovenian law, full compensation of the real value of pecuniary loss suffered is guaranteed to the victims.[63] The actual loss, loss of profit as well as interest may be claimed.[64] Within private enforcement of competition law, only single damages may be awarded.[65] These principles accord fully to the EU pre-directive regime of damages actions for breaches of European antitrust,[66] as well as to the current regime as set out in the new directive. Basing its substance on the CJEU case-law, Article 3 of the new directive states that Member States shall ensure that any natural or legal person who has suffered harm caused by an infringement of competition law is able to claim and to obtain full compensation for that harm. It adds that full compensation shall place a person who has suffered harm in the position in which that person would have been had the infringement not been committed, and it shall therefore cover the right to compensation for actual loss and for loss of profit, plus payment of interest, but

62 For further details, see *Jadek Pensa* in *Juhart et al.: CO Commentary*, pp. 665–683, 795–819; *Plavšak* in *Juhart et al.: CO Commentary*, pp. 683–742; *Ahtik & Vlahek: Določanje odškodnin v primeru kršitev antitrusta*.

63 See *Plavšak* in *Juhart et al.: CO Commentary*, pp. 755–760, 942–990; *Jadek Pensa* in *Juhart et al.: CO Commentary*, pp. 919–921. Non-pecuniary damages may also be claimed under CO, but within the field of antitrust that is unlikely.

64 See *Plavšak* in *Juhart et al.: CO Commentary*, pp. 755–760; *Ahtik & Vlahek: Določanje odškodnin v primeru kršitev antitrusta*.

65 Slovenian tort law is based on the principle of full compensation and single damages. Only in exceptional cases, damages exceeding single damages may be awarded. According to the Copyright and Related Rights Act, for example, treble damages may be awarded if the act was breached intentionally or in gross negligence.

66 See *Vlahek* in *Grilc et al.: PRCA-1 Commentary*, pp. 495–500; *Ahtik & Vlahek: Določanje odškodnin v primeru kršitev antitrusta*.

shall not lead to overcompensation, whether by means of punitive, multiple or other types of damages.

3.3. QUANTIFICATION OF HARM

Quantification of harm is regulated in Article 17 of the new directive. So far, this issue has been addressed only by EU soft-law, i.e. Commission *Communication on quantifying harm in actions for damages based on breaches of Article 101 or 102 of the TFEU* of 2013[67] accompanied by the *Practical guide on quantifying harm in actions for damages based on breaches of Article 101 or 102 TFEU.*[68] Article 17/1 of the new directive states that Member States shall ensure that neither the burden nor the standard of proof required for the quantification of harm renders the exercise of the right to damages practically impossible or excessively difficult. Member States shall also ensure that national courts are empowered, in accordance with national procedures, to estimate the amount of harm if it is established that a claimant suffered harm but it is practically impossible or excessively difficult to precisely quantify the harm suffered on the basis of the available evidence. It will be most interesting to see to what extent and how these provisions are implemented into Slovenian legislation.

Under Slovenian rules of civil procedure, the burden of proof (*onus probandi*) rests upon the party raising an issue (more precisely, the party obliged to raise an issue – *onus proferendi*).[69] There are also some explicit rules concerning shifting of the burden of proof (for example, in a tort case, a claimant must establish the facts concerning the harmful act, the causal link and the damage; however, Article 131 of the CO sets out a presumption that the wrongdoer is liable, and it is thus the defendant who must prove the lack of his or her fault in a case concerning the damages),[70] but do not apply with regard to harm and its amount.

In Slovenia, the standard of proof (describing the amount and quality of evidence required to discharge a burden of proof) is very high.[71] Pursuant to Article 215 of the CPrA, the judge should decide according to the rules on the burden of proof (the burden rests upon the party who raises an issue) if he or she cannot reliably establish the existence/non-existence of the disputed fact. The

---

67 Communication from the Commission on quantifying harm in actions for damages based on breaches of Article 101 or 102 of the Treaty on the Functioning of the European Union, (2013/C 167/07), C(2013) 3440, available at (in English): <http://eur-lex.europa.eu/LexUriServ/LexUriServ.do?uri=OJ:C:2013:167:0019:0021:EN:PDF> (13 July 2015). Other documents on which the communication is based, are available at (in English): http://ec.europa.eu/competition/antitrust/actionsdamages/documents.html (13 July 2015).

68 SWD(2013) 205, available at (in English): <http://ec.europa.eu/competition/antitrust/actionsdamages/quantification_guide_en.pdf> (13 July 2015).

69 *Galič: Civil Procedure, Slovenia*, p. 174.

70 *Ibidem.*

71 *Ibid.*, p. 175.

judge must be (practically) convinced (persuaded) about the existence of a certain fact, if not, he or she should find against the party whom a burden of proof for this fact rests upon (thus, even if the court finds it more probable – but still not beyond the doubt of a reasonable person – that this fact actually exists).[72] Article 216/1 of the CPrA provides that when the liability of a party is established, and only the amount in question remains in dispute, a court may, in exceptional circumstances, use judicial discretion to establish the missing facts.[73] The court may act in such manner if unreasonable difficulties would ensue the determination of these facts through means of evidence; for example, the cost of evidence would be entirely disproportionate to the value of the claim.[74] It is important to note that in such cases, judicial discretion is applied to establish the facts (e.g., the amount of damages) and not to interpret the law (e.g., the notion of"just satisfaction").[75] This discretion should, however, by no means be a safe harbour for the judges who are unwilling or unable to determine through means of evidence objectively easily determinable facts.

In recent years, the Slovenian courts have started tackling with quantification of damages in antitrust cases. One of the seminal (and much debated among legal practitioners) judgments as regards the burden of proof and the method of quantification of damages in antitrust cases was the judgment of the High Court in Ljubljana issued in May 2013 in the ABM v. Telekom Slovenije case presented below.[76] In applying Article 216/1 of the CPrA, the High Court stressed that in antitrust damages cases it is focal that the parties[77] reveal to the court and prove all relevant facts on their business activities. Unless they do so, the court is faced with the so-called "cognitive crisis". The method of quantification applied by the High Court (using, *inter alia*, the infringer's profit as the claimant's profit in the but-for scenario) was later confirmed by the Supreme Court of RS.[78]

According to Article 17/2 of the new directive, Member States shall ensure that it shall be presumed that cartel infringements cause harm, and that the infringer shall have the right to rebut this presumption. Paragraph 47 of the preamble to the directive clarifies that in order to remedy the information

---

72 *Ibidem*. As further pointed out by Galič, in the doctrine as well as in case law, the harshness of the high standard of proof (combined with a very limited scope of pre-trial production of evidence and a very limited access to evidence in the possession of the opponent) is sometimes rectified by shifting a burden of proof. Some authors also try to relax the standard of proof and propose a solution that a standard of proof in a civil case should not, as Article 215 of the CPrA could imply, be practically identical as the one in criminal cases (i.e. beyond reasonable doubt), and opt for a clearly overwhelming degree of probability to be sufficient in a civil case. *Galič: Civil Procedure, Slovenia*, p. 175.

73 *Galič: Civil Procedure, Slovenia*, p. 176.

74 *Ibid.*, pp. 176–177.

75 *Ibid.*, p. 177.

76 No. I Cpg 125/2013 of 28 May 2013 (in particular para. 16 ff).

77 Even the defendant if certain facts favouring the claimant who cannot prove the damage are within the defendant's "cognitive sphere" and thus for him to rely to and prove.

78 No. III Ips 98/2013 of 23 May 2014 (in particular para. 36 ff).

asymmetry and some of the difficulties associated with quantifying antitrust harm, and to ensure the effectiveness of claims for damages, it is appropriate to presume that in the case of a cartel infringement, such infringement resulted in harm, in particular via a price effect. It further explains that depending on the facts of the case this means that the cartel has resulted in a rise in price, or prevented a lowering of prices which would otherwise have occurred but for the infringement. It adds that this presumption should not cover the concrete amount of harm – this will obviously (at least in principle) still have to be proven by the plaintiff (unless in the scenario where the court itself, not the plaintiff, will estimate the amount of harm that has rebuttedly occurred, enabling the plaintiff to be awarded damages without proving harm or its amount).

An entirely new and (at least to my knowledge) previously not much debated rule is set out in Article 17/3 of the new directive which states that Member States shall ensure that, in proceedings relating to an action for damages, a national competition authority shall be able, if it deems it appropriate, to assist on the determination of the amount of damages upon request of a national court. It will be interesting to see if and to what extent Slovenian courts will opt for such assistance and thus attract an administrative body in judicial proceedings as some sort of *amicus curiae*.[79]

3.4. SCOPE OF THE VICTIMS SEEKING DAMAGES

The scope of the victims seeking damages is not limited under Slovenian law. In practice, however, it is mainly competitors that are filing damages actions against (alleged or actual) antitrust infringers. As has been explained above,[80] damages class and representative actions within competition law have to date not been possible in Slovenia. It is yet to be seen if and what kind of collective redress will be available under Slovenian antitrust damages regime following the European Commission's *Recommendation of 11 June 2013 on common principles for injunctive and compensatory collective redress mechanisms in the Member States concerning violations of rights granted under Union Law.*

3.5. PASSING-ON

Rules on passing-on of overcharges as set out in Chapter IV of the new directive will also have to be implemented into the PRCA-1. Although Slovenian (general) legislation already accords to the basic rule that compensation of harm can be

---

79 For further details as to amicus curie regime regulated in Article 15 of Regulation 1/2003 and Article 63 of the PRCA-1, see *Vlahek: Amicus curiae....*

80 See *supra* chapter on legal standing in antitrust private enforcement cases.

claimed by anyone who suffered it, irrespective of whether they are direct or indirect purchasers, that the defendant may invoke the passing-on defence, etc., detailed substantive as well as procedural rules regarding passing-on of overcharges will plausibly have to be inserted into the PRCA-1 in order to implement the directive accordingly in the antitrust-specific legislation. Guidelines for national courts on how to estimate the share of the overcharge which was passed on to the indirect purchaser that will have to be issued by the Commission in accordance with Article 16 of the new directive will undoubtedly be of additional assistance to Slovenian courts. With regard to passing-on it is worth mentioning that the directive did (wisely) not include the provision of Article 12/2 of the directive proposal of 11 June 2013 according to which the defendant could not be able to invoke the passing-on defence insofar as the overcharge has been passed on to persons at the next level of the supply chain for whom it is legally impossible to claim compensation for their harm. Such provision, if inserted into the directive, would enable direct purchasers that have passed-on the overcharge, to be awarded such overcharge solely because otherwise the defendant might not be awarded to return the overcharge to indirect purchasers. Such provision would be in contradiction with the basic concepts of the law of obligations.

3.6. FAULT

Article 62/1 of the PRCA-1 explicitly establishes tort liability for infringements of Slovenian and/or European antitrust: *Anyone intentionally or negligently breaching Article 6 or 9 of the PRCA-1 or Article 101 or 102 TFEU, is liable for the damage sustained by that.* As the concept of liability for damages stemming from unlawful conduct represents a core concept of Slovenian civil law enshrined already in the CO, additional specific stipulation in the PRCA-1 of tort liability for antitrust breaches was not indispensable. It is, however, important in a declaratory manner as it signals to all potential offenders of damages claims they might face next to all public enforcement measures available under Slovenian and European legislation.

When claiming damages according to Slovenian law, the plaintiff will have to show that the following elements of tort liability based on fault have been met: (i) the defendant has breached Article 6 or 9 of the PRCA-1 or Article 101 or 102 TFEU; (ii) the plaintiff has sustained a loss; and (iii) there is a causal link between the breach and the loss sustained; while (iv) the defendant's fault, i.e. that it committed a wrongful act intentionally or negligently, will be presumed according to Article 131 of the CO as Slovenian legislation adopts the concept of fault liability with shifted burden of proof concerning fault. The alleging party need not prove that the defendant acted wrongfully. On the contrary, the alleged wrongdoer has to prove the absence of his or her fault, otherwise the fault is presumed.[81] Other elements of liability are to be proven by the alleging party. In competition law cases, proving that the defendant who breached competition legislation was not at fault will pose serious obstacles to the defendants. The Commission, however, has proposed in its White Paper as well as in its first draft directive that to the extent that Member States require, in addition to proof of an infringement of Article 101 or 102 TFEU, fault to be proven in actions for damages, they shall ensure that, once an injured party has established such an infringement, the infringer is liable for damages unless he shows that he could not reasonably have been aware that his conduct distorted competition. The latest text of the new directive, however, does not address the issue of fault offering thereby various interpretations, e.g. that it is for the Member States to regulate this question, that fault is not a relevant element in antitrust damages liability, that the infringer is irrefutably deemed liable for damages caused by the infringement, etc.

3.6. JOINT AND SEVERAL LIABILITY OF INFRINGERS

The new directive stipulates *a novo* joint and several liability of infringers. It states in Article 11/1 that Member States shall ensure that undertakings which have infringed competition law through joint behaviour are jointly and severally liable for the harm caused by the infringement so that each of those undertakings is bound to compensate for the harm in full, and the injured party has the right to require full compensation from any of them until he or she has been fully compensated. A general rule on joint and several liability for damages is already set out in Article 186 of the CO and corresponds to the basic rule set out in Article 11/1 of the new directive. Article 11/2 of the directive, however, states that where the infringer is a SME pursuant to the definition in Commission *Recommendation of 6 May 2003 concerning the definition of micro, small and medium-sized enterprises*,[82] it shall be liable only to its own direct and indirect purchasers if its market share in the relevant market was below 5% at any time during the infringement, and the application of the normal rules of joint and several liability would irretrievably jeopardise its economic viability and cause its assets to lose all their value. This exception to the joint and several liability of the SME shall, however, not apply if the SME led the infringement or coerced

81 Article 131/1 of the CO states that any person inflicting damage on another shall be obliged to reimburse it, unless it proves that the damage was incurred without any culpability. That only *culpa levis* is presumed cannot be derived from the CO, but was explained on the joined session of the highest courts of the former Yugoslavia in 1980. In cases outside *culpa levis*, fault is presumed only if a statute expressly states so or if that can be undoubtedly derived from the purpose of a given provision. See *Jadek Pensa* in *Juhart et al.: CO Commentary*, pp. 796 and 801.

82 2003/361/EC, available at (in English): <http://eur-lex.europa.eu/LexUriServ/LexUriServ.do?uri=OJ:L:2003:124:0036:0041:en:PDF> (13 July 2015).

other undertakings to participate in the infringement, or it has previously been found to have infringed competition law (Article 11/3).

According to Article 11/4 of the new directive, Member States shall also ensure that an immunity recipient is jointly and severally liable (only) to its direct or indirect purchasers or providers, while it is liable to other injured parties only where full compensation cannot be obtained from the other undertakings that were involved in the same infringement of competition law, whereby Member States shall ensure that the limitation period in these cases is reasonable and sufficient to allow injured parties to bring the actions against the immunity recipients. Article 11/5 of the new directive further states that Member States shall ensure that an infringing undertaking may recover a contribution from any other infringing undertaking, the amount of which shall be determined in the light of their relative responsibility for the harm caused by the infringement, while the amount of contribution of an undertaking which has been granted immunity from fines by a competition authority under a leniency programme shall not exceed the amount of the harm it caused to its own direct or indirect purchasers or providers.

Finally, according to Article 11/6 of the new directive, Member States shall ensure that, to the extent the infringement of competition law caused harm to injured parties other than the direct or indirect purchasers or providers of the infringing undertakings, the amount of contribution of the immunity recipient shall be determined in the light of its relative responsibility for that harm. These rules will have to be implemented accordingly into the PRCA-1.

3.7. EFFECT OF NCAS' DECISIONS

Damages actions may be filed as stand-alone actions or as follow-on actions. In the latter case, the plaintiffs decide to wait on the competition authority to issue a decision finding an infringement, and institute damages proceedings with the national courts only afterwards. Such follow-on actions enable the plaintiffs to refer to the competition authority's decision as regards the finding of an infringement. Inspired by Article 16 of Regulation 1/2003, Article 62/2 of the PRCA-1 alleviates the plaintiff's position regarding the burden of proving that rules on competition (be it European or Slovenian) had been breached as it provides that (without prejudice to the rights and obligations under Article 267 TFEU) the national courts assessing damages claims are bound by final decisions issued by the PAPC and the European Commission finding an infringement. Thus, in such cases, the plaintiffs need only prove that they have sustained loss, that the defendant was at fault, and that there is a causal link between the infringement and the loss sustained. It is important to note that, at least with regard to cases of European antitrust breaches, Article 62/2 of the PRCA-1 is to be read in conjunction with Article 16/1[83] of Regulation 1/2003 which sets out additional rules to be observed by the courts that have not been copied in the PRCA-1.[84] It is to be underscored that already prior to inserting Article 62/2 into the PRCA-1, Slovenian courts were in principle bound by final administrative acts, such as the CPO's final decision. This was stressed also by the High Court in Ljubljana in its judgment of 21 November 2013 in the *Blitz v Kolosej* case.[85]

The new directive provides for a novel set of rules regulating the effect of Member States' NCAs' decisions. Article 9/1 thus states that Member States shall ensure that an infringement of competition law found by a final decision of a NCA or a review court is deemed to be irrefutably established for the purposes of an action for damages brought before their national courts under Article 101 or 102 of the Treaty or under national competition law (whereby this provision is without prejudice to the rights and obligations under Article 267 TFEU). This rule was laid down in Article 62/2 of the PRCA-1 by Slovenian legislature already in 2008. Article 9/2 of the new directive, however, adds that Member States shall ensure that a final decision of a NCA or a review court given in another Member State may, in accordance with their respective national law, be presented before their national courts as at least *prima facie* evidence that an infringement of competition law has occurred and, as appropriate, may be assessed along with any other material brought by the parties. In order to implement Article 9/2 of the new directive, Article 62/2 of the PRCA-1 will have to be amended accordingly.

In Slovenia, the plaintiffs have been filing damages actions mostly as stand-alone actions. The CPO was often inefficient in the assessment of cases. Once it finally issued decisions, the undertakings as a rule have instituted lengthy court review proceedings. In order to avoid any time allowed under the statute of limitations from running out, the parties have decided to file lawsuits alleging all elements of tort liability. Should the competition authority during such time issue a final and binding decision finding the infringement, the courts would be bound by such decision, otherwise they would have to assess the alleged

83 *1. When national courts rule on agreements, decisions or practices under Article 81 or Article 82 of the Treaty which are already the subject of a Commission decision, they cannot take decisions running counter to the decision adopted by the Commission. They must also avoid giving decisions which would conflict with a decision contemplated by the Commission in proceedings it has initiated. To that effect, the national court may assess whether it is necessary to stay its proceedings. This obligation is without prejudice to the rights and obligations under Article 234 of the Treaty. 2. When competition authorities of the Member States rule on agreements, decisions or practices under Article 81 or Article 82 of the Treaty which are already the subject of a Commission decision, they cannot take decisions which would run counter to the decision adopted by the Commission.*

84 For further details, see *Vlahek* in *Grilc: PRCA -1Commentary*, pp. 504–510.

85 For further details, see *Sever: Vezanost nacionalnega sodišča*… For further details on the case, see *infra* the last chapter of this paper.

infringement as well. As in practice the courts are usually reluctant to cope with the assessment of the alleged anticompetitive practices, they tend to stall the damages proceedings and await for the competition authority's decision to become final and binding. It is important to note that in some cases in which private lawsuits are pending, the CPO has terminated administrative proceedings according to Article 40 of the PRCA-1 as it had not found that an infringement had taken place. In such decisions, the competition authority does not find that there was no infringement (such a decision would enable the courts to dismiss the damages claims), it merely establishes that it had not found the infringement leaving the courts with the task of fully assessing the undertakings' practices. However, as the competition authority itself was unable to find an infringement, it is plausible to expect the courts to decide in favour of the defendants.

4. DISCLOSURE OF EVIDENCE

Chapter II of the new directive (Articles 5–8) sets out detailed rules on disclosure of evidence in private antitrust lawsuits. Article 5 lays down the rules on disclosure of evidence by the defendant and by third parties, whereas Articles 6 and 7 regulate disclosure of evidence contained in the NCA's file. Article 8 requires the Member States to empower the courts to effectively impose penalties on parties, third parties and their legal representatives in case they breach their duties as to disclosure of evidence. The penalties that can be imposed by national courts must be effective, proportionate and dissuasive, and shall include, with regard to the behaviour of a party to proceedings for an action for damages, the possibility to draw adverse inferences, such as presuming the relevant issue to be proven or dismissing claims and defences in whole or in part, and the possibility to order the payment of costs.

According to Galič, Article 5 of the new directive adopts a middle-way solution between the full scale US style discovery, and the strict traditional civil law discovery regime.[86] Articles 6 and 7 of the new directive try to eliminate a possible hurdle for a successful leniency programme (and thus for a successful public enforcement of antitrust) stemming from the fear of potential leniency applicants that their leniency statements could assist the victims of the infringements in claiming damages from them.[87] In cases of application of Articles 101 or 102 TFEU, the CJEU's interpretation in *Pfleiderer*[88] and *Donau Chemie*[89] is of some, albeit vague assistance to the undertakings in determining

86 *Galič: Disclosure of Documents in Private Antitrust Enforcement Litigation.*
87 For details as to leniency programme in Slovenia, see *Podobnik: Program prizanesljivosti....*
88 C-360/09 *Pfleiderer AG v Bundeskartellamt.*
89 C-536/11 *Bundeswettbewerbsbehörde v Donau Chemie AG and others.*

the plausibility that access to leniency statements will be granted by the national court. The new directive regulates the questions of access to leniency statements more unambiguously and enables the undertakings to decide with more certainty as to future development of their case to apply for leniency or not. In Slovenia, there is no direct regulation of access to PAPC's leniency documents for the purposes of civil law enforcement. The Decree on the procedure for granting immunity from fines and reduction of fines in cartel cases states only that leniency applications are deemed business secrets,[90] Public Information Access Act[91] and its provisions on exceptions to grant access,[92] as well as general provisions of the CPrA[93] would thus be applied.[94] It is yet to be seen how this issue is tackled with by Slovenian undertakings and authorities until the directive is implemented.

Galič states with regard to the new European regime of disclosure in antitrust damages cases that: "[*t*]*he creation of EU-wide litigation disclosure mechanism in the Antitrust Damages Directive will* [...] *inevitably have to have general impacts for civil procedure law in Slovenia*[...]"[95] and that "[*i*]*n Slovenia, a transposition of the Directive's litigation disclosure mechanism will require a fundamental change in the very key procedural principles.*"[96] After making an in-depth analysis of Slovenian rules on disclosure, he concludes that "[...] *it is true that the transposition of the litigation disclosure mechanism of the Antitrust Damages Directive will undermine the existing principles of Slovenian civil procedure. This however goes on the account of the fact that with regard to disclosure of evidence, the Slovenian law is outdated and is partially based on erroneous premises. Therefore the required transposition of the Directive's requirements should therefore be perceived as a positive step. This step will however will be successful only if a general reassessment of the disclosure of evidence in Slovenian civil procedure law will follow.*"[97] This signals the need for very deliberate legislative steps that are to be taken within the project of implementation of the new directive. Not only Article 62 of the PRCA-1, but other pieces of legislation, too, will have to be amended in order to implement the directive accordingly. Where appropriate, the process of implementation of the directive should serve also for reforming relevant aspects of Slovenian law outside the sphere of private enforcement of antitrust.

---

90 Article 6 of the Decree.

91 Sl. *Zakon o dostopu do informacij javnega značaja (ZDIJZ)*, Official Gazette RS, No. 24/03, with further amendments.

92 Article 6 of the Act.

93 Articles 227–229 and 231–234 of the CPrA.

94 In its Judgment No. I Cpg 708/2013 of 21 November 2013 in *T2 v Telekom Slovenije*, the High Court of Ljubljana stated that the PRCA-1 provisions on access to the SCPA file apply only to the CPO administrative proceedings, not to private enforcement proceedings.

95 *Galič: Disclosure of Documents in Private Antitrust Enforcement Litigation.*

96 *Ibidem.*

97 *Ibidem.*

5. LIMITATION

Another antitrust-specific provision of the PRCA-1 is Article 62/3 reflecting the CJEU's reasoning in *Manfredi* as well as the European Commission's ideas entailed in its White Paper as regards the effect of the initiation of administrative infringement proceedings on the limitation period for damages claims. The PRCA-1 provides that the limitation period (for damages claims only)[98] is suspended while public enforcement of competition rules by the PAPC or the Commission (and review courts) is still ongoing. In its White Paper of 2008, however, the Commission preferred the option of a new limitation period starting once the competition authority or a review court issues an infringement decision, over the option of suspending the limitation period. In the withdrawn draft directive of 2009 on rules governing damages actions for infringements of European antitrust, the Commission opted for any of these options. As it had announced already in its White Paper, the Commission has also suggested that the national rules allow victims sufficient time to bring an action after they became aware of the infringement and the harm it caused; that they prevent a limitation period from starting to run before the day on which a continuous or repeated infringement ceases; and that they allow victims at least two years to bring an action after a final finding of the infringement by a competition authority or a review court. The new directive regulates the questions of limitation in Article 10 providing rules on when the limitation period begins to run, the duration of the limitation period and the circumstances under which the period is interrupted or suspended. It states that the limitation period shall not begin to run before the infringement has ceased and the claimant knows, or can reasonably be expected to know the behaviour and the fact that it constitutes an infringement of competition law; the fact that the infringement caused harm to him; and the identity of the infringing undertaking. The limitation period for bringing an action for damages shall be at least five years. Member States shall ensure that the limitation period is suspended or, depending on national law, interrupted, if a competition authority takes action for the purpose of the investigation or proceedings in respect of an infringement of competition law to which the action for damages relates, whereby the suspension shall end at the earliest one year after the infringement decision has become final or the proceedings are otherwise terminated. The provisions of Article 62/3 of the PRCA-1 will therefore also have to be amended in order to implement Article 10 of the new directive accordingly. Until then, CJEU's case-law, Article 62/3 of the PRCA-1 and general national rules on the statute of limitations as set out in the CO apply.

98 As in cases of overcharges, for example, the claim based on unjustified enrichment will most possibly be filed, it is not clear whether rules of Article 62 dealing explicitly with damages claims could be applied. This should be addressed by the legislator as well.

The CO is the basic law regulating limitation and (cogent) limitation periods for bringing a claim.[99] Once the statute of limitation runs out the right to claim performance ceases (but the debtor may still perform his or her obligation voluntarily, the creditor's right itself does therefore not cease).[100] Limitation applies only if the other party in proceedings refers to it, the courts must therefore not take account of limitation *ex officio*.[101] General limitation period is five years, while with regard to claims arising from commercial contracts, limitation period is three years.[102] Limitation period for damages claims[103] is three years as of when the victim became aware of the damage and the person causing damage, and the claim must be brought within five years as of when the damage had actually occurred. If the damage is caused by contractual breach, the limitation period is that as set out for contractual claims. Unless the law provides otherwise, the limitation period starts to run the first day after the creditor had the right to claim the performance, or after the debtor had breached his or her duty not to act.[104] The CO sets out also detailed rules on the suspension and the interruption of limitation.[105] One of the basic rules is that limitation is not interrupted by merely addressing a claim to the debtor. In order to interrupt limitation, the creditor must file an action with the courts or other competent institution.

It should be stressed that Article 62/3 of the PRCA-1 which entered into force on 26 April 2008, poses uncertainties as to its temporal application as prior to its entry into force, suspension of limitation during the public enforcement proceedings was not set out. In cases where the limitation period started to run (but has not yet lapsed) already prior to entry into force of Article 62/3 of the PRCA-1, it is disputed in business practice whether Article 62/3 enabling suspension of limitation can be activated in such cases or not. In contrast to Article 22 of the new directive, the PRCA-1 did not provide for any specific transitional provision in that regard, it states merely that the act enters into force the 15th day after its publication, i.e. on 26 April 2008.[106] If Article 62/3 cannot be activated (perhaps by referring to prohibition of the so-called apparent or quasi retroactivity by (somehow, but how?) showing legitimate expectation that

99 Articles 335–370 CO.

100 Under Slovenian law, there is a distinction between limitation and so-called preclusion, the latter denoting situations in which a right itself ceases to exist (Article 345 of the CO). According to the predominant view of the courts and legal theory, the courts must take account of preclusion *ex officio*.

101 Article 335 of the CO. Once the limitation period runs out, the debtor may, however, renounce the limitation (Articles 340 – 341 of the CO).

102 Article 349 of the CO.

103 Article 352 of the CO. Specific provisions for damages caused by criminal acts and corruption are set out in Articles 353 and 354 of the CO.

104 Article 336 of the CO.

105 Articles 358–370 of the CO.

106 Article 84 of the PRCA-1.

the rule was not going to be amended, limitation takes place irrespective of any administrative proceedings pending after 26 April 2008.[107] If it is to be applied, then the only possible interpretation could be that limitation is suspended only as of 26 April 2008 (respecting at least the prohibition of the so-called real or full retroactivity) until the finality of the administrative decision when the rest of the period continues to run. It is yet to be seen how Slovenian courts will tackle with this issue which is obviously relevant also in the already mentioned (so far out-of-court) case of Telekom Slovenije d.d. and its ISDN/ADSL infringement.[108]

6. COOPERATION OF NATIONAL COURTS WITH NCAS

Article 62/4 of the PRCA-1 obliges Slovenian courts to inform the PAPC of all damages actions for infringements of Slovenian or European antitrust as soon as they are filed. It reflects the general regime of cooperation between the courts and the PAPC as set out in Article 63/1 of the PRCA-1. Article 63 of the PRCA-1 was introduced into Slovenian legislation in order to regulate in detail and to upgrade to a certain extent the *amicus curiae* regime set out in Regulation 1/2003 and in the Commission *Notice on cooperation of the commission and national courts when applying European antitrust*,[109] providing for a cooperation of national courts applying European antitrust with NCAs and the European Commission.[110] It is to be noted that Article 63/1 of the PRCA-1 does not provide

107 Article 155 of the Slovenian Constitution provides that laws and other regulations and general legal acts cannot have retroactive effect. Only a law may establish that certain of its provisions have retroactive effect, if this is required in the public interest and provided that no acquired rights are infringed thereby. Where the new rule applies *ex nunc* only, this is not a case of real retroactivity, but a case of the so-called quasi retroactivity, which exists when a legal norm refers to the current legal relations that have been established before the law was effective, but are not yet completed. Although the quasi retroactive legislation nominally only affects the future, this subsequently undermines the acquired rights in a way that was unforeseen at the time of concluding the legal transaction. Quasi retroactivity thus violates the principle of protection of legitimate expectations, which is an essential component of the rule of law set out in Article 2 of the Constitution. This principle guarantees that the state will not deteriorate an individual's legal situation arbitrarily, i.e. without a proper reason based on prevailing and legitimate public interest. Quasi retroactive measures are therefore prohibited, unless any such measure is justified by clearly demonstrable overriding reasons of public interest. *Šturm et al.: Komentar URS*, pp. 1040, 57. See, for example, also the following case of Slovenian Constitutional Court: U-I-382/02–14 of 15 April 2004.

108 See *supra* chapter on legal standing in antitrust private enforcement cases.

109 Commission Notice on the co-operation between the Commission and the courts of the EU Member States in the application of Articles 81 and 82 EC, Official Journal C 101, 27.04.2004, p. 54–64.

110 For further details, see *Vlahek: Amicus curiae...*; *Vlahek* in *Grilc: PRCA-1 Commentary*, pp. 516, 525–526; *Vlahek: Reforma antitrusta v Evropski uniji.*

for any such cooperation between the PAPC and the courts when the courts apply Slovenian antitrust, while the special provision of Article 62/4 of the PRCA-1 that is applicable (only) to damages actions, requests the courts to inform PAPC of all antitrust damages actions, not only of those for infringements of EU antitrust.

According to Article 63/6 of the PRCA-1, Slovenian courts applying European antitrust must also forward to the PAPC and to the European Commission all court decisions issued applying European antitrust (Article 63/6). Although some proceedings applying European antitrust have been initiated and have in some cases ended already a couple of years ago, such cooperation has taken place only recently as until 2015, the European Commission's database on private enforcement of antitrust in the Member States did not show any Slovenian cases.[111] According to Article 63/2 and Article 63/5, the courts have to inform the PAPC and the parties of any opinion of the European Commission delivered to them in accordance with Article 15/3 or Article 15/1 of Regulation 1/2003. Further, under Article 15/3 of Regulation 1/2003, the PAPC itself may provide Slovenian courts applying European antitrust with a non-binding *amicus curiae* opinion on the application of European antitrust – this form of cooperation is regulated in detail in Article 63/3 of the PRCA-1 whereby in contrast to Article 15 of Regulation 1/2003 as interpreted by the CJEU in *X BV*,[112] the PRCA-1 does not differentiate between the substance of the opinion of the Commission on one hand, and the substance of the opinion of the PAPC on the other.[113] Article 63/4 of the PRCA-1 further states that the Commission and the PAPC may forward their written opinion any time until the judgment is rendered. To my knowledge, no *amicus curiae* opinion has so far been issued to Slovenian courts, plausibly also no other type of cooperation has so far taken place. Article 63/7 of the PRCA-1 states that the PAPC may be used as a communications channel between the Slovenian courts and the European Commission for the purposes of *amicus curiae* cooperation between the courts and the Commission.[114]

111 <http://ec.europa.eu/competition/elojade/antitrust/nationalcourts/> (13 July 2015). 19 decisions of the Supreme Court of RS issued in administrative dispute proceedings (reviewing the CPO/PAPC decisions) are currently published (8 from 2014, 9 from 2013, 1 from 2011 and 1 from 2009). No decisions dealing with private enforcement of antitrust are on the list (possibly because only Slovenian antitrust was applied in such cases).

112 C-429/07 *Inspecteur van de Belastingdienst v. X BV.*

113 See *Vlahek: Amicus curiae....*

114 According to the available information, it is the judiciary that has eventually started informing the Commission of the relevant judgments after that was not done by the CPA/PAPC despite its commitment to do so. It is to be presumed that direct contact between the courts and the Commission will be retained also with other forms of cooperation provided for in Article 15 of Regulation 1/2003.

7. CONSENSUAL DISPUTE RESOLUTION

The new directive also addresses the issue of potential consensual resolution of competition law damages cases and their effects on damages actions and the setting of fines. Article 18/1 states that Member States shall ensure that the limitation period for bringing an action for damages is suspended for the duration of the consensual dispute resolution process where the suspension shall apply only with regard to those parties that are or were involved or represented in the consensual dispute resolution (it is to be noted that Slovenian version of Article 18 of the directive as well as paragraph 49 of its Preamble incorrectly use the word *pretrganje* (interruption) instead of *zadržanje* (suspension) which is used in the English version of the text). Paragraph 48 of the preamble explains that Article 18 refers to "consensual dispute resolution mechanisms, such as out-of-court settlements (including those where a judge can declare a settlement binding), arbitration, mediation or conciliation", and emphasises that the directive is meant to facilitate the use of such mechanisms and increase their effectiveness.

Under Slovenian law, limitation period is interrupted (Sl. *pretrgano*; it starts running anew), its run is not merely suspended (Sl. *zadržano*; it does not run during the suspension) by filing a lawsuit or by performing any other act against the debtor before the court or other competent authority in order to determine, secure or collect a claim.[115] Limitation period can therefore not be interrupted by any activity oriented to enforcing the claim, but only by activities initiated before a competent authority.[116] According to theory and court practice, filing a request for arbitration or statement of claim in arbitration proceedings equals filing a claim with the court.[117] Such conclusion can be derived from both Article 365 of the CO as well as Article 38 of the Arbitration Act[118] stating that as regards the parties, arbitration award has the effect of a final and binding court judgment. It is thus not clear whether Article 18/1 of the new directive requiring suspension of limitation during any consensual dispute resolution process (including arbitration as ensues from paragraph 48 of the Preamble to the directive) is to be applied also to arbitration.

A specific provision on limitation periods is set out in Article 17 of the Mediation in Civil and Commercial Matters Act[119] stating that limitation periods are suspended (not interrupted as in the case of court or arbitration

115 Articles 365 and 369 of the CO.

116 Judgment of the Supreme Court of RS No. III Ips 91/2004 of 31 January 2006.

117 *Damjan: Učinek mediacije na tek rokov*, p. 40. Confirmed, *inter alia*, by the following judgments: Judgment of High Court in Celje No. VSC Cp 1488/2001 of 30 May 2002; Judgment of the Supreme Court of RS No. III Ips 91/2004 of 31 January 2006.

118 Sl. *Zakon o arbitraži (ZArbit)*, Official Gazette RS, No. 45/08.

119 Sl. *Zakon o mediaciji v civilnih in gospodarskih zadevah (ZMCGZ)*, Official Gazette RS, No. 56/08.

proceedings or other proceedings before the competent authority as set out in Article 365 of the CO) during mediation proceedings (whereby mediation proceedings are defined in Article 3 as proceedings in which the parties voluntarily and with assistance of a neutral third person (mediator) attempt to reach an amicable settlement of their dispute arising out of or in connection to a contractual or other legal relationship, irrespective of how such proceedings are named or referred to (mediation, conciliation, dispute intervention, or similar). Such regulation corresponds to the aim of Article 18/1 of the new directive, but it can be presumed that specific provisions will nevertheless be inserted into the PRCA-1 in order to regulate antitrust-specific issues at one place.

Article 18/2 of the new directive further states that, without prejudice to provisions of national law in matters of arbitration, Member States shall ensure that national courts seized of an action for damages may suspend (here, too, the Slovenian text of the directive as well of paragraph 50 of the Preamble is incorrect as it uses the term *pretrganje* instead of *prekinitev*) proceedings where the parties to those proceedings are involved in consensual dispute resolution concerning the claim covered by that action for damages. The suspension in these cases shall not be longer than two years. Article 305b of the CPrA states that if both parties agree to try to resolve their dispute through a scheme of ADR (out-of-court or court-annexed),[120] the court suspends the litigation (for maximum of three months). Article 15 of the Act on Alternative Dispute Resolution in Judicial Matters[121] similarly states that in cases where the parties agree that they will try to solve the dispute by means of judicial alternative dispute resolution regulated in that act, the court may suspend the court proceedings (Sl. *prekinitev postopka*) for a maximum time of three months, and refer the parties to such dispute resolution.[122] Further, Article 19 of the Act on Alternative Dispute Resolution in Judicial Matters authorises the court to suspend its proceedings for a maximum time of three months if it decides (on its own initiative according to the circumstances of each case) to refer the parties to mediation organised within the court. In addition, Article 209 of the CPrA enables the parties to agree that the court proceedings are stayed (Sl. *mirovanje postopka*) until any of the parties moves for the continuation thereof, whereby such a motion cannot be made until three months have lapsed since the day when the proceedings were stayed. If none of the parties has moved for the continuation of the proceedings within four months from the day when they

120 *Galič: Civil Procedure, Slovenia*, p. 159. Galič explains that the CPrA acknowledges to a limited extent also the forms of out-of-court ADR – irrespective of the fact whether these are performed independently from the court or whether they concern the programmes of ADR established as court-annexed. *Galič: Civil Procedure, Slovenia*, p. 114.

121 Sl. *Zakon o alternativnem reševanju sodnih sporov (ZARSS)*, Official Gazette RS, No. 97/09, with further amendments.

122 Sl. *Zakon o alternativnem reševanju sodnih sporov (ZARSS)*, Official Gazette RS, No. 97/09 with further amendments.

were stayed, the action is deemed to be withdrawn.[123] The new rules of Article 18/2 of the directive differ to some extent from the rules already laid down in Slovenian legislation, and will thus have to be implemented anew into Slovenian legislation, presumably into the PRCA-1.

Article 18/3 of the new directive states that a competition authority may consider that compensation paid as a result of a consensual settlement and prior to its decision imposing a fine to be a mitigating factor in the setting thereof. The Slovenian minor offences legislation (the Minor Offences Act[124] which applies subsidiarily to the PRCA-1) states that when determining the fine, the following circumstances of the case are in particular to be taken into account by the authority: the level of the offender's liability for the offence, the offender's incentives for committing the offence, the level of threat to or of breach of the insured interest, the circumstances in which the offence was committed, former lifestyle of the offender, his or her personal circumstances, his or her conduct after committing the offence, in particular whether he or she has recompensated the damage. Slovenian legislation therefore already pays due regard to the fact that the offender has repaid damages to the victims of the infringement (though not mentioning consensual settlement explicitly).[125]

8. NULLITY OF RESTRICTIVE AGREEMENTS AND DECISIONS

Questions of nullity are covered in Articles 86–93 of the CO. The basic principle, enshrined in Article 86/1 of the CO, reads as follows: *A contract that contravenes the constitution, mandatory rules or moral principles shall be null and void if the purpose of the contravened rule does not assign any other sanction or if the law does not prescribe otherwise for the case in question.* Violations of Articles 6 and 9 of the PRCA-1 and of Articles 101/1 and 102 TFEU undoubtedly present a contravention to compulsory regulations. It is, however, to be noted that when deliberating on such cases, Slovenian courts will not need to apply Article 86/1 of the CO as the consequence of nullity for agreements that represent restrictive business practices stems directly from the wording of Article 6/1 of the PRCA-1 (*Agreements..., decisions ... and concerted practices ... are prohibited and null*) as well as from Article 101/2 TFEU (*Any agreements or decisions prohibited pursuant to this article shall be automatically void.*). After finding an infringement of European and/or Slovenian antitrust, the CPO has in the past often declared in the operative parts of its decisions (i.e. in ordering (dispositive)

123 *Galič: Civil Procedure, Slovenia*, p. 160.

124 Sl. *Zakon o prekrških (ZP-1)*, Official Gazette RS, No. 7/03, with further amendments.

125 For further details as to criminal enforcement of antitrust in Slovenia, see *Fatur & Podobnik & Vlahek: Competition Law – Slovenia*, Part I, Ch. 5, §3.

parts) that an agreement of undertakings or a decision of associations of undertakings *is prohibited and null.*[126]

According to Article 92 of the CO, the proceedings for nullity may be instituted *ex officio* or at the request of any person with vested interest in the declaration of nullity.[127] According to Article 93 of the CO, the right to invoke nullity does not expire. The decision on nullity is of a declaratory character and has *erga omnes* effects. In addition, Article 90 of the CO stipulates that a null and void contract cannot become valid if the prohibition or other cause of nullity later ceases.

Consequences of nullity are covered by Article 87/1 of the CO. If a contract is null and void, each contracting party must return everything that was received on the basis of such contract; otherwise, adequate monetary equivalent must be provided. In addition, Article 87/2 of the CO states that when a contract is null and void because it contravenes fundamental moral principles, the court may refuse to grant restitutionary relief to the party tainted by turpitude.

There are no specific provisions on interim measures within private competition enforcement proceedings (Article 38 of the PRCA-1 applies only to interim measures issued by the PAPC), therefore general rules on interim measures (in the form of provisional orders),[128] regulated in the Enforcement and Securing of Civil Claims Act[129] apply.

9. OBSTACLES TO EFFECTIVE PRIVATE ENFORCEMENT OF ANTITRUST IN SLOVENIA

In recent years, antitrust damages actions and other forms of relief have been intensified in Slovenia. Court proceedings have almost exclusively been initiated by competitors of undertakings that have allegedly abused their dominant position on the relevant markets, although consumers and other customers of the infringing undertakings are also slowly starting to realise of their legal rights and procedural steps to enforce them. Telekom Slovenije d.d. being a leading national telecommunications service operator, is by far the most

126 See, for example, the CPO's decision in the *Institute of Public Health Maribor/DDD, Dezinfekcija, dezinsekcija, deratizacija, d.o.o.* case, finding that the agreement on bid-rigging on tenders issued by the *Public Economic Institute for Commodity Reserves* concluded between the *Institute of Public Health Maribor* and a commercial company *DDD, Dezinfekcija, dezinsekcija, deratizacija, d.o.o.* was prohibited and null.

127 Accordingly, Article 181 of the CPrA states that any party with legal interest may bring an action at any time for the purpose of determining the existence or nonexistence of a legal relationship. See *Galič: Civil Procedure, Slovenia*, pp. 89 – 90.

128 Sl. *začasna odredba.*

129 Sl. *Zakon o izvršbi in zavarovanju (ZIZ)*, Official Gazette RS, No. 51/98, with further amendments.

targeted undertaking with other telecommunications operators filing damages actions against it claiming it had abused its dominant position by predatory pricing, margin squeeze, tying etc. In some cases, they were unsuccessful,[130] while in some cases the courts have awarded them damages.[131] In some cases, the plaintiffs have settled with the other party.[132] The majority of the cases, however, are still pending[133] as the proceedings are lengthy and mostly inefficient. The judges are faced with complex competition law issues they have never practiced before and are, so it seems, somewhat intimidated by them. Even in cases where the judges are bound by the PAPC's findings that the undertakings have breached competition law, and must therefore assess only the loss sustained, the defendant's fault and causal link between the breach and the damage caused, they are somewhat reluctant to tackle the cases. They are also assailed with the parties' briefs, which are at times full of vague and unsubstantiated arguments. Although the 1999 and 2008 reforms of Slovenian civil procedure introduced restrictions on late factual allegations and evidence (as of the 1999 reform, the parties may assert new facts and evidence at the first session of the main hearing at the latest;[134] while as of the 2008 reform, the parties are obliged to file preparatory briefs (if filed on their own motion) in sufficient time for them to be served on the other party with adequate time before the date that has been set for the main hearing so that the main hearing will not have to be re-scheduled, while the judges have the discretionary power to require before or on the main hearing that parties make submissions and clarifications concerning facts, evidence and legal positions in the time limits set by the court – in these cases, the court may, however, allow also for briefs submitted after the relevant time limits have passed if the party shows justified reasons caused the default or if the judge is of the opinion that admission of belated submissions would not significantly delay the proceedings),[135] the parties in practice file tens of preparatory briefs what leads to prolongation of proceedings for months or, sadly, years if the judges are passive. Instead of performing their "substantive procedural guidance" efficiently, i.e. taking the active role in the proceedings by asking appropriate questions and promoting

---

130 See, for example, the following cases presented *infra*: *T2 v. Telekom Slovenije, Sinfonika v. Telekom Slovenije, Akton v. Telekom Slovenije.*

131 See, for example, the following cases presented *infra*: *Tušmobil v. Telekom Slovenije, ABM v Telekom Slovenije, S5 vleka ladij v. Luka Koper.*

132 See, for example, the following cases presented *infra*: *WWI v. Mobitel, Si.mobil v. Telekom Slovenije.*

133 See, for example, the following cases presented *infra*: *T2 v. Telekom Slovenije, Quantum v. Telekom Slovenije, Akton v. Telekom Slovenije, Amis v. Telekom Slovenije, Blitz v. Kolosej, Euromedia MB v. Pošta Slovenije.*

134 Save in cases the parties were not able to submit them at the first main hearing through no fault of their own. The same restrictions apply to new facts and evidence which a party wishes to rely on at the appellate stage of proceedings. *Galič: (In)compatibility of Procedural Preclusions ...*, p. 224.

135 *Galič: (In)compatibility of Procedural Preclusions ...*, pp. 224–228.

clarification, and preparing diligently for the main hearing by studying *ex ante* carefully the file and performing an in-depth legal analysis of the case, judges unfortunately often remain passive up to the main hearing (or even all up to the stage after the hearing is closed and they start drafting the judgment) and end up with unmanageable files posing threat to good quality of their decision-making.[136]

As Galič has put it describing the 1999 and 2008 reforms of Slovenian civil procedure and their effects in practice: "*A judge who is himself not diligently prepared for the case cannot effectively exercise his powers in directing the parties to give further clarifications and supplementations, nor can he decide whether conditions for disregarding new facts and evidence are fulfilled. In addition, sanctions for belated submission of facts and means of evidence may not be imposed in cases where the court itself has delayed the proceedings because of insufficient judicial clarification and case management. [...] It [...] might not come as a surprise that the system of preclusions is opposed not only by numerous attorneys but by certain judges as well. In fact, instruments that were introduced by the 2008 reform and designed to enable a comprehensive preparation for the trial are still insufficiently used in practice. These tools require diligent preparation before the trial, thus good knowledge of the file and a serious preliminary legal analysis by both the judge as well as the attorneys. However, such a preparation cannot be expected from a judge who cannot get rid himself of the old habit of having "the first serious look" at the file only at the first hearing and only then truly starting to work on the case. Inevitably, such a judge will neither be able to correctly apply the statutory provisions concerning binding time limits nor will he be able to exercise his duty to pose appropriate questions and promote clarification at the preparatory stage of proceedings.*"[137] Sadly, such situations often seem present in private enforcement of competition law cases. If one scans through the cases relating to private enforcement of competition law that were or are pending before Slovenian courts and focuses on the time-frames of their handling,[138] one sees an alarming situation. The reasons for that surely do not lie solely in the personal attitude of individual judges towards case-handling and decision-making, but are manifold and comprise also the backlogs typical for Slovenian judiciary; the over-burdening of Slovenian judges with solving cases not enabling them to focus enough on individual cases, to perform their in-depth legal analysis and to educate themselves in the field required for proper decision-making; lack of specialisation of judges, etc.

---

136 Cf. *Galič: Civil procedure, Slovenia*, pp. 111–112, and *Galič: (In)compatibility of Procedural Preclusions ...*, pp. 229–233.

137 *Galič: (In)compatibility of Procedural Preclusions ...*, pp. 233–234.

138 Case-law is analysed *infra*.

In order to handle competition law cases efficiently and with confidence, some of the judges have in the last couple of years been taking part in competition law education and training programmes supported financially by the European Commission and organised by various institutions throughout the Member States.[139] It is important that the courts take their role in applying competition law and/or awarding damages for competition law breaches seriously. Damages claims present an important tool in enforcement of competition law. Besides having a preventive effect on all actual and potential offenders, they also strengthen the awareness of the importance of competition within consumer and business environment. The court system in Slovenia should also, if possible, adapt to attaining this goal by providing for specialised courts in competition matters with highly motivated judges relieved of all workload not falling within the ambit of competition law. Reintroduction of panel-decision making in antitrust private enforcement cases at first instance courts might be helpful in guaranteeing proficiency of the judgements.

The judges should be granted enough time to analyze the cases, the sessions of the hearing should be concentrated as much as possible in order to enable the judges to focus in depth on one case at a time and to issue decisions within a reasonable time. One step towards attaining this goal has been made in 2013 at the District Court in Ljubljana (where the majority of competition-law related damages lawsuits are filed) as three judges were specifically assigned to deal with competition law cases (surprisingly not excluding at the same time their assessment of other commercial disputes, but nevertheless removing the minimum caseload requirement to a certain extent),[140] but it is only a small step towards efficient and expertly proficient judicial assessment of competition law cases. One should, however, not forget the importance of proper decision making in administrative review proceedings where, as the law stands now, the Administrative Court of RS reviews the PAPC's decisions, while the Supreme Court of RS is an appellate administrative review court in these cases. Due to the binding effect of the PAPC's decisions as regards unlawfulness of the defendants'

---

139 In Slovenia, Institute for Comparative Law at the Faculty of Law in Ljubljana (IPP-PF, <www.ipp-pf.si/> (13 July 2015)) has thus far been successful organizing workshops, seminars and conferences for Slovenian and Croatian judges applying national and European antitrust (<www.konkurencnopravo.eu> (13 July 2015)).

140 Decree of the President of the District Court in Ljubljana No. Su 9/2013 of 8 May 2013, available at (in Slovene): <www.sodisce.si/mma_bin.php?static_id=20130508151033> (13 July 2015). Prior to such re-organization, more judges of the District Court in Ljubljana were assessing competition law cases. Given the fact that the current judges handling competition law cases have to my information not been disburdened of handling cases within other legal fields within their jurisdiction, this means that in terms of quantity, less judges are appointed to deal with competition law cases. Hopefully, the implemented measure coupled with disburdening the judges of the quantity restraints as to the number of cases solved each year will nevertheless guarantee for a better decision-making in these cases.

conduct, it is of utmost significance that the judges taking part in administrative review proceedings, too, are proficient in antitrust.

10. SELECTED CASE-LAW OF PRIVATE ENFORCEMENT OF ANTITRUST IN SLOVENIA

Civil law actions within the ambit of competition law that have been initiated in Slovenia are concerned mainly with the abuses of dominant position in the telecommunications sector. At least one lawsuit, however, refers to the abuse in the postal services sector, one in the cinematographic sector, and one in the maritime transport sector. The list of cases presented below is not exhaustive but entails the majority of antitrust private enforcement cases that were or are pending before Slovenian courts. They are mostly damages actions, while in some cases, the plaintiffs are the defendant's contractual partners claiming nullity of their agreements and consequently requesting repayment of the overcharges (as well as the damage sustained). According to available information, no private lawsuits alleging abuses in other sectors, or alleging breaches of Article 101 TFEU and/or Article 6 of the PRCA-1, have been filed by the time of submission of this paper.

It is to be underscored that due to the lack of full and transparent database of case-law of Slovenian judiciary (as well as of the PAPC), information as to the selected case-law was partly gathered from publicly available press announcements and media news on the internet. Judgments and decrees issued by Slovenian courts are unfortunately not generally available on the internet as only anonymised more important judgments of the high courts, the Supreme Court of RS and the Administrative Court of RS are published, while the first instance courts' judgments are unfortunately not available online.[141] Only a small portion of the key decisions of the Supreme Court of RS is available in English.[142] It must be noted that Article 61.a of the PRCA-1 requesting the PAPC to publish on its website all judicial review decisions is still not applied by the PAPC, while Slovenian courts have only recently (i.e. 11 years after the entry into force of Regulation 1/2003) set up a cooperation mechanism with the European Commission by forwarding it copies of judgments applying European antitrust as required by Article 15/2 of Regulation 1/2003. The case-law is presented to my best knowledge and understanding of the facts, legal issues and the procedural steps of the cases taking thereby due account of the complexity of the cases as well as the scope and type of sources of information used in the analysis. Hopefully, the presentation will serve as a basis for further research of the cases

---

141 Some of the decisions may also be obtained directly by the competent courts via the Public Information Access Act.

142 <www.sodisce.si/znanje/supreme_court_key_decisions/> (13 July 2015).

enabling the reader to form his or her own opinion on the quality of administrative decisions issued by the CPO/PAPC, of judgments rendered in administrative review proceedings, and of judgments rendered in private damages lawsuits and other proceedings.

10.1. *WWI v. MOBITEL*

In May 2005, Western Wireless Int. d.o.o. (WWI) which was doing its business in Slovenia under the trademark Vega (having approx. 30.000 users, i.e. 2% market share at the time), filed a damages claim against Mobitel d.d. and the Republic of Slovenia with the District court in Ljubljana claiming that there is no market regulation in Slovenia enabling state-owned Mobitel d.d. to act anti-competitively.[143]

It requested damages in the enormous amount of SIT 48,8 billion (EUR 203,9 million) for the loss of its business. Mobitel d.d., on the other hand, sued WWI for SIT 106 million (EUR 442.330) requesting payment of the services it had rendered to WWI. All the parties' actions against one another were eventually withdrawn as the parties concluded an out-of-court settlement in April 2006. WWI's 191 base stations with corresponding technical equipment were also sold to Mobitel d.d. for EUR 2,5 million, while 135 base stations were bought from WWI by Si.mobil d.d. also for EUR 2,5 million. Vega eventually ceased operating in June 2006.[144]

The case is also known for the lawsuit between Telekom Slovenije d.d. and the legal office that had represented Mobitel d.d. and the Republic of Slovenia in the WWI dispute. Filing the lawsuit in April 2008, the office requested Telekom Slovenije d.d. to pay an award amounting to approx. EUR 5 million as was agreed in the Agreement on legal representation, concluded between the parties and the Republic of Slovenia for soliciting services for representation in the WWI case.[145] According to the agreement, the success fee was to be set at 1,5% of WWI's claim. Telekom Slovenije d.d. supposedly claimed that they were in fact not successful due to the office's representation (if at all as they had settled). In January 2011, the High Court in Ljubljana set aside the first instance judgment of awarding the plaintiff approx. EUR 70.000 with interest, and returned the case back to the District Court in Ljubljana.[146] In March 2012, the District Court in Ljubljana issued the second judgment in the same case awarding the plaintiff approx. EUR 2,5 million (EUR 1,547,371.23 with statutory interest in arrears as of 9 April 2008 onwards, and the amount of EUR 256,873.26 EUR and the

143 <www.delo.si/clanek/o65764> (13 July 2015); <www.finance.si/121791/Vega-to%C5%BEi-dr%C5%BEavo-Mobitel-in-APEK> (13 July 2015).

144 <www.delo.si/clanek/o132166> (13 July 2015).

145 <http://seonet.ljse.si/Default.aspx?doc=SEARCH&doc_id=31428> (13 July 2015).

146 Decision No. I Cpg 1283/2010 of 6 January 2011.

statutory interest in arrears as of the expiry of the date for the fulfilment of the obligations).[147] The parties have appealed again. In October 2013, the High Court in Ljubljana issued a judgment itself and awarded the plaintiff EUR 397.541,95 (representing 13% of the agreed fee that amounted to EUR 3.058.015,00 as their share in success of their client) plus interest in the amount of EUR 81.406,29 plus 20% VAT on the principal amount plus interest plus part of the defendant's costs of first instance and appeal proceedings.[148] No information as to the parties' further procedural steps is available to me.

10.2. *SI.MOBIL v. TELEKOM SLOVENIJE, TUŠMOBIL v. TELEKOM SLOVENIJE*

In 2011, Slovenian second and third largest mobile telephony operators (Si.mobil d.d. and Tušmobil d.o.o.) filed stand-alone damages actions against Mobitel d.d. (merged by acquisition with Telekom Slovenije d.d. in June 2011) for its alleged abuse of dominant position on the retail market of mobile telecommunications services by using predatory pricing within its mobile subscription package *Itak Džabest.* Si.mobil d.d. is seeking damages in the amount of EUR 286,392 million,[149] while Tušmobil d.o.o. in the amount of EUR 86 million.[150] The plaintiffs decided to file stand-alone actions as the CPO had not issued its decisions within reasonable period, i.e. in two years after it had initiated the proceedings in 2009. As it was anticipated, the national court had awaited the CPO's decision which was issued in February 2012,[151] and had not assessed the infringement on its own. In November 2013, the Supreme Court of RS (acting as review court) set aside the CPO decision concluding that the decision was burdened by incorrect application of the substantive law, significant procedural irregularities, and incomplete finding of facts, and returned the case back to the CPA for re-assessment in accordance with the Supreme Court's guidelines laid down in its judgment.[152] Si.mobil and Telekom Slovenije settled on 29 December 2014.[153]

The first lawsuit by Tušmobil d.o.o. (Tuš Telekom d.o.o. at the time) against Telekom Slovenije d.d. was filed in 2007 whereby the plaintiff was requesting

---

147 Judgment No. VII Pg 390/2011 of 6 March 2012; <http://seonet.ljse.si/Default.aspx?doc=SEARCH&doc_id=47898> (13 July 2015).

148 Judgment No. I Cpg 678/2012 of 9 October 2013; <http://seonet.ljse.si/?doc_id=53182> (13 July 2015).

149 <http://seonet.ljse.si/Default.aspx?doc=SEARCH&doc_id=47048> (13 July 2015).

150 <http://seonet.ljse.si/Default.aspx?doc=SEARCH&doc_id=46902> (13 July 2015).

151 The CPO's Decision No. 306-14/2009-239.

152 Judgment No. G 9/2012-28 of 26 November 2013; <http://seonet.ljse.si/Default.aspx?doc=SEARCH&doc_id=53393> (13 July 2015).

153 <www.times.si/gospodarstvo/telekom-slovenije-in-simobil-sta-se-poravnala--c05f2a96f1-bfa89a19bf.html> (13 July 2015).

damages in the amount of EUR 21.466.641,85 (presumably with interest amounting altogether to EUR 28,2 million as stated in the media) alleging abuse of Telekom Slovenije's dominant position by favouring SiOL d.o.o.[154] (its wholly owned subsidiary), and violation of provisions of sectoral legislation.[155] On 5 May 2015, Telekom Slovenije received the judgment of the District Court in Ljubljana dated 13 February 2015 awarding Tušmobil damages in the amount of approx. EUR 1,7 million (plus interest from 11 September 2007 until the payment), while it dismissed the action with regard to the rest of the claim.[156]

It is important to note with regard to *Itak Džabest* that on 4 April 2011 Si. mobil d.d. filed a nullity action on the basis of Article 263 TFEU against the European Commission seeking the annulment of its Decision No. C(2011) 355 final of 24 January 2011 in Case No. COMP/39.707 Si.mobil/Mobitel.[157] Si.mobil was arguing that the Commission failed to investigate the abuse of dominant position by Mobitel d.d. as required by Regulation 1/2003 and the Commission Notice on cooperation within the ECN. In August 2009, Si.mobil d.d. informed the Commission of the Mobitel's practices asking it to institute infringement proceedings as the CPO had not issued the decision within the time limit set out in the PRCA-1, and as obviously the Commission is the best placed authority to assess Mobitel's practices. It has been relying also on the General Court's reasoning in *Automec*[158] claiming the existence of the Community interest requiring its involvement in the assessment of the case, as well as on the Commission's Guidelines on its enforcement priorities in applying Article 102 TFEU to abusive exclusionary conduct by dominant undertakings[159] where the Commission has envisaged cases such as the one at hand as its enforcement priority.

As the Commission had rejected Si.mobil d.d.'s complaint finding that there is no sufficient degree of European Union interest for conducting a further investigation into the alleged infringements,[160] Si.mobil d.d. was suing in

---

154 Established in 1999 by Telekom Slovenije d.d. and merged by acquisition with Telekom Slovenije d.d. in 2007.

155 <http://seonet.ljse.si/Default.aspx?doc=SEARCH&doc_id=28489> (13 July 2015); <http://seonet.ljse.si/Default.aspx?doc=SEARCH&doc_id=28381> (13 July 2015); <www.dnevnik.si/posel/novice/1042418370> (13 July 2015); www.finance.si/312543/Vro%C4%8Da-razprava-Tu%C5%A1-Telekom-proti-Telekomu (13 July 2015).

156 <www.telekom.si/o-podjetju/za-vlagatelje/javne-objave/Telekom-Slovenije-dd-prejel-sodbo-v-gospodarskem-sporu-tozece-stranke-Tusmobil-doo-zoper-Telekom-Slovenije-dd> (13 July 2015).

157 T-201/11 *Si.mobil telekomunikacijske storitve d.d. v Commission*, available at (in English): <http://curia.europa.eu/juris/document/document.jsf?text=&docid=82201&pageIndex=0&doclang=EN&mode=lst&dir=&occ=first&part=1&cid=702592> (13 July 2015).

158 T-24/90 *Automec v Commission.*

159 Communication from the Commission – Guidance on the Commission's enforcement priorities in applying Article 82 of the EC Treaty to abusive exclusionary conduct by dominant undertakings (2009/C 45/02).

160 See: <http://ec.europa.eu/competition/antitrust/cases/dec_docs/39707/39707_98_3.pdf> (13 July 2015).

Luxembourg. The European Commission was supported by the Republic of Slovenia and by Telekom Slovenije d.d. On 24 February 2012, Tušmobil d.o.o. sought leave to intervene in support of the form of order sought by Si.mobil d.d. Its action was dismissed on 16 November 2012 by the President of the Fifth Chamber of the General Court.[161]

The General Court issued a decision on 17 December 2014 dismissing Si. mobil d.d.'s action and ordering Si.mobil d.d. to bear its own costs and to pay the costs incurred by the Commission and by Telekom Slovenije d.d., while the Republic of Slovenia is to bear its own costs. As ensues from the CJEU's case-law database, an appeal has not been lodged with the Court.

10.3. *T2 v. TELEKOM SLOVENIJE*

In 2007, one of the internet service providers (T2 d.o.o.) filed a lawsuit with the District Court in Ljubljana against Telekom Slovenije d.d. claiming that it had abused its dominant position by discriminating between T2 d.o.o. and its downstream market competitor SiOL d.o.o. (wholly owned subsidiary of Telekom Slovenije d.d.). According to T2 d.o.o., discriminatory abuse manifested itself in delays in providing services to T2 d.o.o. resulting in certain amount of customers switching to SiOL d.o.o. from T2 d.o.o. T2 d.o.o. sought pecuniary (in the form of *damnum emergens* and *lucrum cessans*) and non-pecuniary damages in the amount of approx. EUR 204 million (EUR 129.556.756,00 of principal, plus approx. EUR 74 million of interest plus other charges). The plaintiff, however, was not willing to reveal its documentation proving the loss as this would allegedly reveal its business secrets.

On 21 January 2013, the court conducted the first session of the main hearing and after reviewing the circumstances of the case, also concluded the hearing. The court found that T2 did not submit evidence on the amount of loss claimed, and adopted a decision that evidence is to be gathered by access into the documents the plaintiff and the defendant submitted to the court in evidence of their claims. The court also decided that the decision be submitted in writing. The judge eventually rejected the claim and obliged the plaintiff to recover the defendant its costs in the amount of 27.197,22 EUR with interest.[162] As with other competition law cases, here, too, the court was allegedly swamped with thousands of pages of documentation. Had the judge tackled (or was able to tackle) the case actively and confidently from the start and directed the parties'

---

161 See: <http://curia.europa.eu/juris/document/document.jsf?text=&docid=130722&pageIndex=0&doclang=en&mode=lst&dir=&occ=first&part=1&cid=16042> (13 July 2015).

162 Judgment No. 8 Pg 54/2007; <http://seonet.ljse.si/Default.aspx?doc=SEARCH&doc_id=53369> (13 July 2015); <http://seonet.ljse.si/Default.aspx?doc=SEARCH&doc_id=50942> (13 July 2015); <http://seonet.ljse.si/Default.aspx?doc=SEARCH&doc_id=50605> (13 July 2015).

submissions within its material procedural guidance, the file would have in the end perhaps been easier to cope with and could be solved sooner than in five years.

The plaintiff appealed to the High Court in Ljubljana claiming that the court of first instance had issued a judgment of surprise. It stated that the information it provided was detailed enough to enable the court to estimate the loss of profit, and that otherwise the court should had requested it to provide relevant documentation. It reiterated its statement that the relevant documentation was not revealed because it contained business secrets. It further stated that its other evidence (witness and expert evidence) was unjustifiably rejected by the court.

The high court rejected the appeal and upheld the first instance court judgment in November 2013 obliging the plaintiff to pay to the defendant additional EUR 2.091,66 of its costs of the appeal proceedings.[163] Referring to relevant Slovenian as well as foreign (in particular German and Austrian) legislation, legal theory and court practice, the high court elaborated in detail on how loss of profit is to be proven and quantified, as well as on the possibility of (Slovenian) courts to estimate harm. It emphasised that the estimation of loss of profit must be based on well-grounded expectations, and that it is the plaintiff who is to reveal the basis for such estimation and bears the burden of asserting facts and adducing evidence. It also stated that in determining loss of profit, the profit that could not be acquired due to the infringer's act, but would otherwise be acquired, is of relevance, and that in cases where the plaintiff continued with its activity the loss of profit is to be calculated as a difference between the hypothetical profit but the infringement and the actual profit acquired by the plaintiff. If the victim is claiming loss of profit, it must at least claim that it would have acquired it in a certain period, and show the amount of actual acquired profit. The latter was in the court's opinion not done by T2. Its assertions and evidence offered were too indefinite and inappropriate. In assessing the lower court judgment, the high court found that the plaintiff was even asked by the defendant and the court on several occasions to provide relevant evidence as to the amount of loss of profit (although it is for the plaintiff to provide such evidence by itself) but refused to do so. The high court decided that all other evidence was consequently rejected by the court of first instance. With regard to business secrets, the high court stressed that the plaintiff must provide detailed information as to which evidence should be deemed business secret and why. In court's view, T2 failed to do so. The court also stated that in any event, the plaintiff could designate as business secrets only the more recent and not all

163 Judgment No. I Cpg 708/2013 of 21 November 2013, available at (in Slovene); <http://sodnapraksa.si/?q=I%20Cpg%20708/2013&database[SOVS]=SOVS&database[IESP]=IESP&_submit=i%C5%A1%C4%8Di&page=0&id=2012032113063477> (13 July 2015). It is to be underscored that Slovenian judiciary (same goes for many lawyers) often (also in this case in the keyword section of the case) wrongfully uses the term "unfair competition" (Sl. *nelojalna konkurenca*) to denote restriction of competition (Sl. *omejevanje konkurence*).

accounting statements, as in the telecommunications sector business relations have changed after the period from which the (belatedly)[164] offered plaintiff's evidence stemmed from.

The court also emphasised that the possibility of the courts to estimate harm as set out in Article 216 of the CPrA (drafted under the influence of Article 287 of German ZPO) does not mean that the courts can determine harm arbitrarily by rule of thumb, but have to observe the evidence that does not on its own give exact determination but nevertheless clears the matter to a certain extent. The plaintiff is still the one with the claim and burden of proof. The court thereby stressed that a lawsuit may be used as a tool for recovering damages, but may also be abused by the plaintiffs to obtain damages to which they are not entitled, and that the court must thus give equal opportunity to the plaintiff to claim and provide evidence, and the defendant to defend itself against the plaintiff's allegations.

In its statement of claim, the plaintiff was referring also to the 2013 Commission Communication on quantifying harm, as well as on the 2013 Draft Directive on antitrust damages. The district court as well as the high court stressed that neither of these documents are binding on the courts and that the courts are to apply only the binding legislation in force and are prevented from playing a role of the legislator by interpreting the legislation arbitrarily outside the interpretation offered by the legislation itself.

In January 2014, the plaintiff filed an extraordinary remedy of revision to the Supreme Court of RS. The case is still pending.

10.4. *SINFONIKA v. TELEKOM SLOVENIJE*

One of the rare cases where a final and binding decision has already been issued is the *Sinfonika v. Telekom Slovenije*. Sinfonika d.d., an electronic telecommunications undertaking (in bankruptcy) filed a lawsuit against Telekom Slovenije d.d. for its alleged abuse of dominant position by introducing a central office exchange service (Centrex) with predatory prices, high switching costs, etc. The claim was EUR 354,440.41 plus interests and was rejected by the District Court in Ljubljana in 2010 stating that while the grounds for liability for damages (the abuse of dominant position) were provided, the plaintiff failed to provide evidence it had suffered damage.[165] The decision was upheld by the High Court in Ljubljana in 2011.[166]

164 According to Article 286 of the CPrA, the parties can assert new facts and evidence until (including) the first session of the main hearing. *Galič, Civil Procedure, Slovenia*, p. 107.

165 <http://seonet.ljse.si/Default.aspx?doc=SEARCH&doc_id=42643> (13 July 2015).

166 <http://seonet.ljse.si/Default.aspx?doc=SEARCH&doc_id=45339> (13 July 2015).

Another lawsuit in the same case was initiated by Sinfonika against Telekom Slovenije d.d. in December 2007 requesting EUR 34.347.627 EUR with interest.[167] In part (approx. EUR 1,7 million), Sinfonika d.d. withdrew the lawsuit, while with regard to the rest of the claim, the court determined in 2011 that at the time Sinfonika d.d. had filed the suit, the statute of limitations had already lapsed.[168] It therefore ruled in the defendant's favour and rejected the plaintiff's claim. In January 2012, the High Court in Ljubljana upheld the first instance decision.[169]

Of particular interest with regard to this case is the fact that the District State Prosecutor's Office opened a criminal case against Telekom Slovenije d.d. and its CEO charging them with committing an unlawful act of creating a monopolistic position according to Article 231 of the Penal Code,[170] during the period between 19 April 2001 and 31 December 2003 by concluding subscription contracts for Centrex telecommunication services. Criminal procedure started on the grounds of the legal complaint made by distributors of in house switchboards who have also claimed in the proceeding that because of this behaviour they were damaged for the total amount of EUR 12,202,753.68. In January 2009, the District Court of Ljubljana dismissed the indictment proposal. It decided that the act, which was the subject of the indictment, is not a criminal act.[171]

10.5. *ABM v. TELEKOM SLOVENIJE*

Administrative infringement proceedings against Telekom Slovenije d.d. started already in September 1999 on request by ABM d.o.o. (at that time, the PRCA of 1999 enabled initiation of administrative proceedings upon request)[172] who claimed, inter alia, that Telekom Slovenije d.d. abused its dominant position by refusing to include the ABM d.o.o.'s CDs for internet access in its "ISDN 3000" packages without just cause giving preference to the CDs offered by SiOL d.o.o. being a subsidiary of Telekom Slovenije d.d. After lengthy administrative and court review proceedings, the abusive practice of Telekom Slovenije d.d. was finally confirmed in 2007 by the Administrative Court of RS and in 2008 by the Supreme Court of RS that rejected the defendant's revision.[173] The first CPO

167 <http://seonet.ljse.si/Default.aspx?doc=SEARCH&doc_id=29884> (13 July 2015).

168 <http://seonet.ljse.si/?doc_id=45479> (13 July 2015).

169 <http://seonet.ljse.si/Default.aspx?doc=SEARCH&doc_id=47271> (13 July 2015).

170 For details on criminal enforcement of antitrust in Slovenia, see *Fatur & Podobnik & Vlahek: Competition Law – Slovenia*, Part I, Ch. 5, §3.

171 <http://seonet.ljse.si/Default.aspx?doc=SEARCH&doc_id=35131> (13 July 2015).

172 For details on administrative proceedings before the CPA/PAPC, see *Fatur & Podobnik & Vlahek: Competition Law – Slovenia*, Part I, Ch. 5, §1, and Part III, Ch. 1.

173 See <www.abm.si/uvk/odlocba-UVK-2000.htm> (13 July 2015). It ensues from the Supreme Court's damages decision analysed *infra* that the CPO issued a partial decision (No. 3073–

decision finding the infringement was issued already in 2000, but was set aside by the review court (Administrative Court of RS at the time) in 2002. After that, another decision was issued by the CPO in 2004 finding an infringement and was confirmed by the Administrative Court of RS in 2007 that did, *inter alia*, not accept Telekom Slovenije's argument that ABM could had offered its CDs to customers on its own without requesting Telekom Slovenije to add them to its ISDN packages; that the relevant market was defined incorrectly as market for fixed voice telephony, etc. In 2007, Telekom Slovenije d.d. filed an extraordinary remedy of revision to the Supreme Court which was rejected by the Supreme Court in December 2008 stressing (by referring also to the CJEU's case-law)[174] that abuse can take place also in cases where the conduct constituting abuse took place on the market for fixed voice telephony, while the effects of the conduct are shown on the market of internet services (retail), while the question of essential facility was according to the available data not discussed at any of the stages.[175] Telekom Slovenije d.d. also unsuccessfully filed two constitutional complaints to the Constitutional Court of RS in 2008 and 2009.

With regard to other illegal acts alleged by the ABM, the CPO eventually terminated the proceedings on the basis of Article 40 of the PRCA-1 enabling the CPO to terminate proceedings also if special circumstances of the case show that proceedings would not be reasonable. ABM contested the CPO's order of January 2011[176] with the Supreme Court of RS claiming that the CPO should have assessed the alleged breach and not merely terminate the proceedings as, *inter alia*, that would be helpful to the damages proceedings pending before the District Court of Ljubljana as well as to the evolution of court practice and legal standards with regard to the alleged breaches. Concurring with the CPO's argumentation leading to termination of administrative proceedings, the Supreme Court dismissed the ABM's claim in June 2013.[177] It emphasised, however, that the plaintiff may still prove the breach in damages proceedings and that there is plenty of relevant case-law of the European Commission and the CJEU available to the parties to formulate their argumentation before the competent authorities. It added that issuing a decision in the case at hand would

---

9/02–4) on 4 May 2004. The Administrative Court of RS dismissed Telekom's action against the CPO decision on 5 September 2007 (No. U 1155/2044), while the Supreme Court of RS dismissed Telekom's revision on 16 December 2008.

174 Stressing that as at the relevant time, Slovenia had not yet joined the EU, reference to CJEU's (ECJ's at the time) case-law is made only for reasons of comparative analysis of the issue in question.

175 Judgment No. X Ips 749/2007 of 16 December 2008, available at (in Slovene): <http://sodnapraksa.si/?q=X%20Ips%20749/2007&database[SOVS]=SOVS&_submit=i%C5%A1%C4%8Di&page=0&id=2010040815242459> (13 July 2015).

176 Order No. 3073–9/2002–90 of 3 January 2011.

177 Decree No. 2/2011 of 11 June 2013, available at (in Slovene): <http://sodnapraksa.si/?q=62%20zpomk-1&database[SOVS]=SOVS&_submit=i%C5%A1%C4%8Di&page=0&id=2012032113055532> (13 July 2015).

not have any positive public effect nor effects on the evolution of competition law related legal standards as the market of narrowband internet has to date become obsolete.

Already in 2002, ABM d.o.o. filed damages action seeking EUR 4,2 million for a loss sustained due to abusive behaviour of Telekom Slovenije d.d. The loss was determined as loss of profit which would be obtained by the plaintiff during the period of infringement (approx. EUR 360.000), plus market value of these customers at the moment the damages claim was filed with the court (approx. EUR 3,8 million). In March 2012, the District Court in Ljubljana awarded ABM d.o.o. damages in the amount of EUR 2,3 million plus interest (while it dismissed the rest of the claim requesting the court to oblige Telekom to insert ABM d.o.o.'s CDs into its packages or pay approx. EUR 4.000 for each day of non-performance). The requested ABM d.o.o.'s amount for damages was lowered by the court on the basis of an expert's opinion quantifying the damages. It is noteworthy that the judge had allegedly mentioned before closing the hearing that in competition law cases damages may be awarded also by use of equitable considerations.[178] That corresponds to the Commission's reasoning in its White Paper, its *Draft Guidance Paper on quantifying of harm in actions for damages based on breaches of the EU antitrust rules*[179] as well as to the latest *Communication from the Commission on quantifying harm in actions for damages based on breaches of Article 101 or 102 of the Treaty on the Functioning of the European Union.*[180] In September 2012, both parties appealed to the High Court in Ljubljana which lowered the amount of damages to approx. EUR 62.000 (approx. EUR 9.700 for lost profit, approx. EUR 6.200 for interest, and approx. EUR 46.000 for the "market value of the customers on the date the action was filed", where data on SiOL's profit and customer value was used). The court applied Article 216 of the CPrA enabling it to use in exceptional circumstances judicial discretion to establish the missing facts when the liability of a party is established, and only the amount in question remains in dispute. The High Court repeated the CPO's findings that approx. 37.800 customers were obtained by SiOL d.o.o. during Telekom Slovenije d.d.'s abuse (1 January 1999 – 30 September 2002), and that one SiOL's customer has market value of EUR 177,91, but it found that the fair share of ABM on these customers would have been only 0,7% (AMB d.o.o. claimed 50%, while the first instance court determined a 28% share on the basis of an expert opinion).[181]

178 <www.delo.si/gospodarstvo/podjetja/tozbe-proti-telekomu-vendarle-napredujejo.html> (13 July 2015).

179 <http://ec.europa.eu/competition/consultations/2011_actions_damages/draft_guidance_paper_en.pdf> (13 July 2015).

180 2013/C 167/07.

181 Data obtained at: <http://damijan.org/2013/07/04/sodisca-so-sramota-te-drzave/> (13 July 2015), the judgments are unfortunately not available online.

The extraordinary remedy of revision was filed to the Supreme Court by ABM d.o.o. and the Supreme Court issued a decision in May 2014 amending the second instance decision and ordering itself Telekom Slovenije d.d. to pay to the plaintiff EUR 941.262,26 plus interest,[182] while each party is to cover its own costs of proceedings. The Supreme Court was of the opinion that the but-for scenario was not properly constructed by the High Court as regards the number of customers ABM would have obtained but for the infringement. In determining the percentage of customers ABM would have in a hypothetical scenario, the High Court estimated that SiOL's customers would be dispersed between all competitors on the market, while the Supreme Court found it most likely that only a couple, but not the majority of competitors would obtain SiOL's share.[183] It estimated that AMB's share would be 5,5% (2.077 customers) which was the share of the group to which ABM was part before the infringement. The Supreme Court increased this number to 4.235 customers as it estimated that ABM would be more successful in gaining customers in the initial period as other competitors would prepare their CDs with delay. It calculated that the loss of profit amounted to EUR 187.813,41, while the loss of market value of the customers (representing a capitalised future loss of profit) amounted to EUR 753.448,85. It is to be stressed that in determining ABM's loss of profit and loss of customer market value, the Supreme Court (as well as the High Court and the first instance court) did not estimate the profit AMB would have gained and the market value ABM's customers would have had, but had instead used data on SiOL's profit per customer and market value of SiOL's customer arguing that this was most appropriate given the circumstances of the case where the defendant abused its dominant position by favouring SiOL, and the availability of the data and the quality of the available data.

Determining victim's loss using the infringer's actual profit and not the victim's profit in a but-for scenario is to my knowledge a unicum in Slovenian tort law, but the Supreme Court explained (unfortunately not providing for an in-depth analysis of this issue – in particular having regard to the importance of its judgment) that Slovenian law does not set out how the loss is to be determined and that in particular in antitrust cases, determination of loss by using the infringer's data is appropriate due to the difficulties in determining loss in such cases. Referring to Austrian and German legislation as well as to Oxera's study of

182 Judgment No. III Ips 98/2013 of 23 May 2014.

183 Referring to expert opinion, SiOL would have had 27.051 customers, while the rest of 10.708 customers would be dispersed between other competitors. The Supreme Court stated that since offering CDs to customers does not require substantial financial means, a certain part of SiOL's competitors would for sure decide to offer their CDs in telekom's packages, but that not all competitors would decide that as competitors have different marketing strategies and use different tactics to enter the market. Beside that, higher the number of competitors deciding to add the CDs, the lower the incentive to do that. An indication that not all competitors would have decided for this step is in the opinion of the Supreme Court also the fact that only ABM was requesting Telekom Slovenije to add its CDs to its packages.

2009, the Supreme Court stated that such calculation of loss is available also in comparative law and literature. Despite taking into account the possibility of merely estimating the amount of harm by the courts, it is surprising how much the amounts of damages awarded by the High Court and the Supreme Court differ as a result of merely making different estimations as to the percentage of customers ABM would obtain but for the infringement (while all other relevant parts of their assessment of the case were identical). This is an indication of how unpredictable is the outcome of estimation of harm in antitrust damages cases by the courts.[184]

10.6. *QUANTUM v. TELEKOM SLOVENIJE*

On 15 July 2014, Telekom Slovenije d.d. received a lawsuit from the District Court of Ljubljana[185] lodged by a company Quantum d.o.o. claiming the payment of damages in the amount of EUR 450.000,00 due to the abuse of dominant position by Telekom Slovenije. The plaintiff alleges that during 1994 and 1998, Telekom Slovenije did not enable it to charge calls to internet hubs through user access via the 9xxx call number range according to the local tariff rate, due to which Quantum allegedly incurred damages. Telekom Slovenije has announced that it will submit a defence plea within the statutory time-limit and in the course of the proceedings prove the claim to be completely unfounded.[186]

The lawsuit is a follow-on lawsuit. In 1997, the CPO found the abuse of Telekom Slovenije d.d. (by discriminating Quantum and K2.net in comparison to Telekom's SiOL d.o.o.). Telekom Slovenije attacked the decision and in 2003, the parties (Telekom Slovenije and the CPO) agreed to settle, but the Supreme State Prosecutor attacked the settlement at the Supreme Court of RS that quashed the settlement in 2004.[187] The decision of the CPO was eventually confirmed by the District Court in Ljubljana in 2010, by the appellate High Court in Ljubljana and finally by the Supreme Court of RS in 2012. At that time, judicial review proceedings were three-stage as the PCA of 1993 provided for an unusual judicial review mechanism by filing an action in civil proceedings.[188]

It can be speculated that the defendant will refer to the statute of limitations for damages claims as under the CO, the limitation period for damages claims is three years as of when the victim became aware of the damage and the person

---

184 See also *Vlahek: Nova Direktiva 2014/104....*

185 Case No. IV Pg 1356/2014.

186 <http://seonet.ljse.si/Default.aspx?doc=SEARCH&doc_id=55178> (13 July 2015).

187 <www.24ur.com/novice/gospodarstvo/sodisce-znova-zavrnilo-tozbo-telekoma-proti-uvk.html> (13 July 2015).

188 Article 25 of PCA of 1993. Such system enabled three-stage judicial proceedings in contrast to two-stage judicial proceedings in force between 1999 and 2008 (and as of 2013), and to merely single-stage judicial proceedings in force between 2008 and 2013.

causing damage, and the claim must be brought within five years as of when the damage had actually occurred.[189] Given the fact that the breach was to occur in the nineties, the damage was most possibly sustained (and the plaintiff informed of the perpetrator and of the damage) around that time. Prior to 2008 when the PRCA-1 entered into force regulating in Article 62/3 the effects of pending administrative (and judicial review) proceedings on the limitation periods (stating that limitation does not run as of initiation of administrative proceedings before the SCPA or the Commission up until these proceedings are finally resolved), no such rule existed under Slovenian law. Based on a speculation that damages occurred way back in the nineties, it can be speculated that the claim will be dismissed on the grounds that the statute of limitation has already run out way before the new system regulating issues of limitation in competition law cases was enforced.

10.7. *AKTON v. TELEKOM SLOVENIJE*

In 2010, Akton d.o.o. filed a lawsuit with the District Court in Ljubljana against Telekom Slovenije d.d. alleging abuse of a dominant position by Mobitel d.d. (now Telekom Slovenije d.d.) with regard to performing its services of transferring international mobile voice calls on number blocks +386 43 and +386 49 to international switchboard, and requesting damages in the amount of nearly EUR 7 million.[190]

At the time relevant for the dispute (as well as at the time of writing this paper), Kosovo did not have its own national dialling code due to political and diplomatic reasons which prevented it to become a member of the UN and to be thus able to obtain a national code by the ITU. As regards mobile voice calls, it used foreign codes which were Monaco's +377 code and Slovenia's +386 code. IPKO Telecommunications LLC (owned by Telekom Slovenije) was successful in bidding for the second mobile phone network operator in Kosovo, the first being Vala Mobile owned by PTK Posta dhe Telekomunikacioni i Kosovës, SH.A. For the purposes of operating the Kosovo mobile network, IPKO uses the +386 43 and +386 49 number blocks while Vala uses blocks with the prefix +377. Slovenian Post and Electronic Communications Agency (PECA)[191] assigned the +386 43 and +386 49 blocks to Mobitel enabling it to transfer calls on +386 43 and +386 49 to international switchboard. For doing that, Mobitel charged its business partners non-regulated prices. In Kosovo, IPKO terminated international mobile voice calls that were transferred to it.

189 For further details on limitation periods under Slovenian law, see *supra* chapter Regulation of private enforcement of antitrust in Slovenia, III, 1, (ix).

190 Case No. IV Pg 4477/2012.

191 Renamed to Agency for Communication Networks and Services of the Republic of Slovenia on 22 January 2014.

Akton (and Si.Mobil that intervened next to Akton before the CPO but had eventually not filed any civil lawsuits in this regard) objected to Mobitel's contractual terms for transferring calls to international switchboard claiming that such activity is in fact termination of calls in Mobitel's public mobile communications network that is regulated by the PECA and on that basis already contracted for by the parties concerned on the basis of the PECA's decisions. Akton also stated that Mobitel discriminated competitors of Telekom Slovenije to whom Mobitel also provided its services while Telekom Slovenije's competitors were forced to terminate calls via other operators what was less favourable to them. Akton further claimed that terminating calls in +386 43 and +386 49 is an essential precondition for transferring calls on these numbers, and that in any event, the prices charged by Mobitel were excessive. Mobitel, on the other hand, claimed that transferring calls for Kosovo cannot be equalled to (regulated) termination of calls in its public network, that calls to Kosovo are not even terminated in its public network (but in IPKO's network in Kosovo where jurisdiction is vested with Kosovar, not Slovenian authorities), and that it as a result legally offered to the plaintiffs its services of transferring calls for Kosovo on the basis of signing additional agreements with non-regulated and non-excessive prices.

In 2009, the PECA issued a decree finding that calls to +386 43 and +306 49 are not terminated in the public mobile phone network of Mobitel d.d.[192] and that regulation of termination of calls in IPKO's network (which is an individual network separate of the Mobitel's public mobile network in Slovenia, a network with its own customers) lies with the Kosovar authorities, emphasising thereby that the fact that IPKO uses the blocks assigned to Mobitel is irrelevant as to these findings.

In 2009, Akton and Si.Mobil filed a complaint with the CPO that initiated proceedings against Mobitel in March 2010 in order to find whether Mobitel breached Articles 9 of the PRCA-1 and Article 102 TFEU. By issuing a decree on commencing the proceedings, the CPO also issued a decree on interim measures imposing Mobitel mandated access to number blocks under equal and non-discriminatory technical and commercial terms in 60 days as of receipt of such demand, etc., but in April 2010, the decree was set aside by the Supreme Court of RS for breaching the principle of *audiatur et altera pars.*[193] In 2012, the proceedings against Mobitel were terminated by the CPO in accordance with Article 40 of the PRCA-1 stating that the SCPA terminates the proceedings if it does not find an infringement, or if special circumstances of the case show that proceedings would not be reasonable.[194] The CPO found, inter alia, that Mobitel does offer access to the two number blocks. It decided not to test whether

192 Decree No. 06012-7/2009-14 of 2 November 2009.

193 Decree No. G 8/2010-17 of 20 April 2010.

194 Decision No. 306-94/2009-227 of 13 February 2012.

Mobitel's prices were excessive as such analysis would be too burdensome given the possible non-appreciable impact a decision finding that prices were excessive would have on the market. It further stated that the sole fact that prices are high does not represent threat to undertakings that they would be forced to leave the market as they could pass on these costs to the operator seeking their activities.

In 2010, Akton has supposedly complained against Mobitel as well as against the PECA also to the European Commission[195] and to the Slovenian Commission for the Prevention of Corruption. Despite the outcome before the PECA and the CPO, Akton decided to file damages actions basing its claims on the abuse which was not established by the CPO. The civil damages case is still pending with the first instance District Court in Ljubljana.

Another damages lawsuit is pending between Telekom Slovenije and Akton before the District Court of Ljubljana. Although it is not a lawsuit within the ambit of antitrust private enforcement, it is being analysed here as it concerns the transfer of international voice calls to Kosovo. In April 2014, Telekom Slovenije (and the persons responsible) received a lawsuit filed by Akton requesting damages in the amount of over EUR 2,4 million with interest alleging that unlawful actions by Telekom Slovenije caused the plaintiff to suffer and damaged its reputation.[196] The lawsuit is in relation to the criminal complaint filed with the police authorities in 2011 by Telekom Slovenije against the plaintiff, who was in a pre-trial investigation suspected of committing a criminal offence of commercial fraud by its alleged illegal activities in transferring mobile voice calls to Kosovo that had allegedly caused harm to Telekom Slovenije and to end-users of mobile telephony.[197] Based on the report of the Slovenian National Bureau of Investigation (that has, inter alia, performed a dawn raid at the premises of Akton in 2011), the state prosecutor terminated the proceedings in 2013. The civil law case is still pending.

A further lawsuit for EUR 1,5 million (later increased to approx. EUR 2,6 million) was filed by Akton against Telekom Slovenije, this time alleging Telekom Slovenije's abuse by charging prices for termination of calls in Slovenia that were higher than those set by the PECA. Akton requested Telekom Slovenije to repay it the sums charged above the set prices. The District Court in Ljubljana fully rejected the claim in November 2014 and ordered the plaintiff to refund the defendant the costs in the amount of approx. 25.000 EUR.[198]

195 <www.telecompaper.com/news/akton-complains-to-ec-over-mobitel--763483> (13 July 2015); <www.finance.si/290834/Mobitel-odira-konkurenco-APEK-pa-ob-tem-mi%C5%BEi> (13 July 2015).

196 <http://seonet.ljse.si/Default.aspx?doc=SEARCH&doc_id=54357> (13 July 2015);<www.dnevnik.si/posel/novice/1042504116> (13 July 2015).

197 <www.mojmikro.si/news/akton_tozi_telekom_slovenije_za_2_4_milijona_evrov> (13 July 2015).

198 Judgment No. IV Pg 4477/2012 of 19 November 2014. See <http://seonet.ljse.si/default_en.aspx?doc=SEARCH&doc_id=56453> (13 July 2015).

10.8. *AMIS v. TELEKOM SLOVENIJE*

In May 2008, Telekom Slovenije d.d. received a lawsuit from Amis d.o.o. for the payment of damages in the amount of nearly EUR 57 million arising out of the alleged breaches of the PRCA of 1999 and the Electronic Communications Act.[199] It had allegedly abused its dominant position in the inter-operator broadband access market, in the unbundled local loop and sub-loop access market, and in the fiber-optics connections to collocations spaces market.[200] Administrative proceedings before the CPA as well as civil court proceedings in this case are to my knowledge still pending.[201]

In another case, Telekom Slovenije and Amis settled for SIT 343.565.000 (i.e. EUR 1,43 million) before the CPO's decision finding the abuse became final and before Amis had filed damages actions against Telekom Slovenije. In 2004, the CPO found (on the basis of a complaint by Medinet d.o.o. (now AMIS d.o.o.)) an abuse of Telekom Slovenije on the market for wholesale bitstream (ADSL) access as Telekom Slovenije was setting different prices for its SiOL on one hand and for SiOL's competition on the other putting the latter in a less favourable competitive position than SiOL.[202]

10.9. *BLITZ v. KOLOSEJ*

Administrative proceedings against Kolosej kinematografi d.o.o., an undertaking operating cinemas, were initiated in 2006 upon request by Blitz Film & Video Distribution d.o.o., an undertaking engaged in film distribution. The CPO established in July 2007 that Kolosej abused its dominant position on the market of cinematographic movie screening in three Slovenian cities (Ljubljana, Koper and Maribor) and their closest suburbs as of 6 March 2004 at least up to 10 February 2005 by discriminating its movie distributor Blitz.[203] It also requested Kolosej to refrain from such activity, and ordered the publication of the operative part of the decision in the OJ of RS. Kolosej instituted judicial review proceedings. The Administrative Court of RS as the review court of first

---

199 Sl. *Zakon o elektronskih komunikacijah (ZEKom)*, Official Gazette RS, No. 43/04, with further amendments (replaced in 2012 by *ZEKom-1*).

200 <http://seonet.ljse.si/Default.aspx?doc=SEARCH&doc_id=31979> (13 July 2015).

201 <www.dnevnik.si/posel/novice/avk-v-zdruzitev-postopkov-alternativnih-operaterjev-proti-telekomu> (13 July 2015); www.24ur.com/akton-tozi-telekom-slovenije-za-2-4-milijona-evrov.html (13 July 2015); <www.rtvslo.si/gospodarstvo/telekom-slovenije-caka-vecmili jonska-odskodninska-tozba-zadeve-ne-komentirajo/320640> (13 July 2015).

202 Decision No. 3072–14/02–62 od 19 November 2004, available at (in Slovene): <www.varstvo-konkurence.si/fileadmin/varstvo-konkurence.si/pageuploads/ijz018.pdf> (13 July 2015).

203 Decision No. 306–6672006–52 of 26 July 2007; available at (in Slovene): <www.varstvo-konkurence.si/fileadmin/varstvo-konkurence.si/pageuploads/informacija_javnega_znacaja/ijz108.pdf> (13 July 2015).

instance rejected in 2009 Kolosej's claim[204] who then instituted revision proceedings with the Supreme Court of RS. The Supreme Court allowed the revision but found it unfounded in October 2010.[205]

Already in 2008 (after the CPO had issued the decision but before the decision had become final), Blitz initiated court proceedings with the District Court in Ljubljana claiming EUR 943.449,69 of damages sustained by the infringement.[206] The relevant Article at that time was Article 44 of the PRCA of 1999 (the currently valid Article 62 of the PRCA-1 of 2008 was not yet in force) stating merely that anyone sustaining a loss as a consequence of competition law infringement could seek damages in accordance with the general rules of obligations. In April 2012, the District Court issued an interlocutory judgment finding (only) that with regard to a part of films the plaintiff's claim is substantiated as regards the issue of liability (in part, it rejected the claim as unsubstantiated), but it did not decide on the amount of damages.[207] According to Slovenian civil procedure, the court may issue interlocutory judgment (on its own motion) when it finds it appropriate to decide first on the issue of liability and reserve the decision on the amount of damages (or purchase price etc.) for the time after the decision on liability becomes final. Such judgment may be appealed against, and while the appeal is pending, the court may not continue the proceedings with a determination of the amount of damages. But when the interlocutory judgment becomes final, it binds the court in the subsequent stages of procedure – thus, when determining the amount of damages (but it has no binding effect for possible later litigations, based on the same occurrence, for example, when further damages are sought in a second action).[208] It may be appropriate to render an interlocutory judgment when the defendant disputes both the liability and the amount sought, and when the case is of such nature that the question of liability is not straight-forward (and it is therefore useful to wait for this determination to be confirmed by the appellate court) and the evidence proceedings concerning the amount of damages would be lengthy and costly.[209]

Both parties appealed to the High Court in Ljubljana. In November 2013, the High Court upheld the appeals, quashed the judgment and remitted the case for a retrial providing the first instance court with substantial guidance as to proper procedural and substantive handling of the case.[210] In its statement of ground, the High Court focused on the following relevant issues of the case: (i) can the

204 Judgment No. U 1853/2007.

205 Judgment No. X Ips 45/2010 of 26 October 2010, available at (in Slovene): <www.sodisce.si/vsrs/odlocitve/2010040815253610/> (13 July 2015).

206 <www.rtvslo.si/kultura/film/blitz-vlozil-tozbo-proti-kcloseju/154230> (13 July 2015).

207 Judgment No. VI Pg 2154/2011 of 4 April 2013.

208 *Galič: Civil Procedure, Slovenia*, pp. 127 – 128.

209 *Ibidem.*

210 Decree No. I Cpg 870/2012 of 29 November 2013.

court issue an interlocutory decision with regard to a part of claim while the rest of claim is rejected; (ii) do factual circumstances of the abuse (e.g. with regard to which films the abuse was determined) form part of the operative part of the judgment or are to be included in the statement of ground only; (iii) where the claimant did not prove certain facts (i.e. that certain claimant's offers to play films were rejected by the defendant) on which it based its claim, while the defendant most plausibly has such information, is the claim to be rejected by the court due to lack of proof (without at least specifically reminding the claimant to provide such proof), or must the defendant itself provide the information in order to be deemed credible by the court; (iv) the effect of the CPO's finding of infringement in private enforcement proceedings in the period prior to 2008 when the PRCA of 1999 did not set out the binding effect of final CPO decisions; (v) the effect of the CPO's finding of infringement in private enforcement proceedings where damages are requested also for defendant's acts that were not assessed by the CPO (but may correspond to the pattern of the defendant's acts assessed by the CPO); (vi) whether administrative proceedings before the CPO or the European Commission are anyhow relevant as to the question when the limitation period starts to run (or are relevant – as set out as of 2008 in Article 62 of the PRCA-1 merely in the sense that during such proceedings the limitation (that has already started to run irrespective of such proceedings) is stayed); etc.

The case is most possibly still pending with the court of first instance that must take all procedural steps and determine all questions in dispute which have been pointed out in the High Court's decree.[211] It is, however, not bound by the legal opinion, expressed in the decision of the appellate court.[212] Thus, it may insist on its original legal position (and, of course, risk that an appeal against its judgment will be successful again).[213]

10.10. *EUROMEDIA MB v. POŠTA SLOVENIJE*

In May 2008, the CPO issued a decision accepting five years' term commitments by *Pošta Slovenije* who in the view of the CPO probably breached Articles 9 of the PRCA-1 and 82 TEC[214] by, inter alia, discriminating agents ordering

211 Article 362 of the CPrA.

212 Article 11 of the Courts Act.

213 *Galič, Civil Procedure, Slovenia*, p. 142.

214 After an order initiating antitrust proceedings has been issued, the undertaking may offer commitments in order to avoid that any anticompetitive situation on the market is established by the PAPC. The commitments may be offered to the PAPC within the time-limit for replying to its statement of objections. If the offered commitments are acceptable for the PAPC, it issues a decision making those commitments binding on the undertaking(s) concerned. By doing that, the PAPC merely finds that there are no longer grounds for action, it does not, however, decide on the infringement. For further details on commitments under Slovenian law, see Grilc in *Grilc et al.: PRCA-1 Commentary*, pp. 393–405.

dissemination of unsolicited mail *vis-à-vis* its direct customers, inserting in its contracts non-compete clauses or clauses on exclusive dealing.[215]

Being one of the providers of unsolicited mail distribution, Euromedia MB d.o.o. filed a claim with the District Court in Ljubljana against Pošta Slovenije requesting approx. EUR 8 million of loss of profit.[216] It also urged the PAPC to reopen the proceedings against Pošta Slovenije. In April 2013, the court appointed an expert to determine whether predatory pricing had in fact occurred and whether the loss (and, if, in what amount) was sustained by the plaintiff.[217] To my knowledge, the case is still pending. It will be interesting to see how the court will tackle with the fact that the CPO accepted commitments and did not issue a decision finding the abuse. Some media, however, report that the judge is supposedly awaiting the PAPC's possible decision on reopening the proceedings against Pošta Slovenije.[218]

10.11. *S5 VLEKA LADIJ v. LUKA KOPER*

In 2008, the CPO instituted proceedings against Luka Koper d.d. for an alleged breach of Articles 9 of the PRCA-1 and 82 TEC in the form of an abuse of a dominant position on the market of operating port infrastructure by denying undertaking S5 vleka ladij d.o.o. access to and use of port infrastructure.[219] The proceedings were instituted on the basis of information forwarded to the CPO by the S5 vleka ladij d.o.o. that was granted a status of intervener in the case. The CPO issued the decision in October 2009 finding the abuse having the effect of excluding all competition on the markets for towing and mooring services in the port of Koper.

In 2010, S5 vleka ladij filed a claim for EUR 2 million[220] with the District Court of Koper that issued an interlocutory judgment finding that the plaintiff's claim is well-founded regarding the period in which the infringement took place (19 June 2008 – 29 July 2008), while it dismissed the claim as regards the rest of the period claimed by the plaintiff as relevant for awarding damages (30 July 2008–29 June 2009) by stating that at that time the infringement already ended. In February 2013, High Court of Koper rejected the defendant's appeal while it

215 Decision No. 306–35/2005–98 of 28 May 2008, available at (in Slovene): <www.varstvo-konkurence.si/fileadmin/varstvo-konkurence.si/pageuploads/ijz015.pdf> (13 July 2015).

216 <www.dnevnik.si/kronika/izvedenec-bo-ugotavljal-morebitno-cenovno-predatorstvo-poste-slovenije> (13 July 2015).

217 *Ibid.*

218 <https://www.dnevnik.si/1042615702/posel/novice/kraskova-nenavadna-milost-za-posto-slovenije-> (13 July 2015).

219 Decision No. 306–1/2008–84 of 15 October 2009, available at (in Slovene): <www.varstvo-konkurence.si/fileadmin/varstvo-konkurence.si/pageuploads/ijz085.pdf> (13 July 2015).

220 <www.dnevnik.si/kronika/luki-koper-kazen-zaradi-monopolnega-polozaja-pri-vleki-ladij> (13 July 2015).

upheld the plaintiff's appeal finding that the District Court incorrectly refused to take into account the period after 29 July 2008 solely on the ground that during that period the infringement ceased to exist, while the plaintiff was merely claiming that it sustained damage also during the period after the infringement. The High Court therefore referred the case back to the first instance court instructing it to assess this time the plaintiff's claims accordingly as well as to decide on the amount of damages to avoid further delay of the proceedings. The High Court elaborated also on the question of binding effect of the CPO's decision finding the infringement, and on the but-for scenario confirming the first instance court's analysis of whether the plaintiff could and would have launched its business but for the infringement;[221]

BIBLIOGRAPHY

Ahtik, M. and Vlahek, A., Določanje odškodnin v primeru kršitev antitrusta, in: Dnevi slovenskih pravnikov 2011 od 13. do 15. oktobra, Portorož, Podjetje in delo, ISSN 0350-7327, Y. 37, No. 6/7, Ljubljana, GV Založba, 2011, pp. 1344–1359 (cited as: Ahtik & Vlahek: Določanje odškodnin v primeru kršitev antitrusta)

Barličm J. and Grilc, P. and Ilešič, M. and Ilešič, M. and Stražišar, B. and Zabel, B., Zakon o varstvu konkurence s komentarjem, Zakon o trgovini s komentarjem, Gospodarski vestnik, Ljubljana, 1993, ISBN 86-7061-065-5 (cited as: Zabel et al.: PCA of 1993 Commentary)

Betetto, N., Vzorčni postopek, in: Pravni letopis, Inštitut za primerjalno pravo pri Pravni fakulteti v Ljubljani, ISSN 1855-5861, 2011, pp. 231–241, 404–405 (cited as: Betetto: Vzorčni postopek)

Damjan, M., Množični zahtevki zaradi posegov v zdravo življenjsko okolje, in: Pravni letopis, Inštitut za primerjalno pravo pri Pravni fakulteti v Ljubljani, ISSN 1855-5861, 2011, pp. 243–270, 406–407 (cited as: Damjan: Množični zahtevki zaradi posegov v zdravo življenjsko okolje)

Damjan, M., Učinek mediacije na tek rokov, in: Pravnik, Zveza društev pravnikov Slovenije, ISSN 0032-6976, 2008, Y. 63, No. 1/3, pp. 37–62 (cited as: Damjan: Učinek mediacije na tek rokov)

Fatur, A. and Podobnik, K., Competition Law in Western Europe and USA, SI/C, Slovenia/Commentary, Suppl. 318 (February 2011), Kluwer Law International, 2011, ISBN 978-90-654-4904-7 (cited as: Fatur & Podobnik: Competition Law in Western Europe and USA: Slovenia)

Fatur, A. and Podobnik, K., and Vlahek, A.: Competition Law – Slovenia, forthcoming in: Denozza Francesco, Toffoletto Alberto (Eds.), International Encyclopaedia for Competition Law, Kluwer Law International / Wolters Kluwer, Expected date of publication 2015 (cited as: Fatur & Podobnik & Vlahek: Competition Law – Slovenia)

221 Judgment and Decree No. Cpg 216/2012 of 22 February 2013, available at (in Slovene): <http://sodnapraksa.si/?q=varstvo%20konkurence&database[IESP]=IESP&_submit=i%C5%A1%C4%8Di&order=date&direction=desc&page=0&id=2012032113055700> (13 July 2015).

Galič A.,: Skupinske tožbe na področju potrošniškega prava, in: Pravni letopis, Inštitut za primerjalno pravo pri Pravni fakulteti v Ljubljani, ISSN 1855-58612011, pp. 251-229, 402-403 (cited as: Galič: Skupinske tožbe na področju potrošniškega prava)

Galič A.,: (In)compatibility of Procedural Preclusions with the Goals of Civil Justice: An Ongoing Debate in Slovenia, in: Uzelac Alan (Ed.), Goals of Civil Justice and Civil Procedure in Contemporary Judicial Systems, Ius Gentium: Comparative Perspectives on Law and Justice, Vol. 34, Springer, 2014, ISBN 978-3-319-03442-3, pp. 221-243 (cited as: Galič: (In)compatibility of Procedural Preclusions ...)

Galič A., Slovenia, International encyclopaedia of laws, Civil procedure, suppl. 49, The Hague, Kluwer Law International, 2008, ISBN 978-90-654-4936-8 (cited as: Galič: Civil Procedure, Slovenia)

Galič A., and Grilc P., and Juhart M. and Zabel B., Zakon o preprečevanju omejevanja konkurence (ZPOmK) s komentarjem, Gospodarski vestnik, Ljubljana, 2000, ISBN 86-7061-228-3 (cited as: Galič et al.: PRCA Commentary)

Galič A.,: Disclosure of Documents in Private Antitrust Enforcement Litigation, Paper presented at International Conference on Harmonisation of Private Antitrust Enforcement: A Central and Eastern European Perspective, Faculty of Law, University of Białystok, Supraśl, 2-4-July 2015 (cited as: Galič: Disclosure of Documents in Private Antitrust Enforcement Litigation)

Grilc, P. and Bratina, T. and Galič, A. and Kerševan, E. and Kocmut, M. and Podobnik, K. and Vlahek, A. and Zabel, B., Zakon o preprečevanju omejevanja konkurence (ZPOmK-1): s komentarjem, (Nova slovenska zakonodaja), 1st edition, Ljubljana, GV Založba, 2009, ISBN 978-961-247-115-6 (cited as: Grilc et al.: PRCA-1 Commentary)

Grilc, P. and Podobnik, K., Das Wettbewerbsrecht in Slowenien, in: Ekey Friedrich L. & Klippel Diethelm & Kotthoff Jost & Meckel Astrid & Grilc Peter & Podobnik Klemen & Brämer Antje: Heidelberger Kommentar zum Wettbewerbsrecht, (Heidelberger Kommentar), 2., neubearbeit. Auflage, Heidelberg, C.F. Müller, cop. 2005. XXV, ISBN 3-8114-3053-X (cited as: Grilc & Podobnik: Das Wettbewerbsrecht in Slowenien)

Juhart, M. and Plavšak, N., (Eds.): Obligacijski zakonik s komentarjem (splošni del), GV Založba, Ljubljana, 2003, ISBN 86-7061-323-9 (cited as: Juhart et al.: CO Commentary)

Podobnik, K., Program prizanesljivosti - novost v slovenski konkurenčnopravni ureditvi, in: Pravni letopis, Inštitut za primerjalno pravo pri Pravni fakulteti v Ljubljani, ISSN 1855-5861, 2009, pp. 205-223 (cited as: Podobnik: Program prizanesljivosti...)

Sever, M., Vezanost nacionalnega sodišča na odločbe Evropske komisije in Urada za varstvo konkurence, in: Pravni letopis, Inštitut za primerjalno pravo pri Pravni fakulteti v Ljubljani, ISSN 1855-5861, 2009, pp. 263-273 (cited as: Sever: Vezanost nacionalnega sodišča...)

Šturm, L. et al.: Komentar Ustave Republike Slovenije, Ljubljana: FDŠ, 2002, ISBN 961-238-053-8 (cited as: Šturm et al.: Komentar Ustave RS)

Ude, L. and Betetto, N. and Galič A., and Rijavec, V. and Wedam-Lukič, D. and Zobec, J: Pravdni postopek: zakon s komentarjem, Uradni list RS, GV Založba, Ljubljana,

2005–2010, ISBN 86-7061-397-2, ISBN 961-204-364-7, ISBN 978-961-247-117-0, ISBN 978-961-247-133-0 (cited as: Ude et al.: CPrA Commentary)

Vlahek, A., Amicus curiae, sodelovanje med slovenskimi sodišči, UVK in Evropsko komisijo v konkurenčnopravnih zadevah, in: Pravosodni bilten, ISSN 1318-1459, 2009, Y. 30, No. 4, pp. 301–330 (cited as: Vlahek: Amicus curiae...)

Vlahek, A., Reforma antitrusta v Evropski uniji, in: Podjetje in delo, ISSN 0350-7327, 2004, Y. 30, No. 2, pp. 230–272 (cited as: Vlahek: Reforma antitrusta v Evropski uniji)

Vlahek, A., Oris odškodnin na področju skupnostnega antitrusta, in: Evro PP, ISSN 0352-0730, Y. 28, No. 11, Ljubljana, GV Založba, 2009, pp. 44–46 (cited as: Vlahek: Oris odškodnin...)

Vlahek, A.,, Kolektivno varstvo v EU, in: Pravna praksa, ISSN 0352-0730, 31 May 2012, Y. 31, No. 21, pp. 16–17, GV Založba (cited as: Vlahek: Kolektivno varstvo v EU)

Vlahek, A., Nova Direktiva 2014/104 o nekaterih pravilih glede odškodninskih zahtevkov in postopka zaradi kršitev evropskega in nacionalnega antitrusta, in: Grilc Peter (Ed.), Izbrani vidiki razvoja slovenskega gospodarskega in civilnega prava od srede 20. stoletja do danes: liber amicorum Bojan Zabel, Pravna fakulteta, Ljubljana 2015, pp. 171–200 (cited as: Vlahek: Nova Direktiva 2014/104...)

CHAPTER 19

ON THE NEED OF EU WIDE BEST PRACTICES IN COMPETITION LAW ENFORCEMENT PROCEEDINGS

Miodrag DORDEVIC

1. INTRODUCTION

In order to establish a system that ensures the competition in the common market is not distorted, Articles 101 and 102 of the Treaty must be applied effectively and uniformly in the European Community. In order to ensure the effective enforcement of the Community competition rules and the proper functioning of the cooperation mechanisms, it is necessary to develop the best practices in international competition law enforcement proceedings.

2. BEST PRACTICES

The best practices should be intended to promote the adoption of procedural safeguards for all types of competition matters, directed at ensuring that due regard is given to the fundamental fairness of the processes by which the competition law is enforced in an increasingly global context. It is essential to embrace the principles of transparency, engagement, confidentiality, due process, non-discrimination and accountability in order to operate effectively. Such principles are essential not only to ensure fairness to firms being investigated, but also to more effectively pursue the policies that underlie competition laws, promote greater respect for competition law, competition authorities and their enforcement decisions.

The best practices would not only ensure procedural fairness for those involved, but would also importantly strengthen vigorous, efficient enforcement of competition laws in a number of respects. For example, frequent and open engagement with firms under investigation enhances the abilities of agencies (enforcing the competition laws) to gather relevant information, increases efficiency by the parties on the issues in which agencies are actually interested, and strengthens the internal deliberations of agencies by enabling them to better understand the firms' arguments, and the facts that support those arguments before, rather than after, the agencies decide whether to recommend formal charges. Providing due process protections to firms under investigation enables competition authorities to ensure their decisions (even if adverse to respondents) to be respected by all parties. Thus, increased procedural fairness can strengthen agency decision-making and increase public confidence in agency decisions, benefiting businesses, competition authorities and the consumers they serve.

3. PROCEDURAL FAIRNESS AND EFFECTIVE ENFORCEMENT

The best practices should not only ensure the procedural fairness, but also would more effectively promote the policies that underlie competition laws. In particular it would promote greater respect for competition law and its enforcement and ensure more efficient utilisation of the enforcement resources of competition authorities worldwide, without jeopardising the legitimate enforcement interests of any jurisdiction. Realisation of these objectives will inevitably require some compromises by the international competition enforcement community, but the increasingly global nature of commerce dictates that competition authorities recognise the need for procedural safeguards that increase the transparency and fairness of their enforcement efforts. Unless different practices are dictated by genuine differences in underlying policy objectives or fundamental statutory constraints, the objective of achieving increased international harmonisation reflected in these "best practices" principles should be followed.

In order to ensure the consistency in the application of the competition rules it is also necessary to ensure that the arrangements are established for cooperation between the national courts and the Commission. This is relevant for all national courts that apply Articles 101 and 102 of the Treaty, whether applying these rules in lawsuits between private parties, acting as public enforcers or as review courts. Namely, it is very important to ensure compliance with the principles of legal certainty and the uniform application of the community competition rules.

4. CONCLUSIONS

In this aspect the role of the courts is essential. The courts, particularly when competition authorities are an administrative body, play or should play a significant role in safeguarding due process. It is important for the courts to ensure antitrust proceedings are conducted in a fair manner. The courts' function as a check and balance of the competition authority enhances not only the credibility of the enforcement action but also basic principles for fairness and rule of law that are hallmarks of a developed and accountable legal system.

BIBLIOGRAPHY

"Council Regulation (EC) No 1/2003 of 16 December 2002 on the implementation of the rules on competition laid down in Articles 81 and 82 of the Treaty".

"Recommended framework for international best practices in competition law enforcement proceedings" prepared by the International Chamber of Commerce (ICC).

"Recommended framework for best practices in international competition law enforcement proceedings" prepared by the United States Council for International Business (USCIB).

INDEX

D

E

F

G

H

R

S

T

U

V

W

www.ingramcontent.com/pod-product-compliance
Ingram Content Group UK Ltd.
Pitfield, Milton Keynes, MK11 3LW, UK
UKHW051918100926
8556IPUK00021B/1250

9 781780 682860